Coolies and Mandarins: China's Protection of Overseas Chinese during the Late Ch'ing Period (1851–1911)

YEN CHING-HWANG

SINGAPORE UNIVERSITY PRESS
NATIONAL UNIVERSITY OF SINGAPORE

© 1985 Singapore University Press
Kent Ridge, Singapore 0511

ISBN 9971-69-087-X (paperback)

Typeset and Printed by Fong & Sons Printers Pte Ltd

Contents

Foreword

The study of the overseas Chinese in Southeast Asia has been bedevilled by some still largely unanswered questions. One that has engaged many scholars has been the slow response of the Ch'ing government to the demand among the Chinese in the southern provinces for increased trading abroad. Less attention, however, has been given to a related question: why did the Ch'ing government appear insensitive to the large-scale population movements out of South China during the middle of the nineteenth century? These movements were dramatic. And the qualitative change in the nature of some Chinese communities abroad, from communities of resident traders, artisans and their local families, to ones dominated by contract labourers meeting the needs of rapidly expanding economies, was in the end equally dramatic. Dr Yen examines the historical and diplomatic background to this question in his study of Ch'ing policy towards the Chinese overseas. He offers no simple answers but provides a scholarly presentation of the main issues that emerged, especially with regard to China's policies during the last decades of the Ch'ing dynasty. In this way, he challenges the picture of official insensitivity which modern Chinese historians sympathetic to overseas Chinese have tended to present.

Dr Yen is particularly well qualified to tackle this controversial subject. His reputation as a fine scholar has been established by his comprehensive and authoritative study of the role of overseas Chinese in the Straits Settlements and the Malay States in support of the 1911 Revolution. That book has been simultaneously translated into Chinese by a Taiwan historian and a group of historians in China and the former has already been published in Taiwan. Dr Yen's knowledge of the overseas Chinese in Southeast Asia is solidly based on two decades of research. He has now, in this new book on Ch'ing policy, extended his research to diplomatic matters pertaining to overseas Chinese in South Africa and the Americas. He has thus provided for the first time in a Western language a comparative perspective on official aspects of overseas Chinese affairs in South-east Asia and other regions of Chinese settlement. It is an illuminating exercise done with the scholarly care we have come to expect from Dr Yen. It tells us about not only what the governments of China and the West were trying to do but also throws new light on the kinds of problems that the Chinese faced when deciding to go east across the Pacific or south across the South China Sea.

Writing from Xiamen, Fujian   **Wang Gungwu**
July 1983

Preface

The reseach for this book began in 1971. At that time, two other scholars were interested in related topics: they were Robert Irick, a Ph.D. candidate at Harvard University, and Sing-wu Wang, the Chief Librarian of the Orientalia of the Australian National Library, Canberra. Irick was interested in Ch'ing policy towards coolie trade, while Wang worked on Chinese emigration in the nineteenth century, with a special interest to the emigration to Australia. Subsequently, Wang and Irick have had their books published. My study is broader in scope and wider in areas than Irick's and Wang's. I wanted to find out what essentially constituted Ch'ing overseas Chinese policy, how the policy was implemented and why it failed. Although this book deals with all overseas Chinese, its main focus is on the Chinese communities in Southeast Asia and the United States.

I collected published materials from various Australian libraries and libraries in Singapore and Malaysia. I especially benefited from excellent collections of the Orientalia of the Australian National Library, the Oriental Library of the Australian National University, Canberra, and the Oriental Library of the Sydney University, Sydney. The materials collected from the above libraries laid a good foundation for the project. In 1974 I had a one-year study leave in Southeast Asia, Hong Kong and Taiwan which gave me access to the Ch'ing archives kept in Taiwan. The most important one was the Tsungli Yamen and Wai Wu Pu Archives kept in the Institute of Modern History, Academia Sinica, Taipei. At the Palace Museum, Taipei, I discovered the gazettes of the Ministry of Education and the Ministry of Commerce of late Ch'ing period entitled *Hsueh-pu kuan-pao* and *Shang-wu kuan-pao*. Both gazettes are very useful for the project.

The first draft of this book was completed in 1978. But I was not happy with it because I felt that I had not exhausted source materials related to the topic and had also not been able to visit the Chinese communities in the United States and Canada about which

I had written. A six-month study leave in 1979 enabled me to visit
Britain and North America. In London I worked in the Department
of Oriental Manuscripts and Documents of the British Library,
Russel Square; the Library of the School of Oriental and African
Studies; the Principal Library of London University; and the
Public Record Office in Kew Gardens. In North America, I visited
the Harvard-Yenching Library and the Houghton Library of Har-
vard University; the East Asian Library of the Columbia Univer-
sity; the Library of the Historical Society, New York; the National
Archives of the United States, Washington, D.C.; the Congress
Libraries, Washington, D.C.; the Library of the University of
Toronto, Toronto; the Libraries of the University of British Col-
umbia, Vancouver; and the Library of the University of Victoria,
B.C., Canada; the East Asian Library and the Bancroft Library of
the University of California, Berkeley; the Library of the Hoover
Institution, Stanford University, Stanford, California; and the
Library of the University of Hawaii, Honolulu.

In these Libraries I had the opportunity to examine some original
records of British and American archives connected with the topic.
In London, in the British Library, I perused some old Chinese
newspapers relating to the activities in the Chinese communities in
Singapore and Malaya. In the Public Record Office, I examined in
detail the Foreign Office Records and Colonial Office Records connected with the topic, in particular, the correspondence of the
Chinese Minister in London to the British Foreign Secretary in the
period between 1877 and 1912. In the United States, I was excited
to have the opportunity to examine the original records of the
Bureau of Immigration from 1877 to 1891, and the correspondence
between the Chinese Ministers in Washington and the Secretary of
State in the period between 1879 and 1906. The records of the
Bureau of Immigration, the so-called Segregated Chinese Records,
consist of reports and correspondence of American immigration officials in dealing with Chinese immigrants; they are contained in six
large boxes, unclassified, and have so far not been microfilmed.

Moreover, I had the opportunity to examine some old Chinese
newspapers published in the United States between 1856 and 1912.
Among them, the *Chung Sai Yat Bao*, deposited in the Bancroft
Library of the University of California, Berkeley, and the *Sun
Chung Kwock Bo (New China Daily News)*, deposited in the
Library of the University of Hawaii, are most useful. Apart from
this I had the opportunity to inspect the original records of the
Chinese Consolidated Benevolent Association of Victoria, British

Columbia, deposited in the Library of the University of Victoria, B.C., Canada. The Chinese Consolidated Benevolent Association of Victoria was the leading organisation among Chinese communities in Canada during the period under study, its records deserve special attention from scholars.

I also inspected the sites of various Chinese communities in the United States and Canada, and observed their way of life and talked to some of the local Chinese about the writing of overseas Chinese history. The visual impact on me was tremendous. Not only did it give me more confidence in writing about the communities, but it also gave me insight into the problems of the communities about one hundred years ago.

The new materials collected during my 1979 trip have been extremely helpful in the revision of my first draft.

In the course of writing I received help from various people. I would like to thank the librarians of the following institutions: The Barr Smith Library of the University of Adelaide, Adelaide; the Orientalia of the Australian National Library and the Oriental Library of the Australian National University, Canberra; the Oriental Library of the Sydney University, Sydney; the Oriental Library of the University of Melbourne, Melbourne; the library of the University of Malaya, Kuala Lumpur; the library of the National University of Singapore; the library of Nanyang University; the National Library of Singapore, Singapore; the Fung P'eng Shan Library of the University of Hong Kong, the library of the Chinese University of Hong Kong, Hong Kong; the Institute of Modern History, Academia Sinica and the Palace Museum Library, Taipei, Taiwan; and also the libraries in Britain, United States and Canada, mentioned earlier.

I would like to thank Professor Wang Gungwu of the Australian National University for his advice and the Foreword for the book. I am indebted to my colleagues, Dr. Robert Dare and Dr. Stephen Large, and my friend Dr. Michael Godley of Monash University, for their efforts in improving the manuscript. I am grateful to Mrs. Beverly Arnold of the History Department and Mrs. Jenifer Jefferies of the Centre for Asian Studies for typing the manuscript.

Finally, I wish to thank my wife, Kwee Ying, for her understanding and encouragement.

Department of History,   **Yen Ching-hwang**
University of Adelaide

Introduction

In the study of Ch'ing history, China's policy towards its overseas subjects has received little attention from scholars in either the Chinese speaking or the English speaking worlds. The neglect of this field had been mainly due to the belief that overseas Chinese history is peripheral to the study of modern Chinese history, and that overseas Chinese had little or no impact on the development of China. This is a false belief. Michael Godley's *The Mandarin-Capitalists from Nanyang* (Cambridge, 1981) and my early work *The Overseas Chinese and the 1911 Revolution* (Oxford, Kuala Lumpur, 1976) have demonstrated clearly that overseas Chinese had an important role to play in the late Ch'ing modernisation and the 1911 revolution.

The subject is also important for an understanding of the relationship between China and foreign Powers, for overseas Chinese became an important issue of China's diplomacy, and it occupied a significant portion of the time of Chinese diplomats; it affected China's attitude towards foreigners and the whole range of Sino-Western relations. In short, the protection of overseas Chinese which formed the main part of late Ch'ing policy towards its overseas subjects, was a major issue of China's foreign policy.

Since the middle of the nineteenth century, China had been the target of Western expansion and a market for industrial goods. Chinese people became consumers of opium and Western products, and were exploited by foreign imperialists. The fate of overseas Chinese was not much better; they were used as an important source of cheap labour and were discriminated against.

From one perspective, overseas Chinese were men and losers of the two worlds. They lived in one but carried the burden of the two. On the other hand, they were discriminated against by foreigners because they carried the culture and values of the old China; they were invariably regarded as culturally undesirable and racially inferior, and they bore the brunt of attacks on China. On the other hand, they lived and experienced something new and different from the old Confucian culture, and because they had received some foreign influence, they were regarded by their home government as potentially dangerous.

Of course, China's policy towards overseas Chinese was not influenced just by cultural bias; it was also influenced by history and its bad experience with some overseas Chinese during the Opium War period. Before the Opium War, the number of overseas Chinese was rather insignificant. They were ignored by the Ch'ing government as "deserters" or "political conspirators". The opening of the Treaty ports in the 1840s quickened the process of Chinese emigration, and exposed Chinese in the coastal provinces to the new economic opportunities overseas. The discoveries of gold fields in California and later in Australia, and the new economic developments in the European colonies in Southeast Asia, stirred the aspirations and imaginations of many poverty-stricken peasants. Many of them saw the opportunities overseas for earning a livelihood, and for a short-cut to personal economic advancement. They were prepared to risk imperial penalties to emigrate overseas.

The opening of the Treaty ports also exposed millions of poor peasants to foreign exploitaion. The shortage of labour in the new world as the result of the abolition of the slave trade in the 1830s made China an alternative source of cheap labour. Treaty ports together with Macao and Hong Kong became a hotbed for the activities of labour contractors and their lackeys. Thousands upon thousands of poor peasants who were popularly known in the West as "coolies" were induced or sold to the new world.

The increase in the number of overseas Chinese, either through contract labour or free emigration, created some problems for the Ch'ing government. Many were ill-treated or killed in foreign lands, and in the 1870s their treatment became an international scandal. The Ch'ing government might not have much feeling for the coolies; nevertheless, the scandals injured its pride and undermined its international status. This new reality compelled the Ch'ing government to take some protective measures to protect overseas Chinese.

Much of this book is concerned with the ways in which the Ch'ing government dealt with its overseas subjects and these are the best indicators of the attitude and policy of the Ch'ing government. This study begins with a broad survey of China's overseas Chinese policy prior to 1850. Chapter 1 examines the formation of the prohibition and non-protection policy towards overseas Chinese dur-

ing the Sung, Yuan, Ming and early Ch'ing period, and suggests
that Ch'ing non-protection policy grew out of the past, particularly
the policy of the Ming.

Chapters 2 and 3 illustrate the process of change of the Ch'ing
government's attitude in the second half of the nineteeth century.
The exodus of hundreds and thousands of Chinese coolies, the
ordeal of the coolies during voyages abroad and their miseries in
foreign lands forced the Ch'ing government to look more closely at
problems related to the protection of its subjects overseas. No matter how the government viewed the issue, the humiliation suffered
by the coolies shattered the image of China as a whole. In dealing
with the problems of the coolies, the government was compelled to
re-examine its attitude towards emigration and overseas Chinese.
This led it to question some of the basic assumptions on which its
traditional policies were based, and to change its hostile attitude
towards overseas Chinese.

At the time when the Ch'ing government changed its hostile attitude towards emigration and overseas Chinese, China came out of
its diplomatic shell and joined the family of nations in the 1870s.
The sending of diplomatic representatives facilitated the application of the new attitude, and also had enormous impact on the
ultimate change of the policy in 1893. Following the stationing of
Chinese diplomats in foreign capitals, Chinese consulates were
established in many countries where overseas Chinese sojourned.
For the first time, the Ch'ing government had official contacts with
its overseas subjects. Chinese consulates enabled the government to
collect reliable information about overseas Chinese, including their
wealth, hopes and aspirations. At the same time, the consuls could
act to protect overseas Chinese. The details of this diplomatic expansion in overseas Chinese communities are fully discussed in
Chapter 4.

The years between 1873 and 1893 were a transitional period from
the change of the old to the new policy. On the one hand, the new
commitment of protecting overseas Chinese led Chinese diplomats
to fight injustices suffered by overseas Chinese in foreign lands;
but, on the other, the government in Peking lacked sustained enthusiasm and efforts to support these fights. The protection of the
Chinese in the United States is the best example illustrating the problems of protecting overseas Chinese during this period. Chapter5
considers this dilemma.

Although the conditions for a change of policy were ripe in the

1880s, it was not until 1893 when Hsueh Fu-ch'eng memorialised the Court that the old emigration law was officially abolished. Hsueh, the Chinese Minister in London, and Huang Tsun-hsien, the Chinese Consul-General for the Straits Settlements, belonged to the group of reformer-diplomats who advocated institutional reform and modernisation along Western lines. They saw the wealth and expertise of overseas Chinese as useful assets in China's economic modernisation. Their joint effort officially changed the policies on emigration and overseas Chinese. An examination of the roles of Hsueh and Huang in changing the policy is found in Chapter 6. This chapter also examines the unfolding of the new policy in China after 1893 and argues that on balance the new policy did not work well. The provincial officials in China paid only lip service to the new policy and their prejudices against the returned overseas Chinese had never substantially changed. Worst of all, the officials together with local bullies still regarded the returned subjects as a source of graft, and attempted to squeeze money out of their victims. This prevented a large number of overseas Chinese merchants from returning or investing in China. This chapter suggests that the well-entrenched, corrupt practices and deeply-rooted prejudices of the Chinese officials were the main causes for the failure of the implementation of the new policy in China.

The new policy also became a crucial test for the protection of overseas Chinese abroad. Chapter 7 shows that the Tsungli Yamen and later the Wai Wu Pu had demonstrated a fresh attitude and taken positive steps to co-ordinate an active protection policy of the overseas Chinese. Many Chinese diplomats gave considerable attention to this task, particularly to the Chinese in the United States where the protection was especially needed. Although the result was not good, the efforts of several diplomats such as Wu T'ing-fang and Liang Ch'eng, were commendable. Of course, the failure of this new protection policy abroad cannot be simply attributed to the weakness of the Ch'ing government, policies of various imperialist Powers were also to be blamed.

1
Legacy of the Past

THE POLICIES OF THE SUNG AND YUAN DYNASTIES

The Policies of Northern and Southern Sung Dynasties

There was little thought given to overseas Chinese before the Sung Dynasty. Although China's international trade had been substantially developed since the seventh century,[1] and while Chinese from Fukien and Kwangtung provinces had increasingly settled in Formosa and the neighbouring P'eng-hu islands (Pescadores),[2] no policy was formed to deal with them. This was probably due to the fact that there was an insignificant number of overseas subjects, though it could have been that the matter was considered too trivial to bother the Court. But the founding of the Sung Dynasty in 960 witnessed an expansion of overseas contacts, particularly with countries in Southeast Asia. The restoration of peace in South China and the new dynasty's southward military conquest provided good conditions for further development in trade.[3] Indeed some of the traders stayed abroad for several years in order to establish commercial footholds in coastal Southeast Asia. Thus these sojourners are generally considered the first generation of the overseas Chinese in the region, and their settlements later formed the centres of overseas Chinese communities.

China's interest in Southeast Asia continued to grow when, after the northern part of China was lost to Chin Tartars, the government was forced to shift its seat to Lin An (modern Hangchow) in the southeast of China. The loss of vast territory meant a great

---

[1] A good study of China's early trade in the South China Sea is by Wang Gungwu, "The Nanhai Trade: A Study of the Early History of Chinese Trade in the South China Sea", in *Journal of Malayan Branch of the Royal Asiatic Society*, vol. 31, pt. 2 (June, 1958), pp. 1–135 (independent issue).

[2] See Ta Chen, *Chinese Migrations, With Special Reference to Labor Conditions* (Taipei, 1967, reprint edition), p. 4.

[3] Eberhard, W., *A History of China* (London, 1960), pp. 208–209.

1

reduction in revenue, and this compelled the government to look to overseas trade as compensation. Commerce became the lifeline of the empire and the capital the entrepôt. By the end of the dynasty it was claimed that in the main street of the capital city "there is not a single person who is not in trade. . . ."[4]

Of course government policy was not alone responsible for the development of international trade during the Southern Sung period; there were other factors helping to bring about this change. The development of maritime technology was particularly important. Chinese and Arab observers agreed that Chinese ships were the largest in the South China Sea and the Indian Ocean. The Chinese ships, built mostly in Ch'uan-chou and Canton had as many as 1,000 crew members.[5] Size alone testified to the advances in Chinese shipbuilding. Large vessels also gave a greater sense of personal and financial security as did the introduction of the compass — a Chinese invention — in 1119.[6]

The popularity of T'ien-hui,[7] a seafaring goddess, was another factor in helping to develop China's overseas trade. Although technological advances played an obvious part, there was no guarantee of absolute safety in the voyage. A goddess who was considered to be the protector of all seafaring people and was believed to have possessed supernatural power in rescuing victims helped to remove the fear of overseas trips, and encouraged more people to engage in lucrative overseas trade. The conferring of titles on the goddess by the Sung court testified to the popular belief that she was omnipotent.[8]

---

[4]Wu Tzu-mu, *Meng-liang lu*, p. 239, quoted in Colin Jeffcott, "Government and the Distribution System in Sung Cities", in *Papers on Far Eastern History*, no. 2 (Sept., 1970), p. 119.

[5]See Yule, *Cathay and the Way Thither*, vol. 4, pp. 25-26, Chou Chu-fei, *Ling-wai tai-ta*, vol. 6; Chen Kao-hua & Wu Tai, *Sung Yuan shih-ch'i te hai-wai mo-i* (China's Overseas Trade during the Sung and Yuan Periods) (T'ientsin, 1981), pp. 26-27.

[6]It was first recorded in Chu Huo, *P'ing-chou ko-t'an*, in the first year of the Hsuan-ho reign of the Hui Tsung emperor of the Northern Sung Dynasty. See Chu Huo, *P'ing-chou ko-t'an*, (Shang Wu, Shanghai, 1941), p. 18.

[7]T'ien Hui was also known as T'ien H'ou, T'ien H'ou Sheng Mu and Ma Tsu. She was the most popular goddess worshipped by the Chinese in Fukien, Kwangtung, Chekiang and Taiwan. For the worship of T'ien Hui and the spread of overseas Chinese in Southeast Asia, see Han Huai-chun, "T'ien H'ou Sheng Mu yu hua-chiao te nan-chin", in *Nan-yang hsueh-pao* (Journal of South Seas Society), vol. 2, no. 2, pp. 51-73.

[8]In 1156, the goddess was first bestowed with the title of "Ling-hui fu-jen"; in

An important development in China's overseas trade during the Northern and Southern Sung periods was the consolidation of a system known as *Shih-p'o-ssu* (Inspectorate of Commerce). First founded in the T'ang Dynasty on an experimental basis it had gradually degenerated into a coveted source of graft and exaction.[9] Its revival and reorganisation on a permanent basis by the Sung government demonstrated the importance of maritime commerce. Separate inspectorates were established at four important coastal ports — Canton, Ch'uan-chou, Ningpo and Hangchow — and were staffed by full-time officials.[10] Institutionalisation paved the way for a policy towards overseas Chinese. Never before had Chinese officials had the opportunity to have direct contacts with both Chinese and foreign traders who could provide reliable information about conditions abroad. The acquisition of such knowledge by officials is best illustrated by the book *Chu Fan Chih* (Records of Various Foreign Nations) compiled by an Inspector of Foreign Trade at Ch'uan-chou named Chao Ju-kua in 1225.[11] Chao who kept in close touch with merchants from India, Persia, Syria and other Arab countries which traded at many ports in the Persian Gulf and Southeast Asia before coming to China, obtained much valuable data about foreign lands.[12] His reports thus helped the

---

1158, "Chao-ying" and "Ch'ung-fu" titles were added to her honour. In 1190, she was upgraded to "Hui-ling t'ien-hui". See Ting po-kuei, "Ken-shan shun-chi sheng-hui miao chi", in *Che-chiang t'ung-chih*, vol. 271.

[9]During the T'ang period, some of the inspectors of foreign trade were eunuchs who, traditionally, had a reputation for corruption. See *Hsin T'ang Shu* (New T'ang History), vol. 126, "Biography of Lu Huai-shen [Huan]".

[10]For details of the Inspectorate of Foreign Trade during the Sung period, see Fujita Toyohachi entitled "Sung-tai shih-p'o ssu chi shih-p'o t'iao li", in Fujita Toyohachi, *Chung-kuo nan-hai ku-tai chiao-t'ung ts'ung-k'ao* (Studies on Ancient Chinese Relations with the Nan-hai) (Shanghai, 1936) (Chinese translation by Ho Chien-min), pp. 239–341.

[11]*Chu Fan Chih* was one of the first few Chinese records about countries in Southeast Asia and those in coastal areas of the Indian Ocean. There are many editions with slight variations. The best is the one revised and annotated by Feng Ch'eng-chun, a noted Chinese scholar, published in Shanghai in 1930. The book was translated into English by F. Hirth and W.W. Rockhill, and published in 1911. See F. Hirth & W.W. Rockhill (translated and edited). *Chau Ju-Kua: His Work on the Chinese and Arab Trade in the Twelfth and Thirteenth Centuries, Entitled Chu-fan-chi* (Oriental Press, Amsterdam, 1966).

[12]See Chao Ju-kua, annotated by Feng Ch'eng-chun, *Chu Fan Chih chiao-chu* (Records of Various Foreign Nations with Annotations) (Peking, 1956), pp. 1–90.

Sung government formulate a policy in dealing with overseas trade as well as overseas Chinese.

Under the *Shih-p'o-ssu* system, the Inspectors were charged with responsibility for collecting dues, supervising foreign merchants who temporarily resided in China,[13] and controlling Chinese traders involved in overseas trade. Permits known as "kung-chien"[14] were issued to prospective merchants who had to comply with established rules; they were forbidden to trade with certain countries hostile to China; they were prohibited from exporting arms and Chinese currency; and they were required to return to their port of departure. Those who failed to comply or left without permits were liable to punishment and the confiscation of their goods. This system was first introduced in 989 during the reign of Emperor T'ai Tsung of the Northern Sung Dynasty,[15] and was maintained with some alterations throughout the period of Northern and Southern Sung Dynasties.

This system, particularly under the Southern Sung, was designed mainly for national security. All the ships had to declare their destinations and the nature of their cargo before permits were granted. As the Southern Sung government depended on the navy for her defence against the Chin invaders (Jurchen), any shipment of weapons and war materials to her enemy would threaten her security. It was in this context that a restrictive policy was developed. However, the permit system contained no specification of the length of time allowable overseas, nor was there any provision prohibiting Chinese traders from staying overseas temporarily.

The absence of prohibitive provisions was the result of expediency rather than the inability of the government to control the movements of the Chinese traders. As overseas trade grew increasingly important in terms of revenue, any stringent measure against the movement of the traders would harm the public purse. As a result, some Chinese traders took the opportunity to establish com-

---

[13]For the functions of the Shih-p'o-ssu system, see Sun Pao, *T'ang Sung Yuan hai-shang shang-yueh cheng-ts'e* (Overseas Commercial Policy of the T'ang, Sung and Yuan Dynasties) (Taipei, 1969), pp. 25–56.

[14]Kung-chien was also known as "kung-p'in" or "kung-chi".

[15]A decree was issued in that year to the effect that merchants who wished to trade overseas had to report to the Inspector of Foreign Trade in Chekiang, and to acquire permits before their departure, violators would punished with their goods confiscated. See *Sung Hui Yao*, chih-kuan, vol. 44, under the fifth moon of the second year of tuan-kung.

mercial footholds in Southeast Asia and Japan. A few even settled permanently overseas, mixed with natives but retained Chinese names and culture.[16] They monopolised certain trade between China and foreign countries, gained the trust of the native rulers, and became leaders of early Sino-foreign trade. Mao Hsu of Java, Chu Jen-ch'ung, Chou Wen-teh, Chou Wen-i, Ch'en Wen-yu, Sun Chung and Li Ch'ung of Japan were among the best known overseas Chinese trade leaders of the time.[17]

Yüan Policy

The number of the overseas Chinese, particularly in Southeast Asia, increased substantially during the Y ›uan period (1280–1368). This was confirmed by two Chinese travellers, Chou Ta-kuan and Wang Ta-yuan. Chou was a member of the Chinese mission sent by the Yuan Court to demand homage from the King of Cambodia (Chen-la). In his vivid description of the kingdom he mentioned the overseas Chinese. Many of them married local women, and were held in great respect.[18] Wang Ta-yuan who had visited several ports in Southeast Asia in the 1330s, reported the activities of Chinese traders in his famous book *Tao-i chih-lueh* (a summary of the records regarding the barbarians of the islands).[19] They had been active in the trade between China and Southeast Asian countries; they had established commercial outposts in the region, and had

---

[16]Chao Ju-kua recorded that when Chinese were killed by natives of Chan Ch'eng (Champa), the murderers were to be apprehended and beheaded; Chao Ju-kua also mentioned that Chinese script was used by the king of San-fu-ch'i (Srivijaya) for correspondence with China. These facts point to the existence of overseas Chinese who mixed with natives and retained the Chinese language and culture. See Chao Ju-kua, annotated by Feng Ch'eng-chun, *Chu Fan Chih chiao-chu* (Records of Various Foreign Nations with Annotations) (Shanghai, 1930), reprint, 1956, pp. 3, 12.

[17]See *Sung Shih* (A History of Sung Dynasty), vol. 489, "Che-p'o kuo chuan" (Biography of Java); see also Hua Ch'iao Chih pien-ch'uan wei-yuan-hui (ed.), *Hua Ch'iao Chih Tsung Chih* (Taipei, 1956), pp. 26, 34.

[18]See Chou Ta-kuan, *Chen-la feng-t'u chi* The Topography of Cambodia) (annotated by P. Pelliot) in Po-hsi-ho (P. Pelliot) *et al.*, translated by Feng Ch'eng-chun, *Shih-ti ts'ung-k'ao* (Research and Notes on History and Geography) (Shang Wu, Taipei, 1962), pp. 90–91, 101.

[19]Wang Ta-yuan was a native of Nanchang of the Kiangsi province. In 1330 and 1337, he visited Southeast Asia on board Chinese merchant ships which called at many ports in the region. The result of his visits was the publication of his famous book *Tao-I chih-lueh* in 1349. See Wang Ta-yuan, annotated by Su chi-ch'in, *Tao-i chih-lueh chiao shih* (Chung Hua, Peking, 1981), "Introduction", pp. 9–11.

mixed with the natives.[20] The impression had been confirmed later by Ma Huan who accompanied Admiral Cheng Ho to Southeast Asia in 1413. He claimed that there was a large Chinese village near Tu-pan on the island of Java comprising more than a thousand families. The village headman was from Kwangtung and the majority of the population were from the same province or Southern Fukien (the districts of Chang-chou and Ch'uan-chou).[21] Traditionally, Chinese favoured the large family system, and a family commonly consisted of eight or more people. If we take an average figure of eight, the Chinese village in Java alone probably had 8,000 to 10,000 people.

The substantial increase of the overseas Chinese population in Southeast Asia was of course partly the result of the continuing development of trade between China and the region; more and more Chinese traders remained overseas because of their business connections. But the most important factor for the influx was a political one. The fall of the Southern Sung Dynasty saw the flight of Chinese loyalists who refused to surrender to the Mongols. They took their families and relatives to mainland Southeast Asia, particularly to Annam and Champa.[22] Some of them even attempted to raise a local army to recapture the lost territories in China.[23] Their unsuccessful attempts to recover their lost motherland compelled them to live permanently overseas. In a parallel development the conquering Mongols inflicted great harm on the southern Chinese who had resisted them tenaciously. Raping, pillaging and burning were frequent, and tens of thousands of the southern Chinese were massacred. Once victorious the Mongol government adopted a high-handed policy towards the Chinese in Fukien and Kwangtung. They were forced to pay heavy taxes and to serve hard labour.[24] In Fukien, a "T'uan-she" system (Community Security)

---

[20]*Ibid.*, pp. 213–14, 227.

[21]See Ma Huan, annotated by Feng Ch'eng-chun, *Ying-yai shen-lan chiao-chu* (Chung Hua, Peking, 1955), pp. 8–9.

[22]See Ch'en Chu-t'ung, "Yuan-tai chung-hua min-tsu hai-wai fa-chan k'ao" (Notes on Overseas Expansion of the Chinese during the Yuan Dynasty), pt. 2, in *Chih-nan hsueh-pao* (Journal of Chih-nan University) (Shanghai, 1937), vol. 2, no. 2, pp. 123–24.

[23]Famous among them was Shen Ching-chih who fled to Champa and requested the king of Champa to help him restore the fallen nation, but his request was kindly rejected. Shen settled and died there. *Ibid.*

[24]See Ch'en Chu-t'ung, "Yuan-tai chung-hua min-tsu hai-wai fa-chan k'ao", pt. 1, in *Chih-nan hsueh-pao*, vol. 2, no. 1, pp. 137–39.

was established with the aim of suppressing potential rural resistance. Village defense buildings were razed to the ground, bridges were destroyed, and graveyards were dug up.[25] One result of this revenge was the exodus of a large number of the Fukienese and Kwangtung residents to Southeast Asia. Many formed independent Chinese settlements which retained their Chinese culture and identities.[26]

The substantial increase of anti-Mongol elements in the overseas Chinese communities in Southeast Asia did not attract the attention of the Yuan Court, presumably because the aggregate number was still small, and because the overseas communities did not pose any direct threat to the national security of the new dynasty. As a result, there was no specific Yuan policy dealing with the overseas Chinese. Like the Sung Dynasty the successor encouraged foreign trade and reaped enormous benefits from it. The new government restored the operation of the Shih-p'o-ssu system soon after its conquest of the South, and added another three new inspectorates in Ch'ing-yuan, Shanghai, and Kan-p'u.[27] The Yuan Dynasty also adopted the "Permit system" (kung-yen or kung-p'in)[28] and improved it. Under this system, leaders of ships were required to apply for permits from the Inspectors, and five guarantors were needed. Applicants now had to state the nature and destination of their trade, to list the names of the crew and to provide other detailed information about the ship and its provisions. Ships were prohibited from bringing out contraband or bringing back criminals or spies. Those who failed to comply would be punished together with their guarantors.[29] This new permit system was of course more effective in the control of Chinese overseas traders. The collective security (the use of guarantors) deterred any undesirable behaviour on the part of the traders. The prohibition of bringing back criminals or spies was probably intended to stop any subversive activities by the overseas Chinese who were hostile to the new regime.

---

[25]*Ibid.*, p. 139.

[26]See Ch'en Chu-t'ung, *op. cit.*, pt. 2, in *Chin-nan hsueh-pao*, vol. 2, no. 2, pp. 137–39.

[27]See *Yüan Shih* (History of Yuan Dynasty), vol. 94, "Shih ho chih" item shih-po.

[28]Kung-yen was the permit issued to larger ships, while Kung-p'in was issued to smaller ships.

[29]See *Sung Hui Yao*, chih-kuan, vol. 44; see also Sun Pao, *T'ang Sung Yuan hai-shang shang-yeh cheng-ts'e*, p. 28.

THE POLICY OF THE MING DYNASTY

The Seafaring Prohibition of the Early Ming Period

The founding of the Ming Dynasty in 1368 saw a dramatic change in China's policy towards foreign trade, and there emerged a new policy dealing with overseas Chinese. The founder of the new dynasty, Chu Yuan-chang, also known as the Hung-wu Emperor, had doubts about the benefits of the Mongol-sponsored international trade. The southeast coast of China where overseas trade converged was one of the last parts added to the empire. It was controlled by Chang Shih-ch'eng and Fang Kuo-chen, two contenders for the throne. Both were known to have connections with pirates, and their followers still commanded influence in the coastal regions after they were defeated.[30] Another obvious threat to the new dynasty was Japanese pirates who were known as "Wo-k'ou" (dwarf pirates). They were active along the coast line of Fukien and Kwangtung, plundering and burning to their hearts' content.[31] What was most threatening was the possibility of cooperation between these two groups; their activities would seriously undermine the foundation of the new empire if left uncurbed. Thus the security of the new dynasty seemed to outweigh any economic benefit from overseas trade. The Hung-wu Emperor did not hesitate to end the private foreign trade which he suspected was, in any case, connected with the rebels and pirates.

The first blanket prohibition was decreed in 1371, less than four years after the founding of the new dynasty. It banned all coastal subjects from going overseas privately.[32] Brief but firm, the decree reflected the fact that the Emperor was determined to do something about rebels and pirates but did not know how. Nonetheless, the prohibition was reaffirmed and amplified in 1381 and 1397:

1. Those who carry contraband (including cattle, military materials, iron, copper coins, silk and cotton goods) overseas are liable to punishment of 100 heavy blows, their goods to be

---

[30]For the connections between Chang Shih-ch'eng, Fang Kuo-chen, and the coastal pirates, see *Ming Shih* (History of Ming Dynasty), vol. 123, biographies of Chang Shih-ch'eng and Fang Kuo-chen; *Ming-shih chi-shih pen-mo*, vol. 55.

[31]For details of the threat of Japanese pirates during early Ming period, see Ch'en Wen-shih, *Ming hung-wu chia-ching chien te hai-chin cheng-ts'e* (The Sea-Faring Prohibition Policy in the Early Ming Dynasty) (Taipei, 1966), chapter 1, section 2, pp. 6–11.

[32]See *Ming Tai-tsu shih-lu*, vol. 70.

confiscated; those who sell human beings and arms overseas are to be hung; those who leak out military secrets are to be beheaded.

2. Any gentry members, military personnel and ordinary subjects who built two-masted ships without permits, carry contraband overseas, trade with foreign countries, and collaborate with pirates, are to be treated as rebels and beheaded. Their heads are to be hung up for display, and members of their families are to be sent off to the frontier for hard labour. Those who build two-masted ships illegally and sell the ships to foreigners are to be punished as those who have carried arms overseas. The leader is to be beheaded, and the rest are to be sent off to the frontier for hard labour. Those who hire out their ships for travel overseas and share the illicit foreign goods, and those who collaborate with people going overseas and buy the illicit foreign goods, are liable to be sent off to the frontier for hard labour.

3. Those who gang together to build ships illegally and carry silk goods overseas, and those who trade with Japan, are liable to the following punishments: the leader is to be chained and sent to the malaria-infested region for hard labour permanently; the followers are to be chained and sent to the frontier for hard labour.

4. Any military personnel and ordinary subject of the coastal region who trade privately with Japan and sell contraband to the Japanese king or his subordinates, are to be punished as rebels. The leaders are to be executed with their heads hung up for display, the followers are to be sent off to the malaria-infested area for hard labour.[33]

These rules were designed primarily to cut off military supply to the Japanese pirates and end the trade with Japan. As negotiations with Japan over the piracy broke down in 1381, the Emperor Hung-wu saw the need of tightening the seafaring prohibition in order to solve the knotty problem of Japanese piracy. Moreover, the reinforcement of the prohibition would also cut off the economic support from the coastal anti-dynastic rebels.

[33]See *Ta Ming Li* (The Statute of the Ming Dynasty), vol. 15, "Ping Li" 3, vol. 8 "Hu Li" 5; *Ta Ming Hui Tien*, vol. 167 "Kuan Li"; *Huang Ming Shih Fa Lu*, vol. 75; see also Ch'en Wen-shih, *op. cit.*, pp. 35-37.

Promulgation of these laws did not automatically mean the success of the prohibition policy. Effective implementation still depended on how well the government could obtain the cooperation of its officials and people. A positive measure was needed to keep the officials informed. This led to the adoption of the "Shou Kao" system under which neighbours and villagers were required to report illegal traders to the local yamen. Those who reported the crime were rewarded with a portion of the forfeited goods.[34] Although the "Shou Kao" system helped apprehend offenders, it did not completely end the illicit trade. A more effective means was to eliminate its markets in China. Thus a decree was issued in 1394 (the twenty-seventh year of Hung-wu) to ban the circulation of foreign goods among the populace.[35]

The prohibition of private trading overseas was also a means of achieving a state monopoly of foreign goods. A "Kung-p'o" (Tribute-bearing) system was established. Under this system, foreign countries that wished to trade with China had to go through political channels, i.e. to establish political relations with China before they were allowed to trade. They would have to submit themselves as junior members to China, the head of the family of nations in East Asia. Their kings would accept China's investitures, and send tributes to China at fixed periods. The tributary system however, between China and Southeast Asian states of course began earlier than the Ming Dynasty. In the pre-Ming period, tribute bearers were allowed private commercial activities while they were in China. But in the Hung-wu reign of the Ming Dynasty, private transactions by the tribute bearers were strictly prohibited, and the goods had to be sold through official channels.[36]

The impact of the introduction of the seafaring prohibition policy during the Hung-wu reign was profound and lasting. It initiated a stringent policy under which the Chinese of the coastal areas and the overseas Chinese suffered for several centuries; it stifled Chinese private commercial activities and the growth of commercial capitalism.

---

[34]*Ibid.*; see also Chang Wei-hua, *Ming-tai hai-wai mao-i chien-lun* (An Introduction to the Study of Overseas Trade of the Ming Dynasty) (Shanghai, 1955), p. 17.

[35]See *T'ai-tsu hung-wu shih-lu*, vol. 231, 1st moon of 27th year of the Hung-wu reign.

[36]For details of the "Kung-p'o" system during the early Ming period, see Ch'en Wen-Shih, *Ming hung-wu chia-ching chien te hai-chin cheng-ts'e*, chapter 2, pp. 41–76.

The prohibition policy did not end with the death of the Hung-wu Emperor. Ironically the Yung-lo Emperor who emerged to become a strong, independent-minded and a far-sighted ruler, continued this policy.[37] His reign was a great age for China's maritime activities. The seven visits of Admiral Cheng Ho (from 1405 to 1433) with the largest fleets ever despatched overseas, were taken as a landmark in the expansion of China's sea power.[38] The period also saw a vigorous growth in China's foreign trade; many foreign traders flocked to China bringing a great variety of goods, and some of the ports in southeastern China became busy entrepôts of East-West trade.

Yet Chinese private traders played little or no part in this flourishing activity for they were still excluded by law from participating in foreign trade. Those who dared to take risks were punished, and further restrictions were imposed on them. In 1404, the second year after ascending the throne, the Yung-lo Emperor decreed that all private ships in the coastal regions had to flatten their bows in an attempt to prevent illegal shipping activities in the Fukien province.[39]

This seemingly contradictory imperial policy was intended to consolidate the state monopoly of foreign trade at the expense of private traders. As the economy of the new dynasty began to show signs of prosperity after three and a half decades of political stability, the demand for foreign luxury goods by the members of the ruling class increased enormously. The existing "Tribute-bearing" system could not meet the increasing demand. At the same time, the recovering economy gave rise to a surplus of agricultural and handicraft products. Foreign markets needed to be expanded to maintain the luxurious way of life of the ruling class.

---

[37]Yung-lo Emperor usurped the throne from his nephew, Chien-wen Emperor, to become the third monarch of the Ming Dynasty. He ruled from 1403 to 1424.

[38]For an excellent interpretation of the ideas and background leading to the Cheng Ho expeditions, see Wang Gungwu, "Early Ming Relations with Southeast Asia — A Background Essay", in J.K. Fairbank (ed.), *The Chinese World Order: Traditional China's Foreign Relations* (Cambridge, Mass., 1968), pp. 34–62; Wang Gungwu, "China and Southeast Asia 1402–1424", in J. Chen & N. Tarling (eds.), *Social History of China and Southeast Asia* (Cambridge, 1970), pp. 375–401; see also Wang Gungwu, *Community and Nation: Essays on Southeast Asia and the Chinese* (Heinemann, Sydney 1981), pp. 28–80.

[39]See *Ming T'ai-tsung shih-lu*, vol. 27, the 2nd moon of 2nd year of the Yung-lo reign.

Economic considerations therefore seem to have been the prime mover behind the Yung-lo Emperor's drive for the expansion of overseas trade. With a greater incentive, a new state monopoly was established. The old "Tribute-bearing" system was strengthened and expanded, the quantity of the "tributes" increased, restrictions were reduced, and foreign private traders were encouraged to carry goods to China. The government achieved a monopoly in buying, distributing and consuming most of the imported goods. It also took the initiative in developing foreign markets for Chinese goods. Agents were sent overseas to purchase foreign goods directly. Even before the departure of Admiral Cheng Ho's fleet, Chinese missions specially sent by the Yung-lo Emperor had already toured several countries of Southeast Asia carrying news of the new order as well as collecting market information.[40]

Cheng Ho's seven voyages to Southeast Asia and into the Indian Ocean had a profound impact on China's commercial expansion, and as attempts to carry out the new state monopoly policy they were unprecedented. The fleet carried large quantities of Chinese products such as silk, porcelain and camphor in exchange for products such as jade, elephant trunk, rhinoceros horn, spices and precious stones.[41] Because these ships were laden with all kinds of treasure, they were generally known as "Treasure ships" (Pao Ch'uan).[42] The direct exchange of Chinese products for foreign goods eliminated the profit of the middlemen, and further ensured the enormous profit for the Ming government.

Relaxation of the Seafaring Prohibition Policy during the Late Ming Period

The seafaring prohibition policy was generally maintained after the death of the Emperor Yung-lo in 1424.[43] But this policy was gradually relaxed in the last seventy or eighty years of the Ming rule. Private traders were allowed to go overseas under the govern-

---

[40]See *Ming T'ai-tsung shih-lu*, vol. 12, pt. 1; vols. 17, 22, 23, 24, 34 and 38.

[41]See *Ming Shih* (History of the Ming Dynasty), vol. 304, "Cheng Ho chuan" (Biography of Cheng Ho); Ma Huan, annotated by Feng Ch'eng-chun, *Ying-yai sheng-lan chiao-chu*, pp. 1–72; Fei Hsin, annotated by Feng Ch'eng-chun, *Hsing-cha sheng-lan chiao-chu*, pp. 1–43; Hsu Yu-hu, *Cheng Ho p'ing-chuan* (A Critical Biography of Cheng Ho) (Taipei).

[42]For a detailed study of the "Treasure ship", see Pao Tsun-p'eng, *Cheng Ho hsia hsi-yang chih pao-ch'uan k'ao* (On the Ships of Cheng Ho) (Taipei, 1963).

[43]See Chang Wei-hua, *Ming-tai hai-wai mao-i chien-lun*, pp. 34–46.

ment's supervision. The government established a "yin-p'iao" system similar to the "kung-chien" or "kung-yen" procedures adopted during the Sung and Yüan Dynasties. Under this system, intending traders were required to obtain "yin-p'iao" from the government. Personal details and details of the shipments were to be recorded.[44] Both domestic and external forces appear to have combined to bring about this change. Domestically, the government's monopolistic land policy forced many investors to shift their capital from land to commerce and handicraft industry.[45] The result of this was the growing surplus of consumer and luxury products. Yet the restricted domestic markets could not absorb this increasing surplus, and the stimulus from foreign markets was needed to push the economic development a step further. The wealthy gentry who invested their capital in commerce and the handicraft industry tended to come from the coastal provinces of southeast China where economic production and transport converged.

These gentry-merchants were more likely to be involved in the illicit foreign trade which became so profitable under the prohibitive edicts. The growth of commerce and the handicraft industry immensely increased the power of the gentry-merchants. On the one hand, they used their wealth to influence provincial officials through whom they made their demand for the removal of the ban. The lifting of the prohibition in 1567 (the first year of the Lung-ch'ing Emperor) came as a result of the efforts of the Governor of the Fukien province, T'u Che-min, and can be taken as an indication of the influence of the gentry-merchants.[46] On the other hand, they organised large scale illicit trade in defiance of the law. They bribed local officials to avoid being caught, and established firm relationships with the officials through social contacts. With the connivance of these local officials, they made the enforcement of the prohibition law impossible, and effectively undermined the sea-faring restriction policy.[47]

The external force that contributed to the change of China's

---

[44]*Ibid.*, p. 50.

[45]*Ibid.*, chapter 2, pp. 10–12.

[46]See Chang Hsieh, *Tung-hsi yang-k'ao* (Taipei, 1962, Reprint), vol. 7, "hsiang-hsui k'ao".

[47]For a discussion of the role of gentry-merchants in undermining the traditional seafaring prohibition, see Ng Chin-keong, "Gentry-Merchants and Peasant-Peddlers — The Response of the South Fukienese to the Offshore Trading Opportunities 1522–1566", in *Nanyang University Journal*, vol. VII (1973), pp. 161–75.

traditional seafaring policy came from the impact of the West. The Portuguese led the way for the expansion of European power in Asia. In 1488, Bartolomeu Dias rounded the Cape of Good Hope. Ten years later, another Portuguese, Vasco da Gama, reached the southwest coast of India, the first stop on mainland Asia. The Portuguese soon defeated the Arab fleets, and secured a certain degree of control over the Arabian sea. In 1510, they secured a base on the small island of Goa on the west coast of India. The following year, under the command of the able Alfonso de Albuquerque, they conquered the strategic port of Malacca on the west coast of Malay Peninsula. The power of the Portuguese spread rapidly in Southeast and East Asia. They proceeded to control the Moluccas Islands which were prized for their spices, and the Portuguese arrived in China in 1514 with the hope of tapping the rich resources of the Chinese tea and silk trade. By 1557, the Portuguese had firmly established themselves in the China trade, and had secured Macao on the southeast coast of China as the centre of their operations.

Following in the footsteps of the Portuguese to Asia came the Dutch and British. They were latecomers on the scene, but their power spread more rapidly than the Portuguese, partly because they possessed stronger fleets and were more efficiently organised. The British East India Company and the Dutch East India Company channelled huge amounts of capital into trading and military operations in Asia, and wrested strategic ports and colonies from the Portuguese. In the last forty years of the Ming Dynasty (1604–1644), the British firmly established themselves in India, while the Dutch controlled many parts of the islands of the East Indian Archipelago. Moreover, the Dutch had occupied the P'eng-hu Islands (Pescadores Islands) in the Taiwan Straits and the southern part of Taiwan Island, and were developing these places as their centres of trade with China and Japan.[48]

There were two implications of this European expansion in Asia. Firstly, the presence of the European Powers broke the monopoly of Asian trade hitherto enjoyed by the Moslem traders from Persia, India and Southeast Asia. The end of this monopoly pushed up the price of China's products in international market. This induced more private Chinese traders to seek a share in such a lucrative business. At the same time, the existence of a Portuguese trade centre at Macao and the Dutch centre at Taiwan induced many Chinese

---

[48]See Chang Wei-hua, *op. cit.*, pp. 47–49.

to become involved in foreign trade. This contributed directly to the breakdown of the seafaring prohibition. Secondly, the control of the East-West trade routes and some Southeast Asian countries by the European powers undermined China's monopoly system, "the Kung P'o". China was no longer able to obtain foreign luxury goods directly from southeast countries at reasonable prices. The shortage of supply of luxury goods affected the lifestyle of members of the Chinese upper class. Lifting the seafaring prohibition would encourage private trade as a source of foreign luxury goods at a reasonable cost.

The lifting of the seafaring ban contributed, to a certain extent, to the prosperity of coastal China during the late Ming period.

Formation of Image of the Overseas Chinese during the Ming Period

Who constituted the majority of the overseas Chinese during the Ming period? What was their relationship with their home government? How was their negative image formed during this period? These are the questions to be explored in the following pages. The first group of the overseas Chinese seems to have consisted mainly of the descendants of the Chinese fugitives who escaped the scourge of the Mongols after the fall of the Southern Sung Dynasty. There is no evidence to suggest that they returned to China after the Mongols were driven out of their homeland. They survived and prospered overseas and developed their own identities while preserving many elements of Chinese culture. Under the strict seafaring prohibition policy, their contacts with China must have been minimal. They were mentioned sometimes in the official and semi-official records as "T'ao-min" (fugitives).[49] But they attracted little or no attention from the Ming government, because they posed no threat to China and were numerically insignificant. The term "fugitive" was meant not only that they had deserted the Celestial empire, but also that they had run away from Chinese civilisation. It was in this context that the image of the overseas Chinese as "deserters" emerged.

The second group of the overseas Chinese consisted mainly of pirates, smugglers, criminals and those who were without means of earning a living. All of them were grouped together under the com-

---

[49]See *Ming Shih*, vols. 324 and 325; Ma Huan, annotated by Feng Ch'eng-chun, *Ying-yai sheng-lan Chiao-chu*, p. 16.

mon term of "Tsui-huan" (criminals) and the image of overseas Chinese as "criminals" thus emerged in the official records of the Ming Dynasty. Among these, the most feared and hated by the government were the pirates who occupied strategic points on the trade routes and pillaged ships. Their activities posed a direct threat to the state monopoly system.

When the Ming naval power was at its peak, these pirates were suppressed. The suppression of the pirate Ch'en Tsu-i in 1407 was the best known case in early Ming official records. Ch'en had several thousands of followers and commanded a number of ships. He occupied Palembang and pillaged the surrounding areas, and threatened the trade between China and Southeast Asia. He was given amnesty by Admiral Cheng Ho who commanded a strong fleet consisting of more than 28,000 men. Ch'en pretended to accept the amnesty and plotted to counter-attack. His plot failed and he was captured and beheaded. More than five thousand of his followers were killed.[50] The suppression of Ch'en Tsu-i was one of the most exciting episodes in the legendary Seven Expeditions of Admiral Cheng Ho to the Western Ocean (Southeast Asia and Indian Sea). This drama, together with other similar stories[51] helped to perpetuate the "criminal image" of the overseas Chinese in official circles in the early Ming period.

But when the Dynasty was on the decline, it had difficulty suppressing piracy. Then its fear of these "overseas Chinese pirates" or "pirates turned into overseas Chinese" increased. In Ming eyes, they devastated coastal provinces, connived sometimes with the feared Japanese pirates, undermined the state trade monopoly system, and threatened the security of the empire. And there was some cause for the fear. The best known of these pirates, Lin Feng and Lin Tao-ch'ien, plundered the coastal provinces of Fukien and Kwangtung and fought the local forces. Lin Feng fled to the Philippines with his fleet and fought another war with the Spanish.[52] Lin

---

[50]See *Ming Shih*, vol. 304, "Cheng Ho chuan" (The Biography of Admiral Cheng Ho); *Ming shih-lu*, "Ch'eng-tsu shih-lu", vol. 56; see also L.Y. Chiu, "Chi Ming shih chung-kuo jen tsai tung-nan-ya chih shih-li" (The Influence of the Chinese in Southeast Asia during the Ming Period), in L.Y. Chiu, *Ming-shih lun-chi* (Ming History: Seven Studies) (Hong Kong, 1975), pp. 51–52.

[51]The amnesty given to another Chinese pirate, Liang Tao-ming, of Palembang by the Emperor Yung-lo was also well-known in Ming official records. See *Ming Shih*, vol. 324, "San-fu-ch'i chuan" (The Record of Sri Vijaya).

[52]See *Ming shih-lu*, "Shen-tsung wan-li shih-lu", vols. 13 and 46; see also L.Y. Chiu, *op. cit.*, pp. 56–58.

Tao-ch'ien fled to Pattani on the southern part of Thailand and established himself there.[53] The activities of the two Lins and others like them further strengthened the "criminal image" of overseas Chinese during the second half of the Ming Dynasty.

There were other overseas Chinese that attracted the attention of the Ming Court. This group consisted of those who fled or went overseas for various reasons and served as officials to foreign countries. Because of their knowledge of China and their ability to speak Chinese and a foreign tongue, they were given positions as interpreters (T'ung-shih), helping and advising foreign governments in dealing with China. In those countries which had cordial political relations with China, they were given positions in control of tributary missions to China. In Thailand, for instance, many Chinese served in this capacity. Ch'en T́zu-jen was the chief official of the Siamese mission to China in 1381. Ts'eng Shou-hsien was twice the chief official of Siamese missions in 1405 and 1410. Huang Tzu-shun, another Chinese, was the official in charge of the Siamese mission of 1427. The best known overseas Chinese official in Thailand, however, was Hsueh Wen-pin, who held high rank in the Siamese Court, and was the assistant official in charge of the Siamese mission to China in 1477.[54]

In the kingdom of Malacca, Hsiao Ming-chu served as an interpreter for the tributary mission sent to China in 1508.[55] Some of these officials of the tributary missions wore foreign clothes, adopted foreign names, and spoke foreign languages. They excited the suspicion of Ming officials once their real identities had been revealed. From the point of view of the Chinese government, these people degraded themselves by rendering service to foreign countries. The act of adopting foreign names and clothes was despicable by the standard of Confucian ethics for they had betrayed their tradition for material gains. These overseas Chinese were of course used by foreign countries to the best advantage. They spoke Chinese dialects and knew conditions in China well including how

---

[53]See *Ming shih-lu*, "Shen-tsung shih-lu", vols. 79 and 99; see also Hsu Yun-tsiao, "Lin Tao-ch'ien lueh chi po-ni k'ao", in *Tung-fa tsa-chih*, vol. 32, pt. 1, also Hsu Yun-tsiao, *Pei Ta Nien Shih* (A History of Pattani) (Singapore, 1946), pp. 112–21; *Ch'ao-chou fu-chih* (The Gazette of Ch'ao-chou Prefecture), vol. 38, "Lin Tao-ch'ien chuan" (A Biography of Lin Tao-ch'ien).

[54]See Hua-ch'iao chih p'ien-ch'uan wei-yuan-hui (ed.), *Hua-ch'iao chih tsung-chih* (Taipei, 1956), p. 69.

[55]See *Ming Shih*, vol. 325, "Ma-la-chia chuan" (Biography of Malacca).

to bribe officials to assure profitable transactions. Any advantage to foreigners meant loss of profit to the Ming government. But the most important concern of the regime was their political allegiance. If they were loyal to the countries they served, they could not simultaneously be trusted by China. Because their prime loyalty lay in the foreign countries, they were likely to betray China if they had to. Of course the worst possibility was that their services would be used by countries hostile to China. The harm they could then do would be enormous; they could act as spies or as guides for foreign invaders. This was why the Ming Court tended to treat them with suspicion, and regarded them as potential "traitors to the Chinese" (Han-chien). Thus the "traitors" image of overseas Chinese began to develop.

These images of "deserters", "criminals" and "potential traitors", together with the traditional bias against merchants, formed the basis of Ming's hostile policy towards overseas Chinese. Any overseas Chinese who returned to China were apprehended and punished.[56] In the late Ming period when the seafaring prohibition was finally lifted, the hostility towards overseas Chinese was diluted only to the extent of indifference; no protection was given to them overseas.

This non-protection policy was clearly demonstrated in the government's attitude towards the massacre of the Chinese in the Philippines in 1603. The massacre was rooted partly in socio-economic conflict between local Chinese and the Spanish, and partly in the Spanish fear of being ousted by China from the Philippines. It was precipitated by the arrival of a Chinese mission which was said to have been despatched by the Ming Emperor to claim a gold mountain in the islands. Acting under suspicion and fear, the Spanish together with Filipinos and Japanese began the mass killing of more than 25,000 Chinese.[57] Despite the magnitude of the massacre — it almost wiped out the entire Chinese community in Manila — the Chinese government displayed little sympathy. The

---

[56]An overseas Chinese named Sung Su-ch'ing who acted as the chief official of a Japanese tributary mission arrived in China in 1510. When his identity was revealed, the local Chinese officials were thinking of apprehending him for going overseas illegally. See Ch'en Wen-shih, *Ming hung-wu chiang-ching chien te hai-chin cheng-ts'e*, p. 115.

[57]For the full story of this massacre, see Chang Hsieh, *Tung-hsi-yang k'ao* (A Study of the Eastern and Western Oceans) (reprint, Taipei, 1962), 5:3b–6a; see also Victor Purcell, *The Chinese in Southeast Asia* (London, 1965), pp. 513–14.

indifferent attitude of high authority was probably best summed up by Hsu Hsueh-chu, the Governor of Fukien province, in his memorial to the Court. He stressed that "they were scum, ungrateful to China, to their homeland, their parents and ancestors, for they failed to return to China for the new year. Such people were to be deemed of little worth. . . ."[58] This memorial was full of Confucian words, moralistic and paternalistic. It repeatedly emphasised that the overseas Chinese were worthless and ungrateful to the motherland. It therefore recommended to the emperor that China should not wage a war against Spain on behalf of those unworthy overseas Chinese.[59] Whether this document should be interpreted as rhetoric intended to disguise China's military ineptitude is a matter of controversy, but it clearly demonstrated China's non-protective stand towards the overseas Chinese.

THE POLICY OF THE CH'ING DYNASTY PRIOR TO 1850

Early Ch'ing Policies and the Negative Image of Overseas Chinese

The Manchus inherited the prejudice as well as the policy towards overseas Chinese from the Ming Dynasty. The tarnished image of overseas Chinese as "deserters", "criminals" and "potential traitors" were taken over by the early Ch'ing rulers. This image was soon transformed into a new image of "political criminals", "conspirators" and "rebels", for in the first four decades after the Manchu conquest of North China in 1644, the overseas Chinese in Southeast Asia were directly involved in the resistance movement on the southeast coast of China. The leader of the movement, Cheng Ch'eng-kung (known in the West as Koxinga), seems to have enlisted the support of the overseas Chinese, particularly from Vietnam, Cambodia and Siam.[60] It is claimed that Koxinga's naval power was partly drawn from Nanyang (Southeast Asia)

---

[58]For the full text of this memorial, see Ch'en Tzu-lung (ed.), *Huang Ming ching-shih wen p'ien* (Essays on Statesmenship of the Royal Ming Dynasty) (reprint, Taipei, 1964), vol. 26, pp. 633–39; see also Ng Chin-keong, "The Fukienese Maritime Trade in the Second Half of the Ming Period — Government Policy and Elite Groups' Attitude", in *Nanyang University Journal*, vol. 5 (Singapore, 1971), pp. 99–100.

[59]*Ibid.*

[60]See Ch'en Ch'in-ho, "Ching-t'su Cheng Ch'eng-kung ch'an-pu chih i-chih Nan-ch'i" (The Emigration of the Remnants of Cheng Ch'eng-kung's forces to South Vietnam), in *Hsin-ya Hsueh-pao* (Hong Kong), vol. 5, pt. 1, pp. 433–57; vol. 8, pt. 2, pp. 413–59.

shipping, and financed from the profits of the Nanyang trade.[61] Of course those overseas Chinese who supported Koxinga made no apology for their involvement. They saw the Manchus as alien usurpers and as the oppressors of the Han Chinese, and the support for Koxinga was seen as an act of patriotism to save the Han Chinese from the oppressive Manchu rule. The government countered the overseas Chinese involvement by introducing stringent laws against private overseas trade. In 1656 (thirteenth year of the Emperor Shun-chih), a decree was proclaimed that ". . . traders who go overseas privately and trade or supply the rebels with provisions will be beheaded, and their goods confiscated. Properties of the violators will be given to the informants as reward. Local officials who fail to investigate and apprehend the violators will be sacked and punished with heavy penalties, the Pao-chia[62] officials who fail to expose the crime will face capital punishment".[63] This law was reaffirmed in 1661 (eighteenth year of the Emperor Shun-chih).[64] The use of the death penalty and collective punishment had effectively put a stop to private overseas trade with the result that the commercial activities of the overseas Chinese in Southeast Asia were greatly affected.

Even after the suppression of Koxinga's regime in 1683 and the lifting of the ban on overseas trade, the Ch'ing government's fear of overseas Chinese as "political criminals", "conspirators" and "rebels" still existed. In 1712, for instance, Emperor K'ang-hsi decreed that ". . . those who stayed overseas permanently are liable to capital punishment, and will be extradited from foreign countries by the provincial governors for prompt beheading".[65] The fear was based on the assumption that overseas Chinese would continue to support the "rebels" who fled overseas after Koxinga's regime fell. Although the remnants of the rebels posed little or no direct military threat to the Ch'ing government, they could still

---

[61]See Wang Gungwu, *A Short History of the Nanyang Chinese* (Singapore, 1959), p. 13.

[62]Pao-chia was a system of rural control adopted by the governments of the Ming and Ch'ing Dynasties. For details, see Kung-chuan Hsiao, *Rural China: Imperial Control in the Nineteenth Century* (Seattle, 1960), pp. 43-83.

[63]See *Ch'in-ting Ta-ch'ing hui-tien shih-li*, original vol. 776, p. 10; reprint (Taipei, 1963), vol. 19, p. 14951.

[64]*Ibid.*

[65]See *Huang-ch'ao t'ung-tien*, vol. 80, "hsing-chih", quoted in Hua-ch'iao-chih pien-ts'uan wei-yuan-hui (ed.), *Hua-ch'iao-chih tsung-chih* (Taipei, 1956), p. 95.

hatch anti-Manchu conspiracies among overseas Chinese, and could infiltrate China's coastal population through their secret activities. To what extent this fear was well grounded is difficult to judge. However, the Ch'ing government seems to have taken it very seriously. Of course not all overseas Chinese were supporters or sympathisers of the rebels; many were apolitical and were only interested in trade. Some of them were probably prevented from returning to China by the warfare between Ch'ing and Koxinga armies, or by the sea prohibition law introduced by the Shun-chih Emperor. To separate the genuine traders from rebels, a decree was proclaimed to the effect that ". . . Fukienese who have settled overseas are permitted to catch boats to return to their home provinces, and the owners of the boats must act as guarantors. After returning to China, they are to be handed over by the local officials to their relatives for custody. If the returned persons are found to be untruthful and of bad character, they are to be sent off to malaria-infested areas for hard labour; those who do not respond to this amnesty and sneak back into the empire later will be sentenced to death once they are apprehended".[66] As a result of this amnesty, about two thousand overseas Chinese were reported to have returned to their home provinces of Fukien and Chekiang within three years after the amnesty was declared.[67] In the opinion of the government, those who had taken advantage of the opportunity were innocent people, and those who had decided to stay behind were likely to be undesirable elements.

The government's fear of political conspiracy seems to have been relaxed after the amnesty, but its prejudice against overseas Chinese remained. This signifies a retreat from the prevailing image of overseas Chinese as "political criminals", "conspirators" and "rebels" to the old image of "deserters", an image that had no political connotation. But the government's uneasiness was demonstrated in later Yung-cheng Emperor's decrees. The first of 1727 stated that "I believe that the majority of those who go overseas are undesirable elements. If they are allowed to go as they wish without any time restriction, they will become more undesirable, and will encourage more people to follow suit. A time limit must be imposed thereafter, and those who do not return within the period

---

[66]See *Ta-ch'ing lu-li hui-t'ung hsin-ts'uan*, vol. 19, pp. 1732-33.
[67]See *Ch'in-ting ta-ch'ing hui-tien shih-li*, original vol. 776; reprint (Taipei, 1963), p. 14953.

allowable, will never be allowed to return. . . ."[68] The second decree of 1728 reiterated that ". . . those who go overseas and fail to return are those who willingly remain in foreign lands. Those who emigrate without permission will not be allowed to return. . . ."[69] The Ch'ing government was obviously obsessed with the thought that its subjects were prepared to stay overseas for material gain. As it became more and more sinicised, it increasingly assumed a Confucian moralistic and paternalistic outlook. It feared that these materialistically-oriented "deserters" would set bad examples for others to follow.

It seems clear that the Ch'ing government took a hardline attitude towards these "deserters". Although they were not to be extradited from overseas for punishment, they were to be treated as "deserters" and punished in another way. Because they had not fulfilled the obligations towards their country, clans and families, they had already forfeited their rights to protection; even if they risked massacre by foreigners, the government would have no mercy for them, and would not intervene on their behalf. This was most clearly reflected in the attitude of the Emperor Ch'ien-lung towards the Dutch massacre of the Chinese in Java in 1740. In his reply to the memorial of the Governor of Fukien, Ch'ih-ning, who reported the tragedy to him, he asserted that ". . . these people are deserters of the celestial empire, they deserted their ancestral tombs and sought benefits overseas, and the Court is not interested in them. . . ."[70]

The Opium War and the Rise of the "Traitors" Image

The image of overseas Chinese as "deserters" did not soften over time, and in fact hardened. This image was further tarnished by the first major conflict between China and the West in the mid-nineteenth century. China at the beginning of the nineteenth century when the "Traitors" image was being formed, began to show signs of weakness: its power and influence declined; it failed to curb opium smuggling and to stop the drain of silver bullion as a result of intensive opium smuggling activities. The term "Han-chien"

---

[68]See *Huang-ch'ao t'ung-tien*, vol. 80, hsing-chih.

[69]*Ibid.*

[70]See *Hua-ch'iao chih tsung-chih*, p. 96; see also Huang Fu-luan, *Hua-ch'iao yu Chung-kuo ke-ming* (Overseas Chinese and Chinese Revolutions) (Hong Kong, 1955), p. 33.

literally means "the traitor of the Han race". When the term first appeared in the period before the Opium War, it was applied mainly to the Cantonese who collaborated with British merchants in opium smuggling activities. The assumption was that these people betrayed their national interests to the foreigners, and as they were of Han Chinese descent, they were therefore termed "Han-chien". However, those so-called "Han-chien" were never properly tried and found guilty of selling national secrets to the foreigners. They suffered only because of a strong official belief that those who liaised with foreigners must have done something evil to the empire, and were punishable by law.[71] In fact, there was no way to find out what actual relationship existed between these suspected "Han-chien" and the foreigners. The official logic was that all suspected "Han-chien" could speak a "barbarian" language, and the ability to speak a "barbarian" language required constant contacts with foreigners. At the same time, to learn a "barbarian" language one must have won the confidence of the foreigners. If these people had the confidence of and had frequent contacts with the foreigners, they must be prepared to provide the foreigners with information which could be detrimental to the empire. Since Chinese officials had a vague concept of overseas Chinese, this "traitors" image had quickly spilled over to them. The suspicion of overseas Chinese was not entirely unfounded, for it was they who had contacts with foreigners and who could speak a "barbarian" language, and who were likely to co-operate with foreigners.

The activities of these "traitors" were much feared and hated by Chinese officials before and during the Opium War. In 1815, the Governor-General of Kwangtung and Kwangsi, Chiang Yu-tien, accused the "Han-chien" of being the prime agents in the distribution of opium in China.[72] This view was shared later by Commis-

---

[71] For instance, in 1814, a Cantonese merchant named Li Huai-yen of the Nan-hai district, was punished for his private liaisoning with foreigners. Li worked in a British company, and acted as a broker for the company to purchase tea from interior China. See "Memorial of the Governor-General of Kwangtung and Kwangsi, Chiang Yu-t'ien and the Governor of Kwangtung, Tung Chiao-tseng, to the court dated 16th day of 19th year of Chia-ch'ing reign", "Deposition of Li Huai-yen", in Ku-kung po-wu-yen (ed.), *Ch'ing-tai wai-chiao shih-liao* (Palace Museum ed.) *Sources on Diplomatic History of China during the Chia Ch'ing reign* (Peking, 1932), vol. 4, pp. 2–22.

[72] See "Memorial of Chiang Yu-t'ien and Tung Chiao-tseng to the Court dated

sioner Lin Tse-hsu who was appointed by the Emperor to suppress the opium trade. Lin stated quite categorically that it was "the connivance of the local treacherous subjects with foreigners that the smuggling of opium had become increasingly widespread, and its bad effect had deepened. . . ."[73] Lin also held the view that successful apprehension of the "Han-chien" would solve the problem of opium smuggling. He thus considered apprehension of these traitors as the first task of his commission, and instructed Kwangtung officials not to conceal the culprits.[74]

The "traitors" were believed to be active in helping invaders in the course of the Opium War. They were accused of being partly responsible for China's defeat. They were alleged to have served the British invaders as guides and interpreters, to have done intelligence work for the enemy, and even to having helped the enemy in military campaigns. A group of "traitors" who served in Captain Elliot's early military campaign as guides was led by Huang Chou and Cheng Ah-erh. Huang and Cheng were natives of Hsiang Shan, the district next to the Portuguese colony, Macao. Both had been in business in Bombay and became friends of the British, and were thus hired by Elliot at Canton in 1841 to serve on an English warship.[75] In the later campaign when Sir Henry Portinger took over the command, another group of Chinese was engaged as guides. Eight or ten of them served in each warship, and were under the control of two leading "traitors" Su Wang, and Liu Hsiang, both were natives of P'an Yu, a neighbouring district of Canton.[76]

The "traitors" were charged with serving as a channel of intelligence to the enemy. The specific charge was that they helped the enemy to obtain and to read Chinese official documents which presumably helped the British invaders conduct the war more effi ciently. In July 1842, Ch'i-ying, the Manchu plenipotentiary, com-

---

21st day of 2nd moon of 20th year of Emperor Chia Ch'ing (March, 1815) relating to the new rules and regulations for suppressing opium smoking", *ibid.*, p. 29.

[73]See Lin Tse-hsu, "Official instruction to apprehend 'Han-chien' dated 11th day of 1st moon of 19th year of Tao-kuang reign (24 February 1839)", in Lin Tse-hsu, *Lin Tse-hsu chi: kung-tu* (Collected Works of Lin Tse-hsu: Official Correspondence) (Peking, 1963), p. 47.

[74]*Ibid.*

[75]See "Memorial of Military Commander of Taiwan Town, Ta Hung-ah, and the Judicial Commissioner of Taiwan Circuits, Yao Ying, to the Court", in *Ts'ou-pan i-wu shih-mo*, Tao-kuang reign, vol. 59, pp. 13a–14b.

[76]*Ibid.*, pp. 14b–15a.

plained to the Court that the British had "every day read *Ching-pao (Peking Gazette)*", and asked for a thorough investigation and apprehension of the persons responsible.[77] The Emperor in reply denounced the collaborators as "traitors", and instructed provincial governors to apprehend and execute them on the spot.[78]

The "traitors" were also charged with having directly helped the enemy in battle. At the end of 1841 when the Manchu generals planned to launch a counterattack on Hong Kong, occupied by the British in January of the same year, they learned that the enemy had gathered some few thousands "traitors" to help defend the island.[79] In the battle of Cha-p'u (May, 1842) on the coast of Hangchow Bay, "traitors" guided the British to attack from the rear with the result that many Chinese soldiers were killed and wounded.[80] In July 1842 after the British occupied Chinkiang city (Chen Chiang) at the lower reaches of the Yangtze River, "black devils" (Indian) and "traitors" were sent as spies to find shortcuts into the interior of Kiangsu province, but the Ch'ing army guarding Hsin Feng town, an essential pass to the interior, forced many of them into the river.[81] In the same month, when the British fleet withdrew from Chinkiang and sailed northwards upstream, "black devils" and Chinese "traitors" together with "white devils" again patrolled the city, and about two thousands of them were left inside the city to cover the rear of the enemy as they withdrew.[82]

All these charges seem to be well-founded. The "traitors" did help the British in various stages of the war, but their role in China's defeat was exaggerated by the Ch'ing government. China would still have been defeated had they not existed. It is clear that the Ch'ing government wanted to blame the "traitors" to be at least partly responsible for its defeat. Thus, they were used as

---

[77]See "Memorial of Ch'i-ying to the Court", in *Ts'ou-pan i-wu shih-mo*, Tao-kuang reign, vol. 54, p. 37b.

[78]*Ibid.*

[79]It was claimed that the leaders of these traitors were Lu A-ching, Teng Ah-fu, Ho Ah-su and Shih Yu-sheng. See "Memorial of the Rebel-pacifying General, I Shan and others to the Court", in *Ts'ou-pan i-wu shih-mo*, Tao-kuang reign, vol. 37, pp. 33–34.

[80]See "Memorial of Yang-wei General, I Ching, and others to the Court", in *Ts'ou-pan i-wu shih-mo*, Tao-kuang reign, vol. 57, pp. 38a–46a, particularly p. 41a.

[81]See "Memorial of Provincial Commander-in-Chief of Szechwan, Ch'i Shen, to the Court", in *Ts'ou-pan i-wu shih-mo*, Tao-kuang reign, vol. 57, pp. 28b–29a.

[82]*Ibid.*

scapegoats for military defeats by the local generals who had no
better reason than this in trying to get away from severe imperial
punishments. To the Court, acknowledging defeat without any excuse would not only mean humiliation beyond redemption, but
would also be interpreted by some as loss of its mandate of heaven
which could pave the way for internal rebellion. In this context, the
accusation that the "traitors" daily helped the enemy to read the
Peking Gazette can therefore be interpreted as an attempt by the
Ch'ing government to find a scapegoat rather than admit the inadequacy of its security system. The *Peking Gazette* was not as "confidential" as claimed by a high-ranking official;[83] it was published by
various publishers in Peking under different names for private circulation, and consisted largely of edicts and memorials released by
the throne through the Grand Secretariat.[84] Because of its private
nature, there was no way that the Ch'ing government could prevent
the enemy from acquiring copies of it. Further, as the war was a
contest between the two civilisations and two systems, the British
had mobilised all available resources, including foreign missionaries who could read Chinese. Even without the help of Chinese
"traitors" as alleged by the Ch'ing government, the British were still
able to read the *Peking Gazette* every day and know what actually
went on in China.[85]

The "traitors" not only became increasingly feared and hated by
the Ch'ing authorities, their origins also became more and more
difficult to detect. They could have been the lowly Chinese of
Kwangtung or other coastal provinces, undesirable residents of the

---

[83]In response to the Emperor's edict of apprehending "traitors" who were
responsible for helping the enemy to acquire and read the *Peking Gazette*, the
Governor of Chekiang, Liu Yin-k'o, pledged his determination to carry out the instruction. He remarked that the *Peking Gazette* was "confidential", and should not
be read by the enemy. See "Memorial of Liu Yin-k'o to the Court", in *Tao-kuang
Hsien-feng liang-ch'ao ts'ou-pan i-wu shih-mo pu-i* (The Supplements to the Ts'ou-
pan I-wu shih-mo during the Reigns of Tao-kuang and Hsien-feng) (Taipei, 1966),
pp. 17–18.

[84]See K'o Kung-chen, *Chung-kuo pao-yeh shih* (A History of Chinese Newspapers) (Hong Kong, 1964), pp. 33–34; R.S. Britton, *The Chinese Periodical Press
1800–1912* (Taipei, 1966, reprint), pp. 7–8.

[85]By the time of the Opium War, some foreign missionaries had already been able
to read Chinese documents competently. Moreover, an English periodical named the
Chinese Repository was published in Canton by an American missionary, E.C.
Bridgman. The periodical contained not only missionary news, but also information
about laws, customs and current events in the Ch'ing empire. See K.S. Latourette, *A
History of Christian Missions in China* (Taipei, 1966, reprint), pp. 211–20.

Portuguese colony of Macao, or the bad elements from places outside China such as Malacca, Penang, Batavia and Singapore. Wherever they came from and whoever they were, they shared some common features such as their contacts with foreigners and their ability to speak a foreign language. As pointed out by J.K. Fairbank, the connection of the Chinese "traitors" with the British invaders made the Court suspicious of all who had any intercourse with foreigners, including Chinese officials who were to negotiate with the "barbarians".[86] In a similar way, the connection of the "traitors" with the British made the Ch'ing government suspicious of the loyalty of any overseas Chinese.

The end of the Opium War did not end the "traitors" image, which continued to exist in the post-war period. Although the image underwent some changes, it still retained its basic identity — that of a potential traitor, if not an outright one. The opening of the Treaty ports stimulated the growth of China trade. As opportunities arose, some overseas Chinese from the Straits Settlements (Singapore, Malacca and Penang) were attracted to the Treaty ports. Since many of them spoke the Southern Fukien dialect,[87] they concentrated at the port of Amoy where they mixed easily with the local population. For their protection, they registered with the local British Consulate and constituted a major portion of the registered British subjects in the port. In 1846, twenty-seven out of fifty-three registered British residents were Chinese from British Malaya. In the following year, among thirty-five British residents, sixteen of them were British Chinese. At the end of 1848, the overseas Chinese outnumbered other British subjects in Amoy: there were thirteen British, four British Indians and twenty-six Chinese from the Straits Settlements.[88]

The steady increase of the number of overseas Chinese in the Treaty ports meant growing contact between them and the local Chinese, but this contact was far from a cordial one. It was probably the first time that the Chinese officials had had to deal directly with the problem of the overseas Chinese. From the official point of view, these Chinese were still the subjects of the Celestial empire

---

[86]See J.K. Fairbank, *Trade and Diplomacy on the China Coast: The Opening of the Treaty Ports 1842-1845* (Cambridge, Mass., 1964), p. 89.

[87]Even now, the Southern Fukien dialect is still widely spoken in Singapore, Malacca and Penang.

[88]See *FO* 17/88.

regardless of where they were born. Although they might not be the people who escaped from China and were wanted by the imperial authorities, they were still answerable for the "crime" that their ancestors had committed. Even if these "old accounts" could be forgotten their behaviour in China could not be forgiven. They spoke a "barbarian" tongue, acted like "barbarians", showed little or no respect for Chinese culture and systems, and were proud to be "British Chinese". They were seen by the local officials as pawns of foreign imperialists at a time when China suffered unprecedented humiliation. Some of them acted as interpreters and translators for foreigners,[89] and probably helped the foreigners to collect information on local affairs; some of them were even involved in smuggling and the illicit coolie trade,[90] both of which were punishable by death under the imperial law.[91] More dangerous than breaking the imperial law was their likely connection with secret societies which were traditionally anti-Manchu.[92] Some of them could have had close connections with secret societies in Southeast Asia, or could have served as agents or links with local secret societies. Were these anti-dynastic elements both at home and abroad to join hands, they would be capable of initiating a rebellion which would threaten the security of the empire.

This suspicion was not entirely unfounded. In 1849, a British Chinese from Singapore named Ch'en Ch'ing-hsi (or romanised according to Southern Fukien dialect as Tan King Hee) was proved to be a leader of the Triad in Amoy which was known locally as San Ho Hui (Three Combination Society). Ch'en appeared to be deeply involved in gangsterism — smuggling, extortion, and armed

---

[89]When Captain Gribble was appointed the British consul at Amoy, he had two Cantonese linguists, Ah Foo and A Ping, on his staff as interpreters, both of whom were from Hong Kong. To meet the needs of the local situation, the consul had to recruit two overseas Chinese on his staff. One of them was a native of Amoy who had learned some English in Singapore. See J.K. Fairbank, *Trade and Diplomacy on the China Coast: The Opening of the Treaty Ports 1842–1845*, p. 164.

[90]In August 1846, two British Chinese from Penang were detained at the Amoy Customs on suspicion of smuggling. See *FO* 228/60, T.H. Layton to J.F. Davis dated 2 September 1848.

[91]See *Chinese Repository* (Canton, 1851, reprint, Tokyo), vol. 20, p. 49.

[92]See G. Schlegel, *Thian Ti Hwui: The Hung League or Heaven-Earth League* (Batavia, 1866), pp. 2–3; J.S.M. Ward and W.G. Stirling, *The Hung Society, or The Society of Heaven and Earth* (London, 1925), vol. 1, pp. 2–3; Liu Lien-k'o, *Pang-hui san-pai nien ko-ming shih* (Three Hundred Years' Revolutionary History of the Chinese Secret Societies) (Macao, 1941), pp. 23–24, 40.

robbery, and on one occasion, he had led a gang of twenty people storming a local rice shop, and had beaten up the shopkeepers. Ch'en was arrested and tried, and after the intervention of the British Consul in Amoy, he was deported back to the Straits Settlements.[93] After Ch'en Ch'ing-hsi was deported, his brother Ch'en Ch'ing-hsing (or romanised as Tan King Sing) who worked in the local British consulate as an interpreter, was also identified as a leader of another secret society, Hsiao Tao Hui (Small Dagger Society). Ch'ing-hsing was advised by the British Consul to leave Amoy.[94]

The exposure of the secret society connections of the Ch'en brothers tended to reinforce official suspicion. But the most detestible aspect of the overseas Chinese in the Treaty ports was their use of foreign power to defy imperial law. Since the British government offered legal protection to those Chinese who were British subjects in the Straits Settlements and Hong Kong, many overseas Chinese from these two regions used it to cover their illegal activities. This aroused tremendous misgivings in Chinese official circles in the ports. When foreign protection was used by an overseas Chinese to defy imperial laws, it was seen not just as an attempt to avoid punishment, but it was also viewed as a challenge to the Chinese legal system or even to the political authority of the empire itself. As extraterritoriality was newly imposed on China, Chinese officials experienced great difficulty in enforcing Chinese laws. Many of them felt extremely frustrated because they were compelled by circumstances to bend Chinese laws and to yield to foreigners if the law and foreign extraterritoriality were in direct conflict. Sometimes they had even to swallow their pride to overrule some of their own decisions because of direct foreign intervention. In the late 1840s, there were several cases of convicted "criminals" of British Chinese stock being released after the intervention of the British Consuls.[95] Because the Chinese officials were

---

[93]See FO 228/111B, T.H. Layton to S.G. Bonham dated 15 January 1850.

[94]See FO 228/125, G.G. Sullivan to S.G. Bonham dated 4 January 1851.

[95]In 1846, the case of two Chinese from Penang involved in smuggling in Amoy; in 1847, the case of John Seng Sweey, a Chinese from the Straits Settlements, who was involved in burglary; and in 1849, the cases of Ch'en Ch'ing-hsi and Ch'en Ch'ing-hsing, the brothers who were involved in secret society activities. All of them were released after the intervention of the British Consul in Amoy. See FO 228/60, T.H. Layton to J.F. Davis dated 2 September 1848; FO 228/70, T.H. Layton to J.F. Davis dated 6 February 1847; FO 228/111B, T.H. Layton to S.G. Bonham dated 15 January 1850; FO 228/125, G.G. Sullivan to S.G. Bonham dated 4 January 1851.

torn between Chinese laws and foreign privileges, their frustration
sometimes precipitated a crisis. A case in point is the death of
Ch'en Ch'ing-chen (or romanised in Southern Fukien dialect as
Tan King Chin).

Born in Singapore of a Malay mother, Ch'en read and wrote
English, and was registered with the British consulate in Amoy in
1849 as a British subject. At one stage, he worked under M.C. Morrison, the officer in charge of interpreters at the consulate. Later
Ch'en was recommended by Morrison to work as a secretary with
the Amoy branch of Jardine, Matheson and Company.[96] One contemporary observer believed that at sometime in his life he had
worked for a foreign agency involved in the coolie trade.[97] In 1851,
Ch'en Ch'ing-chen was detained by the local authorities on charges
of being connected with a secret society dealing in opium. Both offences were punishable by death under Chinese law. At the request
of the representative of Jardine, Matheson and Co., the British
Consul, G.G. Sullivan, intervened and demanded a fair trial for
Ch'en. Sullivan also requested the Chinese authorities to charge
Ch'en formally in writing.[98] The officer in charge of Ch'en's case
was Chang Hsi-yu, the Tao-t'ai of Hsing-Ch'uan-Yung Circuit,[99]
who was stationed in Amoy. Chang at first agreed to Sullivan's request, but later changed his mind and ordered Ch'en to be beaten
to death with bamboo canes. Ch'en's corpse was put in a sedan and
sent to the British consulate.[100] The precise reason for the killing of
Ch'en Ch'ing-chen is uncertain. It was probably due to Chang's
toughness in dealing with "bad people" (rebels, gangsters and
other types of criminals) and foreigners;[101] or to his fear of an anti-
dynastic uprising flaring up in Amoy in support of the Taiping
rebels in Kwangsi;[102] or perhaps to his frustration and anger arising

---

[96]See *FO* 17/175, S.G. Bonham to Seu dated January 11, 1851.

[97]See *Chinese Repository*, vol. 20 (1851), p. 49.

[98]*Ibid.*

[99]Tao-t'ai was the officer in charge of a circuit (tao); a circuit controlled some
prefectures. In this case, Amoy was under the jurisdiction of the Hsing-Ch'uan-
Yung Tao-t'ai.

[100]*The Chinese Repository*, vol. 20 (1851), p. 49.

[101]Chang was alleged to have had a conversation with a foreign missionary in
Amoy after he took up his appointment as the Tao-t'ai of Hsing-Ch'uan-Yung Circuit. He claimed that he had a reputation for being tough with "bad people" and
also knew how to deal with foreigners. See *FO* 228/125, G.G. Sullivan to S.G.
Bonham dated 4 January 1851.

[102]Before being transferred to Amoy as the Tao-t'ai of Hsing-Ch'uan-Yung Circuit

from violations of Chinese laws by the British Consul who claimed extraterritoriality for the overseas Chinese. The combination of his toughness, fear and frustration probably prompted him to take such drastic action.

The fate of Ch'en Ch'ing-chen sparked off a diplomatic crisis between Britain and China. The British Consul, G.G. Sullivan, made a strong protest, and accused Chang of violating the treaty rights of British subjects. But Tao-t'ai Chang asserted that Ch'en Ch'ing-chen was in fact a Chinese subject, and should be dealt with in accordance with imperial laws.[103] The dispute had spilled over to the broader issue of the concept and definition of nationality which became a hotly disputed subject between the two countries for many years to come. At the same time, the controversy went to a higher level of the diplomatic hierarchy and gained the attention of the Chinese Imperial Commissioner, Hsu Kuang-chin, and the British Plenipotentiary, S.G. Bonham. With the transfer of Chang Hsi-yu from his position,[104] the case ended without any concrete result,[105] but it laid the foundation for future disputes over the protection of the British Chinese in the Treaty ports.

Unhappy encounters between Ch'ing officials and some British Chinese in Treaty ports reinforced the bad image the overseas Chinese acquired during the Opium War and revived the old prejuices against them. Thus, the label of "potential traitors" was generally applied to all overseas Chinese during the post Opium War period.

---

in late 1850, Chang Hsi-yu was the top officer of the Nanning prefecture of Kwangsi province. He must have been well aware of the Taiping rebels who had already occupied the Yung An city of the Northern part of Kwangsi.

[103]A good discussion on the dispute over Ch'en Ch'ing-chen case is Huang Chia-mo's article entitled "Ying-jen yu Hsia-men hsiao-tao hui shih-chien" (The British and the Small Dagger Uprising in Amoy), in *Chung-yang Yen-chiu-yen chin-tai shih yen-chiu so chi-k'an* (Bulletin of the Institute of Modern History, Academia Sinica) (Taipei, 1978), pp. 309-353.

[104]Although Chang was removed from his position as the Tao-t'ai of Hsing-Ch'uan-Yung Circuit, he had in fact got a promotion. He was promoted to become the Judicial Commissioner of Kansu province (An-ch'a shih). His removal was of course a tactical move on the part of the Ch'ing government. See *FO* 228/125, Chang Hi-yu to G.G. Sullivan (translation) dated February 1851.

[105]Huang Chia-mo, *op. cit.*, pp. 325-28.

2
The Rise of the Coolie Trade

What transformed the Ch'ing government's image of its overseas subjects from "deserters" and "traitors" to "Chinese subjects" and "Chinese merchant-gentry" hinged upon its experience in handling the coolie trade. Tens of thousands of Chinese coolies were shipped overseas without China's official approval, and all this was carried out beyond China's ability to prevent it from occurring.

The handling of the coolie issue compelled the Ch'ing government to examine closely its traditional policy towards its overseas subjects, and the issue of emigration in general. This led it to question some of the basic assumptions on which its traditional policy was based. The plight of Chinese coolies forced the Ch'ing government to change its traditional hostile attitude, and to take positive steps in protecting its overseas subjects. A thorough inquiry into the system of the coolie trade and the miseries that coolies suffered is the prerequisite to the understanding of Ch'ing handling of the coolie problem and the eventual protection of the overseas Chinese.

BACKGROUND AND FACTORS LEADING TO THE COOLIE TRADE

Both international and domestic factors were responsible for the rise of the coolie trade in the mid-nineteenth century. Internationally, the prohibition of the slave trade in the first part of the nineteenth century gave rise to the demand for other types of "slaves" to work in the farms or mines in North America, the West Indies and South America. The Treaty of Ghent of December 1814 obliged Great Britain and the United States to extinguish the inhuman African slave trade. By the terms of the Webster-Ashburton Treaty of 1842, Great Britain and the United States had further agreed to enforce the measure by maintaining joint squadrons off the west coast of Africa. With these steps taken, the slave trade which was the main source of cheap labour for the European colonists in the new continents in the previous century, ceased to exist. The abolition of the slave trade was the triumph of human rights supporters, moral crusaders and Christian clergymen. But it was a self-inflicting measure, from the point of view of the white colonists. What could be done to remedy the situation was to find an alternative source of cheap labour which would guarantee their economic success. To look for the alternative, they soon cast their eyes on the teeming millions of Chinese in the mysterious orient.

Domestic factors were equally important to explain the exodus of Chinese coolies in the mid-nineteenth century. The most important factor was obviously economic. The first component part of the economic factor was overpopulation. According to a modern study, China's population was about 150,000,000 around 1700, to about 313,000,000 in 1794, and it reached the figure of 430,000,000 in 1850.[1] Clearly, the population of China almost tripled in one and a half centuries. The impact of overpopulation was two-fold: heavy pressure on land and inflation. Because of the lack of comparative increase in cultivable land, overpopulation increased the pressure on existing land. This was most clearly reflected in the worsening of the land-population ratio. In 1753 (the eighteenth year of Ch'ien-lung Emperor), land per head was estimated at 3.86 mou, it decreased to 3.56 mou in 1766 (thirty-first year of Ch'ien-lung Emperor), 2.19 mou in 1812 (seventeenth year of Chia-ch'ing Emperor) and 1.86 mou in 1833 (thirteenth year of Tao-kuang Emperor).[2] It had been suggested that 4 mou per person was the requirement to maintain minimum living standard in the same period. If so, the figure in 1833 (1.86) was apparently much lower than the normal requirement.[3]

As land is the main productive factor in any agrarian economy, its scarcity in China created an imbalance in the supply and demand in agricultural products. As a result, inflation occurred. Inflation was most serious in the price of rice which was the main diet of the population of South China. The price of rice began to climb as early as the beginning of the eighteenth century in the later part of

---

[1] See Ping-ti Ho, *Studies on the Population of China, 1386–1953* (Cambridge, Mass., 1959), p. 278.

[2] See Lo Erh-kang, "T'ai-p'ing t'ien-kuo ko-ming ch'ien te jen-k'ou ya-po wen-t'i" (The Population Pressure on the Eve of the Taiping Rebellion), in *Chung-kuo she-hui ching-chi shih chi-k'an*, vol. 8, no. 1, pp. 20–80, especially p. 40.

[3] *Ibid.*

Emperor K'ang-hsi's reign.[4] It continued to increase throughout the century under the rule of both Emperors Yung-cheng and Ch'ien-lung. It became serious at the beginning of the nineteenth century, but turned worse in the middle and the later part of the century. In Hunan province, for instance, the price of a *shih* of rice during the K'ang-hsi period was two to three *ch'ien* (or equivalent to 200–300 *yen*); it increased to four to five *ch'ien* during the Yung-cheng period (1723–35) and five to six *ch'ien* in Ch'ien-lung reign (1736–95).[5] The price rise was obviously there but appeared to be steady. However, the price of rice had jumped dramatically in the middle and at the end of the nineteenth century. The Governor-General of Fukien and Chekiang reported in 1899 that due to various factors, the price of rice in Fukien soared sharply to more than 7,000 *wen* (70 *ch'ien*) per *shih*,[6] an increase of more than ten times over the figure of the Ch'ien-lung period a century earlier.

The second component part of the economic factor was natural calamities caused most frequently by drought and flood. China was a country well-known for its calamities. Statistical evidence suggests that there were droughts in 92 years and floods in 190 during the entire 267 years of the Ch'ing Dynasty.[7] Some of these calamities involved several provinces and affected millions of people. One of the worst drought famines in modern Chinese history was that of 1877–78, which struck four northern provinces of Shensi, Shansi, Honan, Hopei and the eastern coastal province of Shantung. About 5,000,000 to 6,000,000 people were greatly affected.[8] Many of them undoubtedly starved to death, and still millions more were forced to move south in search of food. The frequency and intensity of natural calamities created a tendency for people to migrate overseas, particularly in the two coastal pro-

---

[4]In the 52nd year of Emperor K'ang-hsi, his majesty had already noticed the price of rice was rising. See *Huang-ch'ao wen-hsien t'ung-k'ao*, vol. 2, *t'ien-fu k'ao*, no. 3.

[5]See a memorial of Yang Hsi-fu, the governor of Hunan in the Ch'ien-lung period explaining the causes leading to the rising prices of rice, in *Huang-ch'ao ching-shih wen-p'ien*, vol. 39.

[6]See "Memorial of Hsu Ying-k'uei, the Governor-General of Fukien and Chekiang and the Acting General of Foochow, to the Court dated 16th day of 8th moon of 25th year of Kuang-hsu (20 September 1899)", in *Yu-chi hui-ts'un* (Taipei, 1967), vol. 1.

[7]See Ping-ti Ho, *op. cit.*, p. 229.

[8]*Ibid.*, p. 231.

vinces of Fukien and Kwangtung where contacts with Southeast Asia and other parts of the outside world had long been established.

The third component part of the economic factor was the impact of the opium trade. Since the eighteenth century, Western trade had grown considerably through the system of controlled exchange between the foreign merchants and the semi-official Chinese merchants known as "Cohong" at Canton. It began to exert a serious impact on the Chinese economy, not so much because of the volume of the legitimate trade, but because of the increasing smuggling of opium into China. The volume of this illicit trade increased dramatically, from 4,555 chests worth £1,800,000 in 1800 to 40,000 chests worth £16,000,000 in 1838, about nine times increase in thirty-eight years.[9] Because of its illicit nature, opium gradually drained off Chinese silver, and seriously upset the internal Chinese fiscal system. The Chinese internal currency was based on silver and copper, silver to be used for tax payment and for payment of the officers' salaries; copper was to be used for general transactions, particularly in the local agricultural markets. Traditionally a certain parity was maintained between these two currencies.[10] As a result of the outflow of silver, the internal value of silver to copper was changed from 1:2 to 1:3. This greatly aggravated the financial problems of the vast Chinese peasants, who had to pay tax and rent in silver but received their income in the devaluated copper currency.

Added to these economic factors was a political one. This was mainly confined to rebellions which had greatly shaken the foundation of the Ch'ing empire in the nineteenth century. Many rebellions arose in the eighteenth and nineteenth centuries, among the best known were the White Lotus Insurrection in the Hupei-Szechwan-Shensi border area in 1796; the Nien Rebellion in the Huai river area, southern part of Chihli (Hopei) and western Shantung in the mid-nineteenth century; and the famous Taiping

---

[9]For a study of the opium trade and its economic impact on China, see Hsin-pao Chang, *Commissioner Lin and the Opium War* (Cambridge, Mass., 1964), chapter 2. See also Michael Greenberg, *British Trade and the Opening of China 1800–42* (Cambridge, 1969, reprint), chapter 2.

[10]For a detailed study of traditional Chinese currencies, see Frank H.H. King, *Money and Monetary Policy in China 1845–1895* (Cambridge, Mass., 1965).

Rebellion in the south and central China from 1851 to 1864.[11] The impact of the rebellions on the economy was profound: disruption of economic activities, destruction of farms, and the driving of many of the rural population to coastal cities. The combination of the above factors created a situation of rural destitution; a concentration of population in coastal cities; an oversupply of labour;[12] and a strong desire for migration.

THE COOLIE TRADE IN ACTION

The demand for cheap labour in the new world after the abolition of the slave trade coincided with the opening of China by Britain in the famous Opium War. It would appear later that the British had done an invaluable service to the rise of the coolie trade by the opening of the Treaty ports on the China coast and by acquiring special privileges for the foreigners as a whole. There is no evidence to suggest that Britain went to war with an intention of securing Chinese coolie labour, but later events show that many British nationals were involved in the early coolie trade.

The Rise of the Coolie Agency System

The coolie agency system was the product of the interaction of international, domestic and individual factors. Internationally, European planters and miners, compelled by economic need, were eager to obtain Chinese cheap labour, but they could not get the free supply of it because of the Chinese government's prohibition on emigration; domestically, millions of poverty-stricken Chinese in the war-torn south desired to earn their livelihood overseas, yet they were prohibited to do so. Taking advantage of this situation,

---

[11]For a study of the Taiping Rebellion, see Franz Michael, *The Taiping Rebellion: History and Documents* (University of Washington Press, Seattle and London, 1966), vol. 1, History, Jen Yu-wen, *The Taiping Revolutionary Movement* (Yale University Press, New Haven, 1973).

[12]Oversupply of labour was demonstrated in the low wages of labourers in coastal cities. In Amoy, for instance, wages of all labour was very low. A British consular officer, Dr. Charles A. Winchester, observed in 1852 that "The average wages of all labour at Amoy are very low, and there is not much variation between the rates paid for different kinds, skilled and unskilled. From 80 to 100 cash is the daily hire of an able-bodied man. The highest of these amounts is about equal to 4d". See "Note by Dr. Charles A. Winchester, British Consulate, Amoy, 26 August 1852", in *British Parliamentary Papers: Command Papers (1852–53)*, p. 355, Inclosure 3 in No. 8.

some foreign merchants at the Treaty ports developed a system of supplying coolies to meet the international demand. Under this system, the foreign merchants set up agencies at the ports, and were engaged either by the would-be employers or speculators to supply the needed labourers.[13] They charged commissions on the number of coolies supplied, and set up coolie houses known as "barracoons", at the ports, to collect coolies for overseas countries.[14] In acquiring coolies, they were handicapped by linguistic barriers and by their inability to travel freely in the Chinese interior.

These circumstances forced them to forge a close link with local Chinese crimps popularly known as "coolie brokers" or known in Chinese circles as "Kheh-taus".[15] Although the exact origins of the "Kheh-taus" is uncertain, it can be said that they came into existence in the coastal ports of Fukien and Kwangtung long before the opening of China in the 1840s.[16] Two types of coolie brokers can be discerned: the principal coolie broker and the subordinate coolie broker. The former was attached to the foreign coolie agencies[17] and the latter appeared to be under the control of the former.[18] As the

---

[13]See P.C. Campbell, *Chinese Coolie Emigration to Countries Within the British Empire* (London, 1923, reprint, Taipei, 1970), p. 95.

[14]See "Dr. Bowring to the Earl Malmesbury dated 3 August 1852", in *British Parliamentary Papers: Command Papers (1852–53)*, pp. 347–48, no. 5.

[15]The term "Kheh-tau" is romanised according to southern Fukien dialect, it is an equivalent to Mandarin "K'e-t'ou". "Kheh" means guest, and "tau" means head. In the eyes of Chinese, emigrants were considered as new guests, and thus the headmen who guided the emigrants was called "Kheh-tau".

[16]Because of its southern Fukien origins, the term "Kheh-tau", probably at the beginning, referred to those headmen who had arranged the illegal emigrants to Formosa from southern Fukien ports. A Ch'ing imperial statute was enacted in 1740 to punish those "Kheh-taus" who smuggled illegal emigrants to Formosa and Macao. This suggests that the "Kheh-tau" system must have existed at least by the middle of the eighteenth century. See *Ch'in-ting ta-ch'ing hui-tien shih-li* (Collected Statutes of the Great Ch'ing Empire) (Taipei, 1963), vol. 19, pp. 14944–45; or the original text, vol. 775, pp. 15–17.

[17]See "Mr. Harvey (British Special Investigator into the Amoy Riot) to Dr. Bowring" dated 22 December 1852, in *British Parliamentary Papers: Command Papers (1852–53)*, p. 387, Inclosure 7 in No. 14; "Evidence given by Le Tsai, a coolie broker, to the Special Court set up at the British Consulate at Amoy", *ibid.*, p. 405, Inclosure 8 in No. 14.

[18]See "Commander Fishbourne to Captain Massie dated 21 December 1852", *ibid.*, p. 436, Inclosure 1 in No. 17; "Evidence presented to the Special Court held at the British Consulate at Amoy from 13 to 16 December 1852", Appendix A, "Proclamation Issued by the Scholars and Merchants of Amoy", *ibid.*, p. 417, Inclosure 8 in No. 14.

coolie trade was an illegal operation, the brokers tended to come from the members of a lower socio-economic class.[19] Not surprisingly, the members of this class responded more readily than the members of the scholar-gentry or merchant class to the opportunities provided by the foreigners. Being underprivileged, they had no chance to enter officialdom through normal imperial examinations.[20] They were also less influenced by Confucian ideology and this enabled them to deal with the foreigners with less prejudice, furthermore, not being obligated to Confucian morality allowed them to pursue material gains to the utmost. Though many of these brokers were well-off,[21] they possessed little or no social status in the community.[22] What distinguished a principal broker from a subordinate one appeared to depend a great deal on the ability on being able to speak a foreign language and to acquire the confidence of the foreigners.

The intrusion of the West humiliated China but also provided opportunities to acquire wealth for some of its people. The development of China's foreign trade benefited a small group of Chinese known as "Compradors" (Mai-pan) who served as the middlemen in the commercial transactions between China and the West.[23] Like the foreign trade, the rise of coolie trade provided excellent opportunities for those who had linguistic ability and foreign contacts, to make money. It is therefore not surprising that the overseas Chinese from the Straits Settlements and the Cantonese became the principal coolie brokers in the early stage of coolie

---

[19]See "Petition of Lae Chinese, a Chinese woman of Amoy, for compensation for her husband who was killed accidently by the British in the Amoy Riots", *ibid.*, pp. 440–41, Inclosure 5 in No. 17.

[20]In traditional China, members of families of slaves, servants, prostitutes, entertainers and other "mean people" were excluded from the examinations. See Ping-ti Ho, *The Ladder of Success in Imperial China: Aspects of Social Mobility, 1386–1911* (New York, 1964), pp. 18–19; Chung-li Chang, *The Chinese Gentry: Studies on Their Role in Nineteenth-Century Chinese Society* (Seattle, 1955), p. 183.

[21]See "Petition of Lae Chinese, a Chinese woman of Amoy, for compensation for her husband who was killed accidently by the British in the Amoy Riots", in *British Parliamentary Papers: Command Papers (1852–53)*, pp. 440–41, Inclosure 5 in No. 17.

[22]See "Note by Dr. Charles A. Winchester, British Consulate, Amoy dated 26 August 1852", *ibid.*, p. 358, Inclosure 3 in No. 8.

[23]For details on the role of the Compradors in China's foreign trade, see Yen-p'ing Hao, *The Comprador in Nineteenth Century China: Bridge Between East and West* (Cambridge, Mass. 1970).

trade. Loo Kwang-hung and Loo Chang-piao, two natives of Canton, together with Wang Wei-chang, Lin Kin-toan, Lew Shih-new, Le Tsai and Lin Hwan, were some of the principal brokers employed by Tait & Co., and Syme, Muir & Co., the two main coolie agencies in Amoy.[24] Loo Kwang-hung, one of the notorious brokers among them, was said to have been a menial of the lowest class; but through his vile and selfish conduct, he managed to acquire considerable wealth and influence of an unparalleled extent.[25] The size of the principal coolie brokers in Amoy from 1849 to 1852 was small but they were said to have been intimately leagued together.[26] The precise relationship among these principal brokers is difficult to ascertain. They could be relatives, friends, sworn-brothers, or fellow villagers. Loo Kwang-hung and Loo Chang-piao, were said to be either brothers or uncle-nephew.[27] Whatever their actual relationship, it bears the evidence that the traditional bonds such as kinship, common geographical origins and brotherhood had played some part in cementing the principal coolie brokers together.

The key to the success of acquiring coolie emigrants was not with the principal brokers but in the hands of the subordinate brokers. They were a larger group than the principal brokers. In Amoy from 1849 to 1852, they numbered about several hundred.[29] The strength of this group lay not just in its numbers, but also in its function in the coolie trade system. It served as the most important link between the coolies and the coolie suppliers and the system could not have succeeded without its service. Like the principal brokers, the subordinate brokers came mostly from the members of lower classes who had a burning desire to "get rich quick" and who had

---

[24]See "Petition of Le Hien, a Chinese subject in Amoy", in *British Parliamentary Papers: Command Papers (1852-53)*, p. 442, Inclosure 7 in No. 17; "Deposition of Lin Hwan, a Coolie Broker", *ibid.*, p. 429, Inclosure 15 in No. 14.

[25]See "Petition of Lae Chinese", *ibid.*, pp. 440–41, Inclosure 5 in No. 17.

[26]See "Proclamation Issued by the Scholars and Merchants of Amoy", *ibid.*, p. 417, Inclosure 8 in No. 14.

[27]A petitioner, Le Hien, claimed Loo Chang-piao was the nephew of Loo Kwang-hung; while another petitioner, Chin Sha, claimed that Loo Kwang-hung and Loo Chang-piao were brothers. See "Petition of Le Hien", *ibid.*, p. 442, Inclosure 7 in No. 17; "Petition of Chin Sha, a Native of Amoy", *ibid.*, p. 442, Inclosure 8 in No. 17.

[28]See "Proclamation Issued by the Scholars and Merchants of Amoy", *ibid.*, p. 417, Inclosure 8 in No. 14.

few moral constraints.[29] They were directly involved in recruiting coolies: taking orders from the principal brokers; distributing the news about emigration and the terms of contracts.[30]

In recruiting the coolies, they had three trump cards. Firstly, they monopolised the news of emigration and the information about the foreign lands. Versed in local dialects, they also became interpreters of the contents contained in the contracts and could therefore manipulate the prospective emigrants to their advantage. Secondly, they had the financial backing of the principal brokers and the foreign coolie agents which enabled them to satisfy the immediate material needs of the prospective emigrants. Food, clothes and lodgings offered a great attraction to many paupers who roamed the coastal cities seeking for jobs. A contemporary observer noted how the poor in Amoy in 1852 were attracted to such offers. He stated that "One great temptation they [the subordinate brokers] held out is that they at once offer to supply plenty of food and lodgings for the day to every one willing to be mustered, whether he be eventually accepted or not. . . . Fifty cash a day are allowed for each man who comes to the muster, a sum significant to provide him with rice and fish, and he is lodged at night in some ruinous tenement rented by the crimp for a trifle. . . ."[31]

Thirdly, the subordinate brokers held considerable power in the underworld. Coastal provinces in Southeast China were the hotbed for secret society activities. The Triad which was best known in South China and the overseas Chinese communities,[32] was parti-

---

[29]The Proclamation by the Scholars and Merchants of Amoy in 1852 described the subordinate brokers and their activities as ". . . would follow the course of their interest wherever it might lead, without any scruple. They have daily in the country, along the coast, sought about in all directions for persons whom they might entice away, with the end of making gain for themselves by the detriment of others". *Ibid.*

[30]See "Note by Dr. Charles A. Winchester, British Consulate, Amoy dated 26 August 1852", in *British Parliamentary Papers: Command Papers (1852-53)*, pp. 356-57, Inclosure 3 in No. 8.

[31]*Ibid.*

[32]For a study of the activities of the Triad and its branches in the overseas Chinese communities, particularly in Southeast Asia, see G. Schlegel, *Thian Ti Hwui: The Hung League or Heaven-Earth League* (Batavia, 1866); J.S.M. Ward & W.G. Stirling, *The Hung Society, or The Society of Heaven and Earth* (London, 1925), 3 vols.; L. Comber, *Chinese Secret Societies in Malaya: A Survey of the Triad Society from 1800-1900* (Singapore, 1959); M.L. Wynne, *Triad and Tabut: A Survey of the Origin and Diffusion of Chinese and Mohamedan Secret Societies in the Malay Peninsula, 1800-1935* (Singapore, 1941); W. Blythe, *The Impact of Chinese Secret Societies in Malaya* (Kuala Lumpur, 1969). Mak Lau Fong, *The*

cularly active in Fukien and Kwangtung.[33] The rise of the Treaty ports in these regions stimulated its activities, and provided it with additional cover. As a result, the Treaty ports became the paradise for organised crime such as gambling, prostitution, extortion and opium smuggling.[34] The rise of the coolie trade and its highly profitable "enterprise" could not have escaped the attention of the members of the secret societies. The precise relationship between the subordinate brokers and the secret society members is unclear; the brokers could have been members of the secret societies, and vice versa. Whatever the relationship was, both groups had much in common — both belonged to the underworld and had sinister powers over the populace; both depended on secrecy and unlawful means for the livelihood of their members; and both operated outside the law. Because the secret societies penetrated into the life of the lower classes, the brokers found it a perfect organisational tool for their recruitment operation in obtaining information about the prospective emigrants; in enabling them to act promptly to fill the quota they needed; and in enabling them to coerce or kidnap coolies when necessary.[35]

The Rise of the Coolie Trade Centres

The port that emerged as the first centre of the coolie trade was Amoy. Located on the ancient trade route between the Eastern and Western worlds, it gradually replaced the port of Ch'uan-chou to become an important entrepôt of the southeast coast of China. It has an excellent harbour which was hardly surpassed by any other ports in the region.[36] It had a flourishing junk trade with various

Sociology of Secret Societies: A Study of Chinese Secret Societies in Singapore and Peninsular Malaysia (Kuala Lumpur, 1981).

[33]For secret society activities in Kwangtung, see F. Wakeman, Jr., "The Secret Societies of Kwangtung, 1800-1856", and W. Hsieh, "Triads, Salt Smugglers, and Local Uprisings: Observations on the Social and Economic Background of the Waichow Revolution of 1911", in J. Chesneaux (ed.), *Popular Movements and Secret Societies in China 1840-1950* (Stanford, 1972), pp. 29-47, 145-64.

[34]See R. Murphey, *Shanghai: Key to Modern China* (Cambridge, Mass., 1953), pp. 7-11.

[35]See F. Wakeman, "The Secret Societies of Kwangtung, 1800-1856", in J. Chesneaux (ed.), *Popular Movements and Secret Societies in China 1840-1950*, p. 30.

[36]According to Commander R. Collinson of British Army who surveyed the Amoy harbour in 1843, the harbour was superior to others on the east coast of China from Canton to Chusan Archipelago in Chekiang. Its outer area had a good holding ground and was free from gale wind, its inner area was capable of containing

countries in Southeast Asia and Japan.[37] Apart from these advantages, Amoy was not the seat of provincial government, hence, the
mandarins were less powerful than those in Canton and Foochow,
the provincial capitals of Kwangtung and Fukien. Amoy was thus
chosen as the centre for coolie trade. Moreover, the British had
established a solid commercial base there and were on good terms
with local mandarins.[38] Any favours given by the mandarins would
facilitate the operation of the illicit trade.

The first shipment of coolies under contract to foreign lands was
made in 1845, in French vessels, from Amoy to the island of Bourbon.[39] In 1847 a Spanish company induced a body of 800 coolies to
Cuba.[40] In the same year, a European observer reported that Amoy
could supply from its neighbouring districts 50,000 coolies annually.[41] From 1847 to March 1853, Amoy was estimated to have exported 8,281 coolies.[42] The flourishing of the coolie trade at Amoy
could partly be attributed to the factors mentioned earlier, and
partly to the vigorous efforts of several active coolie agencies.
There were six foreign coolie agencies in Amoy, five of them were
British.[43] The principal agencies were the firms of Messrs. Syme,

---

60 to 100 vessels. See Commander R. Collinson, "Servey of the Harbour of Amoy",
in *Chinese Repository*, vol. xii, p. 121.

[37]See Charles Gutzlaff, "Journal of Residence in Siam and a Voyage along the
Coast of China to Manchu Tartary", July 1832, in *Chinese Repository*, vol. 1, p.
97.

[38]See George Smith, *A Narrative of An Exploratory Visit to Each of the Consular
Cities of China and to the Islands of Hong Kong and Chusan* (London, reprint,
Taipei, 1972), vol. 1, pp. 380–93.

[39]See "Note by Dr. Charles A. Winchester, British Consulate, Amoy, dated 26
August 1852", in *British Parliamentary Papers: Command Papers (1852–53)*, p.
353, Inclosure 3 in No. 8.

[40]See H.B. Morse, *The International Relations of the Chinese Empire* (reprint,
Taipei, n.d.), vol. 2, p. 165.

[41]See Anonymous, "Coolie Trade from Amoy in 1847", in *Chinese Repository*,
vol. xvi, p. 208.

[42]The breakdown of this figure is as follows: Havana (from 1847 to March 1853)
2,930, Sydney (from 1848 to March 1853) 3,425, Honolulu (1851 to March 1853)
300, Peru (1852 to March 1853) 404, British West Indies (1852 to March 1853) 812
and California (1852 to March 1853) 410. See "Report of C.W. Bradley Jr., the
American Consul at Amoy, dated 25 March 1853", in *American Diplomatic and
Public Papers: The United States and China* (Wilmington, 1973), Series 1, vol. 17,
The Coolie Trade and Chinese Emigration, pp. 182–84.

[43]These coolie agencies were Hyde, Hodge & Co., Jackson, Robert & Co., Syme,
Muir & Co., Tait & Co., Turner & Co., and Smeird & Co. The first five were British,

and Muir & Co., and Messrs. Tait & Co. Although coolie trade was illegal, the European agents had little regard for Chinese law. Indeed, in their contempt for Chinese authorities, they did not even bother to cover their illegal activities. Syme, Muir & Co. had erected a shed as barracoon in front of its hong (company) building to receive the deceived and kidnapped coolies. The shed was described by Mr. Harvey, the British Special Investigator into the Amoy Riot in 1852, as "disgusting and obnoxious", and its existence was accused by Harvey as "a disgrace to the British name and character in Amoy".[44] Tait and Co., on the other hand, had engaged a vessel, the *Emigrant*, as a receiving depot.[45]

The surprising fact about these European agency firms was their possession of official influence. James Tait, an English merchant who was the proprietor of Tait and Co., and probably the most powerful coolie merchant of the time, became the Spanish Consul at Amoy in 1846. He was also made the Vice-Consul of the Netherlands in 1851 and the Portuguese Consul in 1852.[46] Another Englishman who became the French Consul at Amoy in 1840, later tried unavailingly to become the Peruvian Consul, because Peru at that time was an important country interested in coolie labour. In 1851, Tait recruited the American Consul, Charles W. Bradley as a partner in his company.[47] It was more than a coincidence for the coolie merchants to hold consular positions. The positions were sought partly to facilitate the operation of their illegal activities. With these positions, they could have direct dealings with Chinese authorities, but more important, as the Chinese mandarins in Amoy had little or no experience in dealing with foreigners, and were confused by this merchant consulship system,[48] the positions could be effectively

---

and the last one was Dutch. See Sing-wu Wang, *The Organization of Chinese Emigration 1848–1888* (San Francisco, 1978), Appendix 3, "List of Important Emigration Agents", pp. 355–60.

[44]See "Harvey to Dr. Bowring dated 22 December 1852", in *British Parliamentary Papers: Command Papers (1852–53)*, pp. 387–88, Inclosure 7 in No. 14.

[45]See "Evidence given by several coolies to the Special Court held at the British Consulate in Amoy on 15 December 1852", *ibid.*, pp. 406–10, Inclosure 8 in No. 14.

[46]See J.K. Fairbank, *Trade and Diplomacy on the China Coast: The Opening of the Treaty Ports 1842–1854* (Cambridge, Mass., 1964), pp. 213–14; "Dr. Bowring to the Earl of Malmesbury, Hong Kong, August, 1852", in *British Parliamentary Papers: Command Papers (1852–53)*, p. 348, no. 5.

[47]J.K. Fairbank, *op. cit.*, pp. 213–14.

[48]The merchant consulship system arose as the result of need in controlling non-British foreign subjects in the treaty ports. After the opening of the ports, British

used as a cover for the illicit trade.[49] Under the merchant consulship system, the British government had to issue permission before
a British subject could take up any position as consular representative of other Foreign Powers. The fact that James Tait, the notorious
coolie merchant could become the Consul for Spain, the Netherlands, and Portugal, with the permission of the British government, indicates its tacit approval of the coolie trade.[50]

This British attitude was further revealed in Britain's trade policy
at Amoy in the early days of the opening of the port. John Francis
Davis, the British Superintendent of Trade and the Governor of
Hong Kong, reported in 1847 that business in Amoy was flourishing,
the value of British trade exceeded £72,000, a figure more than triple
the combined amount of the foreign trade of other Treaty ports.[51]
Most of the Amoy trade consisted of supplying coolies to the plantations of Cuba and other West Indian islands.[52] Although Davis
felt the coolie trade was morally wrong, calling it "virtual slave
trading",[53] he nevertheless allowed it to occur and continue. The
condonation of the British authorities helped to stimulate the burgeoning trade in Amoy. British condonation rather than open
encouragement indicates her dilemma in relation to the coolie
trade. On the one hand, the British government still affirmed the
preservation of human dignity in the post slave trade period. On
the other, it was pressed by the economic necessities of the new
Treaty ports, and of its colonies of West Indies — British Guiana,
Trinidad and Jamaica, where the impact of the emancipation of

---

Consuls were asked several times to secure non-British vessels. In some cases they
did so. But this practice had dangerous implications, for the British Consuls lacked
jurisdiction over foreign subjects. In case of serious trouble they could not have
lived up to their responsibility. This practice was ended in the middle of 1844, and it
paved the way for the rise of the merchants consulship system. Under the system,
resident British merchants received commissions from foreign governments to act as
consuls or vice-consuls on their behalf. *Ibid.*, pp. 212-13.

[49]Commenting on coolie merchants and their illicit activities, Dr. Bowring stated
that "The principal shipper of coolies is Mr. Tait, a British subject, who has all the
advantages and influence which his being Spanish, Dutch and Portuguese Consul
give him". See "Dr. Bowring to the Earl of Malmesbury, 3 August
1852", in *British Parliamentary Papers: Command Papers (1852-53)* p. 348, no. 5.

[50]See "Dr. Bowring to the Earl of Malmesbury, Hong Kong, 7 February 1853",
ibid., p. 447, no. 21.

[51]See *FO* 17/123, "Davis to Palmerston dated 29 January 1847".

[52]See *FO* 17/124, "Davis to Palmerston dated 10 March 1847".

[53]*Ibid.*

African slaves was greatly felt. The newly-opened Treaty ports had to depend on foreign trade for their survival. A ban on coolie trade would cripple Amoy's foreign trade, and would undermine the newly-established Treaty Port System. The economic necessity of the West Indies colonies was no less pressing. The tropical climate of these colonies made it possible for the emancipated slaves to earn an easy living without the necessity of regular work on the plantations. Their withdrawal into the interior of the colonies from the coastal plantations caused a serious labour shortage.[54] Attempting to solve this crisis, the plantation owners of the West Indies formed a strong pressure group with the name, West India Committee, and clamoured for "economic justice" from the government.[55] The West India planters latched onto Chinese coolie labour as the alternative source of labour supply, following a private inquiry into the successful use of Chinese labour in the Straits Settlements. The West India Committee lodged its official application to the Colonial Office for the introduction of Chinese coolies into West Indies in July 1843, and gained sympathetic attention from Lord Stanley, then the Secretary of State for the Colonial Office.

However, there had been continual disagreement between the Colonial Office and the West India Committee over various problems arising from the proposed introduction of Chinese coolies. The planters were determined to secure a reliable labour force. Lord Stanley, while admitting their necessity, was concerned with the safeguards to the welfare of the immigrants.[56] The West India planters seemed to have won the day. In June 1848, Lord Grey, the new Secretary of State for Colonies, sounded out the feasibility of inducing Chinese labourers to British colonies from Hong Kong. In the following year, the British government and the West Indies authorities decided to import Chinese coolies into the West Indies.[57] At the end of 1851, the Colonial Land and Emigration Commissioners, under the direction of the Colonial Office, agreed to a scheme of recruiting Chinese coolies for West Indies plantations by Messrs. Hyde, Hodge & Co., a company that was involved

---

[54]See C.C. Chang, "The Chinese in Latin America, A Preliminary Geographical Survey with Special Reference to Cuba and Jamaica" (an unpublished Ph.D. thesis, University of Maryland, 1956), p. 21.

[55]See P.C. Campbell, *Chinese Coolie Emigration*, pp. 86–88.

[56]*Ibid.*, p. 91.

[57]*Ibid.*, pp. 93–99.

in Amoy coolie trade.[58] Thus, the coolie business by private enterprise was given official sanction.[59]

Although the British policy helped to encourage the growth of
the coolie trade in Amoy, the flourishing of the trade was basically
determined by market forces. The demand for coolie labour was
high, and there were many countries competing for it. Cuba and
Peru, the two Latin American countries whose economies were
greatly affected by the emancipation of the African slave labourers,
became keen importers of the coolies. In Cuba, the supply of the
slave labourers to the plantations was reduced by twenty-five per
cent in the period from 1841 to 1846;[60] the ban on the import of the
slaves by the Spanish Colonial Government in the island in January
1845 further dealt a severe blow to the Cuban economy.[61] As a
result, the Cuban sugar industry which depended entirely on the
slave labour, suffered considerable decline in production.[62] Efforts
to import white labourers from Europe failed, which forced the
plantations owners to turn to Chinese coolie labour as the substitute. The Spanish Colonial Government in 1847 was under pressure
to allow the import of "contract labourers", and the result of
which was the arrival of the first shipload of the coolies in Havana,
in June of the same year.[63] The impact of the emancipation of the
slave labourers in Peru was no less severe. Peruvian Independence
in 1825 stimulated economic development, and also brought freedom to 17,000 Negro slaves and led to the prohibition of the import
of slave labourers. The result of these was a serious shortage of
labour.[64] In the early 1840s, the growing demand for guano (bird
manure) in foreign markets stimulated the development of the fer-
tilizer industry in Peru — the digging of guano beds in the coastal
headlands and offshore islands was a labour-intensive operation.
As guano export earning became more and more important in the

[58]See Sing-wu Wang, *The Organization of Chinese Emigration 1848-1888*, p.
357, Appendix 3, "List of Important Emigration Agents".

[59]P.C. Campbell, *op. cit.*, p. 100.

[60]See H.H.S. Aimes, *A History of Slavery in Cuba 1511-1868* (New York, 1967,
reprint), p. 159.

[61]*Ibid.*, pp. 166-72.

[62]See A.L. Valverde, *Estudios Juridicos e Historicos* (Havana, 1918), pp. 23-25,
quoted in C.C. Chang, "The Chinese in Latin America", p. 16.

[63]C.C. Chang, *ibid.*

[64]W. Stuart, *Chinese Bondage in Peru: A History of the Chinese Coolies in Peru,
1849-1874*, p. 5.

national economy, an alternative labour force to the Negro slaves had to be found.[65] To meet the shortage of labour, the Peruvian Congress passed an immigration law in November 1849, to make possible the introduction of Chinese coolies into Peru.[66]

Another strong competitor, Australia, entered into the coolie market under different types of pressure. The transportation of convicts from England to New South Wales ended in May 1840, but the sustained economic growth of the colony depended heavily on a continuous supply of labour. The decrease in convict labour would greatly affect wool production and threaten the general prosperity of the colony.[67] The possibility of importing Asiatic labourers either from India or China was suggested at that time, but it did not gain favourable response from both the Colonial government in New South Wales and the home government in England. However as the scheme of recruiting European labourers ceased to exist in 1845, and because of the rise of wool price in the world market which stimulated wool production in the colony, the need for Asiatic labourers became more urgently felt.[68] Although the capitalists in New South Wales came under different pressure from their counterparts in Cuba and Peru, the need for Chinese coolie labourers was the same. The Australian capitalists arranged through James Tait for the first consignment of 120 coolies who arrived at Sydney on 2 October 1848.[69] Australia thus became a leading competitor for Chinese coolies, in the period between 1848 and 1852, and an estimated 2,666 coolies were shipped there.[70]

Apart from Australia, Cuba and Peru, others were also interested in importing coolies, they were British West Indies, the French colony of Islands of Bourbon, and the Spanish colony of Batangas in the Philippines. The result of this keen competition was the flourishing of the coolie trade in Amoy.[71]

---

[65]*Ibid.*, p. 4.

[66]*Ibid.*, pp. 12–13.

[67]Sing-wu Wang, *The Organization of Chinese Emigration 1848–1888*, chapter 7, "Chinese Emigration to Australia", p. 257.

[68]*Ibid.*, p. 260.

[69]*Ibid.*, p. 261.

[70]See "Note by Charles A. Winchester, Amoy, 26 August 1852", in *British Parliamentary Papers: Command Papers (1852–53)*, p. 354, Inclosure 3 in No. 8.

[71]*Ibid.*

The flourishing coolie trade in Amoy did not last long, it declined abruptly after 1852, and was later replaced by Macao as the centre of the trade. The decline was brought about by the strong reaction of the local residents against the illicit trade which culminated in a serious riot in November 1852. Anti-coolie feeling was gradually built up as the result of growing criminal activities of the coolie brokers. In 1847, a Chinese from Penang named Lee Shun Fah who acted as a crimp for a British coolie firm, was seized by local villagers. They held him responsible for the death of sundry coolies kept below hatches in a typhoon on the emigrant ship *Sophie Frazier*. As Lee was a British subject, he was released after the British Consul intervened.[72]

The incident caused quite a stir in the community, but was suppressed by the local mandarin. Public resentment intensified after 1849 following the stepping up of the criminal activities of the coolie brokers as reflected in the substantial increase of the number of coolies exported from Amoy.[73] But a stability was maintained up to the end of 1852 due to a delicate balance based on a triangular relationship between the general public in Amoy, the local mandarins, and the foreign authorities. The public was restrained by the mandarins who feared the foreigners, but the action of the foreigners was constrained to a certain extent by public feeling. However, when this equilibrium broke down, a crisis developed. The riot in November 1852 was caused immediately by the excessive action of the foreigners in procuring coolies and in pressurising the mandarins to succumb to their authorities. What triggered off the riot was the action of Mr. Syme, a notorious British coolie merchant, who went to rescue a coolie broker from the local police station.[74] The said coolie broker named Lin Hwan was beaten up by the public while he was engaged in decoying coolies, and he was detained in the local police station.[75] On hearing of the broker being

---

[72]See J.K. Fairbank, *Trade and Diplomacy on the China Coast*, p. 216.

[73]In 1849, only 280 coolies were shipped out from Amoy. But this figure sharply increased to 1,000 in 1850, and to 2,066 in 1851. For the first eight months of 1852 when this estimate was taken, the number of the coolies shipped out from Amoy was 1,739. See "Note by Charles A. Winchester, Amoy, 26 August 1852", in *British Parliamentary Papers: Command Papers (1852–53)*, p. 54, Inclosure 3 in No. 8.

[74]See "Mr. Harvey (British Special Investigator into the Amoy Riot) to Dr. Bowring (The Governor of Hong Kong) dated 22 December 1852", *ibid.*, pp. 385–86, Inclosure 7 in No. 14.

[75]See "Deposition of Lin Hwan, Broker, to a Special Court to Investigate into

detained, Syme rushed to the police station to have Lin released, and placed Lin under his own custody.[76]

Syme obviously overstepped his authority. Even under the operation of Extraterritoriality, foreign Consuls were empowered only to try their nationals in accordance with their respective laws, but not to release any suspects detained by the Chinese authorities.[77] Syme was not a Consul, and did not possess even their limited power to intervene in the enforcement of Chinese law. But Syme was a successful businessman who had wide contacts among the foreign diplomats, and was probably powerful in the local underworld; his wealth, influence and power seemed to have led him to believe that he could defy the Chinese law. His action had serious implications — it discredited the Chinese authorities in the eyes of her subjects, and it encouraged the general public to take the law into their own hands. This was because before the incident, the general public who were increasingly infuriated by the criminal activities of the coolie brokers still had some faith in their government's ability to mete out justice, but Syme's action shattered this faith.

Syme's intervention thus precipitated the riot. It was on 21 November 1852 when Syme and his clerk made the second visit to the police station that they were assaulted by an angry crowd, only managing a narrow escape.[78] Soon the crowd grew larger, and it also gained the sympathy of some Chinese soldiers. The sympathy was probably taken by the crowd as a sign of approval of certain authorities, and they quickly displayed their anger on foreigners. Mr. Mackay, a clerk in the coolie firm of Tait and Co. was beaten up, another two Englishmen, Mr. Vallancy and Mr. Walthew who were completely ignorant of what was going on were badly injured.[79] In the following two days, anti-foreign feeling was greatly

---

the Causes of the Amoy Riot, December 1852", *ibid.*, p. 429, Inclosure 15 in No. 14.

[76] See "Harvey to Dr. Bowring dated 22 December 1852", *ibid.*, pp. 385–86, Inclosure 7 in No. 14.

[77] See Article 21 of the Treaty of Wanghia signed by China and the United States of America on 3 July 1844, and ratified on 31 December 1845. In W.F. Mayers, *Treaties Between The Empire of China and Foreign Powers* (London, 1877, reprint Taipei, 1966), pp. 80–81; see also *Chung-wai t'iao-yeh hui-p'ien* (Collections of Sino-Foreign Treaties) (Taipei, 1964), p. 125.

[78] See "Harvey to Dr. Bowring dated 22 December 1852", in *British Parliamentary Papers: Command Papers (1852–53)*, p. 386, Inclosure 7 in No. 14.

[79] *Ibid.*

aroused and tension mounted. Angry relatives and friends of the coolies who were decoyed overseas gathered; a number of vagabonds from neighbouring areas also poured in to plunder; and the shops were closed. The riot climaxed on Wednesday (24 November) where a large crowd gathered in front of Mr. Syme's hong (shop building) demanding the surrender of the broker. Upon refusal, the outraged crowd began to attack the premises, but was repulsed by the fire of the marines from H.M.'s steamer sloop *Salamander*. About ten to twelve Chinese were wounded or killed.[80]

Although the riot was anti-coolie trade in nature, it contained elements of anti-foreignism. Had the riot continued longer and been carried out on a larger scale, it would probably have been selected, like the San-yuan-li Incident,[81] as one of the early heroic acts of anti-imperialism.[82] But as the riot lacked scope and tenacity, it seems to have escaped the attention of the historians of the People's Republic of China. The undercurrent of anti-foreignism went deep into the community when the British occupied Amoy in the course of the Opium War — some misconducts were committed by the invading troops, disorder was created, and people were dislocated.[83] The inhabitants of Amoy, like many other port cities on the south-east coast of China, had carried the war scars with them after the Treaty of Nanking in 1842.

After peace was restored in Amoy, the British still maintained troops on the island of Koolungsoo near Amoy harbour as part of the guarantee of implementation of the treaty clauses.[84] The occupation of Koolungsoo appeared to the local residents not only as a symbol of national humiliation, but also a target for expressing anti-foreign feeling. From the points of view of local traders and

---

[80]See "Acting Consul Backhouse to Dr. Bowring dated 27 November 1852", *ibid.*, pp. 80–81, Inclosure 1 in No. 14.

[81]For a description of San-yuan-li Incident and its interpretation, see Frederic Wakeman Jr., *Strangers at the Gate: Social Disorder in South China 1839–1861* (Berkeley, 1966), pp. 11–41.

[82]For the attitude of Chinese historians towards the San-yuan-li Incident, see the preface to the book edited by Kuang-tung-sheng wen-shih yen-chiu-kuan, *San-yuan-li jen-min k'ang-ying tou-cheng shih-liao* (Historical Materials related to the Struggle of San-yuan-li People against the British) (Peking, 1978), pp. 1–2.

[83]See "Official Reports of Capture of Amoy by Commanders-in-chief Sir Hugh Gough and Sir William Parker dated 5 September 1841", in *The Chinese Repository*, vol. xi (Jan.–Dec. 1842), p. 151.

[84]See W.C. Costin, *Great Britain and China 1833–1860*, p. 101.

gentry, the worst had come after the opening of Amoy as one of the five Treaty ports. The increase of foreign trade carried in foreign ships meant a serious threat to the traditional junk trade between Amoy and Southeast Asia.[85] The coming of Western missionaries and their evangelical activities threatened Confucian values.[86] The presence of Western merchants with their materialistic and inquisitive outlook and their active commercial activities undermined traditional socio-economic order. This fear was gradually crystallised in the criminal activities of the coolie trade. The members of the scholar-gentry class who traditionally regarded themselves as guardians of values and systems of the Confucian society, felt compelled to take some action against the coolie trade. But to what extent did the merchants and scholar-gentry involve themselves in the riot? Did they engineer the riot or did they just help to stir up public feeling which ended in riot?

The lack of scope and tenacity of the riot seems to indicate that it was not an organised act, but a spontaneous reaction against Syme's releasing of a hated coolie broker. However, the involvement of the merchants and scholar-gentry was revealed in the two placards posted up throughout the city of Amoy on 23 November,[87] the day before the attack on the Syme's hong. The placards attracted a large crowd of people and probably influenced their action. The first placard was issued under the name of the merchants and scholars of Amoy and was moderate in tone, it only attacked the criminal activities of the Chinese brokers, recounted the miseries of the victims, and warned people to be alert of the evil practice.[88] Its attack on the foreigners

---

[85]For study of the junk trade between Amoy and the countries in Southeast Asia, particularly with Singapore, see Wong Lin Ken, *The Trade of Singapore 1819–69*, an independent issue in the *Journal of the Malayan Branch of Royal Asiatic Society*, vol. 33, pt. 4 (December, 1960), pp. 106–33.

[86]For Christian missionary activities in Amoy from 1842 to 1846, see "Amoy: memoranda of the Protestant missions from their Commencement. With Notice of the City and Island, Prepared by Resident Missionaries", in *The Chinese Repository*, vol. xv (Jan.–Dec. 1846), pp. 355–61.

[87]See "Evidence given by the Reverend William Chalmers Burns, British subject, missionary in China, to the Special Court held at the British Consulate in Amoy on Monday 13 December 1852", in *British Parliamentary Papers: Command Papers (1852–53)*, p. 392, Inclosure 8 in No. 14.

[88]See "Proclamation issued by the Scholars and Merchants of Amoy", "Evidence presented to the Special Court held at the British Consulate in Amoy from 13 to 16 December 1852", Appendix A, *ibid.*, pp. 417–18, Inclosure 8 in No. 14.

was restrained mentioning only that the "barbarians" had practised the buying and selling of innocent people, subjecting them to cruel treatment.[89] It did not point out that these "barbarians" were partly responsible for the crime committed by their brokers. The second placard which was issued under the name of the inhabitants of the Eighteen Wards (the city of Amoy) had a stronger anti-foreign overtone. The writers accused the "barbarians" of a desire for material gain and complained of their uncontrollable behavior. They emphasised however that they did not seek direct confrontation with the "barbarians". What this placard incited people to do was to boycott the two notorious coolie agencies, Tait and Co., and Syme, Muir and Co., and they threatened that those who failed to comply would be killed, their property seized, and their houses destroyed.[90] It also incited people to take the law in their own hands, advising them to kill any broker seized, instead of turning him over to the authorities.[91]

The source of these placards is unknown, and there is no way to check whether the first placard was really issued by the merchants and scholar-gentry. But what is certain is the fact that some merchants and members of the scholar-gentry must have been involved in the production of these placards, for they were the only people possessing high literacy and who were capable of producing any written work. Although they had expressed their anti-foreign feeling in the placards, they did not seek direct confrontation with the foreigners. They were fully aware of the foreign military might which they had no intention to challenge. This opportunistic attitude probably explains why the riot was restricted in its scope and tenacity.

The port that later replaced Amoy as the centre of the coolie trade was Macao, a Portuguese colony near Canton. Situated on the right bank at the mouth of the estuary of the Pearl river, Macao consists of a small peninsula and two small islands. It is close to Canton which lies in the northern part of the estuary, and to Hong Kong, the newly established British colony. Geographically Macao is sufficiently near the mainland for the flow of trade and the movement of population. The Portuguese, after many vicissitudes, established a

---

[89]*Ibid.*

[90]See "Proclamation issued by the inhabitants of the Eighteen Wards", "Evidence presented to the Special Court held at the British Consulate in Amoy from 13 to 16 December 1852", Appendix B, *ibid.*, p. 418, Inclosure 8 in No. 14.

[91]*Ibid.*

trading station in 1557, paying rental to China until 1849 when it was declared a Portuguese possession, but the declaration was not confirmed until 1887 in a treaty with China.[92] The ambiguous status of Macao provided excellent cover for illegal activities. On the one hand, it enjoyed all the facilities that China could provide, and on the other, it did not have any treaty obligations to be fulfilled. The peculiar international status of Macao does not explain fully its emergence to become the centre of the coolie trade. Internal conditions also favoured its rise. Like Amoy, Macao had extensive trade with Southeast Asian ports like Singapore, Batavia, Penang and Malacca, and also ports in India like Calcutta and Bombay.[93] The existence of this trade network facilitated the shipment of coolie overseas. More important, there existed a powerful underworld that controlled the drug traffic, slave transactions, prostitution and other vices.

In the 1830s Macao appeared to be the paradise for European adventurers, drug smugglers, slave dealers, gamblers and prostitutes.[94] This was indicated in the population composition recorded by a British observer. In 1810 the total population of Macao was 4,049 of which 1,172 were white men, 1,846 were white women, 425 male slaves and 606 female slaves. In 1830, the population increased to 4,628, and the breakdown was 1,202 white men, 2,149 white women, 350 male slaves and 779 female slaves.[95] There is reason to speculate that large numbers of white women were involved in some forms of prostitution which would probably explain the abnormality in the ratio between men and women among the white population. With all its facilities and with government approval, Macao became the logical choice as the centre of coolie trade after the coolie traders had encountered hostilities in Amoy. In Macao, they would have a free hand to carry out their criminal activities without fear of any treaty obligations and hostile local sentiment.

---

[92]See *Chung-wai t'iao-yeh hui-p'ien*, p. 410.

[93]See A.L. Knt, "Contribution to an Historical sketch of the Portuguese settlements in China, principally of Macao; of the Portuguese envoys and ambassadors to China; of the Catholic missions in China; and of the papal legates to China", in *The Chinese Repository*, vol. 1 (May 1832–April 1833), pp. 403-4.

[94]Before the Opium War, Macao was a chain in the European opium-smuggling ring in the Far East. It was also a centre for buying and selling slaves who were kidnapped in China, Japan and other parts of Asia. *Ibid.*, p. 405.

[95]*Ibid.*

Moreover, as Macao became the centre of all vices, coolie traders and international dealers had a more enjoyable social life there.

After the riot in 1852, many coolie merchants shifted their operations from Amoy to Swatow, Hong Kong and Macao. James Tait, the principal coolie supplier in Amoy, moved his receiving ship *The Emigrant* to Namoa, an island off the port of Swatow. He also erected other barracoons on the continent at Swatow to receive coolies.[96] Swatow was a non-treaty port where the foreigners had no treaty right to trade, but their presence was tolerated by the local Chinese authorities. In fact, the absence of the foreign Consuls there gave the coolie merchants a freer hand to carry out their illicit trade. Tait was reported to have obtained approval for recruiting coolies from the local mandarins who were paid one tael per head.[97] For a short period between 1853 and 1855, Swatow seems to have been favoured to be the centre of the coolie trade. But it had its vulnerabilities — the mandarin's favour might not last long, and any excess in recruiting the coolies could provoke a riot like the one in Amoy. At the end of 1855, signs of unrest emerged due to the increasing abuse of the system. The captain of an American coolie ship was rescued by a party of his countrymen from an excited crowd, who accused him of kidnapping and carrying away their kindred — the ship had to leave with an incomplete cargo.[98] The latent anti-coolie sentiment threatened the growth of the coolie trade in Swatow, and explains why Swatow could not compete with Macao, to be the centre of the trade.

Although Hong Kong matched Macao in geographical position, trade potential and social milieu, it lacked the right political climate to become the centre for the coolie trade. Although the British government condoned the activities of the British coolie merchants in Amoy, it was not prepared to let its colony become the centre of the unreputable trade. Some coolie agencies in Amoy moved their operation to Hong Kong in 1853, but their activities were restricted by the enforcement of the Passengers Act of 1852.[99] The chance for

---

[96]See "Dr. Bowring to the Earl of Malmesbury dated 7 February 1853", in *British Parliamentary Papers: Command Papers* (*1852–53*), p. 447, no. 21.

[97]See "Dr. Bowring to the Earl of Malmesbury dated 10 January 1853", *ibid.*, p. 443, no. 18.

[98]See "Sir John Bowring to the Earl of Clarendon dated 2 February 1856", in *FO* 97/102(A) (1856), pp. 1b–2a.

[99]See "Enclosure in the Proclamation issued by the Governor of Hong Kong, S.G. Bonham, dated 28 December 1853", in *British Parliamentary Papers: Command Papers* (*1857–58*), pp. 572–74, no. 43.

Hong Kong to emerge as the coolie trade centre was completely ruled out by the proclamation of the Chinese Passengers Act of 1855, under which emigration officers were empowered to inspect every emigrant ship leaving Hong Kong with a view to ensure that the emigrants had been shipped out voluntarily and the provisions and accommodation had been made suitable.[100] The Hong Kong government further tightened control over the activities of the coolie brokers by licencing them in an Ordinance issued in 1857.[101] Although these government actions had not completely ruined the coolie business in Hong Kong, they invariably drove the coolie agencies to Macao where better conditions were found.

What accounted most for the rise of Macao as the centre of the coolie trade was the attitude of the Portuguese government. Unlike the British government, it did not have any moral scruples, nor did it care for the welfare of the victims. It treated the coolie trade strictly as business, and was interested only in the profit derived from this lucrative trade. Although the Portuguese were the first to arrive in Asia, and had established their outposts in various parts of the South, Southeast and East Asia, their control over the Asian trade was weakened by the arrivals of the Dutch and the British, who seized Portuguese colonies and drove the Portuguese out of some parts of Southeast Asia. The British, who had reaped the enormous profit from the China trade, had waged a war to open up China for her manufactured goods in the East Asian continent.[102] British success in the Opium War and her acquisition of Hong Kong further consolidated its leading position in the East Asian trade. The Portuguese having lost their trading advantage, now tried to regain their lost position. It was in this competitive situation that the Portuguese grabbed the opportunity to develop Macao as the centre of the coolie trade.

Although no evidence is available to suggest that the Portuguese government in Macao had openly encouraged the coolie trade, the fact that it allowed the growth of the barracoons in the colony from

---

[100]See Acts 18 and 19 Victoria C 104, *Great Britain Statutes-at-Large*, vol. 95, pp. 473–81.

[101]See "Enclosure in Ordinance for Licensing and Regulating Passage Brokers dated 3 November 1857", in *British Parliamentary Papers: Command Papers (1856–58)*, pp. 637–38, no. 43.

[102]For a good discussion on the economic intention of the British in waging the Opium War, see M. Greenberg, *British Trade and the Opening of China* (London, 1951).

five in 1856[103] to 300 in 1872[104] is a clear indication of its tacit approval. If the coolie trade was to serve as a Portuguese cutting edge in the competitive East Asian trade, it had to benefit the Portuguese traders directly. There is evidence to suggest that the Portuguese traders in Macao had a large share of the trade, including the buying and selling of women and female children to foreign lands. As early as 1855, there were reports that the Portuguese nationals had monopolised the trade of female children. They established a network of supply in various coastal ports,[105] and were particularly active in Ningpo, a Treaty port on the southeast coast of China, where many female children were kidnapped by their crimps.[106] A Portuguese merchant in Ningpo named Allino da Encarnacao was identified as the leader of this trade; another Portuguese coolie merchant named Joze Vicente Jorge was also identified to be the largest supplier of the Chinese women for foreign countries under contracts.[107] More alarming was the revelation that the Portuguese Consul in Ningpo received pecuniary benefit from these improper transactions.[108] The success of the slave trade of women and female children might also have contributed in part to the concentration of the coolie trade in Macao.

It is difficult to pinpoint precisely when Macao became the centre of the coolie trade. What we can gather from the available evidence is that it probably acquired that status in 1856, which lasted until the suppression of the trade in 1874. This is indicated in the number of the coolies shipped out from Macao. From 1856 to 1864, 15,000 to 20,000 coolies were shipped from that port each year.[109] The

---

[103]See "The anti-coolie placard in Canton, 1856", in *FO* 97/102A(1856), pp. 88a–88b.

[104]See "Sir A.E. Kennedy to the Earl of Kimberley dated 7 June 1872", "Papers relating to the Measures taken to prevent the Fitting out of ships at Hong Kong for the Macao Coolie Trade", in *British Parliamentary Papers: Accounts and Papers*, 1873, no. 75, C.829, p. 1.

[105]See "Sir John Bowring to the Earl of Clarendon dated 19 May 1855", in *FO* 97/101(1855), pp. 62a–62b.

[106]See "Proclamation of the Taotai of Ningpo, Shaoshing and Taechou Circuit to prohibit the purchase of female children, April 1855", in *FO* 97/101 (1855), pp. 64b–65a.

[107]See "Sir John Bowring to the Governor of Macao dated 18 May 1855", in *FO* 97/101(1855), pp. 68a–68b.

[108]*Ibid.*

[109]See "Sir R. Alcock to Lord Stanley dated 21 November 1868", "Correspondence Respecting the Engagement of Chinese Emigrants by British and

figure fluctuated slightly, it exported about 13,675 in 1865, 22,901 in 1866 and 15,579 in 1867, and it declined slightly to about 12,000 each year from 1868 to 1872.[110]

ABUSES IN THE SYSTEM OF COOLIE TRADE

Viewed from a broad historical perspective, the abuse of the coolie recruitment system was an inevitable historical process. The dearth of labour in the British colonies, Cuba and Peru, the high profitability of the trade, and the covetous and rapacious character of the coolie recruiters, all, in combination, ensured that the coolie trade would grow and flourish. Abuse was generally found in the different stages of transaction, from procuring coolies to transporting and receiving them. It was also outright in the methods and manner of acquiring the coolies. As the demand was high and the competition was keen, price was reflected in the market. European agents were highly paid for the quotas provided. In order to meet the quotas, the agents offered the Chinese brokers a high price for each coolie recruited. In Amoy around 1852, for instance, the Chinese brokers were paid at the rate of $3 per coolie, an amount that was more than a monthly pay for honest labour.[111] Under the stimulus of high reward, the brokers resorted to their crooked methods — decoy and kidnapping. The Cuba Commission which was sent by the Ch'ing government to investigate the conditions of the coolies in Cuba, clearly testified that the majority of the coolies who worked in that island before 1874 were decoyed or kidnapped.[112] Gambling and traps were frequently used in the decoying,[113] but the most common one was deceiving. The prospective coolies were attracted by economic opportunities overseas and were told that they could earn high wages and that work conditions would be excellent. Some were even deceived by the brokers with

---

French Subjects, 1865-69'', in *Foreign Office Confidential Prints*, No. 1737-39, p. 30.

[110]See Sing-wu Wang, *The Organization of Chinese Emigration 1848-1888*, p. 138.

[111]See "Dr. Bowring to the Earl of Malmesbury dated 5 January 1853'', in *British Parliamentary Papers: Command Papers (1852-53)*, p. 433, No. 16.

[112]See *Chinese Emigration: Report of the Commission Sent by China to Ascertain the Condition of Chinese Coolies in Cuba 1874* (The Imperial Maritime Customs Press, Shanghai, 1876, reprint, Ch'eng-wen Publishing Company, Taipei, 1970, thereafter *The Cuba Commission Report*), pp. 6-8.

[113]For a detailed discussion on this topic, see Sing-wu Wang, *op. cit.*, pp. 59-60.

fancy stories that eight foreign years specified in the contract were equivalent to only four Chinese years.[114] There were many who had no intention of emigrating, but were deceived by the brokers who promised them jobs in the coastal ports, however once they arrived at the barracoons, they were confined and later shipped out of the port against their will.[115]

The whole system of recruitment was under constant pressure of time. Coolie ships arriving in the port for loading were usually subjected to a heavy demurrage, coolies were therefore immediately wanted at any cost.[116] The European agents were under contract to supply the number needed within a certain time, the quotas for the "human cargo" and time schedule were quickly passed to the principal Chinese brokers who in turn pressed the subordinate brokers to supply the number. Failure to deliver the "cargo" within a fixed time would result in a heavy financial penalty.[117] The result of this pressure was kidnapping which seemed to be simple and time-saving to the brokers. Kidnapping was usually conducted by three to five crimps in secluded places like small villages, quiet streets and creeks along the sea-coast.[118] In 1859 and 1860 when the coolie trade was flourishing in the Canton area, the crimps were active in kidnapping along the Pearl river, and it was claimed that Canton was alive with kidnappers.[119] No place was safe either in the fields

---

[114]See the petition of Cheng A-mou and 89 others to the Cuba Commission. *The Cuba Commission Report*, p. 7.

[115]See "Evidence given by several coolies, Chen Po, Chin Gan, Seang Tsoo Sang and Hung Tsaon, to the Special court at the British Consulate, Amoy on 15 December 1852", in *British Parliamentary Papers: Command Paper* (*1852-53*), pp. 407-10, Inclosure 8 in No. 14; "Statements of Wong Ah Faht, Lum Apak and So Ayung, three coolies on board the French ship, La Nouvelle Penelope, to the Magistracy, Hong Kong, 16 May 1871", contained in the "Correspondence respecting the Emigration of Chinese Coolies from Macao", in *British Parliamentary Papers: Accounts and Papers* (*1872*), No. 70, C. 504, pp. 2-5.

[116]See "Mr. Harvey to Dr. Bowring dated 22 December 1852", in *British Parliamentary Papers: Command Papers* (*1852-53*), p. 387, Inclosure 7 in No. 14.

[117]See "A Statement of the Wicked Practice of Decoying and Kidnapping" (translated from Chinese), as Inclosure ? in No. 1 of "Papers relative to the Measures taken to Prevent the Fitting out of Ships at Hong Kong for the Macao Coolie Trade", in *British Parliamentary Papers: Accounts and Papers* (1873), No. 75, C. 829, p. 2.

[118]See "Proclamation issued by the Governor of Kwangtung, Pih-kwei (Po-kuei), dated 9 April 1859", "Correspondence Respecting Emigration 1859-60", in *Foreign Office Confidential Prints*, No. 894, p. 6.

[119]See "Vice Consul to Sir R. Alcock dated 1 November 1866", "Correspondence

or along the river. There were reports of fishing boats having been captured, the men kidnapped and the boats sunk.[120] Tens of thousands of innocent Chinese were kidnapped and carried away by the crimps and were sold as coolies during the second half of the nineteenth century. Undoubtedly, this was one of the most deplorable aspects of the system.

After the prospective coolies were procured, they were sold to the receiving depots which was popularly known as "barracoons". The barracoons were usually secluded and guarded. Once the coolies were thrown into the barracoons, they immediately lost their freedom and were completely cut off from the outside world.[121] The barracoons thus functioned as factories for processing "human commodity" ready for export. The most objectionable aspect of this abuse was the dehumanisation of the human beings. It deprived basic human needs and brutally lowered human dignity. Basic human needs such as food, clothes and lodging were inadequate. The facilities of the barracoons were generally very bad. They were poorly ventilated and their floors were damp. Only mats were spread on the floors for the coolies to sleep on in extremely crowded conditions. One report described the condition of a barracoon in Amoy in 1852 as follows: ". . . the coolies were penned up in numbers from 10 to 12 in a wooden shed, like a slave barracoon, nearly naked, very filthy, and room only sufficient to lie; the space 120 by 24 feet with a bamboo floor near the roof; the number in all about 500. . . ."[122] In the course of processing, the coolies were treated like slaves, they were stripped half-naked, and had to be stamped or numbered to be ready for export. Dr. John Bowring, the Acting Governor of Hong Kong in 1852 had himself witnessed such as ugly scene in the barracoons in Amoy:

. . . hundreds of them gathered together in barracoons, stripped

---

respecting the Engagement of Chinese Emigrants by British and French subjects 1865-9", *ibid.*, No. 1737-9, p. 4.

[120]See "Statement respecting Emigration from China by W. Lobscheid, 1866", *ibid.*, p. 16.

[121]See "Evidence given by Sen Shan and Chang Fang, two coolies from the barracoon of Mr. Syme, to the Special Court held at the British Consulate in Amoy on 15 December 1852", in *British Parliamentary Papers: Command Papers (1852-53)*, pp. 407-8, Inclosure 8 in No. 14.

[122]This report was compiled by Commander Fishbourne of the British steamer *Hermes* which visited Amoy in 1852. See "Dr. Bowring to the Earl of Malmesbury dated 26 November 1852", *ibid.*, pp. 374-75, No. 11.

naked, and stamped or painted with letters C (California), P (Peru) or S (Sandwich Island) on their breasts, according to the destinations for which they were intended.[123]

Apart from depriving the basic human needs and lowering human dignity, the coolies were also subject to brutality such as beating, kicking, whipping and other forms of torture. The coolies who petitioned the Cuba Commission inquiry in 1874 alleged that many of them were beaten, chastised and confined to privies when they were suspected of having tried to escape, or of expressing their unwillingness to go abroad when questioned by the foreign inspectors, or of refusing to sign the contracts.[124]

Similar abuses were found on the voyage. Coolies were crowded together with little space for movement. Usually coolie ships were overloaded, each coolie was allocated a small space to live and sleep, and they were in fact treated as livestock. Overcrowdedness was described by an eye-witness as follows:

> The ship in which I made the voyage from Callao to China was of thirteen hundred tons burden, and her hold was fitted up with bunks for eight hundred Chinese (this ship was obviously overloaded, working on two-ton per coolie ratio, it should have only carried 650 instead of 800). There were two tiers of platforms, one above the other, running entirely around the vessel, and upon them were numbered, in Chinese and Arabic, the space allotted to each man, which was something less than two feet in width and five in length. There was also a double tier of the same running down the centre of the ship, leaving a narrow passage on each side between the bunks. The voyage from Callao to China is made in from sixty to seventy days, but the returning is generally over a hundred, as the winds are contrary.[125]

Overcrowdedness was a major factor causing problems on the ship.

---

[123]See "Dr. Bowring to the Earl of Malmesbury dated 3 August 1852", *ibid.*, p. 2, no. 5.

[124]See the petition of Yeh Fu-chun and 52 others, the petitions of Liang Ah-sheng, Ch'en Lung, Lin A-lieh and Chang Lin-an, in *The Cuba Commission Report*, pp. 9-10.

[125]The eye-witness was Mr. J.B. Steere, an American scientist who, in 1873 made the voyage from Callao, Peru, to China on one of the coolie ships. See "Letter from Mr. Steere to Mr. Bailey, the American Consul in Hong Kong", Inclosure 3 in "Mr. Bailey to Mr. Davis dated 12 September 1873", in U.S. State Department, *Papers Relating to Foreign Relations of the United States*, 1873, vol. 1, pp. 207-8.

Other problems were bad ventilation, frustration, tension and sickness. Although most of the coolies came from South China, they did not speak a common dialect.[126] Communication difficulty tended to create misunderstanding and distrust. As most of the coolies had undergone the process of dehumanisation in the barracoons, tension and frustration had been gradually built up. The tension was aggravated when they were confined in an overcrowded ship. Sometimes the tension burst into fights, scuffle and murder.[127]

Another problem on board was the insufficient supply of fresh water and food. As most coolie ships were overcrowded and the Pacific voyage took more than a hundred days,[128] a shortage of the supply of water and food was inevitable. A strict control over provision was usually taken by the captains of the ships. As a result, many coolies suffered extreme thirst and hunger, and some of them died because of this. In the petitions to the Cuba Commission, many coolies complained of extreme thirst on the voyage, and claimed that two coolies had jumped into the sea because they could no longer endure the suffering.[129]

The most notorious abuse of the system during the voyage was the ill-treatment of the coolies. The Cuba Commission Report had provided much evidence of such ill-treatment. The petition of Li Chao-ch'un and 165 others states:

> When quitting Macao, we proceeded to sea, we were confined in the hold below; some were even shut up in bamboo cages, or chained to iron posts, and a few were indiscriminately selected

---

[126]As the coolies in Macao were mainly brought from Canton, Whampoa and Swatow, they spoke different dialects. The coolies from Swatow area spoke a distinctive Teochew dialect which was unintelligible to those from Canton and Whampoa areas. Even among the coolies from Canton and Whampoa areas, there were regional variations which made communication difficult. For reference to the sources of Macao coolies, see Sing-wu Wang, *The Organization of Chinese Emigration 1848–1888*, p. 138.

[127]Coolies murdering each other took place in one American coolie ship, *Waverly* in October 1855. The ugly scene was recorded as follows: ". . . they had murdered one another. . . . It was an awful sight to look at; some were hanging by the neck, some were shoved down into the tanks, some had their throats cut, and the greater part of them were strangled to death". See John W. Foster, *American Diplomacy in the Orient* (Boston, 1903), p. 271.

[128]See "Letter from Mr. Steere to Mr. Bailey", Inclosure 3 in "Mr. Bailey to Mr. Davis dated 12 September 1873", in U.S. State Department, *Papers Relating to Foreign Relations of the United States, 1873*, vol. 1, p. 208.

[129]*The Cuba Commission Report*, p. 13.

and flogged as a means of intimidating all others; whilst we cannot estimate the deaths that, in all, took place, from sickness, blows, hunger, thirst, or from suicide by leaping into the sea.[130]

Other petitioners also testified to other forms of cruelties and their consequences, such as "one man jumped overboard because he was constantly beaten by the master and the interpreter"; "those who asked for water were beaten and many died of thirst"; "the interpreter was a Portuguese, and constantly kicked us"; "I was chained to the bottom of the hold"; "On board a sailor wounded me with a knife and the scar is still visible".[131] Flogging seems to be the most common punishment that many of the coolies received on the voyage, those who made complaints, disobeyed orders, or stole food and water were flogged publicly on deck as punishment and as a warning to others.[132]

The result of the overcrowdedness, inadequate health care, insufficient supply of necessities and the ill-treatment was high mortality.[133] The busiest coolie trade route from Macao to Callao (a Peruvian seaport), bore such indelible records. In 1850, of 740 coolies who embarked on two ships for Callao, 247 died on the voyage, this represents a mortality rate of more than 33 per cent.[134] On the ship *Empresa* which carried 323 coolies from Amoy to Callao in November 1852, 77 people died at sea, almost 24 per cent of the total.[135] On 20 December 1868, a French ship *Enrique IV* arrived at Callao, 142 of the 458 coolies on the voyage died at sea. This represents a 31 per cent death rate.[136] In 1872, quite a few Peruvian ships arrived at Callao with coolie cargoes, the death toll varied from 12 to 26 per cent.[137] Based on this figure, one can conclude that the system of coolie trade was abused in the stage of transporting coolies and resulted in the loss of innumerable human lives.

The ugliest aspect of the abuses was the cruel treatment of coolies

---

[130]*Ibid.*, p. 12.

[131]*The Cuba Commission Report*, p. 14.

[132]*Ibid.*, pp. 12–17.

[133]For a detailed study on the mortality of the coolie ships, see Sing-wu Wang, *The Organization of Chinese Emigration 1848–1888*, pp. 209–25.

[134]See H.B. Morse, *The International Relations of the Chinese Empire*, vol. 2, p. 172.

[135]See W. Stewart, *Chinese Bondage in Peru*, p. 18.

[136]*Ibid.*, p. 67.

[137]*Ibid.*

in foreign lands. After the coolie ships arrived at destined ports, coolies were passed into the hands of dealers. There is strong evidence to suggest that a few powerful companies and individual dealers monopolised the coolie trade. In Peru, for instance, there were only six companies and individuals who controlled the trade from Macao to Callao.[138] The dealers were usually men of means possessing wealth, status, and influence in the society. Some of them were landowners, manufacturers, plantation or mine owners. They involved themselves in the coolie trade partly to meet their demand for cheap labour, and partly for sheer profit. Due to their close connection with local farming and plantation owning class, the dealers normally had no difficulty in disposing of their "human cargoes".[139] When the local market was over-supplied, open sale of coolies would take place. The sale of coolies, like the sale of slaves, took the similar procedure. An advertisement of the sale of coolies appeared in the local newspapers; coolies were then lined up on deck or a platform together with their possessions and contract papers waiting to be purchased. The prospective buyers would run up and down checking each man's strength and character, and then would bargain for the price.[140]

The open sale system seems to be most popular in Cuba where numerous coolies underwent a most humiliating experience before they reached their masters. From the evidence given to the Cuba Commission by many coolies, we can reconstruct the vivid picture of the horrible experience of the Chinese coolies in Cuba. On landing at Havana, coolies were escorted to barracoons by guards on horseback with whips in their hands, the coolies were treated like herds of cattle, their movements and their meals were carefully watched.[141] They proceeded to quarantine stations for medical check-ups, and their queues or long plait of hair were cut off and they were sent to the coolie market to be disposed of.[142] Presumably, the act of cutting queues by the Cuban authorities was not intended at humiliating the coolies, but was probably due to medical reasons. But the act was taken by the coolies as one of the most in-

---

[138]They were Canevaro and Co., Figari and Son, Maritime Co., Juan Ugarte, Candamoy Campania and Dimaly Filgueira.

[139]W. Stewart, *op. cit.*, p. 80.

[140]*Ibid.*, p. 81.

[141]See the petition of Hsieh Shuang-chiu and 11 others and the petition of Ch'iu Pi-shan and 34 others, in *The Cuba Commission Report*, p. 17.

[142]See the petition of Li Chao-ch'un and 165 others, *ibid.*, p. 18.

sulting acts that foreigners could have done to the Chinese, for most Chinese regarded their hair as being given to them by their parents, and to be an inseparable part of their bodies. The queue which distinguished Chinese from foreigners was taken as a symbol of national pride and an expression of loyalty to the Dynasty.[143] When they were in the market for sale, the coolies were classified into first, second and third grades, according to their strength and physical condition. When the buyers made the selection, the coolies were forced to remove their clothes for inspection. To them, the compulsory removal of clothes in public was another blow to their pride and a further degradation of their bodies.[144]

After being sold, the coolies were quickly brought to farms, plantation estates, factories and mines to face their real masters. Except for a few lucky ones, the majority of them were ruthlessly exploited, badly treated and cruelly punished. They worked for very long hours, at least twelve hours a day, a number of them worked for eighteen to twenty hours. Many coolies who testified to the Cuba Commission stated that they worked from three to four in the morning till midnight.[145] Except for a three-day holiday during

---

[143]The queue originated from the Manchu rule starting in 1644. It was imposed on Han Chinese as a symbol of subjugation. In the early period of the Manchu rule, many Han Chinese regarded the queue as a symbol of enslavement and strongly objected to it. As time passed on, the political significance of the queue was lost, and the queue was regarded by the majority of the Chinese as of their own choice. With increasing contact with the West, the queue distinctively differentiated Chinese from foreigners, and sometimes became the object of derision. In reacting against this, the Chinese became more aware of the queue, and were sensitive towards any ridicule. The overseas Chinese who lived mostly under Western rule, became even more sensitive than their compatriots in China over the issue of the queue. In 1888, for instance, there was a strong feeling in the Chinese community in Singapore against the local police force because policemen used to arrest Chinese suspects by pulling their queues. *Lat Pau*, the leading Chinese newspaper in Singapore, launched an attack on the police force by claiming that the queue was the most important thing in Chinese custom, and was a symbol of national pride. See *Lat Pau*, 31/3/1888, p. 1.

[144]See the petition of Yeh Fu-chun and 52 others, the petition of Chang Ting-chia and 127 others, and the petition of Lin A-pang, in *The Cuba Commission Report*, p. 18.

[145]T'ang Chien and 170 others testified that they had laboured on the sugar plantation from 3 a.m. until midnight, and that on Sundays similar hours were imposed. Chang Chao and 121 others also testified that they had laboured on sugar plantations from 4 a.m. till midnight, and that on Sundays similar hours were enforced. Wen A-chao and 20 others testified that they had laboured from 2 a.m. to midnight. *Ibid.*, pp. 32–34.

the Chinese New Year period, they worked practically seven days a week and thirty days a month.[146] The toil of day and night caused fatigue and low spirits, and their physical condition deteriorated. An American scientist, J.B. Steere who visited Peru in 1873 to collect material in natural history, described the miserable appearance of some coolies he saw in a sugar plantation as follows:

> . . . they were poorly clothed, were very thin in flesh, and looked despondent and despairing as if they did not care whether they lived or died[147]

The coolies were generally paid much less than what was stipulated in the contract, and their wages were paid not in hard cash but in paper money which was frequently eroded by inflation. Many of them found that wages received were in fact lower than what they could have got in China.[148] With this meagre income, the coolies could never have saved enough money to pay their passage back to China, not to mention accumulating wealth overseas.

Apart from the direct economic exploitation, other forms of extraction were also employed. One of these was the monopoly of the sale of sundry goods which most coolies had to acquire, to meet their daily needs. Usually grocery shops were set up near their quarters, by the masters, who compelled the coolies to obtain goods from their shops. Prices were generally higher, and those who attempted to buy goods elsewhere were punished. Through this, extra money was extracted from the coolies. Li Chao-ch'un and P'an To-li, two coolie leaders who testified to the board of the Cuba Commission on how they were exploited financially in the sugar plantations said,

> . . . we are paid $4 (paper money) worth a month, a little more than $1 in silver, and not sufficient even for the additional food and clothes that are indispensable. On each estate there is

---

[146]See W. Stewart, *Chinese Bondage in Peru*, p. 116.

[147]See "Letter from Mr. Steere to Mr. Bailey", Inclosure 3 in "Mr. Bailey to Mr. Davis dated 12 September 1873", in U.S. State Department, *Papers Relating to Foreign Relations of the United States, 1873*, vol. 1, p. 208.

[148]A coolie named Ciang A-lin testified to the Cuba Commission that ". . . although the wages are nominally larger than in China, the paper currency is so much depreciated, and prices are so high, that $8 or $10 do not represent more than $1 or $2 in China". Another coolie Lo A-chi deposed that ". . . in China I found 100 cash daily sufficient for the support of a family, whilst here the cost of living is so great that $1 a day will hardly maintain a single individual". See *The Cuba Commission Report*, p. 35.

a shop belonging to the administrator and others; the things
are of bad quality and very highly priced, but if we attempt to
make a purchase outside, it is said that we are running away,
and we are compelled to work with chained feet. How is it
possible, after the term of service, to have saved enough to pay
for our passage home? . . . if we make purchases at a shop outside the plantation our wages suffer deduction during some
months and we are forced to work with chained feet for a
similar period.[149]

The treatment of the coolies was scandalous. They had never
been properly accommodated. They were crowded together in
enclosed wooden quarters, and in sheds, which were dim, filthy and
badly ventilated. These quarters were lockable, and the coolies
were confined at night. In Peruvian plantations, for instance, the
coolie quarters were known as the "galpon". Sometimes the
galpon was a large shed, sometimes a walled enclosure containing a
number of buildings. Its construction was never very substantial.
Whatever the type of the galpon, it was usually capable of being
locked at night. The coolies were locked up at eight or nine o'clock
in the galpons without water or the most necessary sanitary arrangements.[150] A rationing system was adopted for distributing foods to
the coolies. They were given minimum requirements to keep them
alive. Since rice was the main staple for Chinese, it became the
main item of ration for the coolies. Sometimes a small quantity of
meat and fish was issued on Sunday. In some cases, the coolies
were squeezed further by providing them with cheaper food such as
maize, bananas, sugar cane, sweet potatoes and other local products.[151] The quantity of their rations was sometimes reduced to
save cost and the quality of meat was bad.[152]

The most outrageous treatment of the coolies was raw cruelty. It
ranged from confinement, chained feet, flogging, cutting fingers,
ears and limbs. Although some of the Western laws prohibited the
employers to take disciplinary penalties against the coolies in the
event of repeated offences, the laws were generally disregarded,
and in practice, the employers resorted to whatever cruelties they

---

[149]*Ibid.*, p. 26.

[150]See W. Stewart, *Chinese Bondage in Peru*, p. 98.

[151]See the petition of Chang Ting-chia and 127 others, in *The Cuba Commission Report*, p. 26.

[152]See the petitions of Wang A-chi and Yang Chin, *ibid.*

saw fit.[153] Evidence produced in the enquiry of the Cuba Commission show that on all the plantations on Cuba island the owners had established prisons, to which stock and various implements of punishment were attached, and that the administrator and overseers constantly, at will, made use of hounds, knives, bludgeons and whips, so that the coolies were kept in a constant terror of death.[154] Flogging was the most common and one of the worst forms of cruelty inflicted on the coolies. When coolies were slow at work, or physically incapable of doing certain jobs, or showed signs of any disobedience, or even failed in understanding the instructions of the administrators, they were flogged. The severity of flogging depended very much on the type of offences the coolies committed, and sometimes on the temperament of the administrators and overseers. On some occasions, severe flogging could end in death. Ho A-pa who had only committed a minor offence was severely flogged. He testified to the Cuba Commission that ". . . on one occasion my master who observed me making a cigarette,[155] ordered four Negroes to seize my hands and feet, and I was flogged with a rattan rod so severely that my flesh was lacerated and the bones became visible".[156]

Fan Ssu-ho testified that he had seen a coolie named Chen A-ssu struck for pushing a bundle of cane against an overseer, and it was alleged that the coolie had hung himself.[157] Another coolie, Lu A-chen, also testified that ". . . I have seen men beaten to death, the bodies being afterwards buried, and no report being made to the authorities".[158] Although some coolies were not flogged to death, they ended their lives by committing suicide because they could no longer take the torture of flogging. Hsieh A-sheng testified about such a tragedy to the Cuba Commission. He said,

---

[153]See for instance, the 77th article of the Spanish Royal Decree of 1860 provided that in the event of repeated offences on the part of the labourers, the employer shall report the occurrence to the official designated as protector of Chinese, who shall, if the laws afford the necessary means, prescribe a punishment in accordance with their provisions. *Ibid.*, p. 25.

[154]*Ibid.*

[155]Presumably this coolie tried to save some money by making his own cigarette, and did not consume those packed cigarettes sold in the grocery shop owned by the master.

[156]See the petition of Ho A-pa, in *The Cuba Commission Report*, p. 30.

[157]*Ibid.*, p. 36.

[158]*Ibid.*

". . . with me was a native of Sinning by the name of Chen, and a native of K'aip'ing by the name of Liang. The administrator accused them of cutting grass slowly, and directing four men to hold them in a prostrate position, inflicted with a whip, a flogging which almost killed them. The first afterwards hanged himself, and the second drowned himself".[159]

The testimonies collected by the Cuba Commission have clearly shown that besides those who were flogged to death on the spot and those who died from the effects of wounds, a countless number destroyed themselves by cutting their own throats, by hanging, drowning, poisoning and casting themselves under wheels or into sugar caldrons. Constantly too, when but one or two had committed the crime, ten or twenty longing for death would accuse themselves of the act.[160] The desire to kill themselves and the high suicide rate reflected on the extreme misery of the coolies' lives. As some coolies put it, "our existence is so miserable that the hours seem as days, and the days as years".[161]

Why did the employers treat the coolies so cruelly? It seems to be contradictory that the employers desired to have cheap labour but did not take care of the coolies. One answer to this seemingly contradictory situation was that the employers did not treat the coolies as employees, but as slaves or private properties. This attitude was best expressed by a Peruvian agriculturist who in 1869 marked his forty-eight coolies with a hot iron in the manner formerly done with African slaves.[162] If the Chinese coolies were to be treated as African slaves, they were likewise considered to be sub-human, they therefore needed to be treated like animals if they did not comply with the instructions. American scientist J.B. Steere witnessed in a Peruvian sugar estate in 1873 that about thirty to forty coolies were heavily ironed while they were at work as a punishment of their attempted escape.[163] With this attitude, the cruelties received by the coolies were expected.

---

[159]*Ibid.*

[160]*Ibid.*, p. 40.

[161]See the petition of Wu A-fa and 39 others, *ibid.*

[162]See "Extract from the Lima 'Comercio' of 27 February 1869", Inclosure ? in No. 1, "Correspondence respecting the Emigration of Chinese Coolies from Macao", in *British Parliamentary Papers: Accounts and Papers 1871*, No. 47, C. 403, p. 3.

[163]See "Letter from Mr. Steere to Mr. Bailey", Inclosure 3 in "Mr. Bailey to Mr. Davis dated 12 September 1873", in U.S. State Department, *Papers Relating to Foreign Relations of the United States, 1873*, vol. 1, p. 208.

Perhaps the main reason for the cruel treatment of the coolies was because the employers were motivated by quick returns. Many of them intended to reap the maximum profit at the shortest time. To many employers, the coolies were mere living machines which were disposable and could be replaced at any time. To them, human life had no real value when weighed against profit, therefore the lives and deaths of the coolies were not their prime concern. What they were really concerned with was how to achieve the quickest turn-over of agricultural products which meant higher profit for them. Liu A-lin, one of the coolies who testified to the Commission said, "The administrator is of exceptional cruelty. The owner has told him to flog without restraint, that it matters not if one is beaten to death as ten others can be bought in his place."[164] Hsieh A-ssu also testified that ". . . the owner has urged the administrator and the overseer to flog us. He has said that it matters not if one is beaten to death as he is rich enough to buy ten others".[165] Another coolie, Liu A-jui, continued that ". . . the owner continually urges upon the overseers that a large crop of sugar is the only matter of importance, and that no consideration should be shown to the labourers, as if one be beaten to death ten others can be purchased".[166]

Another reason for the cruel treatment of the coolies was probably a racial one. The decline of the Ch'ing empire and its weakening position in the world community, the starving millions, the throng of work-hungry coolies flooding the international labour market, opium-smoking and foot-binding, female infanticide and other ugly aspects of Chinese society created an unfavourable image of the Chinese overseas. The poor image was further prejudiced by differences in appearance, culture, habits and religion. The coolies looked distinctively different from the Europeans and dressed differently. They spoke unintelligible dialects which were beyond comprehension even to those who had been to China for years. They carried different and rather confusing names, ate rice rather than bread, and celebrated Chinese New Year rather than Christmas. The most despicable aspect of the coolies, in the eyes of many Westerners of the time, was probably their being unconvertible "heathens" who remained pre-eminently

---

[164]See *The Cuba Commission Report*, p. 27.
[165]*Ibid.*
[166]*Ibid.*

Chinese in almost every respect,[167] and who showed no respect for the Christian way of life. These prejudices undoubtedly affected the attitude of the coolie masters who possessed unrestrictive power over the fate of their employees. A comment on the attitude of the members of the lower class towards the coolies in Peru in 1873 reveals that the coolies were placed much lower than the members of the lower class in the social scale and only slightly higher than brutes.[168] If the coolies were generally regarded slightly better than brutes, it seems logical for the coolie masters to treat their employees as "tamed beast" who should be exploited and whipped.

The redemption of the coolies' misery was remote if not impossible. They were first handicapped by the language barrier and were unable to lodge any complaints against the overseers and the masters, to the proper authorities. They were prevented from reaching the authorities by intimidation and severe punishment.[169] Those who could not endure it any longer and were brave enough to bring the matters to the local authorities, were either brushed aside or rebuffed as a result of connivance between the officers and coolie masters.[170] The only hope of redemption, from the point of view of many suffering

---

[167]See "Mr. Jerningham to the Earl of Clarendon dated 9 March 1869", No. 1 in "Correspondence respecting the Emigration of Chinese Coolies from Macao", in *British Parliamentary Papers: Accounts and Papers 1871,* No. 47, C. 403, p. 1.

[168]Commenting on the attitude of the members of the lower class towards the coolies, the *South Pacific Times*, a Peruvian newspaper, wrote: "Every one is aware of the contempt in which the Chinaman is held in this country, however well conducted and respectable he may be, and those whom we should be inclined to class under this category are not a few. Many who affect to despise them could, if they were so disposed, take lessons in cleanliness, sobriety, self-respect, and humanity from most of the hard working emancipated coolies. But the prevailing idea among the lower orders in the towns has been that the Chinaman was created solely for their special benefit, so much lower down in the social scale than themselves, as to be but slightly above the brutes." Quoted in W. Stewart, *Chinese Bondage in Peru*, p. 130.

[169]Ch'en A-shun, a coolie who worked in a Cuba plantation, testified to the Cuba Commission that "on the plantation was a prison in which men were constantly confined and chained. If we went only a few steps beyond the limits of the estate, were seized, flogged and chained, so that there were no means of preferring complaints". Another coolie Huang Hsing deposed that "on the plantation we are constantly chained and beaten, but do not complain to the officials through fear of being subjected to even greater cruelties". See *The Cuba Commission Report*, pp. 23–24.

[170]Much evidence point to such connivance. Yeh Yu deposed to the Cuba Commission that "on the plantation we were constantly beaten. If we complained to the officials, our employers presented them with money, and we were sent back, and after our clothes were removed again flogged". Another coolie Hsieh A-fa testified that "on one occasion, having been flogged with great severity, I laid a complaint

coolies, was the expiry of their contracts which were usually set for eight years. Even this last hope was dashed because most coolie owners had no intention to honour the contract. By hook or by crook, they attempted to prolong the enslavement of the coolies as long as possible. Hu Ju, a coolie leader who told his own experience to the Cuba Commission, claimed ". . . on the expiration of the contract time, a cedula was withheld, and I worked for another two years, under contract, on the same plantation. On the termination I was sent to the depot, which I was hired out for three years. These ended I was sent back to the depot, where I laboured for five years without wages. I then again, during nine years, was hired out under various engagements, returning to the depot at the close of each. . . ."[171] He further stated that "I have been here for twenty-seven years. The inhabitants truly desire to reduce the Chinese into slaves for life."[172] This statement clearly reveals the true intention of the majority of the coolie masters, that is, to enslave their employees for life.

The coolie traders, dealers and owners should take the main blame for the miseries of the coolies in foreign lands. However, part of the blame should be placed on the governments of those countries which allowed large numbers of coolies to be imported. Had they tried to do something about it, many abuses could have been avoided, and the misery of the coolies could have been alleviated. Their failure in protecting the coolies was due to inability rather than inefficiency. The most powerful force operating behind the scene was the interest of the planters and landowners. Through direct participation in government, lobbying and asserting economic pressure on the existing governments, they prevented implementation of any policy which was not favourable to them, or they even manipulated government policies to the best of their interest.[173]

The inability of the foreign governments to protect the coolies removed the possible check on the abuse of the coolie system. The lack of an active protection from the Chinese government allowed the abuse to continue for a long period. To understand this lack, a thorough examination of the Ch'ing government's changing attitude and policies towards the coolie trade is needed.

---

before the officials, but my master by an outlay of money was enabled to bring me back, and then compelled me to labour in irons". *Ibid.*
[171]*Ibid.*, p. 41.
[172]*Ibid.*, p. 9.
[173]See W. Stewart, *Chinese Bondage in Peru*, pp. 12-28.

3
Coolie Trade and Ch'ing Government Policy

CH'ING GOVERNMENT POLICY TOWARDS COOLIE TRADE, 1845-59

The coolie trade began in 1845 and ended in 1874. In the thirty years of its existence, Ch'ing government policy towards it went through two distinctive stages. In the first stage, from 1845 to 1859, the government clung to the traditional policy of prohibiting emigration, and studiously refused to face the problems arising from it; in the second stage, from 1860 to 1874, the government was forced by the Foreign Powers to recognise the right of Chinese subjects to emigrate, distinguished between voluntary emigration and the coolie trade, and attempted to regulate the coolie trade which eventually led to its suppression in 1874.

The Ch'ing government had been very consistent with its restrictive policy up to 1859. Since its early rule in China, prohibitive statutes against emigration had been proclaimed and vigorously implemented. This had effectively prevented any large scale emigration overseas before the Opium War period. But after 1842, the rise of Treaty ports and Hong Kong as centres for foreign trade reduced the government's effective control over the emigration. The beginning of large-scale emigration to Western countries in the later part of the 1840s could not have escaped the attention of the Ch'ing government, but very little action was taken to prevent such exodus. The inaction of the Ch'ing government partly demonstrates its inability to solve the incurable economic problem that compelled numerous Chinese to seek livelihood overseas, and partly reveals its adherence to the traditional policy. The attitude of the Ch'ing Court to the new emigration was to ignore it and refer all cases back to the local officers with instructions to enforce the prohibition.

The main reason behind the Court's attitude is difficult to ascertain. It was possibly due to traditional conservatism, bureaucratic inefficiency, fear of foreign complications, lack of concern for any emigrants, or lack of information upon which the Court could act.

A modern study suggests that the lack of information from below accounted for the inaction of the Court during this period.[1] Whatever the main reason behind the Court's attitude, the problem of enforcing the prohibition fell squarely upon the shoulders of the local officers. They were charged with an impossible task. On the one hand, they were entrusted to enforce a practice that was carried on in ports often not under their firm control and by foreigners whom they dared not antagonise. On the other hand, they were required by the Court to discharge their responsibilities faithfully and vigorously. They were caught between the Court and the foreigners. Like other sensitive issues of the day, vigorous enforcement of the prohibition of emigration would involve foreign disputes, and sometimes could precipitate a war. The fate of those high-ranking officials who had precipitated the crisis over opium served as a warning to those officers who might have entertained the idea of carrying out their duty faithfully.[2]

This obvious dilemma forced many officers to turn to an opportunistic stand of "preserving yourself in the time of difficulty". The attitude of the local officers was therefore to avoid handling the emigration issue, and to tolerate the existence of the coolie trade to the extent that it did not threaten law and order. If they were compelled by circumstances to face the foreigners over the emigration issue, they would seek compromise rather than confrontation; they were prepared to give way to the foreigners as far as their authority was not publicly challenged. In case of a crisis, they attempted to solve the problem together with their superiors, and avoid disturbing the Court.

The Attitude of the Amoy Mandarins

As Amoy was the earliest centre of the coolie trade from 1845 to 1852, the mandarins there had been brought first into the position to deal with the problems of the trade. They closely adhered to the policy of "self-preservation" by ignoring the trade. They pretended

---

[1]See R.L. Irick, "Ch'ing Policy Toward The Coolie Trade 1847–1878", vol. 2, pp. 456–57.

[2]The best known example was Commissioner Lin Tse-hsu who was known of his role in the Opium War. When China was defeated in the war, Lin was used as the scape-goat for the defeat, and was sent to Ili in disgrace. See Hsin-pao Chang, *Commissioner Lin and the Opium War* (Cambridge, Mass., 1964), p. 212.

not to have noticed any of these illegal activities.[3] The fact that the great barracoons where the coolies were loaded and unloaded in Amoy were only yards away from the customhouse, served as a mockery to the mandarins' authority.[4] But the mandarins seem to have possessed the virtue of great tolerance; they would act on the issue only when law and order was threatened. Beneath this non-interference policy lay some practical advantages to the mandarins: to get rid of unwanted surplus of population, to eliminate some undesirable elements, and to obtain pecuniary benefits from the coolie merchants.[5] There being no evidence to suggest that the Amoy mandarins were directly involved in the coolie trade, at best we can claim that they condoned the activities of the coolie merchants.

But when the kidnapping of coolies was rife, and law and order was threatened, the mandarins were obliged to take some action to restore public confidence. Sometimes when encouraged by public support, they took positive steps to deal with the coolie trade. The attitude of the local mandarins towards the Amoy Riot in 1852 is a case in point, as seen in the last chapter when riot broke out in Amoy. The central issue was the kidnapping of the coolies. The worsening kidnapping was of course known to the mandarins who were aware that the powerful British coolie merchants were behind the scene. Fearful of becoming directly involved in confrontation with the foreigners, they refrained from taking any action. But by 1852 when public outcry flared up over the increasing kidnapping of coolies, they were compelled to take some positive actions. A notorious Chinese coolie broker of Syme, Muir and Co. was arrested and punished for the crime.[6] From their point of view, this action was moderate in view of the fact that kidnapping was rife. They did not close down any coolie firm, nor did they arrest any foreign coolie merchant. What they tried to do was to calm public

---

[3]See "Memorandum by the British Acting Interpreter Pedder, Amoy", in *British Parliamentary Papers: Command Papers* (*1852-53*), p. 364, Inclosure 2 in No. 9.

[4]See "Dr. Bowring to the Earl of Malmesbury dated 17 May 1852", *ibid.*, p. 346, No. 2.

[5]See "Note by Dr. Charles A. Winchester, British Consulate, Amoy, 26 August 1852", *ibid.*, p. 354, Inclosure 3 in No. 8.

[6]See "Mr. Harvey to Dr. Bowring dated 22 December 1852", in *British Parliamentary Papers: Command Papers* (*1852-53*), pp. 385-86, Inclosure 7 in No. 14.

indignation and prevent the outbreak of any large-scale anti-foreign riot.

This rather moderate action was however not appreciated by the notorious Mr. Syme, who, together with his aids, forcibly removed the broker from the police station — on action which sparked off the riot.[7]

The response of the Amoy mandarins to the riot was cautious. They realised that they had been dragged into the dangerous area of a possible large-scale conflict. To minimise the danger, they quickly moved to suppress the riot and restore law and order. The sub-prefect of Amoy by the name of Wang issued a proclamation on 25 November (1852), the day after the serious rioting at Syme's hong, appealing to the general public to be calm. He appeased public indignation by claiming that the coolie broker, Lin Hwan, had been brought to justice, and warned vagabonds not to take advantage of the situation to create disturbances.[8] What Wang and other Amoy mandarins feared most was that an agitated public would go all out to destroy foreign hongs and to slaughter foreigners. To prevent that situation occurring, they had to prevent the anti-coolie kidnapping riot from becoming an all-out anti-foreign movement. Accordingly Wang issued a second proclamation on 27 November to prohibit the circulation of placards which contained a strong anti-foreign overtone.[9] He called upon the public to cooperate with the authorities and report to him of any new placards attached to the walls. He also called upon the people not to be misled by rumours, to exercise prudence, and to leave the judgement of right or wrong to the authorities. He warned that those who disregarded the prohibition would be severely punished.[10]

---

[7]*Ibid.*

[8]See "1st Proclamation by Wang, Sub-Prefect of Amoy dated 14th day of 10th moon of 2nd year of Hsien-feng reign (25 November 1852)" (translated from Chinese by W.H. Medhurst, the Chinese Secretary of the British Consulate, Amoy), in *British Parliamentary Papers: Command Papers (1852–53)*, p. 428, Inclosure 13 in No. 14.

[9]See the 2nd placard under the title "Proclamation issued by the Inhabitants of the Eighteen Wards", "Evidence presented to the Special Court held at the British Consulate in Amoy from 13 to 16 December 1852", Appendix B, *Ibid.*, p. 418, Inclosure 8 in No. 14.

[10]See "2nd Proclamation by Wang, Sub-Prefect of Amoy dated 16th day of 10th moon of 2nd year of Hsien-feng reign (27 November 1852)", *Ibid.*, pp. 428–29, Inclosure 14 in No. 14.

To further placate the public fury, Wang issued orders to the police to apprehend the coolie brokers whom he denounced for committing a serious breach of the law.[11] Of course, the law had long been violated by the coolie brokers, but no action had been taken by the mandarins until the riot broke out. This act therefore can be interpreted as Wang's attempt to restore public confidence in the authorities, and to suppress the main cause of the riot.

At the same time, the Amoy mandarins also attempted to stop the coolie trade in the port. The Marine Magistrate who had an interview with the British Special Investigator of the Riot, Mr. Harvey, urged the British authorities to halt the coolie trade carried out by the British nationals, and warned that the lives and properties of British subjects would be endangered if the abuse of the trade was not corrected. He also urged the British authorities to punish the soldiers who had killed four Chinese in the riot.[12] This strong stand indicates that the mandarins were determined to rid the evils of the coolie trade in Amoy. Apart from these steps, the mandarins also referred the issue to the Taot'ai of Hsing-ch'uan-yung and the Governor of Fukien in Foochow for further instructions.[13] What instructions the Amoy mandarins received from their superiors were not known. But as the potential disaster was avoided, the Taot'ai and the Governor who had also adhered to the principle of self-preservation saw no need to disturb the Court, which probably explains why the Amoy Riot did not find its way into the official records of the Ch'ing government.[14]

The Attitude of the Kwangtung Mandarins

As the coolie trade was shifted from Amoy to Swatow, Hong Kong and Macao after 1852, kidnapping became especially concentrated in the province of Kwangtung where the above three ports were located. By 1856, popular hostility was greatly aroused to the

---

[11]See "Official Notice by Wang, Sub-Prefect of Amoy", *ibid.*, pp. 427–28, Inclosure 12 in No. 14.

[12]See "Account of the Interview at the Marine Magistrate on the 14 December 1852", *ibid.*, pp. 426–27, Inclosure 10 in No. 14.

[13]See "Mr. Sinclair (interpreter) to Mr. Harvey (Special Investigator) dated 18 December 1852", *ibid.*, pp. 424–25, Inclosure 9 in No. 14.

[14]Checking through the official diplomatic records of the Hsien-feng reign (1851–61) in the *Ch'ou-pan i-wu shih-mo*, nothing is found in connection with the Amoy Riot. See particularly *Ch'ou-pan i-wu shih-mo*, vol. 6, 2nd year of the Hsien-feng reign (1852).

coolie trade around the Canton area where a large number of innocent people were kidnapped and sold to the barracoons in Macao. Reflecting this public disquiet was the circulation of anti-coolie placards in the city of Canton. One of these placards told the story of a victim, and what he had heard and seen. It was claimed that there were five barracoons in Macao regularly collecting coolies for export.[15] The victim described in detail how innocent people were deceived, kidnapped and sold to the barracoons, and were rushed through the so-called "inspection line".[16] He described the horror of the treatment of these coolies in foreign lands once they were sold to foreign masters. According to him, these victims were "to serve either like baits for fish in catching birds, or as horse and oxen in the labour of reclaiming waste land, or perhaps they are placed in front of armies to be shot down by cannon. I know not what else they are subjected to, but it is enough that they became the slaves of foreigners to be driven about as these list. . . ."[17] It was also alleged that life in the barracoons in Macao was so intolerable that some of the desperate coolies took their own lives. In conclusion, this particular placard warned the residents of Canton to be aware of the evil-doing of the coolie brokers, and to guard their young from being enticed or kidnapped by the crimps.[18]

Much of the information contained in the placard was probably a true description of what actually happened in the Macao barracoons; the story of the fate of the coolies in foreign lands was probably used as a warning to those who desired to emigrate. The placard as a whole could be taken as a concrete expression of public resentment against the burgeoning coolie trade in Macao.

The attitude of the mandarins of the Kwangtung province seems to be more resolute than the attitude of the government of Fukien under whose jurisdiction that Amoy Riot occurred. This was probably because Canton was the seat of the Kwangtung government, and because the provincial government was better informed and could act faster. Although the Kwangtung mandarins had similar tendencies towards "self-preservation", they came under stronger pressure to act on the coolie kidnapping which as it were, occurred

---

[15]See "Translation of a Chinese Placard in Canton respecting Coolie Barracoons at Macao", in *FO* 97/102A(1856), pp. 88a–88b.

[16]*Ibid.*, pp. 88b–90a.

[17]*Ibid.*

[18]*Ibid.*, pp. 90b–91b.

under their eaves. Even before the outburst of public outcry in 1856, the provincial authorities already began checking the spread of the abuse of the coolie trade. At the beginning of 1855, a proclamation was issued under the name of the Governor, forbidding the abduction of innocent people. The Governor noted that these victims were sold to foreign lands to labour like horses and oxen, at that death alone brought them relief.[19] He also noted that the kidnappers were mainly derived from the natives of Shun-te, Tung Kwan (Tung Kuan) and Heang Shan (Hsiang Shan), the neighbouring districts of Macao.[20] The Governor instructed the local authorities to seek out and apprehend these offenders, and called upon the inhabitants and military to support the operation. The criminals once convicted would be punished with utmost rigour of the law.[21]

This is probably the first major official document on the suppression of the coolie trade ever issued by a Chinese high-ranking official since the coolie trade began in 1845. It seems to have little effect in checking the kidnapping activities for it was followed in the same year by a second proclamation issued on 14 April 1856. In this proclamation, the Governor described his outrage by declaring that he was "so exasperated that the hairs upon my head stand erect". He indicated that apprehension of the kidnappers was difficult because they conducted their operations in areas outside his control. He ordered the prefects and magistrates to employ guides to search for them and punish them. A special proclamation was also issued to the militia and people to arrest the kidnappers. After their trial and conviction, the Governor promised to reward the captors according to the number arrested. In this way, he hoped to "exterminate this class of rascals".[22]

The second proclamation re-affirmed both the official and non-official measures stated by the Governor in the first proclamation. His special appeal to the militia and people was indicative of the grave situation of kidnapping that had spurred the government to

---

[19]See "A Proclamation of Forbidding the Abduction of People with the Intention of Obtaining Ransom for Them, or to Transport Them Beyond the Sea, issued in the early part of 1855, re-issued in 1856", in *FO* 97/102A(1856), pp. 84a–85.
[20]*Ibid.*
[21]*Ibid.*, pp. 85a–86a.
[22]See "Parker to Sampson dated 8 September 1856", in *House Report* 443, quoted in R.L. Irick, "Ch'ing Policy Toward The Coolie Trade 1847–1878", vol. 1, pp. 67–68.

seek cooperation from non-official sources. But this action was still confined to the stringent punishment of Chinese nationals, he did not attempt to attack the root of the problem — the activities of the foreign coolie merchants, and the socio-economic problems of the society as a whole. The Governor realised that he had no solid support from the Court, and was well aware that an attack on the foreign merchants could lead to direct confrontation with the Foreign Powers which might precipitate a war. But he also knew that the solution to the socio-economic problems such as overpopulation and starvation was beyond his capacity. There is no evidence to suggest that the Governor's appeal for public support to suppress the coolie trade led to any concrete results.

By contrast, however, the Governor's order to the prefects and magistrates seems to have some effect. The chief magistrate by the name of Hwa proclaimed a stringent prohibition of kidnapping in 1856 in response to the Governor's order. Apart from instructing local police to round up some known coolie brokers, the magistrate ordered the boat people[23] who were involved in the local transport to help arrest the suspects.[24] Failure to comply with the order would result in the seizure of their boats and punishment. The magistrate also claimed that some notorious coolie brokers led by Chin Sing Fa had been arrested and severely punished.[25]

The official and non-official measures taken by the Kwangtung mandarins obviously failed to stop the kidnapping, this was reflected in the continuing growth of the coolie export from Macao after 1856.[26] This failure was predictable. Apart from their "self-preservation" attitude, their power to suppress the kidnapping was restricted because the whole illegal operation was directed from Macao where they had no jurisdiction.[27] Furthermore, the petty

---

[23]These boat people were a floating population on the Pearl river. They lived on boats and spent their entire lives on boats. They obviously were important in water transport, moving people and cargoes. Because of their important role in the local transport, they were called upon to help the government to arrest the coolie kidnappers.

[24]See *FO* 97/102A (1856), pp. 226b–227b.

[25]*Ibid.*, p. 226b.

[26]About 15,000 to 20,000 coolies were shipped from Macao to foreign countries each year from 1856 to 1864. See "Sir R. Alcock to Lord Stanley dated 21 November 1868", "Correspondence Respecting the Engagement of Chinese Emigrants by British and French Subjects, 1865–69", *F.O.C.P.*, No. 1737–39, p. 230.

[27]See "Parker to Sampson dated 8 September 1856", in *House Report* 443,

officials who were entrusted with the job of apprehending the kidnappers, were more inclined to bribery,[28] and were more likely to
be subjected to intimidation by the power of the underworld from
where the kidnappings were carried out.

The Attitude of the Court

Although the coolie trade began in 1845, the Court was not informed of its existence until about a decade later. At the beginning
of 1854, the Governor-General of Kwangtung and Kwangsi, Yeh
Ming-ch'en, memorialised the Court and mentioned the coolie trade
in the context of a possible Sino-American dispute. Yeh informed
His Majesty that a protest had been lodged by the American Consul
against a mutiny in which an American ship was seized by the
Chinese passengers, and the captain was killed. Yeh also stated that
the captured passengers were put on trial and found to be mostly
innocent coolies who, having been deceived by coolie brokers, were
being shipped to foreign lands. He claimed that the ill-treatment
the coolies suffered prompted them to mutiny.[29] This was probably
the first time the Emperor was informed about the coolies and the
coolie brokers, but His Majesty seemed to have taken no interest in
the issue whatsoever. He made no comment on Yeh's memorial,
but only noted that "I have read it".[30]

This indifferent attitude of the Court was further expressed in
1858 when the Emperor commented on the memorial of T'an
T'ing-hsiang, the Governor-General of Chihli, with regard to the
issues of opium smuggling and the coolie trade. T'an informed His
Majesty that the Russian Ambassador had advised the Chinese
government to protest with the British for allowing British nationals to engage in opium smuggling and the coolie trade. The
Russian pinpointed that the trading of coolies was concentrated in
Amoy and other coastal islands.[31] The Emperor's response to this
memorial was indifference. He emphasised that both opium smug-

---

quoted in R.L. Irick, "Ch'ing Policy Toward The Coolie Trade 1847–1878", vol. 1,
pp. 67–68,

[28]Commenting on the proclamation issued by the Chief Magistrate of Nanhai
district, the British Consul in Canton made such a remark to the Governor of Hong
Kong, Sir John Bowring. See "Sir John Bowring to the Earl of Clarendon dated 18
July 1856", in FO 97/102A(1856), pp. 224a–224b.

[29]See Ch'ou-pan i-wu shih-mo, Hsien-feng Period, 7:14a–15a.

[30]Ibid., p. 17a.

[31]Ibid., 21:20b–21a.

gling and trading of coolies were prohibited by law, and the prohibition was to be enforced by the provincial officials concerned.
Thus, there was no need for T'an to specially memorialise on these
matters.[32] The Emperor's attitude towards the coolie trade was
clear to his mandarins — he was simply not interested in the issue.
Perhaps because he was busily occupied with the suppression of the
Taipings and fighting a war with Britain and France at that time, he
had no time for seemingly trivial matters, such as the coolie trade.
If there was any violation of the existing emigration law, it was the
responsibility of the provincial officials to apprehend those wrong-
doers, and he was preferably not to be disturbed.

It was only a year later (1859) that the attention of the Court was
seriously drawn to the problem of the coolie trade. In late July and
early August 1859, tension between foreigners and Chinese in
Shanghai developed to a dangerous level. Communications were at
one point severed and trade came to a standstill. The foreigners
went so far as to deploy troops in anticipation of an assault. The
crisis was caused by attacks upon foreigners in retaliation for their
purchase of kidnapped coolies from Chinese brokers. The crisis in
Shanghai took place at a very delicate time when negotiations to
settle differences over the exchange of the Tientsin Treaty were
under way between the Imperial Commissioner Ho Kuei-ch'ing and
the British Plenipotentiary, Frederic A.W. Bruce. The two con-
secutive riots in July and August not only threatened the lives of the
foreigners,[33] but also affected the negotiations. This was why the
Imperial Commissioner, Ho, had stepped in. He deputed Ch'iao
Sung-nien, a former Taot'ai awaiting appointment in Soochow, to
go to Shanghai to work with the local authorities in pacifying the
populace, repressing violence, and apprehending and executing the

---

[32]*Ibid.*, p. 24b.
[33]Some time prior to the riots, relatives and friends of the kidnapped coolies were
patrolling Yang Ching-pin road, Shanghai, in the hope of intercepting and releasing
their relatives from the coolie ships. On 29 July 1859, following the departure of the
French coolie ship *Gertrude*, the patrols gave vent to their anger by attacking two
British sailors whom someone had identified as kidnappers. One sailor was killed
and the other wounded. When H.N. Lay, the Inspector-General of the Chinese
Maritime Customs, and a British doctor attempted to intervene, the mob turned on
them both. On the following day, another incident also occurred in Shanghai. Six
Siamese sightseers who wandered into the Ch'eng-huang temple while a play was in
progress were attacked by the audience in the fear that they had come to kidnap
coolies. For details, see R.L. Irick, "Ch'ing Policy Toward The Coolie Trade
1847-1878", vol. 1, pp. 80–82.

Chinese who kidnapped coolies for the foreigners; he also despatched a memorial to the Emperor pointing out that the British
representative was using the incident as the pretext for refusing further negotiations on the exchange of the treaties.[34] At the same time
he began to negotiate with the Foreign Powers to suppress the
coolie traffic in the area under his jurisdiction.

The seriousness of the situation prompted the Court to take action. On 22 August 1859, an Imperial edict was issued to the Grand
Council in which the Emperor decreed that "In order that neither
reason nor law be stretched, let orders be immediately issued to
search out the culprits who kidnapped for the barbarians and execute them on the spot, and ascertain the people who attacked and
mistakenly wounded the barbarians, and using the precedents,
punish them as befits their crimes. Let the Governor-General order
the local officials to exert all efforts in arresting the murderers.
They must be arrested and prosecuted. . . ."[35]

This was the first time that the coolie issue had provoked the
Emperor's anger and concern. He was not so much concerned
about the fate of the victims, but about the disruptive influence on
the delicate negotiations on the exchange of the Treaty of Tientsin.
From this point of view, the abuse in the coolie traffic in itself was
not an issue requiring special attention. Rather, he was concerned
that the behaviour of the coolie kidnappers, which had caused the
riots, would threaten the negotiations, thereby jeopardising both
his throne and the safety of the empire. The imperial decree was
very traditional — it gave the most severe punishment to the kidnappers by ordering the culprits to be executed on the spot without
trial. The severity was to serve as the most serious warning to those
who dared to follow suit. At the same time, he delegated his
authority to the provincial Governor-General concerned to apprehend the offenders and to reinforce the prohibition of emigration.[36]

The stern attitude of the Emperor certainly bore results. The
local official in Shanghai charged with the matter, Ch'iao Sung-
nien, apprehended and executed four natives of Ningpo who were

---

[34]"Memorial from Ho Kuei-ch'ing and 2 enclosures to the Court dated 22 August
1859" in *Ch'ou-pan i-wu shih-mo*, Hsien-feng Period, 41:44a–47b, 48b–50a.

[35]See the edict of 22 August 1859, in the *Ch'ou-pan i-wu shih-mo*, Hsien-feng
Period, 41:47a–48b.

[36]*Ibid.*

engaged in the selling of coolies to the foreigners, and their heads were put on public display.[37] In the two memorials received by the Emperor on 18 September and 4 October, respectively, the Imperial Commissioner Ho Kuei-ch'ing had reported that "The Shanghai populace and barbarians are now returned to normal. The local officials are still charged with the speedy arrest of the criminals [involved in the riots] and are to prohibit the export of coolies . . .",[38] and "The culprits involved in the Chinese barbarian controversy have been arrested. The notorious Chinese traitor Ni A-p'ei has also been caught and executed. The Shanghai populace and barbarians are getting along without trouble. . . ."[39]

The Imperial Commissioner, Ho, who was delegated to deal with the aftermath of the Shanghai Riots, took advantage of the occasion to try to stamp out the coolie traffic in that region. The officials under him renewed the prohibition of emigration and took strong measures to stop the kidnapping by beheading principal culprits and displaying their heads on poles as a warning. However, there was still the problem of foreigners. Under the extraterritorial clause of the treaty agreements with the Foreign Powers,[40] China did not have the right to punish the foreigners who were involved in this illegal traffic. It would be extremely unwise for the Chinese officials to try to punish the foreign coolie dealers, for this could result in direct confrontations with foreign consuls, and precipitate another war such as the Arrow Incident.

The only alternative left for the Chinese officials was to try to convince the foreign consuls to prohibit their own subjects from sending ships to China to procure kidnapped coolies. The argument used by the Chinese officials was that the general Chinese populace was outraged by the behaviour of the coolie kidnappers and foreign purchasers, and that the ordinary Chinese people had difficulty in distinguishing the difference among foreigners. As a result, innocent foreigners were killed. Citing the Shanghai Riots as an example that the British nationals were mistakenly wounded while the

---

[37]*Ibid.*, 42:25a–26a; see also R.L. Irick, *op. cit.*, vol. 1, pp. 84–85.

[38]See Memorial of Ho Kuei-ch'ing, 18 September 1859, in *Ch'ou-pan i-wu shih-mo*, Hsien-feng Period, 43:4a–6b.

[39]See memorial of the Imperial Commissioner Ho Kuei-ch'ing, on 4 October 1859, in *Ch'ou-pan i-wu shih-mo*, Hsien-feng Period, 43:17a–19a.

[40]See W.F. Mayers, *Treaties Between The Empire of China and Foreign Powers*, pp. 80–81; see also *Chung-wai tiao-yeh hui-p'ien*, p. 125.

public anger was caused by the French coolie ship, the Chinese officials argued that it would be difficult for the Chinese authorities to guarantee the safety of lives and properties of foreigners in the event of such riots. The only course to prevent repetition of such tragedies was for the foreign consuls to prohibit their nationals from procuring kidnapped coolies.[41] The argument was sound and reasonable. The Chinese officials found a great deal of sympathy and cooperation from the French and Americans. But the British, however, remained adamant and even went so far as to accuse Chinese authorities of inciting the general populace of Shanghai against the foreigners.[42]

The British Policy.

The British government had been very consistent with its policy against the prohibition of Chinese immigrants, although it wanted the abuse of coolie trade stopped. The official British policy was to acquire Chinese cheap labour through a regulated source. In essence, the formation of the British policy was governed by two important considerations: the need for cheap labour in many British colonies and the demand of an influential public opinion in Britain that all forms of slavery in its realm be abolished. These two considerations were in fact contradictory, for the insistence on one would undermine the other. To reconcile these two contradictory positions, the British government adopted a policy of importing Chinese labourers from the Straits Settlements (a British colony) into her other possessions. The reasoning behind was that if the Chinese labourers had already emigrated to the Straits Settlements, they must have been well aware of implications of a labour con tract. Their entering into further contracts, therefore, must be considered to be voluntary. This policy could overcome the opposition of those anti-slavery crusaders as well as to meet the demand of the planters in the colonies. At the end of 1843, licences were issued for

---

[41]See "Ho Kuei-ching chih Hua Jo-han chao-hui dated 9th day of 8th moon of 9th year of Hsien-feng" (Communication from Ho Kuei-ching to John E. Ward, 5 September 1859), in Chu Shih-chia (ed.), *Mei-kuo po-hai hua-kung Shih-liao* (Peking, 1958), p. 17.

[42]See Memorial from Imperial Commissioner Ho Kuei-ch'ing, 18 September 1859, in *Ch'ou-pan i-wu shih-mo*, Hsien-feng Period, 43:4a–6b; also in Earl Swisher, *China's Management of the American Barbarians: A Study of Sino-American Relations, 1841–1861, with Documents* (Yale U.P., New Haven, 1951), p. 627, Document 478.

the introduction of some 2,850 Chinese labourers from the Straits Settlements into British Guiana, Trinidad and Jamaica.[43] But this policy was not put into effect, since the need for labour force in those colonies was met by Indian immigrants as a result of a surprising change of attitude of the Governor-General of India.[44]

The issue of importing Chinese labourers was not reopened until the "Free Trade" crisis of 1846–49. The Sugar Act of 1846 had equalised duties on colonial and foreign sugar. This made a cheap source of labour even more imperative for the colonial planters. Under these new circumstances, both the colonial planters and the British government looked to China. The policy adopted thereafter was to try to negotiate directly with the Chinese government for regulated labour force; at the same time, the colonial planters were allowed to acquire Chinese labourers through private sources but with official supervision. In 1850, permission was given to the planters of Trinidad and British Guiana to import Chinese coolies. To avoid the abuses inherent in the private procurement of coolies, the government decided to supervise the recruitment. E.T. White who had some experience in recruiting Indian immigrants in Calcutta,[45] was appointed as the government's immigration agent in 1851. White's effort in acquiring coolies "legally" in an illegal trade proved to be unsuccessful. He found himself caught between the rules set by the British government and the practice of acquiring coolies that had been going on for years. The British merchants and captains involved in the trade were unwilling to be bound by British regulations. Moreover, he found it almost impossible to secure ships for transporting coolies, for the maximum expense he was authorised to incur for each coolie was far below that paid by other agents. To accomplish his task, White had compromised his position by advising British ships to secure coolies from non-treaty ports which was not in direct violation of treaty agreements with China.[46]

White's failure was inevitable. He had no power to control British merchants and captains who were involved in the trade. At

---

[43]See P.C. Campbell, *Chinese Coolie Emigration to Countries Within the British Empire*, pp. 91–92.

[44]*Ibid.*

[45]E.T. White was the assistant immigration agent of the British government in Calcutta.

[46]See R.L. Irick, "Ch'ing Policy Toward The Coolie Trade 1847–1878", vol. 1, pp. 100–102.

the same time, the illicit trade was so lucrative that only those who were willing to pay high prices would get the supply of coolies. The British government, therefore, had to enter into keen competition for cheap labour with other Western countries. Possessing neither power nor wealth, White's initiatives were destined to fail.

The British policy of seeking a direct approach to the Chinese government for labour supply was equally unsuccessful. Sir John Bowring, the new Governor of Hong Kong and British Plenipotentiary, and one of the most outspoken critics of the abuses of the coolie trade, was the first British high ranking official to attempt to discuss regulated immigration with the Chinese authorities. On 13 February 1854, the British Foreign Secretary, Lord Clarlendon sent the newly appointed Plenipotentiary instructions to seek revision of the existing treaties. One of the proposals was "to regulate, if possible, the emigration of Chinese labourers".[47] However, Bowring's attempt in seeking an interview with Yeh Ming-ch'en, the Governor-General of Kwangtung and Kwangsi and the Imperial Commissioner in charge of dealing with foreigners, was unsuccessful. His trips to Shanghai and Peiho which were intended to negotiate treaty revision with the central government in Peking, also proved to be abortive.[48]

The next British attempt of securing Chinese approval for the right to emigrate by her subjects was made by Lord Elgin in 1857. When the relations between China and Britain was strained by the Arrow Incident at the end of 1856, many British thought another treaty should be forced upon the Chinese. The West Indian authorities seized the opportunity to urge the British government to put pressure on the Chinese government so that they would "be forced or induced to sanction emigration". As a result, the British Minister-Plenipotentiary, the Earl of Elgin was instructed on 20 April 1857 that "The experiment might be worth trying of obtaining formal recognition on the part of the Emperor of the right of all classes of his subjects, male or female, to leave the country if they should be inclined to do so".[49] Lord Elgin raised the subject at the

---

[47]See Lord Clarendon to Dr. Bowring dated 13 February 1854, in H.B. Morse, *The International Relations of the Chinese Empire*, vol. 1, p. 672, Appendix Q, item 6.

[48]For Bowring's trips to Shanghai and Peiho, see W.C. Costin, *Great Britain and China 1833–1860*, pp. 186–94.

[49]See P.C. Campbell, *Chinese Coolie Emigration to Countries Within The British Empire*, p. 112.

Tientsin negotiations, but it was outweighed by other important issues.[50] He decided to give up his insistence upon the issue in the belief that it might be used by the Chinese to delay settlement of other important issues.

CANTON REGULATED EMIGRATION

British failure to acquire Chinese labour was compensated by its success in Canton. During the period of the Arrow War, the British had come to the conclusion that one of the obstacles in advancing its interests in China was the presence of Yeh Ming-ch'en. In much of the British official correspondence, Yeh was frequently described as "intransigence".[51] But Yeh's method of dealing with foreigners had earned him a reputation of toughness and gained immense respect among his colleagues. He was also honoured by the Emperor for his "success" in handling "barbarian affairs".[52] To revenge Yeh's objectionable attitude and to teach the Chinese government another lesson, both British and French envoys, Lord Elgin and Baron Gros, decided to attack and occupy the city of Canton. The attack was launched on 28 December 1857, and the occupation was completed on 5 January 1858 with the capture of Yeh Ming-ch'en, who was shipped to Calcutta.[53] Realising their insufficient strength to rule the province of Kwangtung, the invading forces decided to recognise the existing Chinese government but to appoint an Allied Commission to supervise its activities in Canton. The Commission was composed of both British and French military and civilian personnel, including the British Consul in Canton, Harry S. Parkes.[54] The logical choice of a Chinese official to head the government for the joint administration was Po-kuei, the Governor of Kwangtung who became a prisoner after the fall of Canton. From the Allies point of view, Po-kuei was a more flexible

---

[50]The important issues in the Tientsin negotiations were: the resident minister in Peking, new ports along the Yangtze river, inland travel and indemnity. For details, see Immanuel C.Y. Hsu, *China's Entrance into the Family of Nations: The Diplomatic Phase 1858-1880*, Chapter 3, pp. 46-70.

[51]W.C. Costin, *op. cit.*, pp. 188, 199-201, 202, 259, 268, 313.

[52]The Emperor Tao-kuang had conferred upon Yeh Ming-ch'en the title of Baron of the 1st degree. See *Ch'ou-pan i-wu shih-mo*, Tao-kuang period, 80:15a-16a.

[53]See John Wong, *Yeh Ming-ch'en: Viceroy of Liang Kuang 1852-58* (Cambridge, 1976), pp. 193-97.

[54]See H.B. Morse, *The International Relations of the Chinese Empire*, vol. 1, p. 505.

and realistic person than Yeh Ming-ch'en. More important, Po-kuei was the only Chinese official who had commanded sufficient authority to ensure law and order for the province. His rapid rise in the provincial hierarchy indicated his administrative ability.[55] With these qualifications, Po-kuei was the ideal person to be the Chinese partner in the joint administration. In fact, Po-kuei was forced into such a position by the British and the French, and he was to maintain law and order among the Chinese population, particularly in the areas not directly under the control of the Allied forces.[56]

It was during the Allied occupation of Canton (January 1858 to October 1861) that the first attempt was made to regulate Chinese emigration. The disturbances caused by internal and external wars after 1856 left a large number of Chinese in Kwangtung unemployed. Many of them became bandits or were involved in the lucrative business of kidnapping coolies. Kidnapping was so rife at one stage that local residents in Canton and neighbouring areas lived under constant fear. The British Consul Rutherford Alcock reported in the spring of 1859 that ". . . The acts of violence and fraud connected with the coolie trade at this port have lately reached such a pitch of atrocity that a general feeling of alarm spread through the population, accompanied by the degree of excitement and popular indignation which rendered it no longer possible or

---

[55]In May 1849, Po-kuei was the Provincial Judge of Kwangtung. Several months later he was promoted to be the Provincial Treasurer. On 7 September 1852, he was promoted again to the governorship of Kwangtung, and he held that position up to the fall of Canton into the hands of the Allies in January 1858. See Huang Yen-yu, "Viceroy Yeh Ming-ch'en and the Canton Episode 1856–1861", in *Harvard Journal of Asiatic Studies*, vol. 6, (1941), pp. 37–127, note 126.

[56]The conditions laid before Po-kuei for acceptance were (1) a committee of officials, civil and military of the Allied forces, shall be appointed by the Plenipotentiaries and Commanders-in-chief. Its members will reside at the Governor's yamen, and will assist the Governor to maintain order; (2) beyond the limits of the positions held by the Allied forces, all cases in which Chinese alone are concerned shall be disposed by the Chinese authorities; but the above Committee will take cognizance of all in which foreigners and Chinese are concerned. Offences committed within the limits above indicated will be dealt with under martial law; (3) no proclamation shall be issued by the Governor, nor under his authority by his subordinates, until it shall have been submitted to the Committee aforesaid, and shall have been sealed with their seal; (4) all depots of arms, magazines, and military stores, shall be handed over to the Allied Commanders-in-chief. Po-kuei was at that time the prisoner of the Allied forces, he could only accept or quit. After 24 hours of deliberation, he accepted the conditions and continued his office as the Governor, *ibid.*, Appendix 7, pp. 111–12.

safe for any authority interested in the peace of the place to remain inactive. . . . The intolerable extent and character of evil has thus tended to work its own cure. When no man could leave his own house, even in public thoroughfares and open day, without a danger of being hustled, under false pretences of debt or delinquency, and carried off a prisoner in the hands of crimps, to be sold to the purveyors of coolies at so much a head, and carried off to sea, never again to be heard of, the whole population of the city and adjoining districts were roused to a sense of common peril. . . .''[57]

The activities of the coolie kidnappers greatly attracted the attention of the Allied Commission. It began to work out a new system of regulated emigration which would solve the problem of kidnapping as well as provide reliable labour supply to the plantations in the British colonies. The new system known as the "Canton System", was the product of the effort of Harry S. Parkes and J.G. Austin. Parkes who was known for his part played in the Arrow War, was the former British Consul in Canton, and was appointed as a British representative on the Allied Commission. He was outraged by the abuses in the coolie trade. Austin, the Immigration Agent-General of British Guiana, was entrusted by the British government to initiate an acceptable system of contract emigration to the colony.[58] His arrival in China at the beginning of 1859 was timely, for Parkes and other Allied Commissioners were deliberating on a solution to the coolie kidnapping problem.

The successful introduction of the new system could not have been achieved without the co-operation of the Chinese. The Chinese officials and leading gentry members displayed a spirit of earnestness and co-operation.[59] A reasonable explanation of why they were eager to co-operate is that they also saw the proposed scheme as an effective solution to the kidnapping problem. Although they ran the risk of severe punishment for collaborating with the enemies, they nevertheless wished to show their goodwill to the Allies. As the imperial army failed to protect Canton from falling into the hands of the Allies, they could always claim that they had been coerced into that position by the foreigners.

---

[57]See S. Lane-Poole & F.V. Dickens, *The Life of Sir Harry Parkes* (London, 1894) 1, pp. 192-92.
[58]See P.C. Campbell, *op. cit.*, p. 113.
[59]See S. Lane-poole and F.V. Dickens, *op. cit.*, 1, p. 193.

Introduction of the Canton System

The introduction of the new Canton system began with a proclamation on 6 April 1859. The main message of the proclamation was the right of the people to emigrate. With the new right, people could go overseas without fear of punishment. The proclamation strictly prohibited the kidnapping and the operation of the barracoon system. It cautioned the prospective emigrants to have a full understanding of the working conditions before they signed the contract. It also expressed the government's desire to see that contracts be fairly and justly drawn up and signed on their free will.[60] Surprisingly, this first proclamation was issued neither by the Government of Kwangtung nor the Allied Commission, but from two district magistrates who were evidently familiar with the plan of the new system. Two days later (8 April), Governor Po-kuei confirmed the proclamation. He attacked the practice of kidnapping, condemning it on pain of death and offering rewards for information leading to the arrest of kidnappers. He went on to find justification for Chinese wanting to emigrate, and conceded that voluntary emigration would henceforth be allowed on the condition that "the parties involved consent to the arrangement".[61] The arrangement of the timing of the two proclamations was probably designed to give Po-kuei a convenient excuse for not initiating the new system. If he were to be punished by the Imperial government for allowing people to emigrate, he could have pleaded that it was from the demand below that the system was introduced.

Although the outlines of the new emigration system were contained in the two proclamations, no concrete steps had been immediately taken. The death of Governor Po-kuei on 21 May further delayed its implementation. It was not until the end of October, 1859 that the regulations were promulgated. The regulations were based on the plan of J.G. Austin which was submitted to the Allied Commission on 22 October. Under the recommended new system, an emigration house was to be established; prospective emigrants were required to apply at the emigration house for contract labour in the West Indies; the entire system was to be jointly supervised by

---

[60]See H.F. MacNair, *The Chinese Abroad, Their Position and Protection: A Study in International Law and Relations* (Shanghai, 1926, reprint, Taipei, 1971), pp. 13-14.
[61]P.C. Campbell, *op. cit.*, p. 120.

the British emigration agent and the Chinese officials; joint investigations were to be carried out to ascertain the willingness of the prospective emigrants to go abroad under the terms of the contract; conditions in the emigration houses and on board the coolie ships were to be closely supervised and controlled; and free passage was to be offered to the wives and children of the voluntary emigrants.[62]

A series of informal meetings were held between Parkes who represented the Allied Commission, and the Governor-General Lao Ch'ung-kuang and some of the leaders of the community. On 26 October, five articles of regulation were drafted and submitted to the Governor-General for approval. Two days later (28 October 1859), Lao issued a proclamation confirming the right of Chinese people to emigrate and describing the conditions under which emigration was to be allowed. He stated that "It has been formally intimated to me by the Allied Commissioners that the British government has sent an authorised agent to these provinces to establish an emigration house for the reception of emigrants for the British West Indies. To this end it is proposed that those Chinese who wish to obtain employment in the said colonies should go to the emigration house and there negotiate for themselves all the conditions of service as well as their exact destination, and that these conditions, when accepted by both parties, should be recorded in a formal contract and joint inquiry to be held by the foreign agent and a Chinese officer specially deputed for the purpose, in order that the circumstances of each case may be clearly ascertained and thus all the abuses intent on kidnapping may be eradicated".

He went on to say: "I am also requested by the Allied Commissioners to issue a proclamation on the subject. I have accordingly directed the Financial and Judicial Commissioners of Kwangtung to communicate the establishment of these arrangements to all their respective subordinate authorities and to require them to make the same everywhere known by proclamation; and the said commissioners will also see that the cooperation of the Chinese officers with the foreign emigration agents is duly provided for. And, in addition to the above, I myself proclaim these measures to the poorer classes. . . . Let it be known by you all that those who desire of their own will to go abroad . . . should proceed themselves to the emigration houses . . . when the Chinese officer and the emigration

---

[62]See R.L. Irick, "Ch'ing Policy Toward The Coolie Trade, 1847–1878", vol. 1, p. 115.

agent will carefully . . . ascertain whether they are indeed voluntary emigrants, and not victims to the crafty designs of kidnappers. . . ."[63]

Immediately after the official proclamation, the West Indies agent posted public notices soliciting labourers and describing the conditions under which emigrants would work in the colony. Rules and regulations of the emigration house were also widely published. At the same time Chinese officials were sent into country areas to explain to local leaders that emigration to the British West Indies was permissible and to seek their cooperation. On 10 November 1859, a license was issued to Mr. J.G. Austin, and the first emigration house was soon established under the joint control of Mr. T. Sampson, the local British agent, and a Chinese deputy magistrate.[64]

The centrepiece of the new system was the emigration house. It was to take charge of the whole operation of recruitment — from putting up the posters, to asserting the free will of emigrants, enforcing new rules and regulations, and arranging transportation of the emigrants. The emigration house was therefore to take the place of the barracoon to process the prospective emigrants. Because emigration was made "legal" and public, procurement of emigrants did not need to go underground, and was free from the control of the underworld in which the crimps used to operate. Because the emigration house was licensed and was under the joint supervision of a foreign emigration agent and a Chinese official, potential abuses were effectively prevented.

However, the problem remained of how to get the prospective emigrants to the emigration house. As the new system lacked the middlemen such as crimps, it had to rely on the village elders and gentry members to pass around the reliable information about the emigration.[65] With their special status in the society, their words were likely to be taken into confidence by the prospective emigrants. The sending of Chinese officials into country areas to spread the emigration news contributed in part to the success of the new system, by strengthening the link between the emigration house and the prospective emigrants. News spread through official

---

[63]See C. Clementi, *The Chinese in British Guiana* (Georgetown, 1915), Chapter 4.
[64]See P.C. Campbell, *op. cit.*, pp. 123-24.
[65]*Ibid.*

channel carried special weight among the local leaders who were given a feeling that they were doing something worthwhile for the government and the people.

Although the Canton system achieved a reasonable success by providing needed labour to the British colonies, it failed to eradicate the coolie trade. The existing crimping system was so entrenched that any effective control over it required successful cooperation from all parties concerned, including many countries in the West. Even within the province of Kwangtung, neither the Allied agents nor the Chinese officials could exercise sufficient control over the areas outside Canton. Moreover, the unscrupulous coolie merchants, including many Englishmen, had only paid lip service to the new regulations.[66]

The Enforcement of the Canton System

The enforcement of the Canton system rested partly on the Chinese government in Kwangtung. With its ambiguous status in relation to the Allied and the Peking governments, its power and authority were greatly curtailed. However, the Governor-General Lao Ch'ung-kuang took the initiative to enforce the law. Two days after his approval of the introduction of the regulated emigration, he despatched a fleet of war junks to the Whampoa anchorage. Thirty-six coolie kidnappers were arrested and forty-one victims were released. Eighteen kidnappers were beheaded and eleven received severe punishment. A cruiser was permanently assigned to the area to prevent future traffic between foreign receiving ships and the Chinese crimps.[67]

Lao realised the success of the system depended, to a greater extent, on the cooperation of Foreign Powers other than Britain and France. On 21 November 1859, he sent a copy of the regulations to Oliver H. Perry, the American Consul in Canton, and it was probably at the time that he issued a joint circular to the foreign consuls declaring that the regulations were to be applied to all concerned, and requesting that the consuls not allow their countrymen to collect coolies outside the licensed emigration house at Canton.[68]

But Lao's appeal for cooperation seemed to have little effect on

---

[66]R.L. Irick, *op. cit.*, pp. 118–19.
[67]See P.C. Campbell, *op. cit.*, p. 125.
[68]R.L. Irick, *op. cit.*, vol. 1, p. 120.

the on-going trade. Coolie ships belonging to American, Dutch and Peruvian nationals still anchored off Whampoa collecting coolies. Lao firmly believed that the presence of the coolie ships was the main source of kidnapping activities, and the success or failure of the Canton system depended largely on the control of the receiving ships. Failing to obtain the desired cooperation, he decided to act against an American coolie ship, the *Messenger*, as a warning to others. The *Messenger* was under the control of Captain Benjamin D. Manton, and had been in the vicinity of Whampoa for almost a year collecting coolies to be shipped to Cuba. Despite the warning of the Chinese government, it continued to operate in the said area. Lao had received a report that several hundred coolies were on board. He instructed the customs authorities to refuse port clearance for the *Messenger*. At the same time, he sent an official communication to the American Consul in Canton requesting him to accompany the Chinese officials to inspect the ship. This step was followed by a lengthy communication in which Lao reiterated his belief that the source of the kidnapping was indeed springing from the receiving ships. He informed the Consul that his immediate plan was to bring all the coolies on board to Canton for interrogation. He requested the Consul for co-operation in this action, and concluded by pointing out that such steps were necessary to ensure the function of the Canton system, to restore friendly relations with the Americans, and to eradicate the evil of the kidnapping.[69]

These communications prompted the American Consul to go to Whampoa to take part in the investigation. As a result of the investigation, fifty coolies on board of three American receiving ships were found to be the victims, twenty-eight of them came from the *Messenger*.[70] All of them were turned over to the Canton authorities for rehabilitation. Governor-General Lao Ch'ung-kuang made the *Messenger* issue a test case for the enforcement of the Canton system, and he won the battle. His toughness surprised his colleagues as well as foreign observers. He could have got himself into great trouble if a direct confrontation developed between him and the American representative in China. What had

---

[69]See "The Communication from Lao Ch'ung-kuang to the American Consul Perry" classified as Communication 3, in Chu Shih-chia (ed.), *Mei-kuo po-hai hua-kung shih-liao* (Collection of Historical Materials of American Oppression of Chinese Coolies) (Chung-hua Book Company, 1958, Peking), p. 20.

[70]See R.L. Irick, *op. cit.*, vol. 1, p. 125.

happened earlier to Commissioners Lin Tse-hsu and Yeh Ming-ch'en must have reminded him of the possible consequences. Perhaps his courage came from his firm belief that the evil kidnapping should be eradicated at all cost, even to place his job on the line; or perhaps he felt his action would have firm support of the British representatives whose interests were at stake in the success or failure of the Canton system. Whatever the reasons, Lao had, to a certain extent, successfully enforced the new system, and later extended it to Swatow, another Treaty port which was under the jurisdiction of the Governor-General.

The Reaction of the Court to the Canton System

The introduction of the Canton system was not made known to the Court. Presumably Governor-General Lao saw no need to disturb the Court, particularly inasmuch as the new system was a sharp departure from the existing emigration law. Lao could justify his involvement in the implementation of the Canton system only on the basis of expediency. But Lao's involvement could not escape the notice of the Censors who were traditionally to serve as eyes and ears of the Emperor and to check the power of the bureaucrats.[71] A Censor named Yang Jung-hsu saw it as his duty to report to the Emperor on this anomaly. Yang, a native of Pan-yu district of Kwangtung province,[72] probably obtained the information about the Canton system from a private source. Although he did not attack Lao by name, he severely criticised the Kwangtung officials in his memorial that they not only failed to prevent the kidnapping of the coolies, but also permitted innocent people to "sell themselves". He blamed the Allied oocupation for all ills of the Canton city, including coolie kidnapping. He also blamed the Canton system for the intensification of the criminal activities of the coolie kidnappers and traders.[73] He warned that "if we do not strictly prohibit this evil practice and deal with the kidnappers severely, it will become

---

[71]For a detailed study of the role of Censors in traditional China, see C.O. Hucker, *The Censorial System of Ming China* (Stanford, 1966).

[72]Yang received his Chin-shih degree in 1853, and had been appointed a bachelor in the Department of Study of the Hanlin Academy. After several years service in the capital, he was appointed Censor of the Honan circuit. This memorial was probably written after he had taken up his new post.

[73]See Memorial from Censor Yang Jung-hsu, 2nd day of leap 3rd moon of 10th year of Hsien-feng (22 April 1860), in *Ch'ou-pan i-wu shih-mo*, Hsien-feng Period, 50:1b–2b.

worse day by day and the good people will be harmed . . . the barbarians will be able to obtain more of our people from interior to
use . . . and I fear that in the future it will not be just confined to
Kwangtung only".[74]

Yang obviously presented a rather distorted view to the Emperor
with regard to the Canton system and the behaviour of the local
Chinese officials. He seems to have placed the blame squarely on
both the Allied government and the local Chinese officials for the
unbridled activities of the coolie kidnappers. His general obsession
with the foreigners was clearly expressed in the fear that more and
more Chinese would be utilised by the foreigners. He probably had
in mind that by so doing, China's manpower would be exhausted
and become weakened, while the foreign countries would become
stronger. Yang's memorial was read on 22 April 1860, and the
Emperor immediately issued an edict denouncing the foreigners
and the coolie kidnappers, and ordering an investigation into
Yang's allegation about the Kwangtung mandarins.[75]

The Emperor's strong reaction was not entirely unexpected. He
was angry because he was not informed of the introduction of the
new system which contravened the existing law. He was also angry
because the local officials seemed to have collaborated with the
foreigners. Although he realised that the imperial authority did not
prevail in the city of Canton, he nevertheless expected his mandarins to be loyal to him and to uphold the existing laws. This attitude was clearly reflected in his edict which declared that "if the
Kwangtung officials had acted to apprehend the kidnappers, the
wave of kidnapping could have been curbed. Their action of
punishing Chinese nationals had nothing to do with the foreigners
who should not have interfered at all. Why did not the officials act?
Instead they put out notices permitting people to sell themselves.
. . ."[76] His high expectation of their unreserved loyalty disappointed him when he read about their alleged collaboration with
the foreigners. This was why he wanted those officials who were
responsible for issuing the emigration proclamations to be severely
punished.[77] Although the Emperor was infuriated by the alleged

---

[74]*Ibid.*
[75]See Edict to the Grand Council on 2nd day of leap 3rd moon of 10th year of
Hsien-feng (22 April 1860) in *Ch'ou-pan i-wu shih-mo*, Hsien-feng Period, 50:2b–
3a.
[76]*Ibid.*, p. 3a.
[77]*Ibid.*

action of the Kwangtung mandarins, he nevertheless showed some concern for the abuse of the coolie trade and the fate of the victims. This was clearly indicated in his edict that he wanted the Kwangtung government to strictly prohibit the trade and severely punish the kidnappers in order to prevent the good people from falling prey to the foreigners.[78] Perhaps his change of attitude was partly due to Yang's warning that China would be weakened if the coolie trade continued unchecked.

The man entrusted by the Emperor to investigate Yang's allegations was Ch'i-ling, the Governor of Kwangtung. A Manchu of the Plain Yellow Banner and a collateral relative of the imperial house, Ch'i-ling became the Governor of Kwangtung in October 1859, succeeding Po-kuei. Being a Manchu Bannerman and related to the imperial house, he enjoyed special confidence of the Emperor. After a few months' investigation, Ch'i-ling submitted his report which was not read until 29 August 1860. By this time the Emperor was about to flee Peking and the Allied forces had entered Tientsin. This probably explains why the imperial endorsement was cryptically "noted" and why no further decrees were issued regarding the problem in Kwangtung.[79] Ch'i-ling's investigation confirmed several charges made by Yang such as the Allied occupation was responsible for the increased kidnapping of coolies. His memorial provided more detailed information about the Canton system and its emigration house, but he did not make any judgement on whether it was good or bad; he also indicated that the Governor-General Lao Ch'ung-kuang had cooperated with the foreigners by making a proclamation regarding the right for the common people to emigrate, but again he made no direct charges of treason against Lao.[80]

Ch'i-ling also suggested a plan for rectifying the situation: the offcials in Nan-hai, P'an-yu and Hsiang-shan districts of which the kidnappers appeared to be most active, were to be instructed to lead their's soldiers and gentrty in searching out and arresting the kidnappers, and suppressing the evil practice. Kidnappers were to be executed on the spot. The common people would be prohibited from going to the emigration houses to seek employment overseas

---

[78]*Ibid.*

[79]See R.L. Irick, *op. cit.*, vol. 1, p. 169.

[80]Memorial from Ch'i-ling, 29 August 1860, in *Ch'ou-pan i-wu shih-mo*, Hsien-feng Period, 52:35a–36b.

and those who did would be severely punished. Local officials who did not carry out the new instructions to the best of their ability would be impeached.[81]

Ch'i-ling's memorial was apparently the result of the dilemma in the position he was in, that is, to investigate something he had known but failed to memorialise, and to criticise the foreigners but not to antagonise them. The investigation which by-passed the Governor-General Lao Ch'ung-kuang indicates that the Emperor had special confidence in him, but how to measure up to meet the expectation of the Emperor without implicating himself with the Canton system was a difficult move. Shrewdly, he presented the Emperor with detailed information about the Canton system, and a certain degree of co-operation that Lao Ch'ung-kuang had given to the foreigners, without however revealing the extent to which the Chinese authorities were involved in the emigration activities, for he, as the Governor of Kwangtung, was mainly responsible for whatever happened in that province.

Strictly speaking, the criminal activities of coolie kidnapping came under his jurisdiction rather than that of the Governor-General who was mainly responsible for military matters of the two provinces of Kwangtung and Kwangsi.[82] If it was the case, any further revelation of the deep involvement of the Chinese authorities in the Canton system would have jeopardised his position rather than that of the Governor-General. Ch'i-ling may have been an ardent foe of the Canton system, but he had to take some heat out of the issue in fear of being accused of dereliction of duty.[83] His plan for prohibiting Chinese from going to the emigration houses to seek employment and his proposed enforcement of new instructions by local officials were largely rhetorical, for he knew well he had no power to enforce them as far as the city of Canton was still under the control of the Allied forces. But he presented these proposals mainly for the Court's consumption and in order to calm the Emperor's wrath.

---

[81]*Ibid.*

[82]For details of the functions of Governor and Governor-General, see H.B. Morse, *The Trade and Administration of the Chinese Empire* (Taipei, reprint, 1966), pp. 59–64; Hsieh Poo-ch'ao *The Government of China 1644–1911* (New York, 1966), Chapter 11, pp. 289–320.

[83]R.L. Irick, *op. cit.*, vol. 1, p. 173.

CH'ING GOVERNMENT POLICY TOWARDS THE COOLIE TRADE, 1860–1874

Acquisition of Emigration Rights by the Allied Powers

1860 signified the beginning of a new era in the history of Ch'ing policy towards coolie trade. The new era was brought about not by the Ch'ing government's consciousness of its responsibilities towards its ill-treated subjects, but by the pressure of the Allied forces which humbled the Chinese Court. When the Emperor learned about the Canton system from Yang Jung-hsu's memorial and ordered an investigation into it in April 1860; the Allied expeditionary forces had already begun action in South China as the result of China's refusal of ratification of the Tientsin Treaty signed in 1858. On 22 April 1860, the day before the imperial edict ordering the investigation into the Canton system, Chusan island off the coast of Chekiang province was taken; the Allied forces pushed northwards towards Peking. Between 25 August and 5 September when the Ch'i-ling memorial was read, the situation in Peking became very serious as the Anglo-French Allied forces entered Tientsin. The Emperor's reaction against the Canton system became irrelevant. On 21 September 1860, the Allied forces took Peking, and the Emperor Hsien-feng fled to Jehol. Prince Kung, the youngest brother of the Emperor, was entrusted to negotiate a peace treaty with the British and the French. The fall of Peking thus helped to solve the problem of the right of Chinese people to emigrate, for China was placed in a rather disadvantageous position in the negotiations in the Peking Conventions, and she was forced by situation to comply with many of the new demands.

The inclusion of the emigration clause in the conventions was in fact consistent with the British policy. Lord Elgin had been instructed to discuss it in the Tientsin negotiations, but had not insisted upon it because he felt it might jeopardise his chance of success on other more important issues. The new situation provided the British solid ground to demand the imperial government on the emigrants' right and to implement the Canton experiment on a national scale. The result was the inclusion of the emigration clause in both British and French Conventions in Peking. Article V of the British Convention of Peking signed on 24 October 1860 between Prince Kung and Lord Elgin read:

> As soon as the ratifications of the Treaty of wu-wu year (1858, The Treaty of Tientsin) shall have been exchanged, His Imperial

Majesty the Emperor of China, will, by decree, command the
high authorities of every province to proclaim throughout their
jurisdictions, that Chinese, in choosing to take service in British
colonies or other parts beyond sea, are at perfect liberty to enter
into engagements with British subjects for that purpose, and to
ship themselves and their families on board any British vessels
at the open ports of China; also that the high authorities aforesaid shall, in concert with Her Britannic Majesty's Representative in China, frame such regulations for the protection of
Chinese emigrating as above as the circumstances of the different open ports may demand.[84]

Article IX of the French Convention, signed a day after the British
Convention, on 25 October 1860, contained a similar clause.[85]

Although the treaty clause on emigrants' rights established the
legal basis on which the British and French, and later other Foreign
Powers, could recruit Chinese labour force, it should not be taken
at its face value. To many Chinese, the law prohibiting emigration
was still there, although no longer operative. It still cast a shadow
over many prospective emigrants, and served as a restraint on the
free emigration overseas during this period. It was until 1893 that
the Imperial government took the initiative to abolish the prohibition law and widely publicise it among its subjects. However, it did
remove the psychological protection screen of the Ch'ing government's inability to act. The Court could no longer hide behind the
statutes in dealing with problems arising from the coolie trade.
Thus, it gave rise to a spirit of positiveness in the second stage of
Ch'ing policy towards the coolie trade.

The beginning of the 1860s saw the hopeful signs for the introduction of a uniform controlled emigration scheme and the ending
of the coolie trade. Not only did the Ch'ing Court admit the right
of its subjects to emigrate, but also a general favourable attitude
towards foreigners emerged. The humiliation of China in the hands
of the Anglo-French Allied forces caused the downfall of the anti-
foreign clique in the Court.[86] But the defeat put the pro-foreign

---

[84]See *Chung-wai t'iao-yeh hui-p'ien*, p. 12; W.F. Mayers, *Treaties Between the
Empire of China and Foreign Powers* (Ch'eng-wen Publishing Co., reprint, 1966),
p. 9.

[85]*Chung-wai T'iao-yeh hui-p'ien*, p. 88; W.F. Mayers, *op. cit.*, p. 74.

[86]See a good analysis on the internal political rivalry in the Court during this
period, in Chapter 2 of Masatake Banno, *China and the West 1858-1961: The
Origins of the Tsungli Yamen* (Cambridge, Mass., 1964), pp. 54–92.

party led by Prince Kung and Wen Hsiang in power. With the ascendancy of the new Emperor T'ung-chih in 1862, the power of the pro-foreign party was further consolidated. The unprecedented national humiliation also gave the Court and Prince Kung a fresh opportunity to rethink China's foreign policy. As the coolie trade was a sensitive part in dealing with foreigners, it increasingly received the Court's attention. Moreover, the establishment of the Tsungli Yamen as the *de facto* foreign office in replacement of the Imperial Commissioner system achieved a great breakthrough in China's management of foreign relations.[87] For the first time, China's foreign affairs were dealt with directly by influential princes and ministers. Unlike the previous Imperial Commissioner system, no issue relating to Foreign Powers and foreigners could be pushed around to evade responsibility. The Tsungli Yamen would make decisions over the matters and then make recommendations to the throne for approval,[88] and would facilitate the process of decision making at the Court over the coolie issue.

At the same time, the Anglo-French Allies and other Foreign Powers at Peking showed interest in solving the problems arising from the coolie trade. They seemed to be interested in working out a universal system for recruiting Chinese labour force. The British emigration agent, Mr. Austin, was summoned to Peking to take part in the discussion scheduled in the summer of 1861.[89] A representative of the Tsungli Yamen was also attached to attend the meeting.[90] Had the meeting been successful, the evil of the coolie trade would probably have been eradicated forever. Despite the fact that Austin spent the summer in Peking, no general regulations resulted.

The failure could have been due to a disagreement among the Powers over the handling of a private source of coolie emigration. Unless Spain, Portugal and Peru were obliged to observe the new regulations, any regulation adopted by the leading Foreign Powers would not have any significant effect on the coolie trade system. For Spain had the control of emigration policy over its colony of

---

[87] See Immanuel C.Y. Hsu, *China's Entrance into the Family of Nations*, pp. 107–108.

[88] For the functions of the Tsungli Yamen, see S.M. Meng, *Tsungli Yamen: Its Organization and Functions* (Cambridge, Mass., 1962).

[89] See R.L. Irick, *op. cit.*, vol 1, p. 183.

[90] R.L. Irick, *op. cit.*, vol. 2, Chapter 3, p. 22, note 17.

Cuba which was one of the main markets for coolie labourers; Portugal controlled Macao which gradually developed into the international market for kidnapped coolies; and Peru was also one of the two leading countries obtaining coolies through private channels. Thus, the co-operation of these three countries became the key to the success of eliminating the abuse of the coolie trade. Any adoption of a universal regulation would not only prove futile, but also would jeopardise the interest of the leading Powers.[91]

The hope for a uniform control of Chinese emigration and early elimination of the coolie trade was shattered by the action of the Tsungli Yamen. After the withdrawal of the Allied forces in October 1861, the Kwangtung government quickly let it be known that non-treaty nations would not be allowed to operate in Kwangtung. The local officials based their action on a communication from the Tsungli Yamen, and its subsequent instructions that "hereafter, even though they have a license from the consul, nations which have not exchanged treaties will not be permitted to go into the interior".[92] Whether or not this communication was especially directed against the coolie trade, it was nevertheless used by the local officials to deny the non-treaty nations to rent land, to establish an emigration agency and to recruit labourers. Of course the Chinese government had the right to reject the non-treaty nations from recruiting labourers in Kwangtung. The Chinese government at this stage still saw no benefit in letting its subjects seek a livelihood overseas. From its point of view, the rejection would prevent opening a flood gate for mass emigration and prevent many of its subjects from being sold into slavery in South and Central America.[93] However, this well intended move unwittingly prolonged the operation of the coolie trade. In denying non-treaty nations the right to operate under the Canton system, it forced the

---

[91]Austin remarked in February 1861 after he received the order to go to Peking that "they (the regulations) should be based on government emigration, with special restrictions where private individuals embark in speculation for Cuba. If we are driven into golden competition with the Cuban speculations, . . . I shall press upon Mr. Bruce whether . . . the withdrawal of British emigration would be beneficial to British interests generally. . . ." See C. Clementi, *The Chinese in British Guiana*, pp. 118-9.

[92]See for instance communication from Hsueh Huan of 24 February 1863, in "Tsungli Yamen Archives", Clean Files, French Bureau, 204, Lu-sung-kuo huan-yueh (Treaty Negotiations with Spain), TC2.

[93]See R.L. Irick, *op. cit.*, vol. 1, p. 185.

Cuban and Peruvian planters to rely entirely on the illegal coolie trade. As long as the demand for the illegal supply was high, there would be no chance for the introduction of a uniform controlled emigration scheme.

The Peking Regulations of 1866

The co-existence of the Canton system and the illegal coolie trade proved to be unsatisfactory. The kidnapping of coolies in Kwangtung province was still rife, and it threatened the general social order. This was indicated by the Governor-General of Kwangtung and Kwangsi, Mao Hung-pin, in his memorial to the Court in October 1864. Mao urged the Court to take resolute action against the kidnappers.[94] A meeting was held between the Tsungli Yamen and the Board of Punishment. They proposed to the Emperor that Governor-General Mao's original recommendations for severe punishments — decapitation for the ringleaders and strangulation for followers — be adopted. The throne approved the new measures and instructed Mao to confer with the foreign nations for satisfactory emigration regulations.[95] Hoping to gain better understanding and co-operation with the Foreign Powers, the Tsungli Yamen sent Robert Hart, the Inspector-General of Maritime Customs, to Canton to discuss the regulations with the Governor-General and the Governor. Subsequently both the Governor-General Jui-lin and Hart forwarded a set of draft regulations to the Tsungli Yamen. After further revisions by the Yamen, eighteen articles were presented to the British and French on 7 September 1865.[96] Following long negotiations and compromises, with Sir Robert Hart as the go-between, all parties concerned agreed on twenty-two articles which were to govern Chinese emigration programme. On 5 March 1866, the prepared documents were signed by Prince Kung who was a Grand Councillor and the head of the Tsungli Yamen, and Rutherford Alcock, the new British Minister to China and the French Minister Bellonet. The documents were known as the Peking Regulations, which were to be applied to

---

[94]This memorial is not found in the *Ch'ou-pan i-wu shih-mo*, but part of it was quoted by Prince Kung in 1866. See the memorial of Prince Kung of the Ping-shu 26th day of 1st moon of 5th year of T'ung-chih (12 March 1866), in *Ch'ou-pan i-wu shih-mo*, T'ung-chih reign, vol. 39, p. 4a.

[95]*Ibid.*, p. 4b.

[96]*Ibid.*, p. 5a.

other foreign countries in relation to recruitment of Chinese emigrant labour.[97]

More than five years had elapsed between the signing of the Peking Convention and the signing of the Peking Regulations. Although there was no stipulation in the Peking Convention when regulations should be worked out and a programme be implemented, the slowness of the Peking government in working out emigration regulations invited unfavourable criticism. Commenting on the Peking Regulations, one British author Alexander Michie accused the Chinese government of being indifferent to the cruelties perpetuated on its subjects and its habitual apathy for the welfare of its people. Michie also greatly credited the success of the signing of the Peking Regulations to the British and French.[98] On the other hand, a recent study by R.L. Irick concludes that the Chinese government "lost no time in taking up the problem of emigration regulations".[99]

Both propositions are partially valid. The Chinese government was neither indifferent to the welfare of its people as stated by Michie, nor anxious to act, as described by Irick. The attitude of the Peking government in implementing the emigration clause of the Peking Convention was reluctant but practical. We must remember that the emigration clause was forced on the Chinese government when it had no ground for bargaining with the victorious Allied Powers. As long as there was no pressure put on it, it naturally became passive in the formulating of emigration regulations. Secondly, in the early 1860s, the Peking Court was recovering from the shocks of the loss of the capital to the Allied forces and the death of the Hsien-feng Emperor in 1861. The child Emperor, T'ung-chih, and Prince Kung's group, had just begun to consolidate their power. At that time, the suppression of the Taiping movement was in its final stage. The Court was therefore preoccupied with domestic politics and the coordination of the suppression programme.

Thirdly although the Tsungli Yamen was established at the beginning of 1861 to take charge of foreign affairs, its top priority was given to the implementation of diplomatic representation in

---

[97]See R.L. Irick, *op. cit.*, vol. 1, pp. 195-96.
[98]See Alexander Michie, *The Englishman in China during the Victorian Era* (Edinburgh, 1900), II, pp. 171-74.
[99]R.L. Irick, *op. cit.*, vol. 1, p. 189.

Peking, the opening of inner Treaty ports, and the impact of the opening of the interior of China to foreigners for activities such as anti-missionary activities.[100] Therefore, the issue of implementation of the emigration clause received little attention in the first half of the 1860s. Fourthly, the Canton system continued to function without much complaint from the Kwangtung government until Governor-General Mao Hung-pin's memorial in the fall of 1864. Thus, there was no urgency to implement the emigration clause.

However, the year 1865 signified the beginning of a new era in Ch'ing history. The Taiping regime which threatened the survival of the Dynasty was eventually suppressed in the previous year (1864); Prince Kung and his group had fully consolidated their power at the Court. More importantly, the Dynasty, after so many years of decline, was on the way to recover its strength. In the spirit of restoration, Prince Kung and other statesmen had the time and interest to look at issues of secondary importance such as the implementation of the emigration clause and the protection of prospective emigrants. But certainly, Prince Kung's initial effort was prompted by Governor-General Mao's memorial.

The Tsungli Yamen's communications to the British and French Ministers show a spirit of discernment by identifying two different types of emigrants: emigrants through official channels, and "free emigrants". At the same time, the documents also display a strong concern for the welfare of emigrants not only in the process of recruitment but also in their service overseas. Probably for the first time the Ch'ing government had distinguished the difference among the emigrants. The so-called "free emigrants" were those who went overseas of their own free will and were mainly in pursuance of economic gain. From an official point of view, these people were still more or less semi-legal. Although they would not be prosecuted because of their seeking jobs overseas, they did not deserve protection from the government. This was why the Tsungli Yamen in its communications told the British and French Ministers that it did not bother about these people.[101]

---

[100]Reading through the memorials collected in the *Ch'ou-pan i-wu shih-mo* of the first few years of the T'ung-chih reign, one would conclude that the attention of the Tsungli Yamen was much directed to these few areas.

[101]The communications said that "Wherever they go, whatever the jobs they take for their living, and whether they wish to settle or return to China, all these were up to their own free will, and had nothing to do with the Chinese government". See the

The Tsungli Yamen was much more concerned about the emigrants recruited through the emigration houses in the Treaty ports. Prince Kung pointed out emphatically that these emigrants who were under treaty obligation to work overseas should be treated differently. "Although they are employed by foreigners and received monthly salaries, they are not selling their labour to foreigners, they should be considered as if China were loaning them to foreign countries to use. Therefore, even though they had left their homeland, they are still entitled to protection from the Chinese government."[102] To prevent Chinese labourers from being taken to unknown destinations, or to be resold as slaves, or forced to do unreasonably hard labour, the Yamen proposed that all emigrant ships declare their destinations before leaving the port; after arrival at their destinations, the local officials would be responsible for collecting information from the ships, such as the date of arrival, and the number of labourers arriving. All this information was to be transmitted to the foreign consuls at that particular Treaty port, and then to the local Chinese officials. The local officials of the destination port were obligated to transmit the information to the Chinese officials through the same channel with regard to where the Chinese labourers were sent to; what types of work they did; and whether some of them had died because of illness. The officials of the host country were further obligated to state how many Chinese labourers were willing to stay on and how many would like to return to China after expiry of their contracts.[103]

The Tsungli Yamen also pointed out that the malpractice of prolonging labourers' contracts because of advance payment in money or clothing should be terminated. Thereafter, a maximum reduction of three months wages or three months labour was established to clear all accounts, no matter what had been charged against Chinese labourers. Finally, because all the labourers were uneducated people, they were further handicapped by language problems and were unable to express their grievances if they had any. For this reason, the Yamen would occasionally despatch Chinese officials to investigate the conditions of the labourers. The countries would

communications from the Tsungli Yamen to the British and French ministers, in *Ch'ou-pan i-wu shih-mo*, T'ung-chih reign, vol. 39, p. 6a.

[102]*Ibid.*, p. 6b.

[103]*Ibid.*, pp. 7a–7b.

be expected to treat Chinese envoys with courtesy and not to obstruct their duties.[104] The Tsungli Yamen's positive spirit and its concern for the welfare of emigrants were well embodied in the contents of the Peking Regulations. Of the twenty-two articles, eight major points deserve special attention. Articles 1 and 2 required prospective emigration agents to submit detailed information to the particular foreign consul in the Treaty ports. The information would include how the labour contract was arranged; how the emigration house was managed; and a draft copy of the proposed contract. All these requirements had to be complied with and carefully checked by the said consul and the local Chinese officials, and the good character of the applicant had to be ascertained, before a permit was issued to the agent for setting up an emigration house.

Articles 4 and 6 stated that details of labour contracts and important regulations relating to labour recruitment had to be posted on the door of the emigration house, so that the prospective emigrants would be able to understand them. Further, if the emigration agents wished to send representatives or hire Chinese to recruit labourers in the interior, they were required to submit the contract and related regulations to the consul and local Chinese officials, and a permit would be issued after approval. Their representatives would also receive special permits before they were allowed to go into villages to recruit labourers.

Article 7 stipulated that the Chinese government would send officials to supervise the registering of labourers in the emigration house. The Chinese official together with the emigration agent would witness the registering of names of the prospective emigrants. The emigrants were allowed either to go home or stay in the emigration house to wait for the ships. Article 8 specified that labour contracts should generally contain the following items: the destination and length of engagement; the sum of passage for returning to China after expiry of the contract; the number of working days per year and the number of working hours per day; specification of wages, rations, clothing and other fringe benefits; free medical care; the amount of deduction from wages for remitting money to families in China.

Article 9 limited the length of contract to five years and guaranteed that the emigrants would have funds to return home.

---

[104]*Ibid.*, pp. 7b–8a.

The contract could be renewed for an additional five years at the option of the emigrant. The emigrant would be given half of the return passage money stipulated in the first contract after the signing of the second contract was completed. The return passage would be paid on the expiry of the second contract. Emigrants who became incapable of working due to illness before fulfilment of the terms of their contracts would be paid with return passage and sent back to China. If any dispute arose from this, the emigrants would be allowed to apply to the court for the passage.

Article 10 limited working days to six a week, and a nine and a half hour day. Extra work would not be imposed on the emigrants if they had fulfilled their working time. Any extra work done during the rest hours would be paid, and remuneration would be negotiated between the employers and the emigrants. Articles 12 and 13 stipulated that prospective emigrants would be given four days for reconsidering their application after their names were registered. Contents of the proposed contract would be read to them after the four days in the presence of the Chinese supervisory official. If they genuinely wished to work overseas, they would then be asked to sign the contract. The day before embarkation, emigrants would assemble in the emigration house and be inspected by the Chinese official. The contracts they had signed would be presented to them and be confirmed as genuine copies. Once confirmed, duplicate copies of the contracts would be sent to the consul of the destination country to be put on record. Furthermore, a day before the departure of the ship, a Chinese customs official together with the consul, or his representatives, would check the number of labourers on board. The number would be recorded and cross-checked and signed by the two officials, and the said documents would be sent to both the local consulate and Chinese yamen for future use.

Article 20 stated that emigration ships would comply with certain rules regarding accommodation, food and sanitation on board. The foreign emigration agent would apply to the consul concerned for approval. If a ship was approved by the consul to be suitable to carry emigrants but was rejected by the Chinese supervisory officials, port clearance would not be given by the maritime customs. If that situation arose, the ship would not be allowed to leave, pending further investigation.[105]

---

[105]See *Ch'ou-pan i-wu shih-mo*, T'ung-chih reign, vol. 39, pp. 14a–20b.

The Tsungli Yamen's communications and the new regulations were probably the most important documents that the Ch'ing government had ever promulgated on the issue of emigration. They were certainly the first attempt by the Ch'ing government to regulate emigration on its terms, and to protect the emigrants as it saw fit. It was also the first time that the government considered protection of the emigrants overseas as its duty to its subjects. It was this sense of duty that was later to be extended to the protection of all overseas Chinese abroad. These documents have demonstrated that the Tsungli Yamen had a good grasp of the problems arising from emigration. The eight major points, as discussed, adequately covered the protection of emigrants throughout the whole emigration process — from recruitment of emigrants, to the transportation of the emigrants on ships; their welfare in foreign lands; and their safe return to China.

Implementation of the Peking Regulations

The Peking Regulations appeared to be impressive on paper, but their effectiveness depended very much on the co-operation of foreign consuls in the Treaty ports and foreign officials in the destination countries. The co-operation of the latter was difficult to obtain because there were no Chinese diplomatic representatives in those countries who could check their work. In this respect, China could only hope that they would abide by the regulations that their governments had signed with the Tsungli Yamen.

In actual practice, this would not work. The foreign officials simply brushed aside the regulations and evaded any responsibility assigned to them. They often kept the Chinese government in the dark by simply not reporting to the consuls concerned. The co-operation from foreign consuls in the Treaty ports was also difficult to obtain. The relationship between foreign consuls and Chinese officials in the Treaty ports did not appear to be cordial in the 1860s. Again, the foreign consuls were in the position to manipulate information received, if any, from the officials of the destination countries.

Apart from these, there were technical problems related to the implementation of the Peking Regulations. As pointed out by the French Minister in China to the Tsungli Yamen in his reply to the Yamen's communication, not all the emigrants recruited in the French emigration houses in the Treaty ports went to the French colonies and protectorates. French ships often transported emigrants for countries in South America, which were beyond French jurisdiction. The Minister further pointed out that he could instruct the French emigration agents and shipmasters to abide by the regulations, but he could not instruct the officials of other destination countries to do the same.[106] Part of this technical problem was caused by the lack of regulations binding the particular Power or country to recruit emigrants solely for their own use.

A further shortcoming of the Peking Regulations was the Tsungli Yamen's toleration of the so-called "free emigrants". What the Tsungli Yamen had in mind for the type of "free emigrants" were those who went overseas without the knowledge of the Chinese officials. The Tsungli Yamen expected some Chinese not to go through the official channel of emigration houses, which is why in its communication to the British and French Ministers, it distinguished the two categories of the prospective emigrants.[107] It pointed out quite categorically that those who went away not through official channels would not be protected by the Chinese government. In other words, the Tsungli Yamen would tolerate, although not approve, the private source of emigration. This together with its earlier decisions of not allowing non-treaty nations to participate in government-sponsored emigration unwittingly helped to perpetuate the coolie trade. In retrospect, it is clear that any government sponsored scheme of emigration would not succeed unless the private source of coolie trade was eradicated.

After the signing of the Peking Regulations, the Tsungli Yamen had the document endorsed by the Emperor,[108] and it was sent to the provincial and maritime authorities for enforcement. At the same time, the Yamen set out immediately to secure signatures from other Powers on the document. Prince Kung successfully obtained co-operation from the American government which instructed its consular officials in China to see that American nationals comply with the new regulations.[109] Besides getting U.S. co-operation,

---

[106]See the communication of the French minister to the Tsungli Yamen, in *Ch'ou-pan i-wu shih-mo*, T'ung-chih reign, vol. 39, pp. 12a–12b.

[107]See the communication from the Tsungli Yamen to the British and French ministers, in *Ch'ou-pan i-wu shih-mo*, T'ung-chih reign, vol. 39, pp. 6a–6b.

[108]See Edict of the Emperor T'ung-chih dated 26th day of 1st moon of the fifth year of T'ung Chih (12 March 1866), in *Ch'ou-pan i-wu shih-mo*, T'ung-chih reign, vol. 39.

[109]See U.S. State Department, *Papers Relating to Foreign Relations of the United States, 1866* (Government Printing Office, Washington D.C.), p. 557.

Prince Kung also obtained the concurrence of Belgium, Germany and Russia to the Regulations.[110] This move was part of Prince Kung's overall strategy. By getting the endorsement of the leading Western Powers such as the United States, Russia and Germany, in addition to Britain and France, it was hoped that this would probably produce a chain influence on other Western countries like Spain, Portugal and other small nations which obstinately resisted the giving up of the coolie trade. At the same time, by obligating the leading Powers to the regulations, he hoped to restrict all recruitment of Chinese emigrants in the Treaty ports, and isolate the coolie trade centre to Macao only.[111] If the results had turned out as he had hoped, he would have succeeded in eradicating the evil coolie trade without going into hard battle with Portugal, Spain and Peru.

Eventually the hope for eradicating the coolie trade was dashed by the abrupt change of attitude of the British and French governments. The refusal of both governments to ratify the Regulations was a classic example of power politics and an act of naked hypocrisy. On the one hand, they proclaimed their lofty humanitarian concern for backward nations and the people; on the other hand, they were concerned more about their own interests. While sending missionaries to convert and "civilise" the "heathen Chinese", they condoned and in fact demanded that opium be sold to the vast masses of Chinese. Similarly, while some Western diplomats like R. Alcock and Bellonet were sympathetic with the new measures of the Chinese in protecting its emigrants, their home governments disapproved their actions. For the British government, the main underlying reason for rejecting the Peking Regulations was the protest of the West Indies planters. The British West India Committee, the powerful pressure group, successfully put the pressure on the Foreign Secretary, Lord Carnarvon, and secured a promise from him that the Regulations would not be ratified without revision. The main objection of the planters was the return passage and clauses related thereto. Under the Peking Regulations, each Chinese immigrant would get at the end of five years either a return passage or the value of it. The cost of 100 Chinese labourers would therefore

---

[110]See C. Clementi, *The Chinese in British Guiana*, p. 218.
[111]See Prince Kung's communication to American Chargé d'affaires, S.W. Williams, in U.S. State Dept., *Papers Relating to Foreign Relations of the United States*, 1866, p. 498.

exceed the cost of 100 Indian labourers by nearly £2,000.[112] The acceptance of the repatriation clause in the Regulations would mean substantial capital outlay, and would increase the cost of production of agricultural commodities. The result of this would mean the reduction of the profit margin or would make the commodities uncompetitive in the international market.

Moreover, the planters feared the Peking Regulations would produce bad feeling among the Chinese coolies who were already in the British colonies. There were 12,000 coolies in British Guiana and Trinidad who had been brought there without a stipulation for the return passage. The introduction of new labourers under more favourable terms would produce discontent and jealousy among the old coolies, and would probably lead to a determination on their part to refuse to work unless they were granted with similar advantages.[113]

The French government, had no objection against the repatriation clause, it was more concerned with the length of contracts and working conditions. The reasons are obvious. It did not have colonies like the British where cheap labour was needed. Its interests were closely related to the transportation of Chinese labourers to Spanish America. It was the practice of the Spanish Americans to sign eight-year contracts and work the coolies beyond their endurance. The acceptance of five-year contracts and of improving the coolies working conditions would have resulted in a head-on clash with the interests of the employers of those countries. France could see little prospect of those countries reforming their economic systems in order to take in legitimate emigrants as long as the port of Macao still provided coolies on the old terms.[114] To protect the interests of its coolie shipowners and captains, it had also to protect the interests of coolie employers and speculators, and to insist on the deletion of the two unfavourable regulations.

---

[112]According to a careful calculation, the passage of 100 labourers from India (at £16 per head) would cost £1,600, plus return fare of 15 per cent (presumably the majority of them stayed) to India at £195 (£13 per head); the total cost of passage for 100 Indian labourers would be £1,795. On the other hand, the passage for 100 coolies from China would cost £2,500 (£25 per head), plus return fare of 80 per cent (20 per cent stayed) to China at 1,200 (£15 per head); the total would be £3,700. The difference is £1905. See P.C. Campbell, *Chinese Coolie Emigration*, p. 142.

[113]*Ibid.*

[114]See R.L. Irick, *op. cit.*, vol. 1, p. 220.

The British government was adamant in its demand for alterations of the Regulations. It resorted to intimidatory tactics, and successfully enlisted the support of some Western Powers including Holland, Prussia and Portugal. The result was the redraft of the Regulations, handed to the Tsungli Yamen on 1 April 1868. The redrafted document is a clear evidence of the lack of conscience on the part of the Powers. It was not only a return to the Canton Regulations, but also a return in many respects to the conditions of the regulated coolie trade of the 1850s. All provisions for protecting the emigrant once he left Chinese shores were deleted; much of the power of the Chinese authorities to regulate the emigration establishments in the Treaty ports was reduced; the emigration agents and foreign consuls were given increased power to prevent the Chinese authorities from interfering in the recruitment and embarkation of labourers. Obviously, China's adherence to the 1868 redraft would have been an implicit recognition of the right of these Powers to conduct what was essentially the coolie trade from its own ports.

Contrary to popular belief that the Peking government was apathetic towards the welfare of its subjects, the Tsungli Yamen displayed courage and consistency in resisting the pressure from the Foreign Powers. Prince Kung made it clear that the Chinese government would not accept the 1868 redraft as a substitute for the 1866 Regulations. He found a convenient excuse by stating that the Peking Regulations had been sanctioned by the Emperor and could not be abrogated by the Tsungli Yamen.[115] The only concession that the Peking government was willing to give was to reconsider the repatriation clause for short-term contracts of five years. It was certainly aware that non-ratification annulled the convention insofar as Britain and France were concerned, but it made it clear that if these two countries wanted to recruit Chinese labourers, they must do it on Chinese terms.[116] To reaffirm its stance, instructions were further sent out to the provincial authorities ordering them not to allow emigration except under the 1866 Regulations.

The courage of the Tsungli Yamen in resisting pressure was probably found in part in the general spirit of restoration during the T'ung-chih period. This was in consistence with its stand taken

---

[115]*Ibid.*, p. 228.
[116]R.L. Irick, *op. cit.*, vol. 1, p. 228.

against Russian encroachment of Chinese territories during the Ili Crisis of 1871.[117] The courage could also come from the increasing international outcry against the abuse of the coolie trade; or perhaps it was partly due to Prince Kung's new found secret of using international law to resist the unjust demand of the Powers.[118] Whatever the reasons, the Tsungli Yamen had scored a diplomatic victory over its right to protect its emigrants. In 1868, Britain requested the provincial authorities of Kwangtung to re-open emigration houses in Canton under the pre-1866 conditions — the request was flatly refused. Permission to re-open the French emigration houses was also denied. Britain finally acquiesced and was allowed to re-establish its recruitment agency in early 1873.

Suppression of the Coolie Trade in 1874

When the Tsungli Yamen was fighting to control and to protect its emigrants in the second half of the 1860s, the criminal activities of the coolie kidnappers were intensified in the coastal areas of Kwangtung and Fukien. Governor-General Jui-lin and Governor Chiang I-li of Kwangtung described the worsening situation in late 1866 as follows:

> . . . . In Kwangtung recently the cases of enticing people to go abroad have been occurring more and more frequently. It has reached the point that groups devise means to entice even women and children. As soon as they (those enticed) board the foreign steamships, they are taken to Hong Kong, Macao and other places, where they are resold (to be transported) to

---

[117]For the stand and policy of the Ch'ing government towards Ili Crisis, see Immanuel C.Y. Hsu, *The Ili Crisis: A Study of Sino-Russian Diplomacy* (Oxford, 1965).

[118]In 1864, the new Prussian Minister to China seized three Danish merchant ships off Taku as part of war trophy at the time when Prussia and Denmark were at war in Europe. The Tsungli Yamen protested against the extension of European quarrels to China on the fear that China's indifference on the issue would invite Foreign Powers to claim that area of water as high sea, which, according to Western law, belongs to no country. Quoting Henry Wheaton's *Elements of International Law* in a Chinese translation, Prince Kung insisted that Prussia did not have the right to seize Danish ships in Chinese waters, and refused to receive the Prussian Minister. Because of this, three Danish ships were released. This unprecedented diplomatic victory over a European Power by using international rights probably gave Prince Kung insight into handling of the disputes arising from the Peking Regulations. See Immanuel C.Y. Hsu, *China's Entrance into the Family of Nations: The Diplomatic Phase 1858-1880*, Chapter 9.

various islands, some several ten-thousand li distant. It is impossible to follow and find them. As for the foreigners, they do not know the facts of the deceit and look upon [the kidnapped people] as willing to emigrate. Therefore, the crafty villains consider this to be a good chance to make profits, and one after another are imitating and exceeding the [former practices]. Perhaps they misled [the people] with soft words or openly coerced them; there is nothing strange that has not been tried.[119]

The enticement method certainly was not new, but what was new was the enticement of women and children. The real motive of trapping women and children is uncertain. Probably some forms of work in farms, plantation estates and mines could be undertaken by them, or perhaps some women could be sold overseas as prostitutes.[120] Whatever the motive, the act reflects a desperate move on the part of crimps; healthy male labourers were hard to acquire, the crimps therefore turned to a less attractive source of labour — women and children.

In response to this new wave of coolie kidnapping, Governor-General Jui-lin and Governor Chiang I-li memorialised the throne to authorise them to treat the kidnappers as larcenists, that is, execution would be carried out before authorization was received from the Board of Punishment. Moreover, as soon as an act of deception was discovered — whether those deceived were men, women or children, whether they had been loaded aboard ships or not, or whether the kidnappers were relying on the foreigners for protection or not — the leaders should be summarily decapitated and the followers strangled. The local officials would apprehend the criminals and compile the evidence; the suspects would be sent to the provincial capital for trial before the provincial judge; then the Governor-General and Governor would review the case, and the kidnappers, if found guilty would be summarily executed. As in the case involving larcenists, lists of those executed along with the evidence would be sent to the Board of Punishment only once every three months. The Kwangtung officials also recommended that when the number of cases diminished, they again would memorialise the

---

[119]See memorial from Governor-General Jui-lin and Governor Chiang I-li, 1 December 1866, in Ch'ou-pan i-wu shih-mo, T'ung-chih reign, vol. 45, pp. 54a–56b.

[120]There were few reported cases of enticement of women from China who were sold as prostitutes in brothels in Singapore. See Lat Pau, 26/11/1887, p. 1; 22/3/1888, p. 5; 28/3/1888, p. 1.

throne.[121] The Court approved the stern measures recommended by
Jui-lin and Chiang I-li with an edict issued on 1 December 1866.[122]
The new measures seemed to have little effect. The fact that 15,579
coolies were shipped out from Macao in 1867,[123] the year after the
issue of the edict, demonstrates the inability of the Kwangtung
mandarins to stop the supply line of coolies to Macao. The failure
of the Kwangtung mandarins demonstrates once again that any
effective control over the coolie supply could not succeed without
the co-operation of Western Powers, including those non-treaty nations.

While the Kwangtung mandarins were trying to stamp out the
kidnapping activities, the ill-treatment of coolies during the voyage
and in foreign lands increasingly received international attention,
and created a favourable climate for the suppression of the trade.
The international anti-coolie climate was mainly created by a series
of incidents occurring between 1868 and 1872. The incident occurring in 1868 was connected with branding of forty-eight coolies in
Peru. A Peruvian plantation owner in Callao, fearing that the
coolies might escape, marked them with a hot iron as if they were
slaves.[124] Of course, slave-like treatment of the Chinese in Peru and
Cuba long existed before 1868, what was notorious about this incident was the way the plantation owner blatantly treated his coolies
as African slaves. This was why it received wide publicity in both
local and international newspapers. This incident began to create
some anti-coolie trade feeling among Western diplomats.[125]

Anti-coolie trade feeling was further heightened by several acci-
dents and mutinies of coolie ships between 1870 and 1872. On 4
May 1870, a coolie vessel *Don Juan* flying a Peruvian flag left
Macao with 665 coolies on board. Only two days later, the vessel

---

[121]See "Memorial of Jui-lin and Chiang I-li", in *Ch'ou-pan i-wu shih-mo*, T'ung-
chih reign, 45:54a–56a.

[122]See the edict of the T'ung-chih Emperor of 1st December, 1866, in *Ch'ou-pan
i-wu shih-mo*, T'ung-chih reign, 45:56a.

[123]See "D.B. Robertson to Mr. Hammond dated 15 February 1868", in *F.O.C.P.*,
No. 1737–39, pp. 146–47.

[124]See "D. Narciso Velarde, Portuguese Consul-General in Lima, to Senhor D.M.
Polar, Minister for Foreign Affairs of Peru dated 17 June 1868", Inclosure in No. 1,
"Correspondence respecting the Emigration of Chinese Coolies from Macao", in
British Parliamentary Papers: Accounts & Papers 1871, No. 47, pp. 3–4.

[125]See "Mr. Jerningham to the Earl of Clarendon dated 9 March 1869", *ibid.*,
p. 1; W. Stewart, *Chinese Bondage in Peru*, pp. 148–50.

caught fire, 500 coolies were burned alive or suffocated on the lower deck where they were confined behind iron barriers. Some of the survivors turned up in Hong Kong and received wide publicity.[126] This tragedy was followed in the same year by a mutiny of a French coolie ship *Nouvelle Penelope*. The ship carrying 310 coolies left Macao for Peru on 1 October, the coolies rose in revolt three days later, the captain and several crew members were killed, and the ship was forced to return to Bay Tien-pah, 180 miles south of Macao.[127] In 1872, another two major mutinies occurred on the coolie vessels of the *Maria Luz* and the *Fatchoy*.[128] Among these mutinies, the most widely publicised was the *Maria Luz* affair.

The *Maria Luz* was a Peruvian registered ship under the command of Captain Richardo Herrera, a former Peruvian naval Lieutenant. The ship left Macao on 28 May 1872 with 225 coolies on board. After about a two-week voyage, it was compelled by bad weather to sail into the Japanese port of Yokohama on 10 July.[129] During its anchorage, a coolie jumped overboard and swam to a nearby British ship, the *Iron Duke*. After being rescued, the coolie told his ordeal and the story of ill-treatment on board the coolie

---

[126]See "Earl Granville to Mr. Doria, British chargé d'affaires in Lisbon dated 28 July 1871", and "Mr. Doria to the Marquis d'Avila, Portuguese Foreign Minister dated 8 August 1871", No. 2 and Inclosure in No. 4, "Correspondence respecting Emigration of Chinese Coolies from Macao", in *British Parliamentary Papers: Accounts and Papers, 1872*, No. 70, C. 504, pp. 12–13.

[127]See "Consul Robertson to Mr. Wade, Canton, dated 17 November 1870", Inclosure 1 in No. 8 of "Correspondence respecting the Emigration of Chinese Coolies from Macao", in *British Parliamentary Papers: Accounts and Papers, 1871*, No. 47, C. 403, pp. 7–9.

[128]*Fatchoy* was a German ship flying a Spanish flag, with 1005 coolies on board, and was involved in shipping coolies from Macao to Cuba. The ship left Macao on 26 August 1872. Four days after departure, the coolies attacked the guards, but the mutiny was put down. The coolies were severely punished, many of them were flogged, beaten, their hair was tied to the iron barricade, and about 150 of them were put in iron below deck. When the ship reached Havana, about 80 coolies died on board which represented about 8 per cent in the death toll. This event caused quite a stir internationally. See Inclosures 1 and 2 in "Consul Dunlop (British) to Earl Granville, Havana, dated 24 December 1872", in "Correspondence respecting The Macao Coolie Trade and the Steamer 'Fatchoy'", *British Parliamentary Papers: Accounts and Papers, 1873*, No. 75, C. 797, pp. 3–4.

[129]See R.L. Irick, "Ch'ing Policy Towards The Coolie Trade 1847–1878", vol. 1, p. 261.

ship, and begged for protection. In view of its seriousness, the captain of the *Iron Duke* turned him to the British chargéd'affaires, R.G. Watson, who immediately turned him over to the Japanese authorities. Captain Herrera then went to claim the escaped coolie, with his promise not to inflict any punishment, the coolie was handed over to him and taken on board the *Maria Luz*. Breaking his promise, Herrera flogged the coolie and some others who had attempted to escape. Their cries greatly disturbed those on board of the *Iron Duke*. On learning of this new cruelty, Watson pressed the Japanese government to intervene. At the same time, some other coolies managed to escape to the *Iron Duke*.

In view of this new development, the Japanese authorities held an enquiry into allegations of the maltreatment of passengers. On 22 August, all 230 coolies on board the *Maria Luz* were brought to trial, many of them declared that they were the victims of decoy and kidnapping to which Captain Herrera did not deny. The Captain also admitted that he had cut off the queues of three coolies. Based on this evidence, the court found the Captain guilty of maltreating and restraining the passengers. Under the Japanese law, the Captain was liable for no less than one hundred lashes or one hundred days detention. But taking into consideration the special circumstances and other matters which worked in the Captain's favour, the court decided to pardon him and to allow him to leave with his ship. The coolies were to be turned over to the Chinese authorities.[130]

It was the first time that a coolie ship captain was put on trial and found guilty for his behaviour. Indeed, the trial indirectly found the coolie trade as a system guilty of inhuman activities. Never before had the "illegality" of the coolie trade been so firmly established. More important was the impact of the trial on international opinion. During the course of the trial, details of the abuse of the coolie trade system, the plight of the victims, together with the judgement of the Japanese authorities were published around the world.

The *Maria Luz* affair had profound international repercussions. First, it reached a much wider audience than any other coolie trade scandal, and more and more people were aware of the evil of the coolie trade. Second, it confirmed the alleged abuses in the shipping

---

[130]*Ibid.*, pp. 262–64; W. Stewart, *Chinese Bondage in Peru*, pp. 155–56.

of coolies to foreign lands. People might be cynical about stories of the maltreatment of coolies, but the Japanese court evidence left no doubt in their minds that the abuses were established facts not fantasy; and finally the trial put both Peru and Portugal in the centre of world attention. Peru was criticised for its lack of appropriate legislation to protect the imported coolies, while Portugal which was the only country actively involved in the large-scale export of coolies from its colony in Macao, was blamed for many of the evils connected with the coolie trade. International pressure was thus heightened to bear on both the governments to prohibit the trade.

Although these incidents occurred in different times and places, they invariably served as warning signals to the seriousness of the problem and demonstrated to the world that the abuse of the coolie trade system had reached such an intolerable stage that the victims were prepared to risk their lives in mutinies, and the coolies would continue to revolt if the system was not changed. A serious implication of these incidents was their possible impact on the China scene. News of this kind could provoke strong anti-foreign feeling among Chinese masses, and could lead to a massive killing of Europeans and the halting of trade in China. Realisation of the danger probably helped prompt the United States and Britain to put pressure on the Portuguese government in order to abolish the coolie trade in Macao.[131]

The suppression of the coolie trade in Macao in 1874, has in the past, been attributed to the international pressure brought to bear upon the Portuguese government;[132] little or no mention was given

---

[131]The British government through its embassy in Lisbon, pressured the Portuguese government on several occasions to stop the coolie trade in Macao, and called it as "a disgrace to humanity". See "Sir C. Murray to the Marquis de Sa da Bandeira, Lisbon, 27 May 1869", Inclosure in No. 5, in "Correspondence respecting the Emigration of Chinese Coolies from Macao", in *British Parliamentary Papers: Accounts and Papers, 1871*, No. 47, C. 403, p. 6; "Mr. Doria to the Marquis d'Avila, Lisbon, 8 August 1871", Inclosure ? in No. 4, in "Correspondence respecting the Emigration of Chinese Coolies from Macao", in *British Parliamentary Papers: Accounts and Papers, 1872*, No. 70, C. 504, pp. 13–14; in September 1873, the Consul-General of the United States in Hong Kong, Mr. Bailey, proposed to the British authorities to join forces in bringing pressure on the Portuguese government for the total suppression of the coolie trade in Macao. See "Mr. Bailey to Mr. Davis, Hong Kong, 12 Sept. 1873", in U.S. State Department, *Papers Relating to Foreign Relations of the United States*, 1873, vol. 1, pp. 203–204.

[132]See W. Stewart, *Chinese Bondage in Peru*, pp. 138–59.

to the effort of the Ch'ing government. But the study of Chinese documents reveals that the Ch'ing government played a greater role than has been recognised. The man who carried out much of the actions of the Ch'ing government was Jui-lin, the Governor-General of Kwangtung and Kwangsi. Jui-lin had been involved in the suppression of the coolie kidnapping activities in Kwangtung in 1866–67; his action however did not bear a great deal of result. But his actions in 1872–73 seemed to be much more effective. Perhaps he had better control over the province in the 1872–73 period than in 1866–67 when the society was rehabilitating in the post-Taiping suppression period. Perhaps he became more active in suppressing the coolie trade because he felt that the international anti-coolie climate created at that time was favourable for a total suppression. Whatever the reasons, the strategy adopted by Jui-lin in the period between 1872–73 appears to be practical and effective. He combined the attack on coolie brokers with cutting off the supply of coolies to Macao. In July 1872, he repeatedly ordered his subordinates to apprehend and severely punish those who were involved in the coolie trade.[133] In September, Jui-lin reinforced the rounding-up campaign against coolie brokers. Those who were found guilty of kidnapping of coolies were to be executed on the spot, while those who induced coolies were to be exiled to a border region four thousand miles away.[134] At the same time, he used river patrols to frustrate the coolie supply line. He ordered two warships with Chinese commanders to carry out the task, and the daily steamers between Canton and Macao were under strict inspection.[135]

Jui-lin's new measures forced the coolie merchants in Macao to organise sorties to obtain supply in Lei-chou, Lien-chou and Kao-chou in the remote southwest of the Kwangtung province where the control was relatively weak. In March 1873, after the acting Prefect of Lei-chou reported to him of suspected kidnapping activities of nine foreign ships, Jui-lin immediately despatched Brigadier General Fan Kan-t'ing with a steamship into action. As a result,

---

[133]See "Letter from Jui-lin to Tsungli Yamen, 7 July 1872", in "Tsungli Yamen Archives", clean file, American Bureau, No. 12, "Ta-hsi-yang huan-yueh" (Portuguese Treaty Negotiations), 12th year of T'ung-chih reign.

[134]See "Jui-lin's memorial to the Court on 22nd day (chia-shu) of 8th moon of 11th year of T'ung-chih (24 September 1872)", in *Ch'ou-pan i-wu shih-mo*, T'ung-chih reign, vol. 87, pp. 39b–40b.

[135]See *North China Herald*, 21/9/1872.

two ships with ten crewmembers, a Portuguese coolie merchant named Antonio Lapiola, together with eight kidnapped coolies were taken into custody.[136] In the following month, about twenty ships sailed into the same region in an attempt to recruit coolies. Jui-lin again took stern action. Three ships with nineteen crewmembers, three Portuguese merchants, and sixty kidnapped Chinese were detained.[137]

Jui-lin's new strategy apparently worked well. The rounding-up campaign checked the activities of the Chinese coolie brokers. This gain was consolidated by the attack on the supply line which had practically dried up coolie supply for the barracoons in Macao. In November 1873, the American Chargé d'affaires in Peking, S. Wells Williams, reported to the State Department that "The severe measures adopted by the authorities at Canton to prevent coolies of all kinds going to Macao, in order to stop as much as possible the delivery of those who may have been engaged by contract to go abroad, and the summary execution of all crimps and kidnappers who have been caught, have, I hear, made the business so dangerous and losing that most of the barracoons are empty".[138] Williams' description was probably the true reflection of the desperate situation of the Macao barracoons as a result of the stern action taken by the Ch'ing government.

Jui-lin's stern action received a boost in August 1873 when the British government approved the measures of the Hong Kong government to expel coolie ships. Under the new legislation, Hong Kong was strictly prohibited to be used as a port of call for any coolie ships.[139] On 23 August 1873, only a day after receiving the approval of the new legislation by the home government, Governor

---

[136]See "Letter from Jui-lin to Tsungli Yamen dated 9 June 1873" and "Communication from Jui-lin to Governor Januario of Macao dated 2 May 1873", in "Tsungli Yamen Archives", clean file, American Bureau, No. 12, "Ta-hsi-yang huan-yueh", 12th year of T'ung-chih.

[137]*Ibid.*

[138]See "Mr. Williams to Mr. Fish, Peking, 6 November 1873", in U.S. State Department, Papers Relating to *Foreign Relations of the United States, 1874*, p. 206.

[139]For correspondence between Governor Kennedy and the British Foreign Office with respect to the new measures, and the details of "The Chinese Emigration Ordinance 1873", see Papers relative to the "Measures Taken to Prevent the Fitting out of Ships at Hong Kong for the Macao Coolie Trade", in *British Parliamentary Papers: Accounts and Papers, 1873*, No. 75, C. 829, pp. 5-13.

Kennedy ordered five coolie ships to leave Hong Kong immediately, another two ships were ordered to leave within five and seven days respectively.[140] These coolie ships, in an attempt to refit and obtain provisions, moved to the docks at Whampoa which were controlled mostly by Hong Kong residents. But Jui-lin moved quickly to expel them. Realising the growing international anti-coolie sentiment and the new measures adopted by the Hong Kong government, he was determined to deal with the captains of the coolie ships. He ordered them to leave Whampoa and the adjacent waters and announced that no coolie ship would in the future be allowed to call at the port.[141] The expulsion of the coolie ships from Whampoa and the neighbouring areas dealt another blow to the coolie trade in Macao.

Under international pressure and the cessation of the supply of coolies, the Portuguese government was forced to capitulate. Governor Januario proclaimed on 27 December 1873 the abolition of the coolie trade in Macao, to be effective three months after that date. Thus after about thirty years in existence, the notorious and inhuman coolie trade came to an end on 27 March 1874.[142]

PROTECTION OF THE COOLIES IN CUBA AND PERU, 1872–78

The Cuba Commission and the Protection of the Coolies in Cuba, 1872–78

The sending of the Cuba Commission was an important event in the history of the overseas Chinese. It marked the beginning of Ch'ing concern for its subjects working overseas, and heralded a new era in the government's sympathetic attitude towards overseas Chinese. As the Commission was sent at the end of 1873 during the height of China's fight against the coolie trade, it must be seen as an integral part of China's effort for the total suppression of the trade.

---

[140]See R.L. Irick, "Ch'ing Policy Toward The Coolie Trade 1847–1878", vol. 1, p. 278.

[141]See "Letter from Jui-lin to Tsungli Yamen dated 18 November 1873", in "Tsungli Yamen Archives", clean file, American Bureau, No. 12, "Ta-hsi-yang huan-yueh", 12th year of T'ung-chih.

[142]See "Communication from Governor Januario to Tsungli Yamen dated 30 January 1874", ibid., 13th year of T'ung-chih; W. Stewart, Chinese Bondage in Peru, pp. 53, 159.

The sending of the Commission arose mainly from the dispute over China's rejection of Spanish recruitment of labourers in the Treaty ports in 1872. As the international anti-coolie feeling gained momentum, the Spanish coolie merchants realised that they would have a difficult time ahead in the recruitment of badly needed labourers for the island of Cuba. This prompted them to apply to the Chinese authorities for recruiting Chinese labourers under the proclaimed Peking Regulations.[143] The Spanish application was first approved, but was later turned down because the Tsungli Yamen ministers had read newspaper reports about the ill-treatment of the coolies in Cuba, and the reports had been verified by some foreign diplomats in China.[144] China's rejection prompted the Spanish Minister in China to apply for a compensation of $300,000 incurred by a Spanish merchant in Canton in the abortive recruitment scheme.[145] The dispute hinged upon the allegations of the ill-treatment of the coolies. The Spanish envoy denied the allegations categorically, while the Tsungli Yamen ministers believed the allegations were true. As a result of mediation by the ministers of the five Western Powers (Russia, United States, Britain, France and Germany) in Peking on 1 August, both parties agreed to the sending of a fact-finding mission to Cuba.[146] The Tsungli Yamen recommended Ch'en Lan-pin, then the Special Commissioner of the Chinese Education Mission in the United States,[147] to lead the mission; he was to be assisted by two deputy commissioners, A. Macpherson and A. Huber. Macpherson and Huber were the British

---

[143]See "Memorial from Prince Kung and other Tsungli Yamen ministers to the Court, on Ting-ch'ou day of 8th moon of 12th year of T'ung-chih (22 September 1873)", in *Ch'ou-pan i-wu shih-mo*, T'ung-chih reign, vol. 9, p. 28a.

[144]*Ibid.*

[145]*Ibid.*, p. 28b.

[146]In the meeting on 1 August, 1873, held at the Russian legation, the ministers of the Powers reached the following decisions: the Chinese government was to send one or more delegates to Cuba to investigate the conditions of the coolies there; the Spanish government was to be at liberty to take part in this investigation; the representatives of the Five Powers in Cuba were to assist the Chinese delegates if necessary. See "Mr. Williams to Mr. Fish, Peking, 6 November 1873", in U.S. State Department, *Papers Relating to the Foreign Relations of the United States, 1874,* pp. 203-204.

[147]Ch'en Lan-pin was at that time in the United States. Ch'en was appointed as a co-commissioner to Yung Wing to look after the first Chinese Educational Mission to the United States in 1872. See Yung Wing, *My Life in China and America* (New York, 1909), pp. 181-82.

and French Commissioners of Customs in Hankow and Tientsin respectively, both of them spoke Mandarin and read Chinese well.[148]

The recommendation was approved by the Court on 22 September 1873,[149] and was communicated to the ministers of the Five Powers. The Yamen's move in appointing two British and French representatives was a shrewd one. Both Macpherson and Huber served under Chinese Maritime Customs for years, they were likely to be sympathetic with China's cause. More important, their appointment to the Commission would give it an image of impartiality. In the game of international diplomacy, Prince Kung and the Yamen ministers seem to have realised that the image of impartiality was important for any future findings of the Commission to be endorsed by the Western Powers.[150] Although the Spanish envoy tried to out-manoeuvre the Chinese government by presenting the Tsungli Yamen a protocol in which two Spanish representatives were to assist the Chief Chinese delegate in the Commission, the proposal was rejected by the Yamen.[151] The three-men Commission with its Chinese aides arrived in Havana on 17 March 1874; it visited the local Spanish authorities and the diplomatic representatives of the various Western countries to prepare for the inquiry. The Commission began its work on 20 March and lasted until 2 May. In that six weeks, the Commission conducted the inquiries in barracoons, depots, plantations and jails. It collected many verbal material and 1,176 depositions, and also received 85 petitions supported by 1,665 signatures.[152]

The evidence collected by the Commission confirmed the allegations that the coolies in Cuba were ill-treated. The evidence revealed all aspects of the miserable lives of the coolies from the time they were recruited in China. The depositions and petitions showed that 80 per cent of them were kidnapped or were decoyed; the

---

[148]See "Memorial from Prince Kung and other Tsungli Yamen ministers to the Court, on Ting-ch'ou day of 8th moon of 12th year of T'ung-chih (22 September 1873)", in *Ch'ou-pan i-wu shih-mo*, T'ung-chih reign, vol. 91, pp. 29a–29b.

[148]*Ibid.*

[150]*Ibid.*

[151]See "Mr. Otin to the Yamen, containing a draft of a protocol, dated 9 October 1873", "Foreign Office (Tsungli Yamen) to Mr. Otin, dated 22nd day of 8th moon of 12th year of T'ung-chih (13 October 1873)", in U.S. State Department, *Papers relating to the Foreign Relations of the United States, 1874*, pp. 211–13.

[152]See *The Cuba Commission Report*, pp. 2–4.

mortality rate during the voyage exceeded 10 per cent. On arrival at Havana they were sold into slavery and extreme cruelty was inflicted on them at work which resulted in severe injury or death.[153] The Commission left Havana on 8 May 1874 for the United States to prepare the report. Ch'en Lan-pin was ordered to return to China to present the case in person. The report was completed on 20 October 1874, and was submitted to the Tsungli Yamen at the end of the year. After receiving the report and its attached evidence, the Yamen planned its move. The Spanish claim for compensation no longer remained an issue because China's rejection was justified. What the Yamen was most concerned about was the fate of the coolies in Cuba. Its key objectives were the repatriation of those who had fulfilled the contracts, and the protection of those who remained there. To work towards these objectives, the Yamen on 5 February 1875, forwarded the report with the supporting documents to the ministers of the Five Powers and briefed them on the findings of the Commission in order to put China on a firm ground for negotiations.[154]

At the same time, it widely publicised and distributed the contents of the report in an attempt to project the idea that the Spanish authorities was guilty and responsible for the ill-treatment of the coolies in Cuba. The Yamen also realised that the Portuguese suppression of the coolie trade in Macao at that time greatly strengthened its position in the negotiations, for the Spanish had no way to recruit needed labourers for Cuba except through the official channel. This enabled the Yamen in a series of conventions held in March under the sponsorship of the ministers of the Five Powers to adopt a tough stand in the negotiations with the Spanish envoy. It insisted that the following conditions be complied with before the Spanish be allowed to recruit labourers in China. First, Spain had to return all persons of official or literary ranks; all persons under fifteen and over sixty years of age; all under twenty and over fifty whose contracts had expired; and all women employed as labourers who were not members of the families of male labourers. Second, it had to make compensation for the coolies who had died as a result of cruel treatment. Third, it had to provide free passage

---

[153]*Ibid.*

[154]"See the special note from the Tsungli Yamen dated 5 February 1875, in U.S. State Department, *Papers relating to the Foreign Relations of the United States, 1875*, pp. 298–302.

for those who had fulfilled their contracts and who wished to
return to China, and also make special conditions for labour re-
engagement, lodging and freedom of movement for those who
wished to stay. Fourth, imprisonment and severe punishment by
employers were to be prohibited; all delinquent cases were to be
settled by the Chinese Consul. Fifth, foreign consuls were to be
asked to protect the Chinese coolies until a Chinese Consul was appointed. Sixth, it allowed the establishment of Chinese guilds and
the freedom of labourers to join them.[155]

Armed with concrete evidence, the Tsungli Yamen probably expected a speedy and just settlement with the mediation of the
ministers of the Powers. But it soon became disappointed with the
attitude of the ministers whose partial attitude favoured the
Spanish. Probably this was the first time that China used Western-
type diplomacy to challenge a Western Power. The ministers per-
ceived the danger of China having scored a remarkable victory over
the Spanish on the dispute of the emigration issue. This led them to
adhere to a rather hypocritical policy of "do justice to China
without offending the *amour propre* of Spain",[156] and this thus
indirectly encouraged the Spanish government to be intransigent.
Unfortunately, the negotiations were interrupted by the Margary
Affair,[157] and the frequent change of Spanish envoys in Peking.

The second round of the negotiations was not resumed until the
arrival of the Spanish new minister, Espana, in June 1876. Espana
attempted to exert pressure on China with a new claim of compensation for a Spanish ship alleged to be pirated on Taiwan coast in
1864 — an incident which occurred more than twelve years ago.[158]

---

[155]See Tsungli Yamen's memorandum to the representatives of the Five Powers
dated 4 March 1875, *ibid.*, pp. 307–308.
[156]See R.L. Irick, "Ch'ing Policy Toward The Coolie Trade, 1847–1878", vol. 2,
p. 359.
[157]For Margary Affair, see Chapter 4, Section A.
[158]In early 1864, a Spanish ship, *Sovrana*, was damaged by a storm and pirated on
Taiwan coast. The incident was reported to the Governor of Fukien by the Spanish
Consul in Amoy, but the Tsungli Yamen was not informed until 1866. However, the
Spanish Minister in Peking did not request compensation until 1868, and the Yamen
had instructed for an investigation into the circumstances under which the incident
took place. The issue lapsed until 1874 when the Spanish Minister raised it again in
an attempt to strengthen his position for negotiating a treaty, but it was brushed
aside by the Tsungli Yamen. See "Memorial from Tsungli Yamen to the Court
relating to the plundering of a Spanish ship and the exchange with Spain over the

He even threatened to use force. There were rumours of moving Spanish warships heading for Chinese waters.[159] Facing this new challenge Tsungli Yamen did not capitulate, instead it recommended to the court a war alert in the coastal provinces.[160] The firm stand taken by China, and the successful ratification of the Sino-Peruvian Treaty on emigration in 1876 probably had some bearing on the Spanish envoy who eventually gave in. On 17 November 1877, a treaty containing sixteen items was signed between China and Spain over the emigration issue which had dragged on for six years. China had achieved its main objective of protecting the coolies in Cuba and future labourers to that island. The protection was embodied in the following items of the treaty:

Item 3. Both countries agreed that recruited emigrants to Cuba must be on their free will, no Spanish subjects were allowed to use force or tricky methods to recruit emigrants in China. Any Chinese or Spanish who had violated this agreement should be severely punished in accordance with respective laws.

Item 6. China was to send a consul-general to Havana and consuls to other parts of the island where other foreign consuls were stationed; they were to protect Chinese subjects in the island.

Item 7. Chinese subjects in Cuba were allowed to move freely within and outside the island, and were free to take up any occupation.

Item 9. The Chinese consul-general at Havana would be required to work out regulations with the local officials in order to register the coolies in Cuba and future labourers arriving on the island. The consul-general would issue to Chinese subjects, certificates, which would be examined and recorded by the relevant local authorities. At the same time, the local officials would

---

treaty of Cuba dated 16th day of 10th moon of 3rd year of Kuang-hsu (20 November 1877)", in *Ch'ing-chi wai-chiao shih-liao*, vol. 12, pp. 8a–10b.

[159]A newspaper report claimed that Spain had moved 14 of its 20 warships from Philippines to China for military action. See "Memorial from Tsungli Yamen to the Court relating to movement of Spanish warships heading for China dated 25th day of 12th moon of 2nd year of Kuang-hsu (7 Feburary 1877)", *ibid.*, vol. 8, pp. 37a–38a.

[160]*Ibid.*

provide the consul-general statistics of Chinese subjects and their names, and facilities would be provided for the consul-general to inspect the work-places where Chinese worked.

Item 11. To return persons with a literary background or holding certain ranks, and the relatives of these people, the Spanish government would pay their passage home. The Spanish government would also provide free passage for aged labourers, widows and women to return to China.

Item 12. The Spanish government would press the employers to return those coolies who had fulfilled the contracts which specified a return passage. Those coolies who had fulfilled the contracts which did not guarantee a return passage would be repatriated to China after appropriate arrangement made between the local officials and the Chinese consul-general.

Item 14. Those coolies who had not fulfilled the contracts must complete the term of labour. The new regulations would apply to them. After the ratification of the treaty, all coolies detained in depots would be released and they would be treated as free persons.[161]

In return for the concessions given by the Spanish, the Chinese government allowed Spaniards to recruit labourers freely in China.[162] Of course, this was a departure from the position taken by China in the Peking Regulations in 1866 which emphasised the protection of prospective emigrants in the recruitment process.[163] But given the fact that the Macao coolie trade was suppressed in early 1874, those protective measures contained in the Peking Regulations appeared to be redundant. From this perspective, the concession given to the Spanish was not a high price to pay. The protection of the Cuban coolies was not put into effect until after the treaty was ratified in December 1878.

---

[161]See the Sino-Spanish treaty on Cuban Chinese coolies, in *Ch'ing-chi wai-chiao shih-liao*, vol. 12, pp. 2b–7b.

[162]See item 4 of the Sino-Spanish treaty on Cuban Chinese coolies, *ibid.*, p. 3b.

[163]See *The Peking Regulations of 1866*, in this chapter.

The Protection of the Coolies in Peru, 1873–1876

China's negotiations for a treaty to protect the coolies in Peru was comparatively smoother than the Sino-Spanish negotiations over the Cuban coolies. But from the beginning of the negotiations to the successful ratification of the treaty still took about two and a half years. Throughout the negotiations the Ch'ing government demonstrated its deep concern for the plight and welfare of the coolies in Peru.

The opportunity for negotiating such a treaty arose in 1873 when the Peruvian envoy, Captain Garcia y Garcia, arrived in China to seek a treaty on emigration and trade. Both domestic and international factors compelled the Peruvian government to abandon coolie labour and to seek the supply of free emigrants.[164] The main objective of the Garcia mission was to persuade the Chinese government to sign a treaty for a long term supply of free labourers to Peru. The Peruvian government realised it had a bad reputation in the treatment of coolies, and expected to have difficulty in acquiring a treaty with China. It thus tried to prepare the way for Garcia's negotiations by requesting the American and British ambassadors in Peking to influence China's attitude.

The Tsungli Yamen's initial response was hostile. It informed the Anglo-American envoys that China would have nothing to do with Peru until the Peruvian government had repatriated all Chinese coolies and declared its intention of discontinuing the import of coolies.[165] The Tsungli Yamen's stand was firm and clear. It was well aware at least since the second half of the 1860s of the ill-treatment of the coolies in Peru. These included notorious scandals of branding forty-eight coolies with hot-irons in 1868 and the petitions of the Chinese in Peru, in 1869 and 1871.[166] Further, the *Maria Luz*

---

[164]Among the important domestic factors were the revolts of coolies in the early 1870s, and the economic development of the republic. Internationally Peru came under growing pressure to abandon coolie trade because of the scandals of its ill-treatment of coolies. Besides, the dwindling supply of coolies in the international market also affected Peru's attitude. See W. Stewart, *Chinese Bondage in Peru*, pp. 113–59.

[165]Prince Kung memorialised the court that in July 1873, he received communications from both the American and British envoys in Peking regarding the coming of a Peruvian envoy for negotiating an emigration treaty. See Memorial from Prince Kung and other ministers of Tsungli Yamen, April 1874, in *Ch'ou-pan i-wu shih-mo*, vol. 93, p. 31a.

[166]These two petitions were submitted to the Ch'ing government through

Affair in 1872,[167] seemed to have drawn considerable attention from the Tsungli Yamen and some high ranking officials like Li Hung-chang. The plight of the coolies outraged the Yamen, and contributed mainly to its tough stand.

At the same time the Yamen was also aware that since the suppression of the coolie trade in Macao was in sight, a country like Peru which depended heavily on coolie labour for its prosperity would face a serious crisis if Chinese labour was completely cut off. China therefore could take a tough stand on the issue of protection of the coolies. Accordingly, China was not prepared to negotiate a treaty on emigration with Peru, which was found guilty of illtreating coolies, until the issue of the protection of those coolies was resolved. The Yamen communicated its policy to Li Hung-chang who increasingly assumed duties of negotiating with the foreigners, and was the most likely person to deal with the Peruvian envoy.[168]

The Peruvian envoy arrived in Shanghai on 7 October 1873. With advice from the foreign ministers, he proceeded to Tientsin to see Li Hung-chang. Li received Garcia on 24 October, and next day Li returned Garcia's call. Both meetings concentrated on the illtreatment of the coolies in Peru. Li reiterated Tsungli Yamen's stand of repatriation of all coolies before any treaty would be considered. Quoting the Peruvian Chinese petitions of 1869 and 1871 together with foreign reports, Li charged the Peruvian government of allowing cruelties to be inflicted on the coolies.[169] But Garcia was quick to defend his country by denying all charges of cruelties and declaring that the petitions were full of generalisations which

---

American diplomatic channel. See W. Stewart, *Chinese Bondage in Peru*, pp. 139–41.

[167]The Ch'ing government was informed about the *Maria Luz* Affair by the Japanese consular official in Shanghai in September 1872 when the trial was on. On 6 February 1873, the Acting Governor-General of Liang-kiang, Chang Shu-sheng, memorialised the Court about the affair. The memorial was referred to Tsungli Yamen. See *Ch'ou-pan i-wu shih-mo*, vol. 89, pp. 1b–3b.

[168]See Memorial from Prince Kung and other ministers of Tsungli Yamen, April 1874, in *Ch'ou-pan i-wu shih-mo*, vol. 93, p. 31a.

[169]For details of Li Hung-chang's charges in the meetings with Garcia, see "Tsungli Yamen Archives", clean file, American Bureau, No. 15, "Pi-lu-kuo huanyueh" (Treaty Negotiations with Peru), 12th year of T'ung-chih; Li Hung-chang, *Li Wen-chung kung ch'uan-chi*, I-shu han-kao, vol. 2, pp. 1a–1b: "Memorial from Li Hung-chang to the Court, on 9 December 1873, relating to the negotiations with the Peruvian envoy", in *Ch'ou-pan i-wu shih-mo*, vol. 92, p. 9a.

were not worthy of taking into serious account; while the foreign reports were exaggerations and fabrications. Garcia also pointed out that the return of all coolies would be tantamount to mass deportation of Chinese which was contrary to the Peruvian constitution.[170] Garcia declared that the existing Peruvian government was greatly interested in improving the well-being of the coolies by issuing a series of decrees, and he predicted that once the diplomatic relations had been established between the two countries, the coolies would be protected by Chinese diplomats.[171]

Li Hung-chang was obviously not convinced by Garcia's arguments. The meetings did not bear any result. The second round of talks was scheduled on 7 November, but Garcia did not show up as a protest of his displeasure. On 13 November, another meeting was successfully arranged and both parties met, but neither was prepared to come to any agreement. The Peruvian envoy threatened to leave China at once.[172] At this point, the British Minister, Thomas Wade, intervened. He pointed out to Li Hung-chang that the ministers of the Powers would not be pleased to see Garcia returning to Peru empty-handed, and they would look down on China for not taking the opportunity to protect her subjects in Peru.[173] After consulting with the Tsungli Yamen, Li Hung-chang was prepared to give some concessions to the Peruvian negotiator. He gave up his insistence on the precondition of the repatriation of all coolies, and prepared to start discussing regulations for the protection of the coolies; but he insisted on sending a mission to investigate the conditions of the coolies in Peru.[174] All these proposals were rejected by Garcia — the negotiation was in a deadlock.

With the help of the British envoy, Garcia left Tientsin for Peking at the end of 1873 in the hope of initiating a direct negotiation

---

[170]See W. Stewart, *Chinese Bondage in Peru*, p. 182.

[171]*Ibid.*, p. 183.

[172]See "Memorial from Li Hung-chang to the Court on 9 December 1873 relating to the negotiations with the Peruvian envoy", in *Ch'ou-pan i-wu shih-mo*, vol. 92, p. 9a.

[173]*Ibid.*, p. 9b; "Letter from Li Hung-chang to the Tsungli Yamen dated 25 November 1873", in Li Hung-chang, *Li Wen-chung kung ch'uan-chi*, I-shu han-kao, vol. 2, pp. 8a–10a; "Tsungli Yamen Archives", clean file, American Bureau, No. 15, "Pi-lu-kuo huan-yueh", 12th year of T'ung-chih.

[174]See "Memorial from Li Hung-chang to the Court on 9 December 1873 relating to the negotiations with the Peruvian envoy", in *Ch'ou-pan i-wu shih-mo*, vol. 92, p. 9b.

with the Tsungli Yamen. Although Prince Kung received Garcia, the Prince insisted on the stand taken by Li Hung-chang.[175] No result emanated from this attempt.

The third round of talks between Li Hung-chang and Garcia took place between 1 May and 16 June 1874. The five-month break favoured China. The unsuccessful attempt in Peking reduced Garcia's hope for an early settlement and prompted him to revise his stand. The suppression of the coolie trade in Macao strengthened Li's bargaining position. Further, the help of Western diplomats and the negotiations made between the subordinates of Li and Garcia paved the way for a compromise.[176] In a meeting held on 16 June, Li and Garcia thrashed out the major differences, and on 26 June, a treaty on emigration and trade was officially signed.[177] Five important points contained in the treaty were connected with the protection of coolies and future emigrants. They were:

(1)   China was to send a commission to Peru for the purpose of acquiring a good understanding of the conditions of the coolies. Peru was obliged to provide facilities for the work of the commission.

(2)   Both countries recognised the right of their people to visit and emigrate freely. Both governments agreed to severely punish their respective subjects for using fraud or violence to recruit emigrants from Macao and other Treaty ports.

(3)   Coolies who had served their terms of the contracts and who wished to return to their homeland were allowed to return home.

(4)   There would be an exchange of diplomatic representatives and consular agents for the protection of their respective subjects.

(5)   Chinese subjects in Peru would have equal rights with

---

[175]See Memorial from Prince Kung and other ministers of Tsungli Yamen, April 1874, *ibid.*, vol. 93, p. 31b.

[176]For details of this third round of talks and diplomatic manoeuvering between the two parties, see R.L. Irick, "Ch'ing Policy Toward The Coolie Trade 1847–1878", vol. 2, pp. 399–412; see also "Memorial from Li Hung-chang to the Court on 28 June 1874 relating to the conclusion of a treaty with Peruvian envoy", in *Ch'ou-pan i-wu shih-mo*, vol. 94, pp. 15a–16b.

[177]See *Ch'ou-pan i-wu shih-mo, ibid.*, p. 16a.

Peruvian citizens to appeal to the tribunals for protection of their rights.[178]

The signing of the Sino-Peruvian Treaty could be considered as a minor diplomatic victory for China, particularly for its effort in the protection of the coolies in Peru. Although China did not secure the repatriation of all the coolies, it had gained the promise of return of those coolies who had fulfilled their contracts. It also forced the Peruvian government to punish Peruvian nationals who attempted to recruit Chinese labourers illegally, and would effectively prevent the revival of the newly suppressed coolie trade in Macao or in other Treaty ports. The sending of a Chinese commission would enable China to collect useful information on the actual conditions of the coolies there, while the right of the sending of consuls to Peru would guarantee the protection of the coolies and future emigrants.

The Peruvian government promptly ratified the treaty on 6 October 1874. But the ratification by the Chinese government ran into difficulty. The main reason for China's delay in ratification was the hardening of its attitude on the coolie issue as the result of the negative report of Yung Wing. Yung who was a co-commissioner of Chinese education to the United States, was despatched as the Commissioner of a fact-finding mission to Peru. He spent more than a month in Peru between September and October 1874, and collected much valuable information about the ill-treatment of the coolies. He also took two dozen photographs of Chinese coolies showing how their backs had been lacerated and torn, scarred and disfigured by the lash.[179] This concrete evidence of the cruel treatment of the coolies in Peru together with the revelation of the Cuba Commission report outraged the Tsungli Yamen ministers and Li Hung-chang, and hardened their attitude towards the protection of the coolies. When the new Peruvian envoy, Elmore, arrived in Tientsin on 8 July 1875, for the exchange of ratification, Li Hung-chang told Elmore bluntly that China would not exchange the treaty until some new terms for the protection of the coolies be negotiated.[180] With Li's recommendation, Ting Jih-ch'ang was

---

[178]These points are derived from Li Hung-chang's memorial of 28 June 1874, *ibid.*, pp. 16b–17b; Chung-wai t'iao-yeh hui-p'ien, pp. 450–51; W. Stewart, *Chinese Bondage in Peru*, pp. 196–99.

[179]See Yung Wing, *My Life in China and America*, p. 195.

[180]See "Memorial from Li Hung-chang to the court dated 13th day of 6th moon of

named by the Court as China's plenipotentiary for the exchange of treaty with Peru. In the first meeting with Elmore on 26 July, Ting stated clearly that China would not ratify the treaty unless Elmore provided him with a despatch promising redress and abolition of all ill-treatment. Elmore rejected Ting's demand on the ground that he had no authority to revise the signed treaty.[181] Due to the intervention of the ministers of the Western Powers, particularly the British minister, Thomas Wade, China gave in. The exchange of ratification was completed in February 1876.[182]

Throughout its lengthy negotiations with Spain and Peru over the protection of the coolies, the Ch'ing government had tried to secure the best possible terms for its oppressed subjects, but its attempts were restricted by the intervention of the ministers of the Western Powers. However, the completion of both the Sino-Peruvian Treaty in 1876 and the Sino-Spanish Treaty in 1878 demonstrated amply the determination of the Ch'ing government to protect the coolies. This spirit of protection was later extended to overseas Chinese in other parts of the world.

1st year of Kuang-hsu (15 July 1875) relating to the arrival of the Peruvian envoy at Tientsin'', in *Ch'ing-chi wai-chiao shih-liao*, vol. 1, pp. 30a–30b.

[181]See "Memorial from Li Hung-chang and Ting Jih-chang to the Court dated 10th day of 7th moon of 1st year of Kuang-hsu (10 August 1875) relating to the exchange of treaty with Peruvian envoy", *ibid.*, vol. 2, p. 15a.

[182]*Ibid.*, pp. 15b–17a; W. Stewart, *op. cit.*, p. 204.

4
Diplomatic Representation and Consular Expansion in Overseas Chinese Communities

DIPLOMATIC REPRESENTATION

The sending of the first Chinese envoy to Britain in 1876 marked the beginning of a new era in Chinese diplomatic history. It represented a major breakthrough in Ch'ing foreign relations with the West. It indicated China's acceptance of a system of international relations based on Western practice, and her successful entry into the family of nations. For the first time, the Ch'ing government could deal directly with the British government through its envoy in London rather than the British Minister in Peking. The establishment of this permanent legation was soon followed by other similar missions to the capitals of the United States, Japan, Germany, France and Russia.[1] The speed with which these legations were established reflected a strong desire of the Ch'ing government to grasp the problems arising from international disputes and to curb the growing power of the foreign ministers in Peking. The issue of sending Chinese diplomats abroad was first officially raised by the British government during the negotiations of the Treaty of Tientsin in June 1858, but it was not seriously considered by the Ch'ing government until the end of 1867 on the eve of the revision of the Treaty of Tientsin,[2] the result of which was the sending of the Burlingame mission to the West in 1868 to persuade the Powers not to force modernisation on China.[3] The choice of Anson Burlingame,

---

[1]See Knight Biggerstaff, "The Establishment of Permanent Chinese Diplomatic Missions Abroad", in *The Chinese Social and Political Science Review* (Peking, 1936), 20.1:32–35.

[2]Article 27 of the Treaty of Tientsin signed with Britain in 1858, stipulated that treaty revision might be made at the end of the tenth year (1868). As the time for treaty revision approached, the atmosphere in Chinese officialdom became tense. It was under this atmosphere that many important issues relating to China's foreign relations were discussed; the sending of diplomatic missions abroad was one of them. See *Chung-wai t'iao yeh hui-p'ien*, p. 7; Immanuel C.Y. Hsu, *China's Entrance into the Family of Nations*, pp. 163–64.

[3]For details of the Burlingame mission, see F.W. Williams, *Anson Burlingame*

the retired American Minister in Peking, as China's first roving ambassador to the West, demonstrated China's initiative to overcome a major diplomatic crisis inspite of its lack of suitable personnel for the mission. But this initiative subsided after the mission had achieved remarkable success.[4]

The complacency of the Ch'ing government over the sending of envoys abroad placed China in a disadvantageous position in times of international disputes. The Tientsin Massacre in 1870,[5] and the Formosa Incident in 1874,[6] demonstrated how helpless China was in the negotiations with France and Japan without diplomatic representations in the two countries. The humiliation suffered at the hands of the Japanese in the Formosa Incident could have been avoided had a Chinese envoy been stationed in Tokyo before the event.[7] China's diplomatic disadvantage was further aggravated by

---

and the First Chinese Mission to Foreign Powers (New York, 1912); Knight Biggerstaff, "The Official Chinese Artitude towards the Burlingame Mission", in American Historical Review (July, 1936), 41.4: 682–702; Chih Kang, Ch'u-shih t'ai-hsi chi (The First Mission to the West) (Ch'eng Wen Publishing Co., Taipei, reprint, original 3rd year of Kuang-hsu).

[4]Immanuel C.Y. Hsu, op. cit., p. 170.

[5]The Tientsin Massacre of Western missionaries broke out on 21 June 1870, amidst the growing tension of anti-foreignism. Rumours that French Catholic sisters in Tientsin engaged in kidnapping orphans, in mutilating their bodies, and extracting their hearts and eyes for medicine triggered the massacre. As a result, ten sisters, two priests and two French officials lost their lives, three Russian traders were mistakenly killed, and several churches were burned. This precipitated a crisis between China and France. For details of this event, see J.K. Fairbank, "Patterns behind the Tientsin Massacre", in Harvard Journal of Asiatic Studies (1957), 20: 480–511; P.A. Cohen, China and Christianity: The Missionary Movement and the Growth of Chinese Antiforeignism, 1860–1870 (Cambridge, Mass., 1963), pp. 229–61.

[6]In 1874, Japan sent a military expedition to Formosa to punish the aborigines for killing some shipwrecked sailors from Liu Ch'iu island (Ryukyu). Both China and Japan claimed suzerienty over Liu Ch'iu. The Japanese action caused some concern in Peking. The Court hastily sent Shen Pao-chen, superintendent of the Foochow Dockyard to defend Formosa. After realising its military inferiority and with the mediation of the British Minister to China, Sir Thomas Wade, China retreated by paying half a million taels to the Japanese as compensation for the loss of the Ryukyuan sailors.

[7]Three years before the Formosa Incident, China signed a commercial treaty with Japan in 1871. Articles four and eight provided for the exchange of envoys and consuls between the two countries, but they were not put into effect. After the Formosa Incident, Li Hung-chang advocated sending an envoy to Japan to prevent a similar situation arising in the future. In Li's argument, had a Chinese envoy been posted in Tokyo in 1871, he would have been able to stop the military expedition in

the actions of some foreign ministers at Peking who exceeded their power to settle the disputes. In the 1860s when British missionaries were active in interior China and caused riots, the British diplomats resorted to gunboat diplomacy to obtain local settlements without prior approval from their home government, and sometimes even departed from their government's avowed China policy.[8] The abuse of power by the foreign diplomats was best illustrated by the action taken by Sir Thomas Wade in the Margary Affair in 1875.

Augustus R. Margary, a consular officer in China who was to serve as the guide and interpreter for a British trade expedition to Yunnan province, was murdered by native tribesmen in early 1875. Sir Thomas Wade, the British Minister to China, took advantage of the incident to make excessive demands. Apart from calling for an investigation into the incident and an indemnity for Margary's family, Sir Thomas demanded improvements in audience procedure, better diplomatic etiquette in Peking, reduced transit dues on British goods, an apology mission to England, and the trial of the Acting Viceroy of Yun-kuei (Yunnan and Kueichow provinces) under whose jurisdiction the murder took place.[9] To threaten Peking into submission, Wade withdrew his legation from Peking to Shanghai leaving an impression that diplomatic relations between China and Britain would be severed. At the same time, rumours spread that Britain and Russia had entered into a secret agreement that Britain would advance an army from India to Yunnan while Russia would send another one from Ili.[10] Under these threats the Peking government finally submitted, concluding the Chefoo Convention on 13 September 1876.

Under the agreement, China paid 200,000 taels indemnity, sent an apology mission to England, and agreed to trade concession and a new code of etiquette between Chinese and foreign diplomats.[11] During the negotiations of the Margary Affair, Sir Thomas Wade demonstrated his petulance, aggressiveness and intransigence. Sir

---

the first place, or better still, he would have been able to warn the Chinese government about the Japanese movement. See Li Hung-chang, *Li Wen-chung kung ch'uan-chi* (Complete Works of Li Hung-chang) (Taipei, 1963, reprint), Series 1, "Memorials", 24:27a–b.

[8]P.A. Cohen, *op. cit.*, p. 188.

[9]Immanuel C.Y. Hsu, *op. cit.*, p. 177.

[10]*Ibid.*

[11]See *Ch'ing-chi wai-chiao shih-liao* (Wen Hai, Taipei, 1964, reprint), 7:13–20 (original pages).

Robert Hart, the Inspector-General of Chinese Maritime Customs
who was assisting Li Hung-chang in the negotiations, was infuriated by Wade's uncompromising attitude. He declared that "the
officials at the English Court certainly will not be so intransigent as
Minister Wade", and urged the Chinese government to send an envoy to London to negotiate directly with the British government,
and he volunteered to go with the envoy for the negotiations.[12] Li
Hung-chang, the chief negotiator, came painfully to realise how
helpless China was when confronted with an aggressive foreign
diplomat. If the sending of envoys overseas could better China's
position in international disputes and curb the excessive power of
the foreign diplomats in Peking, then it was imperative for China
to send envoys despite some associated problems.[13] This prompted
Li to recommend strongly to the Tsungli Yamen the establishment
of permanent legations in the West after the Chefoo Convention,
including Britain, France, Russia, Germany, the United States and
Japan.[14]

How important then was a consideration of the protection of
overseas Chinese in this diplomatic breakthrough? The protection
of overseas Chinese seems to have had secondary importance in the
envoy issue. In the early discussion on the issue in 1867, the protection of overseas Chinese was merely mentioned. The Tsungli
Yamen in its recommendation in October 1867 to the Court had
only begun to identify the advantage of enlisting overseas Chinese
service as one of several arguments for supporting the sending of
envoys abroad.[15] But at the end of 1875 when the Yamen recommended to the Court that Ch'en Lan-pin be appointed as the first
envoy to the United States, Spain and Peru, it ranked the protec-

---

[12]Li Hung-chang, *Li Wen-chung kung ch'uan-chi*, 6:2.

[13]These were the problems of finance and finding suitable persons to fill the positions.

[14]See Li Hung-chang, *Li Wen-chung kung ch'uan-chi*, Series III, I-shu han-kao
(Letters to the Tsungli Yamen), 6:27b.

[15]In its secret memorial presented to the Court on 12 October 1867, the Tsungli
Yamen advocated permanent envoys on several grounds. China could (1) circum-
vent and by-pass the foreign ministers in Peking by dealing directly with the foreign
governments; (2) learn the strength and weaknesses of the countries first-hand and
collect important technological data to strengthen its defence; (3) enlist foreign support in disagreements with others; (4) enlist overseas Chinese for service in China;
and (5) spread Chinese civilisation abroad. See R.L. Irick, "Ch'ing Policy Toward
The Coolie Trade 1847–1878", vol. 2, p. 330.

tion of the overseas Chinese as the prime reason for the appointment.[16]

In that short period of eight years, the attitude of the Ch'ing government towards the protection of overseas Chinese underwent substantial change. The change came mainly as a result of petitions from some far-sighted officials and the effect of the Cuba Commission. Ting Jih-ch'ang, one of these officials, showed a remarkable knowledge on overseas Chinese and realised how they could be used to China's advantage. He was impressed by the way in which foreign countries used their overseas subjects, and in 1867 proposed to send officials to protect them and to cultivate their loyalty.[17]

Ting's proposal had little impact at that time partly because the protection issue was not urgent. But international sentiment against the ill-treatment of the Chinese coolies in Peru and Cuba grew between 1868 and 1872, and the attention of the Ch'ing government was thus attracted to the issue. The sending of the Cuba Commission in September 1873 to investigate the conditions of the coolies there was a clear indication of the change in the government's attitude. When the Commission returned to China in late 1874 and submitted its findings on the cruel treatment of the coolies, the government took a very firm stand in its negotiations with Spain over a proposed treaty. The result of which was that the Spanish agreed for the protection of coolies to have a Chinese Consul-General in Havana.[18] Throughout its negotiations with the Spanish, the Tsungli Yamen came to realise that envoys must be sent to protect Chinese immigrants overseas, otherwise the Chinese coolies would continue to be atrociously treated. At the same time Li Hung-chang and Ting Jih-ch'ang, who were charged by the Ch'ing government to negotiate a treaty with the Peruvian representative, came to the same conclusion.[19]

---

[16]See "Memorial from the Tsungli Yamen to the court recommending the appointment of an envoy to the United States, Spain and Peru to protect the Chinese coolies, dated 13th day of 11th moon of the 1st year of Kuang-hsu (11 December 1875)", in *Ch'ing-chi wai-chiao shih-liao*, 4:17a–19a.

[17]See Ting Jih-ch'ang's proposal dated 31 December 1867, in *Ch'ou-pan i-wu shih-mo*, T'ung-chih reign, 55:17a–26a.

[18]See R.L. Irick, "Ch'ing Policy Toward The Coolie Trade 1847–1878", vol. 2, pp. 348–63.

[19]For details of negotiations between Li Hung-chang and the Peruvian representative Captain A.G. Garcia, see R.L. Irick, *op. cit.*, pp. 373–430; see also W. Stewart, *Chinese Bondage in Peru: A History of the Chinese Coolie in Peru 1849–1874*, pp. 175–205.

After signing the treaty with the Peruvian representative, Li Hung-chang memorialised the Court to send an envoy to protect the Chinese coolies. He asserted that only with Chinese envoys overseas could the Chinese coolies be properly protected, for the envoys could then properly enforce the treaty and directly collect complaints and grievances if coolies were ill-treated. Li also emphasised that the protection of overseas Chinese would be the best means of cultivating loyalty among millions of these overseas subjects.[20] Li's memorial undoubtedly reinforced the weight of the protection issue in the sending of envoys abroad. It precipitated the Yamen's submission on the same issue four months later, and prompted the appointment of Ch'en Lan-pin as the first ambassador (minister) to the United States, Spain and Peru. In retrospect, the protection of overseas Chinese, particularly the protection of the coolies in Cuba and Peru, created a sense of urgency among the ministers of the Tsungli Yamen, and altered their priorities in despatching diplomatic representatives.

THE FIRST STAGE OF CONSULAR ESTABLISHMENTS IN OVERSEAS CHINESE COMMUNITIES (1877–83)

Establishment of the First Consulate in Singapore in 1877

The first consulate ever to be established in overseas Chinese communities was in Singapore in 1877. The choice of Singapore rather than Havana (Cuba) or Lima (Peru) was the result of several factors: special circumstance; the vision of Kuo Sung-t'ao; and the availability of consulate personnel. It would seem logical that the first consulate would be established in Havana or Lima, because the protection of the Chinese coolies in Cuba and Peru was most urgently needed. But the establishment of consulates was not under the overall control of the Tsungli Yamen, it was in the hands of individual ambassadors who selected the location as well as the personnel.[21] Although Ch'en Lan-pin was appointed as the first am-

---

[20]See "Memorial of the Governor-General of Chihli Li Hung-chang to the Court urging for the sending of an envoy to Peru to protect Chinese coolies dated 10th day of 7th moon of 1st year of Kuang-hsu (10 August 1875)", in Ch'ing-chi wai-chiao shih-liao, 2:17b–18a.

[21]See the twelve rules and regulations governing diplomatic appointments announced by the Tsungli Yamen in 1875, in Liu Chin-ch'ao (ed.), Ch'ing-ch'ao hsu wen-hsien t'ung-k'ao (Supplementary Encyclopaedia of Historical Records of the Ch'ing Dynasty), vol. 337, "Foreign Relations", no. 1.

bassador to the United States, Spain and Peru in the same year as Kuo Sung-t'ao (1875), Ch'en's establishment of legation in Washington was delayed until 1878, partly because of the uncertainty in Cuba where war was expected to break out between the United States and Spain;[22] and partly the ongoing negotiations between China and Spain over the protection of the Chinese coolies in Cuba resulted in the signing of a special treaty on 17 November 1877.[23] Ch'en's delay in taking up his appointment prevented any early establishment of consulates in Cuba and Peru.

Perhaps the most important factor in leading to the establishment of the first consulate in Singapore was Kuo Sung-t'ao's vision and effort. Kuo was one of the few of his time who saw trade as a basic source of the wealth and power of Western countries. In the early stage of his political career, Kuo demonstrated his remarkable insights into the relationship between trade and foreign expansion. He declared it was trade not territorial ambition that motivated foreigners to extend their activities to China. He advocated diplomacy rather than war to deal with Foreign Powers during the period of confrontation with Britain and France in 1858–60.[24] Because trade was the foundation of a nation, Kuo argued, the Western governments opened up ports and sent out consuls to protect merchants and their commercial activities.[25] Conversely, China was indifferent to trade, and had attempted neither to cultivate the support of merchants nor to protect them. To remedy past mistakes, China should follow the example of the West by giving protection to her merchants who had spread widely overseas and settled there for many generations.[26] From this perspective, Kuo

---

[22]See "Memorial of the Tsungli Yamen to the Court regarding rumour of warfare between the United States and Spain over Cuba dated 14th day of 11th moon of the 1st year of Kuang-hsu (11 December 1875)", in *Ch'ing-chi wai-chiao shih-liao*, vol. 4, pp. 19a–19b.

[23]See "Memorial of the Tsungli Yamen to the Court regarding the signing of a special treaty over the Chinese coolies in Cuba, with treaty clauses, dated 16th day of 10th moon of the 3rd year of Kuang-hsu (20 November 1877)", in *Ch'ing-chi wai-chiao shih-liao*, vol. 12, pp. 1a–10b.

[24]See J.D. Frodsham, *The First Chinese Embassy to the West: The Journal of Kuo Sung-t'ao, Liu Hsi-hung and Chang Te-i* (London, 1974), pp. xxix–xxx; Immanuel C.Y. Hsu, *China's Entrance into the Family of Nations*, p. 180.

[25]"Memorial of Kuo Sung-t'ao to the Court Urging for the establishment of a consulate in Singapore dated 27th day of 8th moon of 3rd year of Kuang-hsu (3 October 1877)", in *Ch'ing-chi wai-chiao shih-liao*, vol. 11, pp. 13b–15a.

[26]*Ibid.*

Sung-t'ao gave Chinese diplomats another meaningful role to play in addition to the protection of coolies, that is to protect overseas Chinese merchants in order to cultivate their support for China's economic modernisation. As many wealthy Chinese merchants had flocked there, Singapore appeared to Kuo to be the ideal place to set up the first consulate in the overseas Chinese communities under his diplomatic control.[27]

Another consideration which led to the establishment of the consulate in Singapore was the discovery of a suitable person, Hu Hsuan-tse (better known as Hoo Ah Kay or Whampoa) for the post of consul. Kuo Sung-t'ao might have heard of Hu's name as early as 1863–66 when he was the Acting Governor of Kwangtung.[28] He must have read about Hu Hsuan-tse in early 1867 when Ting Jih-ch'ang, the Financial Commissioner of Kiangsu,[29] presented his argument in favour of sending diplomats overseas in the great envoy debate. Ting had mentioned Hu Hsuan-tse's surname, and described him as the able leader of more than 100,000 Chinese in Singapore and as the Consul of Russia.[30] Kuo Sung-t'ao might have had some idea of establishing a consulate in Singapore and appointing Hu Hsuan-tse as the first Consul even before his departure for London at the end of 1876. His idea became firm when he met Hu Hsuan-tse in Singapore. Indeed, one source claims that Kuo had already formed the intention of making Hu Consul.[31] Kuo must have been impressed by Hu's wealth and social standing.[32]

---

[27]As Kuo was the first Chinese ambassador to Britain, the Chinese communities in British colonies or protectorates throughout the world would come under his diplomatic control.

[28]See Tu Lien-che, "Kuo Sung-t'ao", in A.W. Hummel, *Eminent Chinese of the Ch'ing Period*, p. 438.

[29]In a short biography of Ting Jih-ch'ang, Professor Fang Chao-ying claims that Ting was promoted to be the Governor of Kiangsu in early 1867, but in Ting's submission to the Court in 12th moon of 6th year of T'ung-chih (January, 1868), Ting was addressed as "Fan Ssu" which was the official designation of Financial Commissioner, that meant Ting was still the Financial Commissioner of Kiangsu when he presented his submission through Li Hung-chang to the Court in early 1868. See Fang Chao-ying, "Ting Jih-ch'ang", in A.W. Hummel, *op. cit.*, p. 722; *Ch'ou-pan i-wu shih-mo*, T'ung-chih reign, vol. 55, pp. 21–26.

[30]See Ting Jih-ch'ang's submission in *Ch'ou-pan i-wu shih-mo*, T'ung-chih reign, vol. 55, p. 22.

[31]See Li Shu-ch'ang, *Feng-shih lun-tun chi* (My Mission to London), p. 1a in Additional Supplement 9 of Series 11 of *Hsiao-fang-hu-chai yu-ti ts'ung-ch'ao*.

[32]Kuo was taken by Hu to visit his famous "Nan Sheng" (Nam Sang in Cantonese) garden where exotic flowers, curious plants, rare birds and animals were col-

Later in recommending Hu to the Tsungli Yamen, Kuo wrote: "The Cantonese Tao-yuan Hu Hsuan-tse is highly respected by the local population. A few years ago when a scuffle broke out between the Cantonese and other dialect groups, Hu Hsuan-tse intervened and restored the peace. Both the British authorities and the merchants place great trust in him. I believe there is definitely no other person more suitable for the post of consul in Singapore."[33]

Kuo apparently had sounded out Hu on the proposed appointment and obtained Hu's agreement to a special arrangement about expenses. Under this arrangement, Hu would receive an initial outlay for the establishment of the consulate but no salary. The office would be maintained by dues and fees collected from the local Chinese population.[34] The arrangement seems to have suited both sides. From Kuo's point of view, the protection of overseas Chinese could be secured at minimum expense to the Ch'ing government which had difficulty in financing the new diplomatic representations. On the other hand, Hu would benefit from the prestige attached to the new office. His entry into the imperial Chinese bureaucracy without going through the competitive examination system would have give him a sense of great achievement, something he might even have dreamt of during his childhood in South China.[35] This special arrangement set the precedent for establishing consulates in the overseas Chinese communities with similar conditions.

Kuo Sung-t'ao and his mission arrived in London on 21 January 1877.[36] He lost no time to work on the issue. He presented his credentials to Queen Victoria at Buckingham palace on 7 February,

---

lected. Kuo was much impressed by the collections which well projected Hu's wealth. See Kuo Sung-t'ao, *Shih-hsi chi-ch'eng* (The Record of an Envoy's Journey to the West), vol. 1, pp. 9a–9b, see also J.D. Frodsham's translation, in *The First Chinese Embassy to the West*, pp. 13–14.

[33]See "Memorial of Kuo Sung-t'ao to the Court Urging for the Establishment of the Singapore Consulate dated 27th day of 8th moon of 3rd year of Kuang-hsu (3 October 1877)", in *Ch'ing-chi wai-chiao shih-liao*, vol. 11, p. 13b.

[34]*Op. cit.*, p. 15a.

[35]Regarding psychological need of overseas Chinese leaders for China's titles and offices, see Yen Ching-hwang, "Ch'ing's Sale of Honours and the Chinese Leadership in Singapore and Malaya 1877–1912", in *Journal of Southeast Asian Studies*, vol. 1, no. 2 (Sept., 1970), pp. 27–31.

[36]See Kuo Sung-t'ao, *Shih-hsi chi-ch'eng*, vol. 2, pp. 28a–29a; J.D. Frodsham, *The First Chinese Embassy to the West*, pp. 77–78; see also *FO* 17/768, "Domestic; Kuo Sung-Tao, Kuo Ta Jen".

and after a little more than two weeks (24 February), he began negotiations with the British government for the establishment of a consulate in Singapore. In his letter to Earl of Denby, British Secretary of State for Foreign Affairs, Kuo pointed out that due to extensive commercial transactions between China and Singapore, and also because of the large number of Chinese residing in that port, the Chinese government intended to appoint a consular agent to look after Chinese interests there.[37] Kuo also pointed out the proposed consular representative was Hu Hsuan-tse (in Kuo's diplomatic note Hu's name was romanised as Hu Hsun-tsih) who was known for his ability and impartiality.[38]

After five months' negotiations, the British government approved in July the proposed consulate in Singapore on a temporary basis, and Hu Hsuan-tse as its first Consul.[39] Kuo memorialised the Court for imperial sanction which was granted on 31 October 1877.[40] The first Chinese consulate ever to be established abroad thus came into being.

Establishment of Consulates in Japan, the United States, Hawaii and Cuba (1878–83)

After Singapore, the second consulate to be established was at Yokohama, Japan, in 1878. Yokohama was an important port in the Sino-Japanese trade, and had attracted many Chinese merchants to do business there. When the first Chinese ambassador to

---

[37]In the Chinese version of Kuo's letter dated 24 February 1877, he pointed out that there were more than hundred thousand Chinese in Singapore, while this figure was not given in the English version. See *FO* 17/768, "Domestic; Kuo Sung-Tao, Kuo Ta Jen", p. 35 (English version), Chinese version attached between pp. 36 and 38.

[38]There is also a slight difference in the description of Hu in Chinese and English versions. The Chinese version only stated that Hu was known of this ability and impartiality; while the English version mentioned that Hu ". . . to be much esteemed by men of all classes, official and civilian, native and foreign". *Ibid.*

[39]See Wen Chung-chi, "The Nineteenth-Century Imperial Chinese Consulate in the Straits Settlements" (M.A. thesis, University of Singapore, 1964), pp. 78–84; "Kuo Sung-t'ao to Earl of Denby dated 2 January 1878" (both Chinese and English), in *FO* 17/794, Jan.-Dec. 1878, pp. 1–16.

[40]See "Memorial of Kuo Sung-t'ao to the Court Urging for the Establishment of the Singapore Consulate dated 27th day of 8th moon of 3rd year of Kuang-hsu (3 October 1877)", in *Ch'ing-chi wai-chiao shih-liao*, vol. 11, pp. 13a–15a; "Memorial of Tsungli Yamen to the Court regarding the Establishment of the Singapore Consulate, dated 25th day of 9th moon of 3rd year of Kuang-hsu (31 October 1877), in *Ch'ing-chi wai-chiao shih-liao*, vol. 11, pp. 30b–32a.

Japan, Ho Ju-chang and his retinue arrived in Tokyo at the end of 1877, Chinese merchants from various ports in Japan, petitioned him for protection. In response to this petition, Ho appointed one of his aides, Fan Chin-p'eng, to be the first Chinese Administrator (Li-shih Kuan) in Yokohama.[41] In June of the same year, another Administrator, Yu Chun was appointed to protect Chinese merchants in Osaka and Kobe.[42] The need for protection of the Chinese in Japan seemed to be a genuine and urgent one. Invariably they had suffered discrimination and ill-treatment at the hands of the Japanese. Suffering of this type was certainly a common experience for all overseas Chinese in the nineteenth century. The Chinese in Japan could not claim any uniqueness in this respect. What appeared to be unique was their experience in the changing Japanese attitude towards the Chinese. The drive for Westernisation in the early era of Meiji Japan radically transformed the Japanese attitude towards the Chinese.

In the pre-Meiji period, the Chinese were held in respect because Japan still looked to China as the model and source of culture. But rapid Westernisation turned many Japanese to the West, and they accepted Western values and culture. On the other hand, as China's power declined in the nineteenth century, they increasingly viewed China as an old, conservative and crumbling empire, and became contemptuous of Chinese culture and Chinese people. The Chinese in Japan were the first who suffered this radical change in the Japanese attitude, and were despised, discriminated against and ill-treated. The suffering of the Chinese in Japan does not seem to have been reflected in official circles until 1875. Four years earlier (at the end of 1871), in the course of discussing the proposed Japanese treaty with the Tsungli Yamen, Li Hung-chang advocated the despatch of an ambassador or consul to Japan partly for defence purposes, and partly for the protection of the local Chinese.[43] The proposal did not eventuate.

---

[41]See "Memorial of Ho Ju-chang to the Court regarding the appointment of administrators in various Japanese ports dated 15th day of 11th moon of 4th year of Kuang-hsu (8 December 1878)", in *Ch'ing-chi wai-chiao shih-liao*, vol. 14, pp. 32b–33b.

[42]*Ibid.*

[43]Although Li did not spell out the intention to protect the overseas Chinese, his wording implied protection. See Li Hung-chang, "A discussion on the exchange of the Japanese Treaty, dated 28th day of 11th moon of 9th year of T'ung-chih (18 January 1871)", in Li Hung-chang, *Li Wen-chung kung ch'uan-chi*, Series III, I-shu han-kao (Letters to the Tsungli Yamen), vol. 1, pp. 10a–11a.

The matter of the protection of the Chinese in Japan did not arise again until 1875 when an unnamed petition by the Chinese merchants in Japan was communicated to the Ch'ing government. The petition condemned the contemptuous Japanese attitude towards the Chinese, and complained of ill-treatment received and of special taxation imposed on the Chinese by the Japanese government.[44] In response to this petition, Li reiterated his previous stand of sending Chinese envoys to Japan. He proposed to the Tsungli Yamen to send an envoy to solve the financial problem. He suggested the despatch of a Chief Administrator (Tsung Li-shih Kuan) to be stationed in one of the three major ports (Yokohama, Kobe and Nagasaki) where the majority of the Chinese population lived. Leaders of the local Chinese communities were to be selected to fill the post of Vice Administrator (Fu Li-shih Kuan). To offset the cost of maintaining the new office, a levy on male adults in the local Chinese population was to be collected. Li further suggested sending one or two warships to cruise these Japanese ports and to back up the authority of the Chinese Administrators.[45] The establishment of the "Administrator" system in Japan seems to have borne the mark of Li Hung-chang's proposal.

The third group of consulates to be established after this was in the United States, Spanish Cuba and Hawaii. Ch'en Lan-pin's delay in taking up his appointment was the main factor in the lateness of establishing consulates in that part of the world. Ch'en left Shanghai on 1 June 1878 for the United States after China had concluded a treaty concerning the coolies in Cuba with the Spanish ambassador to China.[46] Ch'en and his retinue arrived in San Francisco on 27 July after a voyage of about two months. He presented

---

[44] I am unable to find the original petition, but to reconstruct the points from Li Hung-chang's letters to the Tsungli Yamen, see Li Hung-chang, "A discussion on despatching an envoy to Japan dated 25th day of 8th moon of 1st year of Kuang-hsu (24 September 1875)", in Li Hung-chang, *Li Wen-chung kung ch'uan-chi*, I-shu han-kao, vol. 4, pp. 24a–24b.

[45]*Ibid.*

[46]The treaty on Cuban Chinese coolies was initiated by the Tsungli Yamen with the Spanish ambassador to China, at the end of 1875, but the negotiations were interrupted by the Margary Affair. Negotiations resumed after the settlement of the Margary Affair, and both sides agreed to a 16 item treaty signed on 17 November 1877, in Peking. One of the important points of the treaty was the right of the Ch'ing government to send a Consul-General to Havana and consuls to other ports, in order to protect the Chinese coolies. See the memorial of the Tsungli Yamen and the treaty in *Ch'ing-chi wai-chiao shih-liao*, vol. 12, pp. 1a–8a.

his credentials to the President in Washington on 28 September of the same year.[47] The first thing to be done after establishing his legation in Washington was to set up a consulate in San Francisco. His sense of urgency was probably prompted by what he had seen and heard about the Chinese in San Francisco. His arrival at the port was a grandiose one. More than a hundred local Chinese leaders in traditional costume came on board to welcome him and many Chinese residents lined the streets, including some who had travelled a few hundred miles from small towns in California. Chinese shops had also raised dragon flags to greet the distinguished visitor.[48] Ch'en was impressed not only by the warm welcome, but also by the retention by the local Chinese of traditional customs and the Chinese calendar.[49] What worried Ch'en was the anti-Chinese actions of the Irish population in California. He was informed that because of dwindling gold deposits and scarcity of jobs in California, the Irish workers began to feel jealous of the success of the Chinese and took a strong anti-Chinese stand. They assaulted the Chinese, robbed and burnt Chinese properties, and attempted to drive out the Chinese from that state. He was also told that immigrant workers of other nationalities were well protected by their consuls, but the Chinese became victims because of the lack of protection.[50] In view of the urgency, Ch'en appointed his aide Ch'en Shu-t'ang as the Consul-General in San Francisco on 8 November 1878.[51] A local American citizen by the name of Frederic

---

[47]See "Memorial of Ch'en Lan-pin to the Court regarding his arrival in the United States and the presenting of his letter of credence, dated 15th day of 11th moon of 4th year of Kuang-hsu (8 December 1878)", in Ch'ing-chi wai-chiao shih-liao, vol. 14, pp. 31b–32a.

[48]See Ch'en Lan-pin, "Shih Mei chi-lueh" (A Brief Record of an Envoy to the United States), in Hsiao-fang-hu-chia yu-ti ts'ung-ch'ao pu-p'ien, vol. 12, p. 59.

[49]When Ch'en visited the Chinese Associations (hui-kuan) in San Francisco, he was impressed by the Chinese style of decoration in the Associations' buildings. He was further impressed by the Associations' strict rules. Those who did not follow the Chinese calendar and imperial Ch'ing reigns, were refused registration as members, and their complaints were rejected. Ch'en noted in his diary that these humble subjects who earned a living overseas and did not give up the Chinese tradition should be commended. Ibid., p. 61a.

[50]Ibid., p. 60b.

[51]See "Ch'en Lan-pin & Yung Wing to W.M. Evarts dated 8 November 1878", in "Notes from the Chinese Legation in the United States to the Department of State, 1868–1906" (thereafter "Notes from the Chinese Legation"), "The Mission of Ch'en Lan-pin and Yung Wing, September 1878 to December 1881".

A. Bee who had been helping the Chinese to settle disputes, was appointed as the Consul to help Shu-t'ang to discharge his duty.[52]

The success of the establishment of the Consul-General in San Francisco inspired the Chinese in Hawaii to agitate for protection. The local Chinese merchants under the leadership of Ch'en Kuo-fen petitioned Ch'en Lan-pin to send a Consul. In the petition, they expressed their willingness to finance all expenses and the maintenance of the proposed consulate.[53] Although Hawaii at that time was not a part of the United States and did not fall within the sphere of control of Ch'en Lan-pin's ambassadorship, its closeness to the United States and its vital position on the Pacific sea route prompted Ch'en Lan-pin to recommend protection. The ambassador asserted that the presence of a Chinese official would not only protect the local Chinese population against the growing native jealousy of them, but would also help open up an avenue for Chinese immigration.[54] What Ch'en had in mind was that because Hawaii was a rich country on the vital Pacific sea route to the American continents, those Chinese coolies who had difficulty in earning a living in the United States, Cuba or Peru, could retreat to the islands where tens of thousands of poor Chinese immigrants could be accommodated.[55] Probably because the proposed protection was initiated and would be financed by the Chinese merchants, Ch'en Lan-pin was unsure of their real intention and the possible result, and thus recommended to the Tsungli Yamen the establishment of a Commercial Directorate at Honolulu. It was not a full-fledged consulate, and Ch'en Kuo-fen was to be appointed Commercial Director (Shang-Tung).[56]

---

[52]*Ibid.*, "Memorial of Ch'en Lan-pin to the Court relating to the Establishment of a Consulate in San Francisco for the Protection of the Overseas Chinese dated 15th day of 11th moon of 4th year of Kuang-hsu (8 December 1878)", in *Ch'ing-chi wai-chiao shih-liao*, vol. 14, pp. 32a & 32b; regarding the year of setting up the San Francisco consulate, Liu Chin-ch'ao (ed.), *Ch'ing-ch'ao shu wen-hsien t'ung-k'ao* mistakenly put it in the first year of Kuang-hsu (1875), see vol. 337, "Wai-chiao" (Foreign Relations), 1.

[53]See "Memorial of Tsungli Yamen to the Court dated 23rd day of 2nd moon of 5th year of Kuang-hsu (15 March 1879)", in *Ch'ing-chi wai-chiao shih-liao*, vol. 15, p. 7b.

[54]See Liu Chin-ch'ao (ed.), *Ch'ing-ch'ao shu wen-hsien t'ung-k'ao*, vol. 337, "Wai-chiao" 1.

[55]*Ibid.*

[56]The office of "Shang-Tung" (Commercial Director) was seldom found in the

After successful negotiations between Yung Wing, Ch'en's deputy, and the Hawaiian ambassador to the United States, the Commercial Directorate was established at the beginning of 1880.[57] It was upgraded to the status of a consulate after a year's experiment, and Ch'en Kuo-fen was appointed the first Consul.[58]

Although the need to protect the Chinese coolies in Spanish Cuba and Peru was more urgently felt, the establishment of consulates in these two places came later than the consulate in San Francisco. The delay was caused mainly by diplomatic procedure. Consulates in Cuba and Peru could not be established until the ambassador, Ch'en Lan-pin, presented his credentials to the respective governments. Because Ch'en went to Washington first to set up the legation, his trips to Spain and Peru were delayed until April 1879. Accompanied by his retinue, Ch'en set sail from New York on 12 April on board a British ship. He arrived at Madrid after a forty days' voyage, and presented his credentials to the king of Spain on 24 May 1879.[59] While he was setting up an office in Madrid, Ch'en appointed one of his aides, Liu Liang-yuan as the Consul-General for Cuba in the autumn of the same year.[60] Although the despatch of a Consul-General to Cuba for the protection of the Chinese was part of China's right in accordance with the Sino-Spanish treaty on coolies signed in November 1877, Ch'en

---

diplomatic history of the Ch'ing government, presumably the Commercial Director did not have the same power as the Consul. See *Ch'ing-chi wai-chiao shih-liao*, vol. 15, pp. 8a–8b.

[57]The actual date of the establishment of this Commercial Directorate is difficult to decide. In a memorial to the Court dated 16th day of 3rd moon of 7th year of Kuang-hsu (14 April 1881), the Tsungli Yamen stated that the Commercial Directorate had been established for more than a year. According to this, it is reasonable to suggest that it was established in early 1880. See *Ch'ing-chi wai-chiao shih-liao*, vol. 25, pp. 22a–23a; for details about the negotiations between Yung Wing and the Hawaiian ambassador to the United States, see Liu Chin-ch'ao (ed.), *Ch'ing-ch'ao shu wen-hsien t'ung-k'ao*, vol. 337, "Wai-chiao" 1.

[58]See "Memorial of the Tsungli Yamen to the Court regarding the establishment of the consulate in Honolulu dated 16th day of 3rd moon of 7th year of Kuang-hsu (14 April 1881)", in *Ch'ing-chi wai-chiao shih-liao*, vol. 25, p. 23a.

[59]See "Memorial of Ch'en Lan-pin to the Court relating to his arrival in Spain and his presentation of credentials to the king of Spain dated 17th day of 6th moon of 5th year of Kuang-hsu (4 August 1879)", in *Ch'ing-chi wai-chiao shih-liao*, vol. 15, pp. 36b–37a.

[60]See "Memorial of Ch'en Lan-pin to the Court relating to his departure from Spain for Peru dated 4th day of 5th moon of 6th year of Kuang-hsu (11 June 1880)", in *Ch'ing-chi wai-chiao shih-liao*, vol. 21, p. 1a.

feared some disputes might arise from actions taken by the Chinese
Consul-General to enforce treaty rights. This was why he stayed in
Madrid for nearly a year (from 21 May 1879 to 17 April 1880), and
was prepared to argue with the Spanish foreign ministry when the
situation arose. Ch'en's fear was based on his information that the
Spanish treasury depended heavily on the sugar tax collected in
Cuba, and that the huge profit of the Cuban sugar industry
depended on the labour of Chinese coolies.[61] For this reason, Ch'en
expected some trouble after the establishment of the Consulate-
General in Havana.

But things turned out quite unexpectedly: the Chinese Consul-
General worked smoothly with the local officials in Cuba in enforcing the treaty clauses; many Chinese coolies were registered with
the Consulate-General for protection; and the Spanish ambassador
for China who visited the island at that time, did not find the work
of the Chinese Consul-General objectionable.[62] This good working
relationship between the Chinese Consul-General and the Spanish
authorities in Cuba pleased Ch'en Lan-pin, and prompted him to
leave Spain for Peru on 17 April 1880.[63] No record seems to have
been left relating to Ch'en's visit to Peru, nor do we know anything
about the establishment of a consulate there. Presumably, the
absence of Ch'en's memorial to the Court or correspondence with
the Tsungli Yamen indicates the failure of his mission.

The consulate established after the one in Havana, was in New
York in 1883.[64] The selection of New York as a site for a consulate
was a logical one. Although the Chinese were not as numerous

---

[61]*Ibid.*

[62]*Ibid.*, p. 21b.

[63]Ch'en appointed his Counsellor, Li Shu-ch'ang to take charge of the office in
Madrid, and he took eleven retinues with him to sail for Peru. *Ibid.*

[64]There is a confusion about the year of the establishment of the consulate in New
York. The record kept in the archives of the Chinese embassy in Germany claimed it
to be 1879 (the 5th year of Kuang-hsu); while the *Ch'ing-ch'ao shu wen-hsien t'ung-
k'ao* recorded 1882 (the 8th year of Kuang-hsu); but the *Ch'ing-chi wai-chiao shih-
liao* claims 1883 (the 9th year of Kuang-hsu). It appears that the latter is a correct
one. This is supported by the official despatch from the Chinese Minister, Cheng
Tsao-ju to the Secretary of State. See "Cheng Tsao-ju to F.J. Fulinghuysen dated 28
May 1883", in "Notes from the Chinese Legation", "The Mission of Cheng Tsao-
ju". Liu Hsi-hung and others, *Chu Te shih-kuan tang-an ch'ao* (Records of the
Chinese Embassy in Germany) (Taipei, 1966), vol. 1, pp. 563–66; *Ch'ing-ch'ao shu
wen-hsien t'ung-k'ao*, vol. 1, p. 338, "Wai-chiao" 2; *Ch'ing-chi wai-chiao chih-
liao*, vol. 31, pp. 22a–23a.

there as in San Francisco, New York had the second largest Chinese population and the numbers grew steadily. More important, New York was geographically closer to Cuba than San Francisco, and thus became a port of transit for Chinese coolies from Cuba on their way back to China. Furthermore, the government of the United States at that time was in the process of introducing new rules and regulations governing admission of Chinese coolies, and it required Chinese nationals who were exiled from New York to obtain a permit from the Chinese embassy. Those who failed to comply were refused re-entry into the United States. In view of this need, the new Chinese ambassador, Cheng Tsao-ju who succeeded Ch'en Lan-pin in June 1881,[65] memorialised the Court for the establishment of a consulate in New York. He recommended his aide Ou-yang Ming as the first Consul, and Cheng P'eng-chung as interpreter, together with Lai Hung-k'uei as an aide for the new consulate.[66] His recommendation was approved by the Court and the consulate came into being in 1883.[67]

In the early stage of the development of Chinese consulates overseas, it was clear that the overseas Chinese communities selected for that purpose fell into three broad categories: places where protection of coolies was urgently needed, such as Cuba; where the overseas Chinese communities were mature and rich, such as Singapore, San Francisco, Honolulu and New York; and where the communities close to China which might be useful for China's defence, such as those in Japan. The initiative taken by various ambassadors in setting up the consulates indicated their recognition of the potential value of overseas Chinese to China as a whole. On the other hand, many overseas Chinese communities desired to have Chinese guardians. Despite these needs and demands, the Ch'ing government refrained itself from extending diplomatic protection to many overseas Chinese communities, particularly in Southeast Asia. The main reason behind this caution was the lack of finance. In 1875, six per cent of foreign customs

---

[65]See Wai-chiao-pu tang-an tsu-liao ch'u (ed.), *Chung-kuo chu-wai ke ta kung-shih kuan li-jen kuan-chang hsien-ming nien-piao* (Historical table of dates of the Chinese envoys sent overseas) (Taipei, 1969), p. 47.

[66]See "Memorial of Cheng Tsao-ju to the Court relating to the establishment of a consulate in New York dated 10th day of 2nd moon of 9th year of Kuang-hsu (18 March 1883)", in *Ch'ing-chi wai-chiao shih-liao*, vol. 31, pp. 22a–23a.

[67]*Ibid.*

dues was allocated to the funding of the legations overseas.[68] This amount was obviously inadequate to meet the cost of initial establishment. As a result, an extra three per cent of the foreign customs dues was added to the pool in 1878.[69] From the Ch'ing government's point of view, there was a danger of over-expansion in this direction which could put a heavy strain on the treasury. As the government had not yet seen the concrete benefit from the protection of its overseas subjects, massive consular expansion was undesirable. The government's preoccupation with cost was clearly reflected in the Tsungli Yamen's rejection of Kuo Sung-t'ao's proposal to extend consular protection to other Chinese communities in Southeast Asia, apart from Singapore.[70] In fact, Kuo had in mind making Singapore the head office for the protection of the Chinese in Southeast Asia, and establishing a Consulate-General there to control other consulate establishments in the region.[71] Although a consulate was established in Singapore under Hoo Ah Kay (Hu Hsuan-tse), Kuo's ambitious scheme was put aside by the government because of the lack of finance. The government's restrained attitude towards consular expansion was best expressed by the Tsungli Yamen in 1888.

In discussing the call of the Governor-General, Chang Chih-tung, to expand consular representation in Southeast Asia and Oceania, the Yamen pointed out the difficulty in setting up consulates in those countries; it expressed concern over unrestrained expansion which would result in enormous cost to the government. It also criticised the suggestion of private funding of consulates by local

---

[68]See Ch'en Wen-chin, "Ch'ing-chi ch'u-shih ke-kuo shih-ling ching-hui" (Funds for the Chinese legations and consulates during the Ch'ing period 1875-1911), in *Chung-kuo chin-tai ching-chi shih yen-chiu chi-k'an*, vol. 1, no. 1 (Nanking, 1932), pp. 280-81.

[69]Apart from this 9 per cent foreign customs dues, part of the ship tonnage dues of the China Merchants Navigation Company that were held by the customs was added to the fund. The total income from these sources amounted to about 1 million taels annually. *Ibid.*; see also Immanuel C.Y. Hsu, *China's Entrance into the Family of Nations: The Diplomatic Phase 1858-1880*, pp. 194-95.

[70]See "Memorial of the Tsungli Yamen to the court relating to the reply to Kuo Sung-t'ao's memorial for the establishment of a consulate in Singapore dated 25th day of 9th moon of the 3rd year of Kuang-shu (31 October 1887)", in *Ch'ing-chi wai-chiao shih-liao*, vol. 11, p. 31b.

[71]See "Memorial of Kuo Sung-t'ao to the court urging for the establishment of a consulate in Singapore dated 27th day of 8th moon of the 3rd year of Kuang-hsu (3 October 1877)", in *Ch'ing-chi wai-chiao shih-liao*, vol. 11, p. 15a.

Chinese communities, and pointed out that private sources of finance were rather unreliable. In Cuba, it asserted that many Chinese responded fervently and contributed generously to the maintenance of the consulate in the early stage, but their enthusiasm quickly died down and this left the problem for the government to take up.[72] It also reminded the Court that Singapore's case was another example of the fact that the private funding was untenable. The consulate there had collected a few hundred taels from the local Chinese population through dues and fees, but the expenses of the consulate amounted to seven or eight thousand taels.[73]

The Tsungli Yamen was also concerned about the difficulty of finding suitable personnel for consular positions. Career diplomats would take some time to train, and local overseas Chinese like Hoo Ah Kay needed to be properly selected. What the Tsungli Yamen feared most was that unscrupulous overseas Chinese leaders would abuse their position as Consul for personal gains. This in fact would have made the life of ordinary overseas Chinese more miserable, and would have aroused resentment against the imperial government.[74] The Tsungli Yamen's cautious attitude stemmed partly from their traditional suspicion of merchants. As most of the ministers of the Yamen were trained in Confucian classics, their view of merchants was tainted with the Confucian bias against commercialism. To them merchants were greedy, selfish and unscrupulous. The overseas Chinese leaders seemed to fit the picture well because most of them were rich merchants. This cautious attitude was also grounded on the reports of the Chinese emissaries sent to overseas Chinese communities. According to these reports, some Chinese Majoors in the Dutch East Indies were oppressive in treating their compatriots.[75] The Yamen felt that the interests of the overseas Chinese would be better served without consuls but through direct negotiations between the Chinese ambassador and the country concerned.[76]

---

[72]See Liu Chin-ch'ao (ed.), *Ch'ing-ch'ao shu wen-hsien t'ung-k'ao*, vol. 338, "Wai-chiao" 2, k'ao, p. 10798.

[73]*Ibid.*

[74]*Ibid.*

[75]See "Second Report of Wang Yung-ho and Yu Chun on the Commercial Conditions in Southeast Asia dated 2nd day of 3rd moon of 13th year of Kuang-hsu (26 March 1887)", in Liu Hsi-hung *et al.*, *Chu Te Shih-kuan tang-an ch'ao*, vol. 2, pp. 671–86.

[76]See Liu Chin-ch'ao (ed.), *op. cit.*, p. 10798.

THE SECOND STAGE OF ESTABLISHMENT OF
CONSULATES IN OVERSEAS CHINESE COMMUNITIES
(1893-1912)

Chang Chih-tung, Hsueh Fu-ch'eng and the Issue of Consular Expansion in Overseas Chinese Communities

The second stage of the consular expansion began in the early 1890s, the momentum was gathered in the 1880s. The push for expansion came from ambitious high-ranking provincial officials like Chang Chih-tung and far-sighted diplomats like Hsueh Fu-ch'eng. Chang and Hsueh were known for their efforts in changing traditional Ch'ing policy towards the overseas Chinese in 1893, which will be dealt with fully in a separate chapter. Both of them also played an important part in the consular expansion. To them, consular expansion was an integral part of their overall strategy, and was the premium for gaining the loyalty of overseas Chinese. Chang saw the immediate value in defence and finance. As overseas Chinese spread widely over the globe, their support for China was important in times of military conflict with the West. The support given by some Malayan Chinese in 1884 during the Sino-French conflict over Vietnam,[77] demonstrated to him that overseas Chinese could be used in war with the West. But Chang seemed to be interested even more in their economic potential. Of foremost importance was the sending of money to their relatives in China. Chang estimated that this amounted to $20,000,000 annually. The remittances were of incalculable benefit to Kwangtung and Fukien, where the rapidly increasing population caused severe economic strains.[78] At that time, although Chang had no concrete plan of attracting overseas Chinese capital, he appeared to be aware of the wealth of overseas Chinese and of their economic potential to meet China's needs. They could contribute significantly to relief funds which were urgently needed in China to meet natural disasters; they

---

[77]A well-known Chinese Kapitan in Malaya, Chang Keng Kui, (Cheng Ching-kuei in Mandarin, or known as Chung Keng Kwee and Ah Quee) donated 100,000 taels to the Ch'ing government to support the war against the French in Indochina. See "The paper presented to Chang Keng Kui on his 75th birthday by Chang Pi-shih and others", in K'uang Kuo-hsiang, *Pin-ch'eng san-chi* (Hong Kong, 1958), p. 112.

[78]See "Memorial of Chang Chih-tung to the Court relating to the protection of the Overseas Chinese dated 25th day of 2nd moon of 12th year of Kuang-hsu (30 March 1886)", in Chang Chih-tung, *Chang Wen-hsiang kung ch'uan-chi* (Taipei, 1963), vol. 1, pp. 333-34.

could donate money to naval defence programmes for purchasing warships;[79] and they could invest in China to support the ongoing industrial projects of the Self-Strengthening movement. But all these programmes needed an organisation in overseas Chinese communities to coordinate fund raising activities, and consular establishments seemed to be the best answer.

Hsueh Fu-ch'eng took a slightly different stand with regard to the use of overseas Chinese. He appeared to be on a higher plane, thinking not just of the immediate and tangible benefit deriving from overseas Chinese, but of a long term basis for the benefit of China. He certainly appreciated the importance of the overseas Chinese annual remittances about which he learnt in detail when he was on his way to take up his appointment as the Chinese Minister to Britain, France, Italy and Belgium in 1890.[80] But he looked at the overseas Chinese issue from a different perspective. He saw that the wealth and power of the Western countries were built on commerce and military strength. He probably had in mind the way in which the British and the Dutch built their commercial empires in India and the East Indies. If China had followed the Western countries by paying attention to commerce and protecting its merchants overseas, China would likewise have become wealthy and powerful in due course. Hsueh's mercantilist outlook enabled him to make a broad assessment of overseas Chinese on a long term basis.[81] He tried to fit them into the role of Western merchants in China whose drive for profit benefited the mother countries. He used the expression "If the branches, twigs and leaves flourish, and trunk and roots will be firm and secure" to indicate the desirable relationship between overseas Chinese and China.[82] He criticised those who em-

---

[79]See "Memorial of Chang Chih-tung to the Court relating to a scheme to raise funds among Overseas Chinese Merchants for the purchase of merchant-protection warships dated 4th day of 9th moon of 11th year of Kuang-hsu (11 October 1885)", *ibid.*, pp. 302–303.

[80]See Hsueh Fu-cheng, *Ch'u-shih Ying, Fa, I, Pi ssu-kuo jih-chi* (Diary of My Mission to England, France, Italy and Belgium), original, vol. 10, p. 11; in Shen Yun-lung (ed.), *Chin-tai Chung-kuo shih-liao t'sung-k'an*, no. 12 (Taipei, n.d.), p. 32.

[81]For a discussion of Chinese mercantilists in the late Ch'ing period including Hsueh Fu-ch'eng, see Mabel Lee, "Wan-ch'ing te chung-shang chu-i" (Mercantilism in the Late Ch'ing period), in *Chung-yang yen chiu-yen chin-tai shih yen-chiu so chi-k'an* (Taipei, 1972), vol. 3, no. 1, pp. 207–21.

[82]See Hsueh Fu-ch'eng, "To consult the Tsungli Yamen regarding the negotia-

phasised tangible, economic and military benefits from overseas Chinese, as short-sighted.[83] It is clear that this belief in the long-term use of overseas Chinese led Hsueh persistently to champion the change of imperial policy towards overseas Chinese, which resulted in the abolition of the old policy in 1893.

Chang Chih-tung built up a momentum for the change. Chang could claim no expertise in overseas Chinese affairs before 1884. His appointment in that year to the position of Governor-General of Kwangtung and Kwangsi brought him closer to the areas where the majority of overseas Chinese sojourned, and very naturally it attracted him to the overseas Chinese issue. Chang's championship of consular expansion was rooted partly in his general belief that overseas Chinese could be used significantly to the advantage of China. His unorthodox move of calling upon the Chinese in Saigon, Singapore and Penang to sabotage French warships in 1884 showed his diplomatic naivety, but demonstrated his sincere belief that overseas Chinese could be used to defend China.[84] He began to claim expertise on the overseas Chinese affairs in 1885 when he memorialised the Court to build a fleet of warships that would be maintained by overseas Chinese for their own protection.[85] This rather original idea, though difficult to put into practice, did stir some hopes in the concept of forward defence of China's coastal regions. Chang reinforced his claim to expertise in 1886 with Chang Yin-huan, the newly appointed minister to the United States, Peru and Spain, by memorialising the Court to expand consular representation in Southeast Asia. According to their plan, two Consulates-General were to be established in the important locations of the East and West routes of Southeast Asia, presumably one in Singapore and the other in Manila.[86] The Consuls-General

---

tions with the British Foreign Office over consular expansion'', in Hsueh Fu-ch'eng, *Ch'u-shih kung-tu* (Correspondence of My Diplomatic Mission), vol. 1, p. 4.

[83]*Ibid.*

[84]For Chang Chih-tung's call on the Chinese in Saigon, Singapore and Penang to sabotage French warships, see Chang Chih-tung, ''Instruction to coastal inhabitants and overseas Chinese dated 20th day of 7th moon of 10th year of Kuang-hsu (9 September 1844)'', in Chang Chih-tung, *Chang Wen-hsiang kung ch'uan-chi*, vol. 119, kung-tu 34, pp. 15a–15b.

[85]See Chang Chih-tung, ''To urge overseas Chinese merchants to donate funds for the construction of warships dated 4th day of 9th moon of 11th year of Kuang-hsu (11 October 1885)'', in *Chang Wen-hsing kung ch'uan-chi*, vol. 13, pp. 12a–13a.

[86]The memorial did not spell out the actual locations, but judging from the fact

were to be under the control of the Chinese ambassadors in the appropriate European countries, and they were to be entrusted with the jobs of touring around adjacent islands and of recommending upright Chinese leaders for the positions of Vice-Consuls.[87] To cover the cost of maintenance, the two memorialists suggested that Vice-Consuls should be appointed on a voluntary basis but awarded with official titles. Registration and passport fees were to be collected among the local Chinese, part of which would be used to support the proposed new establishments. The rest would be used for supporting Chinese schools and hospitals.[88] The memorial pointed out that consular protection must be widely offered to the overseas Chinese in Southeast Asia before their loyalty could be obtained, and their assistance in the defence of China acquired.

To back up their argument for consular expansion, both Chang Chih-tung and Chang Yih-huan reminded the Court that a petition had been presented by four Philippine Chinese leaders to Chang Yin-huan in Canton in early 1886, and that it was signed by 290 merchants who called upon the Chinese government for consular protection.[89] To show their objectivity in pressing for the move, both the memorialists suggested sending a fact-finding mission to tour Southeast Asia and part of the Oceania before the establishment of the proposed consulates. The mission was to be led by Wang Yung-ho, an Expectant Brigadier[90] and a native of the Lung-ch'i district in Fukien. His assistant was to be the Expectant Prefect Yu Chun, a native of the Hsin-ning district in Kwangtung, who had held a diplomatic position in Japan as the Chinese Consul in Nagasaki.[91]

---

that Singapore and Manila occupied the strategic importance in the traditional West and East routes in Southeast Asia, this assumption is reasonable. Professor Edgar Wickberg has the same assumption. See Chang Chih-tung, "Memorial to the Court relating to the protection of overseas Chinese merchants dated 25th day of 2nd moon of 12th year of Kuang-hsu" (30 March 1886), in *Chang Wen-hsiang kung ch'uan-chi*, vol. 15, tsou-i 15, pp. 11a–11b; Edgar Wickberg, *The Chinese in Philippine Life 1850–1898* (New Haven, 1965), p. 217.

[87]*Chang Wen-hsiang kung ch'uan-chi*, vol. 15, tsou-i, p. 11b.

[88]*Ibid.*

[89]*Ibid.*

[90]"Chi-ming tsung-ping" is translated by Professor Edgar Wickberg as "Brigade-General". I think "Expectant Brigadier" is a more appropriate translation, for Wang Yung-ho at that time was not holding the office of the Brigadier but as a candidate for that office.

[91]Chang Chih-tung, *op. cit.*, pp. 12b–13a.

This was a progressive and realistic scheme, and had it succeeded it would have forged a close link between China and its overseas subjects in Southeast Asia. In retrospect, it is possible to see that it would have laid a solid foundation on which the loyalty of overseas Chinese towards the Ch'ing government could have been developed, and would have placed the government in a better position in checking the growth of the anti-Ch'ing movement in overseas Chinese communities in the later period. Both Changs saw the immediate benefit deriving from consular establishment, particularly in the economic sphere, as they pointed out in the memorial that "the two major aims in establishing consulates are to protect Chinese subjects and to collect donations".[92] Protection was a means to an end, for without overseas Chinese, money would not flow to China. They also saw the usefulness of consulates as a medium through which donations from overseas Chinese could be channelled. Donations such as the flood and famine relief scheme, funds for constructing and maintaining warships etc., would certainly be facilitated by the presence of the Consuls-General and Vice-Consuls. Being physically presented in the overseas Chinese communities, the Consuls-General and Vice-Consuls would effectively establish links with local leaders and radiate their influence over the whole community. The role of the Ch'ing Consul and of the Consuls-General in Singapore in the later period in fund raising vindicated this foresight.[93]

The suggestion of sending an investigative mission to Southeast Asia as a prerequisite for establishing consulates was a shrewd and cautious move on the part of Chang Chih-tung. Although he would like to have demonstrated his foresight to the throne over the overseas Chinese issue, he would not have gone to the extent of rushing into it, for any negative result from his proposed consular expansion would provide ammunition to his political opponents to attack him. As Chang was the rising star on the Chinese political scene in the 1880s,[94] every move would have to be carefully calculated. By

---

[92]Chang Chih-tung, *op. cit.*, p. 10a.

[93]For the role of Ch'ing consul and consul-general in fund-raising activities in Singapore and Malaya during the period between 1889 and 1912, see Yen Ching-hwang, "Ch'ing Sale of Honours and the Chinese Leadership in Singapore and Malaya 1877-1912", in *Journal of Southeast Asian Studies*, vol. 1, no. 2 (September, 1970), pp. 23-24.

[94]Chang Chih-tung was a leader of the "Ch'ing-liu tang" (The Pure Group or Purification Clique) which became politically influential in the 1880s. Chang

sending an investigative mission overseas, Chang could conveniently relegate his direct responsibility to others. Any positive findings of the mission would endorse his credibility. On the other hand, any unfavourable reports from the mission would probably have convinced him to give up his plan. It was in the spirit of a "safe move" that Chang Chih-tung in the joint memorial suggested that the proposed Consuls-General in Southeast Asia were to be partly under his control. His reason was that the Southeast Asian islands were physically closer to Kwangtung than to the European countries where the Chinese ambassadors resided, and any disputes by the Chinese Consuls-General with the local authorities would reach Canton faster for consultation, than London or Madrid.[95] This, to a certain extent, was true. But the real motive of Chang's move was to keep himself informed of what was going on in the overseas Chinese communities in Southeast Asia, and to be directly involved with the administration of overseas Chinese. An influence in the administration of the overseas Chinese in Southeast Asia would not only establish him as an expert on the overseas Chinese affairs, but would also facilitate his fund-raising activities in the region.

The Court approved of Chang Chih-tung's and Chang Yin-huan's suggestion of despatching a fact-finding mission. British, Dutch and Spanish foreign offices were informed of China's intention. Wang Yung-ho and Yu Chun left Canton on 26 August 1886 on board a commercial vessel. The first leg of the visit was to the Philippines and then they proceeded to Singapore, Malacca, Kuala Lumpur, Perak,[96] Penang, Rangoon, Deli (North Sumatra), Batavia, Semarang, Surahbaya, and then to Sydney, Melbourne, Adelaide and Queensland (Brisbane).[97] More than twenty cities or ports

---

achieved rapid promotion in that decade. For a brief biography of Chang in English, see M. Cameron, "Chang Chih-tung", in A.W. Hummel (ed.), *Eminent Chinese of the Ch'ing Period*, pp. 27–32; for references to Ch'ing-liu tang, see L.E. Eastman, *Throne and Mandarins* (Cambridge, Mass., 1967), pp. 26–29; W. Ayers, *Chang Chih-tung and Educational Reform in China* (Cambridge, Mass., 1971), pp. 65–99.

[95]Chang Chih-tung, *op. cit.*, p. 12a.

[96]The names of Kuala Lumpur and Perak were found in the mission's first report to the Chinese Minister to Germany, Holland, France, Italy and Austria, Hsu Ching-ch'eng dated 2nd day of 3rd moon of 13th year of Kuang-hsu (26 March 1887), in Liu Hsi-hung *et al.*, *Chu Te shih-kuan tang-an ch'ao*, vol. 2, p. 668.

[97]See Chang Chih-tung, "Memorial to the Court relating to the proposed protection to overseas Chinese after the fact-finding mission tour to Southeast Asia dated 24th day of 10th moon of 13th year of Kuang-hsu (8 December 1887)", in Chang Chih-tung, *Chang Wen-hsiang kung ch'uan-chi*, vol. 23, tsou-i 23, pp. 9a–9b.

were visited, and the entire trip which was to take eight months took twelve months to complete.[98]

The mission collected a great deal of useful information relating to the conditions of the overseas Chinese in Southeast Asia and Oceania. They were generally despised, ill-treated and discriminated against, except for those in the British Straits Settlements (Singapore, Malacca and Penang). The envoys found the conditions of the Chinese in the Philippines most appalling. Many of the 50,000 Chinese were beaten, robbed or killed. Their properties were damaged, burned, and they were subjected to cheating and extortion by the police and soldiers.[99] The local Filipinos were campaigning for the expulsion of the Chinese coolies, but due to the arrival of the mission, the anti-Chinese campaign came to a halt for a while. The envoys pointed out that the local Chinese had urged for consular protection and had expressed their willingness to raise money for the funding of consular establishment.[100] Wang and Yu found the Chinese in the Dutch East Indies in a similarly distressed condition. The Chinese in Batavia numbered about 74,600, and had to pay heavy taxes to the local government. In addition to income tax, they had to pay property tax, household utensil tax, carriage tax, wedding and funeral taxes.[101] It was claimed by the local Chinese that similar taxes were not imposed on other foreigners.[102] To protect their wealth, some Chinese merchants were forced by the local authorities to take up Dutch citizenship. Both envoys asserted that this practice of forcing the Chinese to become Dutch nationals could become a major problem for China in the future.[103] The Chinese in Semarang and in the neighbouring

---

[98]See Chang Chih-tung, "Supplementary memorial to the Court relating to the proposed protection of overseas Chinese dated 24th day of 10th moon of 13th year of Kuang-hsu (8 December 1887)", *ibid.*, pp. 15a–15b.

[99]*Ibid.*, p. 9b.

[100]*Ibid.*

[101]See the second report of Wang Yung-ho and Yu Chun to the Chinese Minister to Germany, Holland, France, Italy and Austria, Hsu Ching-ch'eng dated 2nd day of 3rd moon of 13th year of Kuang-hsu (26 March 1887), in Liu Hsi-hung *et al.*, *Chu Te shih-kuan tang-an ch'ao*, vol. 2, pp. 671–76.

[102]*Ibid.* Regarding tax grievances of the Chinese in the Dutch East Indies at the turn of the present century, Lea E. Williams pointed out that the Chinese might not have been as heavily taxed as they claimed. See Lea E. Williams, *Overseas Chinese Nationalism: The Genesis of the Pan-Chinese Movement in Indonesia 1900–1916* (Glencoe, 1960), pp. 27–28.

[103]The second report of Wang Yung-ho and Yu Chun, in Liu Hsi-hung *et al.*, *op. cit.*, vol. 2, pp. 671–76.

areas complained to the mission that they suffered additional misery apart from the discrimination and heavy taxes, caused by strict control on their daily movement by the local authorities. They were required to produce a pass wherever they went, and to hold a lamp on their outings at night after 8.00 in the evening. Those who failed to comply with the regulations were punished with two or three months hard labour.[104]

The coolies of Deli in North Sumatra were ranked as the worst treated group among the Chinese in the Dutch East Indies. Their miseries were widely known in the overseas Chinese communities in Southeast Asia. Deli was not included in the schedule of the mission's visit, but while the envoys were visiting Penang, they were convinced of the alleged atrocities on the Chinese coolies and warranted them a special trip.[105] The Chinese in Deli numbered about 50,000 to 60,000 and the majority of them were Teochews. Most coolies there were recruited by brokers in Swatow, and were brought to Singapore or Penang where they were "resold" to Deli.[106] Most of them worked on the tobacco plantations owned by Dutch nationals, and many suffered from cruelty by the owners or overseers. When the envoys arrived at their destination on 17 December 1886, the suspected atrocities had been confirmed. They had the opportunity to interview local Chinese leaders, merchants and coolies, and all agreed that many coolies were ill-treated. One form of ill-treatment was the sacking of coolies as a result of sickness. The victims became either beggars or died of hunger on the roadside. Local Chinese residents who came to the aid of the victims were sometimes accused by the employers of keeping escapees, and this could result in three months' imprisonment.[107] Another cruelty was flogging. Coolies who failed to perform their work satisfactorily or dared to argue with the overseers and owners, were flogged severely. Some floggings resulted in death, but the local Dutch officials condoned the cruel actions. Before the arrival of the mission, a serious case of flogging had taken place. A

---

[104]*Ibid.*, pp. 676–81.

[105]See the third report of Wang Yung-ho and Yu Chun to Hsu Ching-ch'eng (undated, probably from 26 March to 10 May 1887), in Liu Hsi-hung *et al.*, *op. cit.*, vol. 2, pp. 688–93.

[106]See *The Singapore Daily Times*, 11/12/1874, p. 2; "Report of Committee Ap- the Straits Settlements, November, 1876", pp. 2–17, in CO.275/19.

[107]The third report of Wang Yung-ho and Yu Chun, in Liu Hsi-hung *et al.*, *op. cit.*, vol. 2, pp. 693–96.

coolie named Wen Ya-lung was alleged to have been flogged to death by the owner of a tobacco plantation. Wen did not perform his work satisfactorily and had argued with the owner, the result of which was severe flogging and death.[108] Wen's fellow workers petitioned the Chinese Luitenants[109] for justice, but no concrete result followed. The envoys intervened in the case and the local Dutch officials were urged to arrest the owner; however the reply was that the suspect had fled the country.[110] Whatever the truth behind the case, the Dutch authorities had shown their unwillingness to uphold justice, and the Chinese Luitenants appeared to have no power over Dutch nationals.[111]

During their tour of the Dutch colonies in Southeast Asia, the envoys were also struck by the timidity of the Chinese leaders who were appointed by the Dutch as "Ma-yao" (Majoor), "Chia-pi-tan" (Kapitein) and "Lei-chen-lan" (Luitenant).[112] These leaders were supposed to represent the Chinese community and act on its behalf in relation to the Dutch authorities, but due to their delicate relationship with the Dutch, they were unable and unwilling to fight for justice for their compatriots.[113] The inability of the Dutch-appointed Chinese officials to protect their countrymen prompted the envoys to recommend to the Ch'ing government that an im-

---

[108]It was said that Wen Ya-lung did not pick and pack the tobacco in the way that the owner wanted. Wen was hung and flogged. He was given more work and was only allowed to have one cold meal a day. Wen was flogged many times further until his death. *Ibid.*, pp. 696–97.

[109]Chinese leaders in the Dutch East Indies were appointed by the Dutch colonial authorities for the positions of Majoor (Major), Kapitein (Captain) and Luitenant (Lieutenant). Luitenant was the lowest in the Chinese leadership hierarchy. The Chinese term for Luitenant in the report is "Lei-chen-lan".

[110]See the third report of Wang Yung-ho and Yu Chun, in Liu Hsi-hung *et al.*, *op. cit.*, vol. 2, p. 698.

[111]*Ibid.*

[112]When Wang and Yu arrived in Batavia on 6 January 1887 (13th day of 12th moon of 12th year of Kuang-hsu), Chinese Majoors, Kapiteins and Luitenants dared not greet them in fear of inviting the displeasure of the Dutch authorities. It was not until the Dutch officials had received the mission and shown their approval by a meeting with the envoys that the Chinese Majoors, Kapiteins and Luitenants came to meet them. See the second report of Wang Yung-ho and Yu Chun, in Liu Hsi-hung *et al.*, *op. cit.*, vol. 2, pp. 671–76.

[113]*Ibid.*, for a good discussion on these Chinese officials in the Dutch colonial system and their service to the Dutch colonial regime, see Lea E. Williams, *Overseas Chinese Nationalism: The Genesis of the Pan-Chinese Movement in Indonesia 1900–1916*, pp. 124–26.

perial Consul-General be present in Batavia, and Vice-Consuls be appointed among Chinese merchants who could speak out on behalf of the Chinese communities.[114]

The findings of the Wang Yung-ho and Yu Chun mission confirmed the fact that the overseas Chinese needed protection. They furnished Chang Chih-tung with concrete evidence for his idea of consular expansion in Southeast Asia. On the basis of the reports, Chang memorialised the Court for action. His overall plan consisted of three Consulates-General to be established in Manila, Batavia and Sydney. The Consulates-General were to take charge of the Chinese in the neighbouring cities or ports where Vice-Consuls would be selected among upright overseas Chinese leaders.[115] The Consul-General in Sydney, for instance, was to look after the Chinese in Melbourne, Adelaide, Queensland (Brisbane) and New Zealand as well.[116] As the Chinese in the British Straits Settlements and in the Malay states were comparatively better treated, Chang saw no immediate need to upgrade the status of the existing Singapore consulate to Consulate-General, but proposed to appoint a Vice-Consul in Penang which, according to him, produced a great deal of Chinese talent. The Vice-Consul of Penang could help the Chinese Consul in Singapore look after the Chinese in the area. He also proposed appointing a Vice-Consul in Rangoon, Burma, in order to protect the local Chinese as well as for the defence of China's border.[117] Another Vice-Consul was to be appointed in Deli of North Sumatra for the protection of the Chinese coolies.[118] The logic behind this overall plan was clear. The locations for the proposed Consulates-General were the administrative centres of the Spanish, Dutch and British colonies in Southeast Asia and Oceania. The Consuls-General would have access to the highest authorities

---

[114]The second report of Wang Yung-ho and Yu Chun, in Liu Hsi-hung et al., op. cit., vol. 2, pp. 681–86.

[115]See Chang Chih-tung, "Memorial to the Court relating to the proposed protection to overseas Chinese after the fact-finding mission tour to Southeast Asia dated 24th day of 10th moon of 13th year of Kuang-hsu (8 December 1887)", in Chang Chih-tung, Chang Wen-hsiang kung ch'uan-chi, vol. 23, tsou-i, pp. 9b–12a; the same memorial is contained in the Ch'ing-chi wai-chiao shih-liao, vol. 74, pp. 21a–26b.

[116]Chang Chih-tung, op. cit., p. 12a; Ch'ing-chi wai-chiao shih-liao, vol. 74, pp. 24b–25a.

[117]Chang did not really use the word "defence" in his memorial, his expression was "to the benefit of border issue". See Chang Chih-tung, op. cit., p. 10b.

[118]See Ch'ing-chi wai-chiao shih-liao, vol. 74, p. 24a.

in the regions, and could offer protection to the overseas Chinese more promptly. The advantage of this overall plan should be understood not just from the protection point of view, but also from the perspective of controlling the overseas Chinese in these regions. The proposed three Consulates-General together with the existing consulate in Singapore could form an effective diplomatic network. With many vice-consulates under the control of the Consulates-General, the Chinese government would have a very effective command system in the overseas Chinese communities in Southeast Asia and Oceania. Any projects from China such as the proposed warship and fund-raising schemes could be quickly carried out through the Consuls-General and Vice-Consuls. At the same time, the needs and wishes of the overseas communities could be effectively transmitted to the Chinese government through the same channel.

Chang Chih-tung was however a realist. He realised that simultaneous implementation of this plan could cost a huge amount of money, and the cost factor was likely to be the most important consideration in the decisions made on consular expansion by the Tsungli Yamen and the Court. He therefore revised his strategy. Instead of pressing for full implementation of his overall plan, he suggested that a Consulate-General be established in Manila first, in view of the urgency of protection there. He also argued that Manila was geographically close to China, and the overseas Chinese there would be useful for China's coastal defence.[119] Chang also informed the Court that he had discussed the matter with Chang Yin-huan, and agreed to appoint Wang Yung-ho as the first Consul-General in Manila. Chang emphasised that Wang was the most suitable person for the job. Not only was he the head of the fact-finding mission and well-informed about conditions of the Chinese in the Philippines, he was also a native of Fukien who spoke the dialect of the majority of the Chinese there.[120] Chang reiterated his original proposal that the consular establishment be maintained by fees and dues paid by the local Chinese, but suggested that its initial cost and the maintenance fees for the first year be paid out of the regular overseas envoys' funds.[121] He urged the

---

[119]See Chang Chih-tung, *Chang Wen-hsiang kung ch'uan-chi*, vol. 23, tsou-i 23, p. 13a.

[120]*Ibid.*

[121]*Ibid.*, p. 14a; *Ch'ing-chi wai-chiao shih-liao*, vol. 74, pp. 26a–26b.

Court to press the Spanish government for the approval of the proposed Consulate-General in Manila. He intended to use the proposed
Consulate-General as a test case, and if it proved successful, the
next step would be the establishment of various vice-consulates in
the neighbouring areas of Manila and then in the British and Dutch
colonies in Southeast Asia and Oceania.[122] To give sufficient weight
to his proposal, Chang warned that any delay in giving protection
to the overseas Chinese in these regions would bring disaster to
China. He explained that the presence of a few million Chinese
there, and their growing prosperity, would begin to invite jealousy
from the Western Colonial Powers, while if the majority of them
were forced to return, China would be faced with a gigantic problem of feeding and clothing them, and the coastal provinces would
have immense difficulties in coping with millions of roaming inhabitants.[123]

The Tsungli Yamen's reaction to Chang's memorial was a
cautious one. It supported Chang's proposal to set up a consulate-
general in Manila, but opposed his overall plan of massive consular
expansion. The Yamen based its objection on the grounds of three
problems. Firstly, there was the problem of successfully negotiating
for a consulate. It observed that most European Powers were unwilling to approve the proposed consulates because they feared that
the Chinese Consuls would undermine their authority in the colonies. It pointed out that the Wang Yung-ho's mission was initially
rejected by the Dutch government on visiting the East Indies for
fear that the mission would stir up trouble, but due to the repeated
efforts by the Chinese Minister to Holland (Mr. Hsu Ching-ch'eng),
the mission was allowed to go ahead.[124] From the confidential
reports received from the Chinese ministers concerned, tremendous
difficulties were expected in the dealings with the Dutch and
Spanish governments over the consulate issue.[125] Secondly, there
was a problem of finance. Massive consular expansion required
financial backing. The Yamen pointed out the fallacy of Chang's
argument that overseas Chinese funds could substain the consular
establishment. Quoting examples of Cuba and Singapore, it em-

---

[122]See Chang Chih-tung, *op. cit.*, vol. 23, tsou-i 23, p. 13b.

[123]*Ibid.*, p. 12b.

[124]See "Memorial of the Tsungli Yamen to the Court relating to the establishment
of a Consulate-General in Manila dated 2nd day of 2nd moon of the 14th year of
Kuang-hsu (14 March 1888)", in *Ch'ing-chi wai-chiao shih-liao*, vol. 75, p. 19b.

[125]*Ibid.*, pp. 20a–20b.

phasised that overseas Chinese funds were unreliable.[126] The shortage of funds for the diplomatic legations ruled out the possibility of a commitment to massive expansion. Thirdly, the effectiveness of a consulate also became a subject for concern. The Yamen noted that the proposed locations for consular establishment were geographically far away from China and from the Chinese ministers concerned. The Consuls-General would not be able to act effectively in giving protection to the overseas Chinese, because of the delay in correspondence. Moreover, the suggested recruitment of local Chinese leaders for the posts of Vice-Consuls could also create trouble, because any wrong choice of personnel could result in the abuse of the positions and bring disgrace to the imperial government.[127]

Based on the above arguments, the Tsungli Yamen insisted on caution. It also pointed out that if China intended to extend consular protection to her overseas subjects, she should begin with places such as Burma, Thailand and Vietnam which were geographically closer to China and were traditionally within China's sphere of influence; she should not be too much interested in those scattered islands outside her sphere of influence.[128] To conclude, the Yamen recommended to the Court that Chang's proposal of setting up a Consulate-General in Manila should be initiated, and scrapped his idea of massive consular expansion. To protect the overseas Chinese in those areas where consulates had not been established, it suggested that the local Chinese associations elect upright leaders who could liaise with the Chinese ministers concerned; at the same time, the Chinese ministers overseas were to be instructed to deal directly with the European Powers over the protection of the overseas Chinese, in accordance with the treaty agreements.[129]

---

[126]It pointed out that at the initial stage of establishing the consulate in Cuba, the local Chinese donated generously to the maintenance of the consulate, but the enthusiasm quickly died down. In the case of Singapore, the Yamen pointed out that fees and dues collected among Singapore Chinese amounted to only a few hundred taels, but the cost of maintaining the consulate was in the vicinity of 7,000 to 8,000 taels annually. See Liu Chin-ch'ao (ed.), *Ch'ing-ch'ao shu wen-hsien t'ung-k'ao*, vol. 338, wai-chiao 2.

[127]The Memorial of the Tsungli Yamen, in *Ch'ing-chi wai-chiao shih-liao*, vol. 75, p. 20b.

[128]What the Tsungli Yamen referred to here were those places in the Dutch East Indies and probably including Australia and New Zealand as well. *Ibid.*, p. 21a.

[129]*Ibid.*, pp. 21a–21b; Liu Chin-ch'ao, *op. cit.*, vol. 338, wai-chiao 2.

One might wonder why Chang Chih-tung did not get much support for his "grand plan" from his friends in the Tsungli Yamen and from the Grand Council. Since the sacking of the veteran Prince Kung and his close associates from the two top policy making bodies in 1884,[130] the members of the "war party" with which Chang Chih-tung had been closely associated during the Ili and Annam crisis,[131] had assumed power and controlled the two bodies. One would expect Chang Chih-tung to get some solid support from his political allies for his ambitious plan. Although these leaders shared, to a certain extent, Chang's vision of making the overseas Chinese a supporting force for China in these regions,[132] they feared that the massive consular expansion would be conceived by the European Powers as an aggressive move, and would therefore strain China's relations with the Foreign Powers.[133] Another possible explanation for Chang's failure to obtain strong support from the Tsungli Yamen and the Grand Council is the insignificant role played by Prince Ch'ing (I-k'uang). The prince was appointed as the presiding prince of the Tsungli Yamen to succeed Prince Kung. He lacked real power and influence in the ruling circle, and was a man of mediocre ability. He has been described as "the man who had neither personal nor official power, nor desire to take any initiative in China's foreign affairs, but simply wanted to keep his post to increase his personal wealth. . . ."[134] A man of his quality would tend to be timid and conservative, and be unwilling to take any initiative on any issue. Breaking new ground in the protection of overseas Chinese was too much of a risk for him politically, and he no doubt felt safer maintaining the old course.

One might also wonder why Li Hung-chang did not comment on Chang Chih-tung's memorial. Given the fact that Li had a great deal of influence in foreign affairs and was partly in charge of the

---

[130]See S.M. Meng, *The Tsungli Yamen: Its Organization and Functions* (Cambridge, Mass., 1962), pp. 54–55.

[131]See W. Ayers, *Chang Chih-tung and Educational Reform in China*, pp. 78–79; L.E. Eastman, *Throne and Mandarins: China's Search for a Policy during the Sino-French Controversy 1880–1885*, pp. 25–29.

[132]The phrase the Yamen used was "*kuang-hsu fan-li, chieh-lien chung-chih*" (widely established supporting forces, and unite the popular will of the people). See the memorial of the Tsungli Yamen, *op. cit.*, p. 20a.

[133]*Ibid.*, p. 21b.

[134]S.M. Meng, *op. cit.*, p. 55.

newly-established Admiralty (Hai-chun yamen) after 1885,[135] one would expect Chang's overall plan for protecting the overseas Chinese, which had strong implications for both foreign affairs and China's naval defence, to have attracted Li's interest. Moreover, Chang Chih-tung did inform Li about the progress of the investigation mission led by Wang Yung-ho,[136] but there were no comments from Li on Chang's proposal. Li's silence on this issue can be attributed either to his caution on the possible consequences of the consular expansion, or to his displeasure with his potential political rival whom he feared would overtake him over the issue of the protection of overseas Chinese. Whatever the reasons, Li's silence helped to shelve Chang's ambitious plan for a short period.

Although Chang Chih-tung's initiatives did not bear concrete results, the momentum he built up helped to bring forth the second stage of consular expansion in overseas Chinese communities. The beginning of the second stage in the early 1890s saw general signs of confidence in the Dynasty. The humiliation suffered as the result of defeat in the Sino-French war in 1885 had gradually been forgotten; the founding of the Peiyang fleet in 1888 provided China with new confidence in herself; and the transfer of power from the conservative Empress Dowager Tz'u-hsi to the young Emperor Kuang-hsu, generated optimism.[137] It was in the context of growing confidence that the consular expansion was achieved.

Establishment of Consulates in the British Colonies and other Parts of the World

The man who took the lead in the second stage of consular expansion was Hsueh Fu-ch'eng, the new Chinese Minister to Britain,

---

[135]Li was appointed as one of the two deputies to help Prince Ch'un (I-huan) to run the Admiralty. See Chu Shou-p'eng, *Kuang-hsu-ch'ao tung-hua lu*, 9th moon of 11th year of Kuang-hsu (October, 1885), vol. 2, p. 2009.

[136]See Chang Chih-tung, "Cable to Li Hung-chang at Tientsin on 13th day of 10th moon of 12th year of Kuang-hsu (8 November 1886)", in Chang Chih-tung, *Chang Wen-hsiang kung ch'uan-chi*, vol. 127, tien-tu 6, pp. 17a–17b; the same cable is also found in Li Hung-chang, *Li Wen-chung kung ch'uan-chi*, tien-kao, vol. 7, pp. 48b–49a.

[137]Because the Emperor Kuang-hsu reached his maturity, the Empress Dowager Tz'u-hsi, who had been ruling China as the Regent, had to return power to the Emperor. On 26 February 1889, the Emperor was married, and a few days later (4 March) he received power from the Empress Dowager to rule. See Chu Shou-p'eng, *Kuang-hsu-ch'ao tung-hua lu*, 1st moon of 15th year of Kuang-hsu, pp. 2576–80.

France, Italy and Belgium. Hsueh was appointed to that position in April 1889, but did not take up his job in London until about a year later.[138] Hsueh succeeded in establishing consulates in Penang and Hong Kong in 1893. His work for consular expansion was prompted by the proposal of Admiral Ting Ju-ch'ang who visited Singapore and the neighbouring ports in 1890.[139] According to Ting, Chinese merchants were ill-treated and exploited by the local authorities. Due to the lack of consular protection, the Chinese suffered immensely.[140] Ting therefore submitted a report to the Tsungli Yamen and suggested extending consular protection to the Chinese in Penang, Malacca, Johore, Selangor and Perak. He proposed the selecting of upright and wealthy merchants among the local Chinese to fill the positions of Vice-Consuls, who would be under the control of the Consul in Singapore whose status would be upgraded to Consul-General.[141] Ting's proposal was referred to Hsueh Fu-ch'eng by the Yamen for comment. The Yamen's instruction was that if Hsueh was able to obtain approval from the British government, the extension of consular protection to various British colonies would be beneficial to the overseas Chinese.[142] Hsueh acted promptly on the issue. He sent his English Secretary, Sir Halliday Macartney,[143] to find out British attitude. Hsueh's strategy was a shrewd one in comparison with the approaches adopted by his predecessors.[144] Instead of asking for approval for

---

[138]See Hsueh Fu-ch'eng, *Ch'u-shih Ying, Fa, I, Pi ssu-kuo jih-chi*, introduction.

[139]For Ting's visit to Singapore and being greatly welcomed by the local Chinese, see *Lat Pau*, 10/4/1890, p. 2; 14/4/1890, p. 2; 15/4/1890, p. 5; 16/4/1890, p. 2.

[140]See Ting's report to the Tsungli Yamen quoted in Hsueh Fu-ch'eng's correspondence with the Yamen dated 25th day of 8th moon of 16th year of Kuang-hsu (8 October 1890), in Hsueh Fu-ch'eng, *Ch'u-shih kung-tu*, vol. 1, pp. 3a–5b.

[141]*Ibid.*

[142]*Ibid.*

[143]Sir Halliday Macartney (1833–1906) was a Scottish military surgeon and a kinsman of the famous leader of Britain's first mission to China in 1793, Lord Macartney. Macartney was originally on Kuo Sung-t'ao's staff, and had played an important part in Kuo's relations with Britain. He continued to serve as the English Secretary for the Chinese Embassy in London, and had wielded immense influence in the diplomatic relations between China and Britain. This impression is obtained from reading through the despatches between the Chinese Minister and the British Foreign Office contained in *FO* 17.

[144]Both Kuo Sung-t'ao and Tseng Chi-tse, two predecessors of Hsueh Fu-ch'eng in London, had requested British approval of a permanent Singapore consulate on the basis of a specific location. See "Kuo Sung-t'ao to the Earl of Derby dated 24

specific consulate, he requested the British government to grant in principle the right to establish consulates in her colonies. In his despatch to the British Foreign Secretary Marquis of Salisbury, Hsueh pointed out that "China has never at any time repudiated the obligations imposed on her by the law of nations, and her actions, more particularly within the last fifteen years (since 1876), have been regulated by a general and always increasing conformity to it."[145] He also pointed out that foreigners were allowed to reside and carry on commercial activities in more than twenty ports and places in China, and the British government had established consulates or consular agencies in twenty-two of these locations.[146]

In tackling this issue, Hsueh demonstrated a great deal of diplomatic skill. Apart from the official note emphasising the spirit of international law and the principle of reciprocity, he also used the private channel of behind-door negotiations. Macartney who had good contacts in the government circles, was entrusted by Hsueh as go-between to smooth out the issue. He indicated through Macartney that China would persist in fighting for the right to set up consulates in British colonies.[147] The crux of the problem hinged on future consulates in Hong Kong and Melbourne. The British government feared that a consulate in Hong Kong would handicap its administration of the colony which consisted almost entirely of a Chinese population; while a consulate in Melbourne would enhance the anti-Chinese feelings there. To alleviate British fear, Hsueh hinted that China would not press for a consulate in Melbourne at that time, and that he would transfer a veteran diplomat Tso Ping-lung, the Chinese Consul in Singapore, to handle the sensitive post in Hong Kong.[148] Partly due to Hsueh's diplomacy, and partly due to British desire to set up a consular agent in Chinese Turkestan,[149]

February 1877", in *FO* 17/768; "Tseng Chi-tse to the Earl of Granville dated 4 May 1880", in *FO* 17/844.

[145]See "Hsueh Fu-ch'eng to Marquis of Salisbury dated 25 September 1890". This diplomatic note was written in both English and Chinese, and they are kept in the *FO* files. The Chinese note was also reproduced in Hsueh Fu-ch'eng's diary. See *FO* 17/1104, pp. 43–45, 56; Hsueh Fu-ch'eng, *Ch'u-shih Ying, Fa, I, Pi ssu-kuo jih-chi*, vol. 4, pp. 1b–2b.

[146]*Ibid.*

[147]Hsueh Fu-ch'eng's diary, vol. 4, pp. 3a–3b.

[148]*Ibid.*

[149]The British government requested China to set up a consular agency in Chinese Turkestan, the request was considered by the Tsungli Yamen. The British Foreign

the British government agreed to allow China to appoint consuls in British dominions reserving the right to refuse in certain cases;[150] it also agreed to the proposed consulate in Hong Kong, and to upgrade the Chinese consulate in Singapore as Consulate-General for the Straits Settlements.[151] In December 1890, Hsueh was able to report his success to both the Tsungli Yamen and the Commissioner of Northern Ports, Li Hung-chang.[152] The Hong Kong consulate was established in 1891 with Tso Ping-lung as its first Consul, while the consulate in Singapore was upgraded to the status of Consulate-General for the Straits Settlements. The new Consul-General, Huang Tsun-hsien, another veteran diplomat, took up his appointment in Singapore in November 1891.[153] In less than two years (March 1893), Chang Pi-shih, a well-known wealthy Chinese leader, was appointed by Hsueh as the first Chinese Vice-Consul in Penang.[154]

The new consular establishments in Hong Kong and Penang, and the upgrading of the consulate in Singapore represented a major breakthrough in the second stage of Chinese consular expansion. It was followed by many similar establishments in other parts of the world. Its success was due mainly to the foresight, initiative and diplomatic skill of Hsueh Fu-ch'eng. Although Hsueh belonged to the same generation of diplomats as Ch'en Lan-pin and Ho Ju-chang, who were trained in Chinese classics and Confucian philosophy, he did show different qualities from these officer-diplomats. His class background and classical training did not prevent him from looking beyond the horizon of the Confucian world. The geographical proximity of Wu-hsi (Hsueh's birth-place) to Shanghai

---

Office through Macartney asked Hsueh Fu-ch'eng to support such a request. Understandably it was used as a condition for allowing China to appoint its consuls in British dominions. See "Macartney to Sir Thomas Sanderson dated 31 December 1890", in *FO* 17/1104, pp. 75a–75b.

[150]*Ibid.*, p. 77.

[151]See Hsueh Fu-ch'eng, "Despatch to the Tsungli Yamen and the Commissioner of Northern Ports relating to the British approval of establishment of additional consulates dated 1st day of 11th moon of 16th year of Kuang-hsu (12 December 1890)", in Hsueh Fu-ch'eng, *Ch'u-shih kung-tu*, vol. 1, tz'u-wen, pp. 11a–12a.

[152]*Ibid.*

[153]See *Lat Pau*, 9/11/1891, p. 5; *Sing Po*, 9/11/1891, p. 1.

[154]See Hsueh Fu-ch'eng, "Despatch to the Tsungli Yamen relating to the appointment of the Vice-Consul in Penang dated 20th day of 1st moon of 19th year of Kuang-hsu (8 March 1893)", in Hsueh Fu-ch'eng, *Ch'u-shih kung-tu*, vol. 2, tz'u-wen, pp. 25a–25b.

provided Hsueh with excellent opportunities to learn about the West; the Second Anglo-Chinese War (1856–60) and its aftermath had probably awakened Hsueh to the importance of understanding the West and learning how to cope with it.[155] It was probably due to this awakening that Hsueh decided to join Tseng Kuo-fan's secretariat (mu-fu) in 1865, instead of going through the traditional route to mandarin-hood.[156] His service in Tseng Kuo-fan's, and later in Li Hung-chang's mu-fu, between 1867 and 1884, enabled him to be involved directly in the conduct of foreign affairs. He rendered valuable service to Li Hung-chang and made suggestions relating to many important issues, such as the timely despatch of forces to Korea following the riots in Seoul in the summer of 1882.[157]

Although Hsueh was closely associated with Tseng, his approach to foreign policy differed from that of the Self-Strengtheners. He belonged to the group of "Treaty Port Community" whose members consisted of compradores, merchants and entrepreneurs, returned students and some enlightened gentry-members.[158] This group increasingly asserted an influence on China's foreign policy during the last quarter of the nineteenth century. Its diplomatic strategy held the middle ground between the Self-Strengtheners who advocated peaceful and conciliatory pragmatism, and those who were belligerently anti-foreign, represented by the Ch'ing-i (Pure Criticism) group.[159] The members of this group advocated adoption of Western institutions to promote "wealth and power" as well as to defend China. In the 1880s when China was facing mounting pressure from France in Vietnam, and from Japan in Korea, they sought a more aggressive policy of transforming the traditional tribute system into a Chinese colonial empire along Western lines

---

[155]Hsueh was born on 12 April 1838. At the time of the defeat of China in the Second Anglo-Chinese War, he was about 22 years of age. He obtained his Hsiu-ts'ai degree in 1857, but did not continue to pursue his higher degrees in the later years. See To Lien-che, "Hsueh Fu-ch'eng", in A.W. Hummel (ed.), *Eminent Chinese in the Ch'ing Period* (Taipei, reprint, 1970), pp. 331–32.

[156]See K.E. Folsom, *Friends, Guests and Colleagues: The Mu-fu system in the Late Ch'ing China* (Berkeley, 1968), p. 67.

[157]A.W. Hummel (ed.), *op. cit.*, pp. 331–32.

[158]See Louis T. Sigel, "Ch'ing foreign policy and the modern commercial community: T'ang Shao-yi in Korea", in *Papers on Far Eastern History*, no. 13 (Canberra, March 1976), p. 77.

[159]See Lloyd Eastman, "Ch'ing-i and Chinese policy formation during the nineteenth century", in *Journal of Asian Studies*, 24:4 (August, 1965), pp. 595–611.

through the extension of Chinese authority, and the adoption of the techniques of foreign imperialism.[160] It was from this perspective that Hsueh Fu-ch'eng provided a foresight into the issues of consular expansion, and the use of overseas Chinese in general.

When Hsueh Fu-ch'eng was appointed as the Chinese Minister to Britain, France, Italy and Belgium in 1889, he was fifty-one years old. Being a mature and experienced administrator who had considerable insight into foreign affairs, he must have been delighted with the new appointment which would have enabled him to put some of his theory into practice. He realised the importance of his new appointment and was eager to learn more about the secret of the West through personal contact and observation. He aspired to be a great diplomat and to use diplomacy to halt the expansion of British and French influence into China's world.[161] It would be erroneous to suggest that Hsueh masterminded the whole operation which resulted in the breakthrough of the second stage of consular expansion. But one point is certain — he knew how to go about it. He had already made necessary preparations for the job by reading carefully the diaries of Kuo Sung-t'ao and Tseng Chi-tse, his two predecessors in London;[162] he had also read important documents relating to the overseas Chinese problems and consular expansion;[163] he had selected his staff whom he considered to be important for the success of his appointment.

The most outstanding member of his staff was the Counsellor Huang Tsun-hsien, who had considerable experience with the overseas Chinese in San Francisco. Huang's knowledge in diplomacy and overseas Chinese proved later to be crucial to Hsueh's success in his diplomatic career.[164] With his strong determination to go overseas,

---

[160]See Louis T. Sigel, "The Treaty port community and Chinese foreign policy in the 1880s", in *Papers on Far Eastern History*, no. 11 (March, 1975), p. 83.

[161]See Hsueh Fu-ch'eng, "Preface to Ch'u-shih Ying, Fa, I, Pi ssu-kuo jih-chi", in Hsueh Fu-ch'eng, *Ch'u-shih Ying, Fa, I, Pi ssu-kuo jih-chi*, pp. 1–2.

[162]Reference to Kuo's and Tseng's diaries was often found in Hsueh's diary. See Hsueh's diary.

[163]It would appear that Hsueh had read thoroughly Chang Chih-tung's memorials to the Court regarding the plan for consular expansion overseas. In fact, Hsueh did quote Chang's memorial on several occasions. See Hsueh's diary.

[164]For a more detailed discussion on the Hsueh and Huang relationship and their contribution to the change of the traditional overseas Chinese policy, see Chapter 6, "Changes in the Traditional Immigration Policy and Protection of the Returned Overseas Chinese".

Hsueh overcame his long illness at the end of 1889, and set sail for Europe in February 1890. While on his voyage to Europe, he took the opportunity to learn about overseas Chinese by practical observation and direct contact with local Chinese leaders, and gradually formulated the concrete idea of consular expansion. While he was in Hong Kong, he observed and realized the importance of the British colony to the security and law and order of the Kwangtung province, and he noted that he would take the opportunity in the future to press the British government for the establishment of a consulate in Hong Kong.[165] While he was in Singapore, he was very impressed by the wealth of the local Chinese, and contacted some influential Chinese leaders like Tan Kim Ching,[166] whom he considered to be useful for China in the future.[167] He noted that all countries which had consulates in Singapore included Penang and Malacca in their consular jurisdiction; by contrast, the Chinese Consul in Singapore had no power to look after the Chinese residents of other parts of the Straits Settlements. Hsueh considered this to be highly inadequate and believed it should be rectified.[168] His initiative in gaining a profound knowledge of the overseas Chinese issue, was not just confined to direct contact with the overseas Chinese in those ports he visited. He also listened to the advice of experts, such as Huang Tsun-hsien. Huang briefed him in detail about the economic potential of overseas Chinese which seemed to have helped him to decide on the priority of his action when he arrived in London.

In his first memorial to the Court dated 23 October 1890, Hsueh emphasised the importance of diplomacy and its role in upgrading China's international status. He argued that there was a close relationship between the protection of overseas Chinese and the expansion of China's influence.[169] He also indicated that he would take

---

[165]See Hsueh Fu-ch'eng, *Ch'u-shih Ying, Fa, I, Pi ssu-kuo jih-chi*, vol. 1, p. 2b.

[166]Tan Kim Ching (pronounced in Mandarin as Ch'en Chin-chung), was a well-known leader in the Chinese community in Singapore. For a short biography of Tan, see Song Ong Siang, *One Hundred Years' History of the Chinese in Singapore* (Singapore, 1967, reprint), p. 92.

[167]Hsueh also took note that Tan Kim Ching was a multi-millionaire, who had held a prominent Thai office (Siamese Consul). Tan was also known to have donated 10,000 dollars to the coastal defence funds raised by Tso Tsung-t'ang. Hsueh also noted that although Tan did not know the Chinese language, he still wore Chinese costume. See Hsueh Fu-ch'eng, *op. cit.*, vol. 1, pp. 7a–7b.

[168]Hsueh Fu-ch'eng, *op. cit.*, vol. 1, p. 7a.

[169]See "Memorial of Hsueh Fu-ch'eng to the Court relating to diplomatic rela-

the initiative to safeguard China's interests through diplomatic means.[170] This memorial can be taken as Hsueh's policy statement in his diplomatic career. It was in this spirit of taking the initiative that Hsueh contributed greatly to the breakthrough of consular expansion in the second stage.

With the fundamental change in the Ch'ing government's attitude towards the overseas Chinese after 1893,[171] consular expansion received much added impetus. The Tsungli Yamen and other provincial high-ranking officials who were involved in the foreign policy making, no longer argued the need for consular expansion, but discussed rather the means of achieving that aim. This subjective transformation must be accredited to the success of consular expansion at this stage. With regard to the objective situation, there appeared to be no problems for China in extending her consular establishments in the British colonies and protectorates. In 1894, China secured the right to set up a consulate in Rangoon, Burma, through a treaty with Britain over the settlement of the Sino-Burmese border.[172] A Chinese Consulate-General was established in South Africa in 1905 in response to the demand of the local Chinese.[173] Two years later, China secured the right to set up consulates in Australia and New Zealand. On 26 May 1907, the British foreign office approved the request for the establishment of Chinese Consulates-General in Melbourne and Wellington, and Vice-Consulates in Sydney, Fremantle (?, in Chinese text as Fu-si wen-t'o) and Bris-

---

tions with Britain and France dated 10th day of 9th moon of 16th year of Kuang-hsu (23 October 1890)", in *Ch'ing-chi wai-chiao shih-liao*, vol. 83, pp. 21a–22b.

[170]*Ibid.*

[171]For a detailed discussion on the fundamental change of the Ch'ing government attitude, see Chapter 6, "Changes in the Traditional Immigration Policy and Protection of the Returned Overseas Chinese".

[172]See article 13 of the Sino-British treaty over the Burmese border signed in London on 1 March 1894, in *Chung-wai t'iao-yeh h'ui-pien* (Collected Treaties between China and Foreign Countries), p. 20; see also "Memorial of Hsueh Fu-ch'eng to the Court relating to the Burmese border treaty and the appointment of a consul in Rangoon approved by the Court on 9th day of 5th moon of 20th year of Kuang-hsu (12 June 1894)", in *Ch'ing-chi wai-chiao shih-liao*, vol. 91, pp. 5b–6b.

[173]A petition for the establishment of a Chinese consulate by the local Chinese residents led by Ch'en Yung-ch'ao, Huang Kuang-t'ai, Huang Chao-han and others had been sent to the Tsungli Yamen in 1903. In response to this request, the first Chinese Consul-General, Liu Yu-lin was appointed at the end of 1904, and took up his appointment in the following year. See "Tsungli Yamen Archives", the 29th and 30th years of Kuang-hsu, "Ch'u shih Ying-kuo".

bane.[174] The first Chinese Consul-General for Australia arrived in Melbourne in March 1909.[175] In the same year, China also secured the right to set up a Consulate-General in Canada.

In the same period up to the fall of the Ch'ing dynasty (February 1912), Chinese Consulates and Consulates-General were established one after another in many parts of the world. In 1897, a Chinese Consul under the name of trade commissioner was sent to Vladivostok to look after the Chinese in that region of Russia.[176] In July 1898, a temporary Chinese consulate was established in Luzon in the Philippines, and in the following year it was upgraded to Consulate-General and placed on a permanent basis.[177] In the same year, the right to set up Chinese Consulates in Seoul and other trading ports of Korea was acquired in the commercial treaty signed between China and its former protectorate.[178] A similar right was acquired in a commercial treaty with Mexico in the same year.[179] Towards the end of the Dynasty, consular establishments continued to be set up in overseas Chinese communities. In 1909, a Chinese Consul, Lin Lun-chao, was appointed to look after the Chinese immigrants in the German colonies in the Pacific, in particular, the Samoan islands.[180] In the following year, a Chinese Consul for Vancouver, Ou-yang Keng, was appointed to the new position of Consul-General for Panama, the first in Central America.[181] The right of China to establish consulates-general, consulates and

---

[174]See the "Correspondence of the Chinese Counsellor in Britain to the Tsungli Yamen", in "Tsungli Yamen Archives", 33rd year of Kuang-hsu, "Wang Ta-hsieh Li Ching-fang shih-Ying".

[175]C.F. Yong, *New Goldmountain: The Chinese in Australia 1900–1921* (Adelaide, 1977), p. 22.

[176]See *Ch'ing-chi wai-chiao shih-liao*, vol. 125, pp. 18b–19b.

[177]See Edgar Wickberg, *The Chinese in Philippine Life 1850–1898*, p. 233.

[178]See Sino-Korean Commercial Treaty signed on 7th day of 8th moon of 25th year of Kuang-hsu (11 September 1899), article 2, in *Ch'ing-chi wai-chiao shih-liao*, vol. 139, pp. 19a–26a; "Memorial of Hsu Shou-p'eng to the Court urging for additional consuls to protect the Chinese in Korea received and approved by the Court on 28th day of 10th moon of 25th year of Kuang-hsu (1 November 1899)", in *Ch'ing-chi wai-chiao shih-liao*, vol. 141, pp. 7b–8a.

[179]See article 3 of the Sino-Mexican Commercial Treaty signed on 10 December 1899, in *Chung-wai t'iao-yeh h'ui-pien*, p. 484; see also *Ch'ing-chi wai-chiao shih-liao*, vol. 142, pp. 8a–8b.

[180]See *Ch'ing Hsuan-t'ung ch'ao wai-chiao shih-liao* (Foreign Office Records of the Ch'ing Dynasty during the Hsuan-t'ung Reign), vol. 8, p. 49.

[181]See *Ch'ing Hsuan-t'ung ch'ao wai-chiao shih-liao*, vol. 12, pp. 22b–23b.

vice-consulates in the East Indies was obtained from the Dutch government in 1911, but the first Consul-General, Su Jui-chao, did not take up his official appointment in Batavia until August 1912 due to the outbreak of the revolution in China.[182]

The consular establishments in the non-British possessions during this stage were secured either through treaty rights or direct negotiations. The former was simple and straightforward, while the latter involved a great deal of time and difficulties. The Ch'ing government experienced particular difficulty in dealing with Spain and Holland over the consular establishments in their colonies in Southeast Asia. Both Spain and Holland were among the most conservative Colonial Powers in the world, and were well-known for their high-handed policies and their uncompromising attitude towards the people of the colonies. Their main objection to the establishment of Chinese Consulates was based on a general assumption that Chinese diplomats would undermine their rule. The threat of the Chinese Consuls seemed even more real, for their presence would usurp some of the functions of the colonial administrators: would handicap administration of local Chinese communities such as the collection of taxes or lawsuits; and would provide China with a convenient means to conduct gunboat diplomacy.[183] The difficulties that China encountered in dealing with Spain over the establishment of a Chinese Consulate-General in Luzon in the Philippines has been well documented in Edgar Wickberg's excellent book, *The Chinese in Philippine Life 1850–1898*.[184] There is no need to repeat it here. However, China's prolonged negotiations with the Dutch authorities over the consulate issue serve as an excellent case study to illustrate some themes discussed above.

Establishment of the Consulates in Dutch East Indies

China first raised the question of consular establishments with the Dutch Foreign Office in 1882, but did not succeed in signing an agreement over the issue until 1911. The three decades of negotiations were the longest in China's diplomatic history, and while it

---

[182]Lea E. Williams, *Overseas Chinese Nationalism: The Genesis of the Pan-Chinese Movement in Indonesia 1900–1916*, pp. 166–67.

[183]Edgar Wickberg, *The Chinese in Philippine Life 1850–1898*, p. 221.

[184]*Ibid.*, pp. 209–36.

was mainly due to the intransigent attitude of the Dutch, it also suggested vacillation on the part of China. Like many other consular establishments overseas, the proposed Consulate-General in the Dutch East Indies had a certain degree of spontaneity. Given the miserable conditions under which the Chinese in the Dutch East Indies had suffered,[185] it was not surprising that many Chinese desired consular protection. Their desire was much encouraged by the establishment of the consulate in Singapore, and it was conveyed through a petty officer named Li Mien who petitioned Tso Tsung-t'ang, the newly appointed Governor-General of Liang Kiang (Kiangsu and Kiangsi). Li was an Expectant Prefect for Kwangsi province (Kwangsi hou-pu chih-fu). His relations with the Chinese leaders of the Indies is unclear. He did not seem to have visited the Dutch East Indies before he presented his first petition to Tso in early 1882. Perhaps it was because he was a native of Fukien and the majority of the Chinese in the Indies were also Fukienese that he was contacted and used as a medium for the petition to the Chinese officialdom. The reasons why Li Mien petitioned Tso Tsung-t'ang rather than the Tsungli Yamen or the Governor-General of Fukien and Chekiang are uncertain. Perhaps it was because Li knew Tso personally or because Tso had enjoyed a considerable reputation as a good administrator while he was the Governor-General of Fukien and Chekiang between 1863 and 1866.[186] Whatever the reasons, Tso Tsung-t'ang did take a sympathetic view to the petition, and transmitted it to the Tsungli Yamen and to the Chinese Ambassador to Britain and France, Tseng Chi-tse.

Although Tso was sympathetic, he was not sure about the conditions of the Chinese in the Indies, and was particularly dubious about the significance of the Indies Chinese in relation to China's border security, which was much emphasised in Li's petition. To find out the truth, he urged Tseng Chi-tse to instruct the Chinese Consul in Singapore, Tso Ping-lung, to submit a report on the matter.[187] Tso's cautious attitude was an appropriate one. He refrained from

---

[185]For a discussion on the grievances of the Chinese in the Indies in the late nineteenth century, see Lea E. Williams, *Overseas Chinese Nationalism: The Genesis of The Pan-Chinese Movement in Indonesia 1900–1916*, pp. 27–36.

[186]For a short biography of Tso Tsung-t'ang, see Tu Lien-che, "Tso Tsung-t'ang", in A.W. Hummel (ed.), *Eminent Chinese of the Ch'ing Period*, pp. 762–67.

[187]See "Correspondence of the Tsungli Yamen to the Chinese Ambassador for

making any concrete recommendation to the Court on this issue before he had a fuller understanding of the matter as well as its implications. His check on Li's petition was a wise one, for Li had overstated his case in the petition. Probably because Li Mien wanted a quick result, he exaggerated the importance of the Indies Chinese to China's border security.[188] His whole argument for setting up consulates there was centred on the threat posed by Holland to the security of China. Historically, he argued that the Dutch had used the East Indies as a base to launch an attack on the coastal areas of Fukien and Kwangtung, and occupy Taiwan.[189] He revealed that the Dutch were developing Acheh, which was geographically closer than Ke-lo-pa (Batavia, or refer to Java in general) to China, and could pose a direct threat to China's security.[190] Li asserted that there were signs of such threat, and that the Dutch government had recruited many Chinese as well as Europeans into its army. He further suggested that due to the cordial relationship that existed between Holland, Britain and France, there would be a direct threat from the Dutch to the border of China.[191] Although the arguments are not very coherent, this "scare tactic" seems to have had some bearing on the thinking of the coastal defense advocates such as Tso Tsung-t'ang. As the French were encroaching on Vietnam and the British on Burma, this argument of a potential Dutch threat to China's border had stimulated some hard thinking on the part of the Chinese leaders.

Tso Ping-lung's report was in favour of the idea of establishing Chinese consulates in the Dutch East Indies, but it did not support Li Mien's "Dutch threat" theory. His argument was a balanced one which was based on moral, cultural and political factors. As a Confucian diplomat, Tso Ping-lung felt that China had a moral obligation to protect her subjects overseas. Since the majority of the Chinese there were coolies who suffered ill-treatment at the hands of foreigners, the presence of Chinese Consuls would prevent

---

Germany dated 14th day of 6th moon of 8th year of Kuang-hsu (28 July 1882)'', in Liu Hsi-hung *et al.*, *Chu Teh shih-kuan tang-an ch'ao*, vol. 1, pp. 269–70.

[188]Li stated that Ke-lo-pa (Batavia or Java) had a vast territory, and the number of the Chinese there was more than ten times the number of the Chinese in Japan, San Francisco, Peru and Cuba put together. *Ibid.*, p. 267.

[189]*Ibid.*, p. 266.

[190]In actual distance, Acheh is not closer to China than Batavia. Li was either ignorant or had purposely distorted this to support his argument. *Ibid.*

[191]*Ibid.*, p. 269.

cruelties being inflicted on them. Culturally, as Tso argued, the presence of the Consuls would help retain the Chinese identity among the overseas subjects. Because of the lack of contacts with China, the Indies Chinese gradually lost their cultural identity by changing their costumes and customs, and the Chinese Consuls would set good examples for them to follow. Politically the Chinese Consuls could act as government agents and collect information about those countries, as the information could be of great use to China in times of war. Tso emphasised that as international contacts became more frequent, any move made by China would be heeded by foreign countries and if China was ignorant about the real situation of the world, she would be placed in a disadvantageous position in times of international negotiations or war.[192] Tso Ping-lung was neither a politician nor military strategist. His interest in China's security was a reflection of a general concern of every thinking Chinese at the time. What he did was to provide a diplomatic perspective and to point out the close relationship between diplomatic establishments and defense, and how the Chinese diplomats could be used to do "spying work" like most Western diplomats did in China.

Tso Ping-lung had no illusions about the issue, and he expected difficulties arising from the proposed consulates in the Indies. He listed three major obstacles: the difficulty of controlling Westernised Chinese who had already taken up Dutch citizenship; the opposition of the Dutch-appointed Chinese officials such as Majoors; and the opposition of the Dutch authorities.[193] The first problem was connected with the post-establishment period, and was not of great concern before the consulates were established. The second and third should be overcome before the consulates could be established. Tso realised the Dutch-appointed Chinese officials had a vested interest in opposing the establishment of the Chinese Consulates, for the presence of the Chinese diplomats would challenge their authority over the members of the local Chinese communities. Tso also realised that the Dutch authorities would oppose the proposal because they feared interference from Chinese Consuls. However he was optimistic about the issue. In the traditional Confucian moral tone, he asserted that if China could get the right per-

---

[192]See Tso Ping-lung's report dated 16th day of 9th moon of 8th year of Kuang-hsu (27 October 1882), in Liu Hsi-hung *et al.*, *Chu Teh shih-kuan tang-an ch'ao*, vol. 1, pp. 276–78.
[193]*Ibid.*, p. 275.

sons for the job, the problems of controlling the westernised Chinese and overcoming the opposition of the Majoors could be solved.[194] With regard to the opposition of the Dutch authorities, he suggested using international law to put pressure on the Netherlands. He argued that protection of overseas subjects was the right of a sovereign state by the international diplomatic practice, and since the Dutch authorities allowed other countries such as Britain, the United States and France to station their consuls in Batavia, he saw no reason why the Dutch authorities should reject China's request.[195] In concluding his report, Tso Ping-lung suggested a course for action. He proposed to appoint a Consul-General to be stationed in Batavia. The Consul-General was to be responsible for recommending suitable local leaders to fill the posts of consuls in the major cities where the Chinese were centred. The diplomat was to visit various cities once a year to inspect the conditions of the local Chinese.[196]

At the time when Consul Tso Ping-lung was submitting his report, the Chinese Minister to Germany, the Netherlands, Italy and Austria, Li Feng-pao, began to sound out the opinion of the Dutch Foreign Office. The initial reaction was indifferent though not hostile. The Dutch Foreign Minister hinted to Li that a special treaty needed to be negotiated if China wished to set up consulates in the Indies. Li also got the message from a conversation with the Minister that the negotiations for the right to set up consulates would not be easy.[197] Apart from reflecting the attitude of the Dutch authorities on the issue, Li's despatch favoured establishing a consulate in Batavia to look after the local Chinese and the Chinese in the neighbouring areas. If this proved to be successful, similar establishments could be extended to other cities.[198] Although Li supported the establishment of consulates in the Indies in principle, he did not take the initiative to negotiate a special treaty with the Dutch authorities, but left the decision to the Tsungli Yamen.[199]

---

[194]*Ibid.*

[195]*Ibid.*, pp. 275–76.

[196]*Ibid.*, pp. 279–82.

[197]See the despatch of Li Feng-pao to the Tsungli Yamen dated 20th day of 9th moon of 8th year of Kuang-hsu (31 October 1882), in Liu Hsi-hung and others, *Chu Teh shih-kuan tang-an ch'ao*, vol. 1, p. 287.

[198]*Ibid.*, p. 288.

[199]*Ibid.*

The Tsungli Yamen's basic attitude towards the consular expansion at this stage was cautious. Apart from the financial consideration which had been discussed earlier, its lack of a clearly defined policy governing consular establishments was also responsible for the failure for any initiative to be taken in this direction. Because of the lack of such a policy, the Yamen became complacent and wavering, and tended to put aside issues of which difficulties were expected. As soon as it was learnt from Li Feng-pao that any negotiations with the Dutch government over the consulate issue would be tough, it was decided that the issue be put aside for a while.[200]

The failure of this episode was also partly the result of the lack of strong pressure coming from Tso Tsung-t'ang. Although Li Mien presented his second petition to Tso in January 1883 to reinforce his request for the protection of the Chinese in the Indies,[201] his petition came at the wrong time, when Tso was sick. Tso was not only a sick old man, he was also given an important task of quelling the rebellion in southern Shantung towards the end of 1883.[202] Under this circumstance, Tso's lack of effort in pressing the establishment of consulates in the Indies was expected. Tso's busy involvement in the Sino-French conflict in 1884 and of his death in September 1885, shattered the hope of establishment of consulates in the Indies.[203]

Other attempts prior to 1893 were also unsuccessful because of the passive attitude of the Ch'ing government and some of its diplomats.[204] Even the change of the immigration policy in 1893 had no immediate impact on the issue. However, a major step in this direction was taken by Lu Hai-huan between 1897 and 1901 when he was the Chinese Minister to Germany and the Netherlands. Lu began to

---

[200]See the despatch of the Tsungli Yamen to the Chinese Minister to Germany, the Netherlands, Italy and Austria dated 9th day of 1st moon of 9th year of Kuang-hsu (16 February 1883), in Liu Hsi-hung et al., Chu Teh shih-kuan tang-an ch'ao, vol. 1, pp. 291–93.

[201]See the petition of Li Mien to the Governor-General of Liang Kiang, Tso Tsung-t'ang dated 2nd day of 12th moon of 8th year of Kuang-hsu (10 January 1883), ibid., pp. 296–301.

[202]See Tu Lien-che, "Tso Tsung-t'ang", in A.W. Hummel (ed.), Eminent Chinese of the Ch'ing Period 1644–1912, p. 767.

[203]Ibid.

[204]For instance, Chang Chih-tung's grand plan in 1887 for consular expansion in Southeast Asia and Oceania in which a Consulate-General in Batavia was a major part. Chang's grand plan was not accepted by the Tsungli Yamen towards the whole

take an interest in the overseas Chinese affairs while he was a secretary (Chang-ching) of the Tsungli Yamen, and was familiar with the history of "Indies consular case".[205] When Lu was appointed ambassador in early 1897, he was determined to take up the case with the Dutch government. To prepare his negotiations, on his way to Europe, he had a discussion on the issue with Chang Chen-hsun (Chang Pi-shih), then the Acting Chinese Consul-General in Singapore. Chang informed him that it was the Dutch Colonial officers in the Indies who oppressed the local Chinese, and some of the Chinese were treated worse than slaves.[206] After having taken up his appointment, Lu perused the old files of the Chinese embassy in Germany, and found Ch'en Shih-lin's petition which was probably presented to Chang Chih-tung between 1887 and 1890.[207] The petition was referred by Chang to the Tsungli Yamen and the Chinese Minister to Russia, Germany, the Netherlands and Austria for comments. Because of the passive attitude of the Chinese government, it did not evoke any positive response.

The petition called upon the Chinese government to protect her subjects in the Indies by establishing consulates in the area. It listed several areas in which the Chinese had suffered from Dutch oppression. Over-taxation, discrimination in legal matters and migration, movement and trade activities, and cruelty against the Chinese coolies in Deli.[208] Ch'en's petition was a useful document for Lu Hai-huan to work on, for it substantiated the claims made by Chang Pi-shih in Singapore. Since Ch'en was a leading Chinese merchant in Batavia,[209] and was joined by a few local merchants as signatories,[210] his petition would be more reliable than the previous petitions of

---

idea of consular expansion. See Chang Chih-tung, *Chang Wen-hsiang kung ch'uan-chi*, vol. 23, tsou-i, 23, pp. 9b–12a, also in *Ch'ing chi wai-chiao shih-liao*, vol. 74, pp. 21a–26b.

[205]See Chu Shou-p'eng (ed.), *Kuang-hsu-ch'ao tung-hua lu*, vol. 4, p. 192.

[206]*Ibid.*

[207]No actual date was given on the petition. Judging from the context, it was probably presented to Chang Chih-tung during that period to support Chang's scheme of consular expansion in Southeast Asia. See the petition in Liu Hsi-hung *et al.*, *Chu Teh shih-kuan tang-an ch'ao*, vol. 2, pp. 1097–1121; Lu Hai-huan mentioned that he had perused the old files and found the petition. See Chu Shou-p'eng (ed.), *Kuang-hsu-ch'ao tung-hua lu*, vol. 4, p. 192.

[208]Liu Hsi-hung *et al.*, *op. cit.*, pp. 1099–1115.

[209]Ch'en was a native of Hai-ch'eng district of Chang-chou prefecture, Fukien province. *Ibid.*, p. 1097.

[210]Other signatories were Chang Kuo-tung and Huang Feng-ch'ih who were also

Li Mien as far as the information was concerned. At the time when Lu Hai-huan was searching for evidence to fight the case, he received further petitions from the Chinese merchants in the Indies requesting protection. The petitioners refused to disclose their identity in fear of reprisal from the Dutch authorities.[211] These petitions covered the same grounds as those of Ch'en Shih-lin's, but emphasised the urgent need for protection because of the worsening conditions of the Chinese there. The petitions also pointed out that the Chinese Majoors, Kapiteins and Luitenants who were appointed by the Dutch Colonial administration, became extortionate and cruel in the treatment of their compatriots.[212] The petitions seem to have provided Lu with additional ammunition for diplomatic action. But his action was prompted by a report in a Singapore Chinese newspaper about a rebellion of the Chinese mining coolies on Bangka island in the Indies. According to the report, the coolies had long been ill-treated by the Dutch tin miners and their overseers. To oppose the oppression, three hundred coolies rose in rebellion. As a result, many of them were shot or jailed.[213]

The blood of the Chinese mining coolies in Bangka provided Lu with justification for entering direct negotiations with the Dutch authorities for the settlement of the consular issue. The petitions of the Chinese merchants and the news report on the killing in Bangka were translated to back up his demand. The initial reaction of the Dutch Foreign Minister was as expected. He tried to use evasive tactics to ward off any demand. He told Lu that China's proposed consular establishments did not come under his jurisdiction, but instead, under the Department of Colonial Affairs. He assured Lu that the Dutch Colonial administration in the Indies would not treat the Chinese coolies harshly, because they had been living harmoniously in the region for a long time and urged Lu to be cautious not to be misled by rumours; at the same time, he also reminded Lu that any settlement on the consular issue would require a special treaty.[214]

---

the natives of the Hai-ch'eng district; Chang Ying-sheng, Chou Jui-hua, the natives of P'an-yu district of Kuang-chou prefecture, Kwangtung province; *ibid*.

[211]See Chu Shou-p'eng (ed.), *Kuang-hsu-ch'ao tung-hua lu*, vol. 4, 27th year of Kuang-hsu, p. 192.

[212]*Ibid.*, see also Liu Chin-ch'ao (ed.), *Ch'ing-ch'ao shu wen-hsien t'ung-k'ao*, vol. 339, wai-chiao 3, k'ao 10806.

[213]Chu Shou-p'eng, *op. cit.*, pp. 193–94.

[214]*Ibid.*, p. 194.

On Lu's insistence, the Foreign Minister agreed to discuss the matter with his counterpart in the Department of Colonial Affairs. As a result, the Dutch government agreed to send a fact-finding mission to the Indies to investigate the conditions of the Chinese there.[215]

The man who was appointed to head the mission was the Dutch Consul-General in Hong Kong. Presumably he got the job because he had special knowledge of Chinese affairs and had some experience in dealing with the Chinese in Hong Kong. Although Lu Hai-huan attempted to influence the attitude of the head of the mission by sending a letter requesting for an impartial enquiry, his action seems to have been futile. The result of the mission was not entirely unexpected. It had collected a different set of facts which tended to support and justify what the Dutch authorities had done to the local Chinese. Based on the findings of the mission, the Dutch Foreign Office explained to Lu that the claims of ill-treatment of the Chinese contained in the petitions were unfounded; it pointed out that the majority of the 470,000 Chinese in the Indies had taken up Dutch citizenship, and in Java alone, the number of Chinese of Dutch nationality was ten times that of those who had not been converted; it also pointed out that the foreign consuls in the Indies had no jurisdiction over their nationals, but looked after trade only.[216]

The Dutch message was clear. It not only rejected the allegations of ill-treatment, but also implied that the majority of the Chinese in the Indies were Dutch nationals and were of no concern to the Chinese government. It further indicated that no foreign Consuls were allowed to interfere with legal procedures in the Indies, even if China were granted the right to send her consuls there. There would be no chance for Chinese diplomats to meddle in the administration of Dutch law on behalf of their nationals.[217]

Although Lu Hai-huan was a competent diplomat, he was not as shrewd as Hsueh Fu-ch'eng, and his initial negotiations proved to be a wrong step. He allowed the Dutch government to get away easily with the ill-treatment issue and instead, opened up the new issue of "nationality" which was later proved to be a complicated

---

[215]*Ibid.*

[216]See Liu Chin-ch'ao (ed.), *Ch'ing-ch'ao shu wen-hsien t'ung-k'ao*, vol. 339, wai-chiao 3, k'ao 10807.

[217]Chu Shou-p'eng, *op. cit.*, p. 194.

one. Before the despatch of the fact-finding mission, Lu could have
pressed for a joint investigation mission of Dutch and Chinese officials, or for an international mission similar to that of the Cuba
Commission of 1874.[218] Once the seemingly true facts were established by the mission, Lu had little ground to fight for on the
allegations of ill-treatment. Realising the loss of advantage, Lu had
to change his arguments. He pointed out to the Dutch government
that China's request for consular establishments in the Indies was a
legitimate one and was in line with the spirit of international law.
The Dutch government had allowed other countries to set up consulates in the Indies, and China had already established consulates
in Singapore and Luzon. So he saw no reason why China should
not be allowed to have the same right in the Indies. He also pointed
out that China and the Netherlands had had a cordial relationship
for hundreds of years and that China had allowed the Dutch
government to set up consulates in her Treaty ports. It would therefore be reasonable for the Dutch government to reciprocate. He
further argued that the presence of Chinese Consuls in the Indies
would in fact work to the advantage of the Dutch Colonial administration, for some of the Chinese immigrants there were undesirable elements, the Chinese Consuls could assist the Dutch officials
maintain law and order in the Chinese communities. Finally, Lu
assured the Dutch that the Chinese Consuls would follow proper
diplomatic protocol like other foreign Consuls in accordance with
international practice.[219]

Lu's change of tone seems to have pleased the Dutch government
in some ways. The reply of the Dutch Foreign Minister showed
signs of some understanding, and it did not rule out the possibility
of allowing China from establishing consulates in the Indies. While
Lu was deliberating sending a commerce-promotion mission to the
Indies as the first concrete step towards establishing consulates, the
negotiations were disrupted by China's declaration of war against
the Allied Powers in June 1900, as the result of the Boxer Uprising.[220]
When China resumed diplomatic relations with the Powers after
1901, the Dutch Foreign Minister with whom Lu Hai-huan had

---

[218]For an examination of circumstances leading to the appointment of an international mission to investigate into conditions of the Chinese in Cuba, see R.L. Irick,
"Ch'ing Policy Toward The Coolie Trade 1847–1878", vol. 2, pp. 340–46.

[219]Chu Shou-p'eng, *op. cit.*, p. 194.

[220]Kuo T'ing-i, *Chin-tai Chung-kuo shih-shih jih-chi*, vol. 2, pp. 1078–82.

developed a cordial relationship, retired. Furthermore, before the new Dutch Minister was appointed, Lu was transferred back to China.[221]

Carrying his optimism back to China, Lu Hai-huan in early 1902 presented a memorial to the Court urging continuing effort over the consulate issue which he left unfinished, and pressed the Court to demand a consular establishment in the Indies in the forthcoming Sino-Dutch treaty negotiations which arose as part of the post-Boxer settlements.[222] Although his idea was supported by the Wai Wu Pu (Chinese Foreign Office, the successor of the Tsungli Yamen) and was endorsed by the Court, it did not bear any result.[223] Understandably, the idea was rejected by the Dutch negotiators, and as China was the defeated nation, she had little bargaining power to press for any new demand.

In retrospect, much of Lu's optimism was not warranted. Had his negotiations not been disrupted by the rise of the Boxers, had he not been transferred back to China, and had the Dutch Foreign Minister not retired, the consulate issue would still not have been resolved. The Dutch government not only feared the Chinese Consuls' interference in its administration in the Indies, but was also obsessed with the potential spread of Chinese nationalism as the result of the presence of Chinese Consuls. From its point of view, the rise of Chinese nationalism would jeopardise its policy of encouraging the Chinese to take up Dutch citizenship. Its tough stand was shown in its rejection of the "ill-treatment" charges and in its disregard for the spirit of international law. If China wished to get satisfactory results on the consulate issue, she would require more diplomatic skill and a practical issue with which she could force the Dutch to concede to her demand. Judging from this point of view, Lu's optimism was illusory rather than realistic. However, he had started the first round of serious negotiations with the Dutch, and his experience and mistakes provided his successors with useful insights into the problems which would confront them later.

---

[221]Chu Shou-p'eng, *op. cit.*, p. 195; see also Liu Chin-ch'ao (ed.), *Ch'ing-ch'ao shu wen-hsien t'ung-k'ao*, vol. 339, wai-chiao 3, k'ao 10807.

[222]See "Memorial of Lu Hai-huan to the Court of 12th moon of 27th year of Kuang-hsu (January, 1902)", in Chu Shou-p'eng (ed.), *Kuang-hsu ch'ao tung-hua lu*, vol. 4, pp. 191–95, especially p. 195; see also Liu Chin-ch'ao (ed.), *Ch'ing-ch'ao shu wen-hsien t'ung-k'ao*, vol. 339, wai-chiao 3, k'ao 10807.

[223]For the support of the Wai Wu Pu and the endorsement of the Court to Lu's suggestions, see *Ch'ing-chi wai-chiao shih-liao*, vol. 153, pp. 26b–27a.

Lu's setback seems to have had some demoralising effect on the Ch'ing government. For the next six years from 1902 there were no direct negotiations with the Dutch government, but it was during this half of the decade that the Ch'ing government evolved a different strategy in an attempt to solve the problem of the protection of the Indies Chinese. Almost to its surprise, the Ch'ing government found that nationalism grew and developed in the Indies Chinese communities without the presence of Chinese Consuls. The Tiong Hoa Hwe Koan (The Chinese Association) was founded in 1900, and it soon became the focal point for the mobilisation of nationalist sentiment. The organisation set out to promote Chinese nationalism on the basis of Confucianism (reinterpreted by K'ang Yu-wei),[224] and aimed also at breaking down the barriers between Totoks (China-born) and Peranakans (local-born), and among different dialect groups. The keys to the mobilisation of nationalist sentiment were modern education and newspapers. Modern education in the form of modern school became the most important uniting force. As the school used Mandarin as the medium of instruction and had modern contents in its curriculum, it generated a common Chinese identity and helped to break down the barriers among the groups.[225] Modern newspapers, though published in the Malay language instead of Chinese served the same function. They promoted a Chinese cultural identity and spread ideas of nationalism. They also helped to bring different groups of Chinese together.[226] As the Tiong Hoa Hwe Koan held both keys of nationalistic mobilisation, it commanded an increasing influence over the Chinese communities in the Indies as a whole, and it was this influence that attracted the attention of the Ch'ing government.

Although the Tiong Hoa Hwe Koan had inclinations towards reformism expounded by K'ang Yu-wei, it took no clear political stand in supporting the Reformists. It was in this context that the Ch'ing government attempted to exercise control over the Tiong Hoa Hwe Koan and other similar organisations in the Indies. In the Ch'ing

---

[224]For the impact of the re-interpreted Confucianism on the rise of the Tiong Hoa Hwe Koan of Batavia, see Lea E. Williams, *Overseas Chinese Nationalism: The Genesis of the Pan-Chinese Movement in Indonesia 1900–16*, pp. 54–57.

[225]*Ibid.*, p. 70.

[226]For details of the early Peranakan newspapers in the Indies, particularly the first one published in 1901, the *Li Po*, see Leo Suryadinata, *The Pre-World War II Peranakan Chinese Press of Java: A Preliminary Survey* (Ohio, 1971), pp. 10–15.

government's calculations, successful control over these leading social organisations would fulfil its aims of protecting and controlling its subjects in the East Indies without the presence of Chinese Consuls. Thus the strategy adopted was to control rich merchants and teachers in order to control social organisations and schools. The rich merchants formed the backbone of leadership in overseas Chinese communities,[227] and the teachers wielded strong influence in the schools as well as in the communities. The main part of the control mechanism was the honours system. Under this system, overseas Chinese leaders who had done special services for the empire or for the local Chinese communities were awarded with imperial honours.[228] They were recommended to the Court for award by provincial governors or visiting imperial emissaries. To attract the attention of the governors and the imperial emissaries, they had to make substantial monetary donations or had to demonstrate their political loyalty to the Ch'ing government. Although the Ch'ing honours had been freely available for purchase in overseas Chinese communities at the end of the nineteenth century,[229] it seems that the honours conferred by the imperial government had more value than those purchased. Since most rich overseas Chinese merchants were immigrants from poor socio-economic backgrounds, imperial honours greatly satisfied their psychological need and enhanced their prestige and power in the local Chinese communities.[230] They were thus attracted to support the Ch'ing government.

The award of brevet titles to certain rich merchants and teachers

---

[227]See Yong Ching-fatt, "Chinese Leadership in Nineteenth Century Singapore", in *Hsin-she hsueh-pao* (Journal of the Island Society, Singapore), vol. 1, p. 6; Wang Gungwu, "Traditional Leadership in a New Nation", in G. Wijeyawardene (ed.), *Leadership and Authority: A Symposium* (Singapore, 1968), pp. 210–11.

[228]These special services included efforts in raising funds for drought and flood relief in China; in raising funds for coastal defence projects; in donating money to modernisation projects; in raising huge capital for investment in China; and in promoting Chinese or establishing Chinese schools in overseas Chinese communities. See *Lat Pau*, 26/8/1887, p. 2; 5/3/1895, p. 5; *Yu-chi hui-tsun* (The Collected Records of Memorials) (Taipei, 1967), vol. 21, pp. 6412–13, vol. 43, pp. 4969–71, vol. 51, pp. 1487–88; *Ta-ch'ing teh-tsung ching huang-ti shih-lu*, vol. 588, pp. 9b & 14b; Chu Shou-p'eng (ed.), *Kuang-hsu ch'ao tung-hua lu*, vol. 5, p. 39.

[229]See Yen Ching-hwang, "Ch'ing's Sale of Honours and the Chinese Leadership in Singapore and Malaya 1877-1912", in *Journal of Southeast Asian Studies*, vol. 1, no. 2 (September, 1970), p. 21.

[230]*Ibid.*, pp. 24–31.

in the Indies in 1907 bore evidence of the functioning of the control mechanism. Wu Shu-ta, a wealthy merchant in Sumatra who donated 7,000 taels to the Chung Hua Chinese School in Padang was awarded with the title of *Tao-yuan*; Wu Hua-yueh and Huang Chin-hsiung who had donated 2,800 taels each to the same school were awarded with the title of *T'ung-chih*; Lin Yai, the headmaster of the Chung Hua Chinese School in Batavia was awarded with the title of *Chung-shu-k'o chung-shu*; another two teachers of the Chung Hua School of Padang, Sumatra, were awarded with the title of *Han-lin-yuan tien-pu* for their excellent services to the Chinese education. All these awards were recommended by the Governor of Kwang-tung, Ts'en Ch'un-hsüan.[231]

Another major part of the new mechanism was the Chinese Chamber of Commerce. The Chamber was an important organisation used by the Ch'ing government to attract support from the merchants. The first such body was launched in Shanghai in 1902 at the request of Sheng Hsuan-huai, who hoped to use it as a rallying point for the support of the business class and also as a means of administrative control.[232] In 1905, the Ministry of Commerce encouraged the establishment of the Chamber in Peking and other major cities by promulgating guidelines.[233] The Chamber proved to be very effective and was thus extended to overseas Chinese communities to attract the support of rich merchants. The first Chinese Chamber of Commerce in Southeast Asia was established in Singapore in 1906 with the sponsorship of Chang Pi-shih, a renowned overseas Chinese leader who was appointed by the Ch'ing government as the Imperial Commissioner to promote commercial affairs among the Chinese in Southeast Asia.[234] It quickly spread to the

---

[231]See *Hsueh-pu kuan-pao* (The Gazette of the Ministry of Education), vol. 12, 1st day of 12th moon of 32nd year of Kuang-hsu (14 January 1907), pp. 20–22.

[232]See *Shang-wu kuan-pao* (The Gazette of Commercial Affairs, Peking), 1907, vol. 5, pp. 9b–10; see also Michael R. Godley, "The Late Ch'ing Courtship of the Chinese in Southeast Asia", in *Journal of Asian Studies*, vol. 34, no. 2 (February, 1975), p. 376.

[233]Twenty-six items of rules and regulations for establishing chambers of commerce were approved by the Court on 24th day of 11th moon of 29th year of Kuang-hsu (30 December 1904). See "Memorial of the Ministry of Commerce to the Court relating to the Drafted Rules and Regulation for Establishing Chambers of Commerce, approved by the Court of 24th day of 11th moon of 29th year of Kuang-hsu", in *Ta-ch'ing kuang-hsu hsin fa-ling* (New Statutes of the Great Ch'ing Empire during the Kuang-hsu Reign), pp. 30–34.

[234]For the role of Chang Pi-shih in the founding of the Singapore Chinese

Dutch East Indies and to other parts of Southeast Asia. The man who helped to introduce this new mechanism to the Indies was Ch'ien Hsun, the Counsellor of the Chinese Embassy in the Hague.[235] Ch'ien toured the Indies between 1906 and 1907 on his way to Europe to take up his appointment. He arrived in Batavia and found the Chinese there had already planned to establish a chamber of commerce in accordance with the guidelines set by the Ministry of Commerce.[236] As a result of encouragement given by Ch'ien, other Chinese Chambers of Commerce were founded one after another in Batavia, Surahbaya, Semarang and Solo in 1907.[237] A survey of the leaders who were elected to run these organisations shows that all of them held Ch'ing imperial honours,[238] but to what extent their election to the leadership had to depend on the imperial honours is unknown. Their possession of the honours however, clearly revealed two points: they must have possessed reasonable

---

Chamber of Commerce, see "Hsing-chia-po Chung-hua shang-wu tsung-hui teng-chi i-shih-pu" (Minutes of the Chinese Chamber of Commerce of Singapore) (manuscript) vol. 1; *Hsin-chia-po Chung-hua tsung-shang-hui ta-hsa lo-ch'eng chi-nien k'an* (Souvenir of the Opening Ceremony of the Newly Completed Singapore Chinese Chamber of Commerce Building) (Singapore, 1964), p. 150; *Lat Pau*, 19/4/1906, p. 3.

[235]The new embassy in the Hague was established in 1906. The first special Chinese ambassador for the Netherlands, Lu Cheng-hsiang, was appointed on 16 November 1905. Before that year, the position for the Netherlands was also given to the ambassador for Germany, or sometimes to the ambassador for Russia. See Wai-chiao pu tang-an tzu-liao ch'u (ed.), *Chung-kuo chu wai ke ta kung-shih li-jen kuan-chang hsien ming nien-piao* (Chronological Chart of Chinese High-ranking Diplomats to Foreign Countries) (Taipei, 1969), pp. 82–83.

[236]See "Memorial of the Ministry of Commerce to the Court relating to the issue of an official seal to the Chinese Chamber of Commerce of Batavia approved by the Court on 19th day of 5th moon of 33rd year of Kuang-hsu (29 June 1907)", in *Shang-wu kuan-pao*, 1907, vol. 14, kung-tu, pp. 5b–6a.

[237]*Shang-wu kuan-pao*, 1907, vol. 14, kung-tu, pp. 5b–6a, vol. 17, kung-tu, pp. 5–6, vol. 25, kung-tu, pp. 4–5, vol. 33, kung-tu, pp. 6–7.

[238]The Tsungli and deputy Tsungli of the Chinese Chamber of Commerce of Batavia in 1907 were Li Hsing-lien who held a title of Tao-t'ai with feather, and Ch'iu Luan-hsiang who held the position of alternate magistrate of Fukien (Fu-chien pu-yung chih-hsien); in Surahbaya, Huang Chun-hui who had a title of Tao-t'ai, and Chang Chi-an who had a brevet title of five grades (wu-p'in hsien) were elected as Tsungli and deputy Tsungli; in Semarang, Cheng Tsung-hsi who held a Tao-t'ai title was elected as Tsungli, and Chou Ping-hsi who had a brevet title of five grades was elected as his deputy; in Solo, Chang Hsien-hsing who had a title of Tao-t'ai was elected as Tsungli, and Wu Chia-yun who held a title of T'ung-chih was elected his deputy. *Ibid.*

wealth, for without that they would not have been able to purchase these honours and would probably not have been elected to the leadership; and they had shown their inclination to support the Ch'ing government and had valued the prestige that was attached to the honours.

The status of the Chinese Chamber of Commerce in the community was assured by the recognition of the Ch'ing government who had granted it an official seal,[239] that carried a great deal of authority in the eyes of the overseas Chinese. With this assured status, it would not have been much difficulty to move up to the leading position in the community. The professed aims of the Chamber in the Indies were to maintain public interest; to unite various groups; to promote knowledge and learning; to settle disputes; and to protect the interests of the Chinese as a whole.[240] The non-sectarian aims of the Chamber had a wider appeal to the local Chinese communities than the aims of the dialect and clan organisations, and naturally took on a leading position among the social organisations. Its leading status was further consolidated by the power of issuing visas for members who wished to visit China. The power was granted by the Ministry of Agriculture, Industry and Commerce, and was meant to protect the returned overseas Chinese merchants.[241] The visa issued by the Chamber was accepted as being equivalent to the visa issued by the Chinese Consuls

---

[239]See Memorials of the Minister of Agriculture, Industry and Commerce to the Court urging for the granting of official seals to the Chinese Chambers of Commerce in Batavia (29 June 1907), in Surahbaya (29 July 1907), in Semarang (10 October 1907), in Pontianak (30 October 1907) and in Solo (1 January 1908), see *Shang-wu kuan-pao*, vol. 14, pp. 5–6, vol. 17, pp. 5–6, vol. 25, pp. 4–5, vol. 27, pp. 4–5 and vol. 33, pp. 6–7.

[240]See "Pa-ta-wei-ya hua-shang tsung hui shih-pan chang-ch'eng" (The Draft of the Rules and Regulations of the Chinese Chamber of Commerce of Batavia). This draft consists of five chapters, 24 rules and regulations. Chapter 1 deals with the aims of the Chamber, Chapter 2 deals with the name and relationship with China, Chapter 3 deals with the eligibility for membership and external relations with other similar Chinese associations, Chapter 4 deals with subscriptions, and the last chapter deals with the structure of the Chamber, election of the leaders and representation of the dialect groups in the Chamber. See *Shang-wu kuan-pao*, vol. 11, pp. 36–38.

[241]See "Rules and Regulations relating to the issue of visa by the Chinese Chamber of Commerce of Surahbaya", in *Shang-wu kuan-pao*, 1908, vol. 19, pp. 37–38; "Memorial of the Ministry of Commerce to the Court urging for the protection of the returned overseas Chinese merchants dated 4th day of 11th moon of 29th year of Kuang-hsu (22 December 1903)", in *Ta-ch'ing kuang-hsu hsin fa-ling*, vol. 16, pp. 56–57.

overseas.[242] In this respect, the Chamber was elevated almost to the status of a consulate. The Chamber not only had direct contacts with the Ministry of Agriculture, Industry and Commerce, but also served as a liaison agency between the Chinese embassy in the Hague and the local Chinese community.[243] From the embassy's point of view, if the Chamber could smoothly carry out some of the functions of a consulate, the problem of diplomatic representation in the Indies would be partly solved.

But the functions of the Chinese Chamber of Commerce were not carried out as smoothly as the Chinese government would have liked. The Dutch Colonial government in the Indies was quite aware of China's intention, and jealously guarded its rights to control the local Chinese. Although the Chinese government pressed the Dutch to recognise the semi-official status of the Chambers, it seems to have borne little result. At the same time, because of the lack of diplomatic status of the Chambers, the Dutch Foreign Office intercepted correspondence between the Chinese embassy and the Chambers in violation of international diplomatic practice.[244] It was probably for these reasons that the Chinese government came to realise that the Chambers could not be used as effective substitutes for consulates, and thus a resumption of negotiations with the Dutch government over diplomatic representation in the East Indies was needed.

The resumption of negotiations began in August 1908 with an initiative from the Chinese Foreign Office (Wai Wu-pu).[245] The

---

[242]See "Rules and Regulations relating to the issue of visa by the Chinese Chamber of Commerce of Surahbaya", in *Shang-wu kuan pao*, 1908, vol. 19, pp. 37–38. The rules also stated that the returned overseas Chinese merchants who held the visa issued by the Chamber, could go to the local Chinese officials to ask for protection if they were ill-treated by local bullies, or they could leave the case for the Chamber to lodge on their behalf.

[243]No direct evidence is found to support this point. But from the complaints of Lu Cheng-hsiang against the Dutch Foreign Office for its infringement of rights to communicate with the Chinese Chambers of Commerce in the Indies, we can conclude that there was substantial liaison between the embassy and the Chambers. See "Memorial of Lu Cheng-hsiang to the Court dated 20 July 1909", in Tsungli Yamen Archives, 1st year of Hsuan-t'ung, Lu Cheng-hsiang shih Ho (The Mission of Lu Cheng-hsiang to the Netherlands).

[244]*Ibid.*, the same memorial is also found in *Ch'ing Hsuan-t'ung ch'ao wai-chiao shih-liao*, vol. 5, p. 30.

[245]See "Memorial of Wai Wu-Pu to the Court urging for the appointment of a plenipotentiary for the signing of a successfully negotiated treaty with the Netherlands

man who was entrusted with the job was Lu Cheng-hsiang, the
Chinese ambassador to the Netherlands. Lu belonged to the new
generation of Chinese diplomats who were brought up in an environment of mixed Chinese and Western cultures, and had a better
understanding of Western diplomatic practice than their predecessors. As a result of this, they were more inclined to emphasise
diplomatic skill. Like most of his peers, Lu went through the T'ung
Wen Kuan, the official Western Language Institute founded in
1862 in Peking.[246] However, unlike many of his peers, Lu had a
strong missionary background which strengthened his linguistic
ability, deepened his understanding of the West, and made him a
better diplomat. In a little more than a decade, he rose in the diplomatic hierarchy from an interpreter at the Chinese embassy in St.
Petersburg in 1893, to the position of the Chinese Minister to the
Netherlands at the end of 1905.[247] His rapid rise reflected his ability
and his good grasp of the art of diplomacy. In tackling the issue of
diplomatic representation in the Indies, he adopted a different
strategy from his predecessor, Lu Hai-huan. He wanted to establish
evidence of Dutch ill-treatment of the Chinese before he took action. He realised that he could not force the Dutch government to
concede to the issue unless he produced well-substantiated evidence
to support his claims. To this end, he suggested to the Wai Wu-pu
that it send Ch'ien Hsun, a newly-appointed Counsellor to his legation in the Hague, to tour the East Indies on the way to Europe.[248]
Ch'ien's tour in the region between 1906 and 1907 was of great
significance.[249] His trip appears to have been confined only to the

---

over the issue of the establishment of consulates approved on 3rd day of 4th moon
of 3rd year of Hsuan-t'ung (1 May 1911)'', in *Ch'ing Hsuan-t'ung ch'ao wai-chiao
shih-liao*, vol. 20, p. 17.

[246]Lu was trained in T'ung Wen Kuan and specialised in French language and
literature. He graduated from the Institute in 1892. For details of the T'ung Wen
Kuan, see Knight Biggerstaff, ''The Tung Wen Kuan'', in *The Chinese Social and
Political Science Review*, 18 (October, 1934), pp. 307–40; see also the same author,
The Earliest Modern Government Schools in China (Ithaca, 1961), pp. 94–153.

[247]See ''Lu Cheng-hsiang'', in H.L. Boorman & R.C. Howard (ed.), *Biographical
Dictionary of Republican China* (New York, 1968), pp. 441–42.

[248]See ''Despatch of Lu Cheng-hsiang to Wai Wu-pu dated 25th day of 5th moon
of 33rd year of Kuang-hsu (5 July 1907)'', in ''Tsungli Yamen Archives'', Clean file,
''The Mission of Lu Cheng-hsiang and Ch'ien-hsun to the Netherlands, 33rd year of
Kuang-hsu.''

[249]Lea E. Williams suggests in his book that Ch'ien toured the Indies in 1907.
From the available Chinese documents, we can reconstruct more accurately that

big cities in Java like Batavia, Surahbaya, Semarang and Solo, where the majority of the Chinese on the island concentrated. There is no evidence to suggest that he travelled throughout the archipelago.[250]

Ch'ien was received warmly by the local Chinese, and spoke widely with his compatriots from all walks of life. He conveyed the concern of the Ch'ing government for its overseas subjects, encouraged the establishment of Chinese Chambers of Commerce,[251] and promoted Chinese education.[252] He also tried to establish national

---

Ch'ien had toured the Java island in the last two or three months of 1906 and the first two months of 1907. Many of the Chinese documents, including Ch'ien's own memorial briefly stated that Ch'ien had toured Java during the 32nd year of Kuang-hsu (25 January 1906–12 February 1907). The earlier telegram that Ch'ien sent to the Ministry of Agriculture, Industry and Commerce was dated 11th moon of 32nd year of Kuang-hsu (between 16 December 1906 and 13 January 1907), and his other two telegrams to the same Ministry were sent a month later. Based on this evidence, it seems reasonable to suggest that he arrived in Java sometime in October 1906 and left the island in February 1907. See Lea E. Williams, *Overseas Chinese Nationalism: The Genesis of the Pan Chinese Movement in Indonesia 1900–1916*, p. 151; *Shang-wu kuan-pao*, 1907, vol. 14, p. 5, vol. 17, p. 5, vol. 25, p. 4, vol. 33, p. 6; *Ch'ing-chi wai-chiao shih-liao*, vol. 204, p. 19; Ch'ien Hsun, *Erh-erh wu-wu shu*, in Shen Yun-Lung (ed.), *Chin-tai chung-kuo shih-liao ts'ung-k'an*, vol. 54 (Taipei, n.d.), p. 25.

[250]Lea E. Williams also suggests that Ch'ien had toured various parts of the archipelago. But it seems that Ch'ien had only toured the major cities of Java island. Ch'ien's memorial of August 1907 stated quite clearly that he was sent to inspect the conditions of the Chinese education, industry and commerce, of the whole Java island. This statement is confirmed by his telegrams to the Ministry of Agriculture, Industry and Commerce, while he was touring Batavia, Surahbaya, Semarang and Solo. See Lea E. Williams, *op. cit.*, p. 152; "Memorial of Ch'ien Hsun to the Court relating to the conditions of the Chinese in the Dutch East Indies dated 22nd day of 7th moon of 33rd year of Kuang-hsu (30 August 1907)", in *Ch'ing-chi wai-chiao shih-liao*, vol. 204, p. 19, the same memorial is also found in the "Tsungli Yamen Archives", clean file, "The mission of Ch'ien Hsun and Lu Cheng-hsiang, 34th year of Kuang-hsu", and also in Ch'ien Hsun's work, *Erh-erh wu-wu shu*, pp. 25–36.

[251]Ch'ien Hsun's memorial of August 1907, *op. cit.*, *Shang-wu kuan-pao*, 1907, vol. 14, p. 5, vol. 17, p. 5, vol. 25, p. 4, and vol. 33, p. 6.

[252]Ch'ien visited several Chinese schools. He also telegramed the Governor-General of Liang-kiang, Tuan Fang, to found the Chi-nan hsueh t'ang (Chi Nan middle school) in Nanking for educating overseas Chinese students. By finding an outlet for the graduates of the primary school students, Ch'ien indirectly encouraged the development of Chinese education in the region. See Ch'ien's memorial of August 1907, in *Ch'ing-chi wai-chiao shih-liao*, vol. 204, p. 22b, see also Ch'ien Hsun, *Erh-erh wu-wu shu*, p. 32, and "Tsungli Yamen Archives", clean file, "The missions of Ch'ien Hsun and Lu Cheng-hsiang, 34th year of Kuang-hsu".

dignity by flouting the authority of the local Dutch officials.[253] But the most important achievement from a diplomatic point of view, was his success in collecting evidence of Dutch ill-treatment of the Chinese. He received many complaints from them, and probably took down their names and addresses for future reference. He gathered material on how the Chinese coolie system worked in the Indies, and how the system was abused.[254] He further collected information about Dutch discrimination against the Chinese. The discrimination fell into three categories: legal, human movement and taxation. The Dutch degraded the Chinese by having them tried in the "native court" where they had to kneel down in front of the judge, and the Chinese had no right to engage lawyers to defend their cases, while the Europeans and Japanese received different legal treatment.[255] In the aspect of human movement, the Chinese were confined to certain areas to live, and a penalty was imposed on those who spent a night outside the zone. The Chinese who wished to move outside the zones had to obtain passes which were not easily obtainable. They were neither allowed to enter the zones reserved for the indigenous population, nor enter hotels catering especially for Europeans and Japanese. In contrast to the Chinese, the Europeans and Japanese were given a visa which enabled them to tour, trade and live wherever they liked.[256] On taxation, the Chinese had to carry a heavier burden of income tax; the Europeans and Japanese only paid two per cent of their income, while the Chinese had to double the rate. In addition, the Chinese had to pay transport tax.[257] All these seem to be indisputable

---

[253]It was claimed that Ch'ien refused to talk with the Dutch officials except through interpreters, although he was familiar with English. In Semarang he shocked the Dutch and delighted the Chinese by refusing to pay an official call on the local officer. See Lea E. Williams, op. cit., p. 152.

[254]He noted that most Chinese coolies in the Indies were first sold in British Singapore, and then were distributed to other parts of the archipelago. Most of them worked in the tin mines of Bangka and in the tobacco plantations of Deli in Sumatra. Most of the owners of these mines and estates were Dutch. But the cruelty inflicted on the coolies came from overseers, many of whom were undesirable Chinese. See Ch'ien's memorial of August 1907, op. cit.

[255]See Ch'ien's memorial of August 1907, in Ch'ing-chi wai-chiao shih-liao, vol. 204, p. 23a, also in Ch'ien Hsun, Erh-erh wu-wu shu, p. 33, and "Tsungli Yamen Archives", clean file, "The Missions of Ch'ien Hsun and Lu Cheng-hsiang, 34th year of Kuang-hsu."

[256]Ch'ing-chi wai-chiao shih-liao, vol. 204, p. 23b, Ch'ien Hsun, op. cit., p. 34, "Tsungli Yamen Archives", op. cit.

[257]Ibid.

facts,[258] and provided useful evidence for Lu Cheng-hsiang in his negotiations with the Dutch.

On this tour, Ch'ien gained considerable insight into problems with which he dealt with when he took up his appointment in the Hague. One of these problems was the role of Dutch appointed Chinese Kapiteins. A convenient excuse used by the Dutch government to reject China's demand was that the Indies Chinese had been adequately protected by the Kapiteins, and that the Dutch even considered it as a special favour done for the Chinese.[259] Ch'ien must have read the documents of Lu Hai-huan's negotiations with the Dutch, and the petitions sent to the Chinese government by the Indies Chinese; he must also have realised that the Dutch claim of adequate protection was a farce. But to reveal the hypocracies of the Dutch in an appropriate manner, he needed knowledge and evidence. He needed to know how the system functioned, and what actual relationship existed between the Dutch officials and the Chinese Kapiteins. For this purpose he met with the Kapiteins. He even went to the extent of inspecting the files of a Kapitein in order to understand the scope and functions of the system.[260] He also compiled a list of the Kapiteins with their names both in Chinese and in Dutch to avoid confusion.[261] In his calculation, this list was important to provide clear identification of the Kapiteins, and would be useful for future reference. Ch'ien also realised that the Kapitein system originated from the Dutch army ranks,[262] and had been adopted in the Indies for centuries. Due to the hereditary nature of the office, the system deteriorated. The appointees, either through hereditary right or favouritism, were not the best Chinese leaders. Most of them, according to Ch'ien, neither spoke nor read Chinese, nor did they speak the Dutch

---

[258]See Lea E. Williams, *Overseas Chinese Nationalism: The Genesis of the Pan-Chinese Movement in Indonesia 1900–1916*, pp. 27–35.

[259]See Ch'ien Hsun's memorial to the Court of August 1907, in *Ch'ing-chi wai-chiao shih-liao*, vol. 204, p. 21; see also Ch'ien Hsun, *Erh-erh wu-wu shu*, p. 29; "Tsungli Yamen Archives", clean file, "The Missions of Ch'ien Hsun and Lu Cheng-hsiang, 34th year of Kuang-hsu."

[260]*Ibid.*

[261]"Report of Ch'ien Hsun to the Wai Wu Pu relating to the Indies Chinese, received on 23rd day of 9th moon of 33rd year of Kuang-hsu (29 October 1907)", in "Tsungli Yamen Archives", clean file, "The Missions of Lu Cheng-hsiang and Ch'ien Hsun to the Netherlands, 33rd year of Kuang-hsu."

[262]*Ibid.*

language. What they knew was romanised Malay. Because of this, they were unable to communicate adequately with both their fellow Chinese and the Dutch authorities.[263] Their functions, as noted by Ch'ien, had been greatly reduced to merely looking after the registration of marriages, the issue of permits to Chinese after disembarkation at the Indies ports, and the settling of petty disputes.[264]

Ch'ien's findings provided Lu Cheng-hsiang with solid ground for renegotiation with the Dutch government. He thus substantiated his argument that the Indies Chinese were ill-treated, and refuted Dutch claim that the Chinese were adequately protected under the Kapitein system. In addition to Ch'ien's evidence, Lu had another advantage. Due to the development of the tobacco industry in northeast Sumatra, Dutch planters attempted to recruit Chinese labourers from the Fukien province, but had not been successful. The Dutch Minister in Peking was anxious to obtain the co-operation of the Chinese government on this issue.[265] This provided Lu an additional advantage in the negotiations. In the Summer of 1909, the Dutch government agreed to sign a special treaty with China subject to pending legislation on Colonial citizenship.[266] Although the negotiations made some progress, it soon fell into a deadlock because of disagreement over the citizenship of the local-born Chinese (Peranakan) in the Indies.

The East Indian Government Act of 1854 provided an ambivalent national status for the Peranakan Chinese. On the one hand, they were placed on the same level as the indigenous population in legal and administrative matters, in contrast to the privileged position of Europeans; on the other hand, they were given the status of Dutch subjects which carried all the prerogatives of Dutch

---

[263]See Ch'ien Hsun's memorial to the Court of August 1907, in *Ch'ing-chi wai-chiao shih-liao*, vol. 204, pp. 21a–21b; see also Ch'ien Hsun, *Erh-erh wu-wu shu*, pp. 29–30; "Tsungli Yamen Archives", clean file, "The Missions of Ch'ien Hsun and Lu Cheng-hsiang, 34th year of Kuang-hsu (1908)."

[264]*Ibid.*

[265]See Ch'ien Hsun's memorial to the Court of August 1907, in *Ch'ing-chi wai-chiao shih-liao*, vol. 204, p. 20.

[266]See "Memorial of the Wai Wu Pu to the Court relating to the signing of the proposed Sino-Dutch treaty on consular representation, approved on 3rd day of 4th moon of 3rd year of Hsuan-t'ung (1 May 1911)", in *Ch'ing Hsuan-t'ung ch'ao wai-chiao shih-liao*, vol. 20, p. 17b.

citizenship while abroad.[267] But the citizenship law of 1892 classified them as "foreigners".[268]

With the rise of the pan-Chinese nationalist movement in the Indies at the turn of the present century, the Peranakan Chinese became a bone of contention between the Chinese and the Dutch governments. To the Chinese government, the Peranakans possessed number, influence, wealth, and leadership status. Their support was indispensable in the control of the Chinese communities, and was worth cultivating. This policy of cultivating good relationship with the Peranakan Chinese was reflected in the approaches of the Chinese emissaries, including Ch'ien Hsun.[269] To the Dutch government, the Peranakans were potentially loyal Dutch citizens. It feared the loss of their allegiance. To counter the Chinese influence, the ban was lifted on the Peranakans learning the Dutch language, and schools were set up for them. At the same time, Chinese leaders were also appointed on the municipal councils.[270]

Apart from the competition for Peranakan allegiance, both governments also clashed over the principles on which the citizenship law was based. With strong Confucian patriarchial and clanish values, it was not surprising that China adopted the principle of *jus sanguinis* which emphasised blood relationship.[271] Moreover, since China was a country exporting migrants, the principle of blood relationship would help to strengthen the racial and cultural identity of Chinese emigrants, and ease the fear of losing subjects to

---

[267]See Victor Purcell, *The Chinese in Southeast Asia* (O.U.P. London, 1965, second edition), p. 442; D.W. Willmott, *The National Status of the Chinese in Indonesia* (Ithaca, 1961), p. 13.

[268]*Ibid.*

[269]See Ch'ien Hsun's memorial to the Court of August 1907, in *Ch'ing-chi wai-chiao shih-liao*, vol. 204, pp. 19–24, see also Ch'ien Hsun's report to the Wai Wu Pu of October 1907 relating to the Chinese Kapiteins, in "Tsungli Yamen Archives", "The Missions of Lu Cheng-hsiang and Ch'ien Hsun to the Netherlands, the 33rd year of Kuang-hsu (1907)."

[270]In 1908, the first Dutch language school for the Chinese was set up in Batavia and was followed in other cities. A few Chinese had been appointed to Municipal Advisory Councils ever since their establishment during the first decade of the century, and after 1909 the Chinese community was allowed to select some of its own representatives. See Leo Suryadinata, "The Three Major Streams in Peranakan Chinese Politics in Java 1917–1942" (M.A. thesis, Monash University, 1969), p. 12; D.E. Willmott, *op. cit.*, p. 8.

[271]See Donald E. Willmott, *The National Status of the Chinese in Indonesia 1900–1958*, p. 14.

foreign countries.[272] In its citizenship law proclaimed in March 1909, the Chinese government declared that all Chinese of male descent, regardless of their birthplace, were considered to be Chinese subjects.[273] On the other hand, the Dutch government adopted the principle of *jus soli* which emphasised the relationship with the birthplace. Since the Dutch government was on the receiving end of the immigrants, it had a great deal to gain by adopting this principle. In the Netherlands Citizenship Act of February 1910, the Dutch government declared that all persons born in the Indies of parents who were domiciled there, were Dutch subjects even if not Dutch citizens.[274] The stalemate on citizenship issue lasted more than a year from February 1910 to April 1911, and the Chinese negotiator, Lu Cheng-hsiang, was recalled back to Peking in July 1910 as a token of protest against the Dutch government. At the same time, Lu was instructed to continue negotiations with the Dutch ambassador at Peking.[275] The situation worked to the advantage of the Dutch government, for it could enforce its new citizenship law among the Indies Chinese, and create a situation of *fait accompli*. Probably prompted by a claim that the Indies government had begun coercing 300,000 Chinese in Java to take up Dutch citizenship,[276] and realising the loss of ground on the issue, the Chinese government began to give in. With the concession gained

---

[272]See Chueh Ming, "Tseng she ling-shih shuo" (Anonymous "On Increased Consular Representation Overseas") (this article was probably written in 1880s), in Yu Pao-hsien (ed.), *Huang-ch'ao hsu-ai wen-pien* (Collected Essays of the Ch'ing Dynasty), vol. 12, Kuan-chih, in Wu Hsiang-hsiang (ed.), *Chung-kuo shih-hsueh ts'ung-shu* (Taipei, n.d.), no. 21, pp. 1131-35.

[273]See Chapter 1 item 1 of the Citizenship Law, in *Cheng-chih kuan-pao* (Ch'ing Government Gazette), no. 18, p. 171, 10th day of 2nd moon of 1st year of Hsuan-t'ung (31 March 1909).

[274]See Amry Vandenbosch, *The Dutch East Indies* (2nd ed., Berkeley, 1941), pp. 356ff. cited in Victor Purcell, *Chinese in Southeast Asia* (London, 1951), p. 506.

[275]See "Memorial of the Wai Wu Pu to the Court relating to the signing of the proposed Sino-Dutch Treaty on consular representation approved on 3rd day of 4th moon of 3rd year of Hsuan-t'ung (1 May 1911)", in *Ch'ing Hsuan-t'ung ch'ao wai-chiao shih liao*, vol. 20, pp. 18a-18b.

[276]This claim was made by a Chinese leader from Java, Liang Tsu-lu who pleaded to Sheng Hsuan-huai, an influential high-ranking official, for protection. Liang stated that the Indies government had only given the Chinese a month to comply with the citizenship law. See "Telegram of Sheng Hsuan-huai to the Grand Council and the Wai Wu Pu dated 26th day of 5th moon of 2nd year of Hsuan-t'ung (2 July 1910)", in Sheng Hsuan-huai, *Yu-chai ts'un-kao*, vol. 76, Telegram no. 53, pp. 3-4.

from the negotiations that the Peranakan Chinese would be considered as Chinese subjects when they returned to China,[277] Lu Cheng-hsiang signed a treaty with the Dutch ambassador in Peking on 8 May 1911.[278] It was written in French to indicate that there was no room for further disputes,[279] and was to be put into effect four months after having been ratified by the respective governments.[280] The following articles are to be noted:

Article 1   states that the Chinese consul-general, consul, vice-consul, and acting consul could be stationed in ports and cities of the Dutch colonies and protectorates, where other foreign consul-generals, consuls and vice-consuls existed.

Article 2   states that the Chinese consul-general, consul, vice-consul and acting consul are commercial officers, acting to protect the commerce of Chinese subjects. . . .

Article 5   states that records and correspondence of the Chinese consuls are not subject to censorship or search by any Dutch officers or judges.

Article 6   states that the Chinese consul-general, consul, vice-consul and acting consul not being diplomats, are not allowed to communicate directly with the governor or the governor-general of the Dutch colonies and-protectorates except when the matters are of extreme urgency and they could prove that previous communication with subordinate officials had born no result.

Article 8   states that those who hold passports issued or inspected by the Chinese consuls, could not travel or

---

[277]See the memorial of the Wai Wu Pu of 1st May 1911, in *Ch'ing Hsuan-t'ung ch'ao wai-chiao shih-liao*, vol. 20, p. 18b.

[278]See "Memorial of Lu Cheng-hsiang to the Court relating to the signing of the Sino-Dutch Treaty, received on 14th day of 4th moon of 3rd year of Hsuan-t'ung (12 May 1911)", in *Ch'ing Hsuan-t'ung ch'ao wai-chiao shih-liao*, vol. 20, pp. 31a–35b.

[279]See "Memorial of Wai Wu Pu to the Court, received on 3rd day of 4th moon of 3rd year of Hsuan-t'ung (1 May 1911)", *ibid.*, pp. 20a–20b.

[280]See "Memorial of Wai Wu Pu to the Court relating to the signing and ratification of the Sino-Dutch Treaty, approved on 26th day of 4th moon of 3rd year of Hsuan-t'ung (24 May 1911)", *ibid.*, vol. 21, p. 7a.

stay freely in the Dutch colonies or protectorates, and are required to obtain official documents issued by the Dutch officials. The Dutch governments in the colonies and protectorates have the right to detain or deport those who possessed passports issued or inspected by the Chinese consuls.

Article 12   states that when the Chinese die without heirs, the Dutch officials who are in charge of the matter should notify the Chinese consul so as to find suitable beneficiaries for the deceased. . . .[281]

It is clear that the treaty was signed on Dutch terms, Chinese consuls were not considered as diplomats (article 6) but merely China's trade representatives (article 2) looking after the commercial interests of the Chinese subjects. They were not given the right of extra-territoriality which was enjoyed by the foreign Consuls in China (including the Dutch), nor were they given equal status to the Western and Japanese Consuls in the Dutch colonies.

The result could hardly be claimed by China as a diplomatic victory, but in settling a chronic issue China had no choice but to pay a price. How high the price was is a matter of controversy. The claim made by some scholars that China had to pay a high price of relinquishing its claim of jurisdiction over the Peranakans seems to be untenable.[282] The attached notes of the treaty took note that both sides recognised the differences in their citizenship laws, and agreed that if disputes arose in the Dutch colonies, they should be settled in accordance with Dutch laws; but the Dutch government also declared that the Dutch nationals of Chinese descent would be allowed to take up Chinese citizenship while they were in China in accordance with their wishes.[283] Obviously there was no clear

---

[281]See the Sino-Dutch Treaty on consular representations in the Dutch colonies, in *Cheng-chih kuan-pao*, memorial section, 7th day of leap 6th moon of 3rd year of Hsuan-t'ung, (Wen Hai, Taipei edition), vol. 47, pp. 126–31. See also *Ch'ing hsuan-t'ung chao wai-chiao shih-liao*, vol. 21, pp. 7a–13b; and *Chung-wai t'iao-yeh hui-p'ien* (Taipei, 1964), pp. 318–20.

[282]See D.E. Willmott, *The National Status of the Chinese in Indonesia 1900–1958*, p. 16.

[283]See the two attached notes of the Dutch ambassador to China dated separately on 10th and 12th day of 4th moon of 3rd year of Hsuang-t'ung (8 and 10 May 1911), and a note of Lu Cheng-hsiang dated 10th day of 4th moon of 3rd year of Hsuan-t'ung (8 May 1911), in *Cheng-chih kuan-pao*, memorial section, 7th day of

recognition of Dutch rights over the Peranakan Chinese. As correctly pointed out by an eminent Chinese lawyer, Ko Tjay Sing, the Manchu government did not concede its claim to the citizenship of the Peranakans, but merely agreed that the jurisdiction of its consuls should not extend to those persons who were also Dutch subjects according to Dutch law.[284] If this could be considered as a minor victory on the Chinese side, the attached notes did leave some room for the Chinese Consuls to manoeuvre when they took up their appointments in the Indies.

In July 1911, just before the treaty was put into effect, the Chinese Foreign Office recommended to the Court that a Consul-General be appointed to be stationed at Batavia. He would look after the Chinese on West Java island (on the western part of Semarang), Dutch Borneo, Belitung and the surrounding islands; a Consul would be appointed to be stationed in Surahbaya to look after the Chinese on East Java island, (on the eastern part of Semarang),[285] Celebes (Sulawesi), Bali, Lombok and the surrounding islands; another Consul would be stationed at Padang (Pa Tung) to look after the Chinese on the Sumatra island, Bangka and the surrounding islands.[286] The recommendation was approved by the Court on 21 July 1911.[287] The first Consul-General for Dutch East Indies, Su Jui-chao was appointed at the end of the year, but due to the outbreak of the 1911 revolution and the ultimate overthrow of the Ch'ing Dynasty, Su did not take up his appointment in Batavia until August 1912 with new credentials from the new republic.[288]

---

leap 6th moon of 3rd year of Hsuan-t'ung, vol. 47, pp. 129–30; see also *Chung-wai t'iao-yeh hui-p'ien*, pp. 319–20.

[284]See Ko Tjay Sing, "De betekenis van de nota's van 1911 met betrekking tot het onderdaanschap", quoted in D.E. Willmott, *The National Status of the Chinese in Indonesia 1900–1958*, p.16.

[285]Chinese documents put West Java as the eastern part of Semarang, and East Java as the western part of Semarang. These are obvious mistakes. Presumably the Chinese looked at the map from the direction of China. See "Memorial of Wai Wu Pu to the Court relating to the establishment of Consul-General and Consuls in the Dutch East Indies approved on 26th day of leap 6th moon of 3rd year of Hsuan-t'ung (21 July 1911)", in *Cheng-chih kuan-pao*, memorial section, 7th day of leap 6th moon of 3rd year of Hsuan-t'ung, vol. 47, pp. 131–32.

[286]*Ibid.*

[287]*Ibid.*

[288]See L.E. Williams, *Overseas Chinese Nationalism: The Genesis of the Pan-Chinese Movement in Indonesia 1900–1916*, pp. 166–67.

5
Protection of Overseas Chinese Abroad before 1893

CHINESE DIPLOMATS AND THE ISSUE OF THE PROTECTION OF OVERSEAS CHINESE

The protection of overseas Chinese became a major issue of China's diplomacy after the middle of 1870s when Chinese diplomatic representations were established throughout the major countries of the Western world. It also became the focal point of conflict between China and the West. Unlike the issue of Christian missionary activities that created friction in China, the scene of conflict was in the homelands and colonies of certain Western Powers.

Under normal conditions, China's protection of its overseas subjects would be deemed to be its right rather than privilege. But under the Unequal Treaty system, although the treaties entitled Chinese nationals to live freely in certain Western countries,[1] their rights for residence and protection were not automatically accorded, and China had to fight to maintain these rights. Because China was weak and had low international status, it had great difficulties enforcing its treaty rights.

The fault was not just because China was weak, it also failed to take initiatives. This was mainly due to the organisational weaknesses of Ch'ing diplomacy. The founding of the Tsungli Yamen in 1861 was a landmark in China's diplomatic history. Although the Yamen's evolution from an information transmitting centre to a major decision-making body was a great achievement for a Ch'ing institution, it was nevertheless not a full-fledged modern foreign office. Its power of managing China's foreign affairs was shared by provincial authorities, principally the Governor-General of Chihli

---

[1] The right of Chinese to live freely in Britain, France, the United States and their dominions was embodied in the clauses of the Treaty of Nanking concluded between Britain and China in 1842, the Sino-French Treaty of 1858, and the Sino-American Treaty of 1868. See *Chung-wai t'iao-yueh hui-p'ien* (Collection of Treaties signed between China and Foreign Countries) (Taipei, 1964), pp. 5, 76, 131.

who was also the Superintendent of Trade for Northern Ports, and the Governor-General of Liang Kiang who was concurrently holding the position of the Superintendent of Trade for Southern Ports.[2] In addition, Chinese legations overseas also had some say in the conduct of diplomacy. However, the power and authority of these various organisations had never been clearly defined. From one perspective, this multi-faceted organisation of diplomacy can be interpreted as an attempt of the Court to apply the traditional principle of "check and balance". The power of managing diplomacy must be divided and balanced in order to prevent excessive accumulation of power in one institution at the expense of the Court.

The crux of the problem of this multi-faceted authority was inefficient decision making. The Tsungli Yamen, the provincial authorities and overseas legations were placed on almost parallel positions for the conduct of diplomacy. The Yamen had no power to issue instructions either to provincial authorities or overseas legations, it could only advise the emperor to do so. The envoys overseas did not take orders from the Yamen, nor from the provincial governor-generals; they were appointed by the emperor and were directly responsible to him, and they memorialised him on matters of importance. This multi-faceted organisation in diplomacy generated unnecessary competition, jealousy and rivalry, but at the same time, the lack of a strong centralised decision-making body gave rise to complacency and ineptness.

The Tsungli Yamen which served as the principal organisation in advising the emperor, had its own structural weaknesses. It was managed by a controlling board consisting of several ministers who were appointed by the emperor. Holding concurrently important ministerial positions in the central government, these ministers could only give part of their time to attend to the Yamen's business.[3] The Yamen's lack of full-time ministers meant an unprofessional approach to diplomacy and slowness in making its decisions.[4] The secretariat of the Yamen which administered informa-

---

[2]See Tsai Shih-shan, "Reaction to Exclusion: Ch'ing Attitude Toward Overseas Chinese in the United States 1848-1906" (an unpublished Ph.D. dissertation, University of Oregon, June 1970), pp. 22-31.

[3]See S.M. Meng, *The Tsungli Yamen: Its Organisation and Function* (Cambridge, Mass., 1962), p. 27.

[4]This usually involved "buck-passing" and delaying tactics. For a brief discussion on this topic, see Ch'in Kuo-ching, "Ch'ing-tai te wai-wu-pu chi ch'i wen-shu

tion relating to various foreign countries, also suffered the same deficiency. The secretaries of the five bureaus in the secretariat held concurrent posts in other government departments.[5] The secretariat tended to collect outdated information or failed to process information because of the lack of a fulltime staff. The result of which were the poor judgements made by the ministers and ill-advice given to the emperor.

In the period between 1876 and 1893, there was no central coherent policy dealing with the protection of overseas Chinese abroad. The protection was mainly in the hands of Chinese diplomats. The majority of the Chinese ambassadors appointed before 1894 were the "foreign matters" (Yang-wu) experts, yet none of them had received any formal training in foreign languages and international law.[6] Their only qualification was their apprenticeship in dealing with foreigners under Ts'eng Kuo-fan or Li Hung-chang.[7] Of course, they were more knowledgeable about the Western world than most Chinese officials at the time. Their horizon had gone beyond the Confucian world and they knew something about Western culture and institutions, and had had some contacts with foreigners.

Although these Confucian-diplomats had a broader world view than their peers, they had no direct experience in Western education and culture, and therefore held mostly Confucian values and moral standards. They despised those values which were contrary to their own and in this context, their encounter with the West during their stay overseas must have been a traumatic experience. After a long and tiring voyage, they found themselves in a strange milieu. For the first time in their lives, they were confronted with

---

tang-an chih-tu" (The Ch'ing Ministry of Foreign Affairs and Its Correspondence and Archival Systems), in Li Shih Tang An p'ien-chi-pu (ed.), *Li Shih Tang An* (Historical Archives), (Peking), no. 2 (1981), p. 120.

[5]See Tsai Shih-shan, *op. cit.*, p. 17.

[6]See Chow Jen Hwa, *China and Japan: The History of Chinese Diplomatic Missions in Japan 1877–1911* (Singapore, 1975), p. 61. For background of the early Chinese Ministers to the United States of America, see Chan Kim Man, "Mandarins in America: The Early Chinese Ministers to the United States 1878–1907" (an unpublished Ph.D. dissertation, University of Hawaii, 1981), pp. 90–102.

[7]See K.E. Folsom, *Friends, Guests, and Colleagues: The Mu-Fu System in the Late Ch'ing Period* (Berkeley, 1968), pp. 68, 133–41; P.A. Cohen, *Between Tradition and Modernity: Wang T'ao and Reform in Late Ch'ing China* (Cambridge, Mass., 1974), pp. 267–71.

different architectural buildings, bridges, landscapes, people, costumes, and so forth. This strange feeling later deepened and was
provoked to become distaste as they witnessed the free contacts between men and women in the streets and social gatherings.[8] This
distaste for the Western way of life discouraged them to learn
about Western institutions and society.

Apart from this feeling, their handicap in language and international law reinforced their isolation. The lack of a good command
of a foreign language meant they had to depend heavily on interpreters to supply them information about the country in which they
resided, and their contacts with other diplomats were very limited.
Lack of knowledge in international law further meant they had difficulty discerning right or wrong in accordance with international
practice, and their ability to protect overseas Chinese was thus
greatly reduced.

These limitations generated complacency, timidity and pessimism. Ch'en Lan-pin, the first Chinese Minister in Washington, was
described by his deputy, Yung Wing, as timid and without a strong
sense of responsibility in the discharge of his duty.[9] These short-
comings were probably more than flaws in his character, but could
also well be the result of his traumatic experience in his encounter
with the West. Kuo Sung-t'ao, China's first Minister to Britain, felt
pessimistic about the role of Chinese diplomats overseas. This was
because any mistake made by the Chinese diplomats in the negotiations would result in embarrassment and humiliation.[10] He even advised the Court that "talented 'foreign matters' experts should *not*
be posted overseas as ministers, for this would be equivalent to
dumping something useful into a rubbish bin".[11] Kuo's pessimism

---

[8]See for instance, Liu Hsi-hung, the first Chinese vice ambassador to England,
was obviously embarrassed to see the way European women dressed for an audience
with Queen Victoria in Buckingham Palace in March 1877. He commented that "all
the women wore dresses which exposed their bodies, and did not mind being in a
place crowded with men. . . . All the men and women who knew one another shook
hands". Judging from Chinese moral standards of the time, this sight must have
shocked Liu. See *Liu Hsi-hung, Ying-yao jih-chi* (Diary of my Mission to England);
see also J.D. Frodsham (trans.), *The First Chinese Embassy to the West: The Journals of Kuo Sung-t'ao, Liu Hsi-hung and Chang Te-yi* (Oxford, 1974), p. 126.

[9]Yung Hung (Yung Wing), *Hsi-hsueh tung-chan chi* (Wen Hai, Taipei, reprint),
in Shen Yung-lung (ed.), *Chin-tai chung-kuo shih-liao ts'ung-k'an*, no. 95, p. 122.

[10]Kuo Sung-t'ao, "Yi hsiao chia lun yang-wu shu", in *Yang-tzu-shu wu i-chi,
tsou-shu* vol. 12, p. 9a.

[11]*Ibid.*

was again probably the result of a traumatic encounter with the Western world.

In Singapore which was the first port to set up a Chinese consulate, protection of the overseas Chinese was not as crucial. In fact, the Chinese in Singapore were among the fortunate ones who were comparatively well-treated. The protection of the Chinese there was therefore considered to be of minor importance. Apart from collaborating with the British Protector of Chinese in Singapore,[12] relating to the welfare of Chinese immigrants in the Straits Settlements,[13] the Consul spent much of his time promoting Chinese education, literary and cultural activities, and pro-Ch'ing national consciousness.[14]

In Japan, the protection given to the Chinese appeared to be impressive. Under the Sino-Japanese Treaty of 1871,[15] China had acquired the consular jurisdiction which enabled the Chinese to enjoy extraterritoriality, like other foreign nationals in Japan. The Chinese Consuls in Yokohama, Kobe and Nagasaki had the right to try Chinese nationals if the disputes involved the Chinese only. In lawsuits involving both Chinese and Japanese nationals, the official from the plaintiff's country would sit on the tribunal of the court of the defendant's country. For example, if a Chinese criminal case opened in the consulate in Yokohama, the local Japanese district judge would come to the consulate; or to reverse the position, if a Japanese was the defendant in a criminal case, the Chinese consulate would send men to the Japanese court.[16] Apart from this extraterritoriality, Chinese Consuls also acquired concessions from

---

[12]The Protector of Chinese was a British official in charge of Chinese affairs. The Chinese Protectorate was set up in 1877, and the first Protector of Chinese was W.A. Pickering. See R.N. Jackson, *Pickering: Protector of Chinese* (Kuala Lumpur, 1965), pp. 64–91.

[13]See Wen Chung-chi, "The Imperial Chinese Consulate in The Straits Settlements" (an unpublished M.A. thesis, University of Malaya, Singapore, 1964); see also Lin Hsiao-sheng, "Ch'ing-chao Chu Hsing Ling-shih yu hai-hsia chih-min-ti cheng-fu chien te chiu-fen" (The Dispute between the Ch'ing Consul in Singapore and the Colonial government of the Straits Settlements), in Ko' Mu-lin and Ng Chin Keong (eds.), *Hsin-chia-po hua-tsu shih lun-chi* (Papers on the History of the Chinese in Singapore) (Singapore, 1972), p. 16.

[14]See Yen Ching-hwang, "Overseas Chinese Nationalism in Singapore and Malaya 1877-1912" in *Modern Asian Studies*, vol. 16, no. 3 (1982), pp. 410–11.

[15]For the negotiations of this treaty, see Chow Jen Hwa, *China and Japan: The History of Chinese Diplomatic Missions in Japan 1877-1911*, pp. 39–43.

[16]*Ibid.*, pp. 141–42.

the Japanese government for the local Chinese to meet their special needs. In Yokohama, the Japanese government granted a special burial ground and a hospital exclusively for the Chinese at the request of the Chinese Consul.[17]

ANTI-CHINESE MOVEMENT IN THE UNITED STATES

The protection of overseas Chinese during this period was in fact most urgently needed in the United States. Ironically the United States was sympathetic to China's fight for coolie justice in Peru,[18] yet its treatment of the Chinese immigrants in the last two decades of the nineteenth century was an international scandal. The maltreatment of the Chinese, particularly in California, was the result of a long period of a built-up of popular anti-Chinese feeling.

When the Chinese immigrants were first attracted to the gold mines of California in the mid-nineteenth century, they aroused interest and curiosity rather than hostility. Society in the early years of the gold rush was in a state of flux and there were opportunities for everyone. The presence of the Chinese in relatively small numbers posed no direct threat to the interest of the white population. In fact their services as general labourers, laundrymen, carpenters, and cooks were considered to be useful to the growing communities.[19] During this "honeymoon" period, the general public had even praised their industry, quiet nature, cheerfulness and cleanliness.[20] But this friendly attitude towards the Chinese immigrants gradually turned sour as the numbers of Chinese indentured labourers substantially increased,[21] thus posing keen competition to the white population. Most of the Chinese only aimed at making as much money as possible at the shortest period, and were prepared to take on any type of work, and to work for longer hours and less wages. This meant they posed a serious threat to the white population in the labour market.

---

[17]*Ibid.*

[18]See W. Stewart, *Chinese Bondage in Peru: A History of the Chinese Coolies in Peru, 1849-1874*, pp. 138-40.

[19]See M.R. Coolidge, *Chinese Immigration* (Taipei, reprint, 1968), p. 21.

[20]*Ibid.*

[21]According to one estimate, the Chinese in California increased from 58,300 in 1866 to 148,660 in 1876. See E.C. Sandmeyer, *The Anti-Chinese Movement in California* (Urbana, 1973, reprint), p. 17.

This hostility was further aggravated by the appearance of the Chinese — from their complexion and facial structure to their hair styles and dressing and the difference of their language, religion and social behaviour. They spoke an unintelligible language; believed in Buddhism, idol worship and the burning of incense; and they were involved in gambling and opium-smoking. It was natural for the Chinese immigrants to stick together because the majority of them spoke the same dialect and shared common values and customs. They therefore grouped together in cities, towns and mining fields, and they formed pockets of settlements known as "Chinatowns" or "work camps". The appearance of these growing settlements was immense, for it reflected on the growing population of the Chinese, and constantly reminded the white community of the physical presence of the Chinese.[22] Moreover, there was also fear that the Chinese quarters would become the breeding grounds of immorality and this would add to the insecurity and the social disorganisation of the community.[23]

Two common weaknesses of overseas Chinese in the nineteenth century were their indifference towards local affairs and their lack of support from the home government. The early Chinese immigrants in California were no exception. They were mostly engrossed in money making, and made no special effort to learn English in order to understand what went on in the host country. They had no intention to make their voice heard nor were they interested in influencing local politics. In short they were silent bystanders rather than active participants in society and this did not enable them to defend themselves in times of trouble. The lack of support from the home government further crippled their ability to check the growing trend of anti-Chinese feeling in Californian society. This anti-Chinese prejudice had actually been built up gradually over a long period. Even as early as February 1851, at the time when Chinese immigrants were welcomed, there were incidents of the cutting off of queues — the plaited long hair worn by the Chinese, and this was considered to be a serious insult to the Chinese immigrants during the Ch'ing time.[24]

---

[22]See Robert McClellan, *The Heathen Chinese: A Study of American Attitudes Toward China, 1890–1905* (Ohio, 1971), p. 25.

[23]See Gunther Barth, *Bitter Strength: A History of the Chinese in the United States, 1850–1870* (Cambridge, Mass., 1964), p. 131.

[24]The queue was originally imposed on Han Chinese by the Manchu conquerors

By the early 1870s, anti-Chinese feeling had reached explosive proportions. In October 1871 a riot in Los Angeles claimed about nineteen Chinese lives.[25] More seriously, throughout the decade of the 1870s, sporadic anti-Chinese incidents had been transformed into an organised political movement. Against this background was the increase in the 1860s of white immigrants from Europe, particularly from Ireland, into California. By 1870 the Irish alone constituted one-fourth of the 210,000 foreign-born persons in the state.[26] As more and more Irishmen entered the labour market, they felt that their employment opportunities were jeopardised by Chinese immigrants, and as the Chinese were prepared to take on jobs of longer hours for less wages, their bargaining power with employers was greatly reduced. To many Irish workers, the Chinese were a docile tool of the "greedy capitalists", and the cause of their misery.[27] But the Irish immigrants knew how to organise themselves; they formed the Workingmen's Party and used this organisation to achieve their political aims. In 1875, in California, they supported the Democrats and succeeded in overthrowing the rule of a Republican state government. The next year during the presidential election, the Chinese question became the focus of the campaign in California. The Democrats organised mass meetings to press for the expulsion of the Chinese. They accused the Chinese of spreading infectious diseases and vices, and accused them of monopolising any trade they engaged in, and of driving thousands out of employment. They further claimed that the Chinese in San Francisco belonged to a criminal class — gamblers, opium-smokers, blackmailers and thugs, who filled the prisons and were the burden of the taxpayers.[28]

This political agitation against the Chinese was continued by the Workingmen's Party, in the Second Constitutional Convention of California in 1878 and 1879 where a delegation brought up a series of anti-Chinese propositions. These included prohibition on the Chinese to hold property, to trade, to hold citizenship, to bear

---

after 1644, since then many Chinese regarded queues as an inseparate part of their bodies, and took pride in it. Many overseas Chinese would be greatly offended if their queues were pulled by foreigners. See *Lat Pau*, 3/12/1890, p. 1.

[25]Gunther Barth, *op. cit.*, p. 144.
[26]M.R. Coolidge, *Chinese Immigration*, p. 64.
[27]*Ibid.*, p. 116.
[28]*Ibid.*, p. 112.

arms, and to give testimony in courts in cases involving white people.[29] Although most of these proposals were contrary to the
Federal Constitution of the United States and violated the treaty
agreements with China, many were incorporated into Article 19 of
the new State Constitution of California.[30] Article 19 provided
legislative power for the state to regulate the immigration of
paupers, criminals, diseased persons and aliens, and to impose conditions for their residence or removal. It also forbade corporations
to employ "Mongolian" (Chinese) who were barred from public
work. Companies importing Chinese coolies were to be penalised.
At the same time, the Legislature was empowered to remove
Chinese beyond the limits of cities and towns, and to prohibit their
introduction into California.[31]

At the higher level of Federal politics, this anti-Chinese sentiment was also aired in Congress. The coastal states of Western
United States, formed a united front to push their line of driving
out the Chinese. Under the leadership of Senator Sargent and
Senator Mitchell, they vilified the Chinese and attacked the Burlingame Treaty of 1868 which gave Chinese the right to work and live
in the United States. Agitation against the Chinese at this highest
level of politics was highlighted in the winter of 1879 when the representatives of the Pacific states both in Congress and the Senate
nearly succeeded in enacting a bill restricting Chinese immigration
and abrogating the Burlingame Treaty. However due to the veto of
President Hayes, the bill failed to become law.[32]

Parallel to the rise of this organised political movement was the
emergence of organised terrorism against the Chinese in the Pacific
states, especially in California. Terrorism was closely connected
with the Workingmen's Party under the leadership of Denis
Kearney. Their strategy was to terrorise both the Chinese and their
white supporters who were either friends or employers. They extorted, robbed and beat up the Chinese, and resorted to the most
barbaric behaviour of burning Chinese buildings and of killing the
Chinese. In dealing with the white sympathisers of the Chinese the
terrorists combined threat with occasional assassination if the

[29]*Ibid.*, p. 119; see also E.C. Sandmeyer, *The Anti-Chinese Movement in California*, pp. 66–72.
[30]M.R. Coolidge, *op. cit.*, p. 120.
[31]*Ibid.*
[32]*Ibid.*, pp. 127–41.

threat did not take effect. By terrorising the Chinese, they hoped to drive back some Chinese who were frightened for the safety of their lives; by terrorising the white supporters, they hoped to isolate the Chinese and reduce both financial and moral support for the immigrants.

The terrorist movement succeeded in mobilising racist elements in the society and resulted in a large-scale attack on the Chinese in California. Many of the Chinese were driven out from small towns and work camps, their quarters were burned, and some of them were injured or killed. In June of the same year, a violent attack was mounted on the Chinese in Truckee. In February 1877, the employers of the Chinese at Chico in Butte County, received many threatening letters, and a number of buildings were burned. In March, Chinese tenant farmers on the Lemm ranch were attacked, five of them were killed, and their bodies were burned.[23] In July of the same year, riots broke out in San Francisco on an unprecedented scale as the rioters continuously for three days sacked and burned the buildings occupied by the Chinese.[34]

CH'EN LAN-PIN AND THE PROTECTION OF THE AMERICAN CHINESE, 1878–81

It was amidst this growing political opposition and racial violence against the Chinese that Ch'en Lan-pin, the first Chinese Minister to the United States, Peru and Spain, arrived to take up his appointment. When Ch'en and his retinue arrived at San Francisco on 27 July 1878, on his way to Washington, he was briefed by the local Chinese leaders about the situation in California.[35] His concern with the anti-Chinese issue was clearly reflected in his diary entitled "Brief Records of My Mission to the United States of America" (Shih Mei chi-lueh). He was informed that the Irish workers were mainly responsible for the anti-Chinese movement; he was also told that because of the absence of protection from China, the local Chinese became the target for terrorists; and he was informed that white employers were threatened into not employing Chinese, in an attempt to drive out the Chinese altogether.[36]

---

[33]*Ibid.*, pp. 262–63.
[34]*Ibid.*, p. 115.
[35]See Ch'en Lan-pin, "Shih Mei chi-lueh", in *Hsiao-fang-hu chai yu-ti ts'ung ch'ao pu-p'ien* (Taipei, 1962, reprint), vol. 16, pp. 1050–51, original vol. 12, p. 60.
[36]*Ibid.*

Ch'en's sense of urgency on the protection of the overseas Chinese prompted him to move quickly to set up a consulate-general in San Francisco at the end of 1878. He appointed his aide, Ch'en Shu-t'ang as the first consul-general, and an American named Frederick A. Bee (his name in official Chinese records is Fu Lieh Pi) as consul.[37] The appointment of a foreigner to the position of consul was not unusual in Western practice,[38] but in Chinese diplomatic history, it had set a precedent. Ch'en Lan-pin's move in appointing an American as the Chinese Consul in San Francisco was probably based on the belief that the anti-Chinese situation there was grave and would require decisions to be made on the spot. An American who was sympathetic with the Chinese cause and had sufficient local contacts would help ease the deteriorating conditions. Ch'en might have also thought that by setting up a consulate-general in San Francisco, the problem of protecting the overseas Chinese would probably resolve itself. This line of thinking was revealed in the absence of his follow-up remarks about the problem of protecting the overseas Chinese in his diary,[39] and the lack of his memorials to the Court on this issue.[40]

Given this heated anti-Chinese climate, what could Chinese diplomats do to protect the overseas Chinese? They could not defuse the growing anti-Chinese sentiment in the local community, nor could they prevent the anti-Chinese laws being enacted. The only course of action was to protect the victims. The Chinese consulates and consulate-general would have been reduced to merely an information centre collecting data of Chinese victims if the consuls and consuls-general were inactive. But a courageous and tactful consul-general could do more for the overseas Chinese. It was claimed for instance that Huang Tsun-hsien, the Chinese Consul-General of San Francisco from 1882 to 1885, accomplished a great deal more than his predecessors for the local Chinese. He succeeded

---

[37]See "Ch'en Lan-pin and Yung Wing to W.M. Evarts dated 8 November 1878", in "Notes from the Chinese Legations", "The Mission of Ch'en Lan-pin and Yung Wing"; Liu Chin-ch'ao (ed.), *Ch'ing-ch'ao shu wen-hsien t'ung-k'ao*, vol. 337, "Wai-chiao" (Foreign Relations), 1; for details relating to the establishment of the Chinese Consulate-General in San Francisco, see chapter 4, section B.

[38]See J.K. Fairbank, *Trade and Diplomacy on the China Coast: The Opening of the Treaty Ports, 1842-1854*, p. 213.

[39]See Ch'en Lan-pin, "Shih Mei chi-lueh", in *Hsiao-fang-hu chai yu-ti ts'ung-ch'ao pu-p'ien*, vol. 121 (original), pp. 64-77.

[40]See *Ch'ing-chi wai-chiao shih-liao*, vols. 13 to 21.

in freeing some Chinese prisoners who were jailed because they lived in overcrowded homes.[41] At the higher level of diplomacy, the Chinese Minister in Washington could also act on behalf of victims and could press the government of the United States to fulfil its treaty obligations.

Ch'en Lan-pin, who gained his reputation as an experienced diplomat after his famous commission to Cuba to investigate the conditions of the Chinese coolies,[42] took up the issue of the anti-Chinese riot in Colorado with the Secretary of State. The riot took place on 31 October 1880, in Denver, the state capital. The Chinese residents, numbering only 400, constituted an insignificant one percent of the total population of 40,000 of the city.[43] But this insignificant number was not spared from racial violence. Ever since the view that white workers and small businessmen were being injured by unfair Chinese competition had spread throughout California in

---

[41]It was claimed that the law against overcrowding in California at the beginning of the 1880s was designed to deal with the Chinese. Many local Chinese were jailed under such a legislation. Acting on the victims' behalf, Huang Tsun-hsien inspected the jail, and argued that the jail was unfit for human living because it was too crammed, and in line with the law of anti-overcrowdedness, the prisoners should be released. It has also claimed that Huang had won this battle by diplomacy. See Ch'ien Ngo-sun (ed.), "Huang Kung-tu hsien-sheng nien-pu", in Shen Yun-lung (ed.), *Chin-tai chung-kuo shih-liao ts'ung-k'an* (Taipei, 1973), no. 959–60, pp. 78–79; Ssu-t'u mei-t'ang, *Tsu-kuo yu hua-ch'iao* (China and the Overseas Chinese), (Hong Kong, 1956), vol. 2, pp. 45–47. Ssu-t'u mei-t'ang's work must be used with care, for it contains strong political bias and many sweeping generalizations. However, as Ssu-t'u himself was one of the Chinese immigrants at that time, his personal experience is valuable. For Huang's other measures of protecting the Chinese in California, see Noriko Kamachi, "American Influences on Chinese Reform Thought: Huang Tsun-hsien in California, 1882–1885", in *Pacific Historical Review*, vol. XLVII, no. 2 (May, 1978), pp. 289–60; see also Noriko Kamachi, *Reform in China: Huang Tsun-hsien and the Japanese Model* (Cambridge, Mass., 1981), chapter 5.

[42]Ch'en's reputation as an experienced diplomat was recognised by the Tsungli Yamen which recommended him to be appointed as the first Chinese minister to the United States, Spain and Peru. Ch'en's appointment was considered by the Yamen as the most important one among several new diplomatic posts created during that period. See "Memorial of the Tsungli Yamen to the Court recommending the appointment of Envoy to the United States, Spain and Peru to protect the Chinese Coolies dated 13th day of 11th moon of the 1st year of Kuang-hsu (10 December 1875)", in *Ch'ing-chi wai-chiao shih-liao*, vol. 4, pp. 17a–19a.

[43]See "Consul F.A. Bee to Consul-General Chen Shu Tang dated 8 December 1880", in "Notes from the Chinese Legation", "Mission of Ch'en Lan-pin and Yung Wing".

the late 1870s,[44] anti-Chinese feeling had radiated from California to outlying areas like Denver. Agitation for driving out Chinese from Colorado mounted and developed into physical violence against the Chinese. From two o'clock in the afternoon, the mob began to attack the Chinese in the streets. A Chinese named Wong Yan Chung was badly beaten, and a rope was placed around his neck and he was dragged through the streets, only narrowly escaping death. The city police, who failed to control the disturbance, put all the Chinese in jail for three days as a safety measure. As a result of the riot, one Chinese named Lu Yang was killed and several were injured,[45] and about $20,000 to $30,000 worth of properties and belongings were lost.[46]

Ch'en Lan-pin was enraged by the riot, and raised the issue promptly. On 5 November, four days after the riot, he called on the Secretary to make a strong protest, and demanded redress for the victims and more effective protection from the U.S. government for Chinese lives and properties. This stand was reaffirmed in an official note to the Secretary on 10 November.[47] At the same time, Ch'en instructed the Chinese Consul-General at San Francisco to conduct an inquiry into the riot.[48] The response of the government of the United States to the issue was evasive; the Secretary expressed his and the President's "regret", but emphasised the difficulty of the Federal Government in intervening in state affairs.[49] Ch'en was upset by the Secretary's attitude. Based on the evidence collected by Consul Frederic A. Bee who had conducted a thorough investiga-

---

[44]For details of anti-Chinese movement in California during this period, see E.C. Sandmeyer, *The Anti-Chinese Movement in California* (Urbana, 1973), pp. 48-77.

[45]The victim Lu Yang (or romanised as Look Young in the original correspondence) was a worker in a Chinese laundry shop. He was twenty eight years old, married with one son, but his wife and child were in China. Like many other young Chinese emigrants, he had been in the United States for four years and had come from his native district of Ho Shan in the Kwangtung province. See "Consul F.A. Bee to Ch'en Lan-pin dated 1 December 1880" in "Notes from Chinese Legation", "Mission of Ch'en Lan-pin and Yung Wing".

[46]See "Ch'en Lan-pin to Secretary W.M. Evarts dated 10 November 1880", the Chinese version of this note accompanied the English version, *ibid.*; this Chinese note is also found in Chu Shih-chia (ed.), *Mei-kuo po-hai hua-kung shih-liao*, p. 78.

[47]*Ibid.*

[48]See "Ch'en Lan-pin to W.M. Evarts dated 21 January 1881", in "Notes from Chinese Legation", "Mission of Ch'en Lan-pin and Yung Wing".

[49]I have not been able to read the original note of Secretary Evarts to Ch'en Lan-pin, but its main contents were summarized in Ch'en's note. *Ibid.*

tion in Denver,[50] Ch'en sent a strongly-worded despatch to the Secretary on 21 January 1881. He reiterated China's claim for redress, and presented a list of names and an estimated amount of loss as a result of the riot. Accusing the local authorities in Denver of incompetence in protecting the lives and properties of the Chinese, he demanded the government of the United States to punish those who were responsible for the riot.[51] The change of a new Secretary of State did not change the policy of the U.S. government. The new Secretary, James G. Blaine, reiterated his predecessor's stand. Insisting that the local authorities in Denver had rendered adequate protection to the Chinese, he rejected China's claim for payment.[52] Thus Ch'en Lan-pin's protest came to nothing.

INTRODUCTION OF THE FIRST EXCLUSION LAW AGAINST THE CHINESE COOLIES IN 1882

The protection of the overseas Chinese in the United States became even more difficult after 1880. This was because China in the middle of November 1880 had signed a treaty with the United States cancelling the right of its subjects to emigrate to America. The right for Chinese to enter, work and settle in the United States was obtained by the well-known Burlingame mission in July 1868,[53]

---

[50]See "Report of F.A. Bee, Chinese Consul of San Francisco, dated 8 December 1880", *ibid.*, pp. 163–64.

[51]See "Ch'en Lan-pin to Secretary W.M. Evarts dated 21 January 1881", in "Notes from Chinese Legation", "Mission of Ch'en Lan-pin and Yung Wing".

[52]See "James G. Blaine to Ch'en Lan-pin dated 25 March 1881", in *American Diplomatic and Public Papers: The United States and China*, series 2, vol. 12, *The Coolies Trade and Outrages Against the Chinese*, pp. 169–70.

[53]In 1867, amidst the national debate over treaty revision with Britain, China appointed Anson Burlingame, a retiring American ambassador, as China's roving ambassador to the West with the aim of persuading the Powers not to force modernisation on China. Burlingame was accompanied by Chih Kang and Sun Chia-ku, two co-envoys. The first leg of the mission was the United States where Burlingame signed a treaty which allowed China to send consuls and admitted Chinese subjects freely into the United States. For the special credentials given to Burlingame, Chih Kang and Sun Chia-ku by the Emperor T'ung-chi, dated 31 December 1867, see the documents both in Chinese and English kept in "Notes from the Chinese Legation", "The Burlingame Mission". For circumstances leading to the despatch of the Burlingame mission, see Immanuel C.Y. Hsu, *China's Entrance into the Family of Nations: The Diplomatic Phase 1858–1880*, pp. 168–69. For details of the Burlingame treaty, see W.F. Mayers, *Treaties Between the Empire of China and Foreign Powers* (Shanghai, 1907, reprint, Taipei, 1966), pp. 93–95.

and in fact was reciprocal to rights given to American citizens in China. But the Burlingame Treaty came under fierce attack in Congress from the representatives of the Western coastal states.[54] The growing opposition to Chinese emigrants in the Western states forced the U.S. government to seek to revise the Burlingame Treaty. In August 1880, three American envoys led by James B. Angell arrived in China seeking negotiations with the Chinese government.[55] The Ch'ing Court appointed Pao Yun and Li Hung-tsao, two of the Ministers of the Tsungli Yamen, as plenipotentiaries for the negotiations. After a series of offers and counter-offers, a treaty was signed on 17 November 1880.

The treaty contained four clauses, the most important one being the first which allowed the government of the United States to restrict Chinese coolie emigration when it saw fit. Clause two stipulated that Chinese who wished to trade, preach and study, would be freely admitted, and those who were already there would not be affected by the restriction. In clause three the United States reiterated its protection of local Chinese and visitors in the same manner as subjects of other countries.[56] The second and the third clauses were supposed to be concessions to China, but in fact they were merely reiterations of what the Burlingame Treaty had obtained. In retrospect, the conclusion of this treaty provided the U.S. government with the legal basis for restricting, and eventually excluding Chinese immigrants. Because of this treaty, Chinese diplomats in the United States had more difficulties protecting the overseas Chinese. The signing of this unfavourable treaty by China was a result of the combination of three factors: the desire to retain a good relationship with the United States, the lack of expert advice from the Chinese Minister in Washington, and the lack of understanding of the problems of the American Chinese.

At the time when the American envoys arrived, China was on the

---

[54]See M.R. Coolidge, *Chinese Immigration*, pp. 132-37; Tsai Shih-shan, "Reaction to Exclusion: Ch'ing Attitude Toward Overseas Chinese in the United States, 1848-1906", p. 170.

[55]For details of the Angell's mission to China, see Susan A. Capie, "James B. Angell, Minister to China 1880-1881: His Mission and the Chinese Desire for Equal Treaty Rights", in Chung-yang yen-chiu-yuan chin-tai shih yen-chiu-so (ed.), *Chung-yang yen-chiu-yuan chin-tai shih yen-chiu-so chi-k'an*, no. 11 (Taipei, 1982), pp. 273-314.

[56]For details of this treaty, see *Chung-wai t'iao-yueh hui-p'ien*, pp. 132-33; see also *Ch'ing-chi wai-chiao shih-liao*, vol. 24, pp. 12b-13b.

verge of a war with Russia over the Ili issue. The Russians were mobilising their troops and fleet. An imminent arm conflict with Russia forced China to seek friends among other Western Powers. The United States which had been friendly with China was considered vital to China's stand against Russia. The desire for good relations with the United States outweighed the rights of the American Chinese. This line of thought was clearly revealed in a letter by Li Hung-chang to the U.S. Consul-General in Tientsin in which he expressed a willingness to favourably consider U.S. demand for revision of the Burlingame Treaty.[57] As Li Hung-chang was the main figure in the conduct of Chinese foreign policy,[58] his thinking had direct bearing on negotiations with the Americans. On the lack of expert advice, Ch'en Lan-pin was partly to be blamed. Although he had submitted several reports to the Tsungli Yamen pertaining to the anti-Chinese activities of the Irish workers, and the anti-Chinese legislation passed by the state of California and Congress,[59] he had not advised the Yamen as to what course to take to remedy the deteriorating situation; nor had he advised the Yamen on how to deal with the American envoys over the coolie emigration issue. Ch'en's failure in this advisory role was perhaps due to the lack of foresight on the problem of protecting the overseas Chinese in the United States. He probably believed that by setting up consulates and by relying on treaty clauses, the local Chinese would be adequately protected. Further, he had little knowledge of American politics and his understanding of the complexity of the anti-Chinese immigration in the context of federal-state relationship was limited. Moreover, in his three year term as the first Chinese Minister to the United States, Spain and Peru, he had spent more than a year in Madrid to set up an embassy there, and to establish a consulate-general in Cuba.[60]

---

[57]See Susan A. Capie, *op. cit.*, p. 287.

[58]See Tsai Shih-shan, *op. cit.*, pp. 26–27.

[59]See "Memorial of the Tsungli Yamen to the Court relating to the American proposed restriction on Chinese coolies emigration dated 14th day of 10th moon of 6th year of Kuang-hsu (16 November 1880), in *Ch'ing-chi wai-chiao shih-liao*, vol. 24, pp. 8b–9a.

[60]Ch'en stayed in Madrid from 21 May 1879 to 17 April 1880. For details, see "Memorial of Ch'en Lan-pin to the Court relating to his arrival in Spain and of presenting his credentials to the king of Spain dated 17th day of 6th moon of 5th year of Kuang-hsu (4 August 1879)" in *Ch'ing-chi wai-chiao shih-liao*, vol. 15, pp. 36b–37a; "Memorial of Ch'en Lan-pin to the Court relating to his departure from Spain for

Ch'en Lan-pin's failure to provide proper advice placed the Tsungli Yamen in a vulnerable position in its negotiations with the American envoys. Most of the Tsungli Yamen Ministers, including the two plenipotentiaries, Pao Yun and Li Hung-tsao, did not have an overall understanding of the problems facing the Chinese in the United States. They only had vague ideas about the number of Chinese there and how they were treated.[61] Furthermore they knew little about the lives and grievances of the American Chinese, nor did they know very much about the nature of the Chinese community and the value of the trade that existed between the two countries. This ignorance was revealed in a memorial in which the Yamen emphasised that restriction on Chinese emigration to the United States was also in the interest of China.[62] Partly based on this ignorance, the Chinese plenipotentiaries signed the treaty with the American envoys, and the Tsungli Yamen recommended that the Court approve it.[63] However, what the Ministers of the Yamen failed to realise was that by conceding to the American demand, China had unwittingly given away the right of its subjects to emigrate to the United States, and the treaty was used by the government of the United States as a legal basis for introducing Exclusion Laws against the Chinese in the next two and a half decades.

The Restriction Act adopted by Congress in May 1882, passed a death sentence on Chinese emigration to the United States. The Act provided for the exclusion of Chinese labourers for ten years. The "labourers" included skilled and unskilled labourers alike. All Chinese except diplomats were required to be furnished with a certificate from the Chinese government, and any Chinese who failed to comply with the law was to be deported.[64] This first American Exclusion Law against the Chinese which was enacted to carry out

---

Peru dated 4th day of 5th moon of 6th year of Kuang-hsu (11 June 1880)'', in *Ch'ing-chi wai-chiao shih-llao,* vol. 21, pp. 1a–2a.

[62]See ''Memorial of Tsungli Yamen to the Court urging it to appoint plenipotentiaries for negotiations with American envoys approved on 30th day of 7th moon of 6th year of Kuang-hsu (4 September 1880)'', in *Ch'ing-chi wai-chiao shih-liao,* vol. 22, pp. 17a and 17b.

[62]See ''Memorial of the Tsungli Yamen to the Court relating to the American proposed restriction on Chinese coolie emigration dated 14th day of 10th moon of 6th year of Kuang-hsu (16 November 1880)'', in *Ching-chi wai-chiao shih-liao,* vol. 24, p. 9b.

[63]*Ibid.,* pp. 9b–10a.

[64]See M.R. Coolidge, *Chinese Immigration,* p. 183.

the Treaty of 1880, had in fact violated the treaty itself. The U.S. government was obligated by the treaty to allow for the free movement of Chinese subjects other than the coolies, and to accord them with all the rights and privileges which were accorded to citizens of the most favoured nations.[65] Instead of fulfilling the treaty obligations, it passed the law to restrict all Chinese subjects except diplomats.[66]

CHENG TSAO-JU AND THE PROTECTION OF THE AMERICAN CHINESE, 1882–86

In response to the Exclusion Act, Cheng Tsao-ju, who succeeded Ch'en Lan-pin as the Chinese Minister in Washington, lodged strong protests with the U.S. government. Before the Bill was passed in Congress, Cheng had handed the State Department a memorandum pointing out that the proposed exclusion of twenty years for Chinese immigrants was too long, and protested against the inclusion of "skilled labourers" in the Bill, an inclusion which violated the Treaty of 1880. He pointed out further that the livelihood of many Chinese manufacturers in the United States would be threatened if the supply of "skilled labour" was stopped.[67] When the Bill was passed as an Act in May 1882, Cheng was away in Spain. Hearing of the Act he telegramed his First Secretary to protest strongly. He reiterated the points stated in his memorandum, and asserted that the length of time of exclusion, though being reduced from twenty years to ten years, was still too long for the Chinese to bear. He also appealed to the American government to allow Chinese "skilled labourers" to emigrate.[68]

Despite strong protests from the Chinese ambassador, the U.S. government persisted in its stand. It had in fact intensified its anti-

---

[65]See 2nd clause of the Treaty of 1880, in *Ch'ing-chi wai-chiao shih-liao,* vol. 24, pp. 13a and 13b; *Chung-wai t'iao-yueh hui-p'ien,* p. 132.

[66]Commenting on the violation of the treaty, Mary Roberts Coolidge rightly pointed out that "The first restriction law, enacted to carry out the treaty, suspended immigration for a period twice as long as the longest term mentioned in the negotiations, and established a system which greatly hampered the exempt classes of Chinese while visiting in this country". See M.R. Coolidge, *op. cit.,* p. 181.

[67]See "Memorandum dated 1 April 1882", in "Notes from Chinese Legation", "The Mission of Cheng Tsao-ju".

[68]See "Hsu Shau Pang, Chinese Chargé d'affaires, to Frederick Frelinghuysen, Secretary of State, dated 1 June 1882", *ibid.*

Chinese posture by amending the Exclusion Act in 1884. Under the new Act, the control over the exempted class was tightened: the certificates issued by the Chinese diplomats were required to be elaborate and closely supervised; the term "merchant" was defined to exclude hawkers and fishermen involved in the drying and shipping of fish; the certificates issued for travellers had to include the itinerary and financial standing of the person; and the certificates of identification issued by the Chinese government had to be endorsed by U.S. diplomatic officials at the port of departure and were to be produced when required.[69]

The Exclusion Act found many victims. It stopped Chinese immigration completely, and greatly undermined the status of the local Chinese who were supposed to be protected by the treaty. The Act also reinforced regional restrictive laws against the Chinese on the west coast. The unjust treatment of the Chinese in San Francisco exemplified the miseries of the Chinese there. According to the petition sent to the Chinese government during this period, the Chinese in San Francisco had "ten bitternesses" with regard to accommodation; "six unjust items" for laundrymen; and "seven difficulties" for coolies and traders.[70] The most notorious item among the "ten bitternesses" was the enforcement of the Lodging House Ordinance which was commonly known as the "Cubic Air" Ordinance. The ordinance required every lodging house to provide at least five hundred cubic feet of air-space for each adult. Those who failed to comply with the law were fined a maximum penalty of five hundred dollars or three months imprisonment.[71] The ordinance was enacted by the San Francisco Municipality in 1870, but was not enforced in the Chinese quarters until 1873.[72]

Like many overseas Chinese in other parts of the world, the Chinese in San Francisco were used to the habit of close dwelling. As they spoke the same dialects,[73] close dwelling gave them a feel-

---

[69]See M.R. Coolidge, *Chinese Immigration*, p. 185.

[70]See Chang Chih-tung, "Memorial to the Court relating to the killings of the Chinese in San Francisco and requesting the U.S. government to punish the criminals, dated 15th day of 5th moon of 12th year of Kuang-hsu (16 June 1886)", in *Ch'ing-chi wai-chiao shih-liao,* vol. 67, pp. 7a and 7b.

[71]See E.C. Sandmeyer, *The Anti-Chinese Movement in California*, p. 51.

[72]*Ibid.*, pp. 51–52; M.R. Coolidge, *op. cit.*, p. 261.

[73]See Gunther Barth, *Bitter Strength: A History of the Chinese in the United States 1850–1870* (Cambridge, Mass.), pp. 88–89.

ing of togetherness and a sense of security. Further, close dwelling was more economical and increased their capacity to save money. They were therefore willing to share living quarters, and many of them worked, ate and slept together in the crowded shophouses of Chinatown.[74] There was no strong ground for passing the law of space restriction except the argument that overcrowding would lead to filth and would breed diseases.[75] This living habit of the Chinese soon became the target for the ordinance, and many Chinese were thrown into jail because thay failed to comply to the law of space restriction. This fear of mass arrest because of inadequate living space gave rise to a commonly known term "li fang" (Ploughing the House) among the San Francisco Chinese.[76]

Among other "bitternesses" were the imprisonment of temporary boarders. Some of these waiting for ships to return to China took up temporary residence with relatives in San Francisco because they were from other distant towns and mines. The result was that many were put in jail. During the time of imprisonment, many of them contracted diseases because of poor and crowded conditions, and they also suffered the humiliation of having their queues cut off because of the untidiness of their hair.[77]

Among the "six unjust items" applied to Chinese laundrymen were rules requiring the renovation of their wooden laundry houses. This would involve substantial sums of money and would dislocate the staff. Further, rules were made against the wooden awnings used for drying clothes in the Chinese laundryhouses. Complaints were also made about the harassment of arrest and fines imposed on staff.[78]

Among the "seven difficulties" were the difficulties of maintaining business, of resisting robberies and of obtaining official protection. Besides, there were other unforeseen difficulties of working as coolies and traders.[79]

---

[74]This habit of close dwelling was very widespread in overseas Chinese communities in the nineteenth century. This practice still exists in some parts of the Chinese communities in Southeast Asia.

[75]E.C. Sandmeyer, *op. cit.*, p. 51.

[76]See Chang Chih-tung's memorial, in *Ch'ing-chi wai-chiao shih-liao*, vol. 67, p. 7a.

[77]*Ibid.*

[78]*Ibid.*, p. 7b.

[79]*Ibid.*

These "ten bitternesses", "six unjust items" and "seven difficulties" reveal the deprivation of the Chinese under the enforcement of the local and federal restrictive laws. Worst of all was the
fact that the victims were not given the basic democratic right to defend themselves in court, particularly in the state of California
where Chinese testimony was not admitted in cases against Cauca-
sians.[80] The Chinese had to depend entirely on U.S. judiciary for
justice. But because of growing anti-Chinese feeling in the community and the influence of extremist politicians, justice meted out
to the Chinese victims was remote or non-existent.

The introduction of the federal Exclusion Law also intensified
the anti-Chinese movement. Many of the extremists saw their actions "legalised", and under the cover of the law, they attempted
to drive out the Chinese by force and organised demonstrations
which agitated mob violence. This resulted in assault, arson, and
the plundering and killing of the Chinese. On many occasions, the
murderers got away without any punishment. This of course encouraged further violence against the Chinese. It was amidst this
growing anti-Chinese movement that the famous Rock Springs
Massacre occurred in 1885.

The massacre took place in Rock Springs, Wyoming, on 2 September. That morning, a group of thirty white miners demonstrated
through the town. With the support of the anti-Chinese organisation, the Knights of Labour, the group became more agitated and
was determined to take violent action.[81] At two in the afternoon,
the group grew larger and many of them were armed with rifles.
They marched through the main street of the town shouting slogans
and asking for support. They were soon joined by some 150 angry
men and women.[82] They first attacked Chinese railwaymen, and
then marched towards the Chinese quarters. They fired at the
Chinese on sight and indiscriminately attacked Chinese houses.[83]
They killed, burned and plundered. The mob also marched towards

---

[80]See M.R. Coolidge, *Chinese Immigration*, p. 256.

[81]See "Statement of Ralph Zwicky, an eyewitness, dated 18 September 1885", in
Enclosure no. 1, "Cheng Tsao-ju to T.F. Bayard dated 30 November 1885", in
"Notes from Chinese Legation", "The Mission of Cheng Tsao-ju 1881–1885".

[82]*Ibid.*

[83]See "Testimony of W.H. O'Donnell, an eyewitness, dated 19 September,
1885", in Enclosure no. 1, "Cheng Tsao-ju to T.F. Bayard dated 30 November
1885", *ibid.*

the neighbouring mines and killed several Chinese miners. As they ran wild for the rest of the day, the Chinese residents fled to the hills for refuge, and the entire Chinatown was set on fire.[84] The result of the massacre was twenty-eight Chinese killed, fifteen seriously injured; and properties valued about US$147,000 destroyed.[85] The surviving Chinese had fled on 5 September to Evanston, a neighbouring town, but their safety was threatened by some hostile whites. It was not until 9 September, that the U.S. army came to their rescue and escorted them back to Rock Springs.[86]

What triggered off the massacre appears to be the dispute over the allocation of rooms in a coal-pit operated by the Union Pacific Railroad Company in Wyoming Territory. A fight ensued, and a few Chinese were wounded.[87] In fact tension between Chinese and white miners in Rock Springs had been building up for a long time. Since the arrival of the Chinese miners in November 1875,[88] white miners had begun to feel threatened. This was especially so as the number of Chinese miners increased. By the time the massacre broke out, Chinese miners outnumbered white miners by more than two to one, with the figure of 331 to 150.[89] This inevitably gave rise to jealousy, prejudice and ill-feeling.

---

[84]*Ibid.*

[85]See "Report of the Chinese Consul at New York dated 5 October 1885", in Enclosure no. 2, "Cheng Tsao-ju to T.F. Bayard dated 30 November 1885", in "Notes from Chinese Legation", "The Mission of Cheng Tsao-ju"; "Cable from Cheng Tsao-ju to the Tsungli Yamen dated 22nd day of 9th moon of 11th year of Kuang-hsu (29 October 1885)", in *Ch'ing-chi wai-chiao shih-liao*, vol. 61, p. 18.

[86]See "Memorial of Chinese Labourers: Resident at Rock Springs, Wyoming Territory, to the Chinese Consul at New York of the Examining Commission dated 18 September 1885", in Enclosure no. 2, "Cheng Tsao-ju to T.F. Bayard dated 30 November 1885", in "Notes from Chinese Legation", "The Mission of Cheng Tsao-ju"; "Petition of 56 Chinese from A-lu-mei of the Wyoming Territory to the Consul of New York dated 17th day of 8th moon of 11th year of Kuang-hsu (25 September 1885)", in Tsungli Yamen Archives, Ko-lu ch'ing-tang, vol. 273, reproduced in Chu Shih-chia (ed.), *Mei-kuo po-hai hua-kung shih-liao*, pp. 78–79.

[78]See "Testimony of J.H. Dickey", "Statement of R. Zwicky" and "Memorial of Chinese Labourers", in Enclosures nos. 1 & 2, "Cheng Tsao-ju to T.F. Bayard dated 30 November 1885", in "Notes from Chinese Legation", "The Mission of Cheng Tsao-ju".

[88]See "Testimony of O.C. Smith, Postmaster of Rock Springs dated 18 September 1885", in Enclosure no. 1, *ibid.*

[89]See Alexander Saxton, *The Indispensable Enemy: Labor and the Anti-Chinese Movement in California*, p. 202.

The Chinese were not only considered by the white miners as threats to their jobs, but were also seen as presenting a serious obstacle to white unionism, because Chinese miners refused to join the unions, and refused to have anything to do with strikes. This made strikes impossible, and undermined any effort for wage demand.[90] In the eyes of many white miners, the Chinese were guilty of undermining their rights and liberties.[91] In short, the Chinese were seen as the willing tools of the "capitalists" to suppress wage demand, and the Chinese had to be driven out before "wage justice" could be obtained. Underlying this animosity against the Chinese lay the different attitudes between Chinese and white miners towards authority. Under the increasing influence of unionism at the time, the white miners felt they had the "legitimate right" to demand a higher share of profit with the "capitalists", and they had the right to strike in order to achieve this objective. On the other hand, the Chinese were traditionally brought up to respect and fear authority; they were submissive and obedient. The Confucian concept of "mutual responsibility" led them to believe that if they behaved well, their well-being would be looked after by the employers. Further, they did not understand modern unionism, they feared the consequences of being sacked if they became involved in unions or strikes. They therefore rejected the idea of strikes.[92]

The anti-Chinese sentiment in Rock Springs found its concrete expression in the formation of a branch of the Knights of Labour in 1883, two years before the massacre.[93] The Knights of Labour, founded in 1869, was a national organisation fighting mainly for the interests of white labourers.[94] The founding of its branch in Rock Springs became the rallying point for local anti-Chinese elements. Available evidence points to the Knights of Labour as the

---

[90]See "Memorial of Chinese Labourers", "Testimony of W.H. O'donnell", "Testimony of J.H. Dickey" and "Statement of A.C. Beckwith dated 21 September 1885", in Enclosure nos. 1 & 2, "Cheng Tsao-ju to T.F. Bayard dated 30 November 1885", in "Notes from Chinese Legation", "The Mission of Cheng Tsao-ju".

[91]See "Letter from Thomas Neasham, Chairman of Knights of Labour, Denver, to the General Manager and the President of the Union Pacific Railway dated 19 September 1885", in Enclosure no. 2, *ibid.*

[92]See "Memorial of Chinese Laborers", in Enclosure no. 2, *ibid.*

[93]See "Testimony of O.C. Smith" and "Memorial of Chinese Laborers", in Enclosure nos. 1 & 2, *ibid.*

[94]Alexander Saxton, *op. cit.*, p. 40.

main force behind the outbreak of the massacre. In August 1885, anti-Chinese leaflets were widely distributed in the town by the organisation. On the eve of the outrage, the bell of the Knights' building rang, and a meeting for action against the Chinese was called.[95] The white miners who started the fight in the coal-pit were alleged to be members of the Knights,[96] and the Knights had quickly rendered its support for violence.[97]

The involvement of the Knights of Labour is further demonstrated in its action after the massacre. On 19 September, slightly more than two weeks after the event, the Denver's branch of the Knights sent an official letter to the management of the Union Pacific Railroad Company demanding expulsion of the Chinese from all mines operated by the company.[98] Based on such evidence one may even conclude that the massacre was engineered and executed by the Knights and the dispute over allocation of rooms was planned rather than incidental. The massacre was probably meant to form a part of an organised violence to drive out the Chinese from the west coast of the United States, for there were simultaneous attacks and killings of the Chinese in Tacoma and Seattle in the Washington Territory.[99]

The Rock Springs massacre, in retrospect, was an important landmark in China's changing attitude towards protection of its overseas subjects in the United States. It greatly attracted the attention of the Tsungli Yamen and some high ranking officials, and compelled them to take a firmer stand on this issue. The result of this firmer stand was a minor diplomatic victory for China — the United States promised to compensate the victims of the massacre.

---

[95] See "Memorial of Chinese Labourers", in Enclosure no. 2, "Cheng Tsao-ju to T.F. Bayard dated 30 November 1885", in "Notes from Chinese Legation", "The Mission of Cheng Tsao-ju".

[96] See "Report of F.A. Bee, Consul at San Francisco dated 30 September 1885", in Enclosure no. 1, *ibid.*

[97] See "Statement of R. Zwickey", in Enclosure no. 1, *ibid.*

[98] See "Letter from Thomas Neasham, Chairman of Knights of Labor, Denver, to the General Manager and the President of the Union Pacific Railway dated 19 September 1885", in Enclosure no. 2, *ibid.*

[99] For details of anti-Chinese outbreaks in Tacoma and Seattle in 1885–86, see J.L. Karlin, "The Anti-Chinese Outbreak in Tacoma, 1885", in *Pacific Historical Review*, vol. 23 (1954), pp. 271–83; J.L. Karlin, "The Anti-Chinese Outbreaks in Seattle, 1885–1886", in *Pacific Northwest Quarterly*, vol. 39 (April, 1948), pp. 103–30.

The minor victory was mainly due to efforts of the Chinese Minister in Washington and the Governor-General of Kwangtung and Kwangsi, Chang Chih-tung.

The role of Cheng Tsao-ju, the Chinese Minister, was an important one. Little is known about him except that he was a Cantonese.[100] Cheng proved to be a competent diplomat who dared to stand up in defence of China's treaty rights. When he succeeded Ch'en Lan-pin in 1881 as the Chinese Minister for the United States, Peru and Spain, he began to fight for the right to set up a consulate to protect the Chinese in the Spanish colony of the Philippines. He resumed negotiations with the Spanish Foreign Office which was initiated by his predecessor Ch'en Lan-pin. Although Cheng failed in his objective, the failure was due mainly to the intransigence of the Spanish rather than to his incompetence. During the prolonged negotiations, he had demonstrated his diplomatic acumen. He attempted to establish concrete evidence to prove that the Chinese in the Philippines were ill-treated so that he would have a good case in dealing with the Spanish.[101] Cheng further demonstrated his diplomatic skill in handling the Rock Springs Massacre and other associated incidents.

As soon as Cheng received the news of the massacre, he sent his Counsellor to call on the State Department and requested for stern action to quell the situation with troops and to apprehend the murderers. At the same time, he instructed a Chinese mission to proceed immediately to Rock Springs for a thorough investigation.[102] He further requested the State Department to send an official to accompany the Chinese representatives.[103] The move of conducting a post-mortem investigation was a shrewd one. By so doing, concrete evidence would be obtained, and responsibility for the massacre would be firmly established. Cheng realised that without verified

---

[100]See Fang Chao-ying, "Chang Yin-huan", in A.W. Hummel (ed.), *Eminent Chinese of the Ch'ing Period: 1644–1912* (Reprint, Taipei, 1970), p. 62.

[101]See Edgar Wickberg, *The Chinese in Philippine Life 1850–1898* (New Haven), pp. 214–15.

[102]See "Cable of Cheng Tsao-ju to Tsungli Yamen dated 14th day of 8th moon of 11th year of Kuang-hsu (22 September 1885)", original copy is kept at the Historical Archives of the Bureau of National Archives of the People's Republic of China, reproduced in Chu Shih-chia (ed.), *Mei-kuo po-hai hua-kung shih-liao*, p. 110.

[103]See "Cheng Tsao-ju to T.F. Bayard dated 11 September 1885", in "Notes from Chinese Legation", "The Mission of Cheng Tsao-ju".

evidence, China's claim for redress would be legally unsound, and any diplomatic battle in the future would be lost. The Chinese mission consisted of Huang Hsi-ch'uan, the Consul of New York; Colonel Frederick A. Bee, the Chinese Consul of San Francisco; and an interpreter named Tseng Hoy. They arrived in Rock Springs on 18 September. To facilitate the investigation, Colonel Bee was to interview white residents and eyewitnesses, while Huang and Tseng were to collect evidence from the Chinese victims.[104] Colonel Bee managed to collect testimonies from some respectable citizens who witnessed the outrage.[105] Huang Hsi-ch'uan, with the support of American officials, inspected the scene. He ordered the remains of the victims to be disinterred and examined. Fourteen coffins were dug up and opened, and other burial sites were also carefully examined. He found five bodies, the remains of eight recognisable bodies, and the bones and parts of another twelve bodies which were unidentifiable. The bodies of another three who were believed to have been killed, could not be found. He also found that fifteen Chinese had been severely wounded; several of them would later die and several would be disabled for life. He estimated the loss of properties in the riot to be US$147,749.[106] Both Colonel Bee and Huang Hsi-ch'uan then presented their findings to the Chinese Minister at Washington.

After acquiring the necessary evidence and after consultation with his legal adviser, Cheng requested the U.S. government to punish the murderers, and to indemnify the victims. He cabled the Tsungli Yamen and urged it to be firm on the issue,[107] and requested

---

[104]See "Report of F.A. Bee dated 30 September 1885", in Enclosure no. 1, "Cheng Tsao-ju to T.F. Bayard dated 30 November 1885", in "Notes from Chinese Legation", "The Mission of Cheng Tsao-ju".

[105]Bee had encountered some difficulties in collecting testimonies, for those who denounced the outrage publicly were threatened by the anti-Chinese elements. See "Report of F.A. Bee", *ibid.*

[106]See "Report of the Chinese Consul at New York, dated 5 October 1885", and its attached lists of killed, wounded and estimate of property losses, in Enclosure no. 2, "Cheng Tsao-ju to T.J. Bayard dated 30 November 1885", in "Notes from Chinese Legation", "The Mission of Cheng Tsao-ju"; "Cable from Cheng Tsao-ju to the Tsungli Yamen relating to the killing of Chinese coal mining workers dated 22nd day of 9th moon of 11th year of Kuang-hsu (29 October 1885)", in *Ch'ing-chi wai-chiao shih-liao,* vol. 61, pp. 18a and 18b; "Cable from Cheng Tsao-ju to the Tsungli Yamen dated 26th day of 10th moon of 11th year of Kuang-hsu (2 December 1885)", in *Ch'ing-chi wai-chiao shih-liao,* vol. 61, p. 37a.

[107]See the above cable dated 2 December 1885, *ibid.*

information relating to China's payment of indemnity to American victims in China.[108] Cheng obviously had in mind that with this information he would be better equipped to negotiate for indemnity. To further strengthen his position, Cheng cabled Li Hung-chang and Chang Chih-tung for support. Li was influential at the Court — over the Tsungli Yamen and China's foreign policy as a whole, his support would be politically and diplomatically useful. Chang Chih-tung was the Governor-General of Kwangtung and Kwangsi provinces that had the closest relationship with the American Chinese. He was also the rising star in Chinese politics at the time.[109] Cheng calculated that Chang's support would add additional weight to his actions.

Cheng's claim was vigorous and firm, his arguments were logically sound and legally impeachable. His official despatch to Secretary T.F. Bayard dated 30 November 1885 has been hailed by an American scholar as "one of the most dignified, discriminating and logical documents ever presented by a Chinese diplomat before the time of the brilliant Minister Wu (T'ing-fang)".[110] In this document, Cheng emphasised at the outset that the Chinese were innocent, well-behaved and law-abiding. They were not the cause, but the victims, of the massacre.[111] He charged the local authorities for their negligence in duty to suppress the riot, and for allowing the mob to run uncontrolled for twelve continuous hours.[112] Cheng was incensed to read Consul Bee's report that none of the murderers would be brought to trial by the local authorities.[113] He therefore demanded severe punishment for those who were guilty of murder, robbery and arson. He also demanded that victims be indemnified, and U.S. protection for Chinese nationals from similar attacks.[114] He reminded the Secretary that the U.S. government was obligated to

---

[108]See "Cable from Cheng Tsao ju to the Tsungli Yamen dated 14th day of 8th moon of 11th year of Kuang-hsu (22 September 1885)", in Chu Shih-chia (ed.), *op. cit.*, p. 110.

[109]See L.E. Eastman, *Throne and Mandarins: China's Search for a Policy During the Sino-French Controversy 1880–1885*, pp. 206–22.

[110]See M.R. Coolidge, *Chinese Immigration*, pp. 271–72.

[111]See "Despatch from Cheng Tsao-ju to T.F. Bayard dated 30 November 1885" (original), pp. 4–5, in "Notes from Chinese Legation", "The Mission of Cheng Tsao-ju".

[112]*Ibid.*, pp. 5 and 7.

[113]*Ibid.*, p. 6.

[114]*Ibid.*, p. 8.

protect Chinese nationals in the territories under its jurisdiction.[115] Much of the contents of the despatch centred on China's claim for indemnity. Cheng argued that the idea and practice of indemnification came from the West, and that American diplomats had insisted on this practice and had used gunboats to enforce it.[116] He produced facts and figures to show that China had on many occasions indemnified American citizens for losses incurred in riots and violence.[117] He pointed out that the principle of "reciprocal justice and comity" was not only part of international law, but was also embodied in the moral codes of China and the United States.[118] To reinforce his legal claim, Cheng also used the traditional Confucian approach of moral persuasion. He cited the case of U.S. indemnification of the Spanish victims in a riot that had occurred in New Orleans in 1851, as the best example of the United States upholding its high principles of equity and national comity, and urged the United States to maintain its high moral standard.[119] Cheng also implied that if the U.S. government could not concede indemnification as part of its treaty obligation, it could at least do it as a gesture of good will.

Cheng's despatch was ignored by Secretary Bayard for some time. It was not until 19 February 1886 (two and a half months later) that Cheng received the first official reply from the Secretary.[120] It is clear that the Secretary tried to evade any legal and treaty responsibilities on behalf of the U.S. government. He attempted to find excuses by arguing that security was inadequate in Rock Springs because of its remoteness, and the suspected murderers were foreign immigrants who were of different racial stock. He even tried to

---

[115]*Ibid.*, p. 31.

[116]*Ibid.*, p. 23.

[117]*Ibid.*, pp. 18–20; see also "The Chinese Indemnity Claims (by the United States)", in Enclosure no. 3, "Despatch from Cheng Tsao-ju to T.F. Bayard dated 30 November 1885", in "Notes from Chinese Legation", "The Mission of Cheng Tsao-ju".

[118]See the despatch, *ibid.*, p. 14.

[119]*Ibid.*, pp. 26–28.

[120]Cheng reported to the Tsungli Yamen that he did not receive Bayard's reply until 16th day of 1st moon of 12th year of Kuang-hsu (19 February 1886). See "Despatch from Cheng Tsao-ju to the Tsungli Yamen dated 10th day of 4th moon of 12th year of Kuang-hsu (13 May 1886)", in Chu Shih-chia (ed.), *op. cit.*, p. 93. But in a separate despatch to Secretary Bayard, he acknowledged receipt of Bayard's reply dated 18 February 1886. See "Cheng Tsao-ju to T.F. Bayard dated 5 March 1886", in "Notes from Chinese Legation", "The Mission of Cheng Tsao-ju".

shift the blame to the Chinese miners by claiming that their refusal to support strikes was contributory to the riots.[121] He concluded that the victims would not be indemnified in accordance with treaty agreements and American convention, but he pointed out that the claim could be considered specially by grace of the President of the United States in consultation with Congress.[122]

Bayard's reply demonstrated the hypocrisy of the U.S. government. It had forced the Chinese government to fulfil treaty obligations to protect American nationals in China, but attempted to evade its responsibility to protect the Chinese in the United States. Cheng Tsao-ju was quick to point out its hypocrisy and irresponsible attitude, and refuted Bayard's arguments. In another important despatch to the Secretary dated 15 April 1886, he emphasised that the responsibility of protecting Chinese nationals rested squarely on the U.S. Federal government rather than on individual state authorities, for it was the Federal, not the state, that entered into treaty with China.[123] He refuted Bayard's theory that the treaty clauses could not be equally applied to both countries because of different conditions and customs. He argued that the main aim behind the conclusion of the Sino-American treaties was to promote good relationship between the two countries, and both should closely adhere to the specifications of the treaty agreements.[124] He reiterated the principle of reciprocity, and pointed out that the Rock Springs Massacre was a serious case. As the U.S. government failed to protect the lives and properties of the Chinese nationals, China had the legal and treaty right to demand for indemnity.[125]

Cheng's vigorous claim might have contributed in part to the softening of the attitude of the U.S. government towards this issue. But it seems that the threat of Chang Chih-tung in making retaliation against Americans did more to change the American attitude. As the Governor-General of Kwangtung and Kwangsi, where the

---

[121]See "Despatch from Cheng Tsao-ju to the Tsungli Yamen dated 10th day of 4th moon of 12th year of Kuang-hsu (13 May 1886)", in Chu Shih-chia (ed.), op. cit., p. 94.

[122]Ibid.

[123]See "Cheng Tsao-ju to T.F. Bayard dated 15 April 1886", in "Notes from Chinese Legation", "The Mission of Cheng Tsao-ju". The Chinese version of this despatch is found in Chu Shih-chia (ed.), op. cit., pp. 91–93.

[124]Ibid.

[125]Ibid.

majority of the American Chinese originated, Chang naturally became concerned about the Rock Springs Massacre and its implications. He was closely informed by Cheng Tsao-ju about the claim for indemnity and its development. At the same time, Chang Chih-tung also received petitions from the Chinese merchants in San Francisco relating to their miseries in the United States.[126] Prompted by these events, Chang took the initiative to meet with the U.S. Minister in China, Charles Denby, to discuss the problem of protection of the American Chinese. What actually happened in the meeting is uncertain. Chang's own report to the Tsungli Yamen only mentioned that the meeting was cordial, and that the Minister expressed regret that his government was unable to protect Chinese nationals effectively.[127] But Chang was reported by Hong Kong newspapers as having telegramed the Chinese legation in Washington intimidating reprisals against the Americans in Kwangtung unless China's demand was acted upon.[128] Although Chang later denied making such a threat, he had nevertheless communicated a warning to the U.S. Consul in Canton that an unsatisfactory solution to the indemnity claim would provoke the ill-feeling of the people against the Americans in Kwangtung.[129] Judging from his tough stand against Russia and France during the Ili Crisis and the Sino-French conflict over Vietnam in the 1880s,[130] Chang was capable of making such a threat, and was likely to have sent that in-

---

[126]See "Cable from Chang Chih-tung to the Tsungli Yamen dated 20th day of 1st moon of 12th year of Kuang-hsu (23 February 1886)", in Ch'ing-chi wai-chiao shih-liao, vol. 66, p. 12.

[127]Ibid.

[128]See "Telegram from Smithers, U.S. Acting Consul-General in Shanghai, to Charles Denby dated 6 March 1886", Enclosure 1 in no. 109, in U.S. State Department, Papers Relating to Foreign Relations of the United States, 1886 (Washington, 1887), p. 78; "Cable from the Court to Chang Chih-tung dated 4th day of 2nd moon of 12th year of Kuang-hsu (9 March 1886), in Ch'ing-chi wai-chiao shih-liao, vol. 64, p. 9.

[129]See "Communication from Chang Chih-tung to Charles Seymour, U.S. Consul in Canton, dated 11 March 1886", Inclosures in No. 117, in U.S. State Department, Papers Relating to Foreign Relations of the United States, 1886, p. 62.

[130]During the Ili crisis, Chang belonged to the "War Party" advocating military solution to the dispute over Ili with Russia. During the Sino-French war over Vietnam, Chang again advocated military action against the French. See Immanuel C.Y. Hsu, The Ili Crisis, pp. 70–77; W. Ayers, Chang Chih-tung and Educational Reform in China, pp. 85–87; L.E. Eastman, Throne and Mandarins: China's Search for a Policy during the Sino-French Controversy 1880–1885, pp. 98, 195–98.

timidating telegram to support Cheng Tsao-ju's move. It is not important to establish whether the threat was a bluff or a real one, what is relevant is that it probably provoked some serious thoughts in the minds of the President and Congressmen regarding the consequences for refusing to give in to the Chinese demand. It was probably due to this consideration that Congress in June 1886, at the request of the President, appropriated US$150,000 to compensate for the property loss of the Chinese, but there was no indemnity for the twenty-eight lives lost in the massacre.[131]

CHANG YIN-HUAN AND THE PROTECTION OF THE AMERICAN CHINESE, 1886-89

The protection of the overseas Chinese in the United States in the years between 1886 and 1893 was difficult to achieve. Although the killings of the Chinese gradually eased, this period saw the tightening of the legislative grip on the Chinese immigrants exemplified by the Scott Act of 1888 and the Geary Law of 1892. The Chinese Ministers in Washington, Chang Yin-huan and Tsui Kuo-yin, had concentrated their efforts in fighting against these unjust laws.

Chang Yin-huan, a native of Nan-hai, Kwangtung, was an able administrator, an expert on coastal defence and foreign affairs.[132] In 1876 while he was the acting magistrate of Chefoo, he assisted Li Hung-chang in negotiating with the British over the famous Margary Affair.[133] He was appointed a probationary member of the Tsungli Yamen in June 1884.[134] His involvement in the Tsungli Yamen gave him direct access to first-hand reports of Chinese Ministers overseas, and enhanced his knowledge on overseas Chinese affairs. His appointment to the position of Chinese Minister to the United States, Peru and Spain in 1885 in the height of tough negotiations was a clear recognition of his expertise in this area. When Chang arrived in Washington to take up his new appointment in 1886, his predecessor Cheng Tsao-ju was instructed by the Court to help Chang

---

[131]See the document sent by Chang Yin-huan to the Tsungli Yamen relating to the Rock Springs indemnity discussed by Congress, in Tsungli Yamen Archives, ko-lu ch'ing-tang, no. 274.

[132]For details about Chang's career, see Fang Chao-ying, "Chang Yin-huan", A.W. Hummel (ed.), *Eminent Chinese of the Ch'ing Period 1644-1912*, pp. 60–64.

[133]For details of the Margary Affair, see Immanuel C.Y. Hsu, *China's Entrance into the Family of Nations: The Diplomatic Phase 1858-1880*, pp. 176–70.

[134]A.W. Hummel (ed.), *op. cit.*, p. 61.

negotiate the settlements of the Rock Springs Massacre and other anti-Chinese riots.[135] Chang continued Cheng's unfinished work and successfully obtained the indemnity.

In dealing with the anti-Chinese problem in the United States, Chang offered no new solution. He had to implement Cheng Tsao-ju's idea of a self-imposed restriction on Chinese coolie emigration. Cheng in January 1886 presented the Tsungli Yamen a plan for the solution of the anti-Chinese problem in the United States. Cheng considered the main source of trouble to be the resentment of American workers[136] towards Chinese coolies, and this feeling was accentuated by a rapid growth of Chinese coolies in the Western states of America. He believed that a permanent solution to the problem was a self-imposed ban on Chinese emigration.[137] According-ing to his plan, China was to prohibit all coolie emigrants to the United States, including those who returned from the United States and wished to go back. China was to negotiate with the British authorities to help implement the ban — ships leaving Hong Kong for the United States were to be prohibited from carrying coolies. Besides, two measures were to be taken to ensure emigration of genuine Chinese merchants: the U.S. government was to be urged to allow its consul in Hong Kong to issue visas for intending merchants; the intending merchants had to be sponsored by the Chinese merchants in the United States with the approval of the local Chinese Consul-General and had to have the endorsement of the American Consul in Hong Kong.[138] Cheng expected several advantages to accrue from the implementation of this plan. It would prevent ignorant coolies from falling into the clutches of dishonest coolie brokers; it would earn respect from foreigners who despised the Chinese because many Chinese had to eke out their livelihood overseas; it would gain sympathy from the President and the Secretary of State and this would indirectly benefit the American Chinese; it

---

[135]See reference made in Chang Yin-huan's memorial to the Court dated 15th day of 5th moon of 12th year of Kuang-hsu (16 June 1886), in *Ch'ing-chi wai-chiao shih-liao*, vol. 80, p. 27.

[136]Cheng used a term "t'u-jen" (native) to generalise the opposition of American workers to the Chinese coolies. Cheng made no attempt to differentiate terms like "t'u-jen" from "Mei chi kung-jen" (American worker).

[137]See "Correspondence from Cheng Tsao-ju to the Tsungli Yamen dated 16th day of 12th moon of 11th year of Kuang-hsu (20 January 1886)", reproduced in Chu Shih-chia, *Mei-kuo po-hai hua-kung shih-liao*, pp. 130–32.

[138]*Ibid.*

would diminish hostility against the Chinese among the Americans; and it would further ease U.S. resentment towards Chinese merchants.[139]

Cheng's scheme, though possibly diplomatically naive, was an effective way of easing the growing conflict between white workers and the Chinese coolies in the United States. He realised that Chinese diplomats had no gunboats to resort to, and China had no effective means to enforce her treaty rights, and the only alternative was to stop Chinese emigrants from coming into the United States. To provide prospective emigrants with alternative places to earn a livelihood, he suggested they be urged to emigrate to countries like Hawaii, Mexico and Panama.[140]

The Tsungli Yamen accepted Cheng Tsao-ju's proposal and recommended it to the Court. In August 1886, the Yamen informed the U.S. Minister to China, Charles Denby, to that effect. But it pointed out that the scheme should be taken as a protest against the U.S. failure in protecting Chinese nationals. It suggested details of the scheme to be negotiated between the new Chinese Minister in Washington and the Secretary of State.[141]

Chang Yin-huan was thus asked by the Yamen to negotiate a treaty with the U.S. government, and preliminary contact was made in February 1887.[142] Serious negotiations did not begin until 18 March 1887 when Chang called on Bayard and handed him a fifteen-point proposal setting out all the conditions.[143] After sporadic negotiations,[144] both sides reached an agreement, and a treaty was signed

---

[139]*Ibid.*, p. 132.

[140]*Ibid.*, p. 130.

[141]See "Correspondence from Tsungli Yamen to the Minister Denby dated 4th day of 7th moon of 12th year of Kuang-hsu (3 August 1886)", reproduced in Chu Shih-chia (ed.), *Mei-kuo po-hai hua-kung shih-liao*, pp. 120–21.

[142]See Chang Yin-huan, *San-chou jih-chi* (My Diary of the Three Continents) (Kyoto, 1896), vol. 3, pp. 14b–15a, 17th day of 1st moon of 13th year of Kuang-hsu (9 February 1887).

[143]See the document entitled "Negotiations for the Protection of the Chinese in the United States" presented by Chang Yin-huan to Secretary Bayard on 8 March 1887, in "Notes from Chinese Legation", "The Mission of Chang Yin-huan, April 1886 to September 1889"; Chang Yin-huan, *op. cit.*, vol. 3, pp. 53b–54a, 24th day of 2nd moon of 13th year of Kuang-hsu (18 March 1887).

[144]The negotiation stopped for few months after April 1887, because Chang Yin-huan had left Washington for Spain. It resumed again in August 1887 and continued through the year. On 2 March 1888, Chang had a meeting with Secretary Bayard to finalise the agreement which led to the signing of the treaty on 12 March 1888. See

on 12 March 1888. Four important points were included in the treaty. First, Chinese coolies would be totally banned from coming to the United States for twenty years. Second, the ban would not apply to coolies who, in the United States, had parents, wife and children, or property valued at one thousand dollars or more; these coolies would be issued with re-entry permits by the United States authorities. Third, the ban would not apply to Chinese subjects who studied, traded and travelled in the United States; further, Chinese coolies in transit would, as before, also enjoy this privilege. Fourth, Chinese residents in the United States would be given all the rights of the most favoured nation except naturalisation, and the United States reaffirmed its intention "to exert all its power to secure protection to the persons and property of all Chinese subjects in the United States".[145]

The signing of the treaty elicited unfavourable response. Some foreign observers in London considered the new treaty as a scandal committed by China, for the Chinese Minister in Washington had willingly given away treaty rights. The status of the Chinese subjects in the United States, according to these observers, would therefore be reduced lower than that of the subjects of Japan, Korea and Thailand.[146] The signing also gave rise to a wave of protest. The Chinese merchants of San Francisco, Hong Kong and Canton expressed their hostility towards the new treaty. Under the leadership of Ch'en Hsuan-liang, they petitioned Chang Chih-tung and Li Hung-chang to help prevent the Court from ratifying the treaty. The petitioners pointed out the self-imposed ban was a suicidal act and the total prohibition of Chinese coolie emigration would mean the end of the overseas Chinese in the United States. They estimated that each year about three thousand Chinese died in the United States, and few thousands more returned to China. The Chinese population in the United States which was estimated at over one

---

"Chang Yin-huan (Chang Yen Hoon) to T.F. Bayard dated 16 August, 1887", "Chang Yin-huan to Bayard dated 30 January 1888" and "Chang Yin-huan to Bayard dated 3 March 1888", in "Notes from the Chinese Legation", "The Mission of Chang Yin-huan, April 1886 to September 1889".

[145]See "Memorial from Chang Yin-huan to the Court relating to the signing of a treaty with the State Department of the United States dated 8th day of 4th moon of 14th year of Kuang-hsu (18 May 1888)", in Ch'ing-chi wai-chiao shih-liao, vol. 76, pp. 1b–2b; M.R. Coolidge, op. cit., p. 194.

[146]See Li Hung-chang, Li wen-chung kung ch'uan-chi, vol. 5, p. 491.

hundred thousand, would disappear completely after twenty years.[147] They further pointed out that many Chinese merchants in Canton, Hong Kong and San Francisco had depended for much of their business on coolie labourers who obtained their dairy foodstuff, domestic utensils, medicines and clothing from China, and the value of this was estimated to be in the vicinity of ten million taels. The total ban of the Chinese coolie emigration would mean the end of their business and also the loss of ten million taels worth of export for China.[148] The petitioners also warned that if the total ban was to come about and if the American example was followed by other Colonial Powers in Southeast Asia, the result would be a disaster. Hundreds and thousands of coolies would be driven back to Kwangtung and Fukien without the means of acquiring a livelihood. They would become a source of trouble for the empire.[149]

Of course some of the statements in the petitions were exaggerated to impress the Chinese authorities, but most of the points were well founded. A complete ban of Chinese coolie emigration to the United States for twenty years would dwindle the Chinese population there to an insignificant number. It is true to claim that business in Canton and Hong Kong, and to a certain extent China's overseas trade, would be affected as a result of the ban. It is also true that a disaster would be likely to occur if all coolies returned to China. However what had not been disclosed in the petitions was the vested interests of the coolie brokers in Hong Kong and San Francisco who would suffer the most severe loss as a result of the ban. According to one estimate, these coolie brokers would stand to lose up to 500,000 dollars each year if the lucrative coolie trade was stopped.[150] How many of the petitioners were coolie brokers is difficult to ascertain. Chang Yin-huan, later, in defending his sign-

---

[147]The original petition is no longer in existence. The extract of it is contained in Chang Chih-tung's memorial to the Court. See Chang Chih-tung, *Chang Wen-hsiang kung ch'uan-chi*, vol. 1, pp. 495-96.

[148]*Ibid.*

[149]*Ibid.*

[150]Chang Yin-huan stated that each coolie was to pay $170 to coolie brokerage firms in Hong Kong so as to get into the United States. Apart from the cost of $50 passage, the coolie merchants were to reap in profits of at least $100 per head. According to Chang, at least 5,000 coolies were shipped to the United States at that time, and the profit accrued to $500,000 each year. See Chang Yin-huan, "Memorial to the Court dated 29th day of 2nd moon of 15th year of Kuang-hsu (30 March 1889)", in *Ch'ing-chi wai-chiao shih-liao*, vol. 79, p. 29b.

ing of the new treaty claimed that the coolie brokers in Hong Kong were the main force behind the petitions. He claimed that through connection with K'uang Ch'i-chao, an interpreter in the office of the Governor of Kwangtung, they had created public opinion against the new treaty.[151] Chang even claimed that the so called "public outrage" was in fact the work of one person (K'uang Ch'i-chao).[152] Whatever the truth behind Chang's claim, it seems reasonable to suggest that the coolie brokers who stood to lose most, were deeply involved in stirring up "public opinion" against the new treaty.

In response to the petitions and "public opinion", both Li Hung-chang and Chang Chih-tung recommended that the Court not ratify the new treaty. Li reminded the Tsungli Yamen of the "public outrage",[153] while Chang reiterated the petitioners' point of view, and emphasised its implications. Chang reminded the Court that signs of anti-Chinese coolies were shown in "New Gold Mountain" (Melbourne),[154] where Chinese coolies were prohibited from disembarking. If the anti-coolie movement spread to Southeast Asia, the result would be an influx of unemployed coolies roaming in the countryside of the coastal provinces, and the creation of such a situation would greatly threaten the security of the empire.[155] Due to the efforts of Li Hung-chang and Chang Chih-tung, the Court refused to ratify the new treaty.

---

[151]*Ibid.*, p. 30a.

[152]According to Chang Yin-huan, it was K'uang Ch'i-chao who acted on behalf of these coolie brokers to publicise objections in various newspapers, and to organise petitioners. *Ibid.*

[153]See "Correspondence of Li Hung-chang to the Tsungli Yamen relating to the new treaty with the United States over prohibition of Chinese coolies dated 15th day of 6th moon of 15th year of Kuang-hsu (12 July 1889)", in *Ch'ing-chi wai-chiao shih-liao*, vol. 76, p. 14b.

[154]New Gold Mountain is a translation of the Chinese name "Tsin Chin Shan" which generally referred to Melbourne, but more precisely to Ballarat, about 112 miles from Melbourne, where goldfields were discovered. Of course the name "Tsin Chin Shan" was coined in contrast to "Chiu Chin Shan" (Old Gold Mountain) which referred to San Francisco where goldfields were found earlier than that in Australia. For a brief discussion on this term and its early Chinese miners, see C.F. Yong, *New Gold Mountain: The Chinese in Australia 1901–1921* (Raphael Arts, Adelaide, 1977), pp. 1–4.

[155]See Chang Chih-tung, "Memorial to the Court transmitting the petition of Cantonese merchants in relation to the new treaty dated 14th day of 7th moon of 14th year of Kuang-hsu (21 August 1888)", in Chang Chih-tung, *Chang Wen-hsiang kung ch'uan-chi*, vol. 1, p. 496, *tsou-i*, vol. 24, pp. 27a–28b (original).

The repudiation of the new treaty was a severe blow to Chang Yin-huan's effort in solving the anti-Chinese problem in the United States. He must have felt bitter about the whole event, for he was only carrying out the Tsungli Yamen's wishes and Cheng Tsao-ju's idea. In private, he had a different plan for solving the problem. Instead of a self-imposed ban, he intended to encourage the old, sick and unemployed Chinese to return to China. By so doing, he believed he could win some sympathy and reduce the hostility against the Chinese.[156] But Chang had to bear the brunt of criticism when the policy of the Tsungli Yamen was under attack. This seems to have prompted him to memorialise the Court to defend himself.[157]

What the abortive treaty had not done to the Chinese coolie emigrants was done by a new American legislation. On hearing the news about China's refusal in ratifying the treaty, Congress and the Senate passed a new act in September 1888 to prohibit Chinese coolie labourers — this Act being known as the Scott Act.[158] The Act contained all the Americans wanted in the abortive treaty, and stated nothing about the protection of the Chinese in the United States.[159] The Act was a reaction against China's refusal in ratifying the new treaty, but it was also a clear violation of international law — the unilateral action taken by a signatory of a treaty. In particular, the Act was passed on the basis of a newspaper report rather than an official communication from China. The hasty action by the U.S. government was in fact politically motivated. As President Cleveland of the Democrats was seeking a second term in the forthcoming presidential election in which the Chinese coolie emigration would become an important issue, a firm anti-Chinese emigration stand would please the sinophobes and attract more votes in the Pacific coastal states. The President and his close supporters had

---

[156]Chang intended to instruct all Chinese Consuls to publicise and to encourage those people to return to China at a discount fare. See Chang Yin-huan, *san-chou jih-chi*, vol. 3, pp. 15b–16a, on 18th day of 1st moon of 13th year of Kuang-hsu (10 February 1887).

[157]See Chang Yin-huan, "Memorial to the Court dated 29th day of 2nd moon of 15th year of Kuang-hsu (30 March 1889)", in *Ch'ing-chi wai-chiao shih-liao*, vol. 79, pp. 27b–32a.

[158]The Act was named after Mr. Scott of Pennsylvania, chairman of the National Democratic Campaign Committee, who introduced the bill on 3 September 1888.

[159]For details of the Scott Act, see Document 7, "An Act to prohibit the coming of Chinese labourers to the United States, 13 September 1888", in W.L. Tung (ed.), *The Chinese in America 1820–1973* (New York, 1974), pp. 67–69.

rushed the Act through Congress and the Senate before the election campaign started.[160]

The Chinese government reacted strongly against the Scott Act. As soon as the Tsungli Yamen received the despatch from Washington about the passage of the bill by Congress in early September, five Ministers of the Yamen headed by Marquis Tseng Chi-tse called on Minister Denby at Peking to ask for clarification, and expressed their deep concern for the possible impact on the American Chinese who were visiting China.[161] A stern official protest was lodged by Chang Yin-huan with Secretary Bayard on 26 January 1889.[162] Chang characterised the Act as a plain violation of the Treaty of 1880. He claimed that Congress had no right to pass the law which contravened the treaty obligations of the U.S. government. He requested the President to recommend that Congress rescind the Act.[163] Failing to get a reply, he sent the Secretary on 8 July 1889 a lengthy despatch to reinforce his protest. Chang's strongly-worded despatch was partly prompted by the Supreme Court's decision to uphold the Act despite its admission that the Act did contravene the stipulations of the Treaty of 1868 and the Treaty of 1880.[164] He reiterated China's strong opposition to the Act, and reminded the U.S. government that all the Sino-American treaties since 1844 were initiated by the United States for its own benefit.[165] He pointed out that Congressional action could not be justified by U.S. conduct towards other nations, and was taken as an affront to China.[166] He warned that China had the right, in accordance with international practice, to denunciate all existing Sino-American treaties, and to terminate all diplomatic and commercial relations with the United States.[167] He further warned that the government

---

[160]See M.R. Coolidge, *Chinese Immigration*, pp. 194–99.

[161]See "Charles Denby to T.F. Bayard dated 17 September 1888", in U.S. Department of State, *Papers Relating to the Foreign Relations of the United States, 1888*, pp. 350–52.

[162]See "Chang Yin-huan to T.F. Bayard dated 26 January 1889", in "Notes from Chinese Legation", "The Mission of Chang Yin-huan, April 1886 to September 1889".

[163]*Ibid.*

[164]See "Chang Yin-huan to J.G. Blaine dated 8 July 1889", p. 2, in "Notes from Chinese Legation", "The Mission of Chang Yin-huan, April 1886 to September 1889".

[165]*Ibid.*, pp. 4–5.

[166]*Ibid.*, pp. 6–9, 13–17.

[167]*Ibid.*, pp. 10–13.

of the United States would be held responsible for all injuries and damages resulting from the enforcement of the Scott Act.[168]

TSUI KUO-YIN AND THE PROTECTION OF THE AMERICAN CHINESE, 1889-93

As Chang Yin-huan was recalled back to China in September 1889, his successor Tsui Kuo-yin continued the vigorous protest against the Scott Act. Tsui's thirty-two-page despatch had expanded Chang's grounds of argument. He was able to present concrete evidence to the Secretary of the adverse effect on Chinese immigrants who were visiting China; on Chinese coolies who were using U.S. ports for transit;[169] and on the Chinese merchants who had business interests in the United States and the Pacific countries.[170] Tsui recounted the efforts of the Chinese government in the protection of American missionaries and merchants in China,[171] and accused the United States for not reciprocating. He warned that the Chinese government might be forced to take retaliatory action against American nationals if the U.S. government was not prepared to change its course of action.[172]

Despite these strong protests and warnings, no action had been taken by the U.S. government to undo the wrong. The State Department adopted the tactic of delay. Some of the protest notes and queries were not replied after months, and most of the replies were evasive in nature.[173] By so doing, it hoped to produce a sense of doom on the part of the Chinese diplomats, and to create the situation of a fait accompli. Indeed, the Chinese Minister in Washington realised he was fighting a losing battle against the Scott Act. A study of Tsui Kuo-yin's diary reveals a sense of utter helplessness. He was disheartened over the issue of the protection of Chinese

---

[168]*Ibid.*, pp. 18–20.

[169]See "Tsui Kuo-yin to J.G. Blaine dated 26 March 1890", pp. 4–7, in "Notes from Chinese Legation", "The Mission of Tsui Kuo-yin September 1889 to August 1893".

[170]*Ibid.*, pp. 20–22.

[171]*Ibid.*, pp. 10–12.

[172]*Ibid.*, pp. 17–19, 24.

[173]See Tsui Kuo-yin, "Ch'u-shih Mei Jih Pi kuo jih-chi" (Diary of my Mission to the United States of America, Spain and Peru), in *Hsiao-fang-hu chai yu-ti ts'ung-ch'ao*, pu-p'ien, vol. 8 (Taipei, 1964), 24th day of 8th moon of 16th year of Kuang-hsu (7 October 1890).

emigrants. For example, thirty Chinese emigrants arrived in the United States in October 1890 but were sent back by the American authorities to Hong Kong where they had embarked. In the same month, another thirty-two Chinese arrived from Canada, and again they were deported to China.[174] Tsui only mentioned these incidents in passing in his diary, and did not seem to have made any official protest with the Secretary of State.[175]

Although Tsui almost gave up the fight on the protection over the new and returned emigrants, he was firm on the issue of protection for the local Chinese. He took up the issue with the U.S. government and actively tried to alleviate the sufferings of the local Chinese. His effort was a timely response to the continuous anti-Chinese actions in the Western coastal states. On 17 February 1890, the San Francisco Municipal authority issued the order requiring Chinese residents of that city to move their houses and business to a prescribed district within sixty days, and declared it unlawful for the Chinese to reside or do business in that city. Those who failed to comply were to be jailed for up to six months.[176] This Municipal ordinance was obviously the work of the San Francisco Working-men's Party which had been agitating for the expulsion of the local Chinese since 1878.[177] Under the leadership of Mayor I.S. Kalloch, and based on the ordinance for the expulsion of the Chinese, it succeeded in condemning Chinatown as a nuisance. The main charges against Chinatown was that it was filthy, disease-prone and a centre from criminal activities, and its existence posed a threat to the health, morals and prosperity of the city.[178] Some of the charges

---

[174]See Tsui Kuo-yin's Diary, 18th and 22nd days of 9th moon of the 16th year of Kuang-hsu (31 October and 4 November 1890).

[175]Checking through Tsui Kuo-yin's diplomatic notes sent to Secretary J.G. Blaine during this period, nothing was mentioned about these two incidents. See Tsui Kuo-yin's correspondence with Secretary J.G. Blaine from August to December 1890, in "Notes from the Chinese Legation", "The Mission of Tsui Kuo-yin, September 1889 to August 1893".

[176]See Sections 1 to 4 of the ordinance, reproduced in *San Francisco Examiner,* 5 March 1890. This reproduction was enclosed by Pan Kwang-yu, Chinese Chargé d'affaires, in his protest note to the Secretary of State, see "Pang Kwang-yu to J.G. Blaine dated 23 May 1890", in "Notes from the Chinese Legation", "The Mission of Tsui Kuo-yin, September 1889 to August 1893".

[177]See A. Saxton, *The Indispensable Enemy: Labor and the Anti-Chinese Movement in California,* pp. 139–40.

[178]See "Resolutions of Condemnation adopted by the Board of Health (City of San Francisco)", in *Chinatown Declared a Nuisance* (San Francisco, 1880), pp. 2–6.

were probably well-grounded,[179] but some were vicious and were designed to degrade the Chinese as a race. The charge that "a terrible disease such as leprosy is a disease inherent within the Chinese race"[180] had strong racist overtones.

Due to the failure to comply with the new ordinance, many Chinese in San Francisco were arrested and put in jail.[181] When this came about, the Chinese Minister, Tsui Kuo-yin, was in Spain, the Chargé d'affaires, Pang Kwang-yu, served a strong protest with Secretary Blaine and appealed for protection for the San Francisco Chinese;[182] but the reply was evasive. The advice offered by the Secretary was to fight the ordinance in the local court.[183] When the case did come up in court, Tsui had instructed the Chinese Consul-General in San Francisco to get the best legal advice. And on 26 August 1890, the court arrived at a verdict that was in favour of the Chinese. The Municipal ordinance was thus rescinded.[184]

Tsui's more important role in the protection of the local Chinese was his fight against the Geary Law which was passed in May 1892.[185] The essential provisions of the Law were: the strict prohibited entry of the Chinese except for diplomats and their servants; a heavy penalty imposed on illegal Chinese emigrants and on those who helped to bring them to the United States; all Chinese residents were

---

[179]The charges of filth and overcrowding were probably true. According to the Committee of Investigating into the Condition of the Chinatown, in an alley on the east side of Dupont street the water-closets were foul, the sewers stopped up, and the stench of decaying vegetables and human urine was horrible. In many parts of Chinatown, it was common for 12 or more people to eat and sleep in rooms of 8 × 10 and 10 × 12. *Ibid.*, pp. 3–4.

[180]See "Memorial on Chinatown by an Investigating Committee of the Anti-Chinese Council, W.P.C.", in *Chinatown Declared a Nuisance*, p. 14.

[181]See "Pang Kwang-yu to J.G. Blaine dated 23 May 1890", in "Notes from the Chinese Legation", "The Mission of Tsui Kuo-yin, September 1889 to August 1893".

[182]*Ibid.*, also "Pang Kwang-yu to J.G. Blaine dated 7 June 1890", in "Notes from the Chinese Legation", "The Mission of Tsui Kuo-yin, September 1889 to August 1893".

[183]*Ibid.*

[184]See "Memorial of Tsui Kuo-yin to the Court relating to U.S. government's abrogation of new rules against the Chinese in San Francisco dated 17th day of 10th moon of 16th year of Kuang-hsu (28 November 1890), in *Ch'ing-chi wai-chiao shih-liao*, vol. 83, pp. 29a–30a.

[185]Geary Law was named after Thomas J. Geary, Congressman from the State of California, who initiated the bill in Congress.

required to obtain a certificate giving detailed particulars and were required to supply the authorities with photographs.[186] Obviously this Law represented a further step taken by the United States to tighten its control over the Chinese immigration, particularly the illegal immigrants. To justify their action, Thomas Geary and his supporters claimed that the existing legislation was inadequate in preventing illegal Chinese immigration, for there were an alleged 60,000 Chinese who had smuggled themselves into the United States in the decade prior to 1892.[187] This claim of 60,000 illegal Chinese immigrants in the United States could have been true for there were continuous activities of the smuggling of Chinese immigrants from various ports and towns of the United States, particularly from the Canadian border.[188] But what Thomas Geary and his supporters were reluctant to admit was the fact that many of these smuggling activities were carried out with the connivance of American officials.[189] To admit to the connivance of the American officials would tantamount to admitting a flaw in the American political system and the corruptibility of its officials. Whatever the truth behind the claim, the measures contained in the new Law were a serious violation of basic human rights. The requirement for Chinese residents to obtain a certificate with a photograph attached was done only to criminals in the United States. In this sense, the U.S. government could not escape the accusation that it did not

---

[186]See M.R. Coolidge, *Chinese Immigration*, pp. 213-14.

[187]*Ibid.*

[188]See "Report of Inspector S.W. Day of Port Huron to the Special Agent of the Treasury Department at Detroit dated 2 March 1889", "Despatch of Robert J. Stevens, U.S. Consul in Victoria, British Columbia, to W.F. Wharton, Assistant Secretary of State dated 3 December 1889", "Report of the Special Agent of the Treasury Department at Victoria, British Columbia, to the Secretary of Treasury dated 6 February 1890", "Report of James J. Brooks, A Special Agent of the Treasury Department, Vancouver, B.C. to W. Windom, the Secretary of the Treasury dated 10 March 1890", in U.S. National Archives, "Bureau of Immigration, Segregated Chinese Records", "3358 d. File" ca 1877-91, Boxes 5 and 6.

[189]Reports claimed that some customs officials in Port Townsend and Port San Francisco were involved in frauds in issuing certificates to Chinese who paid large sums of money. See "Report of O.L. Spawding, a Special Agent of the Treasury Department at San Francisco, to D. Manning, the Secretary of the Treasury dated 2 November 1885", "Report of H.F. Beecher, a Special Agent of the Treasury Department, Port Townsend, to C.S. Fairchild, the Secretary of the Treasury dated 2 July 1887", *ibid.*, Box 3.

treat the Chinese as normal human beings, but in the same category as dangerous criminals.

Tsui's job in countering the Geary Law was an extremely difficult one. When the bill was debated in both Congress and Senate, Tsui resorted to active lobbying among some Congressmen and Senators who were sympathetic to China's cause.[190] After the bill was passed by the two Houses, waiting to be signed to become law, he lodged a vehement protest with the Secretary of State. He declared that the bill was worse than the Scott Act, and it denied the Chinese the right of bail in habeas corpus suits, and violated many articles of the Treaty of 1880.[191] Quoting the words of a Senator, he accused the bill to be "in contrary to all American law principles and practice, it was unquestionably an act of barbarous legislation".[192] He called upon the President to examine the outright violation of the treaty stipulations by the bill, and appealed to him not to approve it.[193] After the bill became law, Tsui further declared that "the statute of 1892 is a violation of every principle of justice, equity, reason and fair-dealing between friendly Powers".[194] Tsui also backed his words with action. On several occasions he called on the Secretary of State to express China's displeasure and attempted to persuade the Secretary to do something.[195] On one occasion, he, together with a leader of the Chinese community in San Francisco, Ch'en Ta-chao, argued with the Secretary over the issue of registering the Chinese.[196] Tsui's persistent stand together with the strong protest made by the Tsungli Yamen with the U.S. ambassador in Peking, might have had some impact on the attitude of the U.S. government. Many Chinese who failed to comply with the new Law to register had not been arrested or deported. This led Tsui to claim

---

[190]See Tsui Kuo-yin's Diary, 24th day of 1st moon to 28th day of 1st moon of 18th year of Kuang-hsu (22 to 26 February 1892).

[191]See "Tsui Kuo-yin to J.G. Blaine dated 5 May 1892", in "Notes from the Chinese Legation", "The Mission of Tsui Kuo-yin, September 1889 to August 1893".

[192]*Ibid.*

[193]*Ibid.*

[194]See M.R. Coolidge, *op. cit.*, p. 221.

[195]See "Tsui Kuo-yin to J.G. Blaine dated 22 March 1892", in "Notes from the Chinese Legation", "The Mission of Tsui Kuo-yin, September 1889 to August 1893".

[196]See Tsui Kuo-yin's diary, 26th day of leap 6th moon of the 18th year of Kuang-hsu (18 August 1892).

that it was due to his efforts and the Yamen's instructions that the American attitude had been softened.[197] Tsui's claim for much of the credit is however an exaggeration; the delay in enforcing the new Law was due mainly to a technical problem and the high cost involved.[198] Whatever the truth behind Tsui's claim, he had done his best to protect the interests of the American Chinese.

During his term as the Chinese Minister for the United States, Spain and Peru, Tsui had learned the impact of power in the politics of international relations. The weaker partner of the treaty signatories had little or no power to enforce her rights. He seemed to have learned something about American politics. Unlike China where ordinary people had no say in politics, the American people wielded a great deal of influence over national policy through their votes. From this perspective, he lamented Chinese indifference in local politics. He discovered that Chinese unwillingness to take up American citizenship was the main cause of their misery, and suggested that this had deprived the Chinese of votes, and had placed them in a vulnerable position, thus making them the victims of political agitation during times of election.[199] Tsui's "discovery" may not be the real root of the problem, but his attempt to find out the basic cause was an expression of enthusiasm in solving the knotty problem in the interest of the American Chinese.

To sum up, the protection of overseas Chinese before 1893 generally lacked coherence. The action was mainly taken by the diplomats concerned, and on many occasions, they acted on their own initiatives. There was a general lack of both foresight and a well-coordinated policy by the central government of China. This reduced

---

[197]See "Memorial of Tsui Kuo-yin to the Court relating to his mission to the United States, Spain and Peru dated 4th day of 9th moon of 19th year of Kuang-hsu (13 October 1893)", in *Ch'ing-chi wai-chiao shih-liao*, vol. 88, pp. 1a–1b.

[198]According to one estimate, only 13,242 out of 106,668 Chinese in the United States complied with the new law to register. Only $25,000 left in the Treasury with which to deport 85,000 unregistered Chinese. As the cost of steerage passage for the Chinese was $51 and other expenses at $35 per head, it would cost $7,310,000 to deport all of them. At the same time, it would require the time of three judges from 12 to 15 years to go through legal procedures to deport all these unregistered Chinese. See M.R. Coolidge, *op. cit.*, p. 226.

[199]See Tsui Kuo-yin's Diary, 21st day of 7th moon of 16th year of Kuang-hsu (5 September 1890); "Memorial of Tsui Kuo-yin to the Court relating to his mission to the United States, Spain and Peru dated 4th day of 9th moon of 19th year of Kuang-hsu (13 October 1893)", in *Ch'ing-chi wai-chiao shih-liao*, vol. 88, pp. 1a–1b.

the chances of success of the actions taken by the individual diplomats. But the main cause of the failure of the protection of the American Chinese during this period was the unfriendly attitude of the U.S. government. Under the pressure of internal politics, the U.S. government took advantage of China's weak position and refused to fulfil its treaty obligations to protect Chinese nationals in the United States.

6
Changes in the Traditional Emigration Policy and Protection of Returned Overseas Chinese

CHANGES IN THE TRADITIONAL EMIGRATION POLICY IN 1893

Factors for the Change

The suppression of the coolie trade and the consular expansion had their roles to play in creating a favourable climate for the change of the traditional emigration policy. However the most important immediate factor in ending the age-old rules in 1893 was a realisation of the economic potential of overseas Chinese. The economic potential of overseas Chinese did not attract much attention from Ch'ing officialdom before the 1870s, for up to then, annual remittances to China from overseas Chinese were relatively small.[1] Moreover, there were no direct links between China and its overseas subjects so that information about the economic status of overseas Chinese was hard to acquire. But diplomatic representation and consular expansion from the mid-1870s linked overseas Chinese communities with China, and through the regular reports and diaries of the diplomats,[2] information about the economic position of

---

[1] It is difficult to give an estimate of the annual remittances of overseas Chinese before the 1870s. Fragmentary information is collected relating to regional figures. Writing in 1838, T.J. Newbold estimated that the annual remittances of 3,000 Chinese in Penang to their families in China was in the vicinity of 10,000 spanish dollars. Writing in 1846–47, Siah U Chin, a wealthy Chinese in Singapore, estimated the annual remittances of the Chinese in the Straits Settlements as ranging from 30,000 or 40,000 to 70,000 dollars. See T.J. Newbold, *Political and Statistical Account of the British Settlements in the Straits of Malacca* (London, 1939), vol. 1, p. 11; Siah U Chin, "Annual Remittances by Chinese Immigrants to Their Families in China", in *Journal of Indian Archipelago and Eastern Asia*, vol. 1 (1947), pp. 35–37.

[2] Apart from regular correspondence with the Tsungli Yamen, the early Chinese ambassadors had kept diaries about what they saw and heard in foreign lands. Sometimes they made constructive comments. Their diaries were published by the Ch'ing government for the benefit of the administrators who had not set foot overseas. Diaries of famous diplomats such as Kuo Sung-t'ao, *Shih-hsi chi-ch'eng* (The

overseas Chinese were passed on to the Ch'ing official circles. Information was also passed through special missions sent out by provincial governors either to investigate the conditions of overseas Chinese or to raise money among them.[3] Both types of mission involved the emissaries to live in temporary residences in overseas Chinese communities where they established personal contacts. Through this work, the emissaries were also able to collect reliable information about the financial positions of overseas Chinese.

Based on the information provided by diplomats and special emissaries, some Ch'ing high-ranking officials who had never been overseas before, could arrive at some concrete assessment of the economic potential of overseas Chinese. In a memorial to the Court in 1886, the Governor-General of Kwangtung and Kwangsi, Chang Chih-tung, stated the importance of the annual remittances of the overseas Chinese, estimating that they could reach 20,000,000 dollars (Mexican?).[4] The importance of the overseas Chinese remittances was confirmed by Hsueh Fu-ch'eng, the Chinese Minister to Britain, France, Italy and Belgium, who estimated that the Chinese in America alone had remitted about 8,000,000 taels annually.[5] In purely monetary terms, the remittance was an important sum. The

---

Record of an Envoy's Journey to the West), Ch'en Lan-pin, *Shih Mei chi-lueh* (Brief Record of an Envoy to America) and Hsueh Fu-ch'eng, *Chu shih Ying, Fa, I, Pi ssu-kuo jih-chi* (Diary of My Mission to England, France, Italy and Belgium), asserted tremendous influence on the Chinese officials. For the practice of requiring diplomats to present their regular reports and diaries, see Liu Chin-ch'ao (ed.), *Ch'ing-ch'ao shu wen-hsien t'ung-k'ao*, vol. 339, "Wai-chiao" 3, K'ao, pp. 10804-5.

[3]For special missions sent to investigate and to raise money in overseas Chinese communities, particularly in Southeast Asia, see Liu Chin-ch'ao (ed.), *Ch'ing-ch'ao shu wen-hsien t'ung-k'ao*, vol. 338, "Wai-chiao" 2, K'ao, pp. 10795-7; Yen Ching-hwang, "Ch'ing Sale of Honours and the Chinese Leadership in Singapore and Malaya 1877-1912", in *Journal of the Southeast Asian Studies*, vol. 1, no. 2 (September, 1970), pp. 22-24; Yen Ching-hwang, "The Overseas Chinese and Late Ch'ing Economic Modernization", in *Modern Asian Studies*, vol. 16, no. 2 (1982), pp. 219-20.

[4]See "Memorial of Chang Chih-tung to the Court relating to the protection of overseas Chinese dated 25th day of 2nd moon of 12th year of Kuang-hsu (30 March 1886)", in Chang Chih-tung, *Chang Wen-hsing kung ch'uan-chi* (Taipei, 1963), vol. 1, pp. 333-34.

[5]See Hsueh Fu-ch'eng, "Hai-wai wen-pien", in Hsueh Fu-ch'eng, *Hsueh Fu-ch'eng ch'uan-chi*, vol. 1, p. 7.

estimated 20,000,000 dollars (about 14,400,000 taels)[6] was equivalent to 65 percent of the annual customs dues collected in the early 1890s.[7] The remittance was significant to Ch'ing finance. It was a net gain for China in its foreign exchange, and helped to pay off huge trade deficits, and to stabilise China's currency.

The wealth of overseas Chinese merchants was another source of attraction for the Chinese diplomats and officers. Before going overseas, the Confucian diplomats in the late nineteenth century might have entertained some misconceptions about the status of overseas Chinese, but they were soon struck by the affluence of the local Chinese communities, and the wealth of the merchants. Some of the wealthiest merchants lived in well-designed and well-constructed Chinese-styled mansions,[8] travelled in luxurious carriages, and spent their leisure in beautiful and elegant gardens.[9] Some of them displayed their wealth by collecting "exotics" and curios. Kuo Sung-t'ao, the first Chinese ambassador to Britain, appears to have been impressed by the collection of curios in the garden of Hoo Ah Kay, for in his diary he described a great deal of what he had seen there.[10] This probably helped him to decide to appoint Hoo as the first Chinese Consul in Singapore.

---

[6]In his estimate, Chang Chih-tung did not give a precise equivalence of taels to the 20,000,000 dollars. He only said that the estimate was equivalent to more than ten million taels. If we accept the general exchange rate in the nineteenth century between dollar and tael as 100 to 71.7, we arrive at the amount of 14,000,000 taels. See Chang Chih-tung, *op. cit.*, pp. 333–34; Frank H.H. King, *Money and Monetary Policy in China 1845–1895* (Cambridge, Mass., 1965), p. 88.

[7]Customs dues became the most important tax during the late Ch'ing period. In 1890, the annual collection was 21,987,000 taels, in 1891 — 22,849,000 taels, and in 1892 — 22,680,000 taels. I take 22,000,000 as the figure for working out the percentage. See Liu Chin-ch'ao (ed.), *Ch'ing-ch'ao shu wen-hsieh t'ung-kao*, vol. 31, "Taxation" 3, k'ao 7834.

[8]For instance, a number of mansions were built in Singapore in the second half of the nineteenth century by wealthy merchants. One of these mansions which belonged to a well-known Teochew merchant, Ch'en Hsu-nien, still exists in Singapore. See Chang Ch'ing-chiang. "Ch'en Hsu-nien yu tzu-cheng ti" (Ch'en Hsu-nien and His Mansion), in Lin Hsiao-sheng *et al.*, *Shih-le ku-chi* (The Historical Relics of Singapore) (Singapore, 1975), pp. 225–30.

[9]See for instance, the Shou-ch'uan garden, the villa of a well-known Fukien leader in Singapore, Cheang Hong Lim, which was a venue for social gatherings for some wealthy merchants and well-known literary figures in Singapore. See *Sing Po*, 3/5/1892, p. 1.

[10]See Kuo Sung-t'ao, "Shih-hsi chi-ch'eng" (The Record of An Envoy's Journey to the West), in J.D. Frodsham, *The First Chinese Embassy to the West: The Jour-*

Information about the wealth of overseas Chinese merchants was also collected through the special missions sent overseas. The Wang Yung-ho mission to Southeast Asia and Oceania in 1886 collected a great deal of valuable information,[11] on the basis of which Chang Chih-tung was able to point out to the Court that the Chinese merchants in Singapore controlled eight-tenths of the local business, and that some of the Chinese tin miners in Perak and Selangor were millionaires.[12]

The Chinese diplomats and high-ranking officers were further impressed by donations from rich overseas Chinese merchants. In 1878, the Governor of Fukien, Ting Jih-ch'ang, collected more than 300,000 dollars from the Chinese in Hong Kong and Southeast Asia (mainly from Singapore, Philippines, Thailand and Vietnam); the donation was for the relief of natural calamities in Honan and Shansi.[13] In 1884 when China was engaged in the Sino-French war over the protection of Vietnam, the wealthy Chinese Kapitan of Perak, Cheng Keng Kwee, donated 100,000 dollars (Straits ?) for the naval defence fund.[14] It was also claimed that the Chinese in Singapore contributed more than 200,000 dollars (Straits ?) to the same fund.[15] In 1889 when China was plagued by various calamities, the Chinese in the Straits Settlements and the Federated Malay States donated about 150,000 dollars to the relief funds.[16] Many of

---

nals of Kuo-Sung-t'ao, Liu Hsi-hung and Chang Te-yi (Oxford, Clarendon Press, 1974), pp. 13–14.

[11]See Chapter 4, "Diplomatic Representation and Consular Expansion in the Overseas Chinese Communities".

[12]Chang Chih-tung, "Memorial to the court relating to the proposed protection of the overseas Chinese after the sending of the investigation mission dated 24th day of 10 moon of 13th year of Kuang-hsu (8 December 1887)", in Chang Chih-tung, *Chang Wen-hsiang kung ch'uan-chi*, "memorials" vol. 23, pp. 8–13.

[13]See Li Hung-chang, "Memorial to the court relating to relief fund collection by Ting Jih-ch'ang dated 14th day of 5th moon of 4th year of Kuang-hsu (14 June 1878)", in Li Hung-chang, *Li Wen-chung Kung ch'uan-chi*, vol. 2, p. 285, original "tsou-kao" vol. 31, p. 30.

[14]See K'uang Kuo-hsiang, *Pin-ch'eng san-chi* (Hong Kong, 1958), p. 112.

[15]The claim was made by Hsueh Fu-ch'eng, see Hsueh Fu-ch'eng, *Hsueh Fu-ch'eng ch'uan-chi*, "Hai-wai wen-pien" vol. 1, p. 7.

[16]There were three separate funds collected in the overseas Chinese communities in Southeast Asia in 1889, the fund for the north China calamity, the fund for the relief operation in Kiangsu and Anhwei, and the fund for the relief operation in Shantung. The North China fund collected $80,758 in March from the British colonies in Southeast Asia, while the Kiangsu and Anhwei fund collected 67,604 dollars

these donations were actually payments for the Ch'ing brevet honours,[17] but they invariably demonstrated the wealth of the overseas Chinese merchants, a wealth which could be further tapped by the Ch'ing government.

Hsueh Fu-ch'eng, Huang Tsun-hsien and the Change of the Policy

The men who were instrumental in changing the traditional policy were Huang Tsun-hsien and Hsueh Fu-ch'eng. Huang, a renowned poet[18] and reformer, was a career diplomat.[19] He did not go through the T'ung Wen Kuan, the institution that produced many competent interpreters and diplomats during the late Ch'ing period. Instead he was the product of the traditional education system. But, disenchanted with the examination system, he turned to the study of "Yang-wu" (Foreign Matters).[20] What actually motivated him to turn to "Yang-wu" is uncertain. Under the influence of the Self-Strengthening Movement, he could have been motivated by the lofty aim of serving the nation through the learning of "Foreign Matters", for it was thought to be the essential means of strengthening China. Perhaps his poetic character gave him insight into the problems of the traditional learning, so that "Foreign Matters" would have offered him the prospect of practical use; or perhaps he was simply attracted to "Foreign Matters" because it offered an alternative route to the bureaucracy, another way of getting into prominence and power besides the imperial examinations. Whatever the real motive, his study gained him a reputation and a diplo-

---

mainly from Singapore, Penang, Malacca, Perak, Kuala Lumpur and Seramban. See *Lat Pau*, 16/3/1889, p. 2, 21/5/1889, p. 2.

[17]See Yen Ching-hwang, "Ch'ing Sale of Honours and the Chinese Leadership in Singapore and Malaya 1877–1912", in *Journal of the Southeast Asian Studies*, vol. 1, no. 2 (September, 1970), pp. 20–32.

[18]Liang Ch'i-ch'ao regarded Huang as one of the top three poets in early twentieth-century China. See Liang Ch'i-ch'ao, *Yin-ping-she wen-chi* (Hong Kong, 1955), vol. 4, "Wen-wan", pp. 74–75.

[19]For a short biography of Huang Tsun-hsien in English, see Fang Chao-ying, "Huang Tsun-hsien", in A.W. Hummel (ed.), *Eminent Chinese of the Ch'ing Period* (Taipei, reprint, 1970), pp. 350–51; for a more detailed biographical chronology of Huang in Chinese, see Ch'ien Ngo-sun, "Huang Kung-tu hsien-sheng nien-p'u" (The Biographical Chronology of Huang Tsun-hsien), in Ch'ien Ngo-sun (ed.), *Huang Tsun-hsien shih p'ing-lun* (Comments on the Poetry of Huang Tsun-hsien) (Taipei, 1973).

[20]Huang began to be interested in "Foreign Matters" in 1870, he was at the age of 22. See Ch'ien Ngo-sun, *op. cit.*, p. 69.

matic career. In January 1877, only a few months after his admission to the *chu-jen* degree, Huang was appointed Counsellor to the newly established Chinese embassy in Tokyo.[21] This was the turning point in his life, for it was during this five-year stay in Japan that many of his reform ideas were formulated. He witnessed the dynamism and success of Meiji Japan. This inspired him to write the "History of Japan" (Jih-pen kuo-chih), a work which he hoped would influence the course of Chinese politics.[22] There has been no evidence to suggest that Huang had a special interest in overseas Chinese at that time, his main attention was drawn to the worsening Sino-Japanese relations and the Japanese encroachment on China's protectorates.[23] His interest in overseas Chinese was not developed until he was transferred to San Francisco in 1882 as the Chinese Consul-General.[24] His new appointment brought him into direct contact with the overseas Chinese, and enabled him to understand their problems, grievances and hopes.

Huang's three years in San Francisco coincided with the ugliest period in the history of America's immigration policy. This was when the U.S. government began to implement the Chinese Exclusion Act which was adopted in 1882 to restrict Chinese coolie immigrants.[25] But the Act contained so many ambiguous clauses that almost any Chinese could be excluded.[26] Moreover, the issue of

---

[21]Huang was appointed by Ho Ju-chang, the first Chinese ambassador to Japan. Ho was Hakka from Ta P'u district, while Huang was a Hakka from Mei district, Ho's and Huang's fathers were known to be friends. It was probably because of this connection, plus Huang's reputation in the study of "Foreign Matters" among the Hakkas, that Ho selected him as Counsellor. *Ibid.*, p. 71.

[22]For a detailed discussion of Japanese influence on Huang Tsun-hsien's thought, see Noriko Kamachi, *Reform in China: Huang Tsun-hsien and The Japanese Model* (Cambridge, Mass., 1981), pp. 36–87; for the impact of Huang's 'History of Japan' on Chinese politics, see Jocelyn Milner, "The Reform Ideas of Huang Tsun-hsien's 'History of Japan' and Its Influence on The Hundred Day's Reform", in *Journal of the South Seas Society*, vol. 17 (1961), pt. 2, pp. 49–92.

[23]See Nan Chih-wei, "Huang Tsun-hsien te ching-shih t'sai-lueh ho wen-hsueh t'e-she, in *Journal of the South Seas Society*, vol. 17 (1961), pt. 2, p. 18.

[24]See Ch'ien Ngo-sun, *op. cit.*, p. 78.

[25]For discussion on the Chinese Exclusion Act of 1882, see M.R. Coolidge, *Chinese Immigration* (New York, 1909, reprint, Taipei, 1968), chapter 11, pp. 168–82.

[26]See Noriko Kamachi, "American Influences on Chinese Reform Thought: Huang Tsun-hsien in California, 1882-1885", in *Pacific Historical Review*, vol. XLVII, no. 2 (May, 1978), p. 245.

Chinese immigration increasingly became the focus of political agitation and the tool for certain political groups.[27] As a result, the overseas Chinese in the United States became victims of the new policy: their activities were circumscribed, their treaty rights were infringed, and they were ill-treated by immigration officers and police.[28] Huang sympathised with the overseas Chinese, particularly the coolies,[29] and fought vigorously against the unjust treatment by the American authorities. He defended the treaty rights of the overseas Chinese, in particular their right to re-enter the United States after short visits to China.[30] He took the initiative to acquire the right for the Chinese Consulate-General in San Francisco to issue certificates of identification and passports to the Chinese residents who left for China.[31] Although this right was revoked by the American authorities after more than a year, it greatly helped the Chinese residents to return legally to the United States. In addition to the protection of the Chinese in the United States, Huang also assisted the Chinese in British Columbia, Canada. He offered them advice on how to deal with problems arising from anti-Chinese legislation adopted by the provincial government of British Columbia.[32] His intimate contacts with the Chinese in the United States

---

[27]See A. Saxton, *The Indispensable Enemy: Labor and the Anti-Chinese Movement in California* (Berkeley, 1975, paperback), pp. 179–200.

[28]For ill-treatment of the overseas Chinese in the United States during this period, see correspondence between Chinese Legation and the Department of State, in "Notes From the Chinese Legation", "The Mission of Cheng Tsao-ju".

[29]See Huang Tsun-hsien, "Chu-k'e p'ien" (The Expulsion of the Chinese Emigrants), in Huang Tsun-hsien, *Jen-ching-lu shih-ts'ao chien-chu* (Annotated Poems of the Jen-ching-lu) (Shanghai, 1957), pp. 126–28.

[30]See "Tsai Kwoh Ching (Chargé d'affaires) to F.T. Frelinghuysen (Secretary of State) dated 31 July 1884", and "Tsai Kwoh Ching to F.T. Frelinghuysen dated 4 October 1884", in "Notes From the Chinese Legation", "The Mission of Cheng Tsao-ju"; "Tsai Kwoh Ching to F.T. Frelinghuysen dated 8 October 1884", in U.S. National Archives, "Bureau of Immigration, 3358d File", Ca 1877–91, Box 2; see also Noriko Kamachi, "American Influences on Chinese Reform Thought: Huang Tsun-hsien in California, 1882–1885", in *Pacific Historical Review*, vol. XLVII, no. 2 (May, 1978), pp. 245–51.

[31]See "Hsu Shau Pang (Hsu Shou-p'eng, Chargé d'affaires) to F.T. Frelinghuysen dated 8 June 1882", a public notice in Chinese issued by Huang Tsun-hsien relating to the issue of passports by the Consulate-General, attached to "Hsu Shau Pang to F.T. Frelinghuysen dated 21 June 1882", "Hsu Shau Pang to F.T. Frelinghuysen dated 28 June 1882", in "Notes From the Chinese Legation", "The Mission of Cheng Tsao-ju".

[32]In 1884 (tenth year of Kuang-hsu), in response to a local legislation of levying

and Canada enabled him to realise their economic potential, their desire for protection, and their fear of extortion when they returned to China. His view of the overseas Chinese at this time appears to be a step ahead of the thinking of other Chinese diplomats. His recognition of the need to promote the welfare of his countrymen arose not only from humanitarian considerations and national pride,[33] but also because of their economic contributions.

While in San Francisco, he discovered that an average of $1,200,000 (US$?) was remitted to Canton annually by the local Chinese.[34] This discovery led him to formulate his opinion on the economic importance of the overseas Chinese. It was probably this experience in San Francisco that made him campaign for the abolition of the age-old emigration policy.

The main factors in determining Huang's opposition to the old emigration policy were his appointments as the Counsellor of the Chinese Legation in London in 1890–91 and as Consul-General in Singapore at the end of 1891.[35] But this must be seen in the light of

---

$10 annually on Chinese residents, four representatives of the Chinese community in Victoria, British Columbia, called on Huang and asked for protection. Huang advised them to employ local lawyers to fight against the new law, instead of going through complicated diplomatic channels. This event was recalled in a letter of Huang's in 1891. See "Letter from Huang Tsun-hsien to the Office Bearers of the Chinese Consolidated Benevolent Association of Victoria, British Columbia, dated 2nd day of 7th moon of 17th year of Kuang-hsu (6 August 1891)", (original), in *Chinese Consolidated Benevolent Association of Victoria Archives* (deposited at the University of Victoria, British Columbia), Section 2, "Record of Protest Against Racial Discrimination"; see also *Souvenir Magazine to Commemorate Victoria's Chinese Consolidated Benevolent Association 1884–1959, and Chinese Public School 1899–1959* (in Chinese, Victoria, 1959), section 3, p. 19.

[33]In a letter to the leaders of the Chinese community of Victoria, British Columbia, Huang urged them to help poor Chinese return to China, so that they would not die miserably overseas without proper burial. Huang emphasised that this would prevent the Chinese being sneered at and laughed at by foreigners. See "Letter from Huang Tsun-hsien to the Office Bearers of the Chinese Consolidated Benevolent Association of Victoria dated 10th day of 12th moon of the 10th year (?) of Kuang-hsu (25 January 1885 ?)", in *Souvenir Magazine to Commemorate Victoria's Chinese Consolidated Benevolent Association 1884–1959 and Chinese Public School 1899–1959*, section 3, pp. 9–10.

[34]See Noriko Kamachi, "American Influences on Chinese Reform Thought: Huang Tsun-hsien in California, 1882–1885", in *Pacific Historical Review*, vol. XLVII, no. 2 (May, 1978), p. 256.

[35]Huang left his post in San Francisco on 20 September 1885 (12th day of 8th moon of 11th year of Kuang-hsu) and returned to China for his mother's funeral. He declined to accept the same post when it was offered to him in 1886 by the new Chinese

changing historical events. During the times of his new appointments, the overseas Chinese issue became more important than ever before. Viceroy Chang Chih-tung's policy of extending consular representation to the Chinese communities in Southeast Asia,[36] the use of overseas Chinese for China's coastal defence,[37] and Admiral Ting Ju-ch'ang's memorial to the Court for increased protection for the Southeast Asian Chinese, aroused considerable attention in the Tsungli Yamen and among Chinese diplomats.[38] Thus, Huang's interest in overseas Chinese was rekindled during his term of counsellorship in London (January 1890–September 1891?), for it was at this time that he was repeatedly consulted by Hsueh Fu-ch'eng as the expert on overseas Chinese issues.[39] He was put in charge of most overseas Chinese matters, and corresponded with overseas Chinese organisations including the Chinese Consolidated Benevolent Association of Victoria, British Columbia.[40]

Minister to the United States, Chang Yin-huan. He then spent time completing his "History of Japan" in 1887, which was printed in the following year. At the end of 1889, Huang was appointed by Hsueh Fu-ch'eng, the new Chinese Minister to Britain, France, Italy and Belgium, as Counsellor of the Chinese Legation in London. Because of the outbreak of epidemics in France and Germany, both Hsueh and Huang did not set sail for Europe until January 1890. After about one and a half years service in the London Legation, Huang took up his new appointment as the Chinese Consul-General for the Straits Settlements in Singapore. See "Letter from Huang Tsun-hsien to the Office Bearers of the Chinese Consolidated Benevolent Association of Victoria dated 2nd day of 7th moon of 11th year of Kuang-hsu", in "Chinese Consolidated Benevolent Association of Victoria Archives" (kept in the Library of the University of Victoria, Canada), section 2; Hsueh Fu-ch'eng, *Ch'u-shih Ying, Fa, I, Pi ssu-kuo jih-chi* (Diaries of My Mission to Britain, France, Italy and Belgium), vol. 1, pp. 1–2; Hsueh Fu-ch'eng, *Ch'u-shih kung-tu* (Official Correspondence of My Mission), vol. 1, p. 16.

[36]For a detailed discussion, see Chapter 4, pp. 140ff.

[37]See Chang Chih-tung, "Ch'ien ling ch'iao-shang chien-tzu kou chao hu-shang ping-ch'uan p'ien" (A memorial to persuade overseas Chinese merchants to contribute funds to purchase merchant-protecting warships) dated 4th day of 9th moon of 11th year of Kuang-hsu (11 October 1885)", in Chang Chih-tung, *Chang Wen-hsiang kung ch'uan-chi*, vol. 13, "Tsou-i" 13, pp. 12–13.

[38]The original memorial of Ting Ju-ch'ang is not contained in the *Ch'ing-chi wai-chao shih-liao*, but its main contents are included in Hsueh Fu-ch'eng's correspondence to the Tsungli Yamen dated 25th day of 8th moon of 16th year of Kuang-hsu (8 October 1890), and Hsueh's memorial to the court dated 25th day of 12th moon of 16th year of Kuang-hsu (3 February 1891). See Hsueh Fu-ch'eng, *Ch'u-shih kung-tu*, vol. 1, tz'u-wen, pp. 3a–5b; *Ch'ing-chi wai-chiao shih-liao*, vol. 83, p. 33.

[39]See Hsueh Fu-ch'eng, *Ch'u-shih Ying, Fa, I; Pi jih-chi*, vol. 1, p. 12, vol. 4, p. 1.

[40]See "Letter from Huang Tsun-hsien to the Office Bearers of the Chinese Con-

Huang's claim to expertise on overseas Chinese affairs was further reinforced by his appointment to the position of the Consul-General of the Straits Settlements. After arriving in Singapore in early November 1891,[41] he soon undertook an energetic programme to promote Chinese literary studies,[42] and to get to know the local Chinese whom he had to protect. In early February 1892, only three months after his arrival, he set out to inspect the Chinese communities in Malacca, Selangor, Perak and Penang.[43] Huang's new experience with the Chinese in Singapore and Malaya gave him a different perspective from which to assess the economic potential of overseas Chinese, and gave him considerable insight into the problems confronting overseas Chinese as a whole. In contrast to San Francisco where the Cantonese were the majority group, the Singapore and Malayan Chinese communities were made up of various dialect groups: Fukienese, Teochews, Hakkas, Cantonese and Hainanese. The diversity of the communities aroused his interest. He noticed that it was not the Cantonese, but the Fukienese from Chang-chou and Ch'uan-chou, and the Teochews who controlled much of the local trade and real estate.[44] He also observed that this group of Chinese were more numerous and financially more powerful than those in San Francisco.[45] He must have noticed that the Chinese in San Francisco were mere petty traders, shop-keepers, coolies and small gold-miners,[46] but many of the Chinese in Singapore and Malaya were wealthy entrepôt merchants, ship-owners, real estate

---

solidated Benevolent Association of Victoria, British Columbia, dated 2nd of 7th moon of 17th year of Kuang-hsu (6 August 1891)'' (original), in "Chinese Consolidated Benevolent Association of Victoria Archives", section 2; see also *Souvenir Magazine to Commemorate Victoria's Chinese Consolidated Benevolent Association 1884-1959, and Chinese Public School 1899-1959*, section 3, p. 19.

[41]See *Lat Pau*, 9/11/1891, p. 5.

[42]See *Lat Pau*, 1/1/1892, p. 5; *Sing Po*, 1/1/1892, p. 8.

[43]See *Lat Pau*, 9/2/1892, p. 2; *The Perak Government Gazette* (Taiping, 1893), 26 February 1892, p. 124.

[44]See *Sing Po*, 2/11/1892, p. 1.

[45]*Ibid.*

[46]There is no record of Huang's impression of the Chinese in San Francisco. But from Ch'en Lan-pin's (First Chinese Minister to the United States) description of the Chinese in that city in 1878, we can suggest what kind of impression Huang would have had during his term as the Chinese Consul-General in San Francisco between 1882 and 1885. See Ch'en Lan-pin, "Shih Mei chi-lueh" (Brief Record of My Mission to the United States of America), in *Hsiao-fang-hu chai yu-ti ts'ung-ch'ao pu-p'ien* (Taipei, 1962), vol. 16, pp. 11049-54.

developers, plantation owners and tin-mining magnates.[47] The scale of wealth of the Chinese in this region added an important dimension to Huang's understanding of overseas Chinese. Another valuable asset in his new job was the opportunity to speak directly to the Hakka people. He was a Hakka from Chia-ying prefecture,[48] and found many of his fellow Hakkas (Khehs) in the Straits Settlements,[49] and the Malay States.[50] He also found that the local Hakka population, though not substantial when compared with other dialect groups, were nevertheless organised in associations which served as the main channel for contact.[51] As he

---

[47]Again there is no record of Huang's impression of the Chinese in Singapore and Malaya except from the records of his contemporaries such as the report of Wang Yung-ho and Yu Chun who visited Singapore and Malaya in 1886 on a fact-finding tour, and the description of Singapore by Li Chung-chieh who visited the city in 1887. See the report of Wang Yung-ho and Yu Chun contained in Chang Chih-tung's memorial to the court in 1887, in Chang Chih-tung, *Chang Wen-hsiang kung ch'uan-chi* (Taipei, 1963), vol. 1, pp. 471–73; Li Chung-chieh, *Hsin-chia-po feng-t'u chi* (The Topography of Singapore) (Singapore, 1947), pp. 8–9.

[48]See Fang Chao-ying, "Huang Tsun-hsien", in A.W. Hummel, *Eminent Chinese of the Ch'ing Period*, p. 350; Ch'ien Ngo-sun, "Huang Kung-tu hsien-sheng nien-p'u", in Ch'ien Ngo-sun (ed.), *Huang Tsun-hsien shih p'ing-lun*, p. 63.

[49]In 1891, the Hakka population in the Straits Settlements was 16,736 out of the total Chinese population of 227,989. In the same year, there were 7,402 Hakkas out of the total Chinese population of 121,908 in Singapore where Huang Tsun-hsien was stationed. See "Population of the Straits Settlements", in *The Straits Settlements Blue Book for 1902* (Singapore, 1903), p. 'p 4'; "Population of the Straits Settlements" in *The Straits Settlements Blue Book for 1904* (Singapore, 1905), p. 'p 12'.

[50]In the late nineteenth century, many Hakkas were congregated in Asa and Jelabu in Negri Sembilan, Kuala Lumpur in Selangor, Taiping, Telok Anson and Ipoh in Perak. The concentration of the Hakka population, particularly the Chia-ying Hakkas, was reflected in the founding of several Hakka associations in these areas. The earliest Chia-ying Hakka association named "The Association of the Five Districts of Mei River" (Mei-chiang wu-shu hui-kuan) was founded in Asa in 1826; the second earliest was the "Ying Ho Association" (Ying-ho hui-kuan) of Telok Anson which was founded in 1872; the third was the "Chia Ying Association" of Jelabu founded in 1880; and the fourth was the "Chia Ying Association of Perak" (Pi-li chia-ying hui-kuan) founded in Ipoh in 1900. See *Ma-lai-hsi-ya chia-hsu lien-ho-hui yin-hsi chi-nien* (Souvenir Magazine of Silver Jubilee Celebration of the Federation of the Chia Ying Hakka Associations, Malaysia) (Kluang, 1978 ?), pp. 111–23.

[51]Three Chia Ying associations existed in the Straits Settlements long before the arrival of Huang Tsun-hsien. The Penang "Chia Ying Association" (Chia-ying hui-kuan) was founded in 1801; the "Malacca Ying Ho Association" (Ma-liu-chia ying-ho hui-kuan) was founded in 1821, and the "Singapore Ying Ho Association" (Hsin-chia-po ying-ho hui-kuan) was founded in 1822. For details, see Liu Ko-yin,

was a renowned poet and diplomat, he must have been well-known
to the local Hakka community. His appointment to the position of
the Chinese Consul-General must have been greeted by the Hakkas
with honour and pride.[52] Their respect for him meant that they
would have faith and trust in him. In return Huang acted as their
patron, and established close contacts with them, particularly with
some well-known Hakka leaders. His recommendation of Chang
Chen-hsun (Chang Pi-shih), a wealthy Hakka leader, to the position
of the Chinese Vice-Consul in Penang in 1893,[53] bears the proof of
his close alliance with the Hakka people. Since he talked freely with
them,[54] and listened to their problems, he was able to explore the
inner world of the overseas Chinese more deeply in Malaya than in
San Francisco.[55]

Huang's involvement in raising relief funds for Shansi and

"A History of the Penang Chia Ying Association", manuscript, also in *Souvenir
Magazine of Silver Jubilee Celebration of the Federation of the Chia Ying Hakka
Associations, Malaysia*, pp. 101–102; Chung Shih-chieh, "A Short History of the
Malacca Ying Ho Association", in Chung Shih-chieh (ed.), *Ma-liu-chia ying-ho hui-
kuan i-san-i chou-nien chi-nien t'e-k'an* (Souvenir Magazine of 131st Anniversary
Celebration of the Malacca Ying Ho Association) (Malacca, 1952), pp. 59–98;
Huang Fu-yung, "A Short History of the Singapore Ying Ho Association", in
Hsing-chou ying-ho hui-kuan i-pai ssu-shih-i chou-nien chi-nien t'e-k'an (Souvenir
Magazine of 141st Anniversary Celebration of the Singapore Ying Ho Association)
(Singapore, 1965) pp. 10–12.

[52]This was reflected in a warm welcome given to him during his visit to Malacca
in early 1892. He was given a feast by the Hakka community. He was honoured to
be asked to do Calligraphy for the name plaque of the local Hakka temple named
"San To Miao". See Chung Shih-chieh (ed.), *Ma-liu-chia Ying-ho hui-kuan i-san-i
chou-nien chi-nien t'e-k'an*, p. 65.

[53]See Hsueh Fu-ch'eng, "A Despatch to the Tsungli Yamen concerning the appointment of a Vice Consul in Penang dated 20th day of 1st moon of 19th year of
Kuang-hsu (8 March 1893)", in Hsueh Fu-ch'eng, *Ch'u-shih kung-tu*, vol. 2, pp.
25a–25b.

[54]The Hakka people were sub-divided into Chia-ying Hakkas, Hui-chou Hakkas,
and Ta-p'u Hakkas. Although they had some variations in pronunciations, they
could communicate freely. The same situation still exists in Singapore and Malaysia.

[55]Apart from his own Hakka dialect, Huang Tsun-hsien was able to speak Mandarin which he used to communicate with other Chinese officials and diplomats.
Obviously he had problems in communicating freely with the Chinese in San Francisco who were predominantly the speakers of Cantonese and the dialects of the adjacent districts of Canton. For the composition of different sub-dialect groups
among the Chinese in San Francisco, see Gunther Barth, *Bitter Strength: A History
of the Chinese in the United States, 1850-1870* (Cambridge, Mass., 1964), pp.
77–108.

Honan in the early part of his career in Singapore,[56] also helped him to understand the overseas Chinese better. He noticed that many of them were generous in their contributions to relief funds, and were interested in obtaining Ch'ing brevet titles which were offered as rewards.[57] What puzzled him was their unwillingness to return and to invest in China. Through intimate conversations, he gathered that the main reason for their reluctance to return was the fear of extortion by local bullies and of victimisation by corrupt and unscrupulous officials.[58] Of course a large part of this fear was connected with the existence of the prohibitive emigration policy. Although this policy had not been in operation since 1860, its existence still cast a shadow over all overseas Chinese, for they were regarded as illegal emigrants punishable for their desertion from China. Thus this obsolete emigration policy became the main obstacle impeding the development of a cordial relationship between China and its overseas subjects. It was this discovery that led Huang to campaign for the abolition of the policy.

Of Hsueh Fu-ch'eng who was also interested in overseas Chinese affairs, much has been discussed in Chapter 4. What should be added here is his cordial relationship with Huang Tsun-hsien for this had a direct bearing on the success of their joint efforts to remove the age-old policy. Both Hsueh and Huang were Reformers who shared the same inspiration,[59] and held the view that China should react more aggressively to the challenge of imperialism through diplomacy and through the transformation of China's protectorates into provinces and colonies.[60] They also believed that

---

[56]See *Sing Po*, 2/11/1892, p. 1.

[57]See Huang Tsun-hsien, "Tsung-ling-shih Huang kuan-ch'a pin-kao" (The Submission of Huang Tsun-hsien, the Consul-General to the Chinese Minister Hsueh Fu-ch'eng) in *Sing Po*, 2/11/1892, p. 1; for details of the awards of Ch'ing brevet titles, see Yen Ching-hwang, "Ch'ing's Sale of Honours and the Chinese Leadership in Singapore and Malaya (1877-1912)", in *Journal of Southeast Asian Studies*, vol. 1, no. 2 (September, 1970), pp. 20–23.

[58]Huang Tsun-hsien, *op. cit.*, in *Sing Po*, 2/11/1892, p. 1.

[59]See Paul A. Cohen, *Between Tradition and Modernity: Wang T'ao and Reform in Late Ch'ing China* (Cambridge, Mass., 1974), chapter 9, pp. 244–76.

[60]It was claimed that Huang had suggested to the Tsungli Yamen for making Korea as a province of China so as to prevent the Japanese takeover. See Ch'ien Ngo-sun, *op. cit.*, p. 77. For the attitude of the Treaty Port Community Group to which Hsueh Fu-ch'eng belonged towards this issue, see Louis T. Sigel, "The Treaty Port Community and Chinese Foreign Policy in the 1880s", in *Papers on Far Eastern History*, no. 11 (March, 1975), p. 83.

overseas Chinese should be recruited in the service of China.[61]
Besides, both had a mutual respect for each other's scholarship and
literary achievements.[62] Although Hsueh was Huang's superior in
the diplomatic hierarchy, he seems to have treated Huang not as a
subordinate but as a close friend and adviser. His faith in Huang's
expertise on overseas Chinese led him to accept Huang's full
recommendation for the abolition of the policy.

At the end of 1892, Huang drafted a submission to Hsueh asking
him to memorialise the Court for action.[63] Huang listed all the
reasons why this obsolete policy should be changed. The aim of the
action being to attract overseas Chinese.[64] Based on this document,
Hsueh sent off his famous memorial from London on 29 June 1893.
To convince the Emperor on this issue, he needed to show that the
policy had a historical context, but due to changing circumstances,
it had lost its original purpose and needed to be changed. He stated:

> . . . the prohibition of Chinese going overseas originated in the
> reigns of Emperors Shun-chih (1644–61) and K'ang-hsi (1662–
> 1722). At that time Cheng Ch'eng-kung (Koxinga) and his son
> occupied Taiwan and threatened the security of Kiangsu, Che-
> kiang, Fukien and Kwangtung. They enticed and forced ordin-
> ary people to join them. The prohibition of emigration over-
> seas was duly promulgated because of the widespread unrest
> and the threat of the enemy in the coastal areas. Those
> overseas Fukienese who failed to return and later smuggled
> themselves into China, were liable to capital punishment. . . .
> Since the 22nd year of the Emperor Tao-kuang (1842), China
> had concluded treaties with both Eastern and Western Powers
> and allowed them to trade with China. The first item of the
> Treaty of Chiang-ning (Nanking) stipulated that Chinese and
> British subjects who resided in each other's country would
> receive protection from their respective governments. . . . The

---

[61]This is evident in Hsueh Fu-ch'eng's memorial to the Court in which he quoted
Huang Tsun-hsien's opinion. See Hsueh Fu-ch'eng, *Yung-an ch'uan-chi*, "Hai-wai
wen-p'ien", vol. 1, pp. 18–19.

[62]Hsueh's admiration for Huang is evident in his preface to Huang's book
"History of Japan". See Hsueh Fu-ch'eng, "Jih-pen kuo-chih hsu", in Hsueh Fu-
ch'eng, *Yung-an ch'uan-chi*, "Hai-wai wen-p'ien", vol. 4, pp. 4–5.

[63]The draft was completed while Huang was on holiday in China. It was read
among his friends, and a copy was sent to Singapore. It appears that the draft was
published in *Sing Po*, a leading Chinese newspaper in Singapore, before it was sent
to Hsueh Fu-ch'eng. See *Sing Po*, 2/11/1892, p. 1.

[64]*Ibid.*

protection of overseas Chinese was reiterated in the Treaty with Peru and the Sino-Cuban coolie Agreement; it was reinforced by the establishment of Chinese consulates in various important locations. Nowadays the invention of modern ships and trains has greatly facilitated the communications among countries, and the distance between the Western Powers and our nation has been shortened, they are at our very doorway. We cannot therefore maintain the closed-door policy.

Our holy Dynasty has been ruling China for more than two hundred years. Due to overpopulation, China has been forced to loosen its grip on the prohibition of emigration so that some of its subjects could earn a living overseas. Since the loosening of the control and the change of attitude, returned overseas Chinese have in fact been treated like Chinese who never went abroad. The prohibitive law had itself become obsolete. This is not the result of giving special treatment to the overseas subjects, but as the result of changed circumstances.[65]

Having placed the traditional emigration policy in its historical perspective, Hsueh went on to speak of overseas Chinese pointing out their numerical importance, their wealth and their cultural ties with China, and why they were reluctant to return or invest in China. In introducing the subject of overseas Chinese, Hsueh felt obliged to quote the expert opinion of Huang Tsun-hsien. He said:

In the 17th year of Kuang-hsu (1891), I memorialized the Court to appoint Huang Tsun-hsien as the Consul-General of Singapore [This should be the Consul-General of the Straits Settlements] and instructed him to report to me on the actual conditions of the local Chinese. After a close survey of the emigrant Chinese communities, he has submitted a report to this effect. He said: "The total number of the Chinese in the islands of Southeast Asia amounted to more than one million.[66] The Chinese possess seven tenths of the coastal trade and local real estate, while the Europeans, Arabs and Malays have one tenth each. Among the Chinese, two sevenths are Cantonese, Hainanese and Hakkas, five sevenths are made up of Teochews and Fukienese. . . . The Fukienese are the wealthiest, most of

---

[65] See Hsueh Fu-ch'eng, "Ch'ing ku-ch'u chu-chin chao-lai hua-min shu" (Memorial to the Court requesting the abolition of the old prohibitive law and the solicitation of the overseas Chinese), in Hsueh Fu-ch'eng, *Yung-an ch'uan-chi*, "Hai-wai wen-p'ien", vol. 1, pp. 18–20.

[66] In this context, the Chinese in the islands of Southeast Asia could be just referred to Singapore and Malaya.

them are local-born. Many of them have bought properties
and brought up children. Although the Chinese emigrants have
been residing overseas for more than a hundred years, their
descendants still follow Chinese traditions. They retain the use
of the Chinese calendar, costumes, rites for weddings and
funerals. In recent years, they have been very enthusiastic in
contributing to the relief funds for floods and famines, and
funds for national defence in China. They compete in donations
to the funds in order to obtain awards of brevet titles and ranks
to which they attach great honour. All these reveal their deep
emotional attachment to China. But whenever they are asked
to return to their motherland, they all reply with reluctance
saying that they are afraid of the investigations of officials, extortions of yamen runners, and annoyance of neighbours and
kinsmen. Those who had returned to China with money were
either accused of being connivers with robbers, spies for foreign
countries, smugglers of arms and ammunition to pirates, or
coolie brokers in league with foreign kidnappers. Some of
them had their luggage robbed, their houses dismantled, and
some were blackmailed. Once they are caught, they have no-
where to make a complaint, nor have they anyone to depend
on. This is why they are unwilling to return to their homeland.
Some merchants who did go back to China posed as British or
Dutch subjects to get protection. Some of them even took advantage of their positions to act against the law, but the local
officials did not dare to lay hands on them. To remedy these
defects, the government should publicize that the old prohibitive law is abolished, and the new one is in operation. The
general populace should be informed to this effect and benefit
from it."[67]

Hsueh Fu-ch'eng realised that the change of the traditional policy
would affect not just the Chinese in Southeast Asia whom Huang
Tsun-hsien had referred to, but also the Chinese in other parts of
the world. He needed to show to the Court that he had expert knowledge on overseas Chinese as a whole. He thus endorsed Huang's
line of argument, and added some of his own opinions on the subject. He said:

Huang Tsun-hsien has wide knowledge and keen observation
into the problem of overseas Chinese, his report is thus detailed
and pertinent. . . . There are several million overseas Chinese.

---

[67]Hsueh Fu-ch'eng, *op. cit.*, pp. 18–19.

The majority of the Cantonese abroad are labourers whose customs are lowly and despicable, but they still manage to put some money away after caring for their daily needs. Their remittances to China are responsible for the recent prosperity of certain coastal districts. Many Fukienese are rich merchants. They are harshly treated and even rejected in China. Those of them who are millionaires prefer to remain overseas, and not one out of ten ever returns to China. . . .[68]

How important were the overseas Chinese to China? This was the central question that the Court was most interested in. Hsueh realised he had to emphasise their economic importance in order to convince the Court to accept his proposal. He continued:

By and large the overseas Chinese still have emotional attachment to their motherland, and our nation has no intention to exclude them. But the new regulation regarding the emigration is not widely publicized and made known to the general populace, so that corrupt officials and bad gentry can take advantage of the situation at the expense of those who returned to China. To drive fish into other people's nets, or birds into other people's snares is not a clever policy, but this is what we have been doing. Britain, Holland and other countries have used our subjects to cultivate deserted islands and have succeeded in turning them into prosperous ports. They have made use of us. Instead of seeking alliance with our subjects abroad who have talent and economic potential, we reject them. This means we cannot make use of them. If we take it up now, the situation can still be remedied and we will reap the benefit of it. If not, we will repent forever. . . . Your humble servant sincerely urged Your Majesty to send the memorial to the Tsungli Yamen for discussion, and to work out the best way to protect the overseas Chinese. Could Your Majesty graciously decree to the effect that the traditional prohibitive law has been changed, thereby to put an end to the source of extortion by corrupt officials. The abolition of the law should be made known to general populace through the Governors and Viceroys of the coastal provinces and the Chinese Ministers abroad. At the same time, the Chinese Consuls abroad should be instructed to issue visas to those peaceful and law-abiding subjects who wish to return to China. By so doing, the barriers between people and officials, and between China and the West, could be

---

[68]*Ibid.*, p. 19.

removed, and China's declining support among its overseas subjects could be regained. As a result, those overseas Chinese who are emotionally attached to China would return one after another, and China would benefit from their wealth. Once China is in trouble and needs help, it can depend on its overseas subjects. This is in line with the concept of "if branches flourish, the trunk will be secure".[69]

The memorial was received by the Court on 21 August 1893, and was sent immediately to the Tsungli Yamen for discussion. On 13 September, the Yamen submitted a memorial recommending the official abolition of the old policy. It stated:

.... We believe what Hsueh Fu-ch'eng states is true. The number of Chinese emigrants continues to grow substantially. If we prevent them returning to their homeland, they will be greatly disappointed. We are in favour of Hsueh's proposal, and humbly urge Your Majesty graciously to decree to the Ministry of Jurisdiction that they amend the existing law relating to the punishment of illegal emigrants. The Governors and Viceroys of the coastal provinces are to be instructed to announce widely in prefectures, districts and villages that the old law has been abolished and the new one has been adopted. Except criminals and those profiteers under the disguise of foreign merchants, all law-abiding overseas Chinese, regardless of their length of sojournment or marriage abroad, are welcome to return to China. The Chinese ministers and consuls would issue visas for their legal return. They are welcome to come back to live, and will be treated equally like other Chinese at home. They will also be allowed to go abroad to trade at liberty. Local officials who attempt to blackmail or ill-treat the returned overseas Chinese will be punished by law. This change of policy is in line with the idea of spreading the benevolence of our holy Dynasty. . . ."[70]

On the Yamen's recommendation, the traditional prohibitive policy which had dictated the attitude of Ch'ing officials and which had affected the overseas Chinese for more than two hundred years, was officially changed. This change marked the beginning of a new era, one in which saw the overseas Chinese being protected and courted.

---

[69]*Ibid.*, pp. 19–20.
[70]See Chu Sou-p'eng, *Kuang-hsu-ch'ao tung-hua lu*, vol. 3, p. 3244.

THE ENFORCEMENT OF THE NEW PROTECTION POLICY IN CHINA

Overseas Chinese Response to the New Policy

What emerged after 1893 was an uncoordinated policy without a central enforcing agency. There was no overseas Chinese bureau in the Tsungli Yamen, nor was there a new ministry which could incorporate overseas Chinese affairs into its functions. The absence of a central agency left the enforcement of the new policy mainly in the hands of provincial governors and Chinese diplomats concerned. Those who were interested in overseas Chinese would take initiatives to implement the policy, while the less enthusiastic ones would let the policy take its own course.

Delighted with the introduction of the new policy, Huang Tsun-hsien took initiatives to implement it. He widely publicised the changes in the local Chinese newspapers in Singapore.[71] He also announced that visas would be issued to those who wished to return to China. The visas were to be in three grades: the first grade with a red rim was for top gentry-merchants;[72] the second grade with a purple rim was for ordinary merchants; and the third grade with a blue rim was for coolies.[73] The visas which were available for all the Chinese in Southeast Asia obliged the Chinese officials to protect the returned subjects.

The grading of the visas was not just for administrative convenience, but was also used as a status symbol. Many rich overseas Chinese merchants appreciated this especially since it meant they would get special treatment by Chinese officials in China.[74] Rich merchants were thus encouraged to visit China or invest money there.

There is no evidence to suggest that similar steps were taken by other Chinese diplomats in this early stage of the introduction of

---

[71]See the public notice of the Chinese Consul-General for the Straits Settlements, in *Sing Po*, 2/6/1894, p. 4.

[72]The term "Gentry-merchant" (Shen-shang) was mainly applied to those rich merchants in the overseas Chinese communities.

[73]See the public notice, in *Sing Po*, 2/6/1894, p. 4.

[74]For a discussion on the appreciation of status symbols by the Chinese leaders in Singapore and Malaya during the end of the nineteenth and the beginning of the twentieth centuries, see Yen Ching-hwang, "Ch'ing Sale of Honours and Chinese Leadership in Singapore and Malaya 1877-1912", in *Journal of Southeast Asian Studies*, vol. 1, no. 2 (September, 1970), pp. 20–32.

the new policy. This anomaly in the enforcement was also evident in the moves of the provincial governments. In 1895, the Viceroy of Fukien and Chekiang proclaimed new rules for protecting the returned overseas Chinese. The rules offered protection at the very basic levels, such as safety of life and baggage on arrival at Amoy, freedom from extortion by corrupt customs officials and unscrupulous relatives and kinsmen.[75] This move did not seem to have been followed by the Viceroy of Kwangtung and Kwangsi under whose jurisdiction many of the returned overseas Chinese would be affected. This lack of uniformity had serious repercussions on the implementation of the policy, for it failed to present to overseas Chinese an image of a coherent policy, and this gave rise to uncertainty and confusion.

At this early stage of experimentation, many overseas Chinese, though excited at the change, adopted a cautious attitude. They were not so much sceptical about the sincerity of this new move, but were concerned with its effective implementation. The concern was well expressed in the *Sing Po* editorial in response to the proclamation of the Viceroy of Fukien and Chekiang. The main question posed in the article was how the Fukien provincial government would ensure the proper enforcement of the new rules.[76] There was no watch-dog organisation proposed, much of the implementation of the new rules had to depend on the cooperation and good faith of government officials, local people and relatives and kinsmen of the returned overseas Chinese. Although the new rules allowed the victims to bring the extortionate customs officials, inspectors and runners to the Yamen of the Amoy Circuit (Hsia-men-tao), the time and cost of the lawsuits would effectively prevent this happening.[77]

The *Sing Po* editorial may not represent the majority opinion of all of the overseas Chinese, but the questions raised there expressed the deep-seated fear of many of the overseas Chinese. It also touched the central issue of the problem — the strained relationship between the Chinese officials and the empire's overseas subjects. The

---

[75]There were four rules contained in the Viceroy's proclamation which was reproduced in a leading Chinese newspaper in Singapore, see *Sing Po*, 15/7/1895, p. 4.

[76]See "Shu pao-hu fan-k'e hui-chi chang-ch'eng cha hou" (Comments on the Proclamation of the Rules for the Protection of Returned Overseas Chinese) in *Sing Po*, 16/7/1895, p. 1.

[77]*Ibid.*

traditional relationship between mandarins and subjects was characterised by authoritarianism and paternalism. The mandarins' relationship with the overseas subjects was worse than that, for the paternalistic and authoritarian attitude was reinforced by the prejudice against the "deserters" from the Confucian culture.[78] This was further buttressed by the prohibitive law against the emigrants. Under the operation of the old law, the mandarins invariably regarded the returned overseas Chinese as natural prey and any form of squeeze was justifiable. Although the old law was officially abolished at the end of 1893, this bias against the overseas Chinese was to continue for some time. It was this attitude that partly prevented the new policy from being effectively implemented.

Protection of the Returned Overseas Chinese

How many overseas Chinese visited China and invested in China? How successful was the operation of the new policy in its early stage? There are no figures available to answer these questions, but the fact that the Ch'ing government had to create a new body, the "Merchants Protection Bureau" (Pao-shang-chi) in 1899 to attract overseas Chinese, indicates the policy was not working well in its early stages.[79] Probably then, fewer overseas Chinese returned to China before 1899 than might have been expected.

This move by the Court appears to have been prompted by a memorial from the Fukien Governor, Hsu Ying-kuei in 1899. Hsu suggested establishing a "Merchants Protection Bureau" at Amoy to protect returned Fukienese originating from the prefectures of Chang-chou and Ch'uan-chou.[80] In his proposal, upright gentry members were to be appointed to the directorship of the Bureau. The returned overseas Chinese were to register with the Bureau which had to look after their welfare. It had to arrange for them to go back to their home villages, and investigate and take action on their behalf if they were disturbed.[81] What motivated Hsu Ying-kuei to press for this new body is uncertain. He was probably appalled

---

[78]For a detailed discussion on the changing images and attitudes towards the overseas Chinese, see Yen Ching-hwang, "Ch'ing Changing Images of the Overseas Chinese (1644–1912)", in *Modern Asian Studies*, vol. 15, no. 2 (1981), pp. 261–85.

[79]See *Ta Ch'ing te-tsung ching-huang-ti shih-lu* (Veritable Records of the Emperor Kuang-hsu of the Great Ch'ing Empire), vol. 442, p. 15.

[80]*Ibid.*

[81]*Ibid.*

by the ineffective enforcement of the new rules in Fukien, and believed that something should be done about it;[82] or perhaps he was interested in attracting overseas Chinese capitalists to undertake mining and railway enterprises in Fukien so as to ward off the intrusion of Western and Japanese capital.[83] Whatever the motive, Hsu's proposal was accepted by the Court.[84] On the recommendation of Censor P'an Ch'ing-lan, the Court decreed that Viceroys and Governors of the coastal provinces must follow suit.[85] In the following year (1900), the Kwangtung provincial "Merchants Protection Bureau" was established in Canton,[86] and another regional bureau was set up in Swatow.[87]

The speed of setting up the bureaus indicates the interest in the new mechanism. There was a hope that it would more effectively implement the protection policy. The two major functions of the Bureau were to register the returned overseas Chinese, and to look after their welfare while they were in China.[88] In registering the returned subjects, the Bureau sent out printed forms to various social organisations (Hui-kuan)[89] in overseas Chinese communities. Leaders of these Hui-kuan were asked to help to complete the

---

[82]*Ibid.*

[83]Hsu could have been influenced by the Battle for Concessions waged by Western Powers and Japan in acquiring mining and railway concessions in China. For a discussion of the use of overseas Chinese capital to replace foreign capital in the modernisation of Ch'ing China, see Yen Ching-hwang, "The Overseas Chinese and Late Ch'ing Economic Modernization", in *Modern Asian Studies*, vol. 16, no. 2 (1982), pp. 222–27.

[84]See *Ta Ch'ing te-tsung ching-huang-ti shih-lu*, vol. 442, p. 15.

[85]*Ibid.*, vol. 443, p. 8b.

[86]The office of the Bureau was set up at the Ch'i-ch'ang street outside the T'ai-p'ing gate of the Canton city building. See "Memorial of the Governor of Kwangtung and the Acting Viceroy of Kwangtung and Kwangsi, Te Shou, to the Court", in *Kuang-hsu ch'ao tung-hua lu*, 1st moon of 26th year of Kuang-hsu (February, 1900), vol. 4, pp. 10–11. The same memorial was reproduced in *Jit Shin Pau*, a Chinese newspaper in Singapore, on 21 March 1900, p. 6. Regarding the location of the office of the Bureau, see *Jit Shin Pau*, 27/4/1900, p. 7.

[87]See *Jit Shin Pau*, 19/3/1900, p. 4.

[88]See *Kuang-hsu ch'ao tung-hua lu*, 1st moon of 26th year of Kuang-hsu (February, 1900), vol. 4, pp. 10–11.

[89]The term Hui-kuan conventionally includes the dialect organisations and Chinese Chambers of Commerce. But it could also be used as a general term to include all forms of social organisations in overseas Chinese communities such as clan organisations (known as Tsung-tz'u or Kongsi) and guilds (known as Hang). In my opinion, this term is used here more as a general term.

forms with personal details,[90] and a photo was to be attached. The returning overseas Chinese were required to bring the completed forms and to register with the Bureau on their arrival at the ports.[91] This registration was probably designed to keep a record of visitors and to facilitate the Bureau's administrative work.

In looking after the welfare of the returned emigrants, the Bureau concentrated on the area of receiving complaints and transmitting them to the local officials.[92] The work included helping the returned emigrants go back to their respective home villages.[93] It must be pointed out here that the Bureau was not exclusively established to protect the returned overseas Chinese. It was also entrusted with the work of protecting outgoing emigrants. Relatives of the coolies who had been enticed abroad could complain to the Bureau, which would then contact the leaders of the overseas "Hui-kuan" for investigation. The victims would thus be repatriated to China with the financial help of the Chinese Consuls abroad.[94]

The main functions of the Bureau show that it was not intended to be the main government body for enforcing the new law of protecting the returned overseas Chinese, but rather as a liaison office between the bureaucracy and the populace. It could only influence the officials over the execution of the law.

It appears that the Bureau was run by members of the local gentry. Presumably the gentry spoke the dialects of the returned overseas Chinese, and were in a better position than the officials (who were unlikely to speak the local dialect) to communicate with them, and were thus able to obtain their trust and confidence. The gentry were appointed by the provincial government to the directorship of the Bureau on a voluntary basis, receiving no funds from the government, and thus having to raise funds to pay for its regular expenditure.[95]

Superficially the involvement of the gentry members in the Bureau might seem an example of public-spirited gentry participation in local affairs.[96] But most of the gentry's functions had direct or indi-

---

[90]Personal details included name, age, place of origin, occupation and number of family members. See *Kuang-hsu ch'ao tung-hua, op. cit.*, p. 11.

[91]*Ibid.*

[92]*Ibid.*

[93]See *Ta Ch'ing te-tsung ching-huang-ti shih-lu*, vol. 442, p. 15.

[94]See *Kuang-hsu-ch'ao tung-hua lu, op. cit.*, p. 11.

[95]*Ibid.*

[96]Gentry members during the Ch'ing period were involved in many of the local

rect benefits.[97] This leads one to suspect their seemingly altruistic moves in being involved in the "Merchants Protection Bureau".[98] By becoming involved in the Bureau, they would have the opportunity to contact wealthy overseas Chinese visiting their home villages and perhaps planning to invest in China. They would quickly establish personal relationships through which to influence the wealthy merchants as to the types of enterprises to be undertaken, and these enterprises may have indirectly benefitted them. Sometimes they were sent overseas by the Bureau to solicit funds for the economic development of the home provinces they represented.[99] On such occasions, they would have an even better chance to establish cordial relationships with wealthy overseas Chinese merchants abroad.

Whatever good intentions the government might have had in making this move, the Bureau did not measure up to the government's expectation. In fact it had some inherent weaknesses that undermined its work. Firstly, its character as liaison body meant that it had no power to enforce the law, effective law enforcement had to depend on the influence of its directors. Secondly, as it received no regular government funds to offset running costs, its work was interrupted by shortage of funds, and its efficiency was greatly reduced. Thirdly, as the directorship of the bureau was honourary, it had difficulty in attracting the so-called "upright gentry-merchant" (kung-cheng shen-shang). Those who were prepared to work for nothing; those who had to raise money to meet the running costs were likely to be those who wished to make most use of the position for personal gain.

These internal weaknesses prevented the Bureau from becoming an effective non-government body looking after the returned over-

---

affairs, including the supervision of the financing, construction and operation of public works, the organisation and command of local defense corps, and the establishment and management of local and clan charity organisations. See Chung-li Chang, *The Income of the Chinese Gentry* (Seattle, 1962), p. 43.

[97]*Ibid.*, pp. 43–73.

[98]For instance, the gentry members who were directors of the Kwangtung Provincial Merchants Protection Bureau did not draw any salary from the Bureau. Besides, they had to raise more than 100 taels per month (this could range between 1,500 and 2,000 taels per year) to meet the expenses of the Bureau. See *Kuang-hsu-ch'ao tung-hua-lu*, 1st moon of 26th year of Kuang-hsu (February, 1900), vol. 4, pp. 10–11.

[99]For instance, gentry members like Ch'iu Feng-chia and Wang Hsiao-ch'ang were sent by the Swatow Merchants Protection Bureau to tour Southeast Asian Chinese communities in March 1900. See *Jit Shin Pau*, 19/3/1900, p. 4.

seas Chinese. Worst of all, when the Bureau fell into the hands of unscrupulous persons, it was turned into an organisation for corruption and extortion. This appears to be the case of the Amoy Merchants Protection Bureau, the first of its kind set up in the coastal provinces of China. The mismanagement and extortion became so serious that the Chinese in Penang, Singapore and Luzon were prompted to send a petition to the Ministry of Commerce (Shang-pu) in December 1903.[100] The petitioners made the following charges: the Bureau was run by "urban scoundrels" (Shih-k'uai); complaints of the victims had been brushed aside; sinecure positions had been created in the Bureau; the luggage of returned overseas merchants had not been properly looked after; returned overseas merchants had been extorted in many ways, and there were never any balance sheets issued by the Bureau.[101] These serious charges were not likely to have been made without substance. The petitioners had probably experienced these extortions themselves, or were friends and relatives of the victims. Charges of this kind not only discredited the "Merchants Protection Bureau", but also damaged the image of the imperial government among its overseas subjects.

In fact, even before this petition was sent to the Ministry of Commerce, the notorious Amoy Merchants Protection Bureau had been suspended from its functions and its supervising official, Yen-nien, punished after investigation by Censor Yeh T'i-yen.[102] On the recommendation of the Acting Viceroy of Chekiang and Fukien, Ch'ung Shan, the Bureau was incorporated into the newly proposed Bureau of Commercial Affairs (Shang-wu-chi) which was to select "upright gentry-merchants" to run it.[103]

The response of the Ministry of Commerce to the petition of the merchants of Penang, Singapore and Luzon, was to ensure the pro-

---

[100]The original petition is no longer available, it is contained in part in the memorial of the Ministry of Commerce to the Court dated 4th day of 11th moon of 29th year of Kuang-hsu (22 December 1903), see *Ta-ch'ing kuang-hsu hsin fa-ling* (New Statutes of the Great Ch'ing Empire During the Kuang-hsu Reign), vol. 16, pp. 56–57. The same memorial is also found in *Kuang-hsu-ch'ao tung-hua lu*, 11th moon of 29th year, vol. 5, pp. 129–30.

[101]*Ibid.*

[102]*Ibid.*

[103]See *Ta-ch'ing kuang hsu hsin fa-ling*, vol. 16, p. 56; *Kuang-hsu-ch'ao tung-hua lu, op. cit.*, p. 129.

per functioning of the new Bureau in Amoy. It memorialised the Court for the power to supervise the running of "Merchants Protection Bureaus" in general, and of the Amoy Bureau in particular. This involved the submission of the new rules and regulations for the protection of the returned emigrants, and of the new appointees for various Bureaus.[104]

The Ministry of Commerce which was established in September 1903, was part of the result of the post-Boxer reform programme undertaken by the Empress Dowager. Its main aim was to promote commerce and industry which were considered vital for the re-strengthening of the ailing empire. In the climate of resisting the encroachment of foreign capital at the turn of the present century, the overseas Chinese capital was considered to be important in China's economic modernisation.[105] The Ministry had vested interest to see more overseas Chinese merchants attracted to invest in China. Thus, it was concerned about the safety and welfare of the returned merchants in their home villages. The merchants, after many years of absence from their home villages, faced hostile local bullies and scoundrels who were prepared to resort to extortion and kidnapping. The Ministry learned that some of these merchants were bankrupt only a few months after their return to their home villages.[106] Under these circumstances, the protection by the local officials was crucial for the safety and welfare of the returned merchants, and the key to the success of the protection policy. The Ministry memorialised the Court on the matter in 1903.[107] As a result, an imperial decree was issued in December of the same year to that effect, with a stern warning that those officials who had violated the instruction would be punished.[108]

The effort of the Ministry of Commerce was commendable, but the result was lamentable. Only one and a half years after the 1903 memorial, the new Amoy Bureau of Commercial Affairs became a racket for corrupt officials and unscrupulous gentry. Familiar

---

[104]*Ibid.*

[105]See Yen Ching-hwang, "The Overseas Chinese and Late Ch'ing Economic Modernization", in *Modern Asian Studies*, vol. 16, no. 2 (April, 1982), pp. 222-24; M.R. Godley, *The Mandarin Capitalists from Nanyang: Overseas Chinese Enterprise in the Modernization of China 1893-1911* (Cambridge, 1981), pp. 129-48.

[106]See *Kuang-hsu-ch'ao tung-hua lu, op. cit.*, p. 130.

[107]*Ibid.*

[108]See *Ta-ch'ing te-tsung ching-huang-ti shih-lu*, vol. 523, p. 3a.

features of Ch'ing bureaucracy such as corruption, nepotism, waste-fulness and inefficiency plagued the organisation. The supervising official, Lo Ch'eng-chu, was complacent and bigoted and had his brother Lo K'ang occupying a sinecure position in the Bureau. Fur-thermore, the Bureau collected substantial fees from the returned overseas Chinese,[109] but nothing concrete was done to protect them. As a result the returned merchants were still subjected to harass-ment, bullying and extortions.[110] In view of these repeated abuses, the Ministry of Commerce recommended that its main functions be transferred to the newly established Chinese Chamber of Commerce of Amoy (Hsia-men shang-wu tsung-hui).[111] As the Chamber was a self-governing body, and the leaders were elected to represent local business interests, this move suggests the Ministry had more confid-ence in its ability to look after the welfare of the returned overseas Chinese. The Court promptly approved the Ministry's recommen-dation and issued a decree on 24 July 1905 to that effect.[112]

What enraged the Ministry most was the defiance by some local officials of the 1903 Court decree. The decree clearly held the officials responsible for the well-being of the returned overseas Chinese in their home districts.[113] But many of these officials took no positive step in rendering protection. Some of the unscrupulous ones even connived with local bullies and robbers to take advantage of the returned emigrants. The Ministry had from time to time received complaints from overseas Chinese,[114] but the most serious charges were laid against officials of some southern Fukien districts in 1906. Wang Kuo-jui and Yuan Ying-ch'i, Magistrates of Chao-an and An-hsi districts, were charged with condoning open robberies of the returned overseas Chinese;[115] T'an Tzu-chun, the Magistrate of

---

[109]It was estimated by an official of the Ministry of Commerce who investigated into the Amoy Bureau, that the fees collected from the returned overseas Chinese from Philippines alone amounted to 40,000 or 50,000 dollars. See *Kuang-hsu-ch'ao tung-hua lu*, 6th moon of 31st year (July, 1905), vol. 5, p. 93.

[110]*Ibid.*

[111]*Ibid.*

[112]See *Ta-ch'ing te-tsung ching-huang-ti shih-lu*, vol. 546, p. 13a.

[113]*Ibid.*, vol. 523, p. 3a.

[114]*Ibid.*, vol. 555, p. 2.

[115]See the memorial of the Ministry of Commerce to the Court relating to the punishment of local officials who failed to protect the returned overseas Chinese. This memorial is not found in Ch'ing official records, but fortunately it was reproduced in the *Lat Pau*, a leading Chinese newspaper in Singapore. See *Lat Pau*, 5/7/1906, pp. 3 and 8.

Nan-an district, was accused of using local gangsters on his staff, and of condoning robberies.[116] These serious charges were not made by ordinary Chinese, but by leading merchants such as Goh Siew-tin and Lin Yun-lung, [117] who were influential in overseas Chinese business circles.[118] Realising that any failure to act on grievances of the emigrant leaders would seriously affect the policy of attracting overseas Chinese capital, the Ministry of Commerce memorialised the Court for action against certain officials.[119] Again the Court accepted the recommendation, and ordered the Acting Viceroy of Chekiang and Fukien, Ch'ung Shan, to investigate, and to punish the said officials if the allegations were well-founded.[120]

Despite the efforts of the Ministry of Commerce and the decrees of the Court, the extortion and robbing of the returned overseas Chinese seems not to have eased. In fact, the situation of some areas became worse. Chia-wo-shan, a rural hinterland of Amoy where many overseas Chinese of Southeast Asia originated, reported in 1907 of many cases of robbing of the families of the overseas Chinese. It was claimed that when the Imperial Commissioner, Yang Shih-ch'i, toured Southeast Asia at the end of 1907, he received many complaints from local Chinese relating to frequent robberies in the Chia-wo-shan area.[121] Due to repeated pressure from the Ministry of Agriculture, Industry and Commerce (the successor to the Ministry of Commerce), the Circuit Intendent of Amoy arranged

---

[116]*Ibid.*

[117]Apart from Goh Siew-tin and Lin Yun-lung, other rich merchants who were involved in these petitions were Yeh Ch'ing-chi, Ch'en Tao-te and Lin Sheng. Goh Siew-tin and Yeh Ch'ing-chi were originally from Chao-an district, Lin Yun-lung and Ch'en Tao-te from Nan-an, and Lin Sheng from An-hsi. *Ibid.*

[118]Goh Siew-tin was a well-known merchant in Singapore, a community leader, and was in 1906 the first President of the newly founded Singapore Chinese Chamber of Commerce. For Goh's short biography, see Su Hsiao-hsien (ed.), *Chang chou shih-shu lü Hsing t'ung-hsiang lu* (A Directory of Chang Chou Chinese in Singapore) (Singapore, 1948), p. 59; Song Ong Siang, *One Hundred Years' History of the Chinese in Singapore* (Singapore, reprint, 1967), pp. 143–44; for records of Goh as the first President of the Singapore Chinese Chamber of Commerce, see "Hsin-chia-po chung-hua shang-wu tsung-hui teng-chi i-shih-pu" (minutes of the Singapore Chinese Chamber of Commerce) (manuscript), vol. 1, pp. 2–3; see also *Lat Pau*, 19/4/1906, p. 3.

[119]The memorial of the Ministry of Commerce to the Court, reproduced in *Lat Pau*, 5/7/1906, pp. 3 and 8.

[120]See *Ta-ch'ing te-tsung ching-huang-ti shih-lu*, vol. 559, p. 5.

[121]See *Lat Pau*, 7/5/1908, p. 5.

a special police force to look after the families of the overseas Chinese who had to pay a levy for the maintenance of this force. A commissioner was appointed to investigate the local conditions and to organise the operation. But the commissioner soon got involved in corruption and extortion, and the whole thing turned out to be a farce.[122] The Chia-wo-shan case may not be typical as far as the frequency of robbery is concerned, nevertheless it is a further evidence that the Ch'ing government's policy of protecting the returned overseas Chinese and their families was not working.

Reasons for the Failure of the Protection Policy

One cannot help asking why the policy did not work. What was wrong with Chinese society? Why did the Ch'ing central government fail to enforce the law? These are basic questions, the answers to which would reveal more grievous weaknesses in the Ch'ing bureaucracy and society as a whole. Apart from the traditional paternalistic and oppressive relationship between the mandarins and the people, the main reason for the failure of the enforcement of the protection policy was corruption. Corruption as an in-built system has a long history in Ch'ing China. Confucian ideas of dedication and thrift clashed with the practical requirements of the bureaucracy. If an official wished to effectively discharge his duties, he had to employ a number of private secretaries paying them out of his own pocket; his meagre official renumeration would not allow him to meet the practical needs.[123] The only alternative open to him was to take bribes. Because this was so widespread in the bureaucracy, it became almost socially acceptable during the Ch'ing period.

This corrupt system was reinforced by the prevailing social values which exalted the idea of "Promotion in official rank and enhancement of wealth" (Sheng-kuan fa-ts'ai). Traditionally, "Wealth and honour" (Fu-kuei) were considered to be the highest rewards for scholars, and in fact became the goal of one's life. Those who studied hard and passed the imperial examination expected to be given official positions,[124] from which came honour

---

[122]*Ibid.*

[123]See T'ung-tsu Ch'u, *Local Government in China Under the Ch'ing* (Cambridge, Mass., 1962), pp. 22-32.

[124]It must be pointed out that after the middle of the nineteenth century since the introduction of the sale of office on a large scale, the bureaucracy was overstaffed. Many successful candidates had difficulty in obtaining an official position, and had to wait for a long time to fill a vacancy. For discussion on the importance of the sale

for himself, his family, his clansmen, relatives and friends. Furthermore, he could use his official position to enrich himself. Although bribe-taking was contrary to Confucian principles, the Chinese officials who imbued themselves with Confucian values, managed to resolve the contradiction well.

Ch'ing corrupt practice was further aggravated by the sale of offices and honours in the nineteenth century.[125] The sale became so widespread throughout the empire that it had also extended to include the overseas Chinese.[126] It undermined the principle of merit on which the imperial bureaucracy was based. At the same time, it opened up the bureaucracy to many undesirable elements who considered the acquisition of office as a form of investment and who attempted to squeeze as much as possible out of the people. Thus corruption bred corruption, and evil practices multiplied.

During the late Ch'ing period when the Empress Dowager Tz'u-hsi had tightened her grip on the empire, her personal habit of accumulating wealth opened up vast avenues for corruption.[127] Her notorious chief eunuch, Li Lien-ying, was well-known for his appetite for bribe-taking, and he was accused for his role in the Empress Dowager's misappropriation of naval funds for the reconstruction of the Summer Palace.[128]

In such an environment, everyone in office — from the highest

---

of offices in the Ch'ing bureaucracy, see Hsieh Pao-chao, *The Government of China, 1644-1911* (New York, 1966), pp. 112-13; "The Sale of Official Rank, Adopted by the Government of China for Increasing Its Revenue", in *The Chinese Repository*, vol. 18 (1849), p. 207.

[125]Although the Ch'ien Lung Emperor started the sale of offices and ranks in 1756, the practice did not become important until the Tao Kuang reign. He raised about 6,000,000 taels in 1826 for the Turkestan war. See Hsieh Pao-chao, *The Government of China 1644-1911*, p. 108; Chung-li Chang, *The Chinese Gentry* (Seattle, 1955), p. 105.

[126]See Yen Ching-hwang, "Ch'ing's Sale of Honours and the Chinese Leadership of Singapore and Malaya 1877-1912", in *Journal of Southeast Asian Studies*, vol. 1, no. 2 (September, 1970), pp. 21-22.

[127]See Hsu Hsiao-t'ien, *Ch'ing kung shih-san ch'ao yen-i: Tz'u-hsi t'an-ch'ien* (Hong Kong, n.d.), pp. 182-91; it was claimed that the Empress Dowager left a private treasure amounting to 99,000,000 taels of silver and 1,200,000 taels of gold after her death in 1908. See *North China Herald*, 17 April 1909, cited in H.B. Morse, *The International Relations of the Chinese Empire* (Taipei, reprint 1966), vol. 3, p. 442.

[128]See J.O.P. Bland & E. Backhouse, *China Under The Empress Dowager: Being the History of the Life and Times of Tzu Hsi* (William Heinemann, London, 1914), pp. 64-66.

ranking official in the capital down to the Yamen runner in the district office — was corrupt. Lofty Confucian principles of dedication and serving the community and nation gave way to personal greed. Everyone in the bureaucracy was entangled in a web of protection and graft. Local officials had to squeeze as much as possible from the people they ruled and had to give a portion of their income in the form of presents to superiors and officials in the capital. Failure to do this would either jeopardise his position or reduce his chance of promotion.[129] As for officials at the capital, they had to depend on presents collected from local officials to maintain their luxurious lifestyle. Their ability to maintain influence in official circles in the capital which depended on presents, in turn generated more presents. They sometimes tried to get lucrative positions in provincial government and to lay their hands on wealth.[130]

Under the influence of this in-built corruption, the local officials in Kwangtung and Fukien naturally regarded the returned overseas Chinese as potential spoils, and as a new source of income. Prior to 1893, the returned overseas Chinese were "squeezed" without any complaints because they were illegal emigrants. The introduction of the new policy changed their status, but changed little of the basic attitude of the local officials. The well-entrenched corrupt practices and deep-rooted prejudice against overseas Chinese would take years to change. The new policy and the repeated edicts forced them to comply superficially, but behind every change in name or organisation, the same old "squeeze", the same personal ambition, went on. This basically explains the failure of the enforcement of the new policy.

The failure of the protection policy should also be understood in part in the context of central-provincial rivalry. Since most overseas Chinese came from Kwangtung and Fukien, the two provincial governments considered themselves to be the rightful authorities to run overseas Chinese affairs. Their initiatives to cultivate good relationship with the Chinese in Southeast Asia in the 1870s and 1880s were clear indications of this line of thinking.[131] When the traditional policy was proclaimed null and void in 1893, no organ-

---

[129]See Chang Te-ch'ang, *Ch'ing-chi i-ke ching-kuan te sheng-huo* (Life of a Court Official in the Late Ch'ing Period) (Hong Kong, n.d.), p. 2.

[130]*Ibid.*, pp. 16, 20.

[131]See Yen Ching-hwang, "The Overseas Chinese and Late Ch'ing Economic Modernization", in *Modern Asian Studies*, vol. 16, no. 2 (April, 1982), pp. 219–21.

isations were established to implement the new policy. The creation of the "Merchants Protection Bureau" in 1899 in the provinces was an ad hoc arrangement which did not have a firm status in the bureaucracy. The Bureau's relationship with both the provincial and central bureaucracies was ambiguous — it did not take orders from either of them though it was under the indirect control of the former. The provincial government, particularly at the level of Circuit, jealously guarded its control over the Bureau which meant extra income for the province and its officials. The Ministry of Commerce which emerged to become a formidable force in the central bureaucracy, was anxious to control some mechanisms in the provinces which had direct dealings with merchants and overseas Chinese with whom it rested a great hope for China's modernisation.[132] The failure in controlling the Bureau led the Ministry to act as the critic of the implementation of the new policy. It aired many complaints on behalf of the overseas Chinese, repeatedly attacked the Bureau, and memorialised the Court for redress.[133]

The fact that most complaints went directly to the Ministry rather than the provincial governments testified to the Ministry's popularity with the overseas Chinese, but this further intensified the central-provincial conflict. Not being informed before the complaints reached the Ministry, the provincial governments felt offended by these acts. Further, the efforts of the Ministry to bear on the provincial governments through the Court, enraged them. As a result, the provincial governments only paid lip-service to various edicts, and bore a grudge against the Ministry.

The failure of the Ch'ing government to enforce the new policy had serious implications. Firstly, it lost credibility among the overseas Chinese. If it could not effectively carry out its policy in the territories under its jurisdiction, how could they trust its promises to protect them overseas? Secondly, because of the lack of confidence in the Ch'ing government, overseas Chinese merchants were hesitant to respond to calls for investment in China.

---

[132]See Wellington K.K. Chan, *Merchants, Mandarins and Modern Enterpise in Late Ch'ing China* (Cambridge, Mass., 1977), pp. 197–212.

[133]See "Memorial of the Ministry of Commerce to the Court relating to the Protection of the Returned Overseas Chinese (1903)", in *Ta-ch'ing kuang-hsu hsin fa-ling*, vol. 16, pp. 56–57, the abstract of the same memorial can also be found in *Kuang-hsu-ch'ao tung-hua lu*, 11th moon of 29th year, vol. 5 (Peking), pp. 129–30; "Memorial of the Ministry of Commerce to the Court 1906", reproduced in *Lat Pau*, 5/7/1906, pp. 3 and 8.

7
Protection of Overseas Chinese Abroad after 1893

What emerged after the abolition of the traditional emigration policy in 1893 was a new spirit of protecting overseas Chinese abroad. The new spirit was embodied in the Tsungli Yamen's fresh attitude towards the protection issue. Before 1893, the Yamen was passive, responding mostly to the actions taken by the Chinese diplomats concerned. After 1893, the Yamen demonstrated a greater degree of concern for the destiny of overseas Chinese, and was prepared to take initiative on the issue.[1] With this spirit, the Yamen began to coordinate a new measure of protecting overseas Chinese abroad. This was an integral part of the new overall policy of courting overseas subjects. Under this new policy, more consulates were to be set up in overseas Chinese communities, more active protection was to be given by the Chinese diplomats, and more emissaries were to be sent to tour overseas Chinese communities.[2] Active pro-

---

[1] For example, during the outbreak of the first Sino-Japanese war (1894–95), the Yamen expected that the Chinese in Japan would be greatly disadvantaged after the Chinese diplomatic staff was withdrawn. It took the initiative to arrange protection of the local Chinese by American diplomats in Japan. See "Cable from the Tsungli Yamen to Li Hung-chang relating to the protection of Chinese merchants in Japan dated 17th day of 6th moon of 20th year of Kuang-hsu (19 July 1894)", "Cable from the Tsungli Yamen to the Chinese Minister to the United States, Yang Ju, relating to the request of American protection of the Chinese in Japan dated 25th day of 6th moon of 20th year of Kuang-hsu (27 July 1894)" in *Ch'ing-chi wai-chiao shih-liao*, vol. 93, pp. 4a, 15b–16a.

[2] For consulates set up after 1893, see Chapter 4; four emissaries were sent by the Ch'ing central government to tour the overseas Chinese communities in Southeast Asia during this period. They were the mission of Chang Pi-shih (1905), the mission of Yang Shih-ch'i (1907), the mission of Wang Ta-chen (1909) and the mission of Chao Ch'ung-fan (1911). For details, see *Ta-Ch'ing te-tsung ching-huang-ti shih-lu*, vol. 535, p. 6b, vol. 576, pp. 10b–11a; *Kuang-hsu ch'ao tung-hua lu* (comp. by Chu Shou-p'eng) (Peking, 1958), vol. 5, p. 91; "Wai Wu Pu Archives", 33rd year of Kuang-hsu; *Cheng-chih kuan-pao* (Ch'ing Government Gazettes) (Taipei, 1965), no. 15 (34th year of Kuang-hsu), pp. 515–16, no. 17 (1st year of Hsuan-t'ung), p. 317, no. 42 (3rd year of Huang-t'ung), p. 98; *Penang Sin Pao*, 28/3/1911, p. 3; see also

tection was viewed as a premium for acquiring overseas Chinese capital for the modernisation of China.

The essence of this new protective measure was the maximum use of diplomacy. It did not intend to seek direct confrontation with Western Powers, but to get what China wanted through negotiations and compromise. This new measure was not widely publicised but quietly adopted by the Yamen. It seems reasonable to infer that the return of Prince Kung, the elderly Manchu statesmen, to the Yamen in 1894,[3] might have contributed in part to the adoption of this new move. Prince Kung was an experienced politician who had been the head of the Yamen since its inception in 1861 and was the key figure in handling China's foreign affairs for nearly a quarter of a century until April 1884 when he was dropped from power.[4] His experience in handling the coolie issue in the 1870s was useful in helping to adopt the new measure.

But the new measure failed to achieve its main objective. Its failure was the result of institutional weaknesses, circumstances and imperialism. The weaknesses of the Yamen have been discussed in Chapter 5, and these continued to thwart its works. The Yamen's decline in power in the last few years of the nineteenth century further undermined the working of the new measure. Even after the restructuring of the Yamen into a new Wai Wu Pu (Ministry of Foreign Affairs) in 1901, it was unable to implement the protective measure in a much more vigorous way.

M.R. Godley, *The Mandarin-Capitalists from Nanyang*, pp. 129–39; Chui Kwei-chiang, "Wan Ch'ing kuan-li fang-wen Hsin-chia-po" (The Visits of Chinese Officials to Singapore during the Late Ch'ing Period), in *Journal of South Seas Society*, vol. 29, pts. 1 & 2 (1974), pp. 15–29.

[3]See Ch'ien Shih-p'u (ed.), *Ch'ing-chi hsin she chih-kuun nien-piao* (The Chart of the Newly-established Offices during the Ch'ing Period) (Peking, 1961), p. 10.

[4]See *Kuang-hsu ch'ao t'ung-hua lu*, 3rd moon of 10th year of Kuang-hsu (original), pp. 23–24, (reprint, Peking, 1958), vol. 2, pp. 1675–76; Kuo T'ing-i, *Chin-tai chung-kuo shih-shih jih-chih* (Taipei, 1963), vol. 1, p. 731. For a discussion on Prince Kung's idea and strategy in diplomacy, see Tuan Ch'ang-kuo, "Kung-wang i-hsin te chih-hsueh chi ch'i wai-chiao shih-chien" ("The method for study and idea in diplomacy of Prince Kung"), in *Ku-kung wen-hsien* (Ch'ing Documents at the Palace Museum) (Taipei, 1973), vol. 4, no. 4, pp. 46–48; for the study of Prince Kung's early career and his rise to power in 1861, see J.H. Parker, "The Rise and Decline of I Hsin, Prince Kung, 1858–1865: A Study of the Interaction of Politics and Ideology in Late Imperial China" (unpublished Ph.D. dissertation, Princeton U., 1979).

Late Ch'ing China was to a great extent the victim of circumstances. National disasters came one after another. The defeat of China at the hands of Japan in 1895 was followed by the defeat at the hands of the Powers after the Boxer Uprising in 1900. All these had a devastating effect on the Tsungli Yamen, which dealt mainly with the Foreign Powers. Moreover, as the Yamen's main attention was directed towards these disasters and their impact, the protection of overseas Chinese was not given the highest priority in China's dealing with the foreigners.

These weaknesses and circumstances combined with imperialism to doom the protective measure. The word "imperialism" should not be understood purely in terms of military conquest or socioeconomic penetration, but also in terms of denying justice to a weak nation. As a weak nation, China did not have the military power to back up its claims, and her diplomatic protests became feeble. In the heyday of imperialism in the late nineteenth and early twentieth centuries, China was a victim of imperialist oppression, and her measure of protecting overseas Chinese which inevitably involved in the confrontation with the Western Powers, was bound to fail.

Throughout the period from September 1893 to February 1912, three groups of overseas Chinese who drew much attention of the Tsungli Yamen (later the Wai Wu Pu) were those in the United States, in South Africa and in the Dutch East Indies. Details of the negotiations with the Dutch government over the protection of the Indies Chinese have been discussed in Chapter 4. This chapter is therefore entirely occupied with the story of the protection of the Chinese in the United States and South Africa.

THE PROTECTION OF THE CHINESE IN
THE UNITED STATES

Yang Ju and the Protection of American Chinese
The Tsungli Yamen at the end of 1893 took the initiative to negotiate a treaty with the government of the United States for the protection of the American Chinese. Before the new Minister Yang Ju left for Washington, he was asked by the Yamen to negotiate with the United States for the abrogation of the new registration law. He was also briefed that if the negotiation was not smooth, the Yamen was prepared to use the contents of the abortive Treaty of

1888 as the basis for a new treaty.[5] The Yamen's move was partly in response to the petitions of the Chinese merchants of the United States who pleaded strongly for the Ch'ing government's protection,[6] and was partly stimulated by the new spirit of protecting the overseas Chinese. From the Yamen's point of view, China's refusal to ratify the 1888 Treaty was probably a mistake, for it had prompted the United States to take unilateral action to prohibit Chinese emigration. The result was the worsening of the status of the Chinese in the United States under the operation of the new Exclusion Law. Chinese protests against this law proved to be ineffective. Any new treaty would at least give China some rights to deal with her subjects, even if the new treaty would have to be based on the rejected Treaty of 1888.

With firm instructions from the Tsungli Yamen, Yang Ju began to move on the issue. On 8 November 1893, in his letter to the Secretary of State, he expressed the desire of the Chinese government to settle the problems arising from the enforcement of the Registration Law.[7] An initial negotiation took place on 13 December in which both sides stated their positions. Secretary Gresham insisted on the enforcement of the Registration Law by claiming that it was intended for the benefit of residential Chinese in the United States.[8] At the same time the Secretary also expressed interest in entering into a new treaty with China on the basis of the abortive Treaty.[9] Yang immediately cabled the Yamen for instructions. He was told to secure three important points for the new treaty: to halve the length of time of the prohibition of Chinese emigrants from twenty years to ten years; to obtain the right to extradite criminals; and to insist on signing the new treaty before accepting registration of American

---

[5]For details on the Yamen's suggestion, see "Memorial of the Tsungli Yamen to the Court relating to the re-concluding a Sino-American treaty for the protection of the Chinese coolies in the United States dated 17th day of 12th moon of 19th year of Kuang-hsu (23 January 1894)", in *Ch'ing-chi wai-chiao shih-liao*, vol. 88, p. 24b.

[6]*Ibid.*

[7]See "Yang Ju to W.Q. Gresham dated 8 November 1893" in "Notes from the Chinese Legation", "The Mission of Yang Ju, 31 August 1893 to 26 April 1897".

[8]See "Yang Ju to W.Q. Gresham dated 26 December 1893", *ibid.* "Memorial of Yang Ju to the Court relating to the negotiations with the State Department of the United States over the protection of the Chinese Coolies dated 30th day of 3rd moon of 20th year of Kuang-hsu (4 May 1894)" in *Ch'ing-chi wai-chiao shih-liao*, vol. 89, pp. 32a–32b.

[9]*Ibid.*

Chinese.[10] Yang was further advised to be firm on the issue of registration, and to warn the government of the United States that China would take a counter-measure in registering all American residents in China if it insisted on registering the Chinese before the signing of the treaty.[11] What emerged from the negotiations between Yang Ju and W.Q. Gresham was a compromise: the United States agreed to halve the time of prohibition and China gave in on the issue of registration. Under the new agreement all Chinese labourers residing in the United States had to be registered, and the Chinese government could do the same thing with American labourers in China but not with merchants and missionaries.[12] This point was an obvious victory for the United States for there were hardly any Americans in China who could be classified as labourers. Therefore the right to register American labourers in China was tantamount to nothing.

As the differences between the two parties had been resolved, a treaty was signed between Yang Ju and Gresham in Washington on 17 March 1894. The treaty contains the following six items:

a. The contracting parties agree that for a period of ten years, beginning with the date of the exchange of the ratification of the treaty, the coming of Chinese labourers to the United States shall be absolutely prohibited.

b. The preceding article shall not apply to the return to the United States of any registered Chinese labourer who has a lawful wife, child or parent in the United States, or property therein

---

[10]See "Memorial of the Tsungli Yamen to the Court relating to the re-concluding a Sino-American treaty for the protection of the Chinese coolies in the United States dated 17th day of 12th moon of 19th year of Kuang-hsu (23 January 1894)" in *Ch'ing-chi wai-chiao shih-liao*, vol. 88, pp. 24b–25a; "Memorial of Yang Ju to the Court relating to the negotiations with the State Department of the United States over the protection of the Chinese Coolies dated 30th day of 3rd moon of 20th year of Kuang-hsu (4 May 1894)" in *Ch'ing-chi wai-chiao shih-liao*, vol. 89, p. 32b.

[11]*Ibid.*

[12]The Yamen wanted to register all American nationals in China but this was strongly opposed by Secretary Gresham. Yang had to give in on this point before any progress could be made. See "Memorial of Yang Ju to the Court relating to the negotiations with the State Department of the United States over the protection of the Chinese Coolies dated 30th day of 3rd moon of 20th year of Kuang-hsu (4 May 1894)" in *Ch'ing-chi wai-chiao shih-liao*, vol. 89, pp. 33a–33b; see also the draft of the proposed treaty presented by Yang Ju to Gresham, article 5, "Yang Ju to Gresham dated 22 February 1894" in "Notes from Chinese Legation", "The Mission of Yang Ju, 31 August 1893 to 26 April 1897".

of the value of 1,000 dollars, or debts of like amount due him
and pending settlement.[13]

c. The provisions of this Convention shall not affect the right at
present enjoyed by Chinese subjects, being officials, teachers,
students, merchants or travellers for curiosity or for pleasure
. . . It is also agreed that Chinese labourers shall continue to
enjoy the privilege of transit across the territory of the United
States in the course of their journey to or from other countries, subject to such regulations by the government of the
United States as may be necessary to prevent said privilege of
transit from being abused.

d. In pursuance of Article III of the Immigration Treaty between
the United States and China, signed at Peking on the 17th day
of November, 1880, it is hereby understood and agreed that
Chinese labourers or Chinese of any other class, either permanently or temporarily residing in the United States, shall have
for the protection of their persons and property all rights that
are given by the laws of the United States to citizens of the
most favoured nation, excepting the right to become natural-
ized citizens. And the government of the United States reaf-
firms its obligation, as to the persons and property of all
Chinese subjects in the United States.

e. The government of the United States, having by an Act of the
Congress, approved May 5, 1892, as amended by an Act approved November 3, 1893, required all Chinese labourers lawfully within the limits of the United States before the passage
of the first-named Act to be registered as in said Acts, and
reciprocally the government of the United States recognizes
the right of the government of China to enact and enforce
similar laws or regulations for the registration, free of charge,
of all labourers, skilled or unskilled (not merchants as defined
by said Acts of Congress), citizens of the United States in
China, whether residing within or without the Treaty ports.
And the government of the United States agrees that within
12 months from the date of the exchange of the ratifications
of this Convention, and annually thereafter, it will furnish to

---

[13]For details explaining the application of this provision, see G.E.O. Hertslet &
E. Parkes (eds.), *Great Britain and China: and between China and Foreign Powers*
(London, 1908), vol. 1, pp. 563–64.

the government of China registers or reports showing the full name, age, occupation and number or place of residence of all other citizens of the United States, including missionaries residing both within and without the Treaty ports of China, not including, however, diplomatic and other officers of the United States residing or travelling in China upon official business, together with their body and household servants.

f. This Convention shall remain in force for a period of 10 years beginning with the date of the exchange of ratification, and, if six months before the expiration of the said period of 10 years, neither government shall have formally given notice of its final termination to the other, it shall remain in force for another like period of 10 years.[14]

The treaty endorsed most of the American gains in the Scott and Geary Acts, but also gave China some concessions such as a ten-year limit on the operation of the Exclusion Law, re-affirmation of the protection of the Chinese residents in the United States, and the right of transit for the Chinese coolies in Canada and Central America. One may ask why the United States signed a new treaty which did not offer her extra gains? The answer to this question is twofold: firstly, a treaty would restore the image of the United States as a democratic Power which respected international law, because her image had been tarnished by her unilateral action against Chinese immigrants after 1888; secondly, a treaty would obligate China to help control illegal Chinese emigrants smuggled into the United States, because the enforcement of the Scott and Geary Acts had revealed the inadequacy in the control of illegal Chinese immigrants without the co-operation of the Chinese government.[15]

---

[14]*Ibid.*, vol. 1, pp. 563–65; the Chinese version of this treaty is found in Appendix of Yang Ju's memorial to the Court dated 27th day of 2nd moon of 21st year of Kuang-hsu (23 March 1895) in *Ch'ing-chi wai-chiao shih-liao*, vol. 107, pp. 32a–35b; also in *Chung-wai t'iao-yueh hui-pien* (Collection of Treaties Signed between China and Foreign Countries) (Taipei, 1964), pp. 133–34, an abbreviated version of this treaty is also found in Liu Chin-ch'ao (ed.), *Ch'ing-ch'ao shu wen-hsien T'ung-k'ao*, vol. 355, "wai-chiao" 19, k'ao 10993.

[15]For the inadequacy of the control on illegal Chinese immigrants, particularly smuggling from the Canadian border into the United States, see "Report of Inspector S.W. Day of Port Huron to Special Agent of the Treasury Department at Detroit dated 2 March 1889", and the "Report of the Special Agent of the Treasury Department at Victoria, British Columbia, to the Secretary of Treasury dated 6 February 1890", in U.S. National Archives, "Bureau of Immigration, Segregated Chinese Records", "3358 d. File" ca 1877–91, Boxes 5 & 6.

From the Chinese government's point of view, the signing of the new treaty meant a gain for China and an improvement in the position of the Chinese in the United States. China had failed to protect its subjects from the discriminatory treatment against the Chinese in the Scott and Geary Acts,[16] so any gains through the treaty would be welcome ones. Further, China was planning to divert emigrants from the United States to Mexico where the Chinese were still welcome, and the securing of the transit right for the Chinese emigrants would be crucial for the success of the scheme.

Whatever the gains for both sides, the treaty had produced an immediate effect on the attitude of the Chinese Minister at Washington towards the protection of the local Chinese. Unlike his predecessors, Yang Ju sought a solution to the anti-Chinese problem within the overseas Chinese community. Most of his predecessors saw the overseas Chinese as victims of racism and sought to protect them from unjust treatment. But Yang considered that anti-Chinese feeling was mainly caused by the misbehaviour of the Chinese themselves; the problem, as he saw it, was of their own creation. With this new perspective, Yang attempted to reform the local Chinese community. He pointed out that opium-smoking, gambling and gangsterism were the main causes of ill-feeling against the Chinese and they had caused much trouble within the Chinese community and American society at large.[17]

Yang proposed to ban gambling and gangster activities and suggested that Chinese consuls co-operate with American officials to stamp out these two evils. Offenders were to be punished according to American law and repeated violators were to be deported to China for more severe punishment. In relation to opium-smoking, Yang proposed to urge the government of the United States to prohibit this evil practice and to make clear to the host government that the Chinese government would whole-heartedly support such action.[18] Yang, a Confucian diplomat, also believed that moral per-

---

[16]For the failure of China's protests against the Scott and Geary Acts, see Chang Yin-huan's and Tsui Kuo-yin's correspondence with the State Department in "Notes from the Chinese Legation", "The Mission of Chang Yin-huan, April 1886 to September 1889" and "The Mission of Tsui Kuo-yin, September 1889 to August 1893".

[17]See "Memorial of Yang Ju to the Court relating to an overall policy for dealing with the protection of the Chinese in the United States dated 2nd day of 9th moon of 20th year of Kuang-hsu (30 September 1894)" in Ch'ing-chi wai-chiao shih-liao, vol. 97, pp. 6a–6b.

[18]Ibid., p. 6b.

suasion was a permanent solution to the evil practices of the overseas Chinese. Law could restrain but not change behaviour. From a
long term point of view, he maintained, moral education distinguishing right from wrong, and virtue from evil, was what the overseas Chinese needed. He therefore advocated introducing the
"Hsiang-yueh" lecture system into the overseas Chinese community.[19] He proposed to use Chinese Consuls as lecturers who would
conduct regular lectures on the first and fifteenth days of every
month of the lunar calendar at the halls of local Chinese associations.[20] The consuls were to expound the Amplified Instructions of
the Sacred Edict of the Yung-cheng Emperor (Sheng-yu kuang-
hsun) which contained many of the Confucian values.[21] They were
also to explain the harmfulness of opium-smoking, gambling and
gangsterism and to persuade the overseas Chinese to give them up.
Yang hoped that through moral persuasion the overseas Chinese
could be transformed into useful and law-abiding citizens.[22]

Yang's proposed reform, if it eventuated, would change the
character of the local Chinese community and would produce a
more respectable image of the Chinese in American society. But it

---

[19]The "Hsiang-yueh lecture" system is believed to have been inaugurated by the
Emperor Shun-chih, the first Manchu Emperor in China, with the promulgation of
his Six Maxims of Hortatory Edict (Liu Yu). The Maxims instructed his subjects to
practise virtues and to lead a peaceful life. To promulgate these virtues, a Hsiang-
yueh, who was usually appointed among learned scholars, was to give regular lectures to the village folk. This system was used to control the social behaviour and indirectly, the political behaviour, of vast masses in rural China. For details see Kung-
ch'uan Hsiao, *Rural China: Imperial Control in the Nineteenth Century* (Seattle,
1967), pp. 184–94.

[20]See "Memorial of Yang Ju to the Court relating to an overall policy in dealing
with the protection of the overseas Chinese in the United States dated 2nd day of 9th
moon of 20th year of Kuang-hsu (30 September 1894)" in *Ch'ing-chi wai-chiao shih-
liao*, vol. 97, p. 7a.

[21]To expound the Six Maxims, Emperor K'ang-hsi, son of the Emperor Shun-
chih, promulgated the Sixteen Maxims known as "Sheng-yu". The Emperor Yung-
cheng, son of the Emperor K'ang-hsi, must have thought that even the Sixteen Maxims were too brief for the comprehension of the ignorant masses. He therefore promulgated this Amplified Instructions of the Sacred Edict of 10,000 words. Many of
the Confucian values such as filial piety, loyalty to the clan, propriety and thrift,
obedience to the law, emphasis on cultural works, appeasing neighbours and fellow-
villagers and rejection of false doctrines were included. See Kung-ch'uan Hsiao, *op.
cit.*, pp. 187–88.

[22]See Yang's memorial of 30 September 1894, in *Ch'ing-chi wai-chiao shih-liao*,
vol. 97, p. 7a.

would not solve the problem of the anti-Chinese movement as Yang had hoped. The eradication of the evil practices would only remove the convenient pretext that the American extremists had used against the Chinese. The crux of the problem of the anti-Chinese movement was still mainly economic.

Yang's proposed introduction of the "Hsiang-yueh lecture" system, though it would not directly contribute to the reduction of racial tension between Chinese and Americans, would strengthen China's ideological control over its overseas subjects. Of course, the introduction of that system into overseas Chinese communities was not new at the time when Yang suggested it, for as early as 1881 the "Hsiang-yueh lecture" system had already been practised among the Chinese in Singapore and the Chinese Consul there had patronised its activities.[23] In retrospect, if the system had been successfully carried out among the Chinese in the United States, the Ch'ing government would probably have won the battle against the Reformists and the Revolutionaries for the allegiance of the overseas Chinese in the United States in the period between 1900 and 1911.

Apart from the proposed reform, Yang Ju showed considerable willingness to co-operate with the Americans. He felt China was partly responsible for the tightening of the American laws against local Chinese residents, for China had failed to co-operate in the execution of the previous treaty. Some Chinese diplomats even abused their privileges to defeat the enforcement of the treaty. He cited as an example a notorious Chinese Consul-General of Cuba, T'an Ch'ien-ts'u, who issued merchant visas to thousands of Chinese coolies who had falsified their identities in order to enter the United States of America. T'an was alleged to have scooped a large sum of money for this dishonest operation.[24] Because of the abuses, Yang claimed, the U.S. government had to pass the law to prohibit Chinese indiscriminately.[25] Yang therefore suggested a clamp down on the abuses. He informed the Court that the notorious T'an had been replaced by a new Consul-General, Ho Yen-

---

[23] See Yen Ching-hwang, "Overseas Chinese Nationalism in Singapore and Malaya 1877-1912", in *Modern Asian Studies*, vol. 16, no. 3 (July, 1982), pp. 401-404.

[24] According to Yang, Chinese coolies who intended to falsify their identities would go to Cuba first and pay a sum of money to obtain a merchant's visa from the consulate-general. They would then enter the United States through New York. See Yang's memorial of 30 September 1894, in *Ch'ing-chi wai-chiao shih-liao*, vol. 97, pp. 7a-7b.

[25] *Ibid.*, p. 7a.

sheng, who was instructed to carry out the new policy that business visas would be issued only to *bona fide* merchants.[26] This proposed action of course was intended to clear China's bad reputation and to win back the confidence of the American authorities. With this new confidence, Yang hoped to achieve protection of the Chinese merchants in the United States.

Yang's spirit of co-operation was demonstrated in his willingness to work closely with the American authorities. As soon as he was urged by the Acting Secretary of State to remind Chinese residents in Massachusetts to co-operate with the authorities in the compilation of the state census for 1895, Yang instructed the Chinese Consul-General in San Francisco to notify the residents to that effect.[27] He did not query some questions such as "race and colour" and "native born or foreign born" in the census which could potentially be used by the authorities against the locally born Chinese.[28] He seems to have been unaware of the implications of answering these potentially racist questions.

Yang also sought a solution to China's problem of emigration by diverting its emigrants from the United States. China would have no difficulty in absorbing those who were rejected by the United States, but would have a problem if all the Chinese there were forced to return to their homeland. Moreover, the closure of American doors to Chinese emigration meant the loss of migratory opportunities for many intended emigrants. To remedy this situation Yang proposed to the Tsungli Yamen to find an alternative outlet for Chinese emigrants. He had in mind Mexico, a country geographically close to the United States and one that seemed to welcome Chinese emigrants. According to Yang, Mexico had been very keen to acquire Chinese coolies for its economic development and had been trying unsuccessfully to secure a treaty with China for that purpose.[29] China rejected the Mexican request mainly on the ground of caution. But the worsening situation of the Chinese emi-

---

[26]*Ibid.*, p. 7b.

[27]See a special notice to the Chinese residents in the state of Massachusetts by the Consul-General Li Yung-yew dated 16th day of 5th moon of 21st year of Kuang-hsu (8 June 1895); both the original Chinese and an English translation are found in "Notes from the Chinese Legation", "The Mission of Yang Ju, 31 August 1893 to 26 April 1897".

[28]*Ibid.*

[29]See Yang's memorial of 30 September 1894, in *Ch'ing-chi wai-chiao shih-liao*, vol. 97, p. 7b.

grants in the United States forced China to rethink its previous decision. Yang's predecessor, Tsui Kuo-yin, started negotiations with the Mexican authorities over the emigration issue, but Tsui's transfer from his post in August 1893 brought the negotiations to a halt. Yang proposed to continue Tsui's efforts to secure a treaty with Mexico. He pointed out to the Yamen that Mexico in reality had already become the sanctuary for a few thousand Chinese who had been driven out from the United States.[30] He ensured the Yamen that he would not take any action in signing a treaty with Mexico until an investigation into the conditions of that country by two Chinese emissaries had been completed.[31]

How far Yang's proposed reform had been carried out in the Chinese community is unknown. It seems that Yang's intention of using the reform to solve the anti-Chinese problem in the United States was a failure, for the problem was still there when Yang was transferred to the post of Chinese Minister for Russia, Austria and the Netherlands in April 1897.[32] His scheme of using Mexico to absorb some of the Chinese emigrants was not working either, for he had not successfully secured a treaty with the Mexican authorities owing to some unforeseen factors.[33] A treaty for Chinese emigration to Mexico was signed by his successor, Wu T'ing-fang.

Wu T'ing-fang and the Protection of the American Chinese

The man who succeeded Yang Ju as the Chinese Minister in Washington was Wu T'ing-fang, the famous Chinese diplomat during the late Ch'ing and early Republican periods. Wu was born in

---

[30]*Ibid.*, p. 8b.

[31]The two emissaries sent to investigate conditions in Mexico were Yu Ssu-i, the Chinese Consul-General in Cuba, and Li Yung-yew, the Chinese Consul-General in San Francisco. *Ibid.*, pp. 8a–8b.

[32]One source claims that Yang's transfer was in November 1896; this seems to be a mistake for Yang's mission in the United States was not terminated until 26 April 1897. See Ch'ien Shih-p'u (ed.), *Ch'ing-chi hsin-she chih-kuan nien-piao*, p. 21, "Notes from the Chinese Legation", "The Mission of Yang Ju, 31 August 1893 to 26 April 1897".

[33]Partly due to the Sino-Japanese war (1894–95) which greatly affected China's standing in the world, the Mexican government delayed the signing of a treaty with China. See "Memorial of Yang Ju to the Court relating to the mission investigating the condition of Mexico and the delay of signing of a Sino-Mexican treaty dated 20th day of 7th moon of 21st year of Kuang-hsu (8 September 1895)" in *Ch'ing-chi wai-chiao shih-liao*, vol. 117, pp. 20–24.

Singapore in 1842,[34] the son of a successful overseas Chinese merchant. His father, Wu Yung-chang, was a native of the Hsin Hui
district of Kwangtung province. When T'ing-fang was three years
old, his family returned to China and established residence at Fang-
tsun, an islet in the Pearl River near Canton.[35] After receiving his
early education in classical Chinese, Wu T'ing-fang was sent to
Hong Kong to study in St. Paul's College at the age of fourteen.
After completing his secondary education in 1859, Wu held various
positions in the colony in the next decade, including the position of
an interpreter in the Hong Kong courts. Like many other Chinese
intellectuals of his time, Wu believed that China must reform her
institutions in order to regain her vigour and take her rightful place
in the modern world.[36] In 1874, he left Hong Kong for England to
study law, enrolling at Lincoln's Inn as a student on 27 April 1874
at the age of thirty-one.[37] He was known among his peers by his
Cantonese name, Ng Choy, and was mistakenly known as Mr.
Choy.[38] After three years' study he was called to the bar in January
1877,[39] and became China's first barrister. He then returned to
Hong Kong to practise law, and was later appointed as an acting

---

[34]One source claims that Wu T'ing-fang was born in Batu Berendum of Malacca
in 1842. (See Anonymous, "Wu T'ing-fang po-shih" (Dr. Wu T'ing-fang) in *Ma-
lai-ya ku-kang-chou liu-i tsung-hui t'e-k'an* (Souvenir magazine of Pan Malayan
Ku-kang-chou Six Districts' Association) (Penang, 1964), pt. 2, pp. 37–38. But Linda P. Shin, quoting *Wu Chih-yung po-shih ai-ssu-lu* (Memorial Volume of Dr. Wu
T'ing-fang, Chih-yung was another name of Wu T'ing-fang) claims that Wu was
born in Singapore. The same claim is made by H.L. Boorman and R.C. Howard.
Since the *Memorial Volume of Dr. Wu T'ing-fang* was compiled by Wu T'ing-fang's
son, Wu Ch'ao-shu, after Wu's death, Linda Shin's claim is more reliable. See Linda P. Shin, "China in Transition: The Role of Wu T'ing-fang (1842–1922)" (an unpublished Ph.D. dissertation, University of California, Los Angeles, 1970), pp. 28,
74. H.L. Boorman and R.C. Howard (eds.), *Biographical Dictionary of Republican
China* (New York, 1970), vol. 4, p. 453.

[35]See Linda P. Shin, *op. cit.*, p. 28; H.L. Boorman and R.C. Howard (eds.), *ibid.*

[36]For identifying Wu T'ing-fang as an early Chinese Reformer, see Paul A.
Cohen, *Between Tradition and Modernity: Wang T'ao and Reform in Late Ch'ing
China* (Cambridge, Mass.,1974), pp. 248–76; see also Linda P. Shin, *op. cit.*, pp.
128–57.

[37]In the period at Lincoln's Inn Wu T'ing-fang (Ng Choy) was mistakenly
registered under 'Choy'. See Joseph Foster, *Men at the Bar: A Biographical Hand-
List of the Members of the Various Inns of Court* (London, 1885), p. 85.

[38]See Charles Shaw, *The Inns of Court Calendar: A Record of the Members of
the English Bar — Students* (London, 1877), p. 422.

[39]Joseph Foster, *op. cit.*, p. 85.

magistrate and a member of the Legislative Council of Hong Kong, the first Chinese to occupy that position.[40] In 1882, Wu T'ing-fang was recruited by Li Hung-chang as a legal adviser;[41] using Li Hung-chang's Mu-fu[42] as a stepping stone, Wu climbed up the ladder of Chinese officialdom. He assisted Li Hung-chang during the Li-Ito negotiations of 1885, and served Li on various occasions as adviser in Western and international law. He was appointed the Director of the China Railway Company in 1887 with the task of constructing a rail line between Tientsin and Tangku, and when the line was completed in the following year, he became its first managing director.[43]

Because of his legal knowledge, diplomatic experience and administrative ability, Wu T'ing-fang was appointed the Chinese Minister at Washington in 1897. His education and experience in Hong Kong and London provided him with a new perspective in handling China's diplomacy; his legal training equipped him with knowledge indispensable in international negotiations. His approach to the problem of protecting the Chinese in the United States was therefore different from that of his predecessors. Unlike his predecessors who were mostly Confucian scholars and were more prepared to compromise or give in, Wu was assertive in the defence of China's treaty rights. Because of his wide legal knowledge and a good command of English, he could ". . . meet Western diplomats on their own ground and fight them with their own weapons. . . ."[44] Wu's proven diplomatic skill earned him respect among foreign diplomats and government circles in Washington, yet he failed to gain much ground in the fight against the United States over the protection of the American Chinese. In retrospect, Wu's unsuccess-

---

[40]See H.L. Boorman and R.C. Howard (eds.), *op. cit.*, p. 454.

[41]Li Hung-chang first met Wu T'ing-fang at the end of 1877 and attempted to recruit Wu on his staff. Li strongly recommended to the Tsungli Yamen that Wu be offered a high salary so as to attract him to take up the position but did not succeed. Li eventually succeeded in recruiting Wu in 1882. See "Letter of Li Hung-chang to Tsungli Yamen dated 1st day of 9th moon of 3rd year of Kuang-hsu (7 October 1877)" in Li Hung-chang, *Li Wen-chung kung ch'uan-chi*, "i-shu han-kao", vol. 7, pp. 20-21; H.L. Boorman and R.C. Howard (eds.), *op. cit.*, p. 454; K.E. Folsom, *Friends, Guests and Colleagues: The Mu-Fu System in the Late Ch'ing Period* (Berkeley, 1968), p. 141.

[42]For a study of Li Hung-chang's Mu-fu, see K.E. Folsom, *op. cit.*

[43]See H.L. Boorman and R.C. Howard (eds.), *op. cit.*, p. 454; Linda P. Shin, *op. cit.*, pp. 100-16.

[44]See M.R. Coolidge, *Chinese Immigration*, p. 241.

ful attempt should not be considered as a personal failure, but as a reflection of China's declining international status and of her lack of power to enforce treaty rights.

At the time Wu T'ing-fang was appointed the Chinese Minister in 1897, he might have entertained an ambition to do a better job than his predecessors in the protection of the overseas Chinese. He obviously possessed better qualifications for the task. He was an overseas Chinese, speaking a dialect spoken by the majority of the Chinese in America. In addition, he was trained in the West, familiar with Western law and customs. More importantly, he had ample experience in dealing with foreigners during his service in Li Hung-chang's Mu-fu.[45] He must have assumed that he knew Western thinking and behaviour well and that he had little Confucian tradition to inhibit the success of his new task. But he was soon to find out that his optimism had little foundation.

When Wu T'ing-fang took up his appointment in Washington in April 1897,[46] he was about to face a new problem in the protection of the American Chinese which had not been experienced by his predecessors. With the annexation by the United States of the Kingdom of Hawaii in the summer of 1898 and its control of the Philippine Islands in December 1898, the status of the Chinese in both territories became an issue of great concern to the Chinese government.[47] Soon after the annexation of Hawaii the United States banned Chinese immigration to the Hawaiian Islands, as well as prohibited any Chinese entering the United States from the Islands.[48] Wu T'ing-fang quickly reacted to the American move. He memorialised the Court to restore a Chinese consulate in Hawaii which had ceased to exist for some years.[49] In September 1898 he appointed his aide, Yang Wei-pin to be the new Consul in Honolulu,[50] and the

---

[45]See Linda P. Shin, "China in Transition: The Role of Wu T'ing-fang 1842-1922", chapter 3.

[46]See "Wu T'ing-fang to John Sherman, Secretary of State, dated 27 April 1897" in "Notes from the Chinese Legation", "The Mission of Wu T'ing-fang, April 1897 to March 1903".

[47]See H.F. MacNair, *The Chinese Abroad: Their Position and Protection* (Shanghai, 1933, reprint, Taipei, 1971), pp. 85, 88.

[48]*Ibid.*, p. 85.

[49]See "Memorial of Wu T'ing-fang to the Court relating to the appointment of a Chinese consul in Hawaii which was annexed by the United States dated 30th day of 7th moon of 24th year of Kuang-hsu (15 September 1898)" in *Ch'ing-chi wai-chiao shih-liao*, vol. 134, pp. 20a-20b.

[50]Yang was appointed by Wu on 29th day of 7th moon of 24th year of Kuang-hsu

Consul arrived on 22 October of the same year.[51] The restoration of a consulate in Honolulu was intended to lay the groundwork for his future negotiations with the government of the United States over the protection of the Hawaiian Chinese. He realised that a Chinese Consul was urgently needed there for collecting reliable and up-to-date information. Although he had been in his job for more than a year, Wu was not very familiar with the conditions of the Chinese in Hawaii, who did not really fall under his jurisdiction. Further, he had difficulty in finding up-to-date information about the Hawaiian Chinese in the embassy archives because the consulate in Hawaii had ceased to exist before his arrival in 1897.[52] This lack of information forced him to rely almost entirely on the petition of the Hawaiian Chinese to the Government of the United States as the blueprint of his first official protest about the extension of the Exclusion Law to the Islands.[53]

The protest note was sent to the Secretary of State, John Hay on 12 December 1898. Wu declared at the outset that the extension of

---

(14 September 1898). Obviously Wu appointed Yang to that position before the official approval of the Court. See "The Commission of Yang Wei-ping as Chinese Consul for the Hawaiian Islands dated 29th day of 7th moon of 24th year of Kuang-hsu (14 September 1898), both in Chinese and English, in enclosure of "Wu T'ing-fang to W.R. Day, Secretary of State, dated 15 September 1898" in "Notes from the Chinese Legation", "The Mission of Wu T'ing-fang, April 1897 to March 1903".

[51]See Tin-Yuke Char (compiled and edited), *The Sandalwood Mountains: Readings and Stories of the Early Chinese in Hawaii* (Honolulu, 1975), p. 103.

[52]This is most clearly reflected in Wu's remarks about the Chinese population in Hawaii. In his memorial to the Court relating to the appointment of a Chinese Consul in Hawaii which was written on 2 August 1898 (15th day of 6th moon of 24th year of Kuang-hsu), he mentioned that the Chinese population in Hawaii was about 30,000. But in his protest note to John Hay on 12 December of the same year, he stated that the Chinese population was about 20,000. Evidently the latter figure was based on the statistics provided in the petition of the Hawaiian Chinese to the government of the United States, while the earlier was only a guess. See "Memorial of Wu T'ing-fang to the Court dated 15 September 1898" in *Ch'ing-chi wai-chiao shih-liao*, vol. 134, p. 20b; "The Commission of Yang Wei-ping as Chinese Consul for the Hawaiian Islands", "Wu T'ing-fang to John Hay dated 12 December 1898" and "Memorial and Accompanying Data presented to the United States Commissioners by Chinese Residents in the Hawaiian Islands, 17 August 1898" in "Notes from the Chinese Legation", "The Mission of Wu T'ing-fang, April 1897 to March 1903".

[53]See "Wu T'ing-fang to John Hay dated 12 December 1898" and "Memorial and Accompanying Data presented to the United States Commissioner by Chinese Residents in the Hawaiian Islands, 17 August 1898", *ibid.*

the Exclusion Law to the Hawaiian Chinese would suspend important rights hitherto enjoyed by the local Chinese. He was appalled that the liberal-spirited Congress had to inflict such injustice on such peace-loving people as the Chinese. The picture that Wu depicted of the Chinese was of a community that was law-abiding, well-educated and well-liked by the indigenous Hawaiians. He argued that the majority of the Chinese were local-born or naturalised and had been granted rights to freely visit their homeland, to bring their families to the Islands and to send their children home for education.[54] But Wu realised that his arguments for maintaining Chinese rights and privileges under the new regime had little foundation in international law. He thus turned his arguments to the undesirability of applying the Exclusion Act to the Chinese in Hawaii. He declared that the Chinese government agreed to sign the treaties with the United States in 1880 and 1894 to restrict Chinese immigration because it accepted with the fact that Chinese immigrants had posed serious competition to white labour. But the situation in Hawaii was entirely different; the Chinese immigrants did not compete with the white or native labour and were actually welcomed. The extension of the Exclusion Act to the Islands was therefore unnecessary and unreasonable.[55]

What enraged Wu T'ing-fan most was the fact that the Chinese were singled out for discrimination among the Asian immigrants — the Japanese, Malays and Siamese were not restricted. From this perspective he felt that his countrymen were given not only lower status in relation to immigrants from Europe, but also a status lower than immigrants from places like Malaya and Siam which were traditionally tributary states of China. What this act implied was that the Chinese as a race were considered to be inferior to the Malays and the Siamese. This greatly hurt Wu's national pride and prompted him to press the Secretary of State to clarify U.S. attitudes; he wanted to know whether "the Congress of the United States intended to declare that the Chinese are more objectionable or dangerous as residents than Japanese, Malays, Siamese or other of the Asiatic peoples".[56]

Wu's national pride derived partly from his pride in Chinese civilisation. It is surprising that a man like him who received more

---

[54]See "Wu T'ing-fang to John Hay dated 12 December 1898", pp. 1-3, *ibid.*
[55]*Ibid.*, p. 4.
[56]*Ibid.*, p. 5.

Western education than Chinese should have had so much senti-
mental attachment to Chinese civilisation. Although he was critical
of some Chinese customs and practices, he had never doubted that
China was one of the few great surviving civilisations and that the
Chinese people were a civilised race.[57] He was of course infuriated
at remarks that suggested the Chinese were a "semi-civilised" people
because China was a weak nation.[58] From this perspective, the
American act of discriminating against Chinese was seen as a
hostile one, degrading to the Chinese as a race. This was why he
protested so angrily and declared that "to single out the Chinese
alone for exclusion from the Islands is to lower the whole nation in
the eyes of the world, particularly if there is no discriminating
legislation against any other Asiatic people".[59]

Surprisingly Wu T'ing-fang dropped his fight against the extension of the Exclusion Law to Hawaii after his protest note of 14
February 1899. Perhaps Wu was unsure whether his efforts would
bear any result because the ban was already enforced, or perhaps it
was the problem of protecting Filipino Chinese that shifted his attention.

The fight against the extention of the Exclusion Law to the Philippines arose from an American military order issued on 26 August
1898. As a result of a speedy victory over the Spanish for the control of the Philippines, the American military commander, General
Otis, issued the order prohibiting Chinese immigration to the
islands. Wu unofficially heard something about the order and tried
to get confirmation from the State Department. He also sent the
Secretary a diplomatic note emphasising the special relations that
China had with the Philippines both in immigration and trade. He
urged the American government not to extend the Exclusion Law
to the islands.[60]

The military order, by any standard, was not in harmony with
international practice. Otis had no authority to extend a law to a
newly acquired colony without legislation from the American Con-

---

[57]See Wu T'ing-fang, *America: Through the Spectacles of an Oriental Diplomat*
(New York, 1914), pp. 144–62.

[58]*Ibid.*, p. 163.

[59]See "Wu T'ing-fang to John Hay dated 14 February 1899", p. 4, in "Notes
from the Chinese Legation", "The Mission of Wu T'ing-fang, April 1897 to March
1903".

[60]See "Wu T'ing-fang to John Hay dated 3 February 1899", *ibid.*

gress. But he had done it and the American government tolerated the situation. Because it was an anomaly in international practice, the American government tried to cover up the issue by saying there was no information on the issue.[61] It was not until August 1899 when the Chinese Consul-General in Manila complained to Wu about the enforcement of the Exclusion Law in the Philippines that the American government admitted to Wu the true situation.[62]

Wu lodged a strong protest with the Secretary and through him, with the President and Congress. He charged that the military order was contrary to international law and comity, in violation of the spirit of the existing treaties, and utterly disregarded the friendly relations between China and the United States.[63] He pointed out that the order was a departure from President McKinley's announced policy of leaving the status of the newly acquired possessions unchanged until a decision had been taken by Congress.[64] He claimed that the American military in the Islands had no justification whatsoever for serving a military order on the local Chinese population and had done them great injustice. He finally appealed to the President, with an exalted sense of justice, to disallow the existence of a military commander continuing an unjust and cruel measure against a large group of peace-loving people.[65]

The first two test cases for the military order occurred between September and November 1899. A steamer named *Esmeralda*, with seven hundred Chinese immigrants on board, arrived in the Philippines on 19 September. All of the immigrants carried certificates issued by the Amoy Taot'ai[66] and vised by the American Consul, but were not allowed to land.[67] In November, all the Chinese who had arrived in Manila by ship, whether labourers or merchants, were subjected to investigation, and only former residents were per-

---

[61]See "Wu T'ing-fang to John Hay dated 12 September 1899", p. 2, *ibid.*
[62]*Ibid.*, p. 3.
[63]*Ibid.*, pp. 5–6.
[64]*Ibid.*, p. 6.
[65]*Ibid.*, pp. 6–8.
[66]There was no such official position designated as Amoy Taot'ai; presumably it was the Taotai of Hsing-ch'uan-yung who had the direct control over Amoy. This term, Amoy Taot'ai, was used in the telegram so I retain it here.
[67]See "Telegram from Consul-General Li Yung-yew to Wu T'ing-fang dated 22 September 1899" in "Notes from the Chinese Legation", "The Mission of Wu T'ing-fang, April 1897 to March 1903".

mitted to land.[68] These two cases were cabled by the Chinese Consul-General in Manila, Li Yung-yew, to Wu T'ing-fang, requesting immediate intervention.[69]

As soon as Wu received the second telegram on 15 November, he lodged another protest note with the Secretary of State. He reiterated his objection to the extension of the Exclusion Law to the Filipino Chinese by a military commander as contained in his previous despatch. He most vehemently protested against the act of excluding Chinese merchants who belonged to the exempted class. He denounced the acts as a direct violation of the treaty stipulations of 1894 and unwarranted by the law of the United States. He concluded by demanding that Major General Otis be instructed to cease his actions.[70]

Wu's protests seem to have had some temporary effect on the attitude of the government of the United States. In early December, 1899, Wu was informed by Secretary Hay that General Otis' attention had been drawn to China's protests and the General was instructed not to permit any violation of the treaty.[71] Although Wu had won the victory over the technicality of imposing the Exclusion Law in the Philippines, he failed to prevent the extension of the Law to that colony. His temporary victory was lost when Congress passed a new Act in April 1902 which extended the Exclusion Law to her island territories, and prohibited Chinese labourers from these islands entering the mainland territories of the United States.[72]

Apart from his fights against the extension of the Exclusion Law to Hawaii and the Philippines, Wu T'ing-fang during his first term as the Chinese Minister at Washington (1897-1903) also launched a fierce attack on the government of the United States for its mismanagement of the Exclusion Law. He sent a series of protest notes to Secretary Hay attacking the Treasury Department which was entrusted with the authority to enforce the Law. His main thrust was on a group of immigration officials of the Treasury Department,

---

[68]See "Telegram from the Chinese Consul-General in Manila to Wu T'ing-fang dated 15 November 1899", *ibid.*

[69]See the above two telegrams from the Consul-General in Manila.

[70]See "Wu T'ing-fang to John Hay dated 15 November 1899", *ibid.*

[71]See "John Hay to Wu T'ing-fang dated 5 December 1899", quoted in "Wu T'ing-fang to John Hay dated 14 December 1899", *ibid.*

[72]See D.L. McKee, *Chinese Exclusion versus the Open Door Policy, 1900-1906,* pp. 63-64.

such as collectors of ports, inspectors and inquisitors. He charged that these officials were ". . . generally unfriendly if not positively hostile",[73] and that they constituted ". . . the subordinate authorities of the Treasury Department of the United States to distort the language and defeat the plain intent of the solemn treaty stipulations entered into between the United States and China".[74]

Wu T'ing-fang was a legal man, always careful with words and charges, and was aware of their implications. Yet he made such strong charges. This fact in itself reflects his deep resentment towards them. As an astute observer of American politics, he knew well what was actually going on in American society in relation to the overseas Chinese. He knew that some anti-Chinese elements had infiltrated the Treasury Department and exerted strong influence in the running of the Bureau of Immigration. T.V. Powderly, an anti-Chinese labour leader and a lawyer who helped McKinley's successful campaign for the Presidency in 1896, obtained the post of Commissioner General of Immigration and carried out his anti-Chinese programmes after August 1897.[75] Wu also realised that anti-Chinese prejudice found many sympathisers among junior officials, particularly in California where sinophobia was most acute. From Wu's point of view, these officials had conspired to obstruct the coming of any legal Chinese immigrants and to work for the ultimate expulsion of all Chinese from the United States. Wu was most annoyed by the fact that these officials had hidden behind a legal screen to work for their illicit aims and that they had purposely bent the laws and treaty stipulations to fulfil their goals.[76]

Wu T'ing-fang concentrated his attack on the issues of restricting the immigration of members of the exempted class and the ill-treat-

---

[73]See "Wu to Hay dated 26 December 1900", in *Papers Relating to the Foreign Relations of the United States, 57th Congress 1st Session, House Documents 1901*, p. 64, Document No. 200; see also "Notes from the Chinese Legation", "The Mission of Wu T'ing-fang, April 1897 to March 1903".

[74]See *House Documents 1901, ibid.*, p. 59, Document no. 199; see also "Notes from the Chinese Legation", *ibid.*

[75]For a good detailed work on this topic, see D.L. McKee, *Chinese Exclusion Versus the Open Door Policy 1900–1906*, chapter 2, "The Powderly Exclusion Policy".

[76]This is the impression gained from reading Wu T'ing-fang's correspondence with the Secretary of State in the period between 1897 and 1903. See "Notes from the Chinese Legation", "The Mission of Wu T'ing-fang, April 1897 to March 1903".

ment of Chinese merchants in the United States. By treaty rights, Chinese students and merchants could freely enter the United States.[77] But this right was not respected by Powderly and his supporters who worked consciously and actively for total exclusion of Chinese.[78] Wu T'ing-fang was quick to expose their objective and to defend the rights of Chinese students and merchants. On the issue of students, Wu charged the immigration officials with distorting treaty clauses in order to bar students from entering the United States. He accused them of a lack of respect for treaty rights, and of depriving many *bona fide* students of the chance of study in America.[79] He further accused them of adopting obstructive measures such as challenging reliable credentials and twisting a term of general nature.

Two cases provided Wu grounds for the fight. A student named Yip Wah was prevented from landing at San Francisco on the grounds that he had failed to establish his credentials as a student. The Collector of the Port based his decision on Yip's claim to be an attendant upon the native schools of China and on Yip's declaration that he had no intention of practising as a professional after returning to China.[80] Another student named Tong Tseng, aged fifteen, was denied a landing at Honolulu because he only intended to study in a local Chinese-American school.[81] In both cases, the students had complied with the treaty stipulations by producing proper certificates vised by the American consular officials at the ports of embarkation. Wu lashed out at the American immigration officials on two counts: on the credentials of students and on the definition of the term, "student". Firstly, Wu argued that if the

---

[77]See item C of the Sino-American treaty of 1894, in G.E.P. Hertslet and E. Parkes (eds.), *Great Britain and China: and Between China and Foreign Powers*, vol. 1, pp. 563–65; Ch'ing-chi wai-chiao shih-liao, vol. 107, p. 34a; Chung-wai tiao-yueh hui-pien, p. 133.

[78]See D.L. McKee, *op. cit.*, p. 29.

[79]See "Wu T'ing-fang's memorandum to the President of the United States dated 9 December 1901" in "Notes from the Chinese Legation", "The Mission of Wu T'ing-fang, April 1897 to March 1903"; see also the same memorandum in *Papers Relating to the Foreign Relations of the United States, 57th Congress 1st Session, House Documents 1901*, p. 73, Document No. 218.

[80]See "Wu to Hay dated 30 November 1900", in *House Documents 1901, ibid.*, p. 60, Document No. 199.

[81]See "Wu to Hay dated 28 November 1901", *ibid.*, p. 68, Document No. 214; see also "Notes from the Chinese Legation", "The Mission of Wu T'ing-fang, April 1897 to March 1903".

American consular officials had issued the certificates, a student's credentials had already been established. What he implied was that the American consular officials must have satisfied themselves with the credentials of the applicants before they issued the certificates; once the visas were issued, the American immigration officials should not have objected. Concerning Yip Wah's declaration that he had no intention of practising as a professional after returning to China, Wu told the Americans bluntly that it was none of their business. He declared that "Neither the treaty nor the law has to do with his (Yip Wah) pursuit after he leaves the United States and returns to China. . . ."[82] Secondly, Wu accused the Treasury Department of rigidly defining the term, "student", as "a person who intends to pursue some of the higher branches of study" or "seeks to be fitted for some particular profession or occupation".[83] Wu argued that such a rigid definition was a twist of a term of general nature and was contrary to the spirit of the treaty and had caused immense hardship for prospective students.[84]

On the issue of merchant immigrants, Wu charged that bona fide merchants with slightly defective certificates were refused admission to the United States by Port Collectors on the grounds of failure to comply with requirements.[85] Every effort was made to

---

[82]See "Wu to Hay dated 30 November 1900", in *Papers Relating to the Foreign Relations of the United States, 57th Congress 1st Session, House Documents 1901*, p. 60, Document No. 90.

[83]See "Wu T'ing-fang to John Hay dated 28 November 1901", in "Notes from the Chinese Legation", "The Mission of Wu T'ing-fang, April 1897 to March 1903".

[84]*Ibid.*

[85]Wu claimed that Yee Ah Lum and some thirty other Chinese merchants from Canton came to the United States in August 1899 and were refused admission by the Port Collector of San Francisco on the ground that their certificates were defective. The alleged defect was simply the omission of the particulars relating to the nature and character of their business in the English portion of the certificates, though such particulars were stated in the Chinese portion. Yee and other merchants appealed to the Secretary of the Treasury, but the Secretary sustained the Collector's decision. They were accordingly deported. See "Wu T'ing-fang to John Hay dated 2 October 1899", "Letter from A.L. Herley and Associates (Attorneys for the petitioners) to Wu T'ing-fang dated 20 September 1899", "Petitions from Yee Ah Lum and other Chinese merchants to the Secretary of the Treasury for re-hearing the decision of J.P. Jackson, Collector of Customs, San Francisco", in "Notes from the Chinese Legation", "The Mission of Wu T'ing-fang, April 1897 to March 1903"; "Wu T'ing-fang's memorandum to the President of the United States dated 9 December 1901", *ibid.*, also in *House Documents 1901*, pp. 73–74, Document No. 218.

obstruct the coming of merchants such as denying their right to have an attorney present at the taking of testimony at the port of San Francisco.[86] Wu T'ing-fang was incensed by the denial of a basic democratic right of individuals. He claimed that injustice had been done to the merchant immigrants and protested that ". . . these Chinese subjects, who are ignorant of the law, of the language and of the customs of this country, should be deprived of the benefit of counsel and placed entirely at the mercy of inquisitors".[87]

Wu T'ing-fang also fought for the rights of the American Chinese. The resident Chinese merchants, whose right to visit China and re-enter the United States was stipulated in the Treaty of 1894, invariably suffered ill-treatment at the hands of the immigration officials. Those returning to the United States after a temporary visit to China were generally denied a landing, either because of defective certificates or of doubtful credentials. For instance, in June–July 1901, five Chinese merchants who returned to San Francisco after a short visit to China were denied admission by the Customs Collector on the grounds that they were manufacturers not merchants, and therefore not entitled to admittance. In fact these five merchants had extensive manufacturing and business interests in the country. But their credentials as merchants were picked on as an excuse for debarring them from re-entering the United States.[88] Those who were given appeals were imprisoned in the detention sheds for weeks or months pending a decision. A description of their plight by a contemporary observer is as follows:

> When they do arrive, merchants, labourers are all alike penned up, like a flock of sheep, in a wharf-shed, for many days, and often weeks, at their own expense, and are denied all communication with their own people, while the investigation of their cases moves its slow length along. The right of bail is denied. A man is imprisoned as a criminal who has committed no crime.[89]

---

[86]See "Wu T'ing-fang to John Hay dated 26 December 1900", in "Notes from the Chinese Legation", also in *House Documents 1901*, p. 64, Document No. 200.

[87]*Ibid.*

[88]These five merchants were Wong Chee, Tsoy Nam-tun, Tsoy Kan-yik, Wong Sai-kee and Tang Chee. See "Wu T'ing-fang to John Hay dated 19 July 1901", in "Notes from the Chinese Legation", "The Mission of Wu T'ing-fang, April 1897 to March 1903".

[89]See I.M. Condit, *The Chinaman as We See Him and Fifty Years of Work for Him* (New York, 1900), p. 87.

These wooden sheds were filthy, overcrowded and badly ventilated. They were described by those who experienced them as fit only for pigs and horses.[90] These victims were also denied Chinese witnesses, and their American witnesses were often treated with discourtesy and were put to a lot of inconvenience. When required to sign identification papers, they were compelled to await the pleasure of the Immigration Bureau for examination, and were harassed with all sorts of irrelevant questions from an inspector.[91] If any answer was inconsistent with the statements in the certificates they possessed, suspicion was thus cast on their character, and their admission would be denied and they would be sent back to China.[92]

The merchants together with other resident Chinese were also subject to constant harassment by inspectors, special agents and marshals. These officials who were either supporters or sympathisers of the Exclusion had strong prejudices against the Chinese. They abused their power by creating hardship for the local Chinese. They entered shops and private residences searching for evidence and making arrests without warrants; they detained merchants, wives of merchants and American-born Chinese, requiring them to produce certificates.[93] They sometimes, without any warning, surrounded a Chinese community, herded the Chinese together and demanded immediate evidence of registration certificates. If anyone failed to produce sufficient evidence on the spot, he was placed in confinement until a tedious process of investigation was carried out and his right to remain in the United States was proved to the satisfaction of the officials. The action of a notorious Mr. Izard, a special agent of the Treasury Department, is a good example. Izard was a strong supporter of the policy of the total exclusion of Chinese expounded by Powderly. At the beginning of 1902 when he

---

[90]See an anti-Exclusion novel entitled *K'u She Hui* (The Bitter Society), in Ah Ying, *Fan Mei hua-kung chin-yueh wen-hsueh chi* (Collection of Literature relating to Anti-Exclusion of Chinese Labourers from the United States), p. 15.

[91]See "Wu T'ing-fang to John Hay dated 26 December 1900", in "Notes from the Chinese Legation", also in *House Documents 1901*, p. 64, Document No. 200.

[92]See "Wu T'ing-fang to John Hay dated 10 December 1901", in "Notes from Chinese Legation", also in *House Documents 1901*, p. 82, Document No. 219.

[93]A Chinese Inspector named B.F. Jossey made a number of unwarranted arrests of Chinese in Portland, Oregon, between May and October 1898. See "The Petition of Tong Duck Chung, the President of the Association of Jong Wah (The Chinese Association) of Portland, Oregon, to Wu T'ing-fang dated 14 January 1899", p. 2, in "Notes from the Chinese Legation", "The Mission of Wu T'ing-fang, April 1897 to March 1903".

was stationed in Boston, he had initiated a mass arrest of over five hundred Chinese suspected of being unlawful immigrants. But after a preliminary examination, over four hundred and thirty of them were discharged.[94] After Izard's transfer to New York in July, 1902, he carried out two raids upon the local Chinese communities: one on 24 July in Brooklyn causing the arrest of twenty-nine of them; another on 19 August upon some of the Chinese laundries in New York city, resulting in thirty-nine arrests. Izard managed to get blank warrants, entering the names after the arrests were made. He discounted those certificates produced as falsified and handcuffed the suspects like criminals.[95]

As a believer in Western concepts of the rule of law and the impartiality of bureaucracy, Wu was infuriated by the conduct of these officials who were supposed to enforce the law in a fair manner, but who instead violated the law themselves by making unlawful arrests. The act of entering private residences and making arrests without warrants or with blank warrants was a serious breach of legal procedure. This explains why Wu lodged strong protests against these officials by declaring that ". . . the officials of the government of the United States, to whom is entrusted the enforcement of the laws, treat the Chinese not as subjects of a friendly Power lawfully seeking the benefit of treaty privileges, but as suspected criminals".[96] He demanded that investigations be instituted into these unwarrantable acts as well as into the integrity of these officials.[97]

In the fight to protect the Chinese in the United States, Wu came to realise that conventional diplomatic channels were not sufficient to combat the anti-Chinese elements both inside and outside the bureaucracy and that he must try other unconventional means to achieve his objectives. With his experience in Great Britain, Hong Kong,[98] and the United States, he understood that the political pro-

---

[94]See "Wu T'ing-fang to A.A. Adee, Acting Secretary of State, dated 30 August 1902", pp. 1–2, ibid.

[95]Ibid.

[96]See "Wu to Hay dated 10 December 1901", in Papers Relating to the Foreign Relations of the United States, 57th Congress 1st Session, House Documents 1901, p. 85, Document No. 219.

[97]See "Wu T'ing-fang to A.A. Adee, Acting Secretary of State, dated 30 August 1902", p. 4, in "Notes from the Chinese Legation", "The Mission of Wu T'ing-fang, April 1897 to March 1903".

[98]See Linda P. Shin, "China in Transition: The Role of Wu T'ing-fang 1842–1922", pp. 31–47.

cess in the West was very much influenced by public opinion and pressure groups. Unless he could change the attitude of Americans towards China by influencing public opinion and mobilising the support of some pressure groups, the issue of the protection of the American Chinese could not be satisfactorily resolved.

To influence public opinion, Wu went all out to publicise the importance of Sino-American relationships. He used public platforms to preach the spirit of reciprocity, to emphasise trade opportunities in China for Americans, and to evoke the Christian values of love, equality, honesty and justice. He warned the Americans that if they wanted a share of China's trade, they must treat the Chinese in the United States fairly. On 26 January 1900, at the second annual dinner of the American Asiatic Association, he pointed out that China was the greatest potential market with a 400,000,000 population to be fed, clothed and provided with all the necessities in life.[99] He evoked the spirit of reciprocity and fairness by warning the Americans that if they wanted the patronage of these 400,000,000 people, they must treat Chinese fairly. "You must give and take — not take everything and give nothing. It will not do for you to expect China to keep her door open all the time if you shut the doors on Chinese merchants who come to your gate,"[100] he declared. He further declared that "If you want to have a share of China's trade, a good deal depends upon the kind of treatment you extend to my countrymen in this country, and especially in your new possessions."[101] On 8 February 1900, to an audience of three hundred who were attending the banquet of the Silk Association of America held at Delmonico's, Wu told the members that "If you come to China to buy raw silk from us, we embrace you with open arms. We do not legislate against your coming. Our doors are open to you; we treat you as we treat all other people — not as you treat us."[102] On 26 April of the same year, Wu addressed some thousand manufacturers at their annual banquet in Boston, and again pointed out to them the immense market potential and trade opportunities in China.[103]

---

[99] See "American-Asiatic Dinner: Opportunities China Offers", in *The New York Times*, 27/1/1900, p. 3.

[100] *Ibid.*

[101] *Ibid.*

[102] See "Silk Association Dines: Minister Wu Ting Fang Denounces Partition of China", in *The New York Times*, 9/2/1900, p. 3.

[103] Wu stated that "We need the cotton manufacturers of Lowell and the food product of the West. We have immense natural resources to be developed. We need

Wu, together with his brother-in-law, Ho Yow who was the
Chinese Consul-General in San Francisco, also wrote to American
magazines in an attempt to influence public opinion. They again
reiterated trade opportunity and the principle of reciprocity. In
March 1900, Wu wrote in the *Independent* magazine drawing attention to America's growing trade relationship with China, and the
railway concession obtained by an American company.[104] In another
article in the *North American Review* entitled "Mutual Helpfulness
between China and the United States", he stressed the principle of
reciprocity and declared that "Her (China's) door is wide open to
the people of the United States, but their door is slammed in the
face of her people."[105] Ho Yow in June 1900 in a magazine, *Forum*,
discussed wider opportunities for Americans in China, but warned
that the anti-Chinese policy would destroy these opportunities.[106]

To mobilise the support of pressure groups, Wu was active in
social gatherings: mingling with politicians, meeting manufacturers
and bankers and talking to educationists and church leaders.[107]
Two groups of people whose support Wu was interested in gaining
were those who sympathised with the Chinese and those who had
economic or other interests in China. Among the first group were
religious leaders and intellectual liberals who considered that the
United States was morally wrong to discriminate against and ill-
treat Chinese immigrants. Leaders of religious groups such as Con-
gregationalists, Methodists, Presbyterians (U.S.A.), Reformed
Presbyterians and United Presbyterians who were also concerned
about their work among the Chinese in America, came to Wu's aid.
The Reverend Nathan R. Johnson, a missionary who worked among
the San Francisco Chinese, wrote to President McKinley on 24 May

---

your modern mechanical appliances to supplant the slow processes of production.
Again we have thousands of miles of railroads to be built. We need your rails,
locomotives and iron bridges". See "Manufacturers' Banquet: Chinese Minister's
Plea — Points Out the Ways in Which Chinese Trade can be Secured", in *The New
York Times*, 27/4/1900, p. 3.

[104]See Wu T'ing-fang, "China and the United States", in *Independent* 52 (29
March 1900), p. 754.

[105]See Wu T'ing-fang, "Mutual Helpfulness Between China and the United
States" in *North American Review* 171 (July, 1900) 8, pp. 2–9.

[106]See Ho Yow, "The Attitude of the United States towards the Chinese" in
Forum 29 (June, 1900), p. 397.

[107]Quoted in D.L. McKee, *Chinese Exclusion versus the Open Door Policy 1900–
1906*, pp. 46–47.

1901, charging the U.S. government with violating the treaty with China and the Golden Rule.[108] Mrs. S.L. Baldwin, another missionary, wrote in the *New York Daily Tribune* condemning the anti-Chinese laws as contrary to the Christian spirit of justice, and she challenged the Secretary of State as to whether U.S. policy was guided by the Monroe Doctrine and the Golden Rule.[109] The enthusiastic Reverend Johnson also organised petitions in 1901 from Congregations in various states in an attempt to amend the discriminatory laws against the Chinese. Although he failed to collect the 100,000 signatures he hoped for, his act demonstrated his untiring efforts in support of the Chinese cause.[110]

Among the second group of Wu's supporters in American society were manufacturers, grain growers and investors who were interested either in selling their products or investing capital in China. They grouped together under the flag of the American Asiatic Association which aimed to promote trade and close ties with China. The Association, which came into being in January 1898, actively promoted public interest in China. It published a journal, organised public lectures and invited experts and diplomats to talk about China[111] and soon became an effective lobby for American policy in China.[112] Wu T'ing-fang seems to have secured some support from this group in his fight against the Exclusion Law. On 28 January 1902, the Executive Committee of the American Asiatic Association resolved to set up special funds for swaying public opinion to secure a more liberal treaty with China that would promote trade.[113] In the same month, John Foord, the Vice-President of the Association and a close ally of Wu T'ing-fang, set up his headquarters in Washington to lobby politicians. In February 1902, resolutions and petitions poured in from business groups such as the Portland Chamber of Commerce, the Merchants' Exchange in San Fran-

---

[108]See "Nathan R. Johnson to President McKinley dated 24 May 1901", in U.S. National Archives, "Bureau of Immigration, Segregated Chinese Records" FB 20.

[109]See *New York Daily Tribune*, 21/7/1901, p. 1.

[110]See D.L. McKee, *op. cit.*, p. 49.

[111]For instance, Mr. Charles Denby, U.S. ex-Minister for China, and Wu T'ing-fang were invited as the main speakers of the Association's second annual dinner held on 26 January 1900 at Delmonico's. See *The New York Times*, 27/1/1900, p. 3.

[112]See M.B. Young, *The Rhetoric of Empire: American China Policy, 1895-1901* (Cambridge, Mass., 1968), p. 109.

[113]See D.L. McKee, *Chinese Exclusion versus the Open Door Policy 1900-1906*, p. 50.

cisco, the San Francisco Chamber of Commerce, the Philadelphia Board of Trade, and the New York Chamber of Commerce. All called for moderation concerning Exclusion, stressed the need to allow Chinese merchants to come freely to the United States, and proposed the termination of the Geary Act in 1904 when the existing treaty with China was to expire and be renegotiated.[114]

Although Wu T'ing-fang had some success in the use of these unconventional methods, they were not sufficient to halt the efforts of the anti-Chinese elements both inside and outside the government. Further, the ill-feeling engendered in American society by the Boxer Uprising undercut much of the goodwill that Wu had been trying to create. Wu was fighting an uphill battle.

Perhaps the most important effort of Wu T'ing-fang to protect the American Chinese was his fight to prevent the re-enactment of the Exclusion Law in 1902. The Exclusion Law, which was enforced on 6 May 1882, was re-enacted on 5 May 1892, and was due to expire again on 5 May 1902. Anti-Chinese elements quickly mobilised to fight for its re-enactment. The main force outside the government was the American Federation of Labour. At its annual convention in 1900, it adopted a resolution to strengthen and re-enact the Exclusion Law.[115] The anti-Chinese forces led by the American Federation of Labour began a nationwide campaign for the re-enactment at the end of 1900. They lobbied politicians, published and widely distributed anti-Chinese pamphlets, and organised public lectures. This anti-Chinese force outside the government quickly moved to join hands with the Bureau of Immigration headed by Powderly. The Bureau released information which helped to create negative images of Chinese immigrants, and thus provided the American Federation of Labour with plenty of ammunition to attack the Chinese. In this crusade against Chinese immigration and the re-enactment of the Exclusion Law, the labour movement in California was particularly active. It organised mass rallies and sponsored popular petitions with thousands of signatures to press the President and Congress to re-enact the Exclusion Law.[116] On 6 December 1901, Powderly drafted a harsh bill which was presented to Congress by Representative Julius Kahn of California. The Kahn bill was the most extreme version of seventeen anti-Chinese bills. It

[114]*Ibid.*
[115]See E.C. Sandmeyer, *The Anti-Chinese Movement in California*, p. 106.
[116]See D.L. McKee, *op. cit.*, pp. 55–56.

reflected all the demands of the anti-Chinese elements both inside and outside the government, and contained rigid rulings on the definitions of students and merchants. It also excluded Chinese immigrants from the newly acquired territories of the Philippines and Hawaii, and prohibited Chinese migration from these islands to mainland America.[117]

It was at the height of the clamouring and success of these anti-Chinese forces that Wu T'ing-fang made a serious representation to the U.S. government in an attempt to stop the re-enactment of the Exclusion Law. In this fifty-eight page document Wu effectively presented China's case. Wu began by tracing the history of Sino-American treaties on Chinese immigration. He pointed out that the United States had been delighted to sign the Burlingame Treaty in 1868 granting the free entry of Chinese immigrants, but that it gradually relinquished its treaty responsibility by bowing to the demands of labour unions of the Pacific coastal states. It also took unilateral action to pass a series of Exclusion Laws against Chinese immigrants in the 1880s. In order to save the Executive of the United States from embarrassment, Wu claimed, the Chinese government had three times yielded to the wishes of the United States and concluded with it the amended Treaty of 1894.[118]

Wu stressed that the Chinese government in the Treaties of 1880 and 1894, had co-operated to the best of its ability with the American government over the issue of the prohibition of coolies from the United States, but claimed that this good faith was met with deceit and hostility. The Treasury Department, in accordance with an opinion of the Attorney-General,[119] excluded all Chinese

---

[117]*Ibid.*, pp. 59–60.

[118]See "Wu T'ing-fang to John Hay dated 10 December 1901", pp. 3–9, in "Notes from the Chinese Legation", "The Mission of Wu T'ing-fang, April 1897 to March 1903"; see also *Papers Relating to the Foreign Relations of the United States, 57th Congress 1st Session, House Documents 1901*, Document No. 219, pp 76–78.

[119]Attorney-General Griggs, in an opinion addressed to the Secretary of Treasury dated 15 July 1898, stated that "It may be stated, comprehensively, that the result of the whole body of these laws and decisions thereon is to determine that the true theory is not that all Chinese persons may enter this country who are not forbidden, but that only those are entitled to enter who are expressly allowed". In accordance with this interpretation, the Secretary of the Treasury instructed Collectors of Customs that only five categories of Chinese subjects, officials, teachers, students, merchants and travellers for curiosity or pleasure, be admitted. See "Wu T'ing-fang's memorandum to the President of the United States dated 9 December 1901", in "Notes from the Chinese Legation"; see also *House Documents 1901*, Document No. 218, p. 72.

who were not expressly listed in Article 3 of the Treaty of 1894. These hostile actions taken by the Treasury Department, Wu charged, were "in direct opposition to the treaties (of 1880 and 1894), to the laws of Congress and to the whole history of the events which gave rise to them".[120] Wu then proceeded to list many examples to show how these actions had inflicted tremendous hardships on legal Chinese immigrants.[121]

The central argument of Wu's representation was that the Exclusion Law had failed in original aims, and was not in the best interest of the United States. He charged that labour agitators and "Sandlot" politicians of the Western coastal states had used the Chinese immigration issue as a political football for their own gains and had succeeded in pressurising Congress to pass the Exclusion Law.[122] He challenged the validity of the four assumptions on which the Exclusion Law was enacted. The four assumptions were that the Chinese worked for lower wages than American workmen and therefore caused wages to fall; that 400,000,000 Chinese would overrun the United States if Chinese immigration was not prohibited; that the Chinese did not intend to become U.S. citizens but aimed to return to China after having acquired sufficient wealth; and that the Chinese contributed little to the purchasing power of the community because of their low living standards.[123]

In refuting the claim that the Chinese had caused wages to fall, Wu produced statistics to show that the reverse was the case; wages in California in 1870 (before the restriction of Chinese immigration) were in fact higher than wages in 1898 (sixteen years after the introduction of the first Exclusion Law).[124] To explain this pheno-

---

[120]See "Wu T'ing-fang to John Hay dated 10 December 1901", p. 11 in "Notes from the Chinese Legation", "The Mission of Wu T'ing-fang, April 1897 to March 1903".

[121]Most cases listed here were connected with the ill-treatment of students and merchants; some of these cases have been discussed earlier so they are not repeated. *Ibid.*, pp. 19–26.

[122]*Ibid.*, p. 30.

[123]*Ibid.*, p. 31; see also *House Documents 1901*, Document No. 219, pp. 86–87.

[124]Using the statistics of the fifteenth annual report of the Commissioner of Labour, Wu estimated that the average rate of wages for labour in California in 1870 was $2 per day. Immediately upon the passage of the Act of 1884, the average wages dropped to $1.70 per day. After the enactment of the Geary Law, wages in California declined gradually to $1.59 per day in 1898. See "Wu T'ing-fang to John Hay dated 10 December 1901", *ibid.*, p. 32; also *House Documents 1901*, Document No. 219, p. 87.

menon Wu emphasised that Chinese labour did not compete with American labour as popularly believed, but supplemented American labour and benefitted it.[125] To refute the second assumption Wu pointed out that Chinese people generally disliked travelling and the majority of them did not intend to emigrate. He argued that most European countries did not impose any ban on Chinese immigration, and had rarely found any Chinese immigrants in their lands. He also pointed out that the Chinese who emigrated to the United States only came from a few districts of the coastal province of Kwangtung which had a tradition of immigration. What Wu implied was that the United States would only attract a small section of the Chinese population and that the majority of Chinese would not be interested in emigrating to the United States. The fear of Chinese flooding America was therefore ungrounded.[126]

Wu charged that the claim that the Chinese immigrants were not interested in American citizenship was false. He realised that if this claim was left unrefuted, the myth that the Chinese would not be able to assimilate would be perpetuated. He pointed out that it was American laws rather than Chinese attitudes that prevented their naturalisation. He accused the government of the United States of discriminating against Chinese immigrants in this regard, and suggested that if the Chinese were accorded the privilege, many of them would become U.S. citizens. He further argued that the political apathy of Chinese immigrants should not be taken as a liability but as an asset, for they did not seek to control local politics as European immigrants did.[127] In defending the Chinese against the charges that they had low standards of living, Wu argued that the Chinese habit of thrift was the result of the overcrowded conditions in China. As the environment changed, the Chinese would spend more of their earnings on luxuries. He pointed out that the stan-

---

[125]Wu explained that most Chinese labourers were skilled in those areas in which the United States was deficient. They were mostly agriculturists and laundrymen; they would help to increase economic activity and to supplement American labour. See "Wu T'ing-fang to John Hay dated 10 December 1901", *ibid.*, pp. 32–33; also *House Documents 1901*, Document No. 219, pp. 87–88.

[126]See "Wu T'ing-fang to John Hay dated 10 December 1901", *ibid.*, pp. 34–35; also *House Documents 1901*, Document No. 219, p. 88.

[127]Wu gave examples of how the Swedish and Norwegian immigrants in certain communities in the United States had secured control of local politics. See "Wu T'ing-fang to John Hay dated 10 December 1901", *ibid.*, p. 36; also *House Documents 1901*, Document No. 219, p. 88.

dard of living of the Chinese in the United States would prove not to be as low as popularly believed, were the facts to be gathered by a special commission. He assured Americans that the Chinese were not unlike other people in the matter of spending money: the more they earned, the more they would spend.[128]

After refuting the four basic assumptions about the Chinese immigrants, Wu asserted that Chinese immigrants had a great potential to contribute to this relatively new country, but the Exclusion Law prevented that potential from being developed. In this sense, the Law did not work to the best interests of the United States. Further, Wu pointed out that the worst harm that the Law had done to American interests was the disruption of Sino-American trade relations. The Americans had immense trade interests in China, but they were greatly affected by the introduction of the Exclusion Law. He produced statistics to show that exports to China by the Western coastal states declined from US$7,000,000 in 1872 (before agitation against the Chinese immigrants) to a mere US$123,000 in 1892 (soon after the enactment of the Geary Law)[129] and estimated an export loss for the United States of at least US$200,000,000 in the last three decades.[130]

Wu warned the government of the United States that if the Exclusion Law was to be re-enacted in Congress, Sino-American relationships would be seriously impaired. The two governments could not have the cordial and harmonious intercourse enjoyed before, nor could the commercial relations between the two countries be as extensive, intimate and profitable.[131]

In conclusion, Wu T'ing-fang emphasised China's strong objection to the re-enactment of the Exclusion Law and reminded Congress again that the existing laws were "in violation of justice and humanity, inflicting on Chinese unnecessary hardships and indignities, that they are not in harmony with the treaties, that they work

---

[128]See "Wu T'ing-fang to John Hay dated 10 December 1901", *ibid.*, pp. 37–38; also *House Documents 1901*, Document No. 219, p. 89.

[129]Wu claimed that exports from these coastal states to China fell to US$126,000 in 1876 soon after the commencement of agitation against Chinese immigrants. But as soon as President Hayes vetoed the first anti-Chinese bill, the exports increased to US$9,000,000. *Ibid.*

[130]See "Wu T'ing-fang to John Hay dated 10 December 1901", *ibid.*, p. 39; also *House Documents 1901*, Document No. 219, p. 90.

[131]See "Wu T'ing-fang to John Hay dated 10 December 1901", *ibid.*, p. 43; also *House Documents 1901*, Document No. 219, p. 91.

injury to the interests of both countries. . . .''[132] He finally expressed hope that Congress would deal with this important subject in a spirit of fairness and equity.[133] However, Wu's representation, which was one of the best Chinese diplomatic documents of the time, seems to have had no effect on the attitude of the government of the United States.

At the beginning of 1902, both Congress and Senate held hearings on this important subject. Wu T'ing-fang mobilised as much support as he could. His friend John Foord organised a group of businessmen to attend the sessions and to attack the Kahn bill (also known as the Mitchell-Kahn bill). Clarence Cary, the leader of the American China Development Company which had substantial railway concessions in China,[134] also spoke in favour of China. Another important person to defend China's interests at the hearings was John W. Foster, a former Secretary of State and sometime legal adviser to China. He explained in detail that the Mitchell-Kahn bill was in direct violation of the Sino-American treaties. He was appalled by the current abuses and insults given to Chinese visitors, and warned that future trade with China would be threatened by the bill.[135] During the hearings, both anti-Chinese and pro-Chinese camps tried resourcefully to mobilise public support to achieve their aims, but the anti-Chinese camp appeared to have won the battle. On 12 March 1902, the Senate sub-committee on the Chinese Immigration reported to the Senate in favour of maintaining the Exclusion Law.[136] But Wu T'ing-fang continued to fight on. On 22 March he made a further appeal to Secretary Hay and to Congress in opposing the Mitchell-Kahn bill. He pointed out that the bill in a general way excluded many privileged Chinese from coming to the United States, including bankers, capitalists, commercial agents, scholars, professors, physicians and clergymen.[137]

---

[132]See "Wu T'ing-fang to John Hay dated 10 December 1901", *ibid.*, p. 57; also *House Document 1901*, Document No. 219, p. 96.

[133]See "Wu T'ing-fang to John Hay dated 10 December 1901", *ibid.*, p. 58; also *House Documents 1901*, Document No. 219, p. 97.

[134]This company was established in December 1895. It obtained the famous Canton-Hankow railway concession in April 1898. See Lee En-han, *China's Quest for Railway Autonomy 1904–1911* (Singapore, 1977), pp. 51–58.

[135]See D.L. McKee, *Chinese Exclusion versus the Open Door Policy 1900–1906*, pp. 60–61.

[136]*Ibid.*, p. 62.

[137]See "Wu T'ing-fang to John Hay dated 22 March 1901", p. 3 in "Notes from

He claimed that the bill, instead of alleviating the suffering of the Chinese, added further restrictions and created more miseries for the legal immigrants. He warned that if the bill became law, Chinese merchants would not come to buy goods and students would not come to study.[138]

Again Wu's plea fell on the deaf ears of the majority of Congressmen and Senators who passed the bill at the end of April 1902. On 29 April, immediately after the passing of the bill, Wu sent off another appeal to the President through Secretary Hay, as a last effort in his fight against injustice. He requested the President to veto the bill.[139] His appeal had no influence whatsoever on the President who had, in fact, signed the bill before the arrival of Wu's protest note.[140] This ended Wu's continuous efforts to prevent the re-enactment of the Exclusion Law and its extension to Hawaii and the Philippine Islands.

Wu T'ing-fang had tried his best to fight the re-enactment of the Exclusion Law, but he failed to achieve his objective. His failure was mainly determined by forces which were beyond his control. Anti-Chinese forces both inside and outside the government were entrenched and highly organised, and had immense influence over public opinion and politics. Worst of all, President Theodore Roosevelt, who took over the Presidency in September 1901 after the tragic death of President McKinley, came under intense pressure to endorse Exclusion. The opposing party, the Democratic Party, adopted the platform of continuance and strict enforcement of the Exclusion Law. Political realities dictated his stance.[141] Further, Roosevelt seems to have had little sympathy for Chinese immigrants.[142]

---

the Chinese Legation", "The Mission of Wu T'ing-fang, April 1897 to March 1903"; also in *Papers Relating to the Foreign Relations of the United States, 57th Congress 2nd Session, House Documents 1902*, Document No. 240, p. 211.

[138]See "Wu T'ing-fang to John Hay dated 22 March 1902", pp. 4-7, *Ibid.*; see also *House Documents* 1902, Document No. 240, p. 212.

[139]See "Wu T'ing-fang to John Hay dated 29 April 1902" in "Notes from the Chinese Legation", "The Mission of Wu T'ing-fang, April 1897 to March 1903".

[140]In his reply to Wu T'ing-fang, Secretary Hay stated that the appeal was received by the State Department after the President had signed the bill. See "Hay to Wu dated 30 April 1902" in *Papers Relating to the Foreign Relations of the United States, 57th Congress 2nd Session, House Documents 1902*, Document No. 221, p. 214.

[141]See D.L. McKee, *op. cit.*, pp. 58-59.

[142]See H.K. Beale, *Theodore Roosevelt and the Rise of America to World Power* (Baltimore, 1956), p. 28.

Angry and bitter over the failure, Wu had to sit back and rethink his strategy of protecting the American Chinese. He had exhausted his means of reasoning with the government of the United States in order to persuade it to give up its discriminatory laws against the Chinese immigrants, and had not got anywhere. He took this as a personal failure. Being conversant with international law and Western political systems, he had hoped to be more successful than his predecessors over the protection issue, but events proved to the contrary. He began to realise that individual ability did not make much difference in international diplomacy; it was the power and influence of a nation that really counted. China unfortunately was a weak nation and had very little power to enforce its treaty rights.

What distressed Wu most was not the personal failure and the cruel reality of diplomacy, but the loss of his faith in American justice. Justice was for the strong but not for the weak. Unlike Confucian diplomats who were suspicious of Western standards of justice, Wu had tremendous faith in Western legal systems and their inherent spirit. But this faith was completely shattered after this bitter experience.

The failure of Wu T'ing-fang's efforts was a serious indictment of the United States. As a powerful nation, it passed laws which contradicted its treaty obligations; denied the claims by China for indemnities, and denied the local Chinese justice. But on the other hand, it demonstrated its bullying attitude in dealing with the Chinese government over the riots against the American nationals in China. Its minister in Peking dictated terms for punishments for the rioters, demanded the sacking of the officials who were allegedly responsible, used the threat to get what it wanted, and clamoured for "justice".[143]

The "justice" for the American nationals seems not to be the same "justice" meted out to the Chinese in America who were killed or affected by the anti-Chinese riots. The power seemed to have given the United States the right to determine the standard of "justice".

Wu's disillusionment with the government of the United States over its handling of the Exclusion Law led him to consider other

---

[143]See "Mr. Denby to the Tsungli Yamen dated 21 September 1896", "Mr. Denby to the Tsungli Yamen dated 10 July 1897", in *American Diplomatic and Public Papers: The United States and China*, Series 3 (1894-1905), vol. 11, *Missionary Affairs and Antiforeign Riots*, pp. 326-28, 352-54.

options to protect the overseas Chinese. If the United States could
not be persuaded by reason, retaliation seemed to be the only alternative. In his note to Secretary Hay three weeks after the re-enactment of the Exclusion Law, Wu T'ing-fang warned that if the ban
on certain privileged Chinese into the United States was continued,
the Chinese government would reciprocate by prohibiting the entry
into China of all missionaries, whether clergymen or laymen,
bankers, civil and mining engineers, railroad contractors, builders,
commercial brokers and some merchants.[144]

Wu's threat of reprisal was, in retrospect, an important indication of China's preparedness to fight more resolutely for her treaty
rights and to protect her overseas subjects. This put her on a collision course with the United States over the overseas Chinese issue
which led to the large-scale boycott movement against the United
States in 1905.

Liang Ch'eng and the Protection of the American Chinese

The man who took over Wu T'ing-fang's post in Washington
was Liang Ch'eng who was better known in the West by his courtesy
name, Chen-tung.[145] Liang was born in 1864 in P'an-yu district of
Kwangtung province. Like Wu T'ing-fang, he had a strong Western
educational background. In 1875 Liang was among the group of
teenage students selected to study in the United States under the
supervision of Ch'en Lan-pin and Yung Wing. He was recalled to
China in 1881 and given a job as junior Secretary in the Tsungli
Yamen.[146] In 1885 he was selected as one of the trainee students accompanying the Chinese Minister Chang Yin-huan to the United
States, and worked in the embassy and studied part time. Later he
graduated from Yale University.[147] Being a native of the P'an-yu

---

[144]See "Wu T'ing-fang to John Hay dated 19 May 1902" in "Notes from the
Chinese Legation", "The Mission of Wu T'ing-fang, April 1897 to March 1903";
see also *House Documents 1902*, Document No. 247, p. 216.

[145]In all of his diplomatic despatches to the Secretary of State, Liang signed his
name as Chentung Liang Cheng. See "Notes from the Chinese Legation", "The
Mission of Chentung Liang Cheng April 1903 to June 1906"; see also *Papers
Relating to the Foreign Relations of the United States, 59th Congress 1st Session,
House Documents 1905*, pp. 113–238.

[146]See Lo Hsiang-lin, *Liang Ch'eng te ch'u-shih mei-kuo* (Liang Cheng: Chinese
Minister in Washington 1903–1907) (Hong Kong, 1977), pp. 3–4.

[147]See Liang Chia-pin, "Chi Ch'ing-chi she-li ch'iao-chiao yu chung-mei wen-
chiao chiao-liu" (The Establishment of Overseas Chinese Schools and the Cultural

district, he spoke the dialect of the majority of the Chinese in the United States and could therefore share a great deal of their plight and grievances. Being educated in the United States, he experienced racial prejudice against the Chinese. More importantly, he shared Wu T'ing-fang's idea of using modern diplomacy to protect China's treaty rights and was determined to continue Wu's fight for the protection of the American Chinese.

Meanwhile the growing militancy of the American Chinese toughened the attitude of Liang Ch'eng and the Chinese Foreign Office (Wai Wu Pu) to the protection issue. Being the victims, the American Chinese hated the Exclusion Law and wanted to see the Law discontinued. But part of their hope for the change was dashed by the re-enactment of the Exclusion Law in April 1902; their remaining hope therefore rested on the campaign to stop the Ch'ing government from renewing the Treaty of 1894 which was due to expire at the end of 1904. Realising the critical importance of this campaign the American Chinese formed a united front under the leadership of the Chinese in San Francisco. In October 1903, representatives of all Chinese in the United States met at the Chinese Association (Chung-hua hui-kuan) in San Francisco to work out their strategy. The convention lasted for several days and unanimously agreed to petition the Chinese government to reject the renewal of the Treaty.[148] It was probably the first time that the Chinese of the United States had shown such unity and solidarity. The petition was drafted and polished in the traditional way, and was sent to seven authorities which were directly or indirectly connected with the decision on the renewal of the Treaty, including the Ministry of Foreign Affairs; the Ministry of Commerce; the Chinese Minister in Washington; the former Chinese Minister in Washington and currently a Deputy Minister of Foreign Affairs, Wu T'ing-fang; the Governor-General of Hunan and Hupei, Chang Chih-tung; and

---

and Educational Exchange between China and the United States), in *Hua-ch'iao wen-t'i lun-wen chi* (Essays on Overseas Chinese Matters) (Taipei, 1954).

[148]See Liang Ch'i-ch'ao, "Chi hua-kung chin-yueh" (On the Exclusion Law against Chinese Labourers), as an appendix to Liang Ch'i-ch'ao's *Hsin-ta-lu yu-chi* (Diary of My Trip to the New Continent), p. 47. Both of these Liang's works were reprinted in Shen Yun-lung (ed.), *Chin-tai chung-kuo shih-liao ts'ung-k'an*, vol. 10, nos. 96–97; "Chi hua-kung chin-yueh" was also reprinted in A-ying (ed.), *Fan Mei hua-kung chin-yueh wen-hsueh-chi* (Collection of Literatures on Anti-American Exclusion Law) (Shanghai, 1960), pp. 487–522.

the Governor-General of Kwangtung and Kwangsi, Ts'in Ch'un-hsuan.[149]

The petition began with a review of the history of Sino-American treaties on the prohibition of Chinese coolies, and the sufferings that the Chinese had received under these treaties and the Exclusion Law. It proceeded to analyse the forces behind the making of the Law and asserted that the Sand-lot Party which was made up of urban scoundrels was mainly responsible for whipping up the anti-Chinese feeling and manipulating American politics. It pointed out that the United States was a democratic country and that the American President, government and officials had to comply with the wishes of the people; the Sand-lot Party and the Labour Party (Democrats?)[150] could therefore swing public opinion for their own selfish gains.[151] It also pointed out that not all Americans were anti-Chinese; those who were, the petition claimed, came mainly from the workers of lower class. Among these workers, the Jewish, Italian and German new arrivals were most hostile to the Chinese because of competition and jealousy. The petition continued to explain how the workers used votes and political parties to further their interests.[152] An important message that the petition wished to convey to the Chinese authorities was that only a segment of American society was really against the presence of Chinese coolies. It alleged that many Americans had reservations on this issue and that, in fact, many American merchants and manufacturers favoured Chinese coolies because the Chinese did not agree to strikes. However, owing to the threat of white workers, their sympathy for the coolies had to be restrained.[153]

The main thrust of the petition was the call on the Chinese government for a tougher stand in dealing with the United States. It asserted that a weak nation would always lose and be scorned by the strong if it continued to give in, but would gain respect if it dared

---

[149]See Liang Ch'i-ch'ao, "Chi hua-kung chin-yueh", pp. 56–57, *ibid.*

[150]In Chinese text, the name "Kung Tang" was used. Kung Tang can literally be translated as "Labour Party".

[151]The full text of this petition is included in Liang Ch'i-ch'ao's "Chi hua-kung chin-yueh", thereafter cited as "The Petition". See "The Petition", in Liang Ch'i-ch'ao, *Hsin-ta-lu yu-chi*, pp. 46–47; also in A-ying (ed.), *op. cit.*, pp. 509–10.

[152]See "The Petition" in Liang Ch'i-ch'ao, *op. cit.*, pp. 48–49; also A-ying (ed.), *ibid.*, pp. 510–11.

[153]See "The Petition" in Liang Ch'i-ch'ao, *ibid.*, p. 48; also A-ying (ed.), *ibid.*, p. 510.

to put up resistance. The petition explained that the United States was undergoing a rapid transformation from an agricultural to an industrialised state, and that her ability to control international trade and industry depended largely on the success in controlling the Chinese market. Therefore the Sino-American tariff negotiations were crucial to the United States. The petition urged the Chinese government to take advantage of the ongoing Sino-American trade negotiations currently being held at Shanghai and suggested the use of the tariff as a weapon to gain concessions on the Exclusion issue from the United States.[154]

The petition concluded by warning the government of the possible consequences that would arise if China did not act wisely on the issue. It pointed out that if all Chinese in the United States were driven back home, China would lose 25,000,000 taels(?)[155] annually in remittance and export. But worst of all, if American Exclusion was followed by other Western countries, the result would be repatriation of all overseas Chinese. The loss of an annual income of 50,000,000 to 60,000,000 taels, and a sudden increase of more than a million unemployed overseas Chinese would cripple China's economy, and would plunge China into social and political chaos.[156]

Many of the allegations contained in the petition seemed to be well-founded. Of course the petitioners knew how to use exaggeration and scare tactics to convince the Chinese government to reject the renewal of the treaty. But they were realistic enough to assume that the Chinese government may not be able to get what they wanted — the removal of the Exclusion Law — even if she adopted the strategy recommended in the petition. They therefore listed eight major items requiring urgent attention if the removal of the Exclusion Law could not be realised. These items, which were appended to the petition, included opposition to the extension of the Exclusion Law to Hawaii and the Philippines; the right of non-coolie Chinese to emigrate to the United States; clarification of the definition of "merchants" to avoid abuses;[157] cessation of the ill-

---

[154]See "The Petition" in Liang Ch'i-ch'ao, *ibid.*, p. 49; also A-ying (ed.), *ibid.*, pp. 511–12.

[155]The petition did not indicate its estimate in taels or in U.S. dollars, but reading in context, the estimate seems to be given in taels.

[156]See "The Petition" in Liang Ch'i-ch'ao, *op. cit.*, p. 51; also in A-ying (ed.), *op. cit.*, pp. 513–14.

[157]According to the petitioners, since the 24th year of Kuang-hsu (1898), American authorities refused to classify Chinese restauranteurs as "merchants"; at the time

treatment of Chinese on their arrival;[158] improvement of the visa inspection system; abolition of registering the Chinese; the right of Chinese to transit; and the elimination of ambiguous clauses in previous treaties.[159] These demands were not new to the Chinese Foreign Office for some of them were incorporated in the previous Treaties of 1880 and 1894, and some of them had been issues that Wu T'ing-fang had fought for. But even had China gained all these rights in a new treaty with the United States, what guarantee would China have of their honest implementation? This struck the basic problem of how China could effectively protect her treaty rights. The petitioners well understood that in the heyday of imperialism, might was right and that China could do very little about it. They offered no solution to the problem.

However, some radical Chinese in the United States viewed this problem from a different perspective. They saw the futility of the diplomatic exercise and believed China needed action to back up her protests. They proposed to use boycott as the weapon to bow the American authorities. The idea of boycotting American goods was articulated by a Chinese journalist named Ch'en I-k'an. Ch'en, the chief editorial writer of the *Sun Chung Kwock Bo* (New China Daily News)[160] of Honolulu, expounded his idea in a long article entitled "Suggestions for the Boycott of the Exclusion Law".[161] He

---

when the petition was drafted, the American authorities intended to remove the status of "merchants" from the owners of tobacco, broom and clothes factories. See item 3, the appendix to the petition, Liang Ch'i-ch'ao, *ibid.*, p. 52; also A-ying (ed.), *ibid.*, p. 515.

[158]The petitioners particularly singled out confinement of new arrivals for up to one month in wooden sheds which was a most humiliating experience to many Chinese. See item 4, the appendix to the petition, in Liang Ch'i-ch'ao, *ibid.*, p. 53; also in A-ying (ed.), *ibid.*, p. 516.

[159]See the appendix to the petition in Liang Ch'i-ch'ao, *ibid.*, pp. 52-54; also A-ying (ed.), *ibid.*, pp. 515-18.

[160]The name Sun Chung Kwock Bo was the original English name adopted for this Chinese newspaper in Honolulu. It was obviously romanised according to Cantonese pronunciation. In mandarin it should be romanised as *Hsin Chung Kuo Pao*. See *Sun Chung Kwock Bo* kept in the Library of the University of Hawaii.

[161]See Ch'en I-k'an, "I ti-chih chin-li ch'ih" of 29th year of Kuang-hsu (1903), originally published in the *Sun Chung Kwock Bo*. I have checked through the incomplete copy of this newspaper deposited in the Library of the University of Hawaii and could not find the article. Luckily the article was reprinted in the Reformists' main organ, *Hsin-min ts'ung-pao*, vols. 38 and 39, in the column of "P'ing-lun chih p'ing-lun" (Discussion and Criticism), pp. 1-10 and also in A-ying (ed.), *Fan Mei hua-kung chin-yueh wen-hsueh-chi*, pp. 588-97.

argued that the failure of China's diplomatic protests was not due just to her weak status, but was also the result of disunity among the American Chinese. He explained why Chinese, and not other Asiatic people, were singled out for discrimination by white workers. He claimed that two common charges against Chinese workers were that they were filthy and were prepared to work for lower wages. But the Japanese and Korean workers in the United States who had the same standard of hygiene and working conditions as the Chinese, were spared from discrimination. His answer to this was that the Chinese were disunited and had no concept of co-operation; they simply endured what had been imposed on them. Because of these weaknesses, the Chinese were easily pushed around by Americans. Ch'en further pointed out that Wu T'ing-fang, who was widely respected as an able diplomat, failed to fight the Exclusion Law partly because China had no military power to back him up, and partly because the Chinese in the United States had not supported him with concrete action. To remedy this situation, Ch'en asserted it was necessary to implement a boycott.[162]

Ch'en proposed several practical measures to boycott Americans: merchants should stop buying American goods, Chinese should stop using American products and workers should refuse to unload American goods from foreign ships. To enforce these measures, he suggested that Chinese merchants organise themselves into a body which would elect executives to supervise the sanctions. Those merchants who failed to comply with the sanctions would be punished. To help the vast masses to identify American goods, American brands would be listed both in Chinese and English and would be widely circulated. At the same time, public speeches were to be made to publicise the boycott.[163]

According to Ch'en, the success of the boycott would soften the American authorities and would hit the Labour Party (Democrats?), which strongly supported the demands of white workers. He predicted that once American goods stopped circulating in Chinese markets, many factories in the United States would be closed and thousands of white workers would be unemployed as a result of the

---

[162]See *Hsin-min ts'ung-pao*, *ibid.*, p. 2; also A-ying (ed.), *ibid.*, p. 589.
[163]See *Hsin-min ts'ung-pao*, *ibid.*, pp. 4, 8–9; also A-ying (ed.), *ibid.*, pp. 591 and 595.

boycott. This would bring pressure on the American government to give in to China's demands on the Exclusion issue.[164]

To remove the fear of his compatriots in relation to the Ch'ing government, Ch'en emphasised that the proposed boycott was an expression of patriotism; it would not offend the Ch'ing authorities but instead would help Chinese diplomats to discharge their duties effectively.[165]

Ch'en's appeal was mainly aimed at the Chinese in China. He realised that without mobilisation of the support of all his compatriots at home, any action taken by the American Chinese against the United States would be futile. Ch'en was a follower of K'ang Yu-wei and a leader of the Reformist group in Honolulu.[166] His call for a boycott was generally in line with the Reformist policy of arousing the Chinese masses and of resisting foreign imperialism. Although the ill-treatment of the Chinese in the United States was not seen in the same light as the imperialist encroachments upon China's territory, it was still regarded by the Reformists as a humiliation to the Chinese race and an issue that should be used to arouse patriotism.[167] If the proposed boycott could ignite patriotism and unite the Chinese people, it would be a worthwhile political exercise. The claim that the Reformists were mainly responsible for initiating the boycott movement is probably an exaggeration,[168] but the fact that the *Hsin-min ts'ung-pao*, the Reformists' main propaganda organ, had reprinted Ch'en I-k'an's article for wide circulation, shows the Reformists' endorsement of the idea of boycott.[169] Liang Ch'i-ch'ao, a Reformist national leader, second only to K'ang Yu-wei, also expressed his interest in Ch'en's idea, though he had

---

[164]See *Hsin-min ts'ung-pao, ibid.*, pp. 5–6; also A-ying (ed.), *ibid.*, pp. 591–93.

[165]See *Hsin-min ts'ung-pao, ibid.*, p. 9; also A-ying (ed.), *ibid.*, p. 596.

[166]See Feng Tzu-yu, *Hua-ch'iao ko-ming k'ai-kuo shih* (The Involvement of Overseas Chinese in the 1911 Revolution) (Taipei, 1953), p. 33; Wu Hsien-tzu, *Chung-kuo min-chu hsien-cheng tang shih* (A History of the Chinese Constitutional Party) (San Francisco, 1952), p. 42.

[167]See Ai Shih K'e, "Ai Kuo Lun" (On Patriotism), in *Ch'ing I Pao* (China Discussion) (Reprint, Taipei, n.d.), vol. 1, pp. 327–32.

[168]This claim was made by a Reformist leader Wu Hsien-tzu. Wu claimed that the Constitutional Party (Wei Hsin Hui) in the United States had initiated the call for the abolition of the Exclusion Law. It mobilised more than 100,000 Chinese from various cities in America to petition the Peking government not to renew the Sino-American Treaty in 1904. See Wu Hsien-tzu, *op. cit.*, p. 42.

[169]See *Hsin-min ts'ung-pao*, vols. 38 and 39, column of "Discussion and Criticism", pp. 1–10.

some doubts about its likely success. Liang hoped that the proposed boycott, if successful, would become the forerunner of political movements in China.[170]

The petition of the Chinese of the United States and the radical proposal of Ch'en I-k'an must have toughened Liang Ch'eng's stand on the Exclusion issue. By the end of 1903 Liang must have been very sure that he had the solid support of the American Chinese and potentially, tens of thousands of Chinese in China.

In the meantime, the anti-Chinese movement in the United States achieved a new success. As established by a recent research, the re-enactment of the Exclusion Law in 1902 represented "a significant step forward for the Exclusion forces",[171] for it endorsed the ever-hardening administrative regulations of the Bureau of Immigration under the leadership of T.V. Powderly.[172] This official endorsement gave a boost to the anti-Chinese forces both inside and outside the government that mobilised again for the renewal of the Exclusion Treaty. Since May 1902, Frank P. Sargent had succeeded Powderly to become the head of the Bureau of Immigration and the leader of the anti-Chinese elements within the government. The transfer of the Bureau of Immigration from the Treasury Department to the new Department of Commerce and Labour, in 1903, gave Sargent more power and freedom in the control of immigrants. As he tried to outdo Powderly in anti-Chinese zeal, he vigorously carried out his crusade against the Chinese.[173] Meanwhile the Exclusionists outside the government stirred up Sinophobia by distributing leaflets, organising mass meetings and sending petitions to the government.

Reflecting this upsurge of anti-Chinese feeling was the harsh treatment of the Chinese in the United States and the members of the exempted classes. The Bertillon system, introduced in 1903, was intended only for the Chinese coolies but was applied to merchants and students. The system involved the inspection and measurement of the naked body for identification.[174] The harsh treatment was even applied to Chinese diplomats who should have been immuned

---

[170]See Liang Ch'i-ch'ao, "Chi hua-kung chin-yueh" in Liang Ch'i-ch'ao, *Hsin ta-lu yu chi*, appendix, pp. 56–57.

[171]See D.L. McKee, *Chinese Exclusion Versus the Open Door Policy 1900–1906*, p. 64.

[172]For the role of Powderly in implementing total Exclusion policy, see *ibid.*, pp. 28–36.

[173]*Ibid.*, pp. 67–68.

[174]*Ibid.*, p. 74.

from discrimination in accordance with international practice. Tom Kim Yung, Military Attaché of the Chinese legation in Washington, temporarily on detached service in San Francisco, was brutally beaten by two policemen on the night of 10 September 1903. He was alleged to have struggled with the policemen and was badly bruised. He was handcuffed and put in jail though he claimed diplomatic immunity. Finding it difficult to swallow his pride, Tom committed suicide on 14 September.[175] Chow Tsz-chi, the First Secretary of the Chinese legation, was detained at the Winslow railway station, Arizona, on 26 September 1903,[176] by an immigration inspector. Chow was on his way to San Francisco to investigate the death of Tom Kim Yung. He was abused and humiliated. These incidents represented serious violations of the Exclusion Law, the treaties and normal diplomatic practice. Were the outrageous behaviour of these officials to be left unchallenged, perhaps Liang Ch'eng himself would also become a victim. The threat to his personal pride was not an unreal one, for his brother, Liang Hsun, the Consul-General in Manila, also experienced an unpleasant encounter with American immigration officials. Liang Hsun arrived in San Francisco on 30 September 1903, with his wife, daughter and a maid at the invitation of the Chinese Minister but immigration officials permitted only Liang Hsun himself to land. Although the matter was quickly settled with the Minister's intervention, the incident drove home the seriousness of the situation to the Minister.[177]

Perhaps the harshest treatment of the Chinese in the United States at this time was the mass arrest of the Boston Chinese on 11 October 1903. Suspecting large numbers of illegal immigrants in the midst of the Chinese population in Boston, immigration officials with the

---

[175]See "Chentung Liang Cheng to John Hay dated 30 November 1903" and the "sworn statement of Yee Shim, President of the Chinese Merchants' Association of San Francisco (one of the two witnesses to the incident)", in "Notes from the Chinese Legation", "The Mission of Chentung Liang Cheng, April 1903 to June 1906".

[176]According to Chow, he left the train at Winslow to have breakfast in the station eating-saloon, but was stopped by an immigration inspector who demanded to see his residence certificate. Dissatisfied with Chow's name card as a diplomat, the inspector was alleged to have grasped him by the arm and told him that he was under arrest. Chow protested but was told that "even if you were the Chinese Emperor, I would arrest you". See "Chentung Liang Cheng to John Hay dated 15 December 1903", *ibid.*, also D.L. McKee, *op. cit.*, p. 80.

[177]See *The New York Times*, 30/9/1903, p. 8.

support of the local police made the raid. Two hundred and thirty-four people who failed to produce certificates of residence on the spot were arrested.[178] In the course of the action police brutality was alleged. Many were dragged and "herded like cattle upon wagons or other vehicles to be conveyed to the designated place for detention".[179] It was also alleged that an old man was injured and two of his ribs were broken after a wagon was overthrown owing to overcrowding, and those detained were denied food or drink during their temporary confinement.[180] The Chinese Minister lodged a strong protest with the State Department and condemned what he called ". . . lawless acts committed against the Chinese of this country . . . flagrant violation of treaty obligations, and utter defiance of the constitution and laws of the Federal Government (of the United States).[181]

This mass arrest represented a most daring attempt on the part of the Exclusionists to drive out the Chinese by harassment, but it also enraged the Chinese Minister and hardened his attitude towards the treaty negotiations. In a cable to the Wai Wu Pu at the end of 1903, Liang advocated termination of the existing treaty with the United States. He suggested the re-negotiation of important provisions and urged the government to support his stand.[182] Probably on Liang's advice, the Wai Wu Pu on 24 January 1904 served a note on the American Minister at Peking to the effect that China intended to terminate the treaty which expired in December 1904.[183] On 2 February 1904, Wu T'ing-fang on behalf of the Wai Wu Pu proposed to the Minister (E.H. Conger) that the treaty be extended for another year so that a new treaty could be negotiated after the American pre-

---

[178]This was the official figure given by the government of the United States. Pro-Chinese sources claimed that at least 250 were arrested. Among those arrested, five were immediately deported and forty-five followed later. See "Chentung Liang Cheng to John Hay dated 10 November 1903" in "Notes from the Chinese Legation", "The Mission of Chentung Liang Cheng, April 1903 to June 1906"; see also D.L. McKee, *op. cit.*, pp. 68–69.

[179]See "Chentung Liang Cheng to John Hay dated 10 November 1903", *ibid.*
[180]*Ibid.*
[181]*Ibid.*
[182]See Chang Ts'un-wu, *Kuang-hsu sa-i nien chung mei kung-yueh feng-ch'ao* (The 1905 Sino-American Dispute over the Exclusion Law) (Taipei, 1965), p. 29.
[183]See "Prince Ch'ing to Conger dated 24 January 1904" in *Papers Relating to the Foreign Relations of the United States, 58th Congress 3rd Session, House Documents 1904*, p. 117.

sidential election.[184] As a former Chinese Minister at Washington, Wu knew well that the anti-Chinese issue would be used as a major political platform during the election year and that China's negotiations would be greatly disadvantaged because the President and his government would be under immense pressure from sinophobes.

Wu's proposal was rejected by the United States on the ground of its impracticability. In fact, the Roosevelt Administration was under enormous pressure to extend the treaty.[185] Probably prompted by the serious anti-Chinese situation in the United States, Liang took the initiative to negotiate. He drafted the new treaty provisions and obtained the endorsement of the Wai Wu Pu. On 12 August 1904, the draft treaty was sent to the Secretary of State accompanied by a forty-seven page diplomatic note explaining why China was determined to end the old treaty. The note represented a most vehement attack on the Exclusion policy by the Chinese Minister.

Liang at the outset made clear the Chinese government's stand that the old treaty must be substantially revised in order to provide safeguards for its implementation, and it was the implementation of the treaty that came under his most severe criticism. His indictment was that the government of the United States had allowed its officials to distort treaty provisions to kill the spirit of the treaty, and to counter the original aims of the two governments. He accused the officials of having little regard for treaty obligations and charged that ". . . the treaties are being violated under the cover of enforcing the laws; and the laws are being violated under the cover of enforcing the regulations. The regulations are being enforced without much regard to either the treaties or the laws".[186]

The attack was concentrated on the implementation of the treaty clauses, particularly related to the re-entry of the resident Chinese labourers and admission of the members of the exempted class. Under the Treaty of 1894, Liang declared, a registered labourer could return to the United States after a temporary overseas trip on condition that he had "a lawful wife, child or parent in the U.S., or property therein to the value of one thousand dollars, or debts of like amount due him and pending settlement".[187] But he charged

---

[184]See D.L. McKee, *op. cit.*, p. 84.

[185]*Ibid.*, pp. 87–89.

[186]See "Chentung Liang Cheng to John Hay dated 12 August 1904", p. 3 in "Notes from the Chinese Legation", "The Mission of Chentung Liang Cheng, April 1903 to June 1906".

[187]*Ibid.*, p. 9.

that "this seemingly humane and reasonable provision has proved to be delusion and a snare",[188] for the Chinese treaty right was curtailed by laws and regulations. Furthermore, few of the Chinese labourers could produce legally acceptable documents to prove their marital status or their financial arrangements with their debtors. Liang was infuriated by the lack of guarantee of entry for those registered labourers who possessed return certificates issued by the United States immigration authorities. Some of them had to undergo investigation and interrogation. During the period pending a decision, they were detained in wooden sheds and were denied benefit of counsel. This resulted in severe mental strain and sometimes death.[189]

All these charges seemed to be well-founded. But the denial of the right of re-entry to registered labourers should not entirely be attributed to the efforts of the Exclusionists who controlled the Bureau of Immigration. Cultural differences also had a role to play in the failure of the labourers to claim their right. For instance, Chinese marriage was at that time a community affair, and there was no official document issued to prove the relationship between husband and wife. Therefore, a Chinese labourer who had a wife in the United States could hardly produce legally acceptable documents to prove it. Even if he had some kind of document, it would not have been of great use because it was invariably written in Chinese and the traditional practice of Chinese women keeping their maiden surnames after marriage would have aroused suspicion of fraud.[190] In the implementation of the Law, if the immigration officers were upright and sympathetic, the cultural differences could have been overcome. But as the immigration officials were biased and hostile towards the Chinese, their cultural differences were exploited to disadvantage the registered labourers.

On the issue of the admission of members of the exempted class, Liang was equally critical. He repeated Wu T'ing-fang's charges of distortion of the treaty over this issue by the Attorney-General of the United States, and claimed that the rigidity of that interpreta-

---

[188]*Ibid.*

[189]*Ibid.*, pp. 14–16.

[190]This practice is still retained in China and the Chinese communities in some Southeast Asian countries. The American immigration officers who were brought up in the Western tradition and who had little or no knowledge of Chinese culture, would automatically reject two people with different surnames who claimed to be a married couple.

tion had effectively barred many Chinese from entering the United States. He further charged that those who fell into the right categories of the exempted class — officials, teachers, students, merchants and travellers — had also encountered many difficulties on their arrival. The obstacles were purposely created by the immigration officials who picked on technical faults and clerical mistakes on the certificates.[191] Worst of all, Liang declared, was that a visa issued by the proper American diplomats could still be rejected. The victims of this squabble over credibility among American officials were innocent Chinese.[192]

Although Liang lost confidence in U.S. ability to implement the treaty clauses, he nevertheless tried to remedy the situation by simplifying treaty clauses in order to reduce the scope for misinterpretation. To prevent distortion of the term, "labourers", Article 1 of the draft treaty spelled out that "the word 'labourers' shall be construed to mean both skilled and unskilled labourers, including Chinese employed in mining, fishing, huckstering, peddling and laundry work. . . ."[193] Article 1 also made clear that no Chinese other than labourers should be included in the prohibition.[194]

To ensure the re-entry of the Chinese labourers who were already in the United States, Article 2 proposed that the U.S. government register the labourers and provide them with certificates of residence. Those who wished to make temporary overseas trips were required to deposit their certificates with the nearest Chinese consular officials, and to obtain return certificates issued by the said officials and countersigned by proper American immigration or customs authorities. If they returned to the United States with the certificates within a period of two years, they should be admitted without any trouble.[195]

To protect the rights of the non-labouring Chinese, Article 5 suggested that they should be permitted to enter and reside in any territory of the United States; they should present to the immigration or

[191]See "Chentung Liang Cheng to John Hay dated 12 August 1904", pp. 21–25, in "Notes from the Chinese Legation", "The Mission of Chentung Liang Cheng, April 1903 to June 1906".

[192]*Ibid.*, pp. 25–26.

[193]See "Draft of a Proposed Treaty between China and the United States Relating to the Exclusion of Labourers", p. 1, enclosed in "Chentung Liang Cheng to John Hay dated 12 August 1904", *ibid.*

[194]*Ibid.*

[195]*Ibid.*, pp. 1–2.

customs officials a certificate of identification in both English and Chinese issued by the proper representative of the Chinese government and the visa should be authorised by the representatives of the United States. The authenticated certificates should be taken as conclusive evidence of the holder's legitimate right to enter and reside in the United States.[196]

To prevent ill-treatment of the Chinese, Article 6 affirmed that no Chinese seeking to enter the United States would be held in detention or in prison pending a decision on his case. Any adverse decision by an administrative official affecting the treaty rights of a Chinese subject would be referred to a judicial tribunal of the United States of competent jurisdiction. Furthermore, the Article also made clear that no Chinese subjects residing in the United States would be molested or harassed by domiciliary visits from administrative officials, nor would they be arrested without warrants issued by competent authorities.[197]

Although Liang did not dwell on the issue of prohibition of Chinese labourers from Hawaii and the Philippines in great length in his forty-seven page note,[198] he nevertheless expressed his strong feeling in the provisions of the draft treaty. He reasserted Wu T'ing-fang's stand that the Exclusion Law should not be applied to the newly acquired territories of the United States and insisted that Chinese labourers be allowed to go to Hawaii and the Philippines as determined by local conditions.[199]

As Liang held strong doubts about the sincerity of the United States government in implementing the treaty clauses, he attempted to acquire rights for China to enact laws against American citizens in China. Articles 8 and 9 emphasised the principle of reciprocity and required the United States to endorse it.[200]

The draft treaty, which bore the imprint of Liang Cheng's perception of how to solve the problem of protecting the American Chinese, did not differ from the Treaty of 1894 in aims and spirit.

---

[196]*Ibid.*, pp. 3–4.

[197]*Ibid.*, pp. 4–5.

[198]See "Chentung Liang Cheng to John Hay dated 12 August 1904", p. 8, in "Notes from the Chinese Legation", "The Mission of Chentung Liang Cheng, April 1903 to June 1906".

[199]See Article 4 of the draft treaty, "Draft of a Proposed Treaty between China and the United States Relating to the Exclusion of Labourers", p. 3, *ibid.*

[200]*Ibid.*, pp. 6–7.

It reaffirmed China's agreement to total prohibition of labourers
into mainland United States and reasserted the rights of non-labouring Chinese as well as registered labourers. The difference it would
make was that it removed the ambivalent clauses from the previous
treaty and closed loopholes that created possible abuses.

The initial reaction of the State Department to the draft was
favourable,[201] but as the draft intended to close these loopholes, it
provoked strong objection from the Bureau of Immigration of
which the Exclusionists had a firm control. The Bureau produced a
counterdraft which basically preserved the old treaty as the Bureau
interpreted it. The counterdraft left the term, "labourers", ambiguous, reaffirmed the Exclusionists' stand to exclude all except
those specified in the provisions, and retained the right to detain
Chinese pending a decision on their status.[202] It appears that the
State Department and the Bureau of Immigration differed basically
in their objectives. The Department was willing to settle for a treaty
excluding labourers only, while the Bureau worked for total exclusion of the Chinese. The Exclusionists were quick to mobilise political
support and had the counterdraft accepted by the Roosevelt Administration. The counterdraft was sent to Liang on 29 November
1904, and was referred to Wai Wu Pu for consideration. At the
same time, at the request of Secretary Hay, Liang conducted a
detailed examination of the counterdraft with the American officials
entrusted with the job. The result was his flat rejection of it.[203] With
Wai Wu Pu's endorsement of his stand, Liang, on 7 January 1905,
sent Secretary Hay a second draft together with a statement. Surprisingly his stand had hardened as revealed in these documents.

The second draft gave no concessions to American demands. It
reproduced most of the provisions with some slight modification of
the first draft,[204] and in fact inserted additional clauses to protect the

---

See D.L. McKee, *Chinese Exclusion Versus the Open Door Policy 1900–1906*,
p. 96.

Ibid., p. 97.

See "Chentung Liang Cheng to John Hay dated 7 January 1905", in "Notes
from the Chinese Legation", "The Mission of Chentung Liang Cheng, April 1903
to June 1906".

Compare the second draft with the first one; it appears that Articles 2, 3, 8, 9,
10, 11 and 12 were complete reproductions. See "Second Draft of a Proposed
Treaty between China and the United States Relating to the Exclusion of
Labourers" enclosed in "Chentung Liang Cheng to John Hay dated 7 January
1905", *ibid.*

interests of registered labourers and the members of the exempted class. With respect to the registered labourers, a clause was added to Article 6 to give them the option of having an attorney to represent them when their right of re-entering the United States was questioned.[205] In relation to the members of the exempted class, a special article (Article 7) was added to give them the privilege of sending for their parents, wives or children to enter the United States upon production of a certificate issued by a Chinese Consul.[206] The second draft also reinforced the principle of reciprocity. It went to the extent of inserting a sentence in Article 1 that "Similarly the coming of American labourers to the territory of the Chinese empire shall be absolutely prohibited."[207] This sentence was probably more token than real because no American labourers would go to China to work, but its insertion indicated the desire of the Chinese government to assert the principle of reciprocity. This uncompromising draft was accompanied by a warning of retaliation. Many American bankers, accountants and company directors would be excluded from China if the United States insisted on total exclusion of Chinese.[208]

As the two drafts were the brain child of Liang Cheng, his sincerity and determination to protect the American Chinese cannot be questioned. Since the second draft was flatly rejected by the government of the United States after its delivery, Liang realised that his fight for justice through diplomatic means had failed and thus he began to dwell on the idea of boycott as the only alternative. In his despatch to the Wai Wu Pu in January 1905, he explored the possibility of giving implicit support to the proposed boycott movement by the American Chinese. He commended the boycott of American goods as an effective way to hit Americans, but cautioned the Wai Wu Pu not to be publicly involved. What the Chinese government could do, Liang advised, was to give the green light to merchant associations to go ahead with the boycott without its direct involvement. By so doing, the government would not be responsible for any consequences.[209]

---

[205]*Ibid.*, p. 5.

[206]*Ibid.*, p. 6.

[207]*Ibid.*, p. 1.

[208]See "Chentung Liang Cheng to John Hay dated 7 January 1905", in "Notes from the Chinese Legation", "The Mission of Chentung Liang Cheng, April 1903 to June 1906".

[209]See "Wai Wu Pu Archives", "kung-yueh", "Despatch of the Chinese Minister

How important was Liang's role in the rise of the boycott movement is difficult to ascertain. He made no public speeches, nor did
he donate any money to the movement. What we are certain of is
that he was sympathetic to the boycott. In April 1905, the Acting
Chinese Consul-General in San Francisco issued a proclamation to
clear the rumour that China was about to sign a new treaty on
American terms. The proclamation quoted Liang as saying that
"As your Minister I can no longer bear to see our people unjustly
suffering inequities and indignities visited continually upon them,
as people who cry but cry in vain."[210] This statement was probably
taken by the American Chinese as an expression of Liang's tacit
support for their action. Only two weeks later, an explosive situation for the boycott was created among the Chinese in San Francisco.[211] In his despatch to the Wai Wu Pu on 13 May 1905, Liang
defended the boycott movement which was about to take place and
urged the government not to nip it in the bud. He explained that the
pre-boycott meetings in Shanghai and Hong Kong had begun to affect the attitude of American businessmen and officials who feared
that American goods such as flour, kerosene and cotton cloth
would be greatly hit by the boycott, and that the American share of
the Chinese market would be taken over by British, German and
Japanese suppliers.[212] He then assured the Wai Wu Pu that if China
persisted in its firm stand, the United States would eventually bow
to China's demands.[213]

The details of the boycott movement which had swept through
many parts of China and overseas Chinese communities in 1905
and 1906 are beyond the scope of this study, but it must be emphasised here that the movement had probably helped to change
the attitude of the American government in its implementation of
the Exclusion policy. The status of the Chinese in the United States

---

for the United States, Liang Cheng, received on 13th day of 1st moon of 31st year of
Kuang-hsu (16 February 1905)".

[210]See "Proclamation by Chung, Acting Consul-General for California (San
Francisco ?) on statement by Minister Liang, translated by J. Endicott Gerdner, In-
spector and Interpreter at San Francisco, 30 April 1905", in U.S. National Archives,
"Bureau of Immigration, Segregated Chinese Records", FB 85.

[211]See D.L. McKee, op. cit., p. 104.

[212]See "Wai Wu Pu Archives", "kung-yueh", "Despatch of the Chinese Minister
for the United States, Liang Cheng, received on 4th day of 6th moon of 31st year of
Kuang-hsu (6 July 1905)".

[213]Ibid.

had been improved during the years from 1906 to 1909.[214] In this sense, Liang had indirectly achieved some success in the protection of the American Chinese.

THE PROTECTION OF THE CHINESE IN SOUTH AFRICA

The 1903 Petition for the Protection of the South African Chinese

The problem of protecting the Chinese in South Africa did not arise until 1903 when the Chinese in the Transvaal petitioned the Ch'ing government to set up a consulate in Johannesburg.[215] Prior to that year no effort was made by the local Chinese to establish any official relationship with the home government. In fact, the South African Chinese before 1893 were non-existent as far as the Ch'ing government was concerned, for nothing was mentioned about them in the official records.[216] When the first Chinese arrived in South Africa is unknown; it may have been in the second half of the nineteenth century or earlier. What we can be sure of is the fact that before the Boer War (1899–1902) a number of Chinese were in the Transvaal engaging in trade.[217] The number of Chinese increased during the period between 1899 and 1903: one source claims that more than nine hundred of them arrived in that period.[218] The first petition sent to the Ch'ing government in 1903 claimed that the Chinese population in the Transvaal was several thousands.[219] This figure could have been exaggerated for the purpose of impressing the Ch'ing government to come to their aid. As the free Chinese population there in 1907 was estimated at about 1100,[220] a realistic

---

[214]See W.L. Tung, *The Chinese in America 1820–1973*, p. 24.

[215]See "The Petition of the South African Chinese to the Chinese Minister in London of 1903" in Tsungli Yamen Archives, 29th year of Kuang-hsu, "The Mission of Chang Te-i to England".

[216]Checking through the *Ching-chi wai-chiao shih-liao* and Tsungli Yamen Archives, nothing is found about the Chinese in South Africa before 1903.

[217]See "The Petition of the Chinese of the Transvaal to the Chinese Minister in London, Wang Ta-hsieh, dated 27 September 1906" in *FO* 367/16, Africa, General.

[218]See E.G. Payne, *An Experiment in Alien Labor* (Chicago, 1912), p. 30, quoted in H.F. MacNair, *The Chinese Abroad*, p. 67.

[219]See the 1903 petition in Tsungli Yamen Archives.

[220]In October 1907, in a petition to the Chinese Minister in London, the Chairman of the Transvaal Chinese Association, Leung Quinn, mentioned the free Chinese population in Transvaal was about 1,100. See "The Petition of the Chairman of the Chinese Association, Leung Quinn to the Chinese Minister in London dated 14 October 1907" in *British Parliamentary Papers: Accounts and Papers* (1908), no. 73, Cd. 3887, p. 55.

figure for the year 1903 would be a couple of thousand. Whatever the number was, the majority of the South African Chinese before 1903 appear to have been free emigrants, some of whom were probably attracted by gold and many of whom were laundry workers and traders.[221] Some of them were successful in business and became interested in the quest for social status and honour in order to glorify their ancestors. Like many other overseas Chinese merchants in Southeast Asia,[222] they purchased brevet titles and degrees from agents of the imperial government.[223] Despite their purchase of Ch'ing honours, they had not attempted to establish any official link with the home government.

Like other sections of the population in South Africa, the Chinese suffered the impact of the war. They had to flee the war, their businesses were ruined, and their works dislocated. Many of them had difficulty returning to their old jobs. The worst impact was the hostility of the whites towards the non-whites as a result of the war. The war demobilised the white rural population and drove them to cities to look for jobs, which brought them into direct confrontation with non-white labourers and accentuated the tension of racial relationships. To aggravate the impact of the war, there was a fear among white workers of the proposed introduction of Chinese coolies to meet the labour shortage in the Transvaal mines and industries during the post-Boer War period.[224] Reflecting the mood of the time was the tightening of legislation against Asiatics and increased hostility among white workers towards Chinese and Anglo-Indians. The extremist white workers even threatened to drive all Chinese out of Johannesburg and to take away their rights to trade in any urban towns.[225] The tightening of legislation against Asiatics

---

[221]See H.F. MacNair, *op. cit.*, p. 67.

[222]For the purchase of Ch'ing honours by the Chinese in Singapore and Malaya, see Yen Ching-hwang, "Ch'ing's Sale of Honours and the Chinese Leadership of Singapore and Malaya 1877–1912", in *Journal of Southeast Asian Studies*, vol. 1, no. 2 (1970), pp. 20–32.

[223]Among 34 petitioners signed for the 1903 petition, 20 of them possessed Ch'ing brevet titles and degrees such as *Chou-t'ung*, *Li-kung*, *Hou-pu hsien-ch'eng*, *Chien-sheng* and *Wu-sheng*. See the 1903 petition in Tsungli Yamen Archives.

[224]"For a discussion of the role of Chinese coolie labour in South African economy between 1903 and 1908, see Peter Richardson, "The Recruiting of Chinese Indentured Labour for the South African Gold-Mines, 1903–1908", in *Journal of African History*, vol. 18, no. 1 (1977), pp. 85–108.

[225]See the 1903 Petition in Tsungli Yamen Archives.

and the potential threat to the entire Chinese population constituted the two principal themes of argument in the petition of the
Transvaal Chinese to the Ch'ing government in 1903.[226] The petitioners saw the solution to their problems in the presence of a
Chinese Consul. Aware of the financial constraints of the home
government, the petitioners nominated a European named Chin
Shih-li (Kingsley?) who was on good terms with the local Chinese,
to be the Imperial Consul, and pointed out that a sum of money
had been raised to pay for his salary.[227]

The petition had put South African Chinese on the Chinese official record. Of course petition of this kind was not new to the
Chinese government; what was new was the fact that this one came
out of the blue and it was probably the first time the government
knew of the existence of the South African Chinese and their pressing problems. The Chinese Minister in London, Chang Te-i, was
very much in favour of the proposal. Since the cost of maintaining
a consulate was a major factor inhibiting the expansion of Chinese
consulates overseas, Chang saw that the formula of merchant-
sponsorship, first introduced in Singapore in 1877,[228] could still be
used in South Africa. He promptly transmitted the petition to the
Wai Wu Pu with a strong recommendation for its approval.[229]

The Wai Wu Pu did not respond to Chang's recommendation,
and this seemingly indifferent attitude disappointed the petitioners
as well as Chang Te-i. The Wai Wu Pu seems to have been unsure
at the time of the likely outcome of appointing a European Consul,
or at least unsure of China's right to appoint a consul without prior
British approval;[230] but perhaps the main reason for the delay was

---

[226]*Ibid.*

[227]*Ibid.*

[228]For a detailed discussion of this merchant-sponsorship introduced first in
Singapore and later in Hawaii and some other overseas Chinese communities, see
Chapter 4 of this book.

[229]Chang Te-i received the petition on 27 September 1903 (7th day of 8th moon of
29th year of Kuang-hsu) and the petition was received by the Wai Wu Pu on 28
November 1903 (10th day of 10th moon of 29th year of Kuang-hsu), about two
months later. Given the fact that the correspondence between London and China
took about six weeks, Chang must have transmitted the petition to the Wai Wu Pu
about two weeks after he had received it. See "Chang Te-i to Wai Wu Pu relating to
the petition of the South African Chinese for Consular protection" in "Tsungli
Yamen Archives", "The Mission of Chang Te-i to England", 29th year of Kuang-
hsu (1903).

[230]Owing to Hsueh Fu-ch'eng's efforts, the British government in 1890 agreed to

that the Wai Wu Pu was deliberating on a British proposal to recruit a large number of Chinese coolies for the Transvaal mines.[231] To kill two birds with one stone, the Wai Wu Pu probably wanted to consider the protection of the free Chinese in South Africa in conjunction with the protection of the Chinese coolies.

The Coming of Chinese Coolies and the Establishment of the Chinese Consulate-General in South Africa

The idea of recruiting Chinese coolies for the Transvaal mines grew out of the practical needs of the colony. The Boer War and its impact created a bleak situation in the Transvaal gold mining industry: it faced rising costs (both wages and other working costs), falling output, and declining profits and investment.[232] The mining capitalists looked to Chinese coolies for a solution to their problems. Chinese labour was intended to break wage inflation, to increase output and restore the level of profitability.[233] Upon the recommendation of the Transvaal Labour Commission, a Draft Ordinance was prepared in November 1903 to regulate the importation of foreign labour.[234] It was passed by the Transvaal Legislative

---

allow China to appoint consuls in British dominions reserving the right to refuse in certain cases. Hsueh in December 1890 had communicated the British decision to the Tsungli Yamen. Although South Africa was a part of the British empire, the Wai Wu Pu and the Chinese Minister in London appeared to be unsure of China's right to appoint a consul without British prior approval. See *FO* 17/1104 (1890), p. 77; Hsueh Fu-ch'eng, "Despatch to the Tsungli Yamen and the Commissioner of Northern Ports relating to the British Approval of the establishment of additional consulates dated 1st day of 11th moon of 16th year of Kuang-hsu (12 December 1890)", in Hsueh Fu-ch'eng, Ch'u-shih kung-tu, vol. 1, tz'u wen, pp. 11a–12a; "Chang Ta-jen to the Marquess of Lansdowne, dated 11 February 1904", "Introduction of Chinese Labour into the Transvaal", in *British Parliamentary Papers· Accounts and Papers*, 1904, no. 62, Cd. 1945, p. 3.

[231]See "Prince Ch'ing to Sir E. Satow dated 23 October 1903", "Correspondence Respecting the Introduction of Chinese Labour into the Transvaal", in *British Parliamentary Papers: Accounts and Papers*, 1904, no. 62, Cd. 1945, p. 1.

[232]See Peter Richardson, "The Provision of Chinese Indentured Labour for the Transvaal Gold Mines, 1903–1908" (unpublished Ph.D. thesis, University of London, 1978), chapter 1, pp. 17–29.

[233]See Peter Richardson, "The Recruiting of Chinese Indentured Labour for the South African Gold-Mines, 1903–1908", *Journal of African History*, vol. 18, pt. 1 (1977), pp. 85–108, particularly p. 88.

[234]See "Introduction of Chinese Labour into the Transvaal", in *Foreign Office Confidential Prints*, no. 8583, pp. 1–2.

Council on 30 December 1903, and later sanctioned by the Imperial government in London.[235]

Before the official sanction of the Ordinance, the British government began to sound out the proposal to recruit Chinese coolies from the Chinese Minister in London, Chang Te-i.[236] Chang had transmitted the proposal to the Wai Wu Pu which appeared to be enthusiastic about the proposed scheme. The Wai Wu Pu was interested partly because it offered a good prospect for Chinese coolies, especially since coolies were not welcome in Australia, the United States and Canada.[237] This proposal would partly compensate for the lost opportunities in those countries and the scheme would also provide a challenge to the Wai Wu Pu because it was a temporary contracted-labour emigration, and the Chinese government had a direct responsibility for the successful recruitment and repatriation of the coolies.

The Wai Wu Pu's initial response to the proposal was favourable; it even took the initiative to contact the British Minister in Peking, Sir E. Satow, to express interest, and suggested a convention to negotiate a treaty on the issue.[238]

---

[235]*Ibid.*, also P.C. Campbell, *Chinese Coolie Emigration to Countries Within the British Empire*, p. 176.

[236]In British official records, Chang Te-i was known as Chang Ta-jen. In fact, "Ta-jen" is the transliteration of the Chinese term, "Your Excellency". But this courtesy title was mistaken for Chang Te-i's official name. This error was frequently found in the *FO* in reference to the Chinese Ministers in London; Kuo Sung-t'ao, the first Chinese Minister, was referred to as "Kuo Ta-jen"; Tseng Chi-tse, another famous Chinese Minister, was referred to as "Tseng Ta-jen".

[237]For the anti-Chinese movements and legislations in Australia and in Canada during the 1880s, see "Chinese Immigration: Anti-Chinese Immigration in the British Colonies", in *British Parliamentary Papers: Accounts and Papers*, 1888, no. 73, c. 5448, pp. 1-87; "The Honourable Commissioner Gray's Report Respecting Chinese Immigration in British Columbia"; and "Report of the Royal Commission on Chinese Immigration", in *Third Session of the Fifth Parliament of the Dominion of Canada: Sessional Papers*, vol. 2 (1885); "An Act Respecting Chinese Immigration", in *The Revised Statutes of Canada 1886* (Ottawa, 1887), vol. 1, pp. 975-79; C.F. Yong, *The New Gold Mountain: The Chinese in Australia 1901-1921*, pp. 12-13; Sing-wu Wang, *The Organization of Chinese Emigration 1848-1888, With Special Reference to Chinese Emigration to Australia*, pp. 292-301; for the anti-Chinese movements in the United States, see Chapter 5 of this book.

[238]See "Prince Ch'ing (the Head of the Wai Wu Pu) to Sir E. Satow dated 23 October 1903", in "Correspondence Respecting the Introduction of Chinese Labour into the Transvaal", in *British Parliamentary Papers: Accounts and Papers*, 1904, no. 62, Cd. 1945, p. 1.

In the meantime, the British government further contacted Chang Te-i and invited his comments on the Draft Ordinance.[239] Chang's response to it was favourable; nevertheless, he expressed the Chinese government's concern for the protection of the coolies, and pointed out that China must have the right to appoint consuls or consular agents to look after its emigrants, and listed five points for their protection during and after recruitment.[240]

As initial contacts were successful, both governments proceeded to a convention. Chang Te-i was the plenipotentiary for China, while the Marquess of Lansdowne, Principal Secretary of State for Foreign Affairs, represented Britain in the negotiations. From 1 March to 15 April 1904, seven meetings were held. These protracted meetings hinged on aspects of the protection of the Chinese coolies before and during their shipment from China. China insisted that only British and Chinese ships be allowed to transport the coolies, fearing that a lack of control might lead to abuses; at the same time, China insisted that the coolies could only be recruited through five Treaty ports, while Britain also wanted to import coolies through her colonies in Hong Kong and the Straits Settlements.[241] What China feared about the British proposal was that it might stimulate the smuggling of coolies from China to these colonies and re-open the wound which had healed twenty years ago when the Macao coolie trade was suppressed.[242]

A compromise was soon reached and an agreement was signed in London on 13 May 1904. The Agreement consisted of fifteen articles covering all aspects of contracting the Chinese coolies. On the protection of the coolies during recruitment and shipment, the Agreement seems to have reflected the main spirit of the "Peking Regulations".[243] It guaranteed that the coolies would not be subjected to any decoying, fraud or fall into the hands of the sinister coolie

---

[239]See "The Marquess of Lansdowne to Chang Ta-jen dated 4 February 1904", ibid., p. 3.

[240]See "Chang Ta-jen to the Marquess of Lansdowne dated 11 February 1904", ibid., pp. 3–4.

[241]The Straits Settlements had for years been recruiting coolies in China for works in the tin mines in the Malay states, without paying any fees to the Chinese government and without any restrictions being imposed in regard to the manner of recruitment. See "Introduction of Chinese Labour into the Transvaal" in Foreign Office Confidential Prints, no. 8583, pp. 4–5.

[242]For the suppression of the Macao coolie trade in 1874, see Chapter 3.

[243]For the details of the "Peking Regulations of 1866", see Chapter 3.

brokers.[244] However, the Agreement added a new dimension to the "Peking Regulations" by providing adequate protection for the coolies during their sojourn overseas. It not only entitled China to appoint consuls or vice-consuls to protect the coolies, but also obliged the British government to appoint a special official or officials to look after the interests of the coolies, and ". . . to ensure that the emigrants have free access to the courts of Justice to obtain redress for injuries to his person and property which is secured to all persons, irrespective of race, by the local law".[245] During the term of the contract, the Agreement also guaranteed that the coolies would not be transferred from one employer to another, and postal facilities were to be provided to enable them to communicate with their families in China.[246] On the expiry of the contract, the coolies were to be repatriated to the ports from which they were recruited.[247]

After the Agreement was signed, the Wai Wu Pu memorialised the Court recommending its approval.[248] On 19 June 1904, the first shipment of Chinese coolies arrived at Port Natal (Durban). Between June 1904 and November 1906, 63,296 coolies were shipped from South and North China to South Africa.[249]

Anti-Asiatic Legislation and the Protection of the Chinese in the Transvaal

The main opposition to the importation of Chinese coolies for the Transvaal mines came from white workers and small businessmen.[250] Fearing the threat of the coolie labour, white workers quickly

---

[244]See *ibid.*, also the Agreement entitled "Convention between the United Kingdom and China respecting the Employment of Chinese Labour in British Colonies and Protectorates, signed at London, 13 May 1904", in *British Parliamentary Papers: Accounts and Papers*, 1904, no. 62, Cd. 1956; the Chinese version of this Agreement is found in *Wai Chiao Pao* (Diplomatic News), vol. 91, wen-tu, pp. 5–8.

[245]See Article 9 of the Agreement, *ibid.*

[246]See Articles 10 and 12 of the Agreement, *ibid.*

[247]See Article 11 of the Agreement, *ibid.*

[248]See "Memorial from Wai Wu Pu to the Court relating to the Agreement on recruiting Chinese coolies for South Africa" in *Wai Chiao Pao*, vol. 91, wen-tu, pp. 4–5.

[249]See Peter Richardson, "The Recruiting of Chinese Indentured Labour for the South African Gold-Mines, 1903–1908" in *Journal of African History*, vol. 18, pt. 1 (1977), pp. 85–86.

[250]In the Transvaal, apart from white workers and small businessmen, the native Boers also voiced their objection to the proposal to import Chinese coolies. See J.A. Weeks, "The Controversy over Chinese Labour in the Transvaal" (an unpublished Ph.D. dissertation of the Ohio State University, 1968), pp. 21–24.

voiced their opposition through their unions. In October 1903, the Transvaal Miners Association resolved that "We as a Congress pledge ourselves with the other affiliated bodies in opposing the introduction of Asiatics in this colony until referendum is taken and the population agrees."[251] Some radical workers went a step further in opposing the proposal by organising themselves into a racist organisation known as "The White League" and pledged themselves to fight "all forms of colour and to win the Transvaal for the white men, and the white men alone".[252] The League harassed Asiatic traders and was responsible for driving out some Asiatic shopkeepers in towns along the reef.[253] It also organised mass meetings to express its disquiet and to influence public opinion on the subjects.

In these meetings, racial prejudices against Asiatics were aired. Chinese coolies were described as the "Yellow horror", "a curse" and "evil"; Chinese were considered to be unable to assimilate and were believed likely to congregate into a Chinatown where evil practices like opium-smoking and lawlessness would reign.[254]

Beneath these racial barrages was the fear of the economic impact of the proposed scheme. Coolie labour was generally regarded as a major threat to the well-being of white workers.[255] As white workers and small businessmen had attained high standards of living, they feared they would be unable to compete with the Chinese; the Chinese were industrious and painstaking and were prepared to work longer hours for less wages. This would force many Europeans out of their occupations.[256] Mr. Marriman, a major speaker at one of these mass meetings, warned that if Chinese coolies were admitted, "the next thing is that the Chinaman will break away from that (contract), and he will creep, and his friends will creep into every occupation in this country. He will begin by driving out the white

[251]*Ibid.*, p. 26.
[252]See the extract from *Transvaal Leader*, 2 April 1903, in Enclosure 2 in no. 8, *British Parliamentary Papers: Accounts and Papers*, 1904, no. 61, Cd. 1895, p. 15.
[253]*Ibid.*
[254]See the speeches of Hutchinson and Hoffman, in extracts from "Transvaal Leader", 2 April 1903 and "South African News", 8 December 1903, *ibid.*, pp. 16–19, 172–73.
[255]See the speech of Mr. Quinn, in extract from "Transvaal Leader", 2 April 1903, *ibid.*, p. 19.
[256]See the extract of "South African News", 8 December 1903, *ibid.*, pp. 169–70.

artisan, he will then drive out the small shopkeeper, and he will then put himself on the land".[257]

The workers also feared that the Chinese coolies would be used as a tool by the capitalists to suppress their wage demands and to break up their strikes; some of them even believed the proposed scheme to be a capitalist plot in order to put the power of running the mines solely in the hands of management.[258]

These racial prejudices and the fear of an adverse economic impact were aggravated by disturbances and desertions among the Chinese coolies. Owing to the frustration of language difficulties, misunderstandings, and ill-treatment by white overseers,[259] some coolies rioted or deserted the Transvaal mines. The wandering deserters posed a threat to the security of the white population.[260] These incidents created a bad image for the Chinese and were used by the anti-coolie crusaders to pressurise the government to act against the Asiatics.

Under the growing pressure of white opposition, the Transvaal government in 1906 passed the Asiatic Law Amendment Ordinance No. 29 which amended the Asiatic Law No. 3 of 1885, and revitalised some anti-Asiatic measures. The 1906 Ordinance was basically intended to tighten the control over the movement and economic activities of the Asiatics. The Ordinance consisted of three main points: registration of all Asiatics; registration certificates to be produced on demand; and trading licences not to be granted to Asiatics except upon production of certificates.[261]

The free Chinese in the Transvaal were quick to respond to the Ordinance. On 27 September 1906, they submitted a petition to the Chinese Minister in London, Wang Ta-hsieh, for protection. The petitioners protested against the discriminatory nature of the Or-

---

[257]*Ibid.*

[258]See the speech of Percy Tarbutt, *ibid.*, p. 171.

[259]For details of the ill-treatment of the Chinese coolies and the problems they faced in the Transvaal mines, see the "Report of Mr. Bianchini, a former Compound (Chinese) Manager to the Witwatersrand Gold Mining Company dated 28 October 1905", Enclosure 1 in no. 29 "Sir Somers Vine to Lord Selborne dated 28 October 1905", in *British Parliamentary Papers: Accounts and Papers*, 1906, no. 80, Cd. 2819, pp. 47–55.

[260]See J.A. Weeks, "The Controversy over Chinese Labour in the Transvaal", pp. 84–87, 92–93.

[261]See "The Asiatic Law Amendment Ordinance, No. 29 of 1906", in *British Parliamentary Papers: Accounts and Papers*, 1906, no. 80, Cd. 3251, pp. 4–7.

dinance against Asiatics. The petition centred on their objection to the procedures of registration: Asiatics were required to give thumb impressions; to undress for inspection and to submit to the recording on certificates of special marks on the body.[262] To give the petition special weight, the Chinese in the Transvaal deputed L.M. James, a leading Chinese merchant, to present the petition in person to the Chinese Minister in London.[263]

Acting on the petition, Wang Ta-hsieh quickly took up the issue. On 1 November 1906, he protested to the Foreign Secretary, Sir Edward Grey, and accused the Transvaal government of degrading Chinese subjects by demanding finger impressions; he reminded Sir Edward that British subjects had received favourable treatment in China and requested reciprocal treatment for the Chinese in the Transvaal.[264] Surprisingly Wang only protested against the procedures of registration, and did not demand the dropping of the Registration Law altogether. Perhaps he was acting only on the wishes of the free Chinese who seemed to have been against the manner in which the Transvaal government proposed to register the Chinese. Wang's protest seems not to have borne any immediate result.

In the meantime, the free Chinese in the Transvaal under the leadership of Leung Quinn, became more vocal in resisting registration. Leung, in his capacity as the chairman of the Chinese Association of the Transvaal, petitioned the Chinese Minister again for help. He vehemently attacked the requirement of eighteen finger impressions from Chinese for registration and declared that compliance with it would reduce the Chinese to a level lower than the natives and other coloured people. He indicated to the Minister that the Chinese had decided to defy the Law with full understanding of the consequences of their action.[265]

---

[262]See "Petition of the Chinese Merchants of the Transvaal dated 27 September 1906", in FO 367, no. 16 (1906, Africa — General).

[263]Ibid.

[264]See "Wang Ta-hsieh to Sir Edward Grey dated 1 November 1906" in FO 367/16, Africa, General; Wang Ta-hsieh reiterated his stand again in another communication to the British Foreign Secretary in March, 1907. See "Chinese Minister to Sir E. Grey dated 26 March 1907", "Transvaal: Further Correspondence relating to Legislation Affecting Asiatics in the Transvaal", in British Parliamentary Papers: Accounts and Papers, 1908, no. 73, Cd. 3887, pp. 1–2.

[265]See "Leung Quinn's petition to the Chinese Minister dated 14 October 1907", "Transvaal: Further Correspondence relating to the Legislation Affecting Asiatics in the Transvaal" in British Parliamentary Papers: Accounts and Papers, 1908, no. 73, Cd. 3887.

The reasons for the Chinese objection are obvious. As the Chinese regarded the body as sacred, exposure of the body for inspection was a serious humiliation; finger impressions were reserved for criminals in China and the requirement of eighteen finger impressions was therefore regarded by the Transvaal Chinese as a most humiliating demand. Further, the Chinese were very sensitive about their image in the multi-racial environment of the Transvaal, and feared that the criminal treatment of the Chinese would lower their pride and status in the eyes of the natives and other coloured people.

This daring act of the Transvaal Chinese probably toughened the stand of the Ch'ing government. The new Minister in London, Li Ching-fang appears to have taken a more active part than his predecessor in seeking a solution to the problem. Immediately after his arrival in London, Li sent a protest note to Sir Edward Grey. He pointed out that the requirement of eighteen finger impressions was normally reserved for criminals, and that the imposition of such a demand on the Chinese contradicted British principles of jurisprudence which presumed everyone to be innocent until proven guilty. Li thus urged the British government to suspend that particular section of the Ordinance from operation.[266] Apart from the protest note, Li also called on Sir Edward and criticised the way the Transvaal government was treating the Chinese, and hinted that British ill-treatment of the Transvaal Chinese might provoke strong anti-British feeling in China.[267] On 4 December 1907, Li called at the British Foreign Office again and suggested a compromise formula for solving the problem. He proposed that those who refused to register could return to China by a certain date with compensation from the Transvaal government; and those who did not wish to return were to comply with the new Law.[268]

In the meantime, other Chinese diplomatic channels were used to press for a satisfactory solution to the problem. Prince Ch'ing, the head of the Wai Wu Pu, communicated a strong protest to the British Minister in Peking, Sir J. Jordan. The Prince pointed out that Article 15 of the Labour Convention of 1904 obliged the British government to protect the Transvaal Chinese emigrants, and the imposition of registration on the Chinese there was a

---

[266]See "Li Ching Fang to Sir E. Grey dated 25 November 1907", *ibid.*, pp. 61–62.
[267]See "W. Langley (Under Secretary of Foreign Office) to Sir J. Jordan dated 27 November 1907" in *FO* 367/108 (1908).
[268]See "W. Langley to Sir J. Jordan dated 4 December 1907", *ibid.*

breach of the terms of the Labour Convention.[269] At the same time, the Chinese Consulate-General in South Africa also protested to the Transvaal government on the issue. In a communication with the Governor of the Transvaal, the Acting Consul-General, Liu Ngai, stated the objection of the local Chinese to the procedure of registration, and pointed out that according to Chinese law, only criminals condemned to death or exiled for life were called upon to give finger impressions.[270] Liu Ngai reinforced his stand in another communication to the Governor on 2 December 1907.[271]

Despite China's strong protests, the British government did very little to improve the situation. Both governments seemed headed for a collision. On 14 January 1907, twenty-three Chinese merchants who were involved in resisting registration were arrested by the Transvaal government, and the Chinese community in the Transvaal was in an uproar. A telegram was sent to Li Ching-fang requesting help. On receiving the telegram, Li on 16 January delivered a memorandum to the British Foreign Office and urged the British government to intervene.[272]

At this critical juncture, it appears that the problem of registering Asiatics in the Transvaal could not be resolved solely through diplomatic channels, and the firm attitude of the Asiatics had some direct bearing on the Transvaal government. The Anglo-Indians under the leadership of M.K. Gandhi began agitating for a "passive resistance" movement against the registration.[273] Gandhi together with Leung Quinn formed a united front and started negotiations with the Transvaal government. Under diplomatic pressure and facing the strong resistance of the Asiatics, the Transvaal government gave in and accepted a compromise. Under the compromise

---

[269]See "Prince Ch'ing to Sir J. Jordan dated 30 November 1907" in FO 367/108 (1908).

[270]See "Liu Ngai to the Earl of Selborne dated 20 November 1907", ibid., also in British Parliamentary Papers: Accounts and Papers, 1908, no. 73, Cd. 3887, pp. 78-79.

[271]See "Liu Ngai to the Earl of Selborne dated 2 December 1907" in FO 367/108 (1908); also in British Parliamentary Papers: Accounts and Papers, 1908, no. 73, Cd. 3887, p. 79.

[272]See "The Memorandum of the Chinese minister dated 16 January 1908", in FO 367/108 (1908).

[273]See "The Governor of the Transvaal to the Secretary of State dated 3 February 1908", in British Parliamentary Papers: Accounts and Papers, 1908, no. 73, Cd. 4327, p. 1.

formula, the Chinese and Indians agreed to offer voluntary registration in a body within three months; on its side, the government allowed signatures to be taken from educated, propertied or well-known Asiatics, and finger prints from the rest; no questions to which Asiatics had religious objections were to be pressed.[274]

Although the solution to this anti-Asiatic legislation should not be accredited solely to the efforts of the Chinese diplomats, nevertheless, in the course of negotiations and protests, they had demonstrated a deep concern and determination for the protection of the overseas Chinese in that part of the world.

---

[274]See "Telegrams from the Governor of the Transvaal to the Secretary of State, received on 29 and 30 January 1908" in FO 367/108 (1908).

Conclusion

This study effectively refutes an accepted theory of non-protection of overseas Chinese by the Ch'ing government. The non-protection theory was first spread by the anti-Ch'ing Revolutionaries during the period between 1900 and 1912,[1] and was later perpetuated by certain Republican historians and overseas Chinese who supported the Republic.[2] The theory was used as political propaganda to attack the Ch'ing government and to win the support of overseas Chinese upon whom the Revolutionaries had greatly depended.

The foregoing pages have demonstrated that the Ch'ing government had adopted a positive attitude of protecting overseas Chinese after the suppression of the coolie trade in 1874, as indicated in the protection of the coolies in Cuba and Peru. The realisation of this new attitude contradicted the existing restrictive emigration law against overseas Chinese. It challenged some of the basic assumptions behind the law and helped to lead to the abolition of the law in 1893.

The abolition of the old emigration law brought about a new protection policy towards overseas Chinese in 1893 after which the Ch'ing government and Chinese diplomats became more active in protecting overseas Chinese both at home and abroad. However, despite their efforts, the new policy did not succeed. The failure of the protection policy was the result of interplay between the ineptitude of the Ch'ing government and foreign imperialism. Like many other events, the government's response to the problem of

---

[1] See Chong Shing Yit Pao (the main revolutionary organ in Southeast Asia), 5/9/1907, p. 2; 7/9/1907, p. 2; 23/1/1908, p. 2; see also Yen Ching-hwang, *The Overseas Chinese and the 1911 Revolution: With Special Reference to Singapore and Malaya* (Kuala Lumpur and New York, 1976), pp. 102–103, 200.

[2] See Hua-ch'iao chih p'ien-ch'uan wei-yen-hui (ed.), *Ma-lai-ya hua-ch'iao chih* (A History of the Chinese in Malaya) (Taipei, 1959), p. 90; Ou Ch'ung-hsi (ed.), *Lu Mei san-i tsung-hui-kuan chien-shih* (A Concise History of the Sam Yup Association of San Francisco) (San Francisco, 1975).

overseas Chinese was slow to evolve. It took a few initiatives but failed to sustain them. At a deeper level, as China declined in power, it lacked power to enforce its treaty rights. When China faced this cruel reality in the late nineteenth and early twentieth centuries, Social Darwinism was prevalent; generally the Chinese people were invariably considered an inferior race, not entitled to receive equal treatment. This study has documented that the attitude and policies of the Western imperialist governments were mainly responsible for the failure of the efforts of the Chinese diplomats overseas, in particular Chinese diplomats in Washington.

This study has also established that the Ch'ing overseas Chinese policy had its historical roots in the Ming Dynasty and its cultural roots in Confucianism which refutes the claim by the anti-Ch'ing Revolutionaries that Ch'ing overseas Chinese policy was based mainly on racial considerations. Their theory of Manchu conspiracy against Han Chinese on the overseas Chinese issue is clearly untenable.

Another important fact established by this study is that the overseas Chinese policy constituted a major part of China's foreign policy during the late Ch'ing period. Since the signing of the Peking Treaty in 1860, China was forced to pay more attention to the overseas Chinese issue. After the 1870s the overseas Chinese problem was increasingly intertwined with China's relations with Foreign Powers. Many Chinese diplomats, particularly in the United States, devoted a considerable amount of time to the problems of overseas Chinese, and increasingly the protection of overseas Chinese affected China's diplomatic relations with Foreign Powers. The anti-American movement in 1905 is the best illustration of how the overseas Chinese issue sparked off a major crisis in Sino-American relations.

Glossary

Ah Quee（阿贵）
Amoy（厦门）
An-hsi（安溪）
Annam（安南）

Cantonese（广州人）
Champa（占婆）
Chan Ch'eng（占城）
Chang Chao（张熙）
Chang Chen-hsun（张振勋）
Chang Chih-tung（张之洞）
Chang-ching（章京）
Chang Hsi-yu（张熙宇）
Chang Hsieh（张燮）
Chang Kuo-tung（章国栋）
Chang Lin-an（张林安）
Chang Pi-shih（张弼士）
Chang Shih-ch'eng（张士诚）
Chang Ta-jen（张大人）
Chang Teh-i（张德彝）
Chang Ting-chia（张定加）
Chang Wei-hua（张维华）
Chang Wen-hsiang Kung Ch'uan-chi
　（张文襄公全集）
Chang Yin-huan（张荫桓）
Chang Ying-sheng（张应声）
Changchou（漳州）
Chao-an（诏安）
Chao Ju-kua（赵汝适）
Chao-ying（昭应）
Ch'en A-shun（陈阿顺）
Ch'en A-ssu（陈阿四）
Chen Chiang (Chinkiang)（镇江）
Ch'en Ch'in-ho（陈荆和）
Ch'en Ch'ing-chen (Tan King Chin)
　（陈庆真）
Ch'en Ch'ing-hsi（陈庆喜）
Ch'en Ch'ing-hsing (Tan King Sing)
　（陈庆星）

Ch'en Hsu-nien（陈旭年）
Ch'en Hung-hsun（陈鸿勋）
Ch'en I-k'an（陈仪侃）
Chen-la Feng-t'u Chi（真腊风土记）
Ch'en Lan-pin（陈兰彬）
Ch'en Shih-lin（陈仕林）
Ch'en Shu-t'ang（陈树棠）
Ch'en Ta-chao（陈大照）
Ch'en Tao-te（陈道德）
Ch'en Tsu-i（陈祖义）
Chen-tung（震东）
Ch'en Tzu-jen（陈子仁）
Ch'en Wen-shih（陈文石）
Ch'en Wen-yu（陈文佑）
Cheng Ah-erh（郑阿二）
Cheng A-mou（郑阿茂）
Cheng Ch'eng-kung（郑成功）
Cheng Ching-kuei（郑景贵）
Cheng Ho（郑和）
Cheng Keng Kwee（郑景贵）
Cheng Tsao-ju（郑藻如）
Chi-ming Tsung-ping（记名总兵）
Ch'i-ling（耆龄）
Ch'i-ying（耆英）
Chia-ching（嘉靖）
Chia-ch'ing（嘉庆）
Chia-pi-tan（甲必丹）
Chia-shun（家训）
Chia-ying（嘉应）
Chia-ying Prefecture（嘉应州）
Chiang A-lin（姜阿麟）
Chiang I-li（蒋益澧）
Chiang Yu-t'ien（蒋攸铦）
Ch'iao-kung（侨工）
Ch'iao Sung-nien（乔松年）
Ch'ien（钱）
Ch'ien Hsun（钱恂）
Ch'ien Lung（乾隆）
Chien-sheng（监生）

350

Chih Kang (志刚)
Chih li (直隶)
Chin (金)
Chinese Consolidated Benevolent
  Association of Victoria
  (域多利中华会馆)
Ch'ing-chi wai-chiao shih-liao
  (清季外交史料)
Ch'ing-i (清议)
Ch'ing Ming Festival (清明节)
Ching-pao (京报)
Ch'ing-yuan (厌元)
Chinkiang (Chen Chiang) (镇江)
Ch'iu Feng-chia (邱逢甲)
Chou Jui-hua (周瑞华)
Ch'ou-pan I-wu Shih-mo
  (筹办夷务始末)
Chou-t'ung (州同)
Chou Ta-kuan (周达观)
Chou Wen-i (周文裔)
Chou Wen-teh (周文德)
Chu-chai (猪仔)
Chu Fan Chih (诸蕃志)
Chu Fan Chih Chiao-chu
  (诸蕃志校注)
Chu-jen (举人)
Chu Jen-Ch'ung (朱仁聪)
Chu K'e P'ien (逐客篇)
Chu Shih-chia (朱士嘉)
Ch'u-shih Ying Fa I Pi ssu-kuo
  jih-chih
  (出使英法意比四国日记)
Chu Shou-p'eng (朱寿朋)
Chu Yuan-chang (朱元璋)
Ch'uanchou (泉州)
Ch'ung-fu (崇福)
Chung Hua Chinese School
  (中华学校)
Ch'ung Shan (崇善)
Chung-shu K'o Chung-shu
  (中书科中书)
Cohong (公行)
Coolie (苦力，估俚)

Deli (日里)

Erh-shih Ssu-hsiao (二十四孝)
Expectant Brigadier (记名总兵)
Expectant Prefect (后补知府)

Fan Chin-p'eng (范锦朋)
Fan Ssu (藩司)
Fan Ssu-ho (范四和)
Fang Kuo-chen (方国珍)
Fatchoy (发财)
Fei Hsin (费信)
Feng Ch'eng-chun (冯承钧)
Fu-kuei (富贵)
Fu Li-shih Kuan (副理事官)
Fu-shih Wen-to' (佛士文陀)
Fu Lieh Pi (Frederick A. Bee)
  (傅列祕)
Fukienese (福建人)

Goh Siew-tin (吴寿珍)
Governor-General of Liang Kiang
  (两江总督)

Hai-ch'eng District (海澄县)
Hai-chun Yamen (海军衙门)
Hainanese (海南人)
Hakka (客家)
Han-chien (汉奸)
Hanlin-yuan Tien-pu (翰林院典簿)
Hangchow (杭州)
Ho Ah-pa (何阿八)
Ho Ah-su (何亚苏)
Ho Ju-chang (何如璋)
Ho Kuei-ch'ing (何桂清)
Ho Ping-ti (何炳棣)
Ho Yen-sheng (何彦升)
Hoo Ah Kay (胡亚基)
Hopei (河北)
Hou-pu Hsien-ch'eng (后补县丞)
Hsia-men Shang-wu Tsung-hui
  (厦门商务总会)
Hsiang Shan (香山)
Hsiang-yueh (乡约)
Hsin-chia-po Feng-t'u Chi
  (新加坡风土记)
Hsin-t'un (新邨)
Hsing-cha Sheng-lan Chiao-chu
  (星槎胜览校注)
Hsiao (孝)
Hsiao-chen Hsien Huang-hou
  (孝贞显皇后)
Hsiao-ch'uan Ch'eng Huang-hou
  (孝全成皇后)
Hsiao-fang-hu Chai Yu-ti

Ts'ung-ch'ao Pu-p'ien
（小方壶斋舆地丛钞补编）
Hsiao-i Hsun Huang-hou
（孝仪纯皇后）
Hsiao-k'ang Chang Huang-hou
（孝康章皇后）
Hsiao-kung Jen Huang-hou
（孝恭仁皇后）
Hsiao Ming-chu（肖明举）
Hsiao-sheng Hsien Huang-hou
（孝圣宪皇后）
Hsiao-shu Jui Huang-hou
（孝淑睿皇后）
Hsiao Tao Hui（小刀会）
Hsien-feng（咸丰）
Hsin-ning District（新宁县）
Hsin-she Hsueh-pao（新社学报）
Hsing Ch'uan Yung Circuit
（兴泉永道）
Hsieh Ah-ssu（谢阿四）
Hsieh Shuang-chiu（谢双就）
Hsieh Wen-pin（谢文彬）
Hsu Ching-ch'eng（许景澄）
Hsu Hsueh-chu（徐学聚）
Hsu Kuang-chin（徐广缙）
Hsu Shau Pang（徐寿朋）
Hsu Ying-kuei（许应骙）
Hsu Yun-tsiao（许云樵）
Hsuan-t'ung（宣统）
Hsueh Ah-sheng（薛阿盛）
Hsueh Fu-ch'eng（薛福成）
Hsueh-pu Kuan-pao（学部官报）
Hu Hsuan-tse（胡璇泽）
Hu Ju（胡如）
Hua-ch'iao（华侨）
Hua-ch'iao Shen-shang（华侨绅商）
Hua-jen（华人）
Hua-min（华民）
Hua Shang（华商）
Huang Chin-hsing（黄锦兴）
Huang Chou（黄舟）
Huang Feng-ch'ih（黄凤池）
Huang Hsi-ch'uan（黄锡铨）
Huang Hsing（黄兴）
Huang Kung-tu（黄公度）
Huang Tsun-hsien（黄遵宪）
Huang Tzu-shun（黄子顺）
Hui-kuan（会馆）
Hung League（洪门）

Hung-wu（洪武）

Ipoh（怡保）
I Hsiao Chih T'ien-hsia
（以孝治天下）
I-k'uang（奕劻）
Ili（伊犁）
I Shan（　）
I Ti-chih Chin-li Ch'ih
（拟抵制禁例策）

Jelabu（日叻务）
Jih-pen Kuo-chih（日本国志）
Jit Shin Pau（日新报）
Jui-lin（瑞麟）
Jurchen（女真）

K'aip'ing（开平）
Kan-p'u（澉浦）
K'ang-hsi（康熙）
K'ang Yu-wei（康有为）
Kao-chou（高州）
Ke-lo-pa（噶罗巴）
Kheh = Hakka（客家）
Kheh-taus（客头）
Koolungsoo（鼓浪屿）
Koxinga (Cheng Ch'eng-kung)（国姓爷）
Kuala Lumpur（吉隆坡）
K'uang Ch'i-chao（邝其照）
Kuang-chou Prefecture（广州府）
Kuang-hsu（光绪）
Kuang-hsu-ch'ao Tung-hua lu
（光绪朝东华录）
Kuang-hsu Fan-li, Chieh-lien Chung-
chih（广树藩篱，结联众志）
Ku'ang Kuo-hsiang（邝国祥）
Kueichow（贵州）
Kung-chi（公据）
Kung-chien（公券）
Kung-cheng Shen-shang（公正绅商）
Kung-p'in（公凭）
Kung-po'（贡舶）
Kung-yen（公验）
Kuo Sung-t'ao（郭嵩焘）
Kuo Ta-jen（郭大人）
Kwangsi Hou-pu Chih-fu
（广西后补知府）

Lao Ch'ung-kuang（劳崇光）

Lat Pau（叻报）
Lei-chen-lan（雷珍兰）
Lei-chow（雷州）
Li Chao-ch'un（李肇春）
Li Ching-fang（李经芳）
Li Ch'ung（李充）
Li Chung-chieh（李钟钰）
Li Fang（犁房）
Li Huai-yen（李怀远）
Li Hung-chang（李鸿章）
Li Hung-ch'ao（李鸿藻）
Li Mien（李勉）
Li-shih Kuan（理事官）
Liang A-sheng（梁阿盛）
Liang Ch'eng（梁诚）
Lien-chou（廉州）
Lin A-pang（林阿榜）
Lin An (Modern Hangchow)（临安）
Lin Feng（林凤）
Lin Sheng（林省）
Lin Tao-chi'en（林道乾）
Lin Tse-hsu（林则徐）
Lin Yai（林奎）
Lin Yun-lung（林云龙）
Ling-hui Fu-jen（灵惠夫人）
Lingpo（宁波）
Liu A-jui（刘阿瑞）
Liu A-lin（刘阿林）
Liu Chin-ch'ao（刘锦藻）
Liu Ch'iu（琉球）
Liu Hsi-hung（刘锡鸿）
Liu Hsiang（刘相）
Liu Liang-yuan（刘亮沅）
Liu Lien-k'o（刘联珂）
Liu Yu（六谕）
Lo Ch'eng-chu（骆腾衢）
Lo Erh-kang（罗尔纲）
Lo K'ang（骆康）
Lu A-chen（吕阿珍）
Lu Ah-ching（卢亚景）
Lu Hai-huan（吕海寰）
Lung-ch'i District（龙溪县）
Lung-ch'ing（隆庆）

Ma Huan（马欢）
Ma Lao-liu（马老六）
Ma-liu-chia Ying-ho Hui-kuan
　（马六甲应和会馆）
Ma Tsu（妈祖）

Ma-yao（玛腰）
Mai-pan（买办）
Mao Hsu（毛旭）
Mao Hung-pin（毛鸿宾）
Mei-chiang（梅江）
Mei-chiang Wu-shu Hui-kuan
　（梅江五属会馆）
Mei District（梅县）
Meng liang Lu（梦粱录）
Ming Shih（明史）
Mou（庙）
Mu-fu（幕府）

Nam Sang（南生）
Nan-an（南安）
Nan-hai District（南海县）
Nan Sheng（南生）
Nanning（南宁）
Nanyang（南洋）
Negri Sembilan（森美兰）
New Gold Mountain（新金山）

Ou-yang Keng（欧阳庚）
Ou-yang Ming（欧阳明）

Padang（巴东）
P'an To-li（潘多利）
P'an-yu District（番禺县）
Pao-chia（保甲）
Pao Ch'uan（宝船）
Pao-shang-chi（保商局）
Pao Tsun-p'eng（包遵彭）
Pao Yun（宝鋆）
Penang（槟榔屿，槟城）
P'eng-hu Islands（澎湖群岛）
Perak（吡叻）
Pin Ch'un（斌椿）
Po-kuei（柏贵）
Prince Ch'ing（庆亲王）
Prince Kung（恭亲王）

Rock Springs（洛士丙冷）

San-fu-ch'i (Srivijaya)（三佛齐）
San Ho Hui（三合会）
San-yuan-li（三元里）
Seven Difficulties（七难）
Shang-pu（商部）
Shang-tung（商董）

Shang-wu-chi (商务局)
Shang-wu Kuan-pao (商务官报)
Shanghai (上海)
Shen Ching-chih (沈敬之)
Sheng-kuan Fa-ts'ai (升官发财)
Sheng Hsuan-huai (盛宣怀)
Sheng-yu (圣谕)
Sheng-yu Kuang-hsun (圣谕广训)
Shih (石)
Shih Mei Chi-lueh (使美纪略)
Shih-k'uai (市侩)
Shih-p'o-ssu (市舶司)
Shih Yu-sheng (石玉胜)
Shou-kao (首告)
Shu W'en-hsien T'ung-k'ao
　(续文献通考)
Shun-chih (顺治)
Shun Te (顺德)
Siah U Chin (余有进)
Sing Po (星报)
Six Unjust Items (六不近情理)
Southern Sung (南宋)
Su Jui-chao (苏锐钊)
Su Wang (苏旺)
Sun Chung (孙忠)
Sun Chung Kwock Bo (新中国报)
Sung Dynasty (宋朝)
Sung Su-ch'ing (宋素卿)

Ta-jen (大人)
Ta P'u District. (大埔县)
Taiping (太平)
T'an Ch'ien-ts'u (谭乾初)
Tan Kim Ching (陈金钟)
Tan King Chin (Ch'en Ch'ing-chen)
　(陈庆真)
Tan King Sing (Ch'en Ch'ing-hsing)
　(陈庆星)
T'an Sheng (谭升)
T'an Ti-fa (谭第发)
T'an Tzu-chun (谭子俊)
T'ang Chien (唐建)
Tao-i chih-lueh (岛夷志略)
Tao-kuang (道光)
T'ao-min (逃民)
Taotai (道台)
Tao-yuan (道员)
Telok Anson (安顺)
Ten Bitternesses (十苦)

Teng Ah-fu (邓亚福)
Teochew (潮州人)
Thian Ti Hwui (天地会)
T'ien H'ou (天后)
T'ien H'ou Sheng Mu (天后圣母)
T'ien-hui (天妃)
Ting Jih-ch'ang (丁日昌)
Ting Ju-ch'ang (丁汝昌)
Tiong Hoa Hwe Koan (中华会馆)
Tsai Kwoh Ching (蔡国京)
Tseng Chi-tse (曾纪泽)
Tseng Kuo-fan (曾国藩)
Tseng Shou-hsien (曾寿贤)
Tseng Ta-jen (曾大人)
Tsin Chin Shan (New Gold Mountain)
　(新金山)
Ts'in Ch'un-hsuan (岑春萱)
Tso Ping Lung (左秉隆)
Tso Tsung-t'ang (左宗棠)
Tsui-huan (罪犯)
Tsui Kuo-yin (崔国因)
Tsung Li-shih Kuan (总理事官)
Tsungli Yamen (总理衙门)
T'u Che-min (涂泽民)
Tu-pan (杜板)
Tu Ssu (都司)
T'uan-she (团社)
Tung Chiao-tseng (董教增)
T'ung-chih (同知)
T'ung-chih (同治)
T'ung-chih Reign (同治朝)
Tung Kuan (东筦)
T'ung-shih (通事)
T'ung Wen Kuan (同文馆)
Tz'u-hsi (慈禧)

Wai Wu Pu (外务部)
Wang A chi (工阿纪)
Wang Gungwu (王赓武)
Wang Hsiao-ch'ang (王晓沧)
Wang Kuo-jui (王国瑞)
Wang Sing-wu (王省吾)
Wang Ta-hsieh (汪大燮)
Wang Ta-yen (汪大渊)
Wang Yung Ho (王荣和)
Wen Ya-lung (文亚隆)
Whampoa (黄埔)
White Lotus (白莲)
Wo-k'ou (倭寇)

Wong Lin Ken（黄麟根）
Wu A-fa（吴阿发）
Wu-hsi（无锡）
Wu Hua-yueh（吴华岳）
Wu-sheng（武生）
Wu Shou-chen (see Goh Siew-tin)
　（吴寿珍）
Wu Shu-ta（吴淑达）
Wu T'ing-fang（伍廷芳）

Yamen（衙门）
Yang Chin（杨锦）
Yang Ju（杨儒）
Yang Jung-hsu（杨荣绪）
Yang Shih-ch'i（杨士琦）
Yang Wei-pin（杨蔚彬）
Yang-wu（洋务）
Yeh Ch'ing-chi（叶庆济）
Yeh Fu-chun（叶福君）
Yeh Ming-ch'en（叶名琛）

Yeh T'i-yen（叶题雁）
Yeh Yu（叶由）
Yen Chih-t'ui（颜之推）
Yen Ching-hwang（颜清湟）
Yen-shih Chia-shun（颜氏家训）
Yin-p'iao（引票）
Ying-ho Hui-kuan（应和会馆）
Ying-yai Sheng-lan Chiao-chu
　（瀛涯胜览校注）
Ying-yao Jih-chi（英轺日记）
Yu-chi Hui-ts'un（谕谘汇存）
Yu Chun（余瑃）
Yuan Dynasty（元朝）
Yuan Ying-chi（袁英骐）
Yun-kuei（云贵）
Yunnan（云南）
Yung An City（永安城）
Yung-cheng（雍正）
Yung Hung (Yung Wing)（容闳）
Yung-lo（永乐）
Yung Wing（容闳）

Bibliographical Note

This book is based primarily on the publications and archives of the Ch'ing, British and American governments, and is supplemented by overseas Chinese community records, private records, newspapers and books. Among the Ch'ing official materials, *Ch'ou-pan i-wu shih-mo* (The Complete Account of the Management of Barbarian Affairs for Tao-kuang, Hsien-feng and T'ung-chih Reigns); *Ch'ing-chi wai-chiao shih-liao* (Historical Materials on Foreign Relations in the Late Ch'ing Period); Tsungli Yamen Archives (Archives of the Office for General Management); and the Wai Wu Pu Archives (Archives of the Ministry of Foreign Affairs) are most important.

They consist of tens of thousands of memorials and correspondence of the Ch'ing high-ranking officials and top diplomats, and the edicts of the Court over a wide range of issues connected with China's foreign relations from 1838 to 1912. The information on overseas Chinese are generally fragmentary, and are to be extracted from these massive records. Of secondary importance are *Kuang-hsu ch'ao tung-hua lu* (The Tung-hua Records of the Kuang-hsu Reign); *Ch'ing-ch'ao shu wen-hsien t'ung-k'ao* (Supplementary Encyclopedia of the Ch'ing Dynasty); *Shang-wu kuan-pao* (The Gazette of Commercial Affairs, 1906-1910); *Hsueh-pu kuan-pao* (The Gazette of the Ministry of Education, 1906-1910); and *Shih-erh ch'ao tung-hua lu* (The Tung-hua Records of the Twelve Reigns of the Ch'ing Dynasty). The information on overseas Chinese contained in these records is brief, but invariably expresses the attitude and stand of the Ch'ing government on the issue. It must be pointed out here that *Ch'ing-ch'ao Shu wen-hsien t'ung-k'ao* (compiled by Liu Chin-ch'ao) should be used with care. Some of the dates of the establishment of consulates in overseas Chinese communities in the section on "Wai-chiao" (Foreign Relations) are inaccurate.

Of lesser importance among Ch'ing official documents are *Cheng-chih kuan-pao* (Ch'ing Government Gazettes); *Ta-ch'ing li-ch'ao shih-lu* (Veritable Records of Successive Reigns of the Great Ch'ing Empire); *Ta-ch'ing kuang-hsu hsin fa-ling* (New Statutes of the Great Ch'ing Empire during the Kuang-hsu Reign); *Ch'ing-ch'ao wen-hsien t'ung-k'ao* (Encyclopedia of the Ch'ing Dynasty); *Ch'in-ting Ta-ch'ing hui-tien shih-li* (Cases and Precedents of the Collected Statutes of the Great Ch'ing Empire); *Ch'ing kuang-hsu ch'ao chung-jih chiao-she shih-liao* (Historical

356

Materials on Sino-Japanese Relations during the Kuang-hsu Reign); and *Yu-chi hui-ts'un* (The Collected Records of Memorials). Bits and pieces of information from these documents help to fill the gaps left by other Ch'ing official records.

One item of the Ch'ing official documents deserving special attention is *Chinese Emigration: Report of the Commission Sent by China to Ascertain the Condition of Chinese Coolies in Cuba, 1874*. This is not the original Chinese version circulated by the Tsungli Yamen among top Chinese officials, but the English and French versions printed by the Imperial Maritime Customs Press, Shanghai, in 1876, for foreign consumption, and was reprinted by Ch'eng-wen Publishing Co., Taipei in 1970. However, the report is reliable as far as the evidence is concerned. It contains many quotations from depositions and petitions of the coolies in Cuba. Evidence provided in the report are fully used in Chapter 3.

Among British official materials, the reports prepared by British diplomats and the Governor of Hong Kong contained in the *British Parliamentary Papers* are useful for the study of the coolie trade from 1852 to 1874. Of greater significance are the British Foreign Office Records (FO 17) which contain correspondence between the Chinese Minister in London and the British Foreign Secretary covering the period between 1877 to 1906. This correspondence appeared in both Chinese and English, and contain a great deal of information relating to the protection of the overseas Chinese in British colonies and protectorates. British Foreign Office Records also contain correspondence between the Secretaries of the Foreign and Colonial Offices which provide insight into the British decision making over some issues connected with overseas Chinese. The information contained in the British Foreign Office Confidential Prints is also extremely useful. The reports were prepared for internal consumption of high-ranking officials in the Foreign Office, and they provide insight into British decision making.

Among American official materials, the most useful records are the correspondence between the Chinese Ministers in Washington and the Secretary of the State from 1879 to 1906. This correspondence contains thousands of cases dealing with the protection of the Chinese in the United States. They form the backbone of the two chapters dealing with the protection of the American Chinese. Some of this diplomatic correspondence was reproduced for reference during sessions of Congress and Senate and may be found in the *House Documents* of various Congress sessions. They are entitled *Papers relating to the Foreign Relations of the United States, House Documents*. At the same time, important diplomatic correspondence between the Secretary of State and American chief diplomats overseas were collected and printed by the State Department annually. They are entitled *Papers relating to the Foreign Relations of the United States*. An important section is on China containing correspondence between the American Minister at Peking and the Secretary of the State.

No less important are the records of the Bureau of Immigration. Among the Bureau's records, the Chinese Segregated Records, 3358d file, are most important. This collection contains thousands of unbound documents, correspondence, and pamphlets relating to Chinese immigration, and is kept in six large boxes deposited in the National Archives in Washington D.C. The correspondence among immigration officials and the reports of the special agents of the Bureau discloses the policy and the methods of implementation in dealing with Chinese immigrants. The collection generally reflects the Bureau's stance for total Chinese exclusion.

Official documents and archival materials form the research core of this book, but they have left many gaps which are filled by overseas Chinese community records, private records and newspaper materials. Among the Chinese community records, "The minutes of the Singapore Chinese Chamber of Commerce", the archives of the Chinese Consolidated Benevolent Association of Victoria, Canada, and records of the Sam Yap Association of San Francisco are important. The Singapore Chinese Chamber of Commerce was founded in 1906, and was the leading organisation in the Chinese communities in Singapore and Malaya, and it also enjoyed a semi-official status in relation to the Ch'ing government. Its minutes (in manuscript) have kept detailed records of its activities, including an important section on its relations with China. The Chinese Consolidated Benevolent Association of Victoria was the leading organisation in the Chinese communities in Canada. It established a close link with the Ch'ing government. Its archives, now kept in the Library of the University of Victoria, Victoria, British Columbia, have preserved some important correspondence between the Association and the Chinese embassy in London as well as the Chinese diplomats in the United States. The Sam Yap Association was a powerful regional association among the Chinese in United States; its records have been well preserved and printed in the form of a souvenir magazine entitled *Lu Mei san-i tsung-hua-kuan chien-shih* (A Concise History of the Sam Yap Association of San Franscisco). The records have revealed the attitude of the local Chinese towards Exclusion and the relations between San Francisco Chinese and China.

Among private records, the diaries of certain Chinese diplomats and their writings are important. Kuo Sung-t'ao's *Shih-hsi chi-ch'eng* (The Record of an Envoy's Journey to the West); Hsueh Fu-ch'eng's *Ch'u-shih Ying, Fa, I, Pi ssu-kuo jih-chi* (Diary of My Mission to England, France, Italy and Belgium); Ch'en Lan-pin's *Shih Mei chi-lueh* (Brief Records of My Mission to the United States of America); Tsui Kuo-yin's *Ch'u-shih Mei, Jih, Pi kuo jih-chi* (Diary of My Mission to the United States, Spain and Peru); Chang Yin-huan's *San-chou jih-chi* (Diary of My Missions to the Three Continents); and Ch'ien Hsun's *Erh-erh wu-wu shu* are most useful. These diaries not only recorded important events of their missions, but also provided documents and historical backgrounds to those events. Along with diplomatic diaries are writings of the diplomats. Hsueh Fu-ch'eng's *Ch'u-shih kung-tu, tsou-shu* (Correspondence of My Diplomatic Mission and My Memorials to the Court); Yung Wing's *My Life in China and America* (in English); and Wu T'ing-fang's *America: Through the Spectacles of an Oriental Diplomat* (in English) give further details of some important events relating to the overseas Chinese issue. Apart from the diaries and writings of the diplomats, collections of the works of certain high-ranking Ch'ing officials are also useful. Chang Chih-tung's *Chang Wen-hsiang kung ch'uan-chi* (Complete Works of Chang Chih-tung); Li Hung-chang's *Li Wen-chung kung ch'uan-chi* (Complete Works of Li Hung-chang); and Liu K'un-i's *Liu K'un-i i-chi* (Works of Liu K'un-i, posthumously Collected) provide some insights into the decision making in Chinese high official circle over the issue of overseas Chinese.

There are three types of newspaper materials: those published in the Treaty ports, those published by the Chinese in Southeast Asia, and those published by the Chinese in the United States. Among Treaty port newspapers, *Shen Pao*, *Wai Chiao Pao* and *North China Herald* are important. They occasionally published news about coolie trade and overseas Chinese. Among the Southeast Asian Chinese newspapers, the *Lat Pau*, *Sing Po* and *Jit Shin Pao*, all published in Singapore, provide useful information on overseas Chinese matters. They gave good comments on China's change of the traditional emigration policy in 1893. Among the American Chinese newspapers, San Francisco's *Chung Sai Yat Po* (Chinese Daily Paper) and Honolulu's *Sun Chung Kwock Bo* (New China Daily News) are most important. Both papers provide a great deal of information about Chinese activities in the United States in the late nineteenth and early twentieth centuries. In addition, Reformist newspapers such as *Hsin-min ts'ung-pao*, *Ch'ing I Pao* and *Shih Wu Pao* contain some useful articles on overseas Chinese which reflect the view of the Reformists over the issue of overseas Chinese.

Bibliography

CH'ING OFFICIAL PUBLICATIONS AND ARCHIVAL MATERIALS

Che-chiang t'ung-chih (Gazetteer of the Province of Chekiang), (reprint, 1899 n.p.).

Cheng-chih kuan-pao (Ch'ing Government Gazettes), 47 vols., (Taipei, 1965).

Ch'in-ting Ta-ch'ing hui-tien shih-li (Cases and Precedents of the Collected Statutes of the Great Ch'ing Empire), 24 vols., (reprint, Taipei, 1963).

Chinese Emigration: Report of the Commission Sent by China to Ascertain the Condition of Chinese Coolies in Cuba 1874, (reprint, Taipei, 1970).

Ch'ing-ch'ao shu wen-hsien t'ung-k'ao (Supplementary Encyclopedia of the Ch'ing Dynasty), (compiled by Liu Chin-ch'ao) 400 chuan, 4 vols., (reprint, Shanghai, n.d.).

Ch'ing-ch'ao t'ung-chih (Comprehensive History of Ch'ing Institutions), (Taipei, 1963).

Ch'ing-ch'ao wen-hsien t'ung-k'ao (Encyclopedia of the Ch'ing Dynasty), (Taipei, 1963).

Ch'ing-chi ke-kuo chao-hui mo-lu (Index of Diplomatic Notes between China and Foreign Powers during the Ch'ing Dynasty), 4 vols., (Peking, 1936).

Ch'ing-chi wai-chiao shih-liao: Kuang-hsu ch'ao (Historical Materials on Foreign Relations in the Late Ch'ing Period for the Kuang-hsu Reign) 218 chuan, 6 vols., (reprint, Taipei, 1964).

Ch'ing-chi wai-chiao shih-liao: Hsuan-t'ung ch'ao (Historical Materials on Foreign Relations in the Late Ch'ing Period for the Hsuan-t'ung Reign) 24 chuan, 1 vol., (reprint, Taipei, 1964).

Ch'ing Kuang-hsu ch'ao chung-jih chiao-she shih-liao (Historical Materials on Sino-Japanese Relations during the Kuang-hsu Reign), (Taipei, n.d.).

Ch'ing-mo tui-wai chiao-she t'iao-yueh chi (Collection of Treaties with Foreign Countries during the Late Ch'ing Period), (Taipei, 1963).

Ch'ing Shih (A History of Ch'ing Dynasty), 8 vols., (Taipei, 1961).

Ch'ing-shih kao (A Draft History of the Ch'ing Dynasty), 2 vols., (Shanghai, 1942).

Ch'ing-ts'u chi chung-ch'i tui wai chiao-she t'iao-yueh chi: K'ang Yung Chien Tao Hsien wu-ch'ao t'iao-yueh (Collection of Treaties with Foreign Countries during the Early and Mid-Ch'ing Periods with Special Reference to the Reigns of K'ang-hsi, Yung-cheng, Chien-lung, Tao-kuang and Hsien-feng), (Taipei, 1964).

Ch'ou-pan i-wu shih-mo: Tao-kuang ch'ao (The Complete Account of the Management of Barbarian Affairs for Tao-kuang Reign) 80 chuan, 2 vols., (reprint, Taipei, 1972).

Ch'ou-pan i-wu shih-mo: Hsien-feng ch'ao (The Complete Account of the Management of Barbarian Affairs for Hsien-feng Reign) 80 chuan, 2 vols., (reprint, Taipei, 1972).

Ch'ou-pan i-wu shih-mo: T'ung-chih ch'ao (The Complete Account of the Management of Barbarian Affairs for T'ung-chih Reign) 100 chuan, 3 vols., (reprint, Taipei, 1972).
Chung-wai t'iao-yueh hui-p'ien (Collection of Treaties Signed between China and Foreign Countries), (Taipei, 1964).
Hsin T'ang Shu (New T'ang History) 225 chuan, 3 vols., (reprint, Taipei, 1956).
Hsueh-pu kuan-pao (The Gazette of the Ministry of Education) 1906–1910, (Peking, original, 1906–1910).
Huang-ch'ao (Ch'ing) ching-shih-wen hsu-p'icn (Supplementary Collection of Distinguished Political Essays of the Ch'ing Dynasty), (Shanghai, 1888).
Huang-ch'ao (Ch'ing) ching-shih wen t'ung-p'ien (Collection of Distinguished Political Essays of the Ch'ing Dynasty), (Shanghai, 1901).
Ku-kung wen-hsien (Ch'ing Documents at the Palace Museum), vol. 4, no. 4, (Taipei, 1973).
Kuang-hsu ch'ao tung-hua lu (The T'ung-hua Records of the Kuang-hsu Reign), (Compiled by Chu Shou-p'eng), 5 vols., (Peking, 1958).
Kung-chung tang Kuang-hsu ch'ao tsou-che (Secret Palace Memorials of Kuang-hsu Reign), 25 vols., (Taipei).
Ming Hui Yao (Outline of Political Events of Ming Dynasty) 80 chuan, 2 vols., (reprint, Taipei, 1972).
Ming Shih (A History of Ming Dynasty) 332 chuan, 5 vols., (reprint, Taipei, 1956).
Shang-wu kuan-pao (The Gazette of Commercial Affairs) 1906–1910, (Peking, original, 1906–1910).
Shih-erh-ch'ao tung-hua lu (The Tung-hua Records of the Twelve Reigns of the Ch'ing Dynasty), 30 vols., (reprint, Taipei, 1973).
Sung Hui Yao (Outline of Political Events of the Sung Dynasty), (n.d.).
Sung Shih (A History of Sung Dynasty) 496 chuan, 7 vols., (reprint, Taipei, 1956).
Ta Ch'ing Hsuan-t'ung Hsin-fa-ling (The New Statutes of Great Ch'ing Empire During the Hsuan-t'ung Reign), vols. 1–10, (Shanghai, n.d.).
Ta-ch'ing kuang-hsu hsin fa-ling (New Statutes of the Great Ch'ing Empire during the Kuang-hsu Reign), (Shanghai, n.d.).
Ta-ch'ing li-ch'ao shih-lu (Veritable Records of Successive Reigns of the Great Ch'ing Empire), (Ch'ang Ch'un, 1935).
Ta Ch'ing te-tsung ching-huang-ti shih-lu (Veritable Records of the Emperor Kuang-hsu of the Great Ch'ing Empire), 597 vols., in Ta-Ch'ing li-ch'ao shih-lu (Ch'ang Ch'un, 1935).
Ta'i-tsu hung-wu shih-lu (Veritable Records of the Emperor Ta'i-tsu of Ming Dynasty), (n.d.).
Chung-yang yen-chiu-yuan chin-tai shih yen-chin so (ed.) Tao-kuang Hsien-feng liang-ch'ao ch'ou-pan i-wu shih-mo pu-i (Supplements to the Complete Account of the Management of Barbarian Affairs for the Tao-kuang and Hsien-feng Reigns), (Taipei, 1966).
"Tsungli ke-kuo shih-wu ya-men ch'ing-tang" (The Tsungli Yamen Archives: Clean Files), (unpublished records kept in the Institute of Modern History Academia Sinica, Taipei).

The following sections have been consulted:

1. "Lu-sung-kuo huan-yueh" (Spanish Treaty Negotiations).

2. "Jih-jen huan-yueh" (Spanish Treaty Negotiations).
3. "Ta-hsi-yang huan-yueh" (Portuguese Treaty Negotiations).
4. "Pi-lu-kuo huan-yueh" (Peruvian Treaty Negotiations).
5. "Pi-lu-kuo an" (The Peruvian Case).
6. "Fa-kuo tiao-yueh" (French Treaty).
7. "The Mission of Chang Te-i to England" (29th year of Kuang-hsu).
8. "The Mission of Lu Cheng-hsiang and Ch'ien Hsun to the Netherlands" (33rd year of Kuang-hsu).
9. "The Mission of Ch'ien Hsun and Lu Cheng-hsiang" (34th year of Kuang-hsu).

"Wai Wu Pu tien-tang" (Archives of the Ministry of Foreign Affairs), (Unpublished records kept in the Institute of Modern History, Academia Sinica, Taipei).
Yu-chi hui-ts'un (The Collected Records of Memorials), (Taipei, 1967).
Yuan Shih (A History of Yuan Dynasty) 210 chuan, 3 vols., (reprint, Taipei, 1956).

BRITISH OFFICIAL PUBLICATIONS AND ARCHIVAL MATERIALS

"Correspondence With Superintendent of British Trade in China, upon the Subject of Emigration from that Country, 20 August 1853." In *British Parliamentary Papers: Command Papers 1852–53*, vol. 68.
"Despatches Relating to Chinese Immigrants Recently Introduced into the Colonies of British Guiana and Trinidad, 20 August 1853." In *British Parliamentary Papers: Command Papers 1852–53*, vol. 68.
"General Remarks on Chinese Emigration" by Harry Parkes. In *British Parliamentary Papers: Command Papers 1852–53*, vol. 68.
"Dr. Bowring to the Earl Malmesbury dated 3 August 1852." In *British Parliamentary Papers: Command Papers 1852–53*, no. 5.
"Notes by Dr. Charles A. Winchester, British Consulate, Amoy 26 August 1852." In *British Parliamentary Papers: Command Papers 1852–53*. Inclosure 3 in no. 8.
"Fifteenth General Report of the Colonial Land and Emigration Commissioners, 1855." In *British Parliamentary Papers: Reports from Commissioners* (1854–55), vol. 17.
"Sixteenth General Report of the Emigration Commissioners, 1856." In *British Parliamentary Papers: Reports from Commissioners* (1856) , vol. 24.
"Correspondence on Emigration from Hong Kong and the Chinese Empire to the British West Indies and Foreign Countries." In *British Parliamentary Papers: Command Papers 1857–58*, vol. 43.
"Correspondence on Mortality on Board British Ships with Emigrants from China." In *British Parliamentary Papers: Command Papers 1857–58*, vol. 43.
"Correspondence Respecting Emigration from Canton, 1860." In *British Parliamentary Papers: Command Papers 1860*, vol. 69.
"Correspondence Respecting the Emigration of Chinese Coolies from Macao." In *British Parliamentary Papers: Accounts and Papers 1871*, no. 47, C. 403.
"Correspondence Respecting the Emigration of Chinese Coolies from Macao, in Continuation of Papers presented on the 14 July 1871." In *British Parliamentary Papers: Accounts and Papers 1872*, no. 70, C. 504.
"Papers Relating to Measures taken to Prevent the Fitting out of Ships at Hong Kong for the Macao Coolie Trade." In *British Parliamentary Papers: Accounts and Papers 1873*, no. 75, C. 829.
"Correspondence Respecting the Macao Coolie Trade and the Steamer Fatchoy."

In *British Parliamentary Papers: Accounts and Papers 1873*, no. 75, C. 797.

"Correspondence Respecting the Macao Coolie Trade." In *British Parliamentary Papers: Accounts and Papers 1874*, no. 68, C. 908.

"Correspondence Respecting the Macao Coolie Trade 1874–75." In *British Parliamentary Papers: Accounts and Papers 1875*, no. 78, C. 1212.

"Correspondence Respecting Chinese Immigration into the Australian Colonies." In *British Parliamentary Papers: Accounts and Papers 1888*, no. 73, C. 5448.

"The Extract from South African News, 8 December 1903." In *British Parliamentary Papers: Accounts and Papers 1904*, no. 61, Cd. 1895.

"The Extract from *Transvaal Leader*, 2 April 1903." In Enclosure 2 in no. 8, *British Parliamentary Papers: Accounts and Papers, 1904*, no. 61, Cd. 1895.

"Correspondence Respecting Introduction of Chinese Labour into the Transvaal." In *British Parliamentary Papers: Accounts and Papers 1904*, no. 62, Cd. 1945.

"Convention Between the United Kingdom and China Respecting the Employment of Chinese Labour in British Colonies and Protectorates, signed at London, 13 May 1904." In *British Parliamentary Papers: Accounts and Papers 1904*, no. 62, Cd. 1956.

"Report of Mr. Bianchini, a Former Compound (Chinese) Manager to the Witwatersrand Gold Mining Company dated 28 October 1905." In Enclosure 1 in no. 29, *British Parliamentary Papers: Accounts and Papers 1906*, no. 80, Cd. 2819.

"The Asiatic Law Amendment Ordinance, no. 29, of 1906." In *British Parliamentary Papers: Accounts and Papers 1906*, no. 80, Cd. 3251.

"The Petition of the Chairman of the Chinese Association, Leung Quinn, to the Chinese Minister in London dated 14 October 1907." In *British Parliamentary Papers: Accounts and Papers 1908*, no. 73, Cd. 3887, p. 55.

"Transvaal: Further Correspondence relating to Legislation affecting Asiatics in the Transvaal." In *British Parliamentary Papers: Accounts and Papers 1908*, no. 73, Cd. 3887.

"Correspondence Respecting Emigration 1859–60, China No. 52." In *Foreign Office Confidential Prints*, no. 894.

"Correspondence Respecting the Macao Coolie Trade, 1874." In *Foreign Office Confidential Prints*, no. 2445.

"Correspondence Respecting British Protection to Anglo-Chinese in China." In *Foreign Office Confidential Prints*, no. 5485.

"Memorandum on the Question of Chinese Immigration into the Australian Colonies." In *Foreign Office Confidential Prints*, no. 6018.

"Report on the Chinese Question by E.H. Parker of the China Consular Service, 1888." In *Foreign Office Confidential Prints*, no. 6039.

"Introduction of Chinese Labour into the Transvaal." In *Foreign Office Confidential Prints*, no. 8583.

"Memorandum Respecting the Immigration of Persons into British Dominions, with Special Reference to Chinese Immigrants." In *Foreign Office Confidential Prints*, no. 8893.

"An Act Respecting and Restricting Chinese Immigration (Canada)." In *Foreign Office Confidential Prints*, no. 9277.

"Memorandum Respecting the Wai-Wu Pu." In *Foreign Office Confidential Prints*, no. 9586.

"Memorandum Respecting the Anti-foreign Movement in China in 1909." In *Foreign Office Confidential Prints*, no. 9639.

Foreign Office Records (Originals are kept at the Public Record Office, Kew

Gardens, London) F.O. 17 Series, China, original correspondence. **The following correspondence were consulted:**

1. FO 17/768   1877, "Domestic: Kuo Sung-Tao, Kuo Ta Jen."
2. FO 17/794   1878, "Domestic: Kuo Sung-Tao, Kuo Ta Jen."
3. FO 17/821   1879, "Domestic: Kuo Ta-jen, Marquis Tseng."
4. FO 17/844   1880, "Domestic: Marquis Tseng, Chen, Yuan, Chi."
5. FO 17/869   1881, "Domestic: Marquis Tseng, Chen-Ta-Jen, Fung Yee."
6. FO 17/911   1882, "Domestic: Marquis Tseng."
7. FO 17/1034 1886, "Domestic: Marquis Tseng, Tzuchun, Pan, Lew-Ta-Jen."
8. FO 17/1052 1887, "Domestic: Lew-ta-jen."
9. FO 17/1073 1888, "Domestic: Lew-ta-jen, Sir H. Macartney."
10. FO 17/1104 1890, "Domestic: Lew-ta-jen, Sieh-ta-jen, Sir H. Macartney."
11. FO 17/1120 1891, "Domestic: Sieh-ta-jen."
12. FO 17/1142 1892, "Domestic: Sieh-ta-jen, Sir H. Macartney."
13. FO 17/1166 1893, "Domestic: Sieh-ta-jen, Sir H. Macartney."
14. FO 17/1286 1896, "Domestic: Kung Ta Jen, Sir. H. Macartney."
15. FO 17/1327 1897, "Domestic: Kung Ta Jen, Sir C. Lo Fengluh, Sir H. Macartney."
16. FO 17/1355 1898, "Domestic: Sir C. Lo Fengluh, Sir H. Macartney."
17. FO 17/1397 1899, "Domestic: Sir C. Lo Fengluh, Sir H. Macartney."
18. FO 17/1435 1900, "Domestic: Sir C. Lo Fengluh."
19. FO 17/1498 1901, "Domestic: Sir Lo Fengluh."
20. FO 17/1542 1902, "Domestic: Sir C. Lo Fengluh, Chang Ta-jen, Sir H. Macartney."
21. FO 17/1544 1902, "Domestic: Sir C. Lo Fengluh, Chang Ta-jen, Sir H. Macartney."
22. FO 17/1648 1904, "Domestic: Chang Ta-jen, Sir H. Macartney."
23. FO 17/1652 1904, "Domestic: Chang Ta-jen, various."
24. FO 17/1681 1905, "Domestic: Chang Ta-jen, Sir H. Macartney, Ivan chen."

"Petition of the Chinese Merchants of the Transvaal dated 27 September 1906." In FO 367, no. 16 (1906, Africa — General).
"Wang Ta-hsieh to Sir Edward Grey dated 1 November 1906." In FO 367, no. 16 (1906, Africa — General).
"Report of Committee Appointed to Consider and Take Evidence upon the Condition of Chinese Labourers in the Straits Settlements, November 1876." In CO 275/19.

AMERICAN OFFICIAL PUBLICATIONS AND ARCHIVAL MATERIALS

American Diplomatic and Public Papers: The United States and China, edited by Jules Davids, Scholarly Resources Inc., Wilmington, Delaware.

Series 1, 1842–60:
   vols. 8, 9, 10 and 11, *Extraterritoriality*
   vol. 15, *The Treaties of Tientsin*
   vol. 16, *The Ward Mission*
   vol. 18, *Trade, Currency, and the Opium Trade*
   vol. 19, *Consular Affairs and Trade Reports: Canton and Shanghai*
   vol. 20, *Consular Affairs and Trade Reports: Amoy, Foochow, Hong Kong, Macao and Ningpo*

Series 2, 1861-93:

vol. 3, *The Foreign Powers and China: Great Britain*
vol. 12, *The Coolie Trade and Outrages Against the Chinese*
vol. 13, *Chinese Immigration*
vol. 14, *Antiforeignism in China*
vol. 15, *Trade Affairs and the Opium Question*
vol. 16, *Treaty Ports*
vol. 18, *The Consular Service*

Series 3, 1894-1905:

vol. 8, *Sino-American Relations*
vol. 11, *Missionary Affairs and Antiforeign Riots*
vol. 12, *Consular Affairs and Extraterritoriality*
vol. 13, *Trade and Economic Activities*
vol. 14, *Railroad Building and Financial Affairs*

"Bureau of Immigration, Segregated Chinese Records", "3358 d. File", "Ca 1877-91", Boxes 1 to 6 (National Archives, Washington).

"Bureau of Immigration, Segregated Chinese Records", FB20, FB85, (National Archives, Washington).

"Report of Inspector S.W. Day of Port Huron to the Special Agent of the Treasury Department at Detroit, dated 2 March 1889." In "Bureau of Immigration, Segregated Chinese Records", "3358d. File", ca 1877-91 Boxes 5-6.

"Despatch of Robert J. Stevens, U.S. Consul in Victoria, British Columbia, to W.F. Wharton, Assistant Secretary of State dated 3 December 1889." In "Bureau of Immigration, Segregated Chinese Records", "3358d. File", ca 1877-91 Boxes 5-6.

"Report of the Special Agent of the Treasury Department at Victoria, British Columbia, to the Secretary of Treasury dated 6 February 1890." In "Bureau of Immigration, Segregated Chinese Records", "3358d. File", ca 1877-91 Boxes 5-6.

"Report of James J. Brooks, A Special Agent of the Treasury Department, Vancouver, British Columbia, to W. Windom, the Secretary of the Treasury dated 10 March 1890." In "Bureau of Immigration, Segregated Chinese Records", "3358d. File", ca 1877-91 Boxes 5-6.

"Report of O.L. Spawding, a Special Agent of The Treasury Department at San Francisco, to D. Manning, the Secretary of the Treasury dated 2 November 1885." In "Bureau of Immigration, Segregated Chinese Records", "3358d. File", ca 1877-91 Box 3.

"Report of H.F. Beecher, a Special Agent of the Treasury Department, Port Townsend, to C.S. Fairchild, the Secretary of the Treasury dated 2 July 1887." In "Bureau of Immigration, Segregated Chinese Records", "3358d. File", ca 1877-91 Box 3.

U.S. State Department, Papers Relating to the Foreign Relations of the United States, 1866-88, (Washington D.C., 1867-89).

"Notes from the Chinese Legation in the United States to the Department of State, 1868-1906." (National Archives, Washington.)

"The Mission of Ch'en Lan-pin and Yung Wing." In "Notes from the Chinese Legation in the United States to the Department of State, 1868-1906." (National Archives, Washington.)

"The Mission of Cheng Tsao-ju 1881-1885." In "Notes from the Chinese Legation in the United States to the Department of State 1868-1906." (National Archives, Washington.)

"The Mission of Chang Yin-huan, April 1886 to September 1889." In "Notes from the Chinese Legation in the United States to the Department of State, 1868-1906." (National Archives, Washington.)

"The Mission of Tsui Kuo-yin, September 1889 to August 1893." In "Notes from the Chinese Legation in the United States to the Department of State, 1868-1906." (National Archives, Washington.)

"The Mission of Yang Ju, 31 August 1893 to 26 April 1897." In "Notes from the Chinese Legation in the United States to the Department of State, 1868-1906." (National Archives, Washington.)

"The Mission of Wu T'ing-fang, April 1897 to March 1903." In "Notes from the Chinese Legation in the United States to the Department of State, 1868-1906." (National Archives, Washington.)

"The Mission of Chentung Liang Cheng, April 1903 to June 1906." In "Notes from the Chinese Legation in the United States to the Department of State, 1868-1906." (National Archives, Washington.)

Executive Documents of the House of Representatives for the 1st Session of the 47th Congress 1881-82, (Washington, 1882).

U.S. Congress, "Papers Relating to the Foreign Relations of the United States." 57th Congress 1st Session, House Documents 1901, (Washington, 1902).

U.S. Congress, "Papers Relating to the Foreign Relations of the United States." 57th Congress 2nd Session, House Documents 1902, (Washington, 1903).

U.S. Congress, "Papers Relating to the Foreign Relations of the United States." 58th Congress 3rd Session, House Documents 1904, (Washington, 1905).

U.S. Congress, "Papers Relating to the Foreign Relations of the United States." 59th Congress 1st Session, House Documents 1905, (Washington, 1906).

OVERSEAS CHINESE COMMUNITY RECORDS

"Chia-na-ta wei-to-li-ya chung-hua hui-kuan tang-an chi-lu" (Archives of the Chinese Consolidated Benevolent Association of Victoria, B.C. Canada), (Unpublished records kept in the Library of the University of Victoria, British Columbia, Canada).

Chia-na-ta i-to-li chung-hua hui-kuan ch'eng-li ch'i-shih-wu chou-nien, hua-ch'iao hsueh-hsiao ch'eng-li liu-shih chou-nien chi-nien t'e-k'an (Souvenir Magazine to Commemorate Victoria's Chinese Consolidated Benevolent Association 1884-1959, and Chinese Public School 1899-1959), (Victoria, British Columbia, 1959).

Lee Doe Chuen (Comp.) Ch'uan Chia chung-hua tsung hui-kuan k'ai-k'uang (Inside the Chinese Benevolent Association), (Taipei, 1969).

"Hsin-chia-po chung-hua shang-wu tsung-hui teng-chi i-shih-pu" (Minutes of the Chinese Chamber of Commerce of Singapore), 2 vols. (1906-1912), (Manuscript, Singapore).

Hsin-chia-po chung-hua tsung-shang-hui ta-hsa lo-ch'eng chi-nien k'an (Souvenir of the Opening Ceremony of the Newly Completed Singapore Chinese Chamber of Commerce Building), (Singapore, 1964).

Ma-lai-ya ku-kang-chou liu-i tsung-hui t'e-k'an (Souvenir Magazine of Pan Malayan Ku-kang-chou Six Districts' Association), (Penang, 1964).

Ma-lai-hsi-ya chia-hsu lien-ho-hui yin-hsi chi-nien (Souvenir Magazine of Silver

Jubilee celebration of the Federation of the Chia Ying Hakka Association, Malaysia), (Kluang, 1978).

Ch'en Ku'ang-min (ed.) Mei-chou chih-hsiao to-ch'in t'e-k'an (Gee How Oak Tin Journal, 1964), (Taipei, 1964).

Au Ch'ung-hsi and others (eds.) Lu Mei san-i tsung-hui-kuan Chien-shih (A Concise History of the Sam Yap Association of San Francisco), (San Francisco, 1975).

T'an-hsiang-shan chung-hua tsung-kung-hui (ed.) Hua-kung lai T'an pai chou-nien Chi-nien t'e-k'an (Souvenir Magazine of Centenary Celebration of the Arrival of Chinese Coolies in Hawaii), (Honolulu, n.d.).

Lin Ch'i-chung (Lum Ki Chung) and others (eds.) T'an-hsiang-shan Chung-hua hui-kuan wu-shih chou-nien chi-nien t'e-k'an (The 50th Anniversary of the Establishment of the United Chinese Society Honolulu), (Honolulu, 1934 ?).

T'an-hsiang-shan chung-hua tsung shang-hui Wu-shih chou-nien chi-nien (Chinese Chamber of Commerce of Hawaii, Golden Jubilee), (Honolulu, n.d.).

T'an-hsiang-shan lung-tu ch'ung-shan-t'ang ch'i-shih-wu chou-nien chi-nien t'e-k'an (Souvenir Magazine of 75th Anniversary of the Lung-tu Ch'ung-shan T'ang, Hawaii), (Taipei ?, 1965).

Cheng Tung-meng (ed.) T'an-shan hua-ch'iao (The Chinese of Hawaii), (Honolulu, 1929).

Liu Chen-kuang (Lau Chun Kwong, ed.) T'an-shan hua-ch'iao (The Chinese of Hawaii), vol. 2, (Honolulu, 1936).

NEWSPAPERS

Chin-shan jih-hsin lu (The Golden Hill's News), June–July 1854 (incomplete), (San Francisco, 1854).

Ch'ing I Pao (China Discussion), December 1898–December 1901, 12 vols. (reprint), (Yokohama, Reprint, Taipei, 1967).

Chiu-chin-san t'ang-jen hsin-wen tzu (San Francisco China News), nos. 1–46, July 1874–May 1875, (San Francisco, 1874–1875).

Chiu-shih chun-pao (Pacific Coast Chinese War Cry), (Salvation Army), (San Francisco, n.d.).

Chong Shing Yit Pao (The Chong Shing Daily), 1907–1910, (Singapore, 1907–1910).

Ch'ui-chi Hua Mei hsin-pao (Sui Kee American and Chinese Commercial Newspaper), (weekly, April 1888, incomplete), (San Francisco, 1888).

Chung Sai Yat Po (Oriental and Occidental News), January–July 1906, (Oakland, California, 1906).

Chung-wai hsin-pao (Chinese and Foreign News), September and October 1878, San Francisco, 1878).

Chung-wai hsin-wen chi-jih lu (Chinese and Foreign Weekly News), April 1865–July 1867, (Canton, 1865–67).

Chung-wai sin-pao (Chinese and Foreign Magazine), 1855–57, (Ningpo, 1855–57).

Hsin-min ts'ung-pao (New Citizen Journal), (1902–1907), 96 vols., (Yokohama, 1902–1907).

Hua-jen chi-lu (The Chinese Record), July 1877 to November 1878, (San Francisco, 1877–1878).

Jit Shin Pao (The Jit Shin Daily), March to May 1900, (Singapore, 1900).

Lat Pau (The Straits Daily News), 1888–1906, (Singapore, 1888–1906).

Mei Hua hsin-pao (Chinese American), February 1883, (incomplete), (New York, 1883).

Min Pao (The People's Tribune), nos. 1–26, 4 vols., (Tokyo, 1905–1911, reprint, Peking).

New York Daily Tribune, July 1901, (New York, 1901).

North China Herald, 1870–76, (Shanghai, 1870–76).

Pei-ching hsin-wen hui-pao (Peking Daily News), January to April 1901, 24 vols. (original), 8 vols., (reprint, Peking, 1901, reprint, Taipei, 1969).

San Francisco Examiner, 1890, (San Francisco, 1890).

Shen Pao, From 11th year of T'ung-chih to 13th year of Kuang-hsu (1872–87), 44 vols., (reprint, Taipei, 1965).

Shih-wu Pao (Chinese Progress), August 1896–August 1898, 6 vols., (reprint, Taipei, 1967).

Sing Po (The Singapore Daily News), November 1891–July 1895, (Singapore, 1891–95).

Sun Chung Kwock Bo (New China Daily News), October 1900–December 1906, (Honolulu, 1900–1906).

T'ang-fan hsin-pao (San Francisco Chinese Newspaper), August & September 1876, February & March 1877, November 1885 (incomplete), (San Francisco, 1876–77, 1885).

T'ang-fan kung-pao (The Oriental), September to November 1875 (incomplete), (San Francisco, 1875).

The Chinese Record (A Semi-Monthly Journal), July 1877–November 1878, (San Francisco, 1877–78).

The New York Times, January to April 1900, (New York, 1900).

The Singapore Daily Times, December 1874, (Singapore, 1874).

The Wan Kwok Kung Pau (Chinese Globe Magazine), nos. 301–364, 366–620, 623–47, 672–75, (Shanghai, 1874–82).

Tung-ngai San-luk (The Oriental), January–March 1855, July 1855, May 1856 (incomplete), (San Francisco, 1855–56).

Tung-hsi yang-k'ao mei-yueh t'ung-chi chuan 1833–38, (Singapore & Canton, 1833–38).

Wai Chiao Pao hui-p'ien (Collection of the Diplomatic News), 33 vols., (reprint, Taipei, 1964).

Wen-hsin jih-pao (Chinese World Around), March 1902 (incomplete), (San Francisco, 1902).

PERIODICALS AND HISTORICAL SERIES

B.C. Studies nos. 1–31, (Vancouver, 1968–76).

Chih-nan hsueh-pao (Journal of Chih-nan University), vol. 2, no. 2, (Shanghai, 1937).

Ch'ing-hua hsueh-pao (Journal of Ch'ing Hua University), vols. 7–10, (Peking, 1932–35).

Ch'ing-shih wen-t'i, vol. 1, (St. Louis, 1970–71).

Chung-kuo chin-tai ching-chi shih yen-chiu chi-k'an (Studies in Modern Economic History of China), vol. 1, no. 1, (1932).

Chung-shan ta-hsueh hsueh-pao (Journal of the Sun Yat-sen University), no. 4,

(Canton, 1959).

Chung-yang yen-chiu-yuan chin-tai shih yen-chiu-so chi-k'an (Bulletin of the Institute of Modern History, Academia Sinica), vols. 1–8, (Taipei, 1969–79).

Chung-yang yen-chiu-yuan chin-tai shih yen-chiu so (ed.) Chung-yang yen-chiu-yuan chin-tai shih yen-chiu so chuan-k'an (Monographs of the Institute of Modern History, Academia Sinica), vols. 4–11, (Taipei, 1962–64).

Harvard Journal of Asiatic Studies (1957), no. 20, (Cambridge, Massachusetts, 1957).

Hsia-men ta-hsueh hsueh-pao, she hui k'o-hsueh pan (The Journal of the Amoy University, Version on Social Sciences), no. 1, (Amoy, 1958).

Hsin-she hsueh-pao (Journal of the Island Society, Singapore), vol. 1, (Singapore, 1967).

Hsin-ya hsueh-pao (Journal of the New Asian College of the Chinese University of Hong Kong), (Hong Kong).

Journal of African History, vol. 18, no. 1, (London, 1977).

Journal of Asian Studies, vol. 11 (1952), (Michigan, 1952).

Journal of Indian Archipelago and Eastern Asia, vol. 1 (1847), (Singapore, 1847).

Journal of Royal Asiatic Society, vol. 6, (London, 1841).

Journal of Southeast Asian History, vols. 1–10, (Singapore, 1960–69).

Journal of Southeast Asian Studies, vols. 1–11, (Department of History, University of Singapore, Singapore, 1970–80).

Journal of the Malayan (Malaysian) Branch, Royal Asiatic Society, 39 vols., (Singapore, 1922–66).

Journal of the Straits Branch, Royal Asiatic Society, nos. 1–85, (Singapore, 1878–1922).

Kuo-li T'ai-wan ta-hsueh li-shih hsueh-hsi hsueh-pao (Bulletin of the Department of History, National Taiwan University), (Taipei, 1974).

Li Shih Tang An (Historical Archives), nos. 1–8, (Peking, 1981–82).

Li-shih yen-chiu (Studies in History), no. 1 (1957), (Peking, 1957).

Monumenta Serica: Journal of Oriental Studies, (Los Angeles).

Nan-yang hsueh-pao (Journal of South Seas Society), 16 vols., (Singapore, 1957–1972).

Nanyang Ta-hsueh hsueh-pao (Nanyang University Journal), vols. 5–7, (Nanyang University, Singapore 1971–73).

Papers on Far Eastern History, nos. 3–11, (Canberra, 1971–75).

The American Historical Review, (July 1936), vol. 41, no. 4, (Washington D.C., 1936).

The Chinese Repository, vols. 1–20, (Canton, 1833–51, reprint, Tokyo n.d.).

The Chinese Social and Political Science Review, vol. 20, no. 1, (Peiping, 1936).

The Journal of the Institute of Chinese Studies of the Chinese University of Hong Kong, vols. 4 & 5, (Hong Kong, 1971–72).

The Journal of the Oriental Society of Australia, vol. 3, no. 1, (Sydney, 1965).

The New Asia Journal, vol. 5, no. 1 and vol. 8, no. 2, (Hong Kong, 1960, 1968).

Tung-fang tsa-chih (The Eastern Miscellany), vols. 1–29, (reprint, Taipei, 1971).

United College Journal, vol. 3, (Hong Kong, 1964).

Pacific Historical Review, vol. 6, no. 4, (Berkeley).

Hsiao-fang-hu chai yu-ti ts'ung-ch'ao pu-p'ien, (reprint, Taipei, 1962).

Shen Yun-lung (ed.). Chin-tai chung-kuo shih-liao ts'ung-k'an (Modern Chinese Historical Materials Series), 630 vols., (Taipei).

Wang Yu-li (ed.). Chung-hua wen-shih ts'ung-shu (Series in Chinese Literature and History), (Taipei, n.d.).
Wu Hsiang-hsiang (ed.). Chung-kuo shih-hsueh ts'ung-shu (Chinese Historical Series), (Taipei, n.d.).
_____. Chung-kuo hsien-tai shih ts'ung-k'an (Selected Articles on Contemporary History of China), vols. 1–6, (Taipei, 1950–64).

MEMOIRS, DIARIES, BOOKS, ARTICLES, AND DISSERTATIONS

A-ying, Fan Mei hua-kung chin-yueh wen-hsueh chi (Collections of Literatures relating to Anti Exclusion of Chinese Labourers from the United States), (Peking, 1960).
Amyot, Jacques, S.J. *The Chinese Community of Manila: A Study of Adaptation of Chinese Familism to the Philippine Environment*, (Chicago, 1906).
Anonymous, *Chung-shan wen-hsien* (Documents of the Chung Shan District), 8 vols., Wu Hsiang-hsiang (ed.) Chung-kuo shih-hsueh ts'ung-shu, no. 11, (Taipei, 1965).
Anonymous, "Shu pao-hu fan-k'e hui-chi chang-ch'eng cha hou" (Comments on the Proclamation of Rules for Protection of Returned Overseas Chinese), in Sing Po, 16/7/1895, p. 1.
Anonymous, *Hua-ch'iao wen-t'i lun-wen chi* (Essays on Overseas Chinese Matters), (Taipei, 1954).
Anonymous, *Chung-wai ti'ao-yeh hui-p'ien* (Collection of Sino-Foreign Treaties), (Taipei, 1964).
Anonymous, *Ch'ing-shih lieh-chuan* (Historical biographies of the Ch'ing Dynasty), 10 vols., (Chung-hua, Shanghai, 1958).
Anonymous, *Chinatown Declared a Nuisance*, (San Francisco, 1880).
Anonymous, *Chin-tai pi-mi she-hui shih-liao* (Historical Materials on Modern Secret Societies), (Taipei, 1965).
Anonymous, *Studies in Asian History: Proceedings of Asian History Congress 1961*, (Bombay, 1969).
Anonymous (ed.). Symposium on Historical, Archaeological and Linguistic Studies on South China, Southeast Asia and Hong Kong Region, (Hong Kong, 1967).
Anonymous, "Lin Tao-ch'ien chuan" (A Biography of Lin Tao-ch'ien). In Ch'ao-chou fu-chih (The Gazetteer of Ch'ao-chou Prefecture), vol. 38.
Anonymous, "Biographies of Chang Shih-ch'eng and Fang Kuo-chen." In vol. 123 of Ming Shih.
Anonymous, "Wu T'ing-fang po-shih" (Dr. Wu T'ing-fang) In Ma-lai-ya ku-kang-chou liu-i tsung-hui t'e-k'an, pt. 2, pp. 37–38.
Anonymous, "Official Reports of Capture of Amoy by Commanders-in-Chief, Sir Hugh Gough and Sir William Parker dated 5 September 1841." In the Chinese Repository, vol. XI, (Jan.–Dec. 1842).
Anonymous, "Amoy: Memoranda of the Protestant Missions from their Commencement, With Notice of the City and Island, Prepared by Resident Missionaries." In The Chinese Repository, vol. XV (Jan.–Dec. 1846), pp. 355–61.
Anonymous, Shang-hai hsien-chih (County Gazetteer of Shanghai), (1800, ?, n.p.).
Ai Shih K'e. "Ai Kuo Lun" (On Patriotism). In Ch'ing I Pao, vol. 1, pp. 327–32.
Aimes, H.H.S. *A History of Slavery in Cuba 1511–1868*, (New York, 1967, reprint).
Arensmeyer, L.C. "British Merchant Enterprise and the Chinese Coolie Labour

Trade 1850–1874", (Ph.D. Dissertations, U. of Hawaii, 1979).

Armentrout, L. Eve. "Conflict and Contact between the Chinese and Indigenious Communities in San Francisco, 1900–1911." In *Chinese Historical Society of America* (ed.), *The Life, Influence, and the Role of the Chinese in the United States 1776–1960*, (San Francisco, 1976), pp. 55–70.

Armentrout-Ma, Eve. "A Chinese Association in North America: The Pao-Huang Hui from 1899 to 1904", in *Ch'ing-shih wen-ti*, 3:9 (1978), pp. 91–111.

Assey, Charles. *On the Trade to China and the Indian Archipelago*, (Rodwell and Martin, London, 1819).

Ayers, W. *Chang Chih-tung and Educational Reform in China*, (Cambridge, Massachusetts, 1971).

Banister, T.R. "A History of the External Trade of China 1834–81", China. The Maritime Customs I — Statistical Series, no. 6, Decennial Reports 1922–31, vol. 1, pp. 1–193.

Banno, Masatake. *China and the West 1858–1861: The Origins of the Tsungli Yamen*, (Cambridge, Massachusetts, 1964).

Barnett, S.W. "Protestant Expansion and Chinese Views of the West." In Modern Asian Studies, 6:2 (1972), pp. 129–49.

Barth, Gunther. *Bitter Strength: A History of the Chinese in the United States, 1850–1870*, (Cambridge, Massachusetts, 1964).

Bays, Daniel H. "The Nature of Provincial Political Authority in Late Ch'ing Times: Chang Chih-tung in Canton, 1884–1889", in *Modern Asian Studies*, vol. 4, no. 4 (1970), pp. 325–47.

_____. *China Enters the Twentieth Century: Chang Chih-tung and the Issues of a New Age, 1895–1909* (Ann Arbor, 1978).

Beale, H.K. *Theodore Roosevelt and the Rise of America to World Power*, (Baltimore, 1956).

Bernal, Rafael. "The Chinese Colony in Manila 1570–1770." In Alfonso Felix Jr. (ed.), *The Chinese in the Philippines 1570–1770*, vol. 1, (Manila, 1926), pp. 40–66.

Biggerstaff, K. "The Establishment of Permanent Chinese Diplomatic Missions Abroad." In *The Chinese Social and Political Science Review* (Peiping, 1936), vol. 20, no. 1, pp. 1–41.

_____. "The T'ung Wen Kuan." In *The Chinese Social and Political Science Review*, 18 (October, 1934), pp. 307–40.

_____. *The Earliest Modern Government Schools in China*, (Ithaca, 1961).

_____. "The First Chinese Mission of Investigation sent to Europe." In *Pacific Historical Review*, vol. 6, no. 4, pp. 307–20.

_____. "The Official Chinese Attitude toward the Burlingame Mission." In *American Historical Review*, vol. 41, no. 4, pp. 682–702.

Bland, J.O.P. & Backhouse, E. *China Under the Empress Dowager*, (Philadelphia, 1910).

Blussé, Leonard. "Batavia, 1619–1740: The Rise and Fall of a Chinese Colonial Town." In C.F. Yong (ed.), *Ethnic Chinese in Southeast Asia*, a special issue of the *Journal of Southeast Asian Studies*, vol. 12, no. 1 (March, 1981), pp. 159–78.

Blythe, W. *The Impact of Chinese Secret Societies in Malaya*, (Kuala Lumpur, 1969).

Boorman, H.L. & Howard, R.C. (eds.), *Biographical Dictionary of Republican China*, 4 vols., (New York, 1967–70).

Boxer, C.R. "Notes on Chinese Abroad in the Late Ming and Early Manchu Periods Compiled from Contemporary European Sources 1500–1750." In *T'ien Hsia Monthly*, 9.5 (December, 1939), pp. 447–68.

Britton, R.S. *The Chinese Periodical Press 1800–1912*, (reprint, Taipei, 1966).

Burmester, C.A. *Guide to the Collections of National Library of Australia*, 2 vols., (Canberra, 1977).

Campbell, P.C. *Chinese Coolie Emigration to Countries within the British Empire*, (reprint, Taipei, 1970).

Capie, S.A. "James B. Angell, Minister to China 1880–1881: His Mission and the Chinese Desire for Equal Treaty Rights." In *Chung-yang yen-chiu-yen chin-tai-shih yen-chiu-so chi-k'an*, (Taipei, 1982), no. 11, pp. 273–314.

Cha, Shih-chieh. "Ch'ing kuang-hsu ch'ao ch'ien-ch'i te chi-ke cheng-chih chi-t'uan 1875–1884" (The Political Cliques Prior to the Kuang-hsu Reign). In *Kuo-li t'ai-wan ta-hsueh li-shih hsueh-hsi hsueh-pao*, (Taipei, 1974), no. 1, pp. 19–45.

Chan, Hok-lam. "Chinese Refugees in Annam and Champa at the End of the Sung Dynasty." In *Journal of Southeast Asian History*, vol. 7, no. 2 (September, 1966), pp. 1–10.

Chan, Kim Man. "Mandarins in America: The Early Chinese Ministers to the United States, 1878–1907" (An unpublished Ph.D. dissertation, University of Hawaii, 1981), (microfilm).

Chan, Wellington K.K. *Merchants, Mandarins and Modern Enterprise in Late Ch'ing China*. Monograph no. 79 of Harvard East Asian Monographs, (Cambridge, Massachusetts, 1977).

Chang, Chih-tung. *Chang Wen-hsiang kung ch'uan-chi* (Complete Works of Chang Chih-tung), 6 vols., (Taipei, 1963).

Chang Ch'ing-chiang. "Ch'en Hsu-nien yu tzu-cheng ti" (Ch'en Hsu-nien and His Mansion). In Lin Hsiao-sheng and others (eds.), *Shih-le ku-chi*, (Singapore, 1975), pp. 225–30.

Chang, C.C. "The Chinese in Latin America: A Preliminary Geographical Survey with Special Reference to Cuba and Jamaica", (An unpublished Ph.D. thesis, University of Maryland, 1956).

Chang, Chung-li. *The Income of the Chinese Gentry*, (Seattle, 1962).

———. *The Chinese Gentry: Studies on their Role in Nineteenth-Century Chinese Society*, (Seattle, 1955).

——— and Spector, Stanley (eds.). *Guide to the Memorials of Seven Leading Officials of 19th Century China*, (University of Washington, Seattle, 1955).

Chang, Hui-mei. "Ming-tai chung-kuo jen tsai Hsien-lo chih mo-i" (Chinese Traders in Siam During the Ming Dynasty). In *Wen-shih che hsueh pao*, no. 3 (1951), pp. 161–76.

Chang, Hsieh. *Tung-hsi yang-k'ao* (An Investigation of the Eastern Oceans), (reprint, Taipei, 1962).

Chang, Hsin-pao. *Commissioner Lin and the Opium War*, (Cambridge, Massachusetts, 1964).

Chang I-nan. *Hai-kuo kung-yu chi-lu* (Miscellaneous Collection of a Chinese Diplomat overseas), (Shanghai ?, 1898).

Chang, I-shan. *Min-tai chung-kuo yi ma-lai-ya* (The Relations Between China and Malaya during the Ming Dynasty), (Taipei, 1964).

———. *Tung-nan-ya shih yen-chiu lun-chi* (Collections of Essays on the History of Southeast Asia), (Taipei, 1977).

Chang, P'eng-yuan. "Huang Tsun-hsien te cheng-chih ssu-hsiang chi ch'i tui Liang ch'i-ch'ao te ying-hsiang", (The Political Thought of Huang Tsun-hsien and His Influence on Liang chi-ch'ao). In *Chung-yang yen-chiu-yuan chin-tai-shih yen-chiu-so chi-k'an*, no. 1, pp. 217–37.

Chang, Te-ch'ang. "Ming-tai kuang-chou chih hai-p'o mo-i" (The Sea Trade of Canton during the Ming Dynasty). In *Ch'ing-hua hsueh-pao*, vol. 7, no. 2, (1932).

――――. "Ch'ing-tai ya-p'ien chan-cheng ch'ien chih chung-hsi yen-hai t'ung-shang" (Sino-Western Coastal Trade in the Ch'ing Period Prior to the Opium War). In *Ch'ing-hua hsueh-pao*, no. 10 (1935), pp. 97–145.

――――. Ch'ing-chi i-ke ching-kuan te sheng-huo (Life of a Court official in the Late Ch'ing Dynasty), (Hong Kong, 1970).

Chang, Te-i. "Sui-shih jih-chi" (Diary of an Attache). In Wang Hsi-chi (ed.) *Hsiao-fang-hu chai yu-ti ts'ung-ch'ao*, series 11, pp. 146–58.

――――. *Hang-hai shu-ch'i* (Strange Tales of a Voyage), (Shanghai, 1867).

Chang, Ts'un-wu. *Kuang-hsu sa-i nien chung mei kung-yueh feng-ch'ao* (The 1905 Sino-American Dispute over the Exclusion Law), (Taipei, 1965).

――――. "Wu T'ing-fang shih Mei shih tui chung-nan Mei te wai-chiao yu hu-ch'iao" (Wu T'ing-fang's Diplomacy and Protection of the Chinese in Central and South America during his term as the Chinese Minister to the United States). In *Ssu yu Yen*, vol. 13, no. 1, (1975).

Chang, Wei-hua. *Ming-tai hai-wai mao-i chien-lun* (An Introduction to the Study of Overseas Trade of the Ming Dynasty), (Shanghai, 1955).

Chang, Yin-huan. *San-chou jih-chi* (Diary of My Missions to the Three Continents), (8 chûan, Kyoto, 1896), (kept in Harvard-Yenching Library).

Chao, Feng-t'ien. *Wan Ch'ing wu-shih nien ching-chi ssu-hsiang shih* (Economic Thought During the Last Fifty Years of the Late Ch'ing Period), (Hong Kong, 1968).

Chao Ju-kua. Annotated by Feng Ch'eng-chun, *Chu Fan Chih Chiao-chu* (Records of Various Foreign Nations with Annotations), (Shanghai, 1930, reprint, 1956).

Char, Tin-yuke (compiled and ed.). *The Sandalwood Mountains: Readings and Stories of the Early Chinese in Hawaii*, (Honolulu, 1975).

Ch'en, Ching-ho. *Shih-liu shih-chi chih Fei-li-pin hua-ch'iao* (The Overseas Chinese in the Philippines during the Sixteenth Century), (Hong Kong, 1963).

――――. "Ch'ing-ts'u Cheng Ch'eng-kung ch'an-pu chih i-chih nan-ch'i (The Migration of the Cheng Partisans to South Vietnam), part 1, in *The New Asia Journal*, vol. 5, no. 1, (1960), pp. 433–59.

――――. "Ch'ing-ts'u Cheng Ch'eng-kung ch'an-pu chih i-chih nan-ch'i" (The Migration of the Cheng Partisans to South Vietnam), part 2. In *The New Asia Journal*, vol. 8, no. 2, (August, 1968), pp. 413–85.

Ch'en, Chu-t'ung. "Yuan-tai chung-hua min-tsu hai-wai fa-chan ka'o" (Notes on the Chinese Expansion Overseas during the Yuan Dynasty), pt. 1. In *Chih-nan hsueh-pao*, vol. 2, no. 1, pp. 123–49.

――――. "Yuan-tai chung-hua min-tsu hai-wai fa-chan k'ao" (Notes on Overseas Expansion of the Chinese during the Yuan Dynasty), pt. 2. In *Chih-nan hsueh-pao*, vol. 2, no. 2, (Shanghai, 1937).

Ch'en, Fu-ling (ed.). Huan-hai fu-po ta-shih chi (Major Events in the Ch'ing Bureaucracy), 3 vols. In Shen Yun-lung (ed.), *Chin-tai chung-kuo shih-liao ts'ung-k'an*, no. 289, (Taipei, n.d.).

Chen, Jerome. *China and the West: Society and Culture 1815–1937*, (Hutchinson,

London, 1979).

Ch'en, J. & Tarling, N. (eds.). *Studies in the Social History of China and Southeast Asia*, (Cambridge, 1970).

Ch'en, Ju-chou. *Mei kuo hua-ch'iao nien-chien* (Handbook of the Chinese in America), (New York, 1946).

Ch'en, Kao-hua. "Yüan tai te h'ai-wai mo-i" (Overseas Trade of the Yüan Dynasty"). In *Lishi Yanjiu*, no. 3, (Peking, 1978), pp. 61–69.

_____. *Sung Yuan shih-ch'i te hai-wai mo-i* (China's overseas Trade during the Sung and Yuan dynasties), (T'ientsin, 1981).

Ch'en Lan-pin. "Shih Mei chi-lueh" (Brief Records of My Mission to the United States of America). In *Hsiao-fang-hu chai yu-ti ts'ung-ch'ao pu-p'ien*, (reprint, Taipei, 1962), vol. 16, pp. 1050–51.

Ch'en, Li-t'e. *Chung-kuo hai-wai i-min shih* (A History of Chinese Emigration), (Shanghai, 1946).

Ch'en, Lun-chiung. *Hai-kuo wen-chien lu* (A Record of Things Seen and Heard in the Maritime Countries), (Taipei, 1958).

Ch'en, Pao-shen. "Ch'ang-ch'i-lou tsou-i" (Memorials from the Ch'ang-ch'i Hall). In *Chin-tai chung-kuo shih-liao tsung-k'an fen-lei hsuan-chi*, (Taipei, 1971).

Ch'en, San-ching. "Lueh-lun Ma Chien-chung te wai-chiao ssu-hsiang" (On the Diplomatic Thought of Ma Chien-chung). In Chung-yang yen-chiu-yuan chin-tai shih yen-chiu-so (ed.), *Chung-yang yen-chiu-yuan chin-tai shih yen-chiu-so chi-k'an*, no. 3, pp. 543–55.

Chen, Ta. *Chinese Migration: With Special Reference to Labor Conditions*, (reprint, Taipei, 1967).

_____. *Nan-yang hua-ch'iao yu min yueh she-hui* (Southeast Asian Chinese and the Societies in Fukien and Kwangtung), (Shanghai, 1939).

_____. *Emigrant Communities in South China*, (New York, 1940).

Ch'en, T'ao (po-lan). *Shen-an-chai i-kao* (Works of Shen-an Library, posthumously collected), (Taipei, n.d.).

Ch'en Tzu-lung (ed.) *Huang Ming Ching-shih wen-p'ien* (Essays on Statesmenship of the Royal Ming Dynasty), (reprint, Taipei, 1964).

Ch'en, Wen-chin. "Ch'ing-chi ch'u-shih ke-kuo shih-ling ching-hui" (Funds for the Chinese Legations during the Ch'ing period 1875-1911." In *Chung-kuo chin-tai ching-chi shih yen-chiu chi-k'an*, vol. 1, no. 1, (Nanking, 1932).

_____. "Ch'ing-tai chih Tsungli Yamen chi ch'i ching-fei 1861-1884" (The Tsungli Yamen and Its Funds 1861-84). In *Chung-kuo chin-tai ching-chi shih yen-chiu chi-k'an*, vol. 1, no. 1 (1932), pp. 49–59.

Ch'en, Wen shih. *Ming Hung-Wu chia-ching chien te hai-chin cheng-ch'ih* (The Sea-Faring Prohibition Policy in the Early Ming Dynasty), (Taipei, 1966).

Ch'en, Yen. *Fu-chien t'ung-chih lei-chuan hsuan* (Selected Biographies from the Fukien Provincial Gazetteer), (Taipei, 1964).

Ch'en, Ying. *Hai-ch'eng hsien-chih* (County Gazetteer of Hai-ch'eng), (1762, n.p.).

Cheng, I-sung (ed.). *Yung-ch'un hsien-chih* (County Gazetteer of Yung-ch'un), (1878, n.p.).

Cheng, Kuan-ying, *Sheng-shih wei-yen* (Warnings to a Seemingly Prosperous Age), 14 vols., (Shanghai, ?, 1893).

_____. *Chang Pi-shih chun sheng-p'ing shih-lueh* (A Concise Biography of Chang Pi-shih). In Chin-tai chung-kuo shih-liao ts'ung-k'an, series 75, (Taipei, n.d.).

Cheong, W.E. "Canton and Manila in the Eighteenth Century." In Ch'en, J. & Tarling, N. (eds.), *Studies in the Social History of China and S.E. Asia*, (Cambridge, 1970), pp. 227–46.

_____. *Mandarins and Merchants: Jardine, Matheson & Co., A China Agency of the Early Nineteenth Century*, (Curzon, London, 1979).

Chesneaux, J. (ed.). *Popular Movements and Secret Societies in China 1840–1950*, (Stanford, 1972).

Chi, Madeleine. "Shanghai-Hangchow-Ningpo Railway Loan: A Case Study of the Rights Recovery Movement", in *Modern Asian Studies*, vol. 7, no. 1 (1973), pp. 85–106.

Chiang, Hai Ding. "Sino-British Mercantile Relations in Singapore's Entrepot Trade 1870–1915." In Ch'en, J. & Tarling, N. (eds.), *Studies in the Social History of China and S.E. Asia*, (Cambridge, 1970), pp. 247–66.

Chiang, Hsing-tung. "Ho-lan chih-min-ti chu-i che tui Yin-tu-ni-hsi-ya hua-chiao te po-hai" (The Oppression of the Chinese in Indonesia by the Dutch Colonialists). In *Chung-shan ta-hsueh hsueh-pao*, (Canton, 1959), no. 4, pp. 10–42.

Ch'iao-wu wei-yen-hui ch'iao-wu yen-chiu-she (ed.). *Hua-ch'iao wen-t'i lun-ts'ung* (Essays on Overseas Chinese), (Taipei, n.d.).

Ch'ien, Hsun. Erh-erh wu-wu shu, in Chin-tai chung-kuo shih-liao ts'ung-k'an fen-lei hsuan-chi, (Taipei, 1971).

Ch'ien Ngo-sun (ed.). "Huang Kung-tu hsien-sheng nien-p'u" (The Chronological Records of Huang Tsun-hsien). In Shen Yun-lung (ed.), *Chin-tai chung-kuo shih-liao ts'ung-k'an*, (Taipei, 1973), nos. 959–60.

_____. (ed.), *Huang Tsun-hsien shih p'ing-lun* (Comments on the Poetry of Huang Tsun-hsien), (Taipei, 1973).

Ch'ien, Shih-p'u (ed.). *Ch'ing-chi hsin she chih-kuan nien-piao* (The Chart of the Newly-established offices during the Ch'ing Period), (Peking, 1961).

Chih, Kang. *Ts'u shih t'ai-hsi chi* (Records of My Mission to the Western World). In *Ch'ing-mo min-ts'u shih-liao ts'ung-shu*, no. 38, (Taipei, n.d.).

Ch'in, Kuo-ching. "Ch'ing-tai te wai-wu-pu chi ch'i wen-shu tang-an chih-tu" (The Ching Ministry of Foreign Affairs and Its Correspondence and Archival Systems). In Li Shih Tang An pien-chi-pu (ed.), *Li Shih Tang An* (Historical Archives), (Peking), no. 2 (1981), pp. 119–24.

Chinese Historical Society of America (ed.). *The Life, Influence and the Role of the Chinese in the United States, 1776–1960*, (Chinese Historical Society of America, San Francisco, 1976).

Ch'ing, Ju-chi. *Mei-kuo ch'in hua shih* (American Aggression in China), 2 vols. (San Lien, Peking, 1954).

Ch'iu, Feng-chia. *Ling-yun h'ai-jih lou shih-ch'ao* (Collections of Poems of the Ling-yun h'ai-jih lou). In Shen Yun-lung (ed.), *Chin-tai chung-kuo shih-liao ts'ung-k'an*, vol. 55, no. 547, (Taipei, n.d.).

Ch'iu, I-ch'en. *Ch'ing-tai shih-wen* (Anecdotes of the Ch'ing Dynasty), 10 vols., (n.d., n.p.).

Chiu, L.Y. *Ming-shih lun-chi* (Ming History: Seven Studies), (Hong Kong, 1975).

_____. "Chi Ming shih chung-kuo jen tsai tung-nan-ya chih shih-li" (Chinese Influence in Southeast Asia during the Ming Dynasty). In L.Y. Chiu, *Ming-shih lun-chi*, pp. 51–66.

_____. "The Life and Thought of Sir Kai Ho", (Ph.D. thesis, Department of Oriental Studies, Faculty of Arts, Sydney University, March 1968, 362 pp.).

Choi, Ching-yan. *Chinese Migration and Settlement in Australia* (Sydney U.P. Sydney, 1975).

Chong, Shih-chieh (ed.). *Ma-liu-chia ying-ho hui-kuan i-san-i chou-nien chi-nien t'e-k'an* (Souvenir Magazine of 131st Anniversary Celebration of the Malacca Ying Ho Association), (Malacca, 1952).

Chou Ch'i-fei. *Ling-wai tai-ta* (Answers to the Problems Relating to Places outside Kwangtung), (Shanghai, 1936).

Chou, Chia-mei. *Ch'i-pu-fu chai cheng-shu* (Political Treatises of the Chi'-pu-fu Library), 2 vols., (Taipei, 1972).

Chou, Heng-chung. *Ch'ao-yang hsien-chih* (County Gazetteer of Ch'ao-yang), (1884, n.p.).

Chow, Jen-hwa. *China and Japan: The History of Chinese Diplomatic Missions in Japan 1877–1911*, (Singapore, 1975).

Chou, Shih-hsuan. *Ch'ao-chou fu-chih* (Prefectural Gazetteer of Ch'ao-chou), (1762, n.p.).

Chou Ta-kuan. *Chen-la feng-t'u chi* (The Topography of Cambodia) (Annotated by Hsia Nai, Peking, 1981).

Chu Huo. *P'ing-chou k'o-t'an*, (Shanghai, 1941).

Chu, Pao-chin. *V.K. Wellington Koo: A Case Study of China's Diplomat and Diplomacy of Nationalism, 1912–1966*, (Hong Kong, 1981).

Chu Shih-chia (ed.). *Mei-kuo po-hai hua-kung shih-liao* (Collections of Historical Materials of American Oppression of Chinese Coolies), (Peking, 1958).

_____. *Shih-chiu shih-chi Mei-kuo ch'in hua tang-an shih-liao hsuan-chi* (Selection of Archival Materials relating to the American Aggression in China during the 19th century), 2 vols., (Peking, 1959).

Ch'u, T'ung-tsu. *Local Government in China Under the Ch'ing*, (Cambridge, Massachusetts, 1962).

_____. "Chinese Class Structure and Its Ideology." In J.K. Fairbank (ed.), *Chinese Thought and Institutions*, (Chicago, 1967), pp. 235–50.

Chu, Y.K. *Mei-kuo hua-ch'iao k'ai shih* (A History of the Chinese People in America), (Taipei, 1975).

Chui, Kwei-chiang. "Late Ch'ing's Modern Enterprises and the Chinese in Singapore and Malaya, 1904–1911" (Occasional Paper Series, no. 17, Institute of Humanities and Social Sciences, Nanyang University, Singapore, February, 1976).

_____. *Hsing Ma shih lun-ts'ung* (Essays on the History of Singapore and Malaysia, Singapore, 1977).

Ch'uan, Han-sheng. "Ming-tai chung-yeh hou Ao-men te hai-wai mo-i" (Foreign Trade of Macao after the Middle of Ming Dynasty). In *The Journal of the Institute of Chinese Studies of the Chinese University of Hong Kong*, vol. V, no. 1, (1972), pp. 245–69.

_____. "Chih Ming-chi Chih Ch'ing chung-yeh hsi-shu mei-chou te chung-kuo shih-ho mo-i" (Chinese Silk Trade in the Spanish America between the Ming and the Middle of the Ch'ing Dynasty). In *The Journal of the Institute of Chinese Studies of the Chinese University of Hong Kong*, vol. IV, no. 2 (1971), pp. 345–69.

Chung, Sue Fawn. "The Much Maligned Empress Dowager: A Revisionist Study of the Empress Dowager T'zu-hsi (1835–1908)." In *Modern Asian Studies*, vol. 13, no. 2 (1979), pp. 177–96.

Chung-yang yen-chiu-yuan. *Ming Ch'ing shih-liao keng p'ien* (Historical Materials of the Ming and Ch'ing Periods, Series G), (Taipei, n.d.).

Chung-yang yen-chiu-yuan chin-tai shih yen-chiu-so (ed.). *Chung Mei kuan-hsi shih-liao, T'ung-chih ch'ao* (Source Materials on Sino-American Relations, T'ung

Chih Reign), (Taipei, 1968).

_____. *Chin-tai chung-kuo tui hsi-fang chi lieh-ch'iang jen-shih tzu-liao hui-p'ien* (Source Materials on China's Knowledge and Understanding of the West and the Powers), vol. 1, nos. 1 and 2, (Taipei, 1972).

_____. Chung-yang yen-chin-yuan chin-tai shih yen-chiu-so chi-k'an (Bulletin of the Institute of Modern Chinese History, Academia Sinica), (Taipei).

Clark, H.R. "Consolidation on the South China Frontier: The Development of Ch'uan-chou 699–1126", (Ph.D. Dissertation, U. of Pennsylvania, 1981).

Clementi, C. *The Chinese in British Guiana*, (Georgetown, 1915).

Clyde, Paul H. *United States Policy Toward China: Diplomatic and Public Documents 1839–1939*, (Duke U. Press, Durham, 1940).

Cohen, P.A. *China and Christianity: The Missionary Movement and the Growth of the Chinese Anti-foreignism, 1860–1870*, (Cambridge, Massachusetts, 1963).

_____. *Between Tradition and Modernity: Wang Ta'o and Reform in Late Ch'ing China*, (Cambridge, Massachusetts, 1974).

Conwell, R.H. *Why and How: Why the Chinese Emigrate, and the Means they Adopted for the Purpose of Reaching America*, (Boston, 1871).

Coolidge, M.R. *Chinese Immigration*, (reprint, Taipei, 1968).

Collinson, R. "Survey of the Harbour of Amoy." In *The Chinese Repository*, vol. xii, p. 121.

Comber, L. *Chinese Secret Societies in Malaya: A Survey of the Triad Society from 1800–1900*, (Singapore, 1959).

Contemporary China Institute. *A Bibliography of Chinese Newspapers and Periodicals in European Libraries*, (Cambridge U.P., Cambridge, 1977).

Corcoran, E.J. "Hsueh Fu-ch'eng and China's Self-Strengthening Movement, 1865–1894," (Ph.D. Dissertation, U. of Kansas, 1979).

Costin, W.C. *Great Britain and China 1833–1860*, (reprint, Oxford, 1968).

Cuba Commission. *Chinese Emigration: Report of the Commission sent by China to Ascertain the Condition of Chinese Coolies in Cuba*, (Imperial Maritime Custom Press, Shanghai, 1876).

Cushman, J.W. "Fields from the Sea: Chinese Junk Trade with Siam during the Late Eighteenth and Early Nineteenth Centuries" (Ph.D. Dissertation, Cornell University, 1975).

_____. "Siamese State Trade and the Chinese Go-between, 1767–1855", in C.F. Yong (ed.), Ethnic Chinese in Southeast Asia, a special issue of the *Journal of Southeast Asian Studies*, vol. 12, no. 1 (March, 1981), pp. 46–61.

Dalton, Henry G. *The History of British Guiana, Comprising a General Description of the Colony*, 2 vols. (Longman, London, 1855).

Dennett, Tyler. *Americans in Eastern Asia: A Critical Study of United States' Policy in the Far East in the Nineteenth Century*, (Barnes & Noble, Inc., New York, 1922).

Donnelly, Ivon. "Historical Aspects of Chinese Junks and Maritime Trade." In *The Orient*, 5:10, (May, 1955), pp. 72–85.

Drake, Fred W. *China Charts the World: Hsu chi-yü and His Geography of 1848*, (Cambridge, Massachusetts, 1975).

_____. "A Mid-nineteenth-century Discovery of the Non-Chinese World." In *Modern Asian Studies*, 6:2, (1972), pp. 205–224.

Dulles, Foster Rhea. *China and America: The Story of their Relations since 1784*, (Princeton U.P., Princeton, 1946).

_____. *The Old China Trade*, (Boston, 1930).

Eastman, L.E. *Throne and Mandarins: China's Search for a Policy During the Sino-French Controversy 1880-1885*, (Cambridge, Massachusetts, 1967).

Eberhard, W. *A History of China*, (London, 1960).

_____. "Social Mobility and Migration of South Chinese Families." In *Symposium on Historical Archaeological and Linguistic Studies on Southern China, Southeast Asia and Hong Kong Region*, (Hong Kong, 1967), pp. 137-38.

Elegant, Robert S. *The Dragon's Seed: Peking and the Overseas Chinese*, (New York, 1959).

Elvin, M. and Skinner, G.W. (eds.) *The Chinese City Between Two Worlds*, (Stanford U.P., Stanford, 1974).

Erie, S.P. "The Development of Class and Ethnic Politics in San Francisco, 1870-1910: A Critique of the Pluralist Interpretation," (Ph.D. California, Los Angeles, 1975).

Fallers, L.A. (ed.). *Immigrants and Associations*, (Mouton & Co., The Hague, 1967).

Fang, Chao-ying. "Huang Tsun-hsien." In A.W. Hummel, *Eminent Chinese of the Ch'ing Period*, p. 350.

Fang, Jui-shih. *Ling-hsi kung-tu hui-ts'un* (Collection of Political correspondence of my Administration in Kwangtung), 3 vols. In Shen Yun-lung (ed.), *Chin-tai chung-kuo shih-liao ts'ung-k'an*, no. 263, (Taipei, n.d.).

Fang, I. (Comp.), *Chung-kuo ming-jen ta-tz'u-tien* (A Biographical Dictionary of China), (Shanghai, 1921).

Fairbank, J.K. and Teng Ssu-yû. *Ch'ing Administration: Three Studies*, (Cambridge, Massachusetts, 1961).

Fairbank, J.K. *Chinese Thought and Institutions*, (Chicago, 1967).

_____. *Trade and Diplomacy on China Coast: The Opening of the Treaty Ports 1842-1854*, (Cambridge, Massachusetts, 1964).

_____. "Patterns behind the Tientsin Massacre." In *Harvard Journal of Asiatic Studies*, (1957), no. 20, pp. 480-511.

_____. "The Early Treaty System in the Chinese World Order." In *The Chinese World Order*, (ed. by J.K. Fairbank, Cambridge, Massachusetts, 1968), pp. 257-75.

_____. *The Chinese World Order: Traditional China's Foreign Relations*, (Cambridge, Massachusetts, 1968).

Fei Hsin. Annotated by Feng Ch'eng-chun. Hsing-cha sheng-lan chiao-chu, (Shanghai, 1954).

Felix, Alfonso, Jr. (ed.). *The Chinese in the Philippines 1570-1770*, vol. 1, (Solidaridad Publishing House, Manila, Philippines, 1966).

Feng, Ch'eng-chun. *Chung-kuo Nan-yang chiao-t'ung shih* (A History of Commerce Between China and the South Seas), (Shanghai, 1937).

Feng, Tzu-yu. *Hua-ch'iao ko-ming k'ai-kuo shih* (The Involvement of Overseas Chinese in the 1911 Revolution), (Taipei, 1953).

Feuerwerker, A., Murphy, R. and Wright, M.C. (eds.). *Approaches to Modern Chinese History*, (Berkeley, 1967).

Field, Margaret. "The Chinese Boycott of 1905." In *Papers on China*, no. 11, (1957), pp. 63-98.

FitzGerald, C.P. *The Southern Expansion of the Chinese People*, (Canberra, 1972).

Folsom, K.E. *Friends, Guests, and Colleagues: The Mu-Fu System in the Late Ch'ing Period*, (Berkeley, 1968).

Fonacier, Thomas S. "The Chinese in the Philippines During the American Regime 1898-1946." In *Studies in Asian History: Proceedings of Asian History Congress 1961*, (Bombay, 1969), pp. 117-34.

Foster, J. *Men-At-The-Bar: A Biographical Hand-List of the Members of the Various Inns of Court*, (London, 1885).

Foster, J.W. *American Diplomacy in the Orient*, (Boston, 1903).

Franke, W. *The Reform and Abolition of the Traditional Chinese Examination System*, (Cambridge, Massachusetts, 1968).

Freedman, Maurice. *Chinese Lineage and Society: Fukien and Kwangtung*, (New York, 1966).

_____. *Lineage Organization in Southeastern China*, (London, 1970).

_____. *The Study of Chinese Society*, (Stanford, 1979).

_____. "Immigrants and Associations: Chinese in Nineteenth Century Singapore." In *Comparative Studies in Society and History*, vol. iii, no. 1, (October, 1960), pp. 25-48.

_____. "Overseas Chinese Associations: A Comment." In *Comparative Studies in Society and History*, vol. iii, no. 4, (July, 1961), pp. 478-80.

Freedman, M. and Topley, M. "Religion and Social Realignment among the Chinese in Singapore." In *Journal of Asian Studies*, vol. XXI, no. 1, (November, 1961), pp. 3-23.

Frodsham, J.D. (trans.). *The First Chinese Embassy to the West: The Journals of Kuo Sung-t'ao, Liu Hsi-hung and Chang Te-yi*, (Oxford, 1974).

Fu Yi-ling. "Ming Ch'ing shih-tai chieh-chi kuan-hsi te hsin t'an-so" (A New Inquiry into the Class Relations during the Ming and Ch'ing Dynasties). In *Zhong Guo Shi Yan Jiu*, no. 4, (Peking, 1979), pp. 65-74.

Fujita Toyohachi. *Chung-kuo nan-hai ku-tai chiao-t'ung ts'ung-k'ao* (Studies on Ancient Chinese Relations with the Nan-hai), translated by Ho Chien-min from Japanese into Chinese, (Shanghai, 1936).

Godley, Michael R. "Chang Pi-shih and Nanyang Chinese Involvement in South China's Railroads, 1896-1911." In *Journal of Southeast Asian Studies*, vol. 4, no. 1, (1973), pp. 16-30.

_____. "The Late Ch'ing Courtship of the Chinese in Southeast Asia." In *Journal of Asian Studies*, vol. 34, no. 2, (1975), pp. 361-85.

_____. "Overseas Chinese Entrepreneurs as Reformers: The Case of Chang Pi-shih." In Paul A. Cohen & John E. Schrecker (eds.), *Reform in Nineteenth-Century China*, (Cambridge, Massachusetts, 1976), pp. 49-59.

_____. "China's World's Fair of 1910: Lessons from a Forgotten Event." In *Modern Asian Studies*, vol. 12, no. 3, (1978), pp. 503-22.

_____. The Mandarin-Capitalists from Nanyang: Overseas Chinese Enterprise in *The Modernization of China 1893-1911*, (Cambridge, 1981).

_____. "The Treaty Port Connection: An Essay." In C.F. Yong (ed.), *Ethnic Chinese in Southeast Asia*, A Special Issue of the *Journal of Southeast Asian Studies*, vol. 12, no. 1, (March, 1981), pp. 248-59.

Greenbery, Michael. *British Trade and the Opening of China 1800-42*, (reprint, Cambridge, 1969).

Griffin, Eldon. *Clippers and Consuls: American Consular and Commercial Rela-*

tions With Eastern Asia 1845-60, (reprint, Ch'eng Wen, Taipei, 1972).

Gutzlaff, C. "Journal of Residence in Siam and a Voyage along the Coast of China to Manchu Tartary, July 1832." In *The Chinese Repository*, vol. 1.

Han, Chen-hua. "Lun Cheng Ho hsia hsi-yang te hsing-ch'ih" (On the Characteristics of Admiral Cheng Ho's Expedition to Western Ocean). In Hsia-men hsueh-pao, she-hui k'o-hsueh pan, no. 1, (1958), pp. 172-88.

Han, Huai-chun. "T'ien H'ou Sheng Mu yu hua-ch'iao te nan-chin" (Goddess T'ien H'ou and the Southern Expansion of Overseas Chinese). In Nan-yang hsueh-pao, vol. 2, no. 2, pp. 51-73.

Hao, Yen-ping. *The Comprador in Nineteenth Century China: Bridge Between East and West*, (Cambridge, Massachusetts, 1970).

_____. "Cheng Kuan-ying: The Comprador as Reformer." In *Journal of Asian Studies*, vol. 29, no. 1, (November, 1969), pp. 15-22.

Hertslet, G.E.P. and Parkes, E. (eds.). *Great Britain and China; and Between China and Foreign Powers*, (London, 1908).

Hirth, Friedrich, "The Hoppo-Book of 1753." In *Journal of the North-China Branch of the Royal Asiatic Society*, 17, (1882), pp. 221-35.

Hirth, F. and Rockhill, W.W. *Chau Ju-kua*, (St. Petersburg, 1911).

Ho, Alfred Kuo-liang. "The Grand Council in the Ch'ing Dynasty." In *Journal of Asian Studies*, II, (1952), pp. 167-82.

Ho, Ju-chang. "Ho Sao-chan wen-ch'ao" (Reprints of Literary Works of Ho Ju-chang). In *Wen T'ing-ching, Ch'ar-yang san-chia wen-ch'ao*, pp. 7-124.

_____. *Shih Tung hsu-lueh* (Brief Records of My Mission to Japan). In Shen Yun-lung (ed.), *Chin-tai chung-kuo shih-liao ts'ung-k'an*, no. 582, (Taipei, n.d.).

Ho, Ping-ti. *Studies on the Population of China 1386-1953*, (Cambridge, Massachusetts, 1959).

_____. *The Ladder of Success in Imperial China: Aspects of Social Mobility 1368-1911*, (New York, 1964).

_____. "The Geographical Distribution of Hui-Kuan in Central and Upper Yangtze Provinces — with Special Reference to Inter-regional Migrations." In *Tsing Hua Journal of Chinese Studies*, New Series V no. 2, (December, 1966), pp. 120-52.

Ho, Yow. "The Attitude of the United States towards the Chinese." In *Forum 29*, (June, 1950), p. 387.

H'ou, Hou-p'ei. "Wu-k'ou t'ung-shang i-ch'ien wo-kuo kuo-chi mou-i chih k'ai-k'uang" (China's Overseas Trade Before the Opening of the Treaty Ports). In *The Tsing Hua Journal*, vol. 4, no. 1, (Peking, 1927), pp. 1217-64.

Hsiao I-shan. *Ch'ing-tai t'ung-shih* (A General History of the Ch'ing Dynasty), 5 vols., (Shang Wu, Shanghai, 1927-63).

Hsiao, Kung-ch'uan. *Rural China: Imperial Control in the Nineteenth Century*, (Seattle, 1960).

Hsieh, Pao-chao. *The Government of China 1644-1911*, (New York, 1966).

Hsieh, W. "Triads, Salt Smugglers, and Local Uprisings: Observations on the Social and Economic Background of the Waichow Revolution of 1911." In Chesneaux, J. (ed.), *Popular Movements and Secret Societies in China 1840-1950*, pp. 145-64.

Hsu, Chi-yu. *Yin-huan chih-lueh*, 2 vols. In Wang Yu-li (ed.), *Chung-hua wen-shih ts'ung-shu*, vol. 1, no. 6, (Taipei, n.d.).

Hsu, Ching-ch'eng. *Hsu Chu-yüan hsien-sheng ch'u-shih han kao* (Correspondence of Hsu chu-yuan [Ching-ch'eng] During His Mission Overseas), 14 chüan, (n.d., n.p.).

Hsu, Francis L.K. *Under the Ancestor's Shadow: Chinese Culture and Personality,* (Stanford, 1971).

_____. *The Challenge of the American Dream: The Chinese in the United States,* (Belmont, California, 1971).

Hsu, Hsiao-t'ien. *Ch'ing kung shih-san ch'ao yen-i: Tz'u-hsi t'an-ch'ien* (Popular Stories of Ch'ing Palace During the Reigns of Thirteen Emperors), (Hong Kong, n.d.).

Hsu, Immanuel C.Y. *The Ili Crisis: A Study of Sino-Russian Diplomacy 1871–1881,* (London, 1965).

_____. *China's Entrance into the Family of Nations: The Diplomatic Phase 1858–1880,* (Cambridge, Massachusetts, 1960).

Hsu, K'o (ed.). *Ch'ing Pei lei-ch'ao* (Collection of Short Stories of the Ch'ing Dynasty), 12 vols., (Taipei, 1966).

Hsu, T'i-hsin. *Kuan-liao tzu-pen lun* (On the Bureaucratic Capital), (Shanghai, 1949).

Hsu, Yu-hu. *Cheng Ho p'ing-chuan* (A Critical Biography of Admiral Cheng Ho), (Taipei).

Hsu, Yun-tsiao. *Pei Ta Nien Shih* (A History of Pattani), (Singapore, ?, 1946).

Hsueh, Fu-ch'eng. *Ch'u-shih jih-chi hsu-k'e* (Supplements to my Diary of My Mission to England), 2 vols. In Wang Yu-li (ed.), *Chung-hua wen-shih ts'ung-shu,* no. 4, (Taipei, n.d.).

_____. *Ch'u-shih Ying, Fa, I, Pi ssu-kuo jih-chi* (Diary of My Mission to England, France, Italy and Belgium). In Shen Yun-lung (ed.), *Chin-tai chung-kuo shih-liao ts'ung-k'an,* no. 12, (Taipei, n.d.).

_____. "Ao-ta-li-ya k'o chih-ch'iang so" (Australia Could Become Strong). In *Hsiao-fang-hu chai yu-ti ts'ung-ch'ao pu-p'ien chai-pu-p'ien,* vol. 6, (Taipei, 1964).

_____. "Ch'ing ku-ch'u ch'u-chin chao-lai hua-min shu" (Memorial to the Court Requesting the Abolition of the Old Prohibitive Law and the Solicitation of the Overseas Chinese). In *Hsueh Fu-ch'eng,* "Hai-wai wen-p'ien", vol. 1, pp. 18–20.

_____. *Yung-an Wen-p'ien* (Literary Works of Yung-an), 3 vols. In Shen Yun-lung (ed.), *Chin-tai chung-kuo shih-liao ts'ung-k'an,* no. 943, (Taipei, n.d.).

_____. "Hai-wai wen-p'ien." In *Yung-an wen-p'ien.*

_____. *Hsueh Fu-ch'eng ch'uan-chi* (Complete Works of Hsueh Fu-ch'eng), 2 vols., (Kuang Wen Book Store, n.p., n.d.).

_____. *Ch'u-shih kung-tu, tsou-shu* (Correspondence of My Diplomatic Mission to England and My Memorials to the Court), 2 vols., (Taipei, n.d.).

Hu, Hsien-chin, *The Common Descent Group in China and Its Functions,* (New York, 1948).

Hu, Ying-han. *Wu Hsien-tzu hsien-sheng chuan-chi* (A Biography of Wu Hsien-tzu), (Hong Kong, 1953).

Hua-ch'iao chih pien-ch'uan wei-yuan-hui (ed.). *Hua Ch'iao Chih Tsung Chih,* (Taipei, 1956).

Huang, Cheng-ming et al. *Chung-kuo wai-chiao shih lun-chi* (Symposium on Chinese Diplomatic History), vol. 2, (Taipei, 1957).

Huang, Chia-mo. "Ying-jen yu Hsia-men hsiao-tao hui shih-chien" (The British and the Small Dagger Uprising in Amoy). In *Chung-yang yen-chiu-yen chin-tai shih yen-chiu so chi-k'an* (Bulletin of the Institute of Modern History, Academia Sinica), (Taipei, 1978), pp. 309–53.

Huang Fu-luan. *Hua-ch'iao yu chung-kuo ke-ming* (Overseas Chinese and the 1911 Revolution), (Hong Kong, 1955).

Huang, Fu-yung. *Hsin-chia-po Ying-ho hui-kuan shih-lueh* (A Short History of the Singapore Ying Ho Association). In Lin Chih-kao et al. (eds.), *Hsing-chou ying-ho hui-kuan i-pai ssu-shih-i chou-nien chi-nien t'e-k'an* (Singapore, 1965), pp. 10–12.

Huang, San-te. *Hung-men ko-ming shih* (The Revolutionary History of the Hung League), (San Francisco, 1936).

Huang Tsun-hsien. *Jen-ching-lu shih-ts'ao chien-chu* (Annotated Poems of Jen-Ching-lu), (Shanghai, 1957).

Huang Yen-yu. "Viceroy Yeh Ming-ch'en and the Canton Episode 1856–1861." In *Harvard Journal of Asiatic Studies*, vol. 6, (1941), pp. 37–127.

Hucker, C.O. *The Censorial System of Ming China*, (Stanford, 1966).

Hummel, A.W. *Eminent Chinese of the Ch'ing Period: 1644–1912* (reprint, Taipei, 1970).

Hunter, William C. *Bits of Old China*, (Kegal Paul, Trench & Co., London, 1885 Ch'eng-wen, reprint, Taipei, 1966).

I, Kou. "Tsu shih t'ai-hsi chi" (Records of My Mission to the Western World). In Wang Hsi-ch'i (ed.), *Hsiao-fang-hu chai yu-ti ts'ung-ch'ao*, original, vol. 11, pp. 102–44.

Irick, R.L. "Ch'ing Policy Toward the Coolie Trade 1847–1878" (an unpublished Ph.D. thesis, Harvard University, 1971), 2 vols.

————. *Ch'ing Policy Toward the Coolie Trade* (Chinese Materials Center, Taipei, 1982).

Isaacs, Harold R. *Images of Asia: American Views of China and India,* (Harper, New York, 1972).

Jackson, R.N. *Pickering: Protector of Chinese*, (Kuala Lumpur, 1965).

Janisch, H.N. "The Chinese, the Courts, and the Constitution: A Study of the Legal Issues Raised by Chinese Immigration to the United States, 1850–1902", (J.S.D. Chicago, 1971).

Jeffcott, Colin. "Government and the Distribution System in Sung Cities." In *Papers on Far East History*, no. 2, (September, 1970).

Jen, Yu-wen. *The Taiping Revolutionary Movement*, (New Haven, 1973).

Jones, Susan M. "The Ningpo Pang and Financial Power at Shanghai." In Mark Elvin & G.W. Skinner (eds.), *The Chinese City Between Two Worlds*, (Stanford, 1974), pp. 73–96.

Joseph, P. *Foreign Diplomacy in China, 1894–1900*, (Allen & Unwin, London, 1928).

Kahn, H.L. "The Education of a Prince: The Emperor Learns his Roles." In A. Feuerweaker, R. Murphy & M.C. Wright (eds.), *Approaches to Modern Chinese History*, (Berkeley, 1967), pp. 15–64.

————. *Monarchy in the Emperor's Eyes: Image and Reality in the Ch'ien-lung Reign*, (Cambridge, Massachusetts, 1971).

Kamachi, Noriko. "American Influences on Chinese Reform Thought: Huang Tsun-hsien in California, 1882–1885." In *Pacific Historical Review*, vol. XLVII, no. 2, (May, 1978), pp. 239–60.

_____. *Reform in China: Huang Tsun Hsien and the Japanese Model*, (Cambridge, Massachusetts, 1981).

K'ang-hsi Emperor. *Sheng-yu kuang-hsun* (The Maxims of the Emperor K'ang-hsi, amplified by Emperor Yung-cheng), (1724).

Kao, Hsin (ed.). *Hua-ch'iao wen-t'i lun-ts'ung* (Essays on Overseas Chinese), 2 vols., (Taipei).

Karlin, J.L. "The Anti-Chinese Outbreak in Tacoma, 1885". In *The Pacific Historical Review*, vol. 23, (1954), pp. 271–83.

_____. "The Anti-Chinese Outbreaks in Seattle, 1885–1886." In *Pacific Northwest Quarterly*, vol. 39, (1948), pp. 103–30.

Key, Ray Chong. "Cheng Kuan-ying (1841–1920)." In *Journal of Asian Studies*, vol. 28, no. 2, (February, 1969), pp. 247–67.

Kim, S.S. "Burlingame and the Inauguration of the Co-operative Policy." In *Modern Asian Studies*, 5:4, (1971), pp. 337–54.

King, Frank H.H. *Money and Monetary Policy in China 1845–1895*, (Cambridge, Massachusetts, 1965).

Knt, A.L. "Contribution to an Historical Sketch of the Portuguese Settlements in China, principally of Macao; of the Portuguese Envoys and Ambassadors to China; of the Catholic Missions in China; and of the Papal Legates to China." In *The Chinese Repository*, vol. 1, (May 1832–April 1833).

K'o, Kung-chen. *Chung-kuo pao-yeh shih* (A History of Chinese Newspapers), (Hong Kong, 1964).

K'o Mu-lin and Ng Chin-keong (eds.). *Hsin-chia-po hua-tsu shih lun-chi* (Papers on the History of the Chinese in Singapore), (Singapore, 1972).

Ku, Hung-ming. *Chang Wen-hsiang mu-fu chi-wen* (Anecdotes of My Service Under Chang Chih-tung's mu-fu), (Taipei, 1976).

_____. *Tu-i-ch'ao t'ang wen-chi* (Collection of Literary Works of the Tu-i-ch'ao Hall). In *Chin-tai chung-kuo shih-liao ts'ung-k'an*, series 75, (Taipei, n.d.).

Ku-kung po-wu-yuan (ed.). *Ch'ing-tai wai-chiao shih-liao: Chia Ch'ing Ch'ao* (Sources on Diplomatic History of China during the Chia Ch'ing Reign), (Peking, 1932).

Kuan, Keng-lin. *Ying T'an* (Stories about Japan). In Shen Yun-lung (ed.), *Chin-tai chung-kuo shih-liao ts'ung-k'an*, no. 288, (Taipei, n.d.).

Kuang-chih shu-chi P'ien-chi pu (ed.). *San Hsing Shih shu-tu* (Diplomatic Correspondence of Three Chinese Ambassadors), (Shanghai, 1910).

Ku'ang, Kuo-hsiang. *Pin-ch'eng san-chi* (An Anecdotal History of Penang)(Hong Kong, 1958).

Kuang-tung-sheng wen-shih yen-chiu-kuan, San-yuan-li jen-min k'ang-ying toucheng shih-liao (Historical Materials Related to the Struggle of San-yuan-li People against the British), (Peking, 1978).

Kuei, T'ien-chien (ed.). *Wu shih-yung hsing-shih yu Pi-lu cheng-fu po-lun k'e-li wang-lai wen-tu wen-ta i-kao* (Translation of the Diplomatic Correspondence between Wu T'ing-fang and the Peruvian Government over the Protection of the Peruvian Chinese), (n.d., n.p.).

Kuei, Tsung-yao. "Chung Pi wai-chiao kuan-hsi shih" (A History of Sino-Peruvian Relations). In Huang Cheng-ming et al., *Chung-kuo wai-chiao shih lun-chi*, vol. 2.

Kung, Shien-woo. *Chinese in American Life: Some Aspects of Their History, Status, Problems and Contributions*, (Seattle, 1962).

Kuo, Sung-t'ao. *Yang-tzu-shu wu i-chi* (Works of Kuo Sung-t'ao, Posthumously Collected), 55 vols., (1892, n.p.).

_____. *Shih-hsi chi-ch'eng* (The Record of An Envoy's Journal to the West), 2 chuan, (n.d., n.p.).

_____. "Shih-hsi chi-ch'eng" (The Record of An Envoy's Journey to the West). In J.D. Frodsham (trans.), *The First Chinese Embassy to the West: The Journals of Kuo Sung-t'ao, Liu Hsi-hung and Chang Te-yi* (Oxford, 1974), pp. 1–84.

_____. *Tseng chi-tse & Hsueh, Fu-ch'eng, San Hsing-shih shu-tu* (Correspondence of the Three Ambassadors), (Kuang Chih, Shanghai, 1910).

Kuo, T'ing-i. *Chin-tai chung-kuo shih-shih jih-chi* (Chronological History of Modern China), 2 vols., (Taipei, 1963).

_____. *Kuo Sung-t'ao hsien-sheng nien-p'u* (Chronological Biography of Kuo Sung-t'ao), (Taipei, 1971).

Kuwapara, J. (trans. by Ch'en Yu-ch'ing), *P'u Shou-keng k'ao* (on P'u Shou-keng), (Shanghai, 1929).

_____. (Trans. by Yang Lien), *T'ang Sung mo-i kang yen-ch'iu* (A Study of the Trading Ports of the T'ang and Sung Dynasties), (Shanghai, 1935).

La Fargue, T.E. *China's First Hundred*, (Pullman, Washington, 1942).

Lai, Chuen-yan. "The Chinese Consolidated Benevolent Association in Victoria: Its Origins and Functions." In *B.C. Studies*, no. 15, (Autumn 1972), pp. 53–67.

_____. "Chinese Attempts to Discourage Emigration to Canada: Some Findings from the Chinese Archives in Victoria." In *B.C. Studies*, no. 18, (Summer 1973), pp. 33–49.

_____. "Home County and Clan Origins of Overseas Chinese in Canada in the Early 1880s." In *B.C. Studies*, no. 27, (Autumn 1975), pp. 3–29.

Lamley, Harry J. "Hsieh-Tou: The Pathology of Violence in Southeastern China." In *Ch'ing-shih wen-t'i*, 3:7, (1977), pp. 1–39.

Lancashire, D. "A Confucian Interpretation of History." In *The Journal of the Oriental Society of Australia*, vol. 3, no. 1, (Sydney, 1965), pp. 76–87.

Lane-Poole, S. and Dickens, F.V. *The Life of Sir Harry Parkes*, (London, 1894).

Lang, Olga. *Chinese Family and Society*, (New Haven, 1946).

Latourette, K.S. *A History of Christian Missions in China*, (reprint, Taipei, 1966).

Lee, Din-yi. "Chao-ch'i hua-jen i mei chi An-chi-li ti'ao-yueh chih ch'ien-ting" (The Early Chinese Emigration to America and The Angels' Treaties). In *United College Journal*, vol. 3, (1964), pp. 1–29.

_____. *Chung Mei wai-chiao shih* (A History of Sino-American Relations), vol. 1, (Taipei, 1960).

Lee, Doe-chuen. *Ch'uan chia chung-hua tsung-hui kuan k'ai-k'uang* (Inside the Chinese Benevolent Association: A Report of Some Activities of the Highest Governing Body of the Chinese in Canada), (Taipei, 1969).

Lee, En-han. *China's Quest for Railway Autonomy 1904–1911*, (Singapore: University of Singapore Press, 1977).

_____. "Chung Mei shou-hui yueh-han lu-ch'uan chao-she" (Sino-American Negotiations on the Recovery of Canton-Hankow Railway Rights). In *Bulletin of the Institute of Modern History*, Academia Sinica, (Taipei, 1969), vol. 1, pp. 149–215.

Lee, Kuo-chi. *Chang Chih-tung te wai-chao cheng-ch'ih* (The Foreign Policy of Chang Chih-tung), (Taipei, 1970).

Lee, Mabel. "Wan-ch'ing te chung-shang chu-i" (Mercantilism in the Late Ch'ing Period). In *Chung-yang yen-chiu-yuan chin-tai shih yen-chiu so chi-kan* (Taipei, 1972), vol. 3, no 1, pp. 207–221.

————. "The Development of Exalt Commerce in Late Ch'ing", (Ph.D. thesis, Sydney University).

Lee, Poh Ping. *Chinese Society in Nineteenth Century Singapore* (Kuala Lumpur, 1978).

Lee, Rose Hum. *The Chinese in the United States of America*, (Hong Kong, 1960).

Leigh, Michael B. *The Chinese Community of Sarawak: A Study of Communal Relations*, (Singapore, 1964).

Leonard, Jane. "Chinese Overlordship and Western Penetration in Maritime Asia: A Late Ch'ing Re-appraisal of Chinese Maritime Relations." In *Modern Asian Studies*, 6:2, (1972), pp. 151–74.

Leyden, J. "Intercourse between the Chinese and Malays." In *Chinese Repository*, vol. V.

Li, Chung-chieh. *Hsin-chia-po feng-t'u chi* (The Topography of Singapore), (Singapore, 1947).

Li, Feng-pao. *Shih-te jih-chi* (Diary of My Mission to Germany), (Shanghai, 1936).

Li, Huan (ed.). *Kuo-ch'ao ch'i-hsien lei-cheng ts'u-p'ien* (A Classified Compendium of Eminent Ch'ing Personalities, main series), (1884–1890, n.p.).

Li, Hung-chang. *Li Wen-chung kung ch'uan-chi* (Complete Works of Li Hung-chang), 6 vols., (Taipei, 1962).

Li, Shao-ling. *Ou Ch'i-chia hsien-sheng chuan* (A Biography of Ou Ch-i-chia), (Taipei, 1960).

Li, Shu-ch'ang. *Cho-tsun yuan ts'ung-kao* (Collection of Works from the *Cho-tsun yuan*), 4 vols., (1893, n.p.).

————. "Feng-shih lun-tun chi" (My Mission to London). In *Hsiao-fang-hu-chai yu-ti ts'ung-ch'ao tsai pu-p'ien*, (Taipei, 1964).

————. *Hsi-yang tsa-chi* (Reminiscence of My Missions to Western World), (ch'ang-sha, 1981).

Li, Shu-chi. *Ch'eng-hai hsien-chih* (County Gazetteer of Ch'eng-hai), (1814, n.p.).

Li, Wen-chih. "Ch'ing-tai ya-p'ien chan-cheng ch'ien te ti-tsu, shang-yueh tzu-pen, kao-li-tai yü nung-min sheng-huo" (The Rent, Commercial Capital, Usury and the Life of Peasants in Ch'ing China Prior to the Opium War). In *Chung-kuo Tzu-pen chu-i meng-ya wen-t'i t'ao-lun chi* (San Lien, Peking, 1957), vol. 2, pp. 609–656.

Liang, Ch'i-ch'ao. "Hsin-ta-lu yu-chi" (Diary of My Trip to the New Continent). In Shen Yun-lung (ed.), *Chin-tai chung-kuo shih-liao ts'ung-k'an*, no. 96–97, (Taipei, 1967), pp. 377–490.

————. "Chi hua-kung chin-yueh" (On the Exclusion Laws against Chinese Labourers) as appendix to Liang Ch'i-ch'ao, Hsin-ta-lu yu-chi, pp. 436–90.

————. *Yin-pin-she wen-chi* (Collection of Literary Works of the Yin Pin Library), (Hong Kong, 1955).

————. *Yin-ping-she ho-chi* (Complete Works of the Yin Pin Library), 16 vols., (Shanghai, 1933).

Liang, Chia-pin. *Kuang-tung shih-san h'ang k'ao* (A Study of the Thirteen Hongs of Kwangtung), (Nanking, 1937).

————. "Chi Ch'ing-chi she-li ch'iao-chiao yu chung-mei wen-chiao chiao-liu" (The Establishment of Overseas Chinese Schools and the Cultural and Educational Exchange between China and the United States). In *Hua-ch'iao wen-t'i lun-wen chi*.

Liao, Hsiu-i. "Chao-ch'i hua-jen i-min Mei-kuo yu Chung Mei hu-ch'iao chiao-she" (Early Chinese Emigration to the United States and the Sino-American Negotiations on the Protection of American Chinese), (unpublished thesis — National

Cheng Chih University, Taipei, 1972).

Liao, Shubert S.C. (ed.). *Chinese Participation in Philippine Culture and Economy*, (Manila, 1964).

Lin, Chih-kao et al. (ed.). *Hsing-chou ying-ho hui-kuan i-pai ssu-shih-i chou-nien chi-nien t'e-k'an* (Souvenir Magazine of 141st Anniversary Celebration of the Singapore Ying Ho Association), (Singapore, 1965).

Lin, Hsiao-sheng. "Ch'ing-ch'ao chu Hsing Ling-shih yu hai-hsia chih-min-ti cheng-fu chien te chiu-fen" (The Dispute between the Ch'ing Consul in Singapore and the Colonial Government of the Straits Settlements). In K'o Mu-lin and Ng Chin-keong (eds.), *Hsin-chia-po hua-tsu shih lun-chi* (Papers on the History of the Chinese in Singapore), (Singapore, 1972).

Lin, Hsiao-sheng et al. (ed.). *Shih-le ku-chi* (The Historical Relics of Singapore), (Singapore, 1975).

Lin, Hsueh-tseng. *Ch'uan-chou fu-chi* (Prefectural Gazetteer of Ch'uan-chou), (1612, n.p.).

Lin, Jen-ch'uan. "Min-tai ssu-jen h'ai-shang mo-i shang-jen yu wo-k'ou" (Chinese Private Overseas Traders and The Dwarf Pirates." In *Zhong Guo shi Yan Jiu*, no. 4, (Peking, 1980), pp. 94–108.

Lin, K'un-kuang (comp.). *Chin-men chih* (Gazetteer of Quemoy), (Taipei, 1960).

Lin, Tse-hsu. *Lin Wen-chung kung cheng-shu* (Political Correspondence of Lin Tse-hsu), (Shanghai, 1935).

_____. *Lin Tse-hsu chi: kung-tu* (Collected works of Lin Tse-hsu: official correspondence), (Peking, 1963).

Liu, Ch'eng-yu. "Shih-tsai-t'ang ts'a-i" (Reminiscence of the Shih-tsai Hall). In Shen Yun-lung (ed.), *Chin-tai chung-kuo shih-liao ts'ung-k'an*, no. 717, (Taipei, n.d.).

Liu, Chih-t'ien. *Chung-fei kuan-hsi shih* (A History of Sino-Filipino Relations), (Taipei).

Liu Hsi-hung. "Ying-yao jih-chi" (Diary of My Co-Mission to England). In Wang Hsi-chi (ed.), *Hsiao-fang-hu chai yu-ti ts'ung-ch'ao*, series 11, pp. 160–209.

_____. "Ying-yao ssu-chi" (Private Records of My Co-Mission to England), appended to *Li Feng-pao, Shih-te jih-chi* (Shanghai, 1936).

Liu, Hsi-hung et al. *Chu Te shih-kuan tang-an ch'ao* (Records of the Chinese Embassy in Germany), (reprint, Taipei, 1966).

Liu, Hsiung-hsiang. *Ch'ing-chi ssu-shih nien wai-chiao yu h'ai-fang* (Forty Year's of Diplomacy and Coastal Defence during the Ch'ing Period), (Chungking, 1943).

Liu, Jui-fen. "Liu Chung-ch'eng (Chih-t'ien) tsou-kao" (Memorials of Liu Jui-fen). In Shen Yun-lung (ed.), *Chin-tai chung-kuo shih-liao ts'ung-k'an* no. 603, (Taipei, n.d.).

_____. *Yang-yun-shan chuang ch'uan-chi* (Complete Works of Yang-yun-shan chuang), 8 vols., (Shanghai, ?, 1896).

_____. "Hsi-yao chi-lueh" (Concise Records of My Mission to the West). In *Liu Jui-fen, Yang-yun-shan chuang ch'uan-chi*, (Shanghai, ?, 1896).

Liu, Ko-yin. "Pin-ch'eng chia-ying hui-kuan shih-lueh" (A Short History of the Penang Chia Ying Association), (Manuscript kept by C.H. Yen).

Liu, K'un-i. *Liu K'un-i i-chi* (Works of Liu K'un-i, posthumously collected), 5 vols., (Peking, 1959).

Liu, Lien-k'o. *Pang-hui san-pai nien ko-ming shih* (Three Hundred Years' Revolutionary History of the Chinese Secret Societies), (Macao, 1941).

Liu Wang, Hui-chen. *The Traditional Chinese Clan Rules*, (New York, 1959).

Liu, Yeh-ch'in (ed.). *Chieh-yang hsien-chih* (County Gazetteer of Chieh-yang), (1779, n.p.).

Liu, Yu-chun et al. (eds.). *Chu-tsai hua-kung fang-wen lu* (Interviews with Former Coolies from Indonesia), (Sun Yat-sen University, Canton, 1979).

Lo, Erh-kang. "T'ai-p'ing t'ien-kuo ko-ming ch'ien te jen-k'ou ya-po wen-t'i" (The Population Pressure On The Eve of the Taiping Rebellion). In *Chung-kuo she-hui ching-chi shih chi-k'an*, vol. 8, no. 1, pp. 20–80.

Lo, Hsiang-lin. "Tsui chao chih Hsiang-kang liu-hsueh chih Yung Hung chi ch'i so t'i-ch'ang chih yang-wu" (Yung Wing and His Promotion of Foreign Matters). In *Lo Hsiang-lin, Hsiang-kang yu chung-hsi wen-hua chiao-liu*, chapter 4.

――――. *Hsiang-kang yu chung-hsi wen-hua chiao-liu* (Hong Kong and the Sino-Western Cultural Interfusion), (Hong Kong, 1961).

――――. *Liang Ch'eng te ch'u-shih mei-kuo* (Liang Cheng: Chinese Minister in Washington 1903–1907), (Hong Kong, 1977).

――――. *K'e-chia shih-liao hui-p'ien* (Historical Sources for the Study of Hakkas), (Hong Kong, 1965).

――――. "The Southward Expansion of Chinese Civilization and the Advancement of Learning in Kwantung Province." In *Symposium on Historical Archaeological and Linguistic Studies on South China Southeast Asia and Hong Kong Region*, (Hong Kong, 1967), pp. 139–49.

Lo Hui-min. *Foreign office Confidential Papers Relating to China and Her Neighbouring Countries 1840–1916*, (Mouton & Co., The Hague — Paris, 1969).

Lu, Hai-huan. "Keng-tzu hai-wai chi-shih" (Records of my Overseas Mission in the year 1900). In Shen Yun-lung (ed.), *Chin-tai chung-kuo shih-liao ts'ung-k'an*, no. 6, (Taipei, n.d.).

Lo, Jung-pang. "Intervention in Vietnam: A Case Study of the Foreign Policy of the Early Ming Government." In *Tsing Hua Journal of Chinese Studies*, new series VIII, August 1970, nos. 1 & 2, (Taipei), pp. 154–82.

Los Karl and H.M. Lai (comp.). *Chinese Newspapers Published in North America, 1854–1915*, (Washington, D. C., 1977).

Lu, Pao-ch'ien. *Lun wan Ch'ing liang-kuang te t'ien-ti-hui cheng-ch'uan* (On the Political Regime of the Heaven and Earth Society in Kwangtung and Kwangsi during the Late Ch'ing Period), (Taipei, 1975).

Lu, Shih-ch'iang. *Ting Jih-ch'ang yu chih-chiang yun-tung* (Ting Jih-ch'ang and the Self-Strengthening Movement), (Taipei, 1972).

Lyman, S.M. *Chinese Americans*, (New York, 1974).

――――. "Conflict and the Web of Group Affiliation in San Francisco's Chinatown, 1850–1910." In *Pacific Historical Review*, vol. 43, (1974), pp. 473–99.

Lyman, S.M., Willmott, W.E. and Ho. Berching. "Rules of a Chinese Secret Society in British Columbia." In *Bulletin of the School of Oriental and African Studies*, vol. 27, no. 3, (1964), pp. 530–39.

Ma, Chien-chung. "Shih-k'o-chai chi-yen chi-hsing" (Records of the Shih-k'o Library). In Shen Yun-lung (ed.), *Chin-tai chung-kuo shih-liao ts'ung-k'an*, vol. 16, no. 153, (Taipei, n.d.).

Ma, L. Eve Armentrout. "Urban Chinese at the Sinitic Frontier: Social Organizations in United States' Chinatown, 1849–1898", in *Modern Asian Studies*, vol. 17, no. 1 (1983).

――――. "Fellow-regional Associations in the Ch'ing Dynasty: Organizations in Flux for Mobile People: A Preliminary Survey", in *Modern Asian Studies*, vol. 18, no. 2 (1984), pp. 307–330.

Ma Huan. Annotated by Feng Ch'eng-chun, *Ying-yai sheng-lan chiao-chu*, (Shanghai, 1955).

Mackinnon, Stephen R. *Power and Politics in Late Imperial China: Yuan Shih-kai in Beijing and Tianjin, 1901-1908*, (Berkeley, 1980).

MacNair, H.F. *The Chinese Abroad, Their Position and Protection: A Study in International Law and Relations*, (reprint, Taipei, 1971).

——. *Modern Chinese History: Selected Readings*, (The Commercial Press, reprint, Taipei, 1962).

Mai, Jo-p'eng. *Huang Tsun-hsien chuan* (A Biography of Huang Tsun-hsien), (Shanghai, 1957).

Mak, Lau Fong. *The Sociology of Secret Societies: A Study of Chinese Secret Societies in Singapore and Peninsular Malaysia*, (Kuala Lumpur: OUP, 1981).

Malcolm, Elizabeth L., "The Chinese Repository and Western Literature on China 1800-1850", in *Modern Asian Studies*, vol. 7, no. 2 (1973), pp. 165-78.

Martin, W.A.P. *A Cycle of Cathay*, (Edinburgh, London, 1896).

Mayers, W.F. *Treaties Between the Empire of China and Foreign Powers*, (Shanghai, 1907, reprint, Taipei, 1966).

McClellan, Robert. *The Heathen Chinese: A Study of American Attitudes Toward China, 1890-1905*, (Ohio, 1971).

McKee, Delber L. *Chinese Exclusion Versus the Open Door Policy, 1900-1906*, (Detroit, 1977).

Mei, June. "Socioeconomic Origins of Emigration: Guangdong to California, 1850-1882." In *Modern China*, no. 5, (1979), pp. 463-501.

Meng, S.M. *The Tsungli Yamen: Its Organization and Functions*, (Cambridge, Massachusetts, 1962).

Metzger, Thomas. "The State and Commerce in Imperial China." In *Asian and African Studies*, 6 (1970), pp. 23-46.

——. "Ch'ing Commercial Policy", Ch'ing-shih wen-t'i, 1:3, (February, 1966), pp. 4-10.

Michael, Franz. *The Taiping Rebellion: History and Documents*, (Seattle, 1966).

Michie, Alexander. *The Englishman in China during the Victorian Era*, (Edinburgh, 1900).

Mill, J.V.G. *Ma Huan, Ying-yai Sheng-lan* (The Overall Survey of the Ocean's Shores), (1433), (Cambridge: U.P. Cambridge, 1970).

Miller, S.C. *The Unwelcome Immigrant: The American Image of the Chinese, 1785-1882*, (Berkeley, 1969).

Mitchell, Peter M. "The Limits of Reformism: Wei Yuan's Reaction to Western Intrusion." In *Modern Asian Studies*, 6:2, (1972), pp. 175-204.

Montgomery, W.G. "'The Remonstrance' of Feng Kuei-Fen: A Confucian Search for Change in 19th Century China", (Ph.D. Dissertation, Brown University, 1979).

Moore, A.G. "The Dilemma of Stereotypes: Theodore Roosevelt and China, 1901-1909", (Ph.D. Dissertation, Kent State University, 1978).

Morrison, J.R. *Chinese Commercial Guide*, (Canton, 1834).

Morse, H.B. *The International Relations of the Chinese Empire*, 3 vols., (reprint, Taipei, n.d.).

——. *The Guilds of China*, (Longmans, London, 1933).

Morton, J. *In the Sea of Sterile Mountains: The Chinese in British Columbia*, (J.J. Douglas, Vancouver, 1974).

Murphey, R. *Shanghai: Key to Modern China*, (Cambridge, Massachusetts, 1953).

_____. *The Treaty Ports and China's Modernization: What Went Wrong?* (Michigan Papers, no. 7, Ann Arbor, 1970).

_____. (ed.), Nineteenth Century China: Five Imperialist Perspectives. In *Michigan Papers in Chinese Studies*, no. 13, (Center for Chinese Studies, University of Michigan, Ann Arbor, 1972).

Nan Hui. *Mei ti ch'in hua shih-lu* (Historical Records of American Imperialist Aggression in China), (Hong Kong, 1971).

Nee, Victor G. and de Bary Nee, B. *Longtime California: A Documentary Study of an American Chinatown*, (Boston, 1974).

Newbold, T.J. *Political and Statistical Account of the British Settlements in the Straits of Malacca*, 2 vols., (London, 1939).

Newbold, T.J. and Wilson, F.W. "The Chinese Secret Triad Society of the Tien-ti-hui." In *Journal of Royal Asiatic Society*, vol. VI, pp. 120–58, (London, 1841).

Ng, Chin-keong. "The Fukienese Maritime Trade in the Second Half of the Ming Period — Government Policy and Elite Groups' Attitude." In *Nanyang University Journal*, vol. 5, (1971).

_____. "A Study of the Peasant Society of South Fukien, 1506–1644." In *Nanyang University Journal*, vol. 6, (1972), pp. 189–213.

_____. "Gentry-Merchants and Peasant-Peddlers — The Response of the South Fukienese to the offshore Trading opportunities 1522–1566." In *Nanyang University Journal*, vol. VII, (1973), pp. 161–75.

_____. *Trade and Society: The Amoy Network on the China Coast, 1683–1735* (Singapore U.P., Singapore, 1983).

Nolde, John J. "Xenophobia in Canton, 1842–1849." In *Journal of Oriental Studies*, vol. 13, no. 1, (January, 1975), pp. 1–22.

Ocko, J.K. "Ting Jih-ch'ang and Restoration Kiangsu, 1864–1870: Rhetoric and Reality", (Ph.D. Dissertation, Yale University, 1975).

Ou-yang P'u-chih (ed.). *Liu Chung-ch'eng (K'un-i) i-chi* (Works of Liu K'un-i, posthumously collected), 14 vols. In Shen Yun-lung (ed.), *Chin-tai chung-kuo shih-liao ts'ung-k'an*, vol. 6, (Taipei, n.d.).

Pao, Tsun-p'eng. *Cheng Ho hsia hsi-yang chih pao-ch'uan k'ao* (On the Treasure Ships of Cheng Ho), (Taipei, 1963).

Pao, Tsun-p'eng et al. (ed.). *Chung-kuo chin-tai shih lun-ts'ung* (Series of Essays on Modern Chinese History), vol. 1, no. 7, (Taipei, 1956).

Parker, J.H. "The Rise and Decline of I-Hsin, Prince Kung, 1858–1865: A Study of the Interaction of Politics and Ideology in Late Imperial China", (Ph.D. Dissertation, Princeton, 1979).

Patton, John R. "Minister to the Mandarins: Charles Denby and the Emergence of America's China Policy", (M.A. Florida Atlantic University, 1977).

Paulsen, G.E. "The Gresham-Yang Treaty." In *Pacific Historical Review*, vol. 37, (1968), pp. 281–97.

P'eng, Jen-chieh. *Tung-kuan hsien-chih* (County Gazetteer of Tung-kuan), (1797, n.p.).

P'eng, Tse-i. "Kuo Sung-t'ao chih ch'u-shih Ou-hsi chi ch'i kung-hsien" (The Mission of Kuo Sung-t'ao to the West and its Contribution). In Pao Tsun-p'eng et. al., (eds.), *Chung-kuo chin-tai shih lun-ts'ung*, vol. 1, no. 7, pp. 62–78.

_____. "Ch'ing-tai kuang-tung yang-hang chih-tu te ch'i-yen" (The Rise of the Co-hong in Kwangtung during the Ch'ing Dynasty). In *Li-shih yen-chiu*, no. 1, (1957), pp. 1–24.

Petach, L. "Early Relations of China with Southeast Asia." In *Studies in Asian*

History: Proceedings of Asian History Congress 1961, (Bombay, 1969), pp. 186–90.

Pin, Ch'un. "Ch'eng-cha pi-chi." In Wang Yu-li (ed.), *Chung-hua wen-shih ts'ung-shu*, (Taipei), vol. 98, pp. 330–34.

Porter, Jonathan. "Foreign Affairs (Yang Wu) Expertise in the Late Ch'ing: The Career of Chao Lieh-wen." In *Modern Asian History*, vol. 13, no. 3, 1979), pp. 459–83.

Purcell, Victor. *The Chinese in Southeast Asia*, (London, 1965).

_____. *The Chinese in Malaya*, (Kuala Lumpur, 1967).

Reid, A. "Early Chinese Migration into North Sumatra." In J. Ch'en & N. Tarling (eds.), *Studies in the Social History of China and S.E. Asia*, (Cambridge, 1970), pp. 289–320.

Reid, J.G. *The Manchu Abdication and the Powers, 1908–1912*, (Berkeley, 1935).

Reischauer, Edwin O. "Notes of T'ang Dynasty Sea Routes." In *Harvard Journal of Asiatic Studies*, vol. V, 1940, pp. 142–64.

Rhoads, Edward, J.M. "Merchant Associations in Canton, 1895–1911." In Mark Elvin & G.W. Skinner (eds.), *The Chinese City Between Two Worlds*, (Stanford, 1974), pp. 97–117.

Richardson, Peter. "The Recruiting of Chinese Indentured Labour for the South African Gold-mines, 1903–1908." In *Journal of African History*, vol. 18, no. 1, (1977), pp. 85–108.

_____. "The Provision of Chinese Indentured Labour for the Transvaal Gold Mines, 1903–1908", (an unpublished Ph.D. Thesis, University of London, 1978).

_____. *Chinese Mine Labour in the Transvaal*, (MacMillan, London, 1982).

Ros, H. "Early History of the Steamship in China." In *Studies in Asian History: Proceedings of the Asian History Congress 1961*, (Bombay, 1969), pp. 141–48.

Roth, Arnold. "The California State Supreme Court, 1860–1879: A Legal History", (Ph.D. Dissertation, Southern California, 1973).

Roy, P.E. "The Preservation of the Peace in Vancouver: The Aftermath of the Anti-Chinese Riot of 1887." In *B.C. Studies*, no. 31, (Autumn 1976), pp. 44–59.

Sandmeyer, E.C. *The Anti-Chinese Movement in California*, (reprint, Urbana, 1973).

Saxton, A. *The Indispensable Enemy: Labor and the Anti-Chinese Movement in California*, (Berkeley, 1975).

Schlegal, G. *Thian Ti Hwui: The Hung League or Heaven-Earth League*, (Batavia, 1866).

Schwartz, Benjamin. *In Search of Wealth and Power: Yen Fu and the West*, (Cambridge, Massachusetts, 1964).

Shaw, C. *The Inns of Court Calendar: A Record of the Members of the English Bar — Students*, (London, 1877).

Shen, Chih-ch'i. *Ta-ch'ing lu-li ts'ung-ting t'ung-ts'uan chi-ch'eng* (The Fundamental Laws and Subordinate Statutes of the Ch'ing Dynasty), (1830, n.p.).

Shen, I-yao. *Hai-wai p'ai-hua pai-nien shih* (A Century of Chinese Exclusion Abroad), (Hong Kong, 1970).

Shen, Ting-chun (ed.). *Chang-chou fu-chih* (Prefectural Gazetteer of Chang-chou), (1877, n.p.).

Shen, T'ung-sheng. "Kuang-hsu cheng-yao" (Major Political Events of the Reign of Kuang-hsu Emperor). In Shen Yun-lung, (ed.), *Chin-tai chung-kuo shih-liao ts'ung-k'an*, no. 345, (Taipei, n.d.).

Shen, Yun-lung. "Chi Wu T'ing-fang — i-ke chih-te ching-yang te ssu-fa chieh tien-hsing jen-wu" (Wu T'ing-fang: A Respectable Legal Man). In *Shen Yun-lung, Chin-tai cheng-chih jen-wu lun-ts'ung*, (Taipei, 1965), pp. 132–42.

_____. *Chin-tai cheng-chih jen-wu lun-ts'ung*, (Taipei, 1965).

_____ (ed.). *Chin-tai chung-kuo shih-liao ts'ung-k'an*, vol. 10, nos. 96–97, (Taipei).

_____ (ed.). *Ch'ing-mo min-ts'u shih-liao ts'ung-shu* (Series of Historical Materials on Late Ch'ing and Early Republication Periods), (Taipei).

Sheng, Hsuan-huai. *Yu-chai ts'un-kao* (Collected Works of Sheng Hsuan-huai), 2 vols., (Taipei, 1963).

Shih, Chao-chi. *Shih Chao-chi chao-nien hui-i lu* (Memoirs of the Early Life of Shih Chao-chi), (Taipei, 1967).

Shin, Linda P. "China in Transition: The Role of Wu T'ing-fang (1842–1922)", (an unpublished Ph.D. dissertation, University of California, Los Angeles, 1970).

Shin, Tim Sung Wook. "The Concepts of State (Kuo-chia) and People (Min) in the Late Ching, 1890–1907: The Case of Liang Ch'i-ch'ao, T'an Ssu-t'ung and Huang Tsun-hsien", (Ph.D. Dissertation, California, Berkeley, 1980).

Shou Lo Hsiang-lin chiao-shou lun-wen-chi p'ien-chi wei-yen-hui (ed.). *Shou Lo Hsiang-lin chiao-shou lun-wen chi* (Essays in Chinese Studies Presented to Professor Lo Hsiang-lin on His Retirement from the Chair of Chinese, University of Hong Kong), (Hong Kong, 1970).

Shulman, F.J. *Doctoral Dissertations on China, 1971–1975: A Bibliography of Studies in Western Languages*, (Seattle: University of Washington Press, 1978).

Siah, U Chin. "Annual Remittances by Chinese Immigrants to their Families in China." In *Journal of Indian Archipelago and Eastern Asia*, vol. 1, (1847), pp. 35–37.

Siegelbaum, Lewis H. "Another 'Yellow Peril': Chinese Migrants in the Russian Far East and the Russian Reaction before 1917", in *Modern Asian Studies*, vol. 12, no. 2 (1978), pp. 307–30.

Sigel, Louis T. "The Treaty Port Community and Chinese Foreign Policy in the 1880s." In *Papers on Far Eastern History*, no. 11, (March, 1975).

Skinner, G.W. *Chinese Society in Thailand: An Analytical History*, (Ithaca, 1957).

_____. *The City in Late Imperial China*, (Stanford: Stanford U.P., 1977).

_____. *Leadership and Power in the Chinese Community of Thailand*, (New York, 1958).

Smith, George. *A Narrative of An Exploratory Visit to Each of the Consular Cities of China and to the Islands of Hong Kong and Chusan*, (reprint, Taipei, 1972).

Song, Ong Siang. *One Hundred Years' History of the Chinese in Singapore*, (reprint, Singapore, 1967).

Ssu-t'u, Mei-t'ang. *Tsu-kuo yu hua-ch'iao* (China and the Overseas Chinese), 2 vols., (Hong Kong, 1956).

Stewart, W. *Chinese Bondage in Peru: A History of the Chinese Coolies in Peru 1849–1874*, (Durham, 1951).

Su, Hsiao-hsien (ed.). *Chang-chou shih-shu lu Hsing t'ung-hsiang lu* (A Directory of Chang Chou Chinese in Singapore), (Singapore, 1948).

Su, Hsueh-feng. *Chang Chih-tung yu hu-pei chiao-yu kai-ke* (Chang Chih-tung and the Education Reform in Hupei), (Taipei, 1976).

Sun, Chen-t'ao. *Mei-kuo hua-ch'iao shih-lueh* (A Concise History of the Chinese in the United States), (Taipei, 1962).

Sun, Hui-wen. "Sheng-shih wei-yen te tso-tse — Cheng Kuan-Ying." In *Chung-kuo li-shih hsueh-hui shih-hsueh chi-kan*, vol. 2, (Taipei, 1960), pp. 139–82.

Sun, E-tu Zen. "The Board of Revenue in Nineteenth Century China." In *Harvard Journal of Asiatic Studies*, 24, (1962–63), pp. 175–228.

Sun, Pao. *T'ang Sung Yuan hai-shang shang-yueh cheng-ch'ih* (Overseas Commercial Policy of T'ang, Sung and Yuan Dynasties), (Taipei, 1969).

Sung, Betty Lee. *Mountain of Gold: The Story of the Chinese in America*, (Mac-Millan, New York, 1967).

Suryadinata, Leo. *The Pre-World War II Peranakan Chinese Press of Java: A Preliminary Survey*, (Ohio, 1971).

––––––. "The Three Major Streams in Peranakan Chinese Politics in Java 1917–1942", (M.A. thesis, Monash University, 1969).

Swisher, Earl. *China's Management of the American Barbarians: A Study of Sino-American Relations 1841-1861*, with Documents, (New Haven, 1951).

Tai, Hung-tz'u. *Ch'u-shih chiu-kuo jih-chi* (Diary of My Mission to the Nine Countries), (12 chuan, Peking, 1906).

Tan, Mely Giok-lan. *The Chinese in the United States: Social Mobility and Assimilation*, (Oriental Culture Service, Taipei, 1973).

Tang, E. "The Status in China of Chinese British Subjects from the Straits Settlements 1844–1900." In *Papers on Far Eastern History*, no. 3, (Canberra, March, 1971), pp. 189–209.

T'ang, Wen-chih. *Lu-ching t'ang tsou-shu* (Memorials from the Lu-ching Hall). In Shen Yun-lung, (ed.), *Chin-tai chung-kuo shih-liao ts'ung-k'an*, no. 56, (Taipei, n.d.).

Tarling, N. "The Entrepot at Labuan and the Chinese." In J. Ch'en & N. Tarling (eds.), *Studies in Social History of China and S.E. Asia*, (Cambridge, 1970), pp. 355–73.

Teixeira, Manuel. "The So-called Slave Trade at Macao." In *International Association of Historians of Asia, Second Biennial Conference Proceedings*, (Taipei, 1962), pp. 639–46.

T'ien-hou. *T'ien-hou niang-niang hsien-sheng ling-ch'ien chu-chieh* (The Holy and Inspired Sacrificial Lots of the Queen of Heaven Commented on and Explained), (1830, n.p.).

T'ien, Ju-k'ang. "Tsai-lun shih-ch'i chih shih-chiu shih-chi chung-yeh chung-kuo huan-ch'uan yeh te fa-chan" (Another Study of the Development of the Chinese Junk Trade between the 17th and 19th Centuries). In *Li-shih yen-chiu*, no. 2, (1957), pp. 1–11.

––––––. "Shih-pa shih-chi mo-ch'i chih shih-chiu shih-chi mo-ch'i hsi chia-li-man-tan te-hua-ch'iao kung-ssu ts'u-chih" (Overseas Chinese Kongsi Organization in West Kalimantan during the period between Late 18th and Late 19th centuries). In *Hsia-men ta-hsueh hsueh-pao, she-hui k'o-hsueh pan*, no. 1, (1958), pp. 128–51.

––––––. *The Chinese in Sarawak*, (London, 1953).

––––––. "Chin-tai hua-ch'iao shih te Chieh-tuan wen-t'i." In *Hsia-men ta-hsueh hsueh-pao, she-hui k'o-hsueh pan*, no. 1, (1958), pp. 89–92.

Ting, Tse-min. *Mei-kuo p'ai hua shih* (A History of Anti-Chinese Movement in the United States of America), (Peking, 1952).

Tong, Te-kong. *United States Diplomacy in China, 1844–60*, (Seattle, 1964).

Tou, Chung-i. *Li Hung-chang nien (jih) p'u* (The Chronological Records of Li

Hung-chang), (Kowloon, 1968).

Tsai Che. *Ka'o-ch'a cheng-chih jih-chi* (Diary of My Political Investigating Mission), (Shanghai, ?, 1908).

Tsai, Chen. *Ying-yao jih-chi* (Diary of My Mission to England), (Shanghai, 1903).

Tsai, Chen and T'ang Wen-chih. *Ying-yao jih-chi* (Diary of our Mission to England). In Shen Yun-lung, (ed.), *Chin-tai chung-kuo shih-liao ts'ung-k'an*, no. 734, (Taipei, n.d.).

Ts'ai, Chun. *Pien-lun chi-lueh* (Concise Records of My Debates With Foreigners), (Shanghai, 1894).

Tsai, Jung-fang. "Comprador Ideologists in Modern China: Ho Kai (Ho Ch'i, 1859-1914) and Hu Li-Yuan (1847-1916)", (Ph.D. Dissertation, California, Los Angeles, 1975).

Ts'ai Erh-k'ang (comp.), Lin Lo-chih (trans.). "Li Fu-hsiang (Hung-chang) li-p'ing ou-mei chi" (Li Hung-chang's visits to Europe and America). In Shen Yun-lung (ed.), *Chin-tai chung-kuo shih-liao ts'ung-k'an*, no. 808, (Taipei, n.d.).

Ts'ai, Hung-sheng. "Shih chiu shih-chi hou-ch'i tung-nan-ya te chu-tsai hua-kung" (Chinese Coolie Labourers in Southeast Asia during the Late 19th century). In *Chung-shan ta-hsueh hsueh-pao*, (Canton, 1959), no. 4, pp. 117–34.

Ts'ai, Kuan-lo. *Ch'ing-tai ch'i-pai ming-jen chuan* (Who's who during the Ch'ing Dynasty), 3 vols., (Hong Kong, 1963).

Tsai, Shih-shan Henry. "Reaction to Exclusion: Ch'ing Attitudes Toward Overseas Chinese in the United States, 1848-1906", (an unpublished Ph.D. Dissertation, University of Oregon, 1970), (microfilm).

Ts'ao, Yung-ho. "Chinese Overseas Trade in the Late Ming Period." In *International Association of Historians of Asia, Second Biennial Conference Proceedings*, (Taipei, 1962), pp. 429–83.

Tseng, Chi-tse. *Tseng Hui-min kung shih-hsi jih-chi* (Diary of My Mission to the West), (2 chuan, Shanghai, 1893).

_____. "Tseng Hui-min kung shou-hsieh jih-chi" (The Diary of Tseng Chi-tse). In Wu Hsiang-hsiang (ed.), *Chung-kuo shih-hsueh ts'ung-shu*, no. 13, (Taipei, 1965).

_____. *Tseng Hui-min kung i-chi* (Works of Tseng Chi-tse, posthumously Collected), 17 vols., (Shanghai, ?, 1893).

Tso, Ping-lung. "Report on the Chinese in Indonesia dated 27th October, 1882." In Liu Hsi-hung *et. al.*, *Chu Te shih-kuan tang-an chao*, vol. 1, pp. 276–78.

Tso, Tsung-t'ang. *Tso Wen-hsiang kung ch'uan-chi* (Complete Works of Tso Tsung-t'ang), 6 vols., (Taipei, 1964).

Tsui, Kuo-yin. "Ch'u-shih Mei Jih Pi kuo jih-chi" (Diary of My Mission to the United States of America, Spain and Peru). In Wang Hsi-ch'i (ed.), *Hsiao-fang-hu chai yu-ti ts'ung-ch'ao pu-p'ien*, (Taipei, 1964), vol. 8.

Ts'un-ts'ui hsueh-she (ed.). *Chung-kuo chin san-pai-nien she-hui ching-chi shih lun-chi* (Collection of Essays on Social and Economic History of China in the Late Three Hundred Years), vol. 2, (Hong Kong, 1972).

T'u, K'ai-yu. *Hua Ch'iao* (On Overseas Chinese), (Shanghai, 1935).

Tu, Kuang-wen (comp.). *Ch'iung-chou fu-chih* (Prefectural Gazetteer of Ch'iung-chou), (1890, 44 + 1 chuan, n.p.).

Tu, Lien-che. "Kuo Sung-t'ao." In A.W. Hummel (ed.), *Eminent Chinese of the Ch'ing Period, 1644-1912*, p. 438.

_____. "Tso Tsung-t'ang." In A.W. Hummel (ed.), *Eminent Chinese of the Ch'ing*

Period, 1644–1912, p. 767.

_____. *Kuan-yu chun-chi-ch'u te chien-chih* (On the Establishment of the Chun-chi Ch'u), (Canberra, 1963).

Tuan, Ch'ang-kuo. "Kung-wang I-hsin te chih-hsueh chi ch'i wai-chiao shih-chien" (The Method of Study and Idea in Diplomacy of Prince Kung). In *Ku-kung wen-hsien*, vol. 4, no. 4, pp. 46–48.

Tung, Hsun. "Huan-tu-wo shu-she lao-jen shou-ting nien-p'u" (Chronological Autobiography of Tung Hsun). In Shen Yun-lung (ed.), *Chin-tai chung-kuo shih-liao ts'ung-k'an*, no. 282, (Taipei, n.d.).

Tung, L. *China and Some Phases of International Law*, (London & New York, 1940).

_____. *The Chinese in America 1820–1973*, (New York, 1974).

Uchida, Naosaku. *The Overseas Chinese: Bibliographical Essay Based on the Resources of the Hoover Institution*, (Stanford, 1959).

Van der Sprenkel, S. *Legal Institutions in Manchu China*, (New York, 1966).

Vaughan, J.D. *The Manners and Customs of the Chinese of the Straits Settlements*, (Singapore, 1879).

Viraphol, S. *Tribute and Profit: Sino-Siamese Trade, 1659–1853* (Cambridge, Massachusetts, 1977).

Wai-chiao pu tang-an tzu-liao ch'u (ed.). *Chung-kuo chu wai ke ta kung-shih li-jen kuan-chang hsien-ming nien-piao* (Chronological Chart of Chinese High-ranking Diplomats to Foreign Countries), (Taipei, 1969).

_____. *Chung-kuo wai-chiao chi-kuan li-jen shou-chang hsien-ming nien-piao* (Chronological Chart of the Heads and their titles of Chinese Diplomatic Institutions), (Taipei, 1967).

Wakeman, F. Jr. *Strangers at the Gate: Social Disorder in South China 1839–1861*, (Berkeley, 1966).

_____. "The Secret Societies of Kwangtung 1800–1856." In Chesneaux, J. (ed.), *Popular Movements and Secret Societies in China 1840–1950*, pp. 29–47.

_____. *The Fall of Imperial China*, (The Free Press, New York, 1975).

Wakeman, F. Jr. and Grant, C. (eds.). *Conflict and Control in Late Imperial China* (University of California Press, Berkeley, 1976).

Wang, Chao (narrated). *Te-tsung i-shih* (Some Records of the Emperor Kuang-hsu), (Taipei, 1973).

Wang, Erh-min. "Wan Ch'ing wai-chiao ssu-hsiang te hsing-ch'eng" (An Analysis to the Diplomatic Thought of the Late Ch'ing Period). In Chung-yang yen-chiu-yuan chin-tai shih yen-chiu-so (ed.), *Chung-yang yen-chiu-yuan chin-tai shih yen-chiu-so chi-k'an*, no. 1, pp. 19–46.

_____. *Wan Ch'ing cheng-chih ssu-hsiang shih-lun* (A History of Political Thought during Late Ch'ing China), (Taipei, 1969).

Wang, Gungwu. "The Nanhai Trade: A Study of the Early History of Chinese in the South China Sea." In *Journal of Malayan Branch of the Royal Asiatic Society*, vol. 31, pt. 2, (June, 1958), pp. 1–135, (independent issue).

_____. *A Short History of the Nanyang Chinese*, (Singapore, 1959).

_____. "A Note on the origins of Hua-ch'iao", (A Seminar paper, Department of Far Eastern History, Australian National University).

_____. "The Opening of Relations Between China and Malacca 1403–5." In J. Bastin & R. Roolvink (eds.), *Malayan and Indonesian Studies: Essays Presented to Sir Richard Winstedt* (London, 1964), pp. 87–104.

_____. "Traditional Leadership in a New Nation." In G. Wijeyawardene (ed.), *Leadership and Authority: A Symposium*, (Singapore, 1968), pp. 208–22.

_____. "China and South-East Asia 1402-1424." In J. Ch'en & N. Tarling (eds.), *Studies in the Social History of China and S.E. Asia*, (Cambridge, 1970), pp. 375–401.

_____. *Community and Nation: Essays on Southeast Asia and the Chinese* (Heinemann, Singapore, 1981).

Wang, Hsi-ch'i (ed.). *Hsiao-fang-hu chai yu-ti ts'ung-ch'ao* (reprints of Geographical Works from the Hsiao-fang-hu Library), 16 vols., (Hong Kong, n.d.).

Wang, Hsien-ch'ien (ed.). "Kuo Shih-lang (Sung-ta'o) tsou-shu (Memorials of Kuo Sung-t'ao)." In Shen Yun-lung, (ed.), *Chin-tai chung-kuo shih-liao ts'ung-k'an*, no. 151, (Taipei, n.d.).

_____. *Shih-erh ch'ao tung-hua lu* (The Tung Hua Records of the Twelve Reigns of the Ch'ing Dynasty), (reprint, Taipei, 1973).

Wang, Sing-wu. "The Attitude of the Ching Court toward Chinese Emigration." In *Chinese Culture*, vol. 9, no. 4, (1968), pp. 62–76.

_____. *The Organization of Chinese Emigration 1848-1888*, (San Francisco, 1978).

Wang, Ta-yuan. Annotated by Su chi-ch'in, *Tao-i chih-luch chiao shih*, (Chung Hua, Peking, 1981).

Wang, Tai Peng. "Gentry and Commoners in 16th and 17th century Mercantile China", (an unpublished seminar paper, Department of Far Eastern History, Australian National University, 1978).

_____. "The Word Kongsi: A Note." In *Journal of the Malaysian Branch of the Royal Asiatic Society*, vol. LII, pt. 1, (1979), pp. 102–105.

Wang, Tzu-ch'uan. "Yin-ju tsa-chih." In Wang Yu-li (ed.), *Chung-hua wen-shih ts'ung-shu*, vol. 2, (Taipei, n.d.).

Wang, Tsu-shang. *Tao-hsi-chai jih-chi* (Diary of the Tao-hsi Library), (Shanghai, 1892).

Wang, Yen-chien. "The Secular Trend of Prices during the Ch'ing Period." In *The Journal of the Institute of Chinese Studies of the Chinese University of Hong Kong*, (vol. V, no. 2, December 1972), pp. 347–68.

Wang, Yung-ho and Yu, Chun. "The First Report on the Chinese in Southeast Asia." In Liu Hsi-hung *et al.*, *Chu Te shih-kuan tang-an chao*, vol. 2, pp. 665–71.

_____. "The Second Report on the Chinese in Southeast Asia, March 1887." In Liu Hsi-hung *et al.*, *Chu Te shih-kuan tang-an ch'ao*, vol. 2, pp. 671–76.

_____. "The Third Report on the Chinese in Southeast Asia, March to May 1887." In Liu Hsi-hung *et al.*, *Chu Te shih-kuan tang-an ch'ao*, vol. 2, pp. 688–93.

Ward, J.S.M. and Stirling, W.G. *The Hung Society, or The Society of Heaven and Earth*, 3 vols., (London, 1925).

Watson, James L. "Chattel Slavery in Chinese Peasant Society: A Comparative Analysis", in *Ethnology*, vol. 15, no. 4 (October, 1976), pp. 361–75.

_____. "Hereditary Tenancy and Corporate Landlordism in Traditional China: A Case Study", in *Modern Asian Studies*, vol. 11, no. 2 (1977), pp. 161–82.

Weeks, J.A. "The Controversy over Chinese Labour in the Transvaal" (an unpublished Ph.D. Dissertation, Ohio State University, 1968).

Wen, Chung-chi. "The Nineteenth-Century Imperial Chinese Consulate in the Straits Settlements", (M.A. thesis, University of Singapore, 1964).

Wen, T'ing-ching. *Ch'ar-yang san-chia wen-ch'ao* (Reprints of the Literary Works of Three Hakka Scholars from Ta-p'u district), (1925).

West, Jean-Paul. "Catholic Activities in Kwangtung Province and Chinese Responses 1848-1885", (Ph.D. Dissertation, University of Washington, 1977).

White, Ann B. "The Hong Merchants of Canton", (Ph.D. Dissertation, University of Pennsylvania, 1967).

Wickberg, Edgar. *The Chinese in Philippine Life 1850-1898*, (New Haven, 1965).

Wijeyawardene, G. (ed.). *Leadership and Authority: A Symposium*, (Singapore, 1968).

Williams, F.W. *Anson Burlingame and the First Chinese Mission to Foreign Powers*, (New York, 1912).

Williams, Lea E. *Overseas Chinese Nationalism: The Genesis of the Pan-Chinese Movement in Indonesia 1900-1916*, (Glencoe, 1960).

Williams, S.W. *Chinese Commercial Guide about Coolie Trade*, (reprint, Taipei).

Willmott, D.W. *The National Status of the Chinese in Indonesia*, (Ithaca, 1961).

Willmott, W.E. "Some Aspects of Chinese Communities in British Columbia Towns." In *BC Studies*, no. 1, (Winter 1968-1969), pp. 27-36.

_____, "Chinese Clan Associations in Vancouver." In *Man*, vol. LXIV, (March-April 1964), no. 49, pp. 33-37.

Wills, J.E. Jr. *Peppers, Guns and Parleys: The Dutch East Indian Company and China 1622-1681*, (Harvard U.P., Cambridge, Massachusetts).

Wilson, C.G. *Chinatown Quest: One Hundred Years of Donaldina Cameron House 1874-1974*, (San Francisco, 1974).

Wong, C.S. *A Cycle of Chinese Festivities* (Singapore, 1967).

Wong, John. *Yeh Ming-ch'en: Viceroy of Liang Kuang 1852-58*, (Cambridge, 1976).

Wong, Lin Ken. *The Trade of Singapore 1818-69*, an independent issue in *The Journal of the Malayan Branch of Royal Asiatic Society*, vol. 33, pt. 4.

Wong, Owen Hong-hin. "The Origin and Evolution of the Idea of Establishing Chinese Legation Abroad." In *Journal of Oriental Studies*, 10, (1972), pp. 145-71.

Woon, Y.F. "An Emigrant Community in the Ssu-yi Area, Southeastern China, 1885-1949: A Study in Social Change", in *Modern Asian Studies*, vol. 18, no. 2 (1984), pp. 273-306.

Worthy, E.H., Jr. "Yung Wing in America." In *Pacific Historical Review*, vol. 34, (1965), pp. 265-87.

Wright, Kathleen. *The Other Americans: Minorities in American History*, (Greenwich, Conn., 1969).

Wright, Mary C. *The Last Stand of Chinese Conservatism: The T'ung-chih Restoration 1862-1874*, (Stanford, 1957).

Wu, Hsien-tzu. *Chung-kuo min-chu hsien-cheng tang-shih* (A History of the Chinese Constitutional Party), (San Francisco, 1952).

Wu, Lin-chu (ed.). *Hsiang-shan hsien-chih* (County Gazetteer of Hsiang-shan), (1827, n.p.).

Wu, Shang-ying. *Mei-kuo hua-ch'iao pai-nien chi-shih* (One Hundred Years of the Chinese in the United States and Canada), (Hong Kong, 1954).

Wu, Silas H.L. *Communication and Imperial Control in China*, (Harvard University Press, Cambridge, Massachusetts, 1970).

_____. "The memorial systems of the Ch'ing dynasty 1644-1911." In *Harvard Journal of Asian Studies*, 27, (1967), pp. 7-75.

Wu, T'ien-jen. *Huang Kung-tu hsien-sheng chuan-kao* (A Biography of Huang Tsun-hsien), (Hong Kong, 1972).

Wu, T'ing-fang. *America: Through the Spectacles of an Oriental Diplomat* (New York, 1914).

————. "China and the United States." In *Independent*, 52, (29 March 1900), p. 754.

————. "Mutual Helpfulness Between China and the United States." In *North American Review*, 171, (July, 1900), 8, pp. 2–9.

————. "The Causes of Unpopularity of the Foreigners in China." In *The Annals of the American Academy of Political and Social Science 1901*, vol. XVII, no. 1, pp. 1–14.

Wu, T'ing-kuang (ed.). *Wu T'ing-fang* (A Biography of Wu T'ing-fang), (Shanghai, 1922).

Wu, Tsung-lien. *Hsui-yao pi-chi ssu-chung* (Four Items of Records of a Diplomatic Mission to England), (Taipei, 1972).

Wynne, M.L. *Triad and Tabut: A Survey of the Origin and Diffusion of Chinese and Mohamedan Secret Societies in the Malay Peninsula, 1800–1935*, (Singapore, 1941).

Yang, C.K. *Religion in Chinese Society*, (Berkeley, 1967).

Yeh, Te-hui. *Chueh-mi yao-lu*, 4 vols., (Taipei, 1970).

Yen, Cheng-chun. *Tso Wen-hsiang kung nien-p'u* (The Chronology of Tso Tsung-t'ang), (Taipei, 1971).

Yen, Chih-t'ui (trans. by Ssu-yu Teng), *Yen-shih chia-hsun* (Family Instructions for the Yen Clan), (Leiden, 1968).

Yen, Ching-hwang. "Ch'ing Changing Images of the Overseas Chinese (1644–1912)." In *Modern Asian Studies*, vol. 15, no. 2, (1981), pp. 261–85.

————. "The Overseas Chinese and Late Ch'ing Economic Modernization." In *Modern Asian Studies*, vol. 16, no. 2, (1982), pp. 217–32.

————. "Overseas Chinese Nationalism in Singapore and Malaya 1877–1912." In *Modern Asian Studies*, vol. 16, no. 3, (1982), pp. 397–425.

————. *The Overseas Chinese and the 1911 Revolution: With Special Reference to Singapore and Malaya* (Kuala Lumpur and New York, 1976).

————. "Ch'ing's Sale of Honours and the Chinese Leadership in Singapore and Malaya 1877–1912." In *Journal of Southeast Asian Studies*, vol. 1, no. 2, (September, 1970), pp. 20–32.

Yen, Ho-p'ing. *Ch'ing-chi chu-wai shih-kuan te chien-li* (The Establishment of Chinese Embassies Overseas during the Ch'ing Period), (Taipei, 1975).

Yong, C.F. "Chinese Leadership in Nineteenth Century Singapore." In *Hsin-she hsueh-pao*, (Singapore), vol. 1.

————. *New Gold Mountain: The Chinese in Australia 1900–1921* (Adelaide, 1977).

————. "A Preliminary Study of Chinese Leadership in Singapore 1900–1941." In *Journal of Southeast Asian History*, vol. IX, no. 2, (September, 1968), pp. 258–85.

———— (ed.). *Ethnic Chinese in Southeast Asia*. A special issue of the *Journal of Southeast Asian Studies*, vol. 12, no. 1, (March, 1981).

Young, M.B. *The Rhetoric of Empire: American China Policy, 1895–1901*, (Cambridge, Massachusetts, 1968).

Yu, Ch'i-hsing. "Wu T'ing-fang yu Hsiang-kang chih kuan-hsi" (Wu T'ing-fang and Hong Kong). In *Shou Lo Hsiang-lin chiao-shou lun-wen chi*, pp. 256-78.

Yu, Pao-hsien (ed.). *Huang-ch'ao hsu-ai wen-pien* (Collected Essays of the Ch'ing Dynasty), 8 vols., (Taipei, 1965).

Yu, P'i-Ch'eng. *En-p'ing hsien-chih* (County Gazetteer of En-p'ing), (1934).

Yu, Ssu-yu. *Lou-ch'uan jih-chi* (Diary of My Trip on a Chinese Warship), (Shanghai, ?, 1906).

_____. "Ku-pa chieh-lueh" (A Concise Description of Cuba). In *Hsiao-fang-hu-chai yu-ti ts'ung-ch'ao pu-p'ien tsai pu-p'ien*, (Taipei, 1964), vol. 2.

Yue Wai. "I-liu ling-san nien Fei-li-pin hua-ch'iao ch'an-sha an shih-mo" (A Critical Study of the Massacre of the Chinese in the Philippines in 1603). In *The New Asia Journal*, vol. 9, no. 2, (September, 1970), pp. 97-171.

Yung, Wing. *My Life in China and America*, (New York, 1909).

Yung, Hung (Yung Wing). "Hsi-hsueh tung-chan chi." In Shen Yun-lung (ed.), *Chin-tai chung-kuo shih-liao ts'ung-k'an*, (Taipei), no. 95.

Zo, Kil Young. "Chinese Emigration into the United States, 1850-1880", (Ph.D. Dissertation, Columbia, 1971).

Index